REFERENCE GUIDE TO UNITED STATES MILITARY HISTORY 1945 to the Present

CHARLES REGINALD SHRADER

General Editor

Facts On File®

AN INFOBASE HOLDINGS COMPANY

REFERENCE GUIDE TO UNITED STATES
MILITARY HISTORY: 1945 TO THE PRESENT

Copyright © 1995 by Sachem Publishing Associates, Inc.

Facts On File, Inc.
460 Park Avenue South
New York, NY 10016

Library of Congress Cataloging-in-Publication Data
(Revised for volume 5)
Reference guide to United States military history.

Includes bibliographical references (v. 1, p. 265–268) and index.
Contents: v. [1]. 1607–1815—v. [2]. 1815–1865.—v. [3]. 1865–1919.—v. [4]. 1919–1945
✓1. United States—History. Military—to 1900.
I. Shrader, Charles R.
E181.R34 1991   973   90-25673
ISBN 0-8160-1836-7 (v. 1)
ISBN 0-8160-1837-5 (v. 2)
ISBN 0-8160-1838-3 (v. 3)
ISBN 0-8160-1839-1 (v. 4)
ISBN 0-8160-1840-5 (v. 5)

For other books on the subject(s)
discussed in this book, look in the card
catalog, under the checked headings:

Facts On File books are available at special discounts when purchased in bulk quantities for
businesses, associations, institutions or sales promotions. Please call our Special Sales
Department in New York at 212/683–2244 or 800/322–8755.

Printed in the United States of America

VB VC 10 9 8 7 6 5 4 3 2 1

This book is printed on acid-free paper.

Contents

Text Chapter Authors

Chapter 1	Charles R. Shrader Lieutenant Colonel (Ret.), U.S. Army	Chapters 4 & 5	Carlo d'Este Lieutenant Colonel (Ret.), U.S. Army
Chapters 2 & 6	Lawrence A. Yates, Ph.D. Combat Studies Institute, U.S. Army Command & General Staff College	Chapter 7	Clayton R. Newell Lieutenant Colonel, U.S. Army Chief of Historical Services U.S. Army Center of Military History
Chapter 3	Tommy R. Young II, Ph.D. Deputy Command Historian Air Force Communications Command		

List of Contributors

Leslie H. Belknap
Captain, U.S. Army
U.S. Military Academy

Robert H. Berlin, Ph.D.
Combat Studies Institute
U.S. Army Command and General Staff College

M. Guy Bishop, Ph.D.
Seaver Center for Western History Research
Natural History Museum of Los Angeles County

Philip A. Bossert, Jr.
Captain, U.S. Air Force
U.S. Air Force Academy

Leo J. Daugherty III
Ohio State University

James Sanders Day
Major, U.S. Army
U.S. Military Academy

Gilbert B. Diaz
Major, U.S. Army

George B. Eaton
Major, U.S. Army
U.S. Military Academy

Uzal W. Ent
Brigadier General (Ret.), PNG

Peter R. Faber
Major, U.S. Air Force
Yale University

David Friend

Henry G. Gole
Colonel (Ret.), U.S. Army

Lloyd J. Graybar, Ph.D.
Eastern Kentucky University

Russell A. Hart
Ohio State University

Byron Hayes

Jonathan M. House
Major, U.S. Army

Richard Kehrberg
University of Wisconsin-Madison

Roger D. Launius, Ph.D.
Chief Historian
National Aeronautics and Space Administration

Theodore C. Mataxis
Brigadier General (Ret.), U.S. Army

Kevin McKedy
Major, U.S. Army
U.S. Military Academy

Bettie J. Morden
Colonel (Ret.), U.S. Army

Rod Paschall
Colonel (Ret.), U.S. Army

Michael J. Reed
Captain, U.S. Air Force
U.S. Air Force Academy

Stephen Robinson
Author

Charles R. Shrader
Lieutenant Colonel (Ret.), U.S. Army

Lewis Sorley, Ph.D.

Steve R. Waddell
Texas A&M University

James A. Warren
Author

John F. Wukovits
Woodhaven, Michigan

Introduction

The United States emerged from World War II as the undisputed champion of the Free World. Its military power was approached only by that of the Soviet Union, which soon demonstrated both the will and the physical capacity to impose its Communist ideology and imperial dominion around the world at every opportunity. So great was U.S. power and so depleted were the resources of its allies that, however reluctantly, the United States could not turn away from the responsibility of leading the opposition to Soviet domination. The ensuing 45-year conflict with the Soviet Union shaped U.S. military policy, organization, doctrine, and technological development. The threat of nuclear weapons and the requirement to deploy and maintain military forces around the world had a particularly profound effect.

Thus, the era was one in which U.S. military forces had to be maintained constantly at a size and level of readiness unprecedented in American history. Consequently, U.S. military leaders faced continuing challenges of how best to provide an effective defense of the United States and its allies at the least cost. To meet those challenges successfully required the highest levels of managerial skill, military competence, and technological innovation, as well as enormous material and human resources. In the end, American civilian and military leaders proved equal to the challenges and emerged victorious from a cold war that had too often grown uncomfortably hot. The United States now confronts a multi-polar world in which the political, economic, and military challenges may prove even more complex and demanding. But the country still possesses enormous material and human resources, as well as a long tradition of successfully overcoming great obstacles.

In large part, the history of the United States is a history of its military establishment—the story of U.S. military leaders and the forces they have commanded in peace and war. The *Reference Guide to United States Military History* seeks to provide a fresh perspective on this important story. As with each of the previous four volumes of the *Guide,* this volume comprises a thorough examination of the role of the military and its leaders in American life during a given period. Introduced by a short description of the organization, equipment, and doctrine of U.S. military forces, the narrative portion of the volume includes an extended discussion of the course of events and the development of American military institutions from 1945 to the present. The seven narrative chapters are supplemented by biographical profiles of the military and naval leaders of the period, detailed descriptions of the principal battles and events, and the discussion of special topics. The text of the volume is further enhanced by maps and illustrations depicting the nation's military leaders, military life, battles, and other events. This survey of American history as viewed through the perspective of military activities thus provides a unique reference work for school and library use.

Obviously, every detail of the military history of the United States cannot be addressed even in a five-volume series. The editors of the *Reference Guide to United States Military History* have thus selected for emphasis only those aspects that seem to be most important for understanding the course of American military history and the role of the military in American society. To guide the selection of persons and events for inclusion in the *Guide,* a number of prominent themes and key topics in American military history are stressed repeatedly in all five volumes of the series. These themes and topics represent those that the editors believe to be most important to the development of U.S. military forces and of attitudes toward the military in American society from the colonial period to the present.

Special attention thus is given to such key questions as what should be the role of armed forces in a democratic society and what should be the size, nature, and functions of the American armed forces. Similarly, the themes of citizen (militia) forces versus professional (standing) forces, competition among the various elements of the U.S. military establishment for resources and prestige, and ways in which American attitudes toward such matters have differed in time of peace and in time of crisis are also emphasized. The unique American solutions devised to coordinate military strategy and the organization of forces to meet perceived threats are investigated in some depth. The adaptation of technology to military ends occupies an especially important place in U.S. military history in view of the consistent preference of Americans for substituting technology for manpower and thus receives special attention. Another prominent theme is the perpetual and characteristic failure of the United States to prepare adequately for war during peacetime. The attitudes toward soldiers, sailors, and their leaders displayed by American political leaders and ordinary citizens is another important aspect on which the *Guide* focuses. Throughout the five volumes, special care has been taken to highlight the independent nature of the American soldier and sailor and the conditions under which he or she was required to operate. By repeatedly returning to these themes and topics, we hope to give focus to the series as well as to explain better the course and importance of military affairs in American history.

The scholars who have contributed to this as well as to the other volumes of the *Reference Guide to United States Military History* are among the best of the younger generation of scholars working on the problems of U.S. military, naval, and air-power history. Some are serving military officers; others are civilian historians in government service, professors in colleges and universities, or independent scholars from across the nation. Each contributor was chosen for his or her expertise on a particular topic as well as for the ability to explain complex ideas and events clearly and concisely. Chapter authors are identified in the table of contents and all contributors are recognized in the list of contributors.

The editors have worked diligently to make this volume of the *Reference Guide to United States Military History* as complete, accurate, and readable as possible. It is hoped that we have succeeded and that the users of this and all other volumes of the *Guide* will find the work useful for their purposes regardless of their individual interests and levels of expertise. Errors of fact and interpretation are inevitable in any work of this magnitude. Readers are therefore encouraged to bring any errors to the attention of the editors for correction in subsequent editions.

Charles R. Shrader, Ph.D.
General Editor
Reference Guide to United States Military History

PART I

The Organization of American Armed Forces and Their History

1

The Organization of Military Forces: 1945–1992

In 1945, the euphoria of victory and a naive belief that future conflicts could be contained by the U.S. nuclear monopoly and the United Nations (UN) convinced most Americans that large, modern armed forces were unnecessary. Such illusions were soon dispelled by the emergence of the Soviet Union as a rival superpower challenging the United States and threatening the peace and stability of the Free World. The ensuing 45-year conflict with the Soviet Union, its allies, and its surrogates demonstrated the need to maintain large, expensive, and technologically sophisticated armed forces and consequently shaped U.S. military policy, organization, doctrine, and technological development to an unprecedented degree. After the disintegration of the Soviet empire in the early 1990s, the U.S. Armed Forces turned to the challenge of developing new strategies, force structures, and doctrines suitable for dealing with a multipolar world in which even minor regional powers might obtain weapons of mass destruction and the will to use them.

of Western Europe was the second-most feared eventuality. In reality, more significant threats were posed by the Soviet encouragement of wars of national liberation, instability in the Third World, and the use of surrogates to conduct activities inimical to U.S. interests around the world.

The breakup of the former Soviet Union fundamentally altered the strategic situation and the potential threats to U.S. security. Although some residual uncertainty remains regarding the former Soviet Union, the major threats to the United States now seem to reside in the general political, economic, and social instability of much of the developing world; the proliferation of weapons of mass destruction; and the heavy conventional armament of various regional powers. A new wave of nationalism and religious fundamentalism in the Islamic world has also produced a significant threat in the form of international terrorism. In addition, the international traffic in illegal drugs also poses a threat to vital U.S. national interests. Such threats seem likely to continue well into the 21st century.

THREATS

The threat of expanding international Communism led by the Soviet Union manifested itself in several ways. Clearly the most dangerous was an all-out nuclear attack on the United States, its possessions, or its allies. The major focus of U.S. defense efforts from 1945 to 1990 was to deter nuclear attack or, if deterrence failed, to survive an initial attack, retaliate in kind, and prevail in the long term. The possibility of a full-scale Soviet military ground offensive, with or without the use of nuclear weapons, to gain control

STRATEGIES

In the immediate post-World War II period, the United States relied on its nuclear monopoly and the unproven international peacekeeping powers of the UN to prevent conflict and resolve international disputes. It soon became apparent that such a national strategy was inadequate to contain an aggressive Soviet Union. The explosion of a Soviet atomic bomb in 1949 ended all illusions of a permanent Pax Americana based on a U.S. nuclear monopoly and the negotiated settlement of international conflicts.

The doctrine of "containment" then emerged as the principal strategy for countering Soviet expansionism. However, the forces available to implement such a containment strategy were lacking.

A U.S. National Security Council memorandum (NSC-68) called for a massive national investment in the U.S. Armed Forces to make the policy of containment a reality, but in actuality, the major expansion of these armed forces was prompted by the Korean War rather than by NSC-68. Realizing that the U.S. economy would be debilitated by trying to compete with the Soviet Union in conventional ground and air forces, the strategy of "massive retaliation" with nuclear weapons was evolved as the most cost-effective defense. Massive retaliation was designed to deter armed Soviet aggression of any type by the threat of certain and effective U.S. nuclear retaliation that would utterly destroy the Soviet homeland.

It soon became apparent, however, that the threat of massive retaliation was unsuitable, and in fact ineffective, for countering problems caused by Soviet surrogates or conflicts that clearly did not merit a massive response. Thus, the United States cast off the strategy of massive retaliation in the early 1960s in favor of a strategy of "flexible response," whereby it would maintain military forces, including strategic nuclear forces, capable of responding with measures suitable to the situation all along the spectrum of conflict. Accordingly, the United States reorganized its forces and rethought its tactical doctrines to make such a flexible response possible.

The basic U.S. strategic policy has remained unchanged since about 1960; forces are built and deployed to respond with measured force to a variety of threats. Both nuclear and conventional capabilities have been emphasized in varying proportion over the period. Nuclear deterrence rests on ready nuclear retaliatory forces capable of actual nuclear combat if deterrence fails and supplemented by negotiated arms reductions and arms control. Conventional deterrence and combat capability are provided by strong forward-deployed forces and a flexible, ready central reserve supported by sufficient airlift and sealift to move it rapidly to threatened areas. Timely and accurate intelligence as well as effective command and control of both nuclear and conventional forces is considered essential. Over the years, the United States has also stressed the substitution of technology (particularly air power) for manpower and the augmentation of U.S. security through a system of strong alliances. Mutual defense arrangements and material support to U.S. allies remain particularly important parts of American military strategy.

The changed nature of the threats to U.S. security in the 1990s has led to a reassessment and fundamental realignment of U.S. strategy. The basic shift has been to move from an emphasis on nuclear retaliation and the containment of the Soviet Union by forward deployment of military forces to a policy of power projection in response to crises that may arise anywhere in the world to threaten U.S. interests. Such a strategy places a high value on ready mobile forces capable of moving quickly to trouble spots and of responding effectively to a wide range of situations—from terrorist attacks to full-scale war or revolution. This evolving new strategy relies less on forward-deployed forces than in the past but does not do away with them entirely.

PUBLIC ATTITUDES

In 1945, Americans were tired of war. The immediate response after V-J Day was a sigh of relief and a desire to return to the comfortable isolation of earlier days. Once it became apparent that isolation was no longer possible and that the United States was obliged, like it or not, to take the lead in opposing the spread of Communism and Soviet imperialism, Americans grudgingly acceded to the necessity for maintaining sufficient military strength to protect American interests at home and abroad. The shock of the Korean War brought home the need, and since the early 1950s, the American people have, by and large, willingly borne the burden of massive defense expenditures and a hitherto unprecedented degree of regimentation needed to provide an effective counterweight to the Soviets.

Only during the Vietnam era did the traditional American antimilitarism, coupled with a growing distrust of public officials, boil over to create serious active opposition to ongoing military operations and to the military in general. Amplified by the media, the antiwar protests of the 1960s and the shift in public opinion against the war sapped the political will of the elected leadership and in effect forced the United States to withdraw and abandon its South Vietnamese allies to Communist North Vietnamese domination. The unsatisfactory conclusion of the 10-year conflict in Vietnam is seen by some as the first U.S. military defeat. Although many military mistakes were made, the war was lost, if it was lost at all, not on the battlefield but in the streets of the United States and in the minds of its political leaders.

By the late 1970s, antimilitary feeling began to abate, and the eight years of the Ronald Reagan administration brought renewed public respect and confidence in the armed forces, which were simultaneously rebuilt with the latest equipment. The training and morale of this new all-volunteer force also improved significantly. These rebuilt forces achieved minor successes defending U.S. interests in Grenada in 1983 and Panama in 1989–90 and passed a major test in the Gulf War of 1991. The men and women who fought in Operation Desert Storm were supported by the public to a degree unseen since World War II. Attempts to revive the antiwar movement of the 1960s failed

Ronald Reagan, the 40th president of the United States (1981–89), was most responsible for expanding, modernizing, and raising the morale of the military during his two administrations. (Karl Schumacher, The White House)

dismally, drowned out by the exuberant demonstrations of public support for the troops in the Persian Gulf and, by extension, for the military and civilian leadership of the nation. Once the short and militarily successful campaign was concluded, however, the traditional American disinterest in military affairs reexerted itself.

SOCIAL POLICIES

The U.S. Armed Forces have long served as vehicles of social change. In the 19th century, military service was a means of integrating Irish, German, and other immigrants into U.S. society, and American armed forces have always provided both a refuge from bad economic times and a means of suppressing incipient social revolt. The massive military mobilizations for World Wars I and II brought together Americans from all over the nation and from a wide variety of social strata and ethnic groups. The men and women of the U.S. military were subjected to intensive medical and behavioral testing and intervention. They were also introduced to a disciplined lifestyle and the need to cooperate with others. In the late 1940s, the unsuccessful advocates of universal military training cited the acculturative, public health, and educational benefits to be derived from military service. More recently, the armed forces have served as the overt agent for rehabilitation of citizens in the lower mental test categories in Project 100,000. More important, since World War II, the armed services have been involved in two social movements of great importance: racial integration and sexual equality.

The integration of the armed forces was precipitated by Executive Order No. 9981, signed by Pres. Harry S Truman on June 26, 1948. Truman therein declared that there should be equality of treatment and opportunity for all persons in the armed forces without regard to race, color, religion, or national origin. Segregated all-black units subsequently became a thing of the past. By June 1950, the navy, Marine Corps, and air force had eliminated their all-black units. The process was not completed in the army until 1954 due to the larger numbers involved. Since 1948, black Americans have served in ever-increasing numbers and for the most part have found that the armed forces provide equal treatment and opportunity for all. The armed services have also played a leading role in the positive enforcement of civil rights legislation, including the use of regular and reserve forces to maintain law and order and to enforce the decisions of the courts, the legislature, and the executive branch. Although institutional racism continues to exist, it has been steadily degraded since 1945, and the services have acted forcefully to protect the civil rights of all military personnel both in the services and in the civilian communities surrounding defense installations, many of which are in areas traditionally antipathetic to racial equality.

The armed services have also been, somewhat reluctantly, a path to equality and increased opportunities for women. The status of women in the armed services was recognized by the Women's Armed Services Integration Act of June 12, 1948. The act excluded women from combat roles in the armed services, but the Women's Army Corps (WAC) became a permanent part of the regular army, and the status of women in the other services was also permanently established. The proportion of women in the armed forces has increased dramatically since 1970. In 1971, there were about 13,000 female officers and 30,000 female enlisted personnel on active duty—about 1.6 percent of the total active duty force. In 1990, some 291,000 women were serving on active duty (86,500 in the army, 50,000 in the navy, 10,500 in the Marine Corps, 69,000 in the air force, and 3,000 in the Coast Guard). In all, women represented nearly 11 percent of the total active duty force. Another 30,400 women were serving in the Army National Guard and 102,400 in the army reserve. Since 1970, increased emphasis has also been placed on eliminating institutional barriers to the advancement of women in the armed forces. Women were admitted to the military academies for the first time in the mid-1970s, and more recent legislation and regulations have further opened

Many formerly all-male jobs in the military had been opened to women by the 1980s; here, two drill instructors—one female, one male—stand at attention during a review of their troops. (U.S. Marine Corps)

military careers to women, including the possibility of direct combat service.

DEFENSE EXPENDITURES

U.S. defense budgets plummeted after 1945, reflecting a general optimism about peace, the U.S. nuclear monopoly, and President Truman's desire to fund his "Fair Deal" social programs. From a high of $45 billion in fiscal year 1946, defense spending fell to a postwar low of $11.25 billion in fiscal year 1948. Budgets increased somewhat toward the end of the decade with the adoption of a containment strategy toward the Soviet Union, the Soviet atomic bomb, and obvious deficiencies in the national security forces, but fiscal year 1950 defense outlays were still only $14.4 billion (about 4.4 percent of the gross national product and 27 percent of total federal outlays). The recommendations of NSC-68, and more importantly the Korean War, precipitated significantly increased defense spending in the early 1950s; in fiscal year 1953, defense outlays reached a Korean War peak of $43.4 billion (11.9 percent of the gross national product).

Post-Korean War defense budgets rose, fueled by the high cost of nuclear deterrence. In fiscal year 1949, defense outlays were more than $41 billion, most of which was for sophisticated air and missile systems to carry out and defend against nuclear attack. The supposed "missile gap" of the late 1950s and the Kennedy administration's policy of flexible response initiated increased spending on both nuclear and conventional forces. In fiscal year 1961, the Department of Defense spent $43.3 billion (about half the total federal budget, or about 10 percent of the gross national product). A five-year cost-reduction program initiated by Sec. of Defense Robert S. McNamara in 1962 was stymied by the demands of the 10-year war in Vietnam. Department of Defense outlays in fiscal year 1965 were $45.9 billion (about 6.8 percent of the gross national product); in fiscal year 1970, they amounted to $77.1 billion (about 8.3 percent of the gross national product).

The end of the Vietnam War did not bring significant reductions in defense outlays, which reached $132.8 billion by fiscal year 1980. Defense spending increased substantially during the eight years of the Reagan presidency, with outlays rising from $156.2 billion in fiscal year 1981 to $294.9 billion in fiscal year 1989. However, the changed strategic situation arising from the disintegration of the Soviet Union allowed the Bush administration to reduce defense spending. Fiscal year 1991 defense outlays were $287.5 billion, and plans called for a decline in defense spending of about 3 percent per year through fiscal year 1996. Defense outlays were expected to represent only 3.6 percent of the gross national product in fiscal year 1996 (18 percent of total federal outlays), the lowest level since Pearl Harbor (December 1941).

DEPARTMENT OF DEFENSE

After World War II, it became obvious that some restructuring of the American armed forces would be necessary to provide greater unity and coordination of national security. The army and the already semi-independent air force both supported a thorough unification of the armed forces under a single civilian head and a single military chief of staff, but the navy was strongly opposed to such unification. Navy leaders feared the loss of naval aviation to the air force and the loss of the Marine Corps to the army and thus preferred three coordinated services rather than a single military establishment. After much debate and several high-level studies, a compromise was reached, and it was agreed that the national security establishment should consist of three separate military services that would be coordinated but not unified. In 1946, both the Senate and the House of Representatives merged their military and naval committees to form armed services committees in both houses. The following year, Congress enacted legislation implementing the compromise unification proposal in the National Security Act of 1947, which remains the basis for the current U.S. defense establishment.

The National Security Act of 1947 made the air force a separate and equal service and gave each of the military departments its own cabinet-level civilian secretary with direct access to the president and a seat on the new National Security Council (NSC). The services, comprising what was called the National Military Establishment, were to be coordinated by a secretary of defense who would act as the principal assistant to the president on all national security matters. The NSC—composed of the president, the secretaries of state and defense, the three service secretaries, and the heads of other government agencies appointed by the president—was established to develop and coordinate diplomatic, military, and industrial policies and plans, to recommend integrated national security policy to the president, and to guide the execution of that policy. The act also created the Central Intelligence Agency and continued several other agencies with defense-wide responsibilities.

Although the positions of naval aviation and the Marine Corps within the Department of the Navy were explicitly recognized, the roles and missions of the armed services were not clearly spelled out by the 1947 act. In meetings in March 1948 at Key West, Florida, and Newport, Rhode Island, the secretary of defense and the Joint Chiefs of Staff (JCS) agreed to specific primary and peripheral roles for each of the services. The so-called Key West Agreement was subsequently revised by Department of Defense Reorganization Plan No. 6 in October 1952, but the roles and missions of the services remained essentially unchanged.

Defense Department Organization

A principal weakness of the 1947 National Security Act had been its failure to provide the secretary of defense with a staff and the sufficient means for effectively coordinating the military departments. Consequently, the act was amended in 1949 to enhance the powers of the secretary of defense and to add a deputy secretary of defense. The 1949 amendments also redesignated the National Military Establishment as the Department of Defense (DOD), deprived the military departments of their status as executive departments, and subordinated them to the DOD. The service secretaries thus lost their seats on the NSC as well as their direct access to the president. The powers of the secretary of defense and the roles of the service secretaries were further clarified by the DOD reorganization acts of 1958 and 1986. The 1986 act imposed reductions in the overall number of personnel assigned to the service staffs and required greater integration of the services' civilian and military staffs in certain key areas.

As currently constituted, the DOD is responsible for supporting and defending the United States against all enemies, foreign and domestic; for ensuring, by timely and effective military action, the security of the United States, its possessions, and areas vital to its interests; and for protecting and advancing the national policies and interests of the United States. The civilian secretary of defense is appointed by and reports to the president and is confirmed

by the Senate. He or she is assisted by a deputy secretary, two undersecretaries, a number of assistant secretaries, and other staff officers. The DOD includes the Office of the Secretary of Defense, the DOD inspector general, the organization of the JCS, the unified commands, the four military services (army, navy, marines, and air force), the Coast Guard (only in time of war), 13 defense agencies (notably the Defense Intelligence Agency, the National Security Agency, and the Defense Logistics Agency), and 7 DOD field agencies. In the early 1990s, the DOD controlled about 2,000,000 active duty military personnel, more than 1,600,000 National Guard and reserve personnel, and 1,000,000 civilian employees serving at more than 1,250 major military installations worldwide, including some 870 installations in the United States, 375 installations in 21 foreign countries, and 20 installations in U.S. territories and possessions.

Joint Chiefs of Staff

The role of the JCS was formally recognized in the 1947 National Security Act, which provided that the Joint Chiefs were to be the principal military advisers to the president, the NSC, and the secretary of defense. The Joint Chiefs were also charged with formulating joint plans, establishing unified commands in various areas, and providing those commands with strategic direction. The 1949 amendments added a nonvoting chairman and increased the joint staff from 100 to 210.

The National Security Act of 1947 confirmed the place of the JCS in the operational chain of command, but in 1952, DOD Reorganization Plan No. 6 removed the JCS from the operational chain in favor of a system whereby the secretary of defense, with the advice of the JCS, would appoint one of the military departments to be the executive agent for a particular task. However, the 1958 DOD Reorganization Act eliminated the executive agent system and provided for the assignment of all operational forces to unified or specified commands. The 1958 reorganization marked the end of any direct role in the conduct of military operations by the military services. Henceforth, the operational chain of command for military forces would flow from the president through the secretary of defense and the JCS directly to the various specified and unified commands. The military departments would continue to recruit, train, and equip military forces for assignment to the specified and unified commands but would not control such forces operationally. The 1958 act also gave the chairman of the JCS a vote and again increased the size of the joint staff, from 210 to 400.

Major changes in the organization of the JCS were included in the Goldwater-Nichols DOD Reorganization Act of 1986. The JCS chairman was designated as the principal military adviser to the president and secretary of defense, the position of vice chairman of the JCS was created, the role of the JCS in the formulation of strategy and contingency planning was strengthened, and the joint staff was limited to 1,627 military and civilian personnel while the importance of joint assignments in officer personnel management and promotions was enhanced.

Specified and Unified Commands

A specified command is an operational command composed of forces from a single service with a continuing functional mission. Until 1991, there were two specified commands: the U.S. Army Forces Command, for the land defense of the United States, and the Strategic Air Command (SAC), for conducting strategic nuclear warfare. The SAC was subsequently dissolved.

Unified commands are operational commands under a single commander with a broad continuing mission and are composed of forces from two or more services. At present, there are eight major unified commands. Three are functionally oriented, and five are based on general geographical areas. All have subordinate army, navy, and air force component commands and some control subordinate unified commands. The three functional unified commands are Special Operations Command, Transportation Command, and Space Command. Atlantic Command controls three subordinate unified commands (Iceland Defense Forces, U.S. Forces Azores, and Special Operations Command Atlantic). Pacific Command oversees four subordinate unified commands (Alaskan Command, U.S. Forces Japan, U.S. Forces Korea, and Special Operations Command Pacific). European Command oversees one subordinate unified command (Special Operations Command Europe). The Central Command is responsible for Africa and the Middle East and controls one subordinate unified command (Special Operations Command Central). The Southern Command is responsible for the Caribbean and Latin America.

To meet the needs of U.S. strategy, major elements of military forces are deployed overseas under direction of the unified commands. For example, as of 1990, there were 319,020 U.S. military personnel under the control of European Command. The Pacific Command is by far the largest of the unified commands. As of March 1991, some 383,000 active duty military personnel (nearly 17 percent of the total) were assigned to the Pacific Command, which was responsible for a territory of more than 100,000,000 square miles covering 40 countries and 8 American territories—nearly one half the earth's surface.

ARMY

The army has always been "organized, trained, and equipped primarily for prompt and sustained combat incident to operations on land." Today, the emerging new

strategy of power projection assigns the army five principal roles: (1) maintenance of combat-ready land forces for power projection in response to crises, (2) maintenance of a forward presence in areas of vital interest by permanent stationing overseas of some units and periodic deployment of forces from the continental United States (CONUS) and other bases, (3) maintenance in CONUS of forces to reinforce forward deployed and contingency forces, (4) support to civil authorities, including such activities as disaster relief, emergency assistance, and the interdiction of drugs, and (5) support to allied and friendly nations through peacekeeping, nation-building, and security assistance.

Organization

Following World War II, an attempt was made to restore the army's command and control structure to its prewar size and distribution of power. The powerful Operations Division was eliminated, and the General Staff was reformed with five co-equal divisions. These changes were formally incorporated in the Army Reorganization Act of 1950, which eliminated or revised legislation going as far back as 1812. The act also broadened the authority of the secretary of the army, especially with respect to the chief of staff, whose role in supervising army personnel and units, preparing operational plans, and insuring combat readiness was clarified.

The secretary of the army also received authority in 1950 to determine the number and strength of army combat arms and services. The infantry was retained as the premier combat arm; the field artillery, coast artillery, and antiaircraft artillery were consolidated into one artillery branch; and the armor branch was created as a continuation of cavalry. The Transportation Corps and the Military Police Corps were made permanent, and all medical activities (the Medical, Dental, Army Nurse, Veterinary, Medical Service, and Medical Specialist corps) were consolidated under the Army Medical Service. The resulting lineup of 14 services/branches included the Army Medical Service and the Corps of Engineers, as well as the Adjutant General, Chaplain, Chemical, Signal, Transportation, Quartermaster, Ordnance, Military Police, Finance, Inspector General, Judge Advocate General, and Women's Army corps. In 1971, the Artillery Corps was redivided to form separate field artillery and air defense artillery branches. A Military Intelligence Corps was created in 1962, and a separate Army Air Corps was revived in 1983.

Minor evolutionary changes followed the Korean War, but beginning in 1962, the U.S. Army underwent its most important reorganization since World War II. Perhaps the most striking change was the elimination of the chiefs of the various technical services (the old "bureau chiefs") and the consolidation of their functions under separate field commands. The quartermaster general, the chief of the

Chemical Corps, and the chief of ordnance were eliminated outright. The adjutant general, the chief of finance, the chief of transportation, and the chief signal officer were retained as special staff officers. The position of chief of engineers retained its special status with respect to civil works functions, but only the role of surgeon general emerged unchanged. In 1974, the army staff was reduced by 50 percent, and the most recent restructuring of the army staff resulting from the DOD Reorganization Act of 1986 limited the total number of military and civilian personnel in the Office of the Secretary of the Army and on the army staff to fewer than 3,105. The Goldwater-Nichols Act also called for full integration of certain administrative, financial, and information management functions and led to the merger of various army staff offices with their counterparts in the Office of the Secretary of the Army.

As presently constituted, the Department of the Army consists of the Office of the Secretary of the Army, the Office of the Chief of Staff of the Army, army operating forces assigned to the various unified and specified commands, the National Guard and army reserve, the major army commands, and personnel assigned to joint staffs and other government agencies. At the top of the army's management structure is the civilian secretary of the army. Appointed by the president and confirmed by the Senate, he or she directs and supervises the activities of the army but does not exercise operational control of forces. The secretary of the army reports to the president through the secretary of defense and exercises his or her authority through an undersecretary, a deputy undersecretary, five assistant secretaries (civil works, manpower and reserve affairs, acquisition, installations and logistics, and financial management), a number of other civilian assistants, and the chief of staff of the army.

The chief of staff of the army is the senior uniformed officer of the army and is responsible for its efficiency and readiness. He or she is appointed for a term of four years by the president through the secretary of defense and is confirmed by the Senate. The army chief of staff is a member of the JCS and serves as an adviser to the president, the NSC, the secretary of defense, and the secretary of the army. He or she exercises his or her authority through a vice chief of staff, a director of the army staff, and four deputy chiefs of staff (intelligence, personnel, operations and plans, and logistics). The army staff (Office of the Chief of Staff of the Army) also includes the chief of chaplains, the judge advocate general, the chief of engineers, the surgeon general, the chief of the army reserve, and the chief of the National Guard Bureau.

Major Commands
The Marshall reorganization of 1942 created three major army elements: Army Air Forces (AAF), Army Ground Forces (AGF), and Army Service Forces (ASF). The AAF became an independent service in 1947. ASF was abolished in 1946 and the chiefs of the technical services regained their prewar status as departmental agencies. With the elimination of the technical service chiefs in 1962, a new Army Matériel Command became responsible for research and development, production, and distribution of army supplies, equipment, and services and assumed the command and operational functions formerly held by the chiefs of the technical services.

In 1948, the AGF was redesignated as Army Field Forces (AFF), which in 1950 was assigned responsibility for determining tactical doctrine, controlling the army school system, and supervising army field training. In 1955, the AFF was replaced by the Continental Army Command (CONARC), which was given responsibility for the six continental army areas (which in 1946 had replaced the service commands established in 1942) and the Military District of Washington. CONARC also assumed responsibility for the training of active army and reserve components, planning for the development of the future army and its equipment, and planning and conducting the ground defense of the United States. In the 1962 reorganization, CONARC retained responsibility for training, schools, and unit readiness, but the development of doctrine and equipment was assigned to a new Combat Developments Command.

Sweeping reorganization came in 1972 with the STEADFAST program. CONARC was formally disestablished on Dec. 31, 1973, and its functions were assumed by two new major command headquarters. The new Forces Command (FORSCOM) assumed control of all operational units in the continental United States, as well as responsibility for the readiness of the National Guard and army reserve. The new Training and Doctrine Command (TRADOC) assumed CONARC's responsibility for army schools and also took over the doctrinal development responsibilities of the Combat Developments Command, which was disestablished. TRADOC also took control of the Reserve Officers Training Corps program.

At present, there are four continental army areas, and most army activities are supervised by one of nine major commands: Forces Command, Training and Doctrine Command, Army Matériel Command, Special Operations Command, Intelligence and Security Command, Health Services Command, Information Systems Command, the Corps of Engineers, and the Military District of Washington. Army forces operate overseas as the army component of the unified commands in Europe, the Pacific, Korea, the Caribbean, and the Atlantic. Each of the functional unified commands also has a major army command as a subordinate component. For example, the Military Traffic Management Command is the army component of the U.S. Transportation Command.

Major Active Forces

Although the army's post-World War II goal was a ground and air strength of 1,500,000 men and a reserve structure capable of mobilizing 4,000,000 men in one year, by June 1947, the army had declined to just 684,000 ground troops and 306,000 airmen. By mid-1950, the army had shrunk to only 591,000 officers and men in 10 understrength, skeletonized divisions; 5 regimental combat teams; and a constabulary in Germany. However, with the onset of the Korean War in June 1950, the army rapidly expanded to a peak strength in 1952 of 148,427 officers and 1,447,992 enlisted personnel, including reserve and National Guard personnel called to active duty. During the war, the total number of active divisions rose from 10 to 20, of which only 8 actually served in Korea (but only 6 at any one time). The peak army strength in Korea itself never exceeded 275,000.

Following the Korean War, the reliance on a strategy of massive retaliation emphasizing air power and nuclear weapons led to a reduction in army strength. By 1960, the army had only 870,000 officers and men in 14 divisions. However, under the strategy of flexible response, army strength increased. By 1962, the army had 116,050 officers and 950,354 enlisted personnel and had added 2 active divisions for a total of 16. Even greater expansion followed in the late 1960s to meet the needs of the war in Vietnam. A peak strength was reached in 1968 with 166,173 officers and 1,404,170 enlisted personnel in 19 divisions. Army strength in Vietnam itself peaked at 365,000 officers and soldiers before the program of Vietnamization and U.S. withdrawal began in 1969.

After 1969, army strength and division totals declined sharply to an authorized 785,000 personnel and 13 active divisions in 1973, the lowest level since 1950. In 1974, the army initiated a program to create 3 additional active divisions (for a total of 16) by cutting combat support forces and eliminating headquarters. The 16-division program also called for the National Guard and army reserve to provide "round-out" brigades for the active divisions and thereby further reduced active manpower requirements. By 1980, army strength had fallen to 83,117 officers and 666,425 enlisted personnel, and it hovered around 780,000 officers and enlisted personnel for most of the 1980s, even though the Reagan administration increased the number of divisions to 18 in the active army and 10 in the reserve components.

In 1991, the army consisted of 761,100 active-duty military personnel (including 86,500 women), 1,043,000 National Guard and army reserve personnel (including 132,800 women), and 440,000 civilian employees. Active army combat forces included 7 army and 6 corps headquarters; 18 divisions (4 armored, 6 mechanized infantry, 1 motorized infantry, 1 infantry, 4 light infantry, 1 air assault, and 1 airborne); 5 separate brigades (2 armored, 1 infantry, and 2 infantry-theater defense); 3 armored cavalry regiments; 9 aviation brigades; 9 artillery brigades; 1 theater air defense command; 8 Hawk surface-to-air missile battalions; and 14 surface-to-surface missile battalions, most of which were being phased out.

Significant reductions in both the number of personnel and the number of active divisions were planned in the 1990s. Army forces were to be reduced from 5 corps and 28 active and National Guard divisions in 1991 to 4 corps and 20 divisions by 1996. During the same period, army personnel strength was to drop by more than 400,000 soldiers and the army's civilian work force would be reduced by about 25 percent. The 4-corps/20-division army of 1996 would have 12 active divisions (7 armored, 4 light, and 1 infantry), 6 National Guard divisions (5 armored and 1 light), and 2 cadre divisions (both armored). The cadre divisions would be composed of some 3,000 trained officers and noncommissioned officers versus the 10,000 men in a full division and would be available 12–15 months after mobilization. Four of the active divisions would be forward-deployed (2 in Europe and 2 in the Pacific).

Reserve Forces

After World War II, the United States faced for the first time the possibility of a massive engagement without a period of mobilization. That situation led to the policy of forward deployment of regular forces supported by a rapid mobilization of the National Guard, the Organized Reserve Corps, and, if necessary, a new national army. But by mid-1950, there were only 325,000 personnel in 27 understrength National Guard divisions and only 186,000 more in the Organized Reserve Corps. During the Korean War, Congress imposed a "military obligation" of eight years combined active and reserve duty on all physically and mentally fit males between the ages of 18½ and 26. The Reserve Forces Act of 1955 subsequently reduced the obligation to six years.

In 1952, the Organized Reserve Corps was renamed the U.S. Army Reserve; in 1957, the number of army reserve divisions was cut from 25 to 10. Pres. Dwight D. Eisenhower sought additional cuts in reserve strength to save money, but in 1959, Congress mandated a strength of 700,000 for the army reserve. The reserve forces were also then divided into a ready reserve that could be ordered to active duty by the president and a standby reserve that could be called up only after a congressional declaration of war or national emergency.

The Berlin Crisis and reserve call-up in 1961 demonstrated that the reserve components were not up to par, and in the early 1960s, Secretary of Defense McNamara initiated a thorough revision of the reserve system, including large cuts in the army reserve. His program was actively opposed by Congress, the states, and the various guard and reserve associations, but he ultimately succeeded in reducing the National Guard by four divisions and in eliminating all the army reserve divisions. He actually wished to eliminate organized units in the army reserve altogether but was forced to compromise. In 1965, the selected reserve forces were established consisting of more than 150,000 personnel (119,000 National Guard and 31,000 army reserve) organized into nine National Guard divisions and backup units from the army reserve. Three divisions and six separate brigades were to be maintained at 100 percent strength and were to receive extra training and priority on equipment. After 1967, the units remaining in the army reserve were primarily training, combat support, and combat service support organizations.

As of 1990, there were some 1,043,000 men and women in the National Guard and army reserve. The Army National Guard included 454,600 officers and soldiers (including 30,400 women) organized in 10 divisions, 20 independent brigades, 2 armored cavalry regiments, 1 infantry group (arctic reconnaissance), 20 field artillery brigade headquarters, and more than 135 independent battalions. The army reserve included 588,400 officers and soldiers (including 102,400 women) in the units of the selected ready reserve and in the individual ready reserve, 600 standby reservists, and another 87,300 trained officers and enlisted personnel in the retired reserve. The selected ready reserve was organized in 12 training divisions, 3 training brigades, 3 independent brigades, 3 artillery brigade headquarters, and 74 independent battalions.

Some 228,561 reservists were mobilized for the 1991 Gulf War, and 105,000 actually served in the Gulf. In recent years, about $17 billion of an annual $300 billion defense budget has been dedicated to maintenance of the reserve components. Current plans call for the National Guard and reserve to be cut by 24 percent by 1996, despite strong opposition in Congress and among the members of the reserve components.

Tactical Doctrine and Organization

The army fought the Korean War with much the same tactical doctrine it had employed so successfully in World War II, but after 1953, army doctrine was revised to meet the requirements of a nuclear battlefield, and rapid movement and independent action were emphasized. The Vietnam War posed unique doctrinal challenges that were met by an emphasis on air mobility, counterinsurgency techniques, the use of unconventional forces, and other ad hoc solutions. Doctrinal development in the post-Vietnam period was dominated by the presumed requirement to fight heavily armored Soviet forces in Europe. Accordingly, the emphasis shifted to heavy armored forces well supported by artillery, antitank weapons, and tactical air power with tactical nuclear weapons as a final resort. The current army war-fighting doctrine, developed in the 1980s, is known as "AirLand Battle" and emphasizes the joint and combined

nature of modern war and the need for careful integration of all of the elements of combat power. AirLand Battle, which proved exceptionally effective in the 1991 Gulf War, has as its cardinal principles initiative, agility, synchronization, and depth.

The World War II triangular infantry division underwent some modification in the immediate postwar period. Organic tank and antiaircraft artillery battalions were added, and field artillery batteries were increased from four to six guns. At the regimental level, the cannon and antitank companies were dropped and a tank company, a 4.2-inch mortar company, and 57-millimeter and 75-millimeter recoilless rifle companies were added. Economy drives in the late 1940s forced the army to skeletonize its units, and 9 of the 10 divisions were far understrength. Infantry regiments typically had only 2 of their 3 battalions, and most artillery battalions had only 2 of their 3 firing batteries. Organic armor was generally lacking. Such divisions were brought up to full combat strength of about 17,000 men during the Korean War.

After the Korean War, the army turned its attention to creating tactical organizations suitable for both the nuclear and the nonnuclear battlefield. Such organizations needed to be highly mobile in order to assemble and disperse quickly, required their own tactical nuclear capability, and required that the division's major subordinate elements be able to act independently. The result was the so-called pentomic division in which the three infantry regiments of the triangular division were replaced by five "battle groups" reinforced with artillery and armor support. The typical pentomic division had 13,500 officers and enlisted personnel (rather than 17,000 for the old triangular division). Armored personnel carriers and tactical nuclear weapons were introduced, and the division's fixed and rotary wing aviation assets were increased. Conversion of the army's triangular infantry and airborne divisions began in 1956 and was completed by 1960.

In practice, the pentomic division proved unwieldy and difficult to command. The battle groups also lacked sufficient staying power for truly independent operations. Moreover, the shift from a strategy of massive retaliation to one of flexible response in the early 1960s seemed to require a division structure capable of being tailored to the varied missions it might receive. The need was met by the reorganization objectives army division (ROAD), consisting of three brigade headquarters and a common division base of command and control, artillery, combat support, and combat service support elements. The division base normally consisted of a division headquarters and headquarters company, a military police company, a reconnaissance squadron, 4 field artillery battalions, and engineer, signal, medical, maintenance, and supply and transport battalions. The brigade headquarters were designed to control a variable number of types of combat battalions (infantry, mechanized infantry, armor, airborne infantry). Although, theoretically, the ROAD division might control as many as 15 maneuver battalions, the normal ROAD infantry division had 8 infantry and 2 armor battalions, with a total of nearly 16,000 officers and men. Four types of ROAD divisions (infantry, mechanized, airborne, and armored) were authorized, and conversion of all active and reserve component divisions began in 1962 and was completed in mid-1964.

One new type of division came to prominence during the Vietnam War. The Korean War and the concept of the nuclear battlefield had increased interest in the use of helicopters to improve tactical mobility, and in February 1963, the 11th Air Assault Division was created to test tactics and equipment for a highly mobile infantry division using helicopters in significant numbers for troop and supply transport as well as for combat assault. The tests led directly to the creation of the 1st Cavalry Division (Airmobile) in July 1965 and that unit's immediate deployment to Vietnam, where it served with some success as the first division organized from the ground up according to airmobile doctrine. The 1st Cavalry Division (Airmobile) was authorized 15,787 officers and men, 1,600 ground vehicles (half the normal ROAD infantry division complement), and 428 helicopters. Lighter supporting weapons were provided, and the general support field artillery battalion was replaced with an aerial rocket artillery battalion (rocket-firing helicopters). Other divisions in Vietnam, organized under a modified ROAD format, were heavily reinforced with helicopters and also employed the airmobile doctrine. The airmobile concept, spurred by the Vietnam War, led to increased emphasis on army helicopters, and the number of army helicopters increased from 2,700 in 1960 to 7,000 by mid-1967.

In 1976, army planners began development of a new division structure for the 1980–85 period with the emphasis on heavy armored formations suitable for facing a potential Soviet conventional attack in Western Europe. The resulting division structure, called Division 86, proved far too large and too heavy in the light of subsequent assessments of the improbability of a full-scale Soviet onslaught in Europe. Attention then turned to the creation of lighter, more flexible, and more maneuverable forces that were capable of being transported rapidly from the United States to global trouble spots. The "Army of Excellence" study initiated in late 1983 examined several lighter division formats capable of rapid deployment and highly mobile operations in a variety of terrains. Armored, mechanized infantry, light infantry, airborne infantry, motorized infantry, and air assault variants were developed with the heavier versions (armored and mechanized) consisting of 10 maneuver battalions and the lighter versions consisting of 9 maneuver battalions. The new, lighter, and more flexible

A member of the 1st Cavalry Division (Airmobile), a division created to increase the military's mobility, records on his helmet the days served and the days remaining of his tour of duty in Vietnam. (National Archives)

combat elements were supplemented with a variety of updated combat and combat service support units. Increased aviation, air defense, and chemical capabilities as well as new methods of providing logistical support were introduced, along with a variety of new weapons systems designed to maximize the new division's mobility and firepower.

Under current doctrine, the typical division consists of a division headquarters, 3 brigade headquarters (including 1 reserve component round-out brigade), a mix of 9–10 maneuver battalions (tank, mechanized, infantry, light infantry, airborne, or air assault), 3 artillery battalions, 1 multiple-launch rocket system (MLRS) battery, 1 air defense battalion, 1 aviation brigade, and a variety of combat support and combat service support units. Independent combat brigades normally have a mix of 3 maneuver battalions (tank, mechanized infantry, or infantry) and 1 supporting artillery battalion. Such formations proved themselves well in the lightning war in the deserts of Iraq and Kuwait in the 1991 Gulf War, thereby vindicating the concepts advanced by their creators.

NAVY

The principal role of the Department of the Navy is to "organize, train, and equip Navy and Marine Corps forces to conduct prompt and sustained combat operations at sea, including operations of sea-based aircraft and land-based naval air components." Naval forces seek out and destroy enemy naval forces and suppress enemy sea commerce, gain and maintain naval supremacy, control vital sea areas, protect vital sea lines of communications, establish and maintain local superiority (including air superiority) in an area of naval operations, seize and defend advanced naval bases, and conduct such land and air operations as may be essential to the prosecution of naval campaigns.

Organization

As presently constituted, the Department of the Navy consists of the Office of the Secretary of the Navy; the Office of the Chief of Naval Operations; Headquarters, U.S. Marine Corps; Headquarters, U.S. Coast Guard (in wartime only); the Bureau of Naval Personnel; the naval reserve components; naval operating forces assigned to the various unified and specified commands; forces assigned to the naval shore establishment; and naval personnel assigned to joint staffs and other government agencies. At the top of the navy's management structure is the civilian secretary of the navy. Appointed by the president and confirmed by the Senate, the navy secretary directs and supervises the activities of the navy and Marine Corps (and the Coast Guard in time of war) but does not exercise operational control of forces. He or she reports to the president through the secretary of defense and exercises his or her authority through an undersecretary, a number of other civilian assistants, and the chief of naval operations (CNO).

The CNO is the senior uniformed officer of the navy and is responsible for its efficiency and readiness. He or she is appointed for a term of four years by the president through the secretary of defense and is confirmed by the Senate. The CNO is a member of the JCS and serves as an adviser to the president, the NSC, the secretary of defense, and the secretary of the navy. Since 1960, the CNO has been responsible for the operations as well as the logistical support and administration of naval forces. He or she commands the operating forces of the navy and the naval shore establishment consistent with their assignments to unified and specified commands. The CNO exercises his or her authority through a vice chief of naval operations, four deputy chiefs of naval operations (manpower, personnel, and training; program planning; logistics; and plans, policy, and operations), and three assistant chiefs of naval operations (air warfare, surface warfare, and submarine warfare). The Office of the CNO also includes the Offices

of Naval Intelligence; the Surgeon General; Space, Command, and Control; the Naval Reserve; the Oceanographer; the Chief of Chaplains; Research and Development Requirements; and Test and Evaluation.

Major Commands

There are presently two types of major naval commands: operating forces consisting of combat and support forces assigned to unified or specified commands, and shore establishments under the direct control of the Department of the Navy. As of 1990, the major naval operating forces included the Atlantic and Pacific Fleets, the Military Sealift Command, the Mine Warfare Command, the Naval Reserve Force, the Naval Special Warfare Command, the Operational Test and Evaluation Force, U.S. Naval Forces Europe, U.S. Naval Forces Central Command, and U.S. Naval Forces Southern Command. The principal elements of the naval shore establishment include the Chief of Naval Education and Training, the Naval District of Washington, and Naval Air Systems, Data Automation, Facilities Engineering, Investigative Service, Medical, Intelligence, Military Personnel, Sea Systems, Oceanography, Security Group, Space Command, Supply Systems, Telecommunications, and Space and Naval Warfare Systems commands.

Major Active Forces

The navy ended World War II with 3,400,000 personnel, 1,194 major combat ships, 1,256 amphibious transports, and more than 41,000 aircraft. The navy's postwar program called for a navy reduced to 300,000 officers and enlisted personnel, 370 combat ships, 5,000 other ships, and 8,000 aircraft, but in 1948, there were only 267 major combat ships in the active fleet. By June 1950, the navy's personnel complement had fallen to 380,000 officers and sailors. In the first year of the Korean War, navy personnel strength rose to 730,000 and 300 ships were taken out of mothballs to bring the fleet to around 1,100 vessels of all types. In the mid-1950s, the navy maintained 377,000 officers and sailors, 670 active ships, and around 6,700 aircraft. Although the navy's personnel strength hovered around 600,000 through the 1960s and 1970s, the number of active combat vessels fell steadily.

At the end of fiscal year 1981, the navy had only 12 carriers, 196 surface combat vessels, 41 nuclear ballistic missile submarines, 91 attack submarines, and 66 amphibious ships. A major defense goal of the Reagan administration was to rebuild the navy to 600 ships. The Reagan plan called for 20 to 40 strategic ballistic missile submarines, 15 deployable carrier battle groups, 4 battle groups centered around renovated battleships, 100 nuclear attack submarines, 100 antisubmarine warfare ships, 7 convoy escort groups, 14 mine countermeasures ships, and sufficient am-

LVTs (landing vehicles, tracked) from larger naval vessels bring military troops ashore during a 1960s readiness exercise off the coast of Barrier Island in the South China Sea. (U.S. Navy)

phibious shipping to lift the assault echelons of a marine expeditionary force (MEF), and a marine expeditionary brigade (MEB) simultaneously. By the end of 1988, the navy had 588 of the planned 600 ships. The Bush administration subsequently revised the goal downward to 546 battle-force ships by the end of fiscal year 1991, and further cuts were projected.

In 1990, the navy consisted of 590,000 active-duty naval personnel (including 50,000 women), 240,000 naval reserve personnel, and 360,000 civilian employees organized in four principal fleets (the 2d Fleet in the Atlantic, the 3d in the Pacific, the 6th in the Mediterranean, and the 7th in the Western Pacific). Active strategic naval forces included 624 sea-launched ballistic missiles in 34 SSBN ("strategic submarine ballistic nuclear") nuclear-power ballistic missile submarines. The navy also operated 91 submarines in tactical roles and 2 in other roles. Principal surface combat vessels numbered 220, including the following: 14 aircraft carriers and 13 carrier air wings (each wing had about 86 aircraft); 4 Iowa class battleships equipped with 16-inch guns, Tomahawk sea-launched cruise missiles, and Harpoon surface-to-surface missiles; 43 cruisers; 59 destroyers; and 100 frigates. In addition, the navy operated 30 patrol and coastal combat ships and 29 mine countermeasures vessels. There were also 65 amphibious ships and numerous small landing craft. Strategic sealift was provided by the Military Sealift Command, with 69 active vessels. The 141 support and miscellaneous mission vessels included 56 underway support ships, 41 maintenance and logistics ships, 24 special purpose ships, and 20 survey and research vessels.

Naval aviation assets in 1990 included 120,000 personnel, 1,554 combat aircraft, and 372 helicopters organized into 26 fighter squadrons (4 in the naval reserve); 47 ground attack fighter squadrons (6 in the reserve); 2 electronic intelligence squadrons; 14 electronic countermeasures squadrons (1 in the reserve); 37 land-based maritime reconnaissance squadrons (13 in the reserve); 12 antisubmarine warfare squadrons; 15 airborne early warning squadrons (2 in the reserve); 1 command and control squadron; 5 "Aggressor" training squadrons and 17 training squadrons; and 14 other support squadrons with a variety of mission and support aircraft. Navy helicopter assets included 36 antisubmarine warfare squadrons, 4 mine countermeasures squadrons, 6 miscellaneous support squadrons, and 2 training squadrons.

Reserve Forces

Naval reserve forces in 1990 included 238,100 officers and enlisted personnel in selected reserve units and the individual ready reserve, 10,900 in the standby reserve, and another 28,800 in the retired reserve. Naval reserve surface forces included 50 ships (18 guided missile frigates, 10 frigates, 16 mine countermeasures vessels, 3 amphibious ships, and 3 support/miscellaneous ships), 217 combat aircraft, and 58 armed helicopters.

Further augmentation of the navy is provided by the Coast Guard in wartime and by some 242 reserve strategic sealift vessels, of which 93 are in the ready reserve force, available in 5–20 days. Another 149 ships of questionable seaworthiness are in the National Defense Reserve Fleet. In an emergency, more than 300 ships may be taken up from trade to supplement strategic sealift forces.

Tactical Doctrine and Organization

Since World War II, navy tactical doctrine has focused on the employment of task forces, or battle groups, centered around aircraft carriers or other major surface vessels such as the four battleships renovated and recommissioned in the 1980s. A carrier battle group, for example, might include an aircraft carrier and several cruisers, destroyers, frigates, and submarines for antisubmarine, surface, and air defense of the carrier plus a variety of support ships such as oilers and replenishment ships. The carrier battle group can conduct independent operations for an extended period and can carry out a variety of missions including show of force, support of landing operations and operations ashore, sea control, air superiority, and antisubmarine operations. A carrier will usually have a carrier air wing.

COAST GUARD

The Coast Guard has been a separate military service operating within the Department of Transportation since 1967. It has both peacetime and wartime missions. In peacetime, the Coast Guard enforces U.S. laws and treaties in coastal waters and on the high seas under U.S. jurisdiction. This includes enforcement of U.S. customs laws, the suppression of illegal drug trafficking, control of illegal immigration, enforcement of fisheries laws, and enforcement of the 200-mile economic zone. The Coast Guard also insures the safety of recreational boating, the merchant marine, ports, and the coastal environment; conducts search and rescue operations; and operates 400 lighthouses and 13,000 navigational lights. In time of war, the operational direction of the Coast Guard is assumed by the navy, and the Coast Guard performs additional missions such as U.S. coastal defense, convoy escort, and increased civil maritime control.

Organization

In peacetime, the secretary of transportation is responsible for direction of the Coast Guard and for its readiness to perform its wartime mission. The secretary of transportation, or, in wartime, the secretary of the navy through the CNO, exercises his or her authority through the commandant of the Coast Guard, the service's senior uniformed officer. The commandant—appointed for a term of four years by the president through the secretary of defense and confirmed by the Senate—is responsible for the organization, training, and equipment of the Coast Guard.

Currently, the Coast Guard is organized with an administrative headquarters in Washington, 2 areas of command (Atlantic Area and Pacific Area, each commanded by a vice admiral), 10 districts (commanded by rear admirals), 7 training schools, and 2 maintenance and logistics commands. In 1984, an agreement between the secretary of the navy and the secretary of transportation provided for the assignment of Coast Guard officers, responsible to the commanders of the U.S. Atlantic and Pacific fleets, to command the newly established U.S. Maritime Defense Zones in times of war or national emergency.

Major Commands

Coast Guard strength is about 6,900 officers and 30,000 enlisted personnel (including approximately 3,000 women). Coast Guard assets include 165 patrol vessels (59 offshore, 106 inshore), 13 support and other vessels (including icebreakers), 78 fixed-wing aircraft, and 134 helicopters. The budget for the Coast Guard is about $3 billion. The Coast Guard Reserve numbers about 18,000 officers and enlisted personnel (12,000 selected reserve, 5,500 ready reserve, and 550 standby reserve), or about one-fourth of the total Coast Guard complement and more than half of all Coast Guard port safety and security forces.

MARINE CORPS

The Marine Corps acts as a force in readiness to seize or defend advanced naval bases and conduct land operations essential to the prosecution of a naval campaign. In addition, the Marine Corps provides embassy guards and security detachments for the protection of naval property at shore stations and bases and performs the traditional shipboard security duties. Since the Vietnam War, marines have also been employed in hostage rescue and peacekeeping roles, as in Somalia from late 1992.

Organization

The U.S. Marine Corps (USMC) survived several attempts in the immediate post-World War II period to disband it or meld it with the army. The Marine Corps Bill of June 28, 1952, confirmed the status of the Marine Corps as a separate service within the Department of the Navy with its own specified roles and missions and not less than three combat divisions and three air wings. As presently constituted, the Marine Corps consists of Headquarters, USMC; Fleet Marine Forces assigned to unified commands in both the Atlantic and the Pacific; the major Marine Corps commands; the Marine Corps Reserve; and marine personnel assigned to U.S. diplomatic missions abroad, navy and

During war, the Coast Guard, normally under the U.S. Department of Transportation, is directed by the U.S. Navy for coastal defense purposes. (U.S. Coast Guard/William C. Bradshaw)

joint staff positions, naval and Marine Corps shore facilities, and other government agencies. The major Marine Corps commands are Fleet Marine Force, Atlantic; Fleet Marine Force, Pacific; Marine Corps Air-Ground Combat Center; Marine Corps Combat Developments Command; and Marine Corps Research, Development, and Acquisition Command.

The commandant of the Marine Corps is the senior uniformed officer of the corps. He or she is appointed for a term of four years by the president through the secretary of defense and is confirmed by the Senate. Since 1978, the commandant has served as a full member of the JCS and as an adviser to the president, the NSC, the secretary of defense, and the secretary of the navy. The Marine Corps commandant is co-equal with the CNO in access to the secretary of the navy and the secretary of defense. He or she reports to the secretary of the navy but is responsible to the CNO for the organization, training, and readiness of those Marine Corps elements assigned to the operating forces of the navy.

In the early 1950s, Commandant Gen. Clifton B. Cates sought to reorganize Headquarters, USMC, along general staff lines. His efforts were stymied by Maj. Gen. William P. T. Hill, the powerful head of the USMC Supply Department, but Cates's successor, Gen. Lemuel C. Shepherd, Jr., was successful in bringing about the desired reorganization in the mid-1950s. In the 1970s, Headquarters, USMC, was reorganized along functional lines. The commandant of the Marine Corps now exercises his or her authority through five deputy chiefs of staff (manpower; installations and logistics; plans, policy, and operations; aviation; and reserve affairs) and three assistant chiefs of staff.

Major Active Forces

In August 1945, the Marine Corps numbered 37,664 officers and 447,389 enlisted marines. Demobilization was rapid and drastic, and by the spring of 1950, Marine Corps strength had declined to 74,279 officers and marines. The two marine divisions and two marine aircraft wings were understrength and had little modern equipment. In response to events in Korea, existing marine forces were brought up to strength, and the 3d Marine Division was formed at Camp Pendleton, California, in January 1952. The Marine Corps reached its peak Korean War strength of 18,731 officers and 230,488 enlisted marines in 1953. A maximum of 35,000 marines served in Korea at any one time.

Post-Korean War Marine Corps strength reached its nadir in 1960 at 16,203 officers and 154,418 marines before expanding again to meet the needs of the Vietnam War. The Marine Corps provided helicopters and advisers in

Vietnam from 1962, and marine combat units were committed in March 1965. In all, some 794,000 Americans served as marines during the Vietnam era. The III Marine Amphibious Force in Vietnam reached its peak strength in 1968 with 85,755 officers and men, including attached navy personnel. Overall Marine Corps strength peaked in 1969 with 25,698 officers and 284,073 enlisted marines, but by 1979, Marine Corps strength had declined again to 18,325 officers and 171,675 enlisted personnel.

As of 1990, the Marine Corps had an active duty strength of 195,300 officers and enlisted marines. Some 10,500 women were serving as marines, including those in the Marine Corps Reserve. Active marine combat forces were organized in 3 divisions, 3 force service support groups, and 2 security force battalions (1 each in the Atlantic and the Pacific). Active-duty Marine Corps aviation assets included 3 marine aircraft wings with some 407 combat aircraft and 72 armed helicopters.

Reserve Forces

In the 1950s, the Marine Corps Reserve was reorganized as the 4th Marine Division and the 4th Marine Aircraft Wing and included some 45,000 officers and enlisted personnel. In 1980, the organized units of the Marine Corps Reserve had a budget strength of only 33,600, and actual strength was slightly less, but by 1990, the corps' individual ready reserve and selected reserve had increased to 80,100. Another 1,400 marines were available in the standby reserve and 5,200 more in the retired reserve. The selected reserve forces were organized as the 4th Marine Division, the Force Service Support Group, and the 4th Marine Aircraft Wing, with 96 combat aircraft and 24 armed helicopters.

Women marines, of whom there were more than 10,000 in the early 1990s, clean airplane parts after Operation Desert Storm. (U.S. Army)

Tactical Doctrine and Organization

Since World War II, the Marine Corps has led the way in developing the concept of vertical envelopment. The use of helicopters to land combat forces behind the front lines, thereby avoiding frontal assault of enemy positions, is particularly well suited to solving the problems of amphibious assault in a nuclear environment, and the Marine Corps has developed effective doctrine and tactics for the use of helicopters in combat. The first helicopter landing of a combat unit was made by marines during the Korean War. In September 1951, 224 marines and 17,772 pounds of cargo were inserted by helicopter into a combat area in just four hours.

Marine Corps combat units are organized into air-ground task forces of varying sizes, each capable of limited independent ground action, including amphibious assault landings, raids, and other tactical operations. The largest of these units is the marine expeditionary force (MEF; formerly called a marine amphibious force, or MAF), which consists of about 52,000 marine and navy personnel and some 50 ships. A MEF is commanded by a lieutenant general and is designed to "command, control, direct, plan, and coordinate air-ground operations of assigned forces." Its basic element is the marine division. The typical marine division has about 16,000 officers and men with a headquarters battalion, 3 marine infantry regiments (each of 3 infantry battalions), an artillery regiment, a tank battalion, a reconnaissance battalion, a combat engineer battalion, and an assault amphibian battalion. A MEF also includes a marine aircraft wing, a force serve support group, and other combat support forces.

The marine expeditionary brigade (MEB; formerly called a marine amphibious brigade, or MAB) is of medium size and consists of about 16,000 marine and navy personnel. Commanded by a major general, the MEB is usually composed of a regimental landing team, a marine aircraft group, and a brigade service support group. It may be deployed to marine prepositioning force ships. The marine expeditionary unit (MEU; formerly the marine amphibious unit, or MAU) is the smallest marine air-ground task force and is approximately of battalion size with about 2,000 marine and navy personnel. Commanded by a colonel, the MEU is usually forward-deployed and consists of a battalion landing team, a composite aviation squadron (with two or more types of helicopters), and a service support group.

The marine aircraft wing (MAW) is the basic air combat organization of the Marine Corps and usually contains a mix of aircraft types and missions. A typical MAW consists of a wing headquarters group, eight marine aircraft groups of various types, a tactical electronic warfare squadron, a tactical reconnaissance squadron, and an aerial refueling transport squadron. The typical MAW is composed of about 14,000 marine and navy personnel and op-

In 1967, marines of the 1st Division, ready for combat, land and exit a helicopter during a typical search-and-destroy mission during the Vietnam War. (National Archives)

erates around 250 tactical fixed-wing aircraft and 190 helicopters. Elements of a MAW may be either shore-based or carrier-based. Marine aircraft groups (MAGs) may be component elements of a MAW or operate independently as the aviation element of a MEB. The size and composition of the MAG varies according to its assigned mission. There are 5 basic types of MAGs: support, air control, fighter attack, helicopter, and training. A MAG is usually composed of 2 or more tactical squadrons plus a headquarters and maintenance squadron and an air-base squadron. Depending on the type of aircraft assigned, a squadron may have between 12 and 24 operational aircraft.

AIR FORCE

The role of the U.S. Air Force (USAF) is to organize, train, and equip forces to conduct prompt and sustained combat operations in the air to defend the United States against air attack; gain and maintain general air supremacy; defeat enemy air forces; conduct space operations; control vital air areas; and establish local air superiority. Specific air force missions include strategic bombardment (using both manned bombers and intercontinental ballistic missiles), air superiority, area air defense, close air sup-

port, ground attack, interdiction, reconnaissance, and airlift, as well as other related activities such as air-sea rescue.

Organization

The independent air force advocated by army aviators from 1917 became a reality in 1947. As currently constituted, the Department of the Air Force consists of the Office of the Secretary of the Air Force, the Office of the Chief of Staff of the Air Force, air force reserve components, air force field activities (including major commands, separate operating agencies, and direct reporting units), and air force personnel assigned to joint staffs and other government agencies. At the top of the air force management structure is the civilian secretary of the air force. Appointed by the president and confirmed by the Senate, the air force secretary directs and supervises the activities of the air force but does not exercise operational control of forces. Hc or she reports to the president through the secretary of defense and exercises his or her authority through an undersecretary, a number of civilian assistants, and the chief of staff of the air force (CSAF).

The CSAF is the senior uniformed officer of the air force and is responsible for its efficiency and readiness. He or she is appointed for a term of four years by the president through the secretary of defense and is confirmed by the Senate. The CSAF is a member of the JCS and serves as an adviser to the president, the NSC, the secretary of defense, and the secretary of the air force. The CSAF exercises authority through a vice chief of staff, an assistant vice chief of staff, four deputy chiefs of staff (personnel, programs and resources, plans and operations, and logistics and engineering), and three assistant chiefs of staff (intelligence, studies and analysis, and information systems). The air staff (Office of the CSAF) also includes the Office of Air Force History, the surgeon general, the judge advocate general, the chief of chaplains, the chief of the air force reserve, and the chief of the National Guard Bureau/director of the Air National Guard.

Major Commands

Headquarters, USAF, controls numerous major functional commands, including the Strategic Air Command (SAC), Tactical Air Command (TAC), Military Airlift Command (MAC), Air Training Command, Air Force Communications Command, Air Force Logistics Command, Air Force Systems Command, Air Force Space Command, Electronic Security Command, Alaskan Air Command, and the Air University. Recent decisions promise the elimination of SAC and TAC and the creation of a new Air Combat Command. Major air force overseas commands assigned to unified commands include Pacific Air Forces (PACAF) and U.S. Air Forces in Europe (USAFE) as well as air force component commands in the other unified commands. Numbered air forces (for example, the 7th Air Force based in Korea) control assigned air force units and activities in a given geographical area or with a specific mission.

Major Active Forces

In 1945, the army air force numbered some 2.3 million men and 72,000 aircraft. Despite its newfound prominence as the nation's principal strategic striking force, the air force fell to 300,000 men and 10,000 planes by mid-1947, when the air force became a separate service. In 1948, both the president's Air Policy Commission (Finletter Commission) and Congress's Air Policy Board recommended an air force of 70 groups with 8,100 modern planes and 401,000 uniformed personnel, but President Truman impounded the necessary funds, and by mid-1950, the 411,277 officers and enlisted personnel of the air force were barely sufficient to maintain 48 active wings. During the Korean War, the air force expanded to 143 combat wings. Peak strength was reached in 1953 with 977,593 officers and enlisted personnel. Under President Eisenhower's "New Look" program in the late 1950s, the air force was reduced to 137 wings (54 strategic bomb wings, 38 tactical fighter wings, 34 air defense wings, and 11

troop carrier wings). Like the other services, the air force expanded to meet the needs of the Vietnam War.

In 1990, the air force included some 3,685 combat aircraft (including those assigned to the Air National Guard and air force reserve), 571,000 active-duty personnel (including 69,000 women), 268,000 personnel in the Air National Guard and air force reserve, and 260,000 civilian employees. Air force strategic formations included 6 strategic missile wings with 1,000 ICBMs (intercontinental ballistic missiles)—450 Minuteman IIs; 500 Minuteman IIIs; and 50 Peacekeeper-MXes—and 2 numbered air forces with 8 air divisions and 16 bomber wings operating some 301 bombers, 61 reconnaissance aircraft, 22 command and control aircraft, and 648 aerial tankers. The air force also operated a number of satellites used for strategic reconnaissance and intelligence collection missions.

The strategic aerospace defense of the United States is directed by the U.S. Space Command (a unified command) and by the North American Aerospace Defense Command (a combined U.S.-Canadian joint command). In 1990, air defense forces included a variety of satellite and radar detection, early warning, and tracking systems, and 69 active air force interceptor aircraft organized in a numbered air force with 4 air divisions (15 squadrons). The Air National Guard provided another 9 squadrons with 162 aircraft, and the TAC provided augmentation on call.

Tactical air forces in 1990 included 3,620 aircraft (including 784 in the Air National Guard and 247 in the air force reserve) in 24 active combat wings (94 squadrons of 18 or 24 aircraft each), including 4 interceptor squadrons and 72 fighter/ground attack squadrons. Supporting units included 5 reconnaissance squadrons, 1 airborne early warning wing, 4 electronic warfare squadrons, and 7 tactical air control squadrons.

Transport forces included 343 strategic airlift aircraft in 21 squadrons and 429 tactical airlift aircraft in 12 squadrons. Air force training units included an "Aggressor" squadron and 31 training squadrons. In addition, the active air force included 3 medical evacuation squadrons, 1 weather reconnaissance squadron, 1 trials/weapons training squadron; and 3 wings of ground-launched cruise missiles (BGM-109G), which were being phased out. The air force operated a total of 1,583 training aircraft and 301 unarmed helicopters.

Reserve Forces

The first Air National Guard unit gained federal recognition in June 1946, and since that time, Air National Guard and air force reserve units have maintained a very high level of combat readiness, frequently winning tactical weapons competitions with regular air force units. As of 1990, 306,600 officers and enlisted personnel were serving in the Air National Guard and air force reserve. The Air National Guard of some 116,000 personnel comprised 23 wings (92 squadrons) with 736 aircraft. The air force ready reserve with 136,000 personnel in selected reserve units and the individual ready reserve comprised 21 wings (58 squadrons, 37 with aircraft) with 247 combat aircraft. The air force standby reserve included 17,300 trained individuals and the retired reserve another 54,200.

The air force is augmented by the Civil Air Patrol, a voluntary paramilitary organization with some 68,000 members organized in 52 wings (1,881 units) in 8 geographical regions with 579 aircraft augmented by 8,465 private aircraft. The Civil Reserve Air Fleet, presently consisting of more than 500 commercial aircraft, is also available to the air force under conditions of mobilization or national emergency.

Tactical Doctrine and Organization

After World War II, the newly formed air force quickly laid claim to the foremost strategic mission of the postwar period, the delivery of the atomic bomb. Strategic bombardment has remained a primary focus of air-power doctrine, although the concept of the manned bomber has faced increasing competition from the air force's own missile forces as well as from the navy's carrier-based aircraft and sea-launched ballistic missile forces. The doctrine for the employment of strategic nuclear forces, both as a deterrent and for actual employment if necessary, is an extremely complex matter that relies heavily on plentiful and accurate intelligence, the accuracy of the weapons employed, and the maintenance of a very high state of readiness. The emphasis on strategic nuclear and air superiority missions has frequently led the air force to neglect other important tasks such as close air support and airlift.

Like ground forces, air forces are tailored to fit their assigned missions. The basic air force unit that is self-supporting and capable of independent action is the wing. The wing is generally composed of a primary mission element (for example, the assigned aircraft and crews) and a supporting element (headquarters, staff, and logistical elements). A wing is composed of two or more groups. Groups are composed of two or more squadrons, and squadrons are made up of two or more flights. Flights are the smallest organized unit but may be composed of elements (one or more aircraft). Two to five wings comprise an air division, and two or more air divisions constitute a numbered air force. Numbered air forces are assigned to air commands—for example, to TAC or MAC.

IMPACT OF TECHNOLOGY

The competition between the United States and the Soviet Union accelerated technological change, and technology dominated the post-World War II battlefield to an unprecedented degree. The atomic bomb, jet aircraft, ballistic missiles, satellites, advanced guidance systems, the helicopter, nuclear-powered naval vessels, lasers, fiber optics, and new antibiotics are just a few of the many advances in military technology since 1945. Today, military success largely depends on the success of efforts to invent and adapt such new technology to military purposes and to master its design, manufacture, maintenance, and employment.

Infantry Weapons

Infantry weapons changed little in the 50 years after World War II. Following the Korean War, the M-14 rifle, chambered for the 7.62-millimeter standard NATO (North Atlantic Treaty Organization) cartridge, replaced the trusty M-1 as the standard infantry weapon, and the M-60 machine gun replaced the .30-caliber light machine gun used since before World War II. Acting on the perceived need for an infantry weapon with a high rate of fire and light weight, the army replaced the M-14 with the M-16 (which fires the lighter 5.56-millimeter cartridge) during the Vietnam War. Despite certain disadvantages, the M-16 remains the standard infantry weapon. Two other infantry weapons that came into the inventory in the early 1960s— the 40-millimeter grenade launcher and the claymore mine—also saw extensive use from the Vietnam War era. The .45-caliber automatic pistol, introduced in 1911, was finally replaced in the 1980s by a new 9-millimeter automatic sidearm.

Tanks and Antitank Weapons

The requirement for higher mobility and increased armor protection on the modern battlefield prompted a number of improvements in tank technology. The tanks currently in the army inventory bear little resemblance to their World War II forebears. Heavier and more scientifically advanced armor, automatic loading systems for the heavier caliber main gun, advanced laser fire control systems that permit firing on the move, and increased crew protection and comfort—as well as improved speed, mobility, and mechanical reliability—make the current M-1 Abrams tank far superior to its predecessors. The need for greater mobility and protection also led to increased use of armored personnel carriers. The relatively lightweight amphibious M-113 saw extensive use in Vietnam and is still in use. More recently, the M-2 Bradley Infantry Fighting Vehicle equipped with a 25-millimeter automatic cannon has become the standard infantry personnel carrier.

Antitank weaponry has improved as well. The antitank guns of World War II and the 3.5-inch antitank rocket launcher used in Korea have long since been replaced, first by a series of recoilless rifles and more recently by small, mobile, and highly effective antitank guided missiles, such as the TOW (tube-launched, optically guided, wire-tracked) missile. Increasingly, the armed helicopter—

In 1968, a flame tank sprays napalm (a jellylike chemical substance that sticks to and burns what it contacts) to flush out the enemy. (U.S. Marine Corps)

equipped with sophisticated target acquisition and guidance systems for its antitank missiles and rapid-fire guns—has been utilized in the antitank role.

Artillery Weapons
Since 1945, only marginal improvements, mostly increased range and lower weight, have been made in cannon artillery systems. However, major advances have been made in artillery projectiles. Army efforts to obtain a role on the nuclear battlefield led to the development of nuclear artillery shells. The monster 280-millimeter atomic cannon made a brief appearance in the 1950s but was abandoned with the development of even smaller nuclear rounds for the 8-inch gun and 155-millimeter howitzer. More recently, artillery projectiles with miniaturized radar and laser guidance systems, such as the 155-millimeter Copperhead laser-guided projectile, have served to increase both the accuracy and lethality of artillery fire against all types of targets.

Following the Korean War, the army began to develop surface-to-surface tactical missile systems capable of delivering nuclear as well as conventional warheads. The crude tactical free-rocket systems of the early 1960s have long since been replaced by more accurate, reliable, and effective guided missiles. The modernization programs of the 1970s and 1980s also produced such new rocket artillery weapons as the MLRS (multiple-launch rocket system) and the ATACMS (army tactical missile system). Among the other important artillery developments of the past half-century have been the use of armed helicopters as aerial field artillery, computer-assisted fire control systems, and laser target designation systems.

Air Defense Artillery
The antiaircraft artillery gun systems used in World War II and Korea have been replaced by advanced rapid-fire air defense guns and guided missiles with increased lethality, accuracy, and effectiveness. Local air defense on the battlefield is now provided by the new DIVAD gun and the Patriot missile system. The Stinger surface-to-air missile gives soldiers at the lowest level good protection even against high-performance jet aircraft. At the strategic level, the old air defense missile systems such as Nike-Ajax were phased out in the 1960s and not replaced. In

The Stinger surface-to-air missile is one of the most modern weapons that the military possesses. Here, a Stinger team practices on a trainer—one soldier prepares to fire the missile as the other scans the sky for enemy aircraft. (U.S. Army)

the 1980s, the Reagan administration began development of the Strategic Defense Initiative ("Star Wars"), a complex, sophisticated space-based defense system against ICBMs utilizing lasers, computers, and other advanced technology. SDI has been opposed in both Congress and the scientific community, but several important parts of the complex system have been proven to work effectively, and SDI development continues at a limited pace.

Naval Vessels

Although the navy has greatly benefited from the development of advanced aircraft, electronics, and missiles, the most significant advance in ship design and construction

since 1945 has clearly been nuclear propulsion. The U.S. fleet became the first to use this energy source when the nuclear-powered submarine *Nautilus* got underway on Jan. 17, 1955. The subsequent construction of a nuclear-powered navy was due in large part to the persistent efforts of Rear Adm. Hyman G. Rickover. Today, many U.S. submarines, aircraft carriers, and larger surface combat vessels are nuclear-powered and thus have virtually unlimited range and time on station. Nuclear propulsion has also made possible the development of both the ballistic missile submarine and the supercarrier, which utilizes the mirror landing system, the angled flight deck, and the steam catapult, all invented by the British. Although the American navy has neglected its amphibious shipping in favor of submarines and carriers, the recent emphasis on the rapid deployment of combat forces has resulted in the development of faster, more capable logistical support vessels. At the same time, the extensive use of helicopters prompted the development of the landing platform, helicopter (LPH), essentially a small aircraft carrier.

Aircraft

Tremendous advances have been made in aircraft technology since 1945, particularly in the areas of airframe design, avionics, armament, and survivability, but the principal development since World War II has been jet propulsion. The first B-52 was unveiled in August 1954, and by 1957, the entire U.S. strategic bomber force was jet-powered. The aging B-52 remains the mainstay of the U.S. manned bomber force, being used for both strategic nuclear missions and the support of ground operations with conventional bombs and air-launched cruise missiles. Thus

Since 1955, most of the submarines built have used nuclear propulsion. The nuclear-powered submarine USS Cavalla *is seen above water at its home base in Groton, Connecticut. (U.S. Navy)*

far, attempts to supplant the B-52 have met only limited success. The air force inventory contains a few modern B-71 bombers, and hopes are high that the air force will be able to purchase at least a few of the new B-2 Stealth bombers, a radical flying wing design that passed its initial flight testing in July 1989.

The relatively primitive jet fighters of the Korean War were quickly replaced by more advanced models, including the famous F-4 Phantom, which served so well during the Vietnam War as both an air superiority aircraft and a ground attack aircraft and which is still in service. The latest fighter aircraft include the air force's F-15 and F-16 and the navy's F-14 Tomcat and F-18 Hornet. A new F-22 advanced tactical fighter is under development. The Marine Corps also flies the Harrier, a V/STOL (vertical and short takeoff and landing) aircraft that represents another post-World War II technological advance. Yet another important development in technology is incorporated in the air force F-117A Stealth ground attack fighter that performed flawlessly in the Gulf War. Stealth technology, which is also used in the new B-2 bomber, involves various passive methods for minimizing an aircraft's radar signature.

F-18 Hornet aircraft, carrying cluster bombs and AIM-7 Sparrow, AIM-9 Sidewinder, and AGM-88 HARM missiles, fly in formation during Operation Desert Storm. (U.S. Air Force)

Missiles

With the development of more reliable propellants and improved guidance systems in the 1950s, increased reliance was placed on missiles for the delivery of strategic atomic weapons as well as for the delivery of conventional war-

The B-2 Stealth bomber, in the forefront of technology with its radical wing design that minimizes radar detection, is flight-tested in 1989. (U.S. Air Force)

heads on the battlefield. The air force began active conversion to missiles in 1954, but the launch of a Soviet ICBM in August 1957 and the launching of two Sputnik satellites soon thereafter opened the space and missile age. The United States soon developed the Thor, Atlas, Titan, and Minuteman ICBMs. These early models were later replaced by the more advanced Minuteman II and Minuteman III systems. The first equipment of the MX ICBM system was delivered for testing in 1990, and 50 Peacekeeper-MX ICBMs were soon in service. The air force also developed a number of air-launched cruise missiles and other air-to-surface missiles capable of striking ground targets with great accuracy and effectiveness because of sophisticated guidance systems employing advanced radar, television, infrared, and lasers.

The navy also pressed forward with the development of sea-launched ballistic missiles (SLBMs) in the strategic role. The first Polaris SLBM was deployed in 1960. Second-generation Polaris missiles yielded to the Poseidon, which in turn was surpassed by the more advanced Trident II D-5, accepted into service in 1990. The navy also added a number of antiship missiles (for example, the Harpoon) and sea-launched cruise missiles such as the Tomahawk, which can be equipped with either nuclear or conventional warheads. Conventionally armed Tomahawks fired from ships and able to strike targets far inland with great accuracy played an important role in the Gulf War.

Nuclear, Chemical, and Biological Weapons

Nuclear weapons technology has far surpassed the primitive low-yield weapons dropped on Hiroshima and Nagasaki in 1945. The Soviet explosion of an atomic bomb in 1949 provoked development of a thermonuclear device (hydrogen bomb) in the mid-1950s. Subsequent "improvements" in strategic nuclear weapons have included the so-called neutron bomb, which can kill people with minimal damage to equipment and facilities, and multiple independently targetable reentry vehicles (MIRVs), which provide a means of deploying several independently targeted nuclear warheads on a single ballistic missile.

Although the United States has consistently opposed chemical and biological weapons, such devices have continued to be developed, primarily as a means of developing defensive systems to counteract them. The choking gases and blood agents available (but not used) in World War II have been improved and complemented by a series of deadly nerve agents. Binary chemical munitions, in which the deadly chemical is not produced until two or more less dangerous substances are mixed upon firing, represent a significant technological advance. Improved protective masks, protective suits, and other defensive equipment have also been developed and issued to U.S. forces in the field in response to the threat of enemy chemical and biological capabilities.

Communications

Since 1945, satellites and computer data links have significantly increased the range and speed of strategic communications and intelligence gathering while the transistor has provided a breakthrough in miniaturization leading to lighter, smaller, and more reliable tactical radios. Improved radars and new ground sensors provide better ground surveillance, and infrared and laser technology have produced a variety of effective night vision and sighting devices. Fiber optics and the ground positioning system (GPS) have aided the fantastic improvement of military communications since World War II.

Mobility

Worldwide commitments and the need to deploy reinforcements rapidly have led to significant improvements in strategic mobility while the prospect of a nuclear battlefield and operations in unimproved areas have spurred developments in tactical mobility. At the strategic level, fast jet transports have substantially decreased the time required to move forces, and their larger capacities have even permitted the air movement of tanks and other heavy equipment with ease. At sea, containerization, the development of roll-on/roll-off ships, and, more recently, the development of fast logistics support ships have made possible the rapid movement of U.S. forces worldwide.

Tactical mobility was revolutionized by the advent of the helicopter. From the first tentative use of primitive models in the Korean War, the helicopter quickly evolved into a rapid and effective means of battlefield movement and resupply, as was demonstrated during the Vietnam War. The aging air force C-130 Hercules tactical transport, introduced in 1954, has also significantly improved the ability to support forward forces from unimproved airstrips or by aerial delivery systems. On the ground, a number of improved tracked and wheeled vehicles have increased tactical mobility.

Medical Technology

The helicopter also revolutionized battlefield evacuation and the survival of the wounded. A few helicopters saw limited use in World War II for evacuating sick and wounded soldiers from remote locations. Such use was generally expanded during the Korean War and all but replaced ground evacuation in Vietnam. The result was, of course, to reduce significantly the time it took to get a battlefield casualty to lifesaving treatment. Consequently, the number of wounded soldiers who died was substantially reduced and the chances for avoiding permanent disability or disfigurement considerably improved. The major improvement in battlefield evacuation was accompanied by significant advances in surgery, drugs, and medical science. Penicillin and newer, more effective antibiotics were developed; surgical tools and techniques were advanced;

Medevac helicopters, which came into use during the Vietnam War, were flying first-aid stations that evacuated casualties in record time and greatly reduced the number of lives lost. (National Archives)

and the diagnostic equipment now available to the military surgeon far surpasses anything available in 1945. The surgical laser greatly improved x-ray technology, making diagnosis and treatment more efficient and effective. Recent advances in bioelectronics and biomechanical devices have substantially improved the chances of restoring wounded soldiers to the nearly full use of damaged limbs. Preventive and environmental medicine also progressed, and today, barring the obvious dangers of wartime service, the soldier is far healthier and less likely to die from disease or accident than ever before.

CONCLUSION

The half-century since World War II has been one of unprecedented change for the armed forces of the United

States. An enormous variety of political, economic, social, and technological challenges have been met and overcome. The stresses of conducting active conventional operations, maintaining worldwide readiness for nuclear war, and fighting the bureaucratic battles in Washington—all at the same time—have sometimes threatened to overwhelm U.S. civilian and military leaders and those they lead. The resilient nature of the American character, both military and civilian, as well as the enormous natural resources of the United States have led the nation to a position of unchallenged military superiority and global influence in the last decade of the 20th century. The changes and challenges of the next 50 years promise to be even more demanding, but the solid foundation of sound doctrine, efficient organization, and effective technology established over the past 200 years promises a bright future for the armed forces of the United States.

2

The Cold War: 1945–1960

For most Americans, the end of World War II heralded the defeat of fascism and the advent of an era of global peace based upon liberal principles of democracy and international law. After World War I, the United States had pursued a course of narrow nationalism and, a majority of the public was convinced, had paid the price for its shortsightedness. That mistake would not be repeated after World War II. An intensive wartime campaign to promote a new "League of Nations" bore fruit when the Allied Powers agreed to the creation of the United Nations (UN), an international organization that would restore the world to its natural state of harmony and peace through the mechanisms of international law and collective security. In the future, any nation showing aggressive tendencies would be held in check by the combined efforts of the victorious powers. Having joined together to defeat the Axis challenge, these nations would present a unified front, institutionalized in the UN Security Council, to enforce a just and lasting peace.

Wartime propaganda fostered these unrealistic hopes for the postwar world. It also masked from the American public the concerns for the future shared by students of foreign affairs, policymakers, and military advisers who believed conflict to be inherent in the relations among nations. Fascism might have succumbed to Allied power, but new threats to the international order would inevitably arise in its place. Throughout the greater part of World War II, many officials in Congress and Pres. Franklin D. Roosevelt's administration considered Great Britain, with its determination to restore its prewar empire, the greatest potential threat to world peace, once Germany and Japan capitulated. These fears of British imperialism had diminished by 1945, largely because of Great Britain's economic evisceration by the war and because of various

bilateral agreements that ensured the United States economic and financial advantages in the "special relationship" between the two countries. As the war entered its final year, the Soviet Union had replaced Great Britain as the leading candidate to threaten the postwar peace. Soviet intentions were by no means clear at this point, but Soviet behavior seemed to demonstrate distinctly expansionistic tendencies as political commissars followed in the wake of the Red Army's sweep through Eastern and Central Europe.

Whichever country might threaten the peace to come, strategic planners in the United States agreed on several assumptions. First, the American people could not entrust their security needs solely to the UN Security Council, dominated as it would be by the victorious powers whose individual ambitions had been tempered only imperfectly by the existence of a common enemy. Assuming that a new threat to U.S. security would most likely arise from the Eurasian landmass, strategists posited a network of forward bases overseas from which U.S. air power could engage an enemy on its home turf, far away from the American homeland. News of the atomic bombing of Japan served to intensify the planner's conviction that a strategy of defense in depth and the ability to project power rapidly and effectively was imperative.

CHANGES IN THE SERVICES

This ambitious strategy for the forward defense of U.S. security in the postwar world ran afoul of public opinion and political necessity once World War II ended in September 1945. Reconversion to a peacetime society, which entailed drastic budget cuts in the defense sector, took priority over strategic concerns, thus undermining any attempt the government might have contemplated to acquire extensive base rights in the western Pacific and eastern Atlantic. Furthermore, while prudent statesmen feared the consequences of a precipitous reduction in U.S. military forces, political leaders could not ignore mounting public pressure, bordering on hysteria, for demobilization. The clamor to return men in uniform to their families and a normal life was at times deafening.

Inundated by petitions of family members and the appeals of "Bring Back Daddy" clubs and, by early 1946, faced with demonstrations by war veterans still in uniform overseas that in some cases came close to mutiny, Pres. Harry S Truman and the Congress yielded. Plans for gradual demobilization based on an individual point system translated instead into what Truman himself called the "disintegration" of the armed forces. From a wartime peak of 12,000,000 men and women under arms in June 1945, the number of active-duty servicemen plummeted to barely 1,500,000 two years later, at which time the army and army air force had 991,285 personnel on active duty; the navy, 498,661; and the Marine Corps, 94,225. Accompanying the drastic drop in personnel were numerous camp and base closures together with the destruction, sale, or retirement of ships and other military equipment.

Conscription and Universal Training

Official fears that rapid demobilization would disrupt the domestic economy proved unfounded. Wartime savings precluded the slide back into the prewar Great Depression, while the "G.I. Bill of Rights" passed by Congress in 1944 gave returning veterans an incentive to improve their education, thus temporarily keeping many of them out of the job market. Of more lasting concern, however, was the impact that rapid demobilization would have on the military's ability to perform its peacetime missions, which included occupation duties overseas in both the Far East and Europe and, in the worst case, to fight a war.

The Selective Service System had drafted 10,000,000 men during the war, but the postwar demands for demobilization caused Truman to allow the draft to elapse in March 1947. To replace it, the president and many military experts, including Gens. George C. Marshall and Dwight D. Eisenhower and Sec. of the Navy James Forrestal, advocated a program of universal military training (UMT). Under UMT, all male civilians between 18 and 20 years of age would receive one year of basic military

On May 7, 1945, General Jodl of the German high command signed papers documenting the unconditional surrender of the Germans, thus ending the European phase of World War II. (U.S. Army Military History Institute)

training, after which they would move into a six-year general reserve. In this way, a small active force, backed by the National Guard and organized reserves, would be adequately strengthened by a large pool of UMT-trained civilians. The UMT program, Truman also proclaimed, would promote the "moral and spiritual welfare of our young people."

Opponents of UMT denounced the program as unduly militaristic and, at a time when many thought atomic bombs would decide a future war, irrelevant. Critics also charged that the moral and spiritual fiber of America's youth should remain the responsibility of the family, church, and other nongovernmental bodies. Thus, the administration's UMT plan died, and even the onset of several Cold War crises could not resurrect it. UMT's opponents in Congress, on the other hand, reluctantly endorsed the reinstitution of the draft on a temporary basis when it became apparent that the armed services could not muster enough volunteers to deal with Cold War emergencies. The Selective Service Act of 1948 sought to increase army and Marine Corps strength by 250,000 men. Even this seemed inadequate to many. General Marshall, who, after retiring from the army, became Truman's secretary of state in 1947, complained that it was difficult to talk tough to the Soviets when the United States had fewer than 3 divisions to the Russians' 260. Even so, to the extent that the draft succeeded, it was mainly as an incentive for young men to volunteer. Had it not been for the outbreak of war in Korea in June 1950, the administration and Congress would have allowed the Selective Service System to expire.

Unification of the Armed Services

The recurring problem of manpower was not the only concern of the armed forces in the wake of World War II. There was also the more fundamental and contentious issue of how the military itself should be organized. Having separate departments of the army and the navy, each organized differently and evincing competing, often conflicting goals, seemed to many wasteful and potentially disastrous. Turf battles and other problems of coordination, communication, and cooperation between the army and the navy had plagued much of the war effort, especially in the Pacific. The time had come, critics argued, to merge the two departments into a unified military establishment.

The army had traditionally opposed unification schemes, but the experience of the war, together with political worries over postwar resources, missions, and status, convinced several generals, such as Marshall, that the concept of unification had merit. Thus, even while the war was still in progress, Marshall proposed the creation of a single department of defense that would have four divisions (ground, air, sea, and supplies). The army air force, whose

establishment as an independent service appeared inevitable, supported the army plan. The Department of the Navy, however, became a vocal opponent of unification. Navy officers worried that the navy's unique maritime missions might not be fully appreciated in a organization that, no matter how well unified on paper, would be dominated by a partnership of officers drawn from the army and the army air force. Stigmatizing the War Department's blueprint for unification by comparing it to prewar German and Japanese military institutions, the navy submitted its own plan. Endorsed by Secretary Forrestal, the plan rejected a true merger of the armed services in favor of a "federalist" approach in which each service would retain its own identity while enhancing institutional mechanisms for interservice cooperation.

The National Security Act of 1947 adopted the navy plan. It created the National Military Establishment (NME) under which the army, navy, and the air force (now granted independent status) operated as three separate executive departments, each with its own civilian secretary and staff. A secretary of defense would serve as the president's principal military adviser, but lacking an adequate staff and statutory power, the occupant of the office could only mediate among the departments and the president, while he had no power to resolve interservice rivalry. The Joint Chiefs of Staff (JCS), an ad hoc wartime advisory body, received statutory recognition for the first time. To ensure the NME's role in foreign policy and to provide interagency coordination of that process, the law set up the National Security Council (NSC). The newly created Central Intelligence Agency (CIA) would coordinate the collection and assessment of intelligence and make recommendations to the NSC; a National Security Resources Board took on responsibility for planning and coordinating mobilization policy.

Key West Agreements

The navy's victory in 1947 in the battle over unification did not end the bureaucratic war. Forrestal, who as secretary of the navy had led the fight to emasculate plans for true unification, became the first secretary of defense. In this position, he confronted the considerable shortcomings of the system he had helped to create. Interservice rivalry continued unabated, with each service, especially the air force, lobbying Congress for more money, and with interminable arguments among the three departments over roles and missions. To bring the squabbling under control, Forrestal called a meeting of the service chiefs at Key West, Florida, in 1948. The navy received authorization to develop atomic weapons for naval combat but was denied a strategic air force. The army would be responsible for land operations, while the marines, denied a ground army, were allowed to develop air-ground amphibious forces.

The Air Force became a separate division of the armed services in 1947, and the U.S. Air Force Academy was established in 1951 near Denver, Colorado, to instruct future officers. (U.S. Air Force Academy)

The Key West agreements created neither the consensus nor the harmony that Forrestal sought. The pressures weighing on him as secretary of defense ultimately contributed to his nervous breakdown. After resigning in 1949, he committed suicide. His successor, Louis Johnson, a fund-raiser for Truman in the 1948 presidential campaign, moved to assert the authority and power of the defense secretary. By this time, even the architects of the 1947 law conceded the need for a more centralized military establishment.

The 1949 amendments to the National Security Act replaced the NME with a Department of Defense; increased the defense secretary's staff and his managerial effectiveness, especially in the interservice fights over the budget; rescinded the executive status of the service departments; and approved the position of chairman to the JCS. (The chairman had no vote in the JCS, but he wielded influence as the principal military adviser to the president and to the secretary of defense.) Although far from a perfect solution to centralized control of defense policy and planning, the amendments did remove some of the blatant weaknesses of the existing arrangements.

Military Integration

In the midst of the bureaucratic warfare over unification, President Truman initiated another far-reaching change within the military. During the war, black soldiers had served in segregated units. Some small movement toward integration at war's end did not survive the postwar setting of quotas for black enlistment and the military's imposition of rigid segregation policies. Facing an uphill election campaign in which civil rights would be a prominent issue, Truman in 1948 issued Executive Order No. 9981 for the racial integration of the armed services. This move established the President's Committee on Equality of Treatment and Opportunity in the Armed Forces.

Each service had vehemently opposed integration on the grounds that the military was not in the business of social reform and that white servicemen would react violently to integration, thus lowering unit morale and efficiency. Once Truman issued his executive order, the air force reversed its position and moved with some enthusiasm under its civilian secretary, Stuart Symington, to comply. At the other extreme, the army bitterly fought the measure. But the president and his committee refused to concede, and in 1950, the army abolished its quota system and agreed to base black assignments on need and training. The demand for manpower during the Korean War furthered the process of integration, which the army then extended to U.S. installations in general as well as to units in Europe. By the end of the war in Korea, the army reported that 90 percent of its units were integrated.

ORIGINS OF THE COLD WAR

These dramatic changes in the organization and composition of the postwar military took place amid an increasingly uncertain and dangerous international environment. Soviet behavior in the occupied countries of Eastern and Central Europe in 1945, together with Moscow's seeming obstructionist approach to other issues, had raised concerns among U.S. decision-makers. Initially, Truman tried a mixture of tough talk and conciliatory gestures in his diplomacy with the Russians, but by early 1946, he had begun to doubt the efficacy of this approach as Soviet ambitions appeared to extend to Turkey, Greece, northern Iran, and even Western Europe. Policymakers in Washington raised the critical question: What were the true intentions of the Soviet Union?

During the war, President Roosevelt had regarded Soviet demands for defensible borders through territorial acquisitions as justified in light of Russian history. He and the State Department were willing to concede a Soviet sphere of influence in Eastern Europe after the war, but not the imposition of Communist dictatorships within that sphere. Following Roosevelt's death in April 1945, Truman accepted the interpretation of the U.S. ambassador to the Soviet Union, W. Averell Harriman, who likened the Soviet Union to a world bully that would back down on its more extreme demands if the United States stood up to it. But Truman's subsequent "get tough" initiatives seemed to have a negligible effect on Soviet behavior. During early 1946, however, a new consensus began to emerge in Washington that the Soviet Union was an adversarial power whose expansionistic ambitions could not be thwarted by U.S. diplomacy alone. Whether motivated by Communist ideology, as Forrestal argued, or by the dynamics of totalitarian power, as Soviet specialist George F. Kennan maintained, the Soviet Union sought nothing less than world domination. No responsible policymaker believed that the Soviet Union had the intention or the capability to launch World War III. Rather, Moscow would attempt to extend its influence and control by taking advantage of the political turmoil, economic dislocation, social unrest, and anticolonial nationalism created or exacerbated by the war. With the analogy of Britain's appeasement of Germany at Munich before World War II etched in their minds, U.S. officials called for a policy that would deter, not encourage, aggression and its likely product, war.

The Truman Doctrine

To counter Soviet expansionism, the United States adopted the policy of "containment," a term taken from an article on Soviet conduct by Kennan. Even before the article appeared in July 1947, Truman had erected the first contain-

Dean Acheson, President Truman's secretary of state (1949–53), advocated the use of selective military power against the Soviets and was instrumental in the formulation of the Truman Doctrine and the Marshall Plan. (Library of Congress)

ment barrier, after Great Britain had informed the United States that it no longer had the financial resources to play an active role in the eastern Mediterranean. Fearing that the Soviet Union would fill the vacuum created by the retrenchment of British power in that area, Truman, in a message personally delivered before a joint session of Congress on Mar. 12, 1947, called for U.S. economic and military assistance to Greece and Turkey.

Greece at that time was in the midst of a bloody civil war that pitted Communists in the north against monarchist, right-wing forces in the south. Turkey, for its part, had been under pressure from Moscow to cede territory to the Soviet Union and sign a convention for joint Turkish-Soviet control of the straits leading into the Mediterranean. Truman's plan for aid to these two countries was a masterpiece of realpolitik. The offer of U.S. assistance was limited to a small geographical area and was within the ability of the United States to finance (even a fiscally conservative Republican Congress would support the necessary expenditures). It was, in short, a realistic application of U.S. power. In his speech, however, the president employed rhetoric that gave a universalist slant to his limited goals. Although he did not mention the Soviet Union by name, he declared his belief that "it must be the policy of the United States to support free peoples who are resisting attempted subjugation by armed minorities or outside pressure." Although the United States at that time did not have the resources, nor Truman the inclination, to engage in global containment, the Truman Doctrine provided the philosophical justification for just such a policy at some point in the future.

Greek Civil War

The largest portion of aid allotted under the Truman Doctrine was in the form of military assistance to Greece, where a longstanding and at times violent conflict between monarchists and republicans had erupted into civil war in 1946, some months before a national referendum restored the monarchy whose king had fled German occupation of the country during the war. The Communist party of Greece and its armed forces led the fight against monarchist forces. As the organizers of the most effective resistance movement to the Germans during the war, the Communists had combat experience and expertise in guerrilla warfare. The mountains of northern Greece provided security and a base of operations against government outposts; the Communist states of Albania, Yugoslavia, and Bulgaria provided cross-border sanctuaries and training areas, while mountain towns and villages provided a source of food, recruits, and intelligence. Beginning with fewer than 4,000 fighters, Communist forces grew to more than 20,000 at the peak of the war.

The monarchy, on the other hand, operated under several handicaps. Its armed forces numbered between 140,000 and 170,000, thus enjoying vast numerical superiority over the guerrillas, but were organized into a hodgepodge of regular, home-guard, and police units, most of which were poorly trained, poorly led, and completely unprepared to fight a small-unit guerrilla war requiring mobility and flexibility. Lacking an offensive spirit and suffering from low morale, monarchist forces during the early phases of the war adopted a static defense strategy that left the initiative entirely to the Communists. As for the monarchist government in Athens, it contained fascists and right-wing extremists and had a well-deserved reputation for repression. Despite these shortcomings and excesses, the Truman administration chose to support the monarchy on the grounds that the Soviet Union was actively sponsoring the insurgency (an assumption that remains controversial even today) and that a Communist victory in Greece would bring Soviet influence into the Mediterranean. Furthermore, Truman believed, the United States could exert pressure and flex its economic muscle to push the right wing in Greece toward a more democratic, centrist position.

U.S. military assistance in the form of advisers and equipment began arriving in Greece in mid-1947. No one expected an immediate reversal of the dire fortunes of the government forces, and none occurred. Indeed, well into 1948, the insurgency continued to grow. Meanwhile, to increase the efficacy of U.S. military assistance, Washington authorized the establishment (on Dec. 31, 1947) of the

Joint U.S. Military Advisory and Planning Group (JUSMAPG) for Greece under Maj. Gen. James Van Fleet, soon promoted to lieutenant general. JUSMAPG furnished advice to the Greek government and high command and, over time, assumed virtual operational control of the Greek military. Van Fleet, working with able, high-ranking Greek officers, used this leverage to have incompetents retired and to rebuild, equip, and reorganize government forces in accordance with U.S. doctrine and force structure for heavy divisions. The initial results were not promising. Two large-scale conventional offensives in the spring of 1948 failed to defeat the guerrillas, who retreated to their sanctuaries and returned later resupplied and reinvigorated.

So bleak did the situation appear that the Truman administration considered sending U.S. combat forces to Greece. In early 1948, the JCS recommended against this course of action unless the Soviet Union or one of the Balkan states actually intervened. The JCS appraisal, supported by Secretary of State Marshall, was that, without a military buildup at home, the United States could not sustain military operations or guarantee victory in Greece. A decision to intervene in the Greek civil war was thus deferred pending developments on the battlefield.

The pessimism of 1948 yielded to a more optimistic assessment in 1949, as Greek government forces under more vigorous leadership won decisive victories against the Communist guerrillas. By late summer, in fact, the war was all but over. To the U.S. military, the reasons for victory seemed clear enough. Large units amply supplied with heavy firepower and trained in large-scale conventional operations could simply overpower an insurgency in which the most effective units were 30-man platoons. Certainly, U.S. support helped turn the tide against the Greek Communists. But there were other, sometimes more compelling reasons for the government victory, including internal divisions within the guerrilla movement, Marshal Tito's closing of Yugoslavia's border with Greece as one consequence of the Yugoslav leader's falling out with Soviet leader Joseph Stalin, and, perhaps most important, the decision by the dominant faction in the Greek Communist leadership to jettison guerrilla warfare in favor of conventional operations, thus playing into the hands of U.S. and Greek government strategists.

The Marshall Plan

At the time Truman announced aid to Greece and Turkey, the U.S. government was looking at other areas of the world that might require similar aid. Europe, where recovery from the economic and social dislocations of the war was proceeding much more slowly than anticipated, stood out as the principal candidate. After much study, it fell to Secretary of State Marshall in a speech at Harvard University in June 1947 to announce the willingness of the United States to finance a plan for European recovery. A signifi-

As a special adviser to President Truman, John Foster Dulles, who later served as secretary of state (1953–59) during the Eisenhower administration, arrives in Paris to attend a meeting on the Marshall Plan. (National Archives)

cant condition was that the plan would have to be a cooperative effort, drawn up by the recipient countries themselves.

Great Britain and France took the lead in calling together other European countries to formulate a proposal in response to Marshall's speech. Included in the invitation were the Soviet Union and several Eastern European countries under its virtual control. The Soviets sent representatives to a general meeting held in Paris but soon pulled out, denouncing the U.S. offer as proof of American imperialistic designs on Europe. Policymakers in Washington breathed a sigh of relief; Soviet participation in the plan could have raised complications abroad and ensured an uphill fight to gain congressional approval of the initiative. Without Soviet obstructionism, Western European countries forged a proposal for U.S. assistance, which Truman presented to Congress in December 1947. The administration argued that the plan would promote peace and stability in Europe and prosperity in the United States. After bitter debate, bipartisanship prevailed, and Congress passed the Economic Recovery Program in April 1948.

Over a four-year period, Congress authorized more than $13 billion for what Truman named the Marshall Plan. The desired effects were achieved, as U.S. assistance promoted recovery in Western Europe and in the occupied areas of western Germany. The army looked to the Marshall Plan as a means for reversing the unstable and costly conditions that kept U.S. occupation forces in Central Europe. Since U.S. aid helped stabilize several European governments

and undermine the Communist parties of France and Italy, the Marshall Plan stood, after the Truman Doctrine, as the second pillar of Truman's containment policy. On a less positive note, the plan also accelerated the division of Europe into Communist and anticommunist blocs.

Berlin Blockade

As George Kennan and others predicted, the Soviet Union responded vigorously to the Marshall Plan. The Kremlin further consolidated its hold over Eastern Europe and, in February 1948, helped engineer a coup in Czechoslovakia. A "war scare" rolled over Western Europe and the United States, receded, then rose again when the Soviet Union clamped a blockade on the land routes to Berlin, thus beginning the first major confrontation of the Cold War.

The Allies had divided postwar Germany into U.S., British, French, and Soviet zones of occupation. Berlin, the capital city, was located well inside the Soviet zone in the east and had been similarly divided into four zones. A series of Allied conferences had failed to produce accord on a German peace treaty or the future of Germany in Europe. The United States favored creation of an economically sound Germany, reunited or not, that would play a part in general European recovery and stand as a bulwark against Communist expansion. By the end of 1947, the impasse in negotiations with the Soviet Union caused the Western Allies to contemplate unilateral action to unite the western zones and form a separate "West" German government aligned with Western Europe. Currency reform under the Marshall Plan served as a vehicle to that end. When the United States, Great Britain, and France implemented a similar program in western Berlin, the Soviet Union, on June 23–24, 1948, blocked the land routes through its zone into the divided city.

The Allies had signed written agreements granting access to Berlin by air, but only verbal agreements existed covering the ground routes. The Berlin blockade confronted the West with an agonizing choice. To abandon the city would leave it to the Communists at the expense of U.S. credibility. To challenge the blockade could mean World War III. Truman's advisers were divided on the issue. Gen. Lucius Clay, the U.S. military governor of occupied Germany, claimed that U.S. prestige was at stake and initially advocated sending an armored column down the highway to Berlin. The Soviets, he assured his superiors in Washington, would back down. The army chief of staff, Gen. Omar Bradley, and other military and civilian officials did not want to run the risk that Clay was wrong. Soviet troops vastly outnumbered Western forces in eastern Germany, and the U.S. Air Force did not have the capability in 1948 to launch a strategic air offensive against the Soviet Union. Truman talked tough, saying that the West was "going to stay, period," but, in fact, he deferred making a decision for war or peace. The United

States, he knew, had no formal commitment to defend Berlin.

The Western response combined bluff and expediency. To feed and supply the surrounded Allied garrisons in western Berlin, Truman immediately authorized a partial airlift. The Soviets did not shoot down the aircraft, and the airlift was gradually expanded to bring relief to western Berliners as well. In mid-July, Truman announced that he was sending to England 60 B-29 heavy bombers of the type that had dropped the atomic bombs on Japan. This thinly veiled threat to the Soviet leaders was, in fact, a bluff. The planes were not configured to carry atomic weapons.

The Berlin airlift succeeded beyond all expectations in keeping the city alive. Soviet pilots at times harassed the planes, and some aircraft and crews were lost to weather and other causes. But the great powers averted war. In the meantime, the West continued its preparations to create a federal government in western Germany. Realizing that his gambit had failed, Stalin lifted the blockade in May 1949. President Truman attributed the Soviet reversal to his own tough and decisive actions, which he highly exaggerated. Such boasting was unfortunate. According to historian Daniel Harrington, "He had balanced prudence and resolve during the blockade in a way that could have become a model of crisis management in the nuclear age, had it been properly understood. Instead, Harry Truman's obsession with appearing tough threw away that opportunity and helped enshrine hard-line dogmas in American political culture."

North Atlantic Treaty Organization (NATO)

The "war scare" of 1948 and the Berlin blockade accentuated Western concerns that had been growing since 1947—namely, that U.S. economic aid and a modicum of military assistance would not by themselves ensure European recovery. The sense of insecurity in Western Europe, fostered by the constant threat of Communist subversion and Soviet aggression, had to be overcome before the recipients of U.S. largess could use it productively. In the minds of some European leaders, only a U.S. military commitment to the defense of Western Europe would provide the psychological boost needed to create the sense of security essential for economic recovery.

In March 1948, Great Britain, the Netherlands, Belgium, Luxembourg, and France (France fearing a German revival more than a Soviet attack) had signed the Brussels Pact, a formal recognition that mutual defense was essential to European stability. Without U.S. membership in the pact, however, the alliance lacked credibility. Thus, the signatories entreated the United States to renounce its traditional doctrine of no formal military ties with Europe and to become a full partner in the defense of noncommunist Europe and the northern Atlantic area.

General Omar Bradley, army chief of staff in 1948, soon became head of the newly created Joint Chiefs of Staff (1949) and a five-star general (1950). (U.S. Army)

Many Americans who favored the political unification of Western Europe (to include western Germany) promoted an alliance as a means of furthering their goal. Other Americans vehemently opposed a formal U.S. military commitment outside the Western Hemisphere. Hardcore nationalists cited George Washington's and Thomas Jefferson's admonitions against overseas entanglements and warned against diluting America's sovereignty and ability to act unilaterally. Internationalists, on the other hand, feared that a regional alliance involving Europe would undermine the authority and efficacy of the United Nations. Although the debate was often heated, the outcome was not in doubt. Presidents Roosevelt and Truman had made it clear that, after the experiences of World War II, the United States would not again retreat into "isolationism." Truman's postwar policies, with the support of a bipartisan coalition in Congress, had increased substantially the international responsibilities of the United States.

After a year of tough negotiations, the North Atlantic Treaty was signed in 1949. By terms of the treaty, an attack upon one of the members would be considered an attack against them all, requiring consultations at the very least. Charter members included the United States, the Benelux countries, Great Britain, France, Canada, Portugal, Iceland, Italy, Denmark, and Norway. The U.S. Senate approved the treaty for ratification by a vote of 82 to 13. Later in the year, Congress passed the Military Defense Assistance Act, authorizing $1.3 billion in military aid to treaty countries. The North Atlantic Treaty was not the first postwar regional alliance entered into by the United States, which had signed the Rio Treaty with similar collective security arrangements for the Western Hemisphere in 1948. The North Atlantic Treaty was the most important, however, providing as it did for the forward defense of the United States in an area of the world considered vital to American interests.

Military Spending and Nuclear Strategy

U.S. membership in NATO produced the desired psychological lift in Western Europe, even though the alliance's military strength existed almost entirely on paper. The issue of how the United States could best contribute to the defense of its allies remained unclear. Some strategic thinkers, anticipating U.S. strategic doctrine of the 1950s, believed that Soviet fear of overwhelming retaliation by the U.S. atomic arsenal would alone deter Communist aggression on the Continent. Other Americans, arguing that the disabled economies of Western Europe could not support significant military expenditures, called for the commitment of U.S. conventional forces to Europe.

Truman's budgetary policies determined the answer to the debate, at least during the first year of the alliance. A liberal on social matters, but a fiscal conservative, Truman was determined to balance the federal budget, in large part by cutting defense expenditures to the bone, authorizing only what was essential to safeguard the United States from attack. Even the escalation of the Cold War and pressure from the military services could not budge him on this issue. Thus, from a peak of $81.6 billion at the end of the war, the defense budget under Truman fell to somewhat more than $13 billion by the late 1940s. Although the JCS lobbied for twice the lower amount, Truman imposed a ceiling of $14.4 billion on defense spending for fiscal year 1950 (July 1, 1949–June 30, 1950).

The consequences of defense cuts were predictable. Although Truman, despite rapid postwar demobilization, broke with tradition by maintaining what was for the United States a large peacetime standing military, conventional forces had to make do with skeleton organizations and units, inferior training, and antiquated equipment. Inexorably, U.S. military strategy came to rely increasingly on the atomic bomb to deter war and, if deterrence failed, to achieve victory over an opponent.

By the summer of 1947, defense officials recognized the atomic bomb as the centerpiece of the U.S. arsenal. That

After the end of World War II, the United States continued to research and test its nuclear weapons. In July 1946, atomic-bomb tests were conducted on the evacuated Bikini Atoll in the Pacific Ocean's Marshall Islands. (Joint Task Force I)

this recognition did not come sooner in the aftermath of Hiroshima and Nagasaki, when military thinkers proclaimed a revolution in warfare, is best understood by the lack of data concerning the atomic bomb's capabilities and, more important, a lack of the bombs themselves. Only a handful of military officers knew the exact number of usable bombs. Truman himself did not find out until April 1947. When he did, he was appalled. At that point, the United States had 13 usable nuclear components, as compared to 2 in late 1945 and 9 in mid-1946. A shortage of fissionable material and, until 1948, a technological problem in producing atomic bombs accounted for these seemingly low numbers. Technological breakthroughs ultimately increased the atomic stockpile, but hardly enough by 1949 to be decisive in a strategic air attack against the Soviet Union.

Yet, such an attack is exactly what U.S. military planners envisaged. The next war, it was assumed, would be much like the last one in that the United States would find itself pitted against Eurasian powers and fighting on two fronts. As in World War II, the strategy would be to hold the line in the Pacific while concentrating the main effort on defeating the enemy in Europe. In the first postwar plans, the atomic bomb was seen as a weapon critical to this strategy; by 1949, it was regarded as the decisive weapon. How it could have fulfilled this expectation is not clear, given the small stockpile existing at that time. As for delivering atomic bombs—whatever the number—on the Soviet Union, strategic air power would lead the way.

Revolt of the Admirals

Tight defense budgets and a war-fighting strategy based on an atomic air offensive against an enemy country had a discernible impact on each military service. As some observers proclaimed ground forces to be obsolete or irrelevant in the nuclear era, the army scrambled to define its role on the atomic battlefield. A nuclear attack would come from the air, to be sure, but ground troops would be needed to seize and hold bases from which to bomb the enemy and to occupy the enemy homeland after victory. The argument was valid, of course, and eloquently stated, but hardly catchy enough to ensure the army a large slice of the national defense budget pie.

The lion's share of the defense budget would go to the navy or the air force, whichever one could convince the secretary of defense, the president, and Congress that it could best deliver an atomic payload on target. The resulting interservice rivalry was more bitter and intense than usual. The navy lobbied for a strategic air arm that could be launched with its atomic weapons from a new magnitude of floating airfield, the super-carrier. The air force countered with demands to increase its air groups from 55 to 70 and to build a force of B-36 intercontinental bombers, backed by the B-29 and the B-50, for use by the Strategic Air Command.

There were not enough funds budgeted to satisfy both the navy and the air force. It fell to Secretary of Defense Johnson to decide the winner in the budget sweepstakes, and he sided with the air force, canceling navy plans to build the 65,000–ton super-carrier *United States,* cutting in half the active carrier force to four vessels, and slashing the number of carrier air groups.

Faced with even further budget cuts, the admirals went on the offensive. In congressional hearings in October 1949, navy officers scathingly insisted that the B-36 was vulnerable to fighter attack and, what was more, that the air force's reliance on nuclear deterrence/atomic annihilation was impractical and immoral. Truman and Johnson held firm against this "Revolt of the Admirals." The secretary of the navy resigned in protest, and Johnson relieved the chief of naval operations. The navy viewed the setback as temporary. But before a more damaging round of charge and countercharge could begin, events would conspire to enable each service to "get well."

1949: The Year of Shocks

Truman's insistence on low defense budgets did not prevent the president from frequently referring to the United States as the most powerful nation in the world. Based on U.S. economic might, the boast was true enough. In a complex world, however, power cannot always be translated into effective action, a point on which Truman (if not most policymakers) failed to educate the American public. Taught to expect that there existed no challenge that Americans could not meet, the public in 1949 began to

question the gap between expectation and reality. Postwar hopes for a just and lasting peace confronted the Cold War reality of a Europe divided into two hostile, if not at this point well-armed, camps, in which the unresolved status of western Berlin threatened future crises. In the Far East as well, U.S. power appeared to have had a negligible effect on China's civil war, in which Mao Zedong's Red Army stood poised to bring the most populated country in the world into the Communist bloc. Even at home, spy trials and Communist demonstrations caused many Americans to question the loyalty of public officials in and out of government. Then came the ultimate shock: In September, Truman announced in effect that the Soviet Union had broken the U.S. monopoly on atomic weapons.

Those seeking an answer as to why Truman's Cold War rhetoric suggesting the omnipotence of U.S. power seemed at odds with the rather dismal reality of world affairs often lent an attentive ear to political charlatans who blamed America's alleged foreign policy misfortunes all on Communist infiltration of the highest levels of government. Within a year after the "loss" of China to Communism and the testing of a Soviet atomic device, the name of Joe McCarthy had become a household word as the Republican senator from Wisconsin launched a "witch hunt" for Communists in the State Department and other government agencies, including, finally, the army.

The Truman administration suffered politically from what the president's new secretary of state, Dean Acheson, dubbed the "Revolt of the Primitives." Regardless of the

Taiwanese premier Gen. Chiang Ching-kuo succeeded his father, Chiang Kai-shek, who fled China in 1949 in the face of a Communist takeover and headed a government-in-exile on the island of Taiwan. (Chinese Information Service)

domestic uproar, difficult decisions still had to be made in foreign policy and defense. Truman reacted to the events of 1949 by taking the first tentative steps toward expanding containment programs into the Far East. In the spring of 1950, after the Soviet Union and mainland China had signed a treaty of friendship, the Truman administration began to subsidize the French effort against Communist forces in Indochina and to reassess its hands-off policy concerning the Chinese Nationalist government, which had fled to the island of Taiwan in the wake of the Communist victory on the mainland. Truman also accelerated negotiations of a peace treaty with Japan that would bring America's erstwhile enemy, with its enormous economic potential, into the anticommunist camp. The president further decided to proceed with the development of a hydrogen bomb (H-bomb)—the "super"—many times more powerful than an atomic bomb. Several prominent scientists opposed the decision, but the president and his advisers countered that the United States would be placed in a precarious position if the Soviets developed the H-bomb and the United States did not. Finally, in light of world conditions, Truman asked Acheson to head up a State Department-Defense Department reassessment of U.S. policy in the Cold War.

NSC-68

The results of that reassessment were contained in the top secret National Security Council paper numbered NSC-68, delivered to President Truman in April 1950. NSC-68, heralded by Acheson as one of the most important documents of the Cold War, was, in fact, a culmination of a process that had been underway for some time to identify the nature of the Soviet threat and to prescribe the most effective U.S. response to it. To no one's surprise, NSC-68 defined international Communism directed by the Soviet Union as seeking "to impose its authority over the rest of the world." Containment of that threat was still the recommended response, but now a new twist was added. Whereas early containment measures had focused on the security of Western Europe, future U.S. policy, the paper argued, needed to be commensurate with the challenge; that is, it should respond to Communist aggression throughout the world. To do this effectively, the United States had to retain its lead in nuclear weapons, but also expand its conventional military forces. NSC-68 did not mention the cost of a military buildup, but its authors talked privately of a $40 billion annual defense budget.

The president accepted NSC-68's assessment of the Soviet threat but regarded its recommendations as politically unrealizable and economically unacceptable. Although NSC-68 maintained that the survival of the country took priority over budgetary considerations and although one of Truman's key economic advisers indicated that the country could afford both guns and butter, the president was not

Syngman Rhee was the president of South Korea during the Korean War, in which the United States led a United Nations coalition to oppose Communist aggression. (United Nations)

inclined to alter his commitment to low defense budgets. The document, therefore, was not formally accepted as the national security policy of the United States—not, that is, until North Korea invaded South Korea in June 1950. The U.S. forces Truman committed to the defense of the Republic of Korea (South Korea) initially made a poor showing, the inevitable consequence of postwar inattention. The war and the U.S. military commitment to Europe under NATO mandated increased defense spending. During the Korean War, the annual defense budget exceeded $40 billion, and in September 1950, NSC-68 officially became the basis for U.S. policy in the Cold War.

KOREAN WAR CONSEQUENCES

The impact of the Korean War was felt across the Cold War spectrum. With respect to Western Europe, the United States increased military assistance and, in the winter of 1951, took the momentous step of stationing four U.S. Army divisions on European territory (in addition to the two already there for occupation duty). The U.S. troops could not hope to stop a full-scale Soviet invasion of the West, but they could serve as a tripwire that would likely bring the U.S. nuclear arsenal into play should Moscow be so reckless. Furthermore, under the leadership of General Eisenhower, whom Truman had made the first Supreme Allied Commander of NATO, the alliance began to approximate the efficient military "organization" its title implied. Greece and Turkey, both some distance from the northern Atlantic, joined NATO in 1952 to shore up Western Europe's southern flank. In a more controversial move, West Germany sought entry into the alliance. In 1954, the French, still fearful of a resurgent Germany, vetoed the European Defense Community, a supranational organization in which West German units would have been integrated into the Western defense system. A year later, the political climate changed enough so that West Germany became a full-fledged member of NATO without having to integrate its troops into foreign units. In retaliation, the Soviet Union that year created the Warsaw Pact, which included Soviet satellites in Eastern Europe and the government of East Germany.

If the Korean War spurred the development of NATO, it also accelerated the extension of containment into the Far East. The Truman administration continued to withhold diplomatic recognition from the People's Republic of China and, at the beginning of the war, interposed the U.S. 7th Fleet in the Straits of Formosa to prevent Mao's government from attacking the Chinese Nationalist regime on Taiwan. Of perhaps greater significance, North Korean and Chinese Communist aggression against South Korea reinforced the prewar shift in U.S. policy toward Japan, whose reemergence as a regional economic power the Truman administration had come to endorse.

Toward this goal, Washington stepped up its efforts to forge a peace settlement formally ending the state of war with Japan and securing U.S. bases in that country. The Japanese peace treaty signed by several countries (but not the Soviet Union) in September 1951 and a related defense agreement accomplished these objectives. Countries in the western Pacific that had been ravaged by Japan during World War II signed the peace treaty only after the United States had formally committed itself to their protection. U.S. defense pacts with Australia and New Zealand brought the ANZUS alliance into being, while a bilateral pact was concluded with the Philippines.

In January 1953, Eisenhower, a Republican, replaced Truman, a Democrat, in the White House. Building on the alliance system started under his predecessor, the new president approved a defense agreement with the Republic of Korea as a means of enticing the South Korean president, Syngman Rhee, to accept a negotiated end to the hostilities. The Eisenhower administration also signed a bilateral agreement with the Chinese Nationalist government, thus institutionalizing Truman's nonrecognition policy toward the People's Republic. Rounding out the flurry of "pactomania" in the Far East, the United States

and seven other countries in 1954 created the Southeast Asia Treaty Organization (SEATO), designed to protect the region's weaker states from internal subversion and external aggression.

Concept of Limited War

The Korean War also had a decided impact on thinking about military strategy. The war defied the fundamental assumptions contained in U.S. war plans. U.S. forces found themselves engaged not in World War III but rather in fighting a war limited geographically to the Korean peninsula, limited in the weapons used (Truman and Eisenhower both considered the use of atomic bombs but for various reasons chose not to employ them), and limited during most of the war in terms of U.S. objectives. Before the breakout from the Pusan perimeter by UN forces and after the Chinese intervention in November 1950, the objectives had included the restoration of the prewar status with some minor, but significant, shifts in the demilitarized zone above and below the 38th parallel.

The conduct of the war had presented a dilemma for U.S. policymakers. South Korea was never considered a vital U.S. interest, and after the intervention by the Chinese Communists, Truman often reiterated his position that the United States sought no wider war. Korea, in other words, was not worth the risk of a global conflagration. Yet, if South Korea was not a vital interest, it was important enough to convince the president and his advisers that U.S. inaction in the face of flagrant Soviet-backed aggression would only invite further reckless ventures by the Soviet Union and its allies, perhaps in the Middle East or Western Europe. The situation recalled the reaction of Britain and France to Germany's demands over Czechoslovakia before World War II, and the calamitous effect of giving in to these demands during a meeting at Munich, Germany. The influence of the Munich analogy in June 1950 cannot be underestimated. As the war evolved, combat operations became a means not to win the war militarily, since such an attempt might result in expansion of the conflict to the Chinese mainland and perhaps to Europe, but to exert enough pressure to make the enemy realize the folly of further hostilities, thus forcing the enemy to the peace table, where a political end to the war could be negotiated.

In the wake of the Korean War, euphemistically called a "police action," strategic thinkers developed the concept of "limited war" that would explain what had transpired and offer a guide for the crisis management of similar situations that might arise in the future. The theory of limited war regarded war and peace as a continuum in which military capabilities served primarily as political and diplomatic instruments that national security managers could orchestrate not to attain military victory in the traditional sense but to affect the *intentions* of the combatants and make them amenable to *political* solutions. Adherents of the theory deemed centralized civilian control as essential, not only over policy determinations but over military operations as well. The military had to be kept on a tight leash lest the actions of a local or theater commander jeopardize the political objectives sought by the U.S. government or, worse, escalate a local crisis into a regional or global confrontation.

Military professionals conceded policymaking and the formulation of strategic political goals to the civilian establishment, but they insisted on autonomy in the control of military operations and tactics. Even officers who accepted the need for constraint in Korea spoke against employing in future conflicts a model based on the subordination of military operations to political considerations. They wanted, in short, no more "Korea-type" wars.

The New Look

President Eisenhower agreed, although not necessarily for the same reasons. The former general came into office as a Republican internationalist; that is, he believed in collective security and an active role for the United States in world affairs. Also, despite some loose rhetoric in the 1952 presidential campaign about liberating the enslaved people of Eastern Europe from Communist governments, Eisenhower basically accepted Truman's more reactive containment policy, a policy that Eisenhower himself, as chief of staff of the army and as the commander of NATO, had helped to shape. Soviet-led international Communism, he firmly believed, sought world domination through a variety of means, including subversion, devious diplomacy, indirect aggression, and limited war by proxy. In what analysts term a "zero-sum game," any Communist success was perceived by the Eisenhower administration as a setback for the United States and its allies. Mutual security pacts were one means of coping with Communist aggression and avoiding setbacks. So, too, was the U.S. nuclear deterrent. Another critical element was a strong national economy. Should the United States suffer an economic collapse, international Communism would win the Cold War by default, Eisenhower often stressed.

The president's commitment to a strong economy collided with the high defense budgets implicit in NSC-68 and made reality by the Korean War. Unless there were drastic cuts in military spending, Eisenhower declared, inflation would soar and the United States would spend itself into oblivion. In this sense, he shared the abhorrence of his military advisers to limited wars such as the one in Korea; they were just too expensive. The United States literally could not afford to expand its capabilities to challenge Communist initiatives on every front. From this logic it was but a short step back toward Truman's original strategy of "asymmetrical" containment. The Eisenhower administration would attempt to play U.S. strength against

Communist weakness; to deprive the Communists of the initiative by denying to them the ability to dictate the time, place, and means of the U.S. response to their challenges; to keep the Communists guessing as to how the United States might respond to any act of aggression; and to maintain at home both a credible U.S. military capability and a strong economy.

Labeled the New Look, Eisenhower's concept of containment was set forth in NSC 162/2 of October 1953. Basically a policy of deterrence, it inexorably came to rely heavily on the U.S. nuclear arsenal. A war with the Soviet Union or the People's Republic of China was almost certain to involve nuclear weapons. But the New Look held out the distinct possibility that tactical nuclear weapons, on line by the early 1950s, might be used in local or regional conflicts as well, or even against Soviet and Chinese targets, if allies and conventional U.S. naval and air power could not stop aggression at weak points along the Communist periphery. As NSC 162/2 stated, "in the event of hostilities, the United States will consider nuclear weapons to be available for use as other munitions."

Pres. Dwight D. Eisenhower's 1953 New Look was a policy of deterrence—the United States would not hesitate to use nuclear weapons against Communist aggression if necessary. (Library of Congress)

NUCLEAR WAR ALTERNATIVES

Eisenhower did not rely solely on the threat of "massive retaliation" (a term derived from a speech by Sec. of State John Foster Dulles) to prevent war, lessen Cold War tensions, or manage crises. The president firmly believed that traditional diplomacy could resolve secondary points of contention between East and West, even if it could not eliminate fundamental differences. Eisenhower met with the post-Stalin Soviet leadership at Geneva, Switzerland, in 1955 and with Soviet premier Nikita Khrushchev at Camp David, Maryland, in 1959. Neither summit produced major agreements, but both temporarily lowered Cold War tensions, a consequence not entirely welcomed by all administration members, especially Dulles, who feared that the American public would be lulled into a false sense of security, perhaps to the point of calling on the administration to make concessions to the Communists that Dulles considered unwise.

Thus, while negotiations succeeded in ending the Korean War in 1953 and in obtaining an Austrian peace treaty in 1955, neither side could suspend its distrust of the other to take the risks that might produce agreements on arms limitations or the reunification of Germany. That being the case, the Eisenhower administration, quick to accuse Communists of employing blatantly false propaganda against the Free World, itself often used diplomacy more to score propaganda points, by emphasizing American virtues and the essential goodness of U.S. initiatives, than to seek accord with the other side, which it depicted as inherently evil and by nature disposed to chicanery.

Eisenhower also relied on the system of military alliances to prevent war. The presence of NATO troops would likely deter armed Soviet aggression in Europe, although the United States grew frustrated over the failure of its European partners to contribute what Washington perceived as their fair share to the alliance's conventional capabilities. On the periphery of the Eurasian mass, U.S. promises and military assistance would presumably allow allies to counter Communist subversion and indirect aggression. If the Communists employed military forces in a local or regional crisis, the president could commit U.S. air and naval power against them.

Another instrument Eisenhower could draw upon to fight Communism was the covert operations of the CIA. In Iran in 1953, the agency engineered a coup against a Nationalist leader deemed by the U.S. government to be procommunist. That success was followed a year later by the overthrow of a presumably leftist government in Guatemala, after a small CIA-trained army of Guatemalans entered the country and began an extensive campaign of psychological warfare to convince the country's president that a full-fledged invasion had taken place. The regular

John Foster Dulles (left), *conferring with statesman Adlai Stevenson, coined the term "massive retaliation," referring to one of President Eisenhower's strategies to prevent the Soviets from starting a third world war.* (National Archives)

Guatemalan military overthrew the president, and the United States, praising this "spontaneous uprising" of the people, made the leader of the "invading" army the new president. Only after Eisenhower had left the White House did the American people find out about the CIA's involvement in the affair. The advantage of using covert operations was that they gave the president "deniability" should something go wrong. There was a downside, however, even to success. There was, to begin with, the issue of whether covert operations violated democratic principles. There was also an attitude of superiority among U.S. officials in the wake of Iran and Guatemala, an attitude that such operations could not fail. Thus, when the administration determined that Fidel Castro, who had seized power in Cuba in 1959, was a Communist, the president had few qualms about instructing the CIA to engineer his downfall. The result was the disaster at the Bay of Pigs in 1961 under Eisenhower's successor, Pres. John F. Kennedy.

Pentomic Division

Under a national security strategy based principally on nuclear deterrence, the air force, with its plans for the strategic bombing of the Soviet Union, actually enhanced its position in the defense community. The other services felt the budget knife as Eisenhower slashed the high military spending created by the Korean War. The army, understandably, took the biggest cuts in its budget, which, as in the wake of World War II, prompted it to find a mission on the nuclear battlefield that would help recoup its losses. In the early 1950s, several army studies concluded that, given the Soviet and Chinese practice of massing troops, tactical nuclear weapons could be employed effectively in a general war against either country. To lessen its own vulnerability in an atomic war, the U.S. Army would have to forgo the suicidal concentration of troops and supplies and adapt its doctrine and force structure to dispersed warfare on a fluid battlefield.

In 1956, the army presented plans for converting existing divisions into "pentomic" divisions, capable of employing atomic weapons and fighting atomic war. The new division was composed of five "battle groups." The battle group, according to historian Robert Doughty, "was larger than the previous battalion but smaller than a regiment. Each battle group contained five rifle companies, a combat support company . . . , and a headquarters company. The battle group was directly controlled by the division commander though special task forces of two or more battle groups could be formed under an assistant division commander." Units would be dispersed in a checkerboard fashion to deny the enemy attractive targets for tactical nuclear weapons. Through superior mobility, the groups could converge to launch an attack, then disperse again. "The Army," Doughty concludes, "probably has never experienced a more radical change during peacetime in its thought, doctrine and organization."

Established institutions with entrenched procedures do not adapt well to radical change, and the U.S. Army is no exception. Weapons systems and equipment essential to the success of the pentomic division were not available and could not be produced in a timely way. Reduction of army manpower to 861,964 also hindered implementation of the new concept. By 1959, army leaders were already looking for an alternative to the pentomic division. They ended their search in the early 1960s with the transition to the Reorganized Objectives Army Division (ROAD), a more traditional organization in which combat maneuver battalions and three brigade headquarters were attached to a common division base.

Perennial Crises

The atomic war for which the army and its sister services prepared never materialized, although war scares permeated the decade of the 1950s, thanks to a series of international crises that narrowed the gap between cold war and hot war. A short-lived Soviet "peace offensive" following the death of Stalin in 1953 and the end of the Korean War lessened tensions somewhat, but in the rigid setting of mutual suspicion and firmly held perceptions, little basis existed for détente.

To begin with, neither side would budge on the issue of German reunification, and Khrushchev's periodic threats to sign a separate peace treaty with the East German regime, thus placing Allied access rights in jeopardy, created a dangerous situation in the middle of Europe that would extend into the following decade. In the Far East, in late 1954 and early 1955, the United States stood on the verge

In 1954, French forces under Col. Christian de Castries (shown in his bunker) were losing the battle against the Vietnamese Communists at Dien Bien Phu, but President Eisenhower would not commit U.S. forces to the war. (National Archives)

of war with China over two islands off the Chinese coast, Quemoy and Matsu. Peking vowed to remove Chinese Nationalist troops from the islands by force and, in what was perceived as a prelude to invasion, began shelling Nationalist positions from the mainland. Eisenhower, in a controversial move, determined that the islands were essential to the defense and morale of the U.S.-backed Nationalist government on Taiwan. At one point, the administration prepared to use tactical nuclear weapons against military targets on the mainland, but Mao's government, for a variety of reasons, retreated from a direct military confrontation with the United States. The Quemoy-Matsu crisis erupted again in 1958, with similar inconclusive results.

To the south of China, the French were waging an intense war against Communist-led Viet Minh forces. As French fortunes waned during the disastrous battle of Dien Bien Phu in 1954, France made overtures regarding U.S. intervention. Several of Eisenhower's closest advisers urged him to commit U.S. air and naval power to the struggle, even to the point of using tactical atomic bombs around the isolated French outpost, but the president took a more cautious approach, setting conditions for U.S. military involvement that he suspected neither the U.S. Congress nor the French government could accept.

The president also rejected appeals to intervene in Hungary in 1956. Early that year, Khrushchev had made an emotional speech denouncing the suffering the Soviet people endured during the years of Stalin's dictatorship. Although given in secret, the "de-Stalinization" speech soon became known throughout the world. In Eastern Europe, several Communist leaders regarded Khrushchev's words and other signals from Moscow as an opportunity to lessen the Soviet hold over their countries. There were riots in

Poland, but Soviet concessions and a visit by Khrushchev relieved the tension. In Hungary, however, a Communist reform government threatened to take the country out of the Warsaw Pact. What semblance of toleration the Soviet Union had previously demonstrated snapped and, after pulling Soviet troops out of Budapest, the Soviet Union turned them around in a surprise move and reentered the city. Troops and armor suppressed the revolt by force, and its leader was summoned to Moscow under a promise of safe conduct and was then executed. The duplicity and brutality of the Soviet intervention generated emotional appeals from several quarters for the United States to liberate Hungary. Eisenhower stood firm against such a move, however, implicitly conceding the Soviet sphere of influence in Eastern Europe and coolly calculating that it was not in the interest of the United States to risk World War III in order to free Hungary, however tragic the situation in that country might be.

MIDDLE EAST INTERVENTION

In retrospect, historians have given Eisenhower high marks for the thoughtful manner in which he handled the use of U.S. power during his tenure in office. Only once after Korea did he send U.S. troops abroad on a combat mission: In 1958, the United States intervened in Lebanon in an effort to stabilize what the Eisenhower administration correctly perceived as an increasingly turbulent region.

The creation of Israel in 1948 and the ensuing Arab-Israeli conflict, the breakdown of colonialism in the Middle East and the consequent decline of Western influence, the rise of radical Arab nationalism in the region, and Soviet initiatives to take advantage of anti-Western sentiment all combined to create a high level of instability in the Middle East by the mid-1950s. Eisenhower saw radical Arab nationalism as espoused by Syria and by Egypt's new leader, Gamal Abdel Nasser, as the immediate threat to U.S. interests in the region and to U.S. national security in general. Nasser's anti-Western rhetoric and appeals to Arab unity produced a popular following conceivably capable of overthrowing pro-Western governments in the Middle East and of opening the area to Communist penetration. To avoid this latter possibility, the United States, handicapped in the Arab world because of its strong ties to Israel, helped behind the scenes to create a military alliance, the Baghdad Pact. Its members consisted of Great Britain, Turkey, Iraq, Iran (governed by the Shah of Iran, who had taken control with CIA help), and Pakistan. The agreement among the northern tier states of the Middle East failed to deter the Soviets, who instead of employing military force used promises of economic aid to gain a foothold in the area. Creation of the pact, however, did

succeed in further alienating Nasser, who turned to the Soviet Union for arms and economic assistance.

Displeased with Nasser and his overtures to Communist countries, the United States withdrew support for a high dam on the Aswan River. Soon thereafter, Nasser nationalized the Suez Canal, then under British control. When diplomacy failed to resolve the crisis, Israel struck at Egypt in the Sinai Peninsula, thus providing Great Britain and France (which had its own troubles with Nasser and his Pan-Arab message in its colony of Algeria) with a prearranged pretext for intervention to stop the fighting. In reality, all three countries sought the overthrow of Nasser. The intervention, undertaken without consulting the United States, strained the Western alliance and drew a sharp rebuke from an irate Eisenhower. As Khrushchev levied an empty threat to rain rockets on London and Paris, the United States used its leverage to force the British, French, and Israelis to withdraw from territories they had seized. The Suez Crisis, which occurred simultaneously with the Soviet intervention in Hungary and the U.S. presidential election campaign, virtually ended British influence in the Middle East.

The United States moved to fill the power vacuum before Nasser or Khrushchev could cause a further deterioration of the situation. In 1957, in an effort to bolster pro-American Arab leaders, Eisenhower declared that the United States would help defend any country in the region threatened by Communist aggression. The doctrine of containment now covered the Middle East. The so-called Eisenhower Doctrine received a mixed response from friendly governments, primarily because Arab nationalism, not international Communism, presented the principal threat to their existence. In February 1958, Egypt and Syria formed the United Arab Republic, and tension in the area continued to mount. When a domestic crisis erupted in pro-Western Lebanon that spring, the Eisenhower administration feared Syrian involvement and, consequently, began to consider U.S. intervention. A decision to do so came on July 14, 1958, after pro-Nasser elements in Iraq staged a coup, killing members of Iraq's pro-Western royal family. To prevent a similar occurrence in Lebanon, Eisenhower ordered U.S. forces into the country, while the British sent troops to support a friendly government in Jordan.

The U.S. intervention in Lebanon in 1958 was the first major U.S. contingency operation of the Cold War. The marines expected to enter a combat zone, but when they stormed a beach south of Beirut, they encountered sunbathers and ice-cream vendors, not Syrian regulars. Augmented by U.S. Army units pulled out of Europe, the invasion force at its peak exceeded 5,000. The deployment lasted several months, during which the Americans suffered only one fatality, the victim of a sniper. While diplomats tried to resolve an internal crisis of nightmare

Officers of the United Nations Emergency Force are flown by helicopter into El Arish on the Sinai Peninsula to supervise the withdrawal of Israeli troops in 1957. (United Nations)

proportions involving groups divided by religion, tribal loyalty, ethnic heritage, political allegiance, and a myriad of other factors, U.S. troops performed peacemaking and peacekeeping missions. The U.S. force quickly made the transition from a war-fighting to a constabulary posture, providing a show of force and, with the Lebanese army, conducting patrols to keep the warring factions in Beirut from each other. Before the year was out, a settlement of the crisis had been negotiated, and U.S. units left the country. At the time, Eisenhower received some domestic criticism for intervening in the first place. Historians of the Vietnam War era, however, have commended the president for his deft crisis management in committing U.S. forces to achieve limited and realistic objectives and then removing them from harm's way once those objectives had been attained.

A NEW COLD WAR

As Eisenhower closed out his second term as president, at the beginning of 1961, the Cold War was raging as intensely as ever. A summit conference scheduled for May 1960 collapsed when he refused to apologize to Khrush-chev for spying on the Soviet Union after the Russians had shot down a U.S. U-2 spy aircraft. Khrushchev threatened to retaliate militarily on NATO bases in Turkey, and the world again went through another case of war jitters. But while the superpower rivalry continued unabated, moving toward its apex in the Cuban Missile Crisis of 1962, significant changes were taking place in the international environment. The bipolar pattern of the late 1940s and early 1950s, characterized by two superpowers and their respective clients, was unraveling. Well before it became apparent to the West, the Soviet Union and China were deeply divided over ideological issues and traditional rivalries. As the Sino-Soviet split unfolded, Khrushchev's de-Stalinization campaign created difficulties for Soviet control over Eastern Europe. The trend toward polycentrism in the Communist world was paralleled by developments in the noncommunist camp, where the emergence of a strong Europe and of Japan by the mid-1950s made it more difficult for the United States to assert its leadership unchallenged.

Emerging Nations
The perceived simplicity of a bipolar world was also undermined during the 1950s by the emergence of nations

previously considered on the periphery of the Western-dominated system of Great-Power politics. World War II weakened many of the colonial ties that bound countries in Asia, Africa, and the Middle East to the Western powers. Through peaceful means or violence, colonial areas sought independence, looking to the UN and to the superpowers for support. Those countries that achieved independence proved eager to have a voice in world affairs. Some chose to align themselves with one side or the other in the Cold War; others preferred to remain nonaligned. In either case, neither the United States nor the Soviet Union could ignore their presence and their demands. As a result, by the time Eisenhower left office, U.S. Cold War strategies, which originally concentrated on Soviet ambitions in Europe, had come to embrace virtually the entire world, just as NSC-68 had anticipated.

The Soviet Union and the People's Republic of China sought to take advantage of the anticolonial, anti-Western sentiments that generally accompanied the strong nationalism expressed by leaders of the emerging countries. China, for example, played a prominent role in the Bandung Conference of nonaligned nations in 1955. The Soviet leadership, for its part, launched an economic offensive in the mid-1950s calculated to win friends, even allies, through the promise of economic assistance, so desperately needed in most of the new nations.

The United States reacted to these developments, imposing a Cold War template on the process of decolonization and emerging nationalism. The Soviet economic offensive alarmed the Eisenhower administration, for it appeared

Soviet leader Nikita Krushchev, shown after addressing the United Nations in 1959, constantly tested the Eisenhower Doctrine—a doctrine of containment with the threat of nuclear warfare. (United Nations)

that the Soviet Union could "leapfrog" the system of military alliances designed to contain Communism and, through economic aid and support for "wars of liberation," tilt the balance of power in the Cold War against the United States and its friends and allies. Yet, despite this concern, U.S. statesmen found themselves in a disadvantageous position. They could not readily embrace Nationalist leaders who publicly denounced Western imperialism, appeared openly friendly to the Soviet Union or China, and adopted socialistic programs to further economic development. When the United States did offer economic assistance to emerging nations, it was often through private organizations and with conditions that offended the sensibilities of leaders determined to demonstrate their new independence. Furthermore, the Eisenhower administration's preference for dealing with anticommunist Nationalist leaders often resulted in U.S. support for individuals out of touch with the desires and needs of large segments of their own societies. How to devise a more effective approach to what many in the West labeled the "Third World" would quickly become a political issue in American domestic politics.

Balance of Terror

The domestic debate over U.S. policy toward the Third World was accompanied by another aimed at Eisenhower's New Look. Both the Soviet Union and the United States had acquired the H-bomb in the early 1950s, but only the latter, with its intercontinental bombers, had the means to deliver it effectively over great distances. The Soviets, too, had long-range bombers, but had deliberately refrained from expanding or upgrading the force in order to give priority to the development of missiles capable of delivering nuclear warheads anywhere in the world. In August 1957, the Soviets became the first of the superpowers to test an intercontinental ballistic missile (ICBM) successfully: Two months later, the Russians used their advanced rocketry to launch *Sputnik I*, a man-made satellite.

The satellite launch sent shock waves through the United States, as panicked Americans confronted their true vulnerability in the nuclear age. Ill-founded opinions concerning the inferiority of American to Russian science and technology and public speculation about the United States being on the wrong side of a missile gap fueled the panic. Pressure mounted on Eisenhower to increase defense spending, but the president refused to yield, aware as he was from U-2 flights and other intelligence sources that the Soviets enjoyed no strategic advantage over the United States, whose own missile program was proceeding apace. Historian Stephen Ambrose has described Eisenhower's levelheaded response to the often irrational cries for more defense spending as the president's finest hour.

The arrival of the missile age did, however, raise valid questions regarding the soundness of the New Look strat-

1 NOVEMBER 1962
MRBM LAUNCH SITE 2
SAN CRISTOBAL

MISSILE-READY TENT

FUEL TRAILERS

FORMER LAUNCH POSITIONS

FORMER LOCATION OF MISSILE-READY TENTS

By 1960, the policy of deterrence did not hold the threat that it previously had—the Soviets had a substantial nuclear missile arsenal and were supplying their ally Cuba, as President Kennedy discovered in 1962. (U.S. Air Force)

egy. Each superpower now had the weapons and the means of delivering them to inflict unacceptable damage on the other. As a result, mutual deterrence was reinforced, making a nuclear exchange unthinkable and, thus, less likely. However, mutual deterrence also meant that the primary emphasis that the United States placed on its nuclear arsenal to deter all forms of aggression lost much of its credibility. Would, for example, a U.S. president order a nuclear attack on Moscow in retaliation for some form of Communist aggression in the Middle East, or even in Europe, if he knew that the United States would come under nuclear attack in return? Critics of the New Look thought not. U.S. nuclear weapons might avert nuclear war, they conceded, but they could no longer deter (if, in fact, they ever had) other forms of Communist aggression such as insurgency, limited war by proxy, and subversion.

Confronted with these threats, a U.S. president acting according to the New Look and facing Soviet missiles would have but one pair of options: nuclear war or surrender. A new, more flexible strategy was needed, the critics argued, one that would allow the United States and its allies to respond effectively to Communist initiatives without resorting to nuclear war.

Eisenhower regarded criticism of the New Look as ill-founded. The deliberate ambiguity of the New Look had, he believed, kept the Soviets guessing as to the circumstances under which the United States would use its nuclear weapons, thus making the Kremlin more cautious than it might otherwise have been. When Communist aggression had occurred, the United States had responded effectively and without resort to nuclear warfare. Korea, Iran, Guatemala, Quemoy and Matsu, and Lebanon served as proof of this point. Yet, the critics would not be stilled, including Kennedy, Eisenhower's successor. As the United States entered a new decade, the Cold War had become vastly more complex and seemed to many to re-quire new approaches. Kennedy's inauguration as president in January 1961 paved the way for a new Cold War strategy and new U.S. initiatives.

3

The Korean War: 1950–1953

The immediate origins of the Korean War lay in a series of events at the end of World War II. Korea had been annexed by Japan in 1910, an action that went unquestioned by the nations of the world. Not until Japan attacked the United States on Dec. 7, 1941, did the United States acknowledge that Korea had been an early victim of Japanese aggression in the Far East.

At the Cairo Conference in December 1943, the United States, China, and Great Britain proclaimed that they were determined that Korea eventually would become free and independent. The United States, feeling that the military occupation of Korea by a single power would be a serious mistake, called for an international administration. The administrative body would consist of representatives from the United States, Great Britain, China, and the Soviet Union. At the Yalta Conference in February 1945, Pres. Franklin D. Roosevelt suggested to Soviet leader Joseph Stalin that an international trusteeship be established to prepare Korea for independence after the defeat of Japan. Although Stalin appeared agreeable to the suggestion, the Soviet Union took no formal action on the proposal. At the Potsdam Conference (July 27–Aug. 2, 1945), the Allies again affirmed their intent to follow the Cairo pronouncement. When the Soviet Union declared war on Japan on Aug. 8, 1945, the Soviets announced that they would abide by the Potsdam pronouncement.

POST-WORLD WAR II KOREA

The sudden surrender of Japan negated the plan to administer Korea jointly and to avoid dividing it into military occupation zones. The U.S. Joint Chiefs of Staff (JCS) proposed that the Russians receive the surrender of the Japanese forces north of the 38th parallel and that the

United States accept the surrender of the Japanese south of that line. The Soviet chiefs of staff accepted the U.S. proposal without hesitation. While the United States considered the partition of Korea only a temporary and undesirable expedient, the Soviets were more than willing to see Korea divided. By December 1945, the United States had received reports that the Soviets were erecting fortifications on their side of the demarcation line. During the same month, the Soviets and the United States agreed to establish a Joint American-Soviet Commission to represent the two military commands in Korea. The intention was to have the joint commission work to help the Koreans form a provisional government; but despite this intention, nothing could be resolved concerning the eventual overall fate of Korea.

Finally, in September 1947, the United States requested that the United Nations (UN) address the problem of Korean unification. Although the Soviet Union objected, the UN General Assembly decided that a national government for Korea should be established following a general election. To supervise the election, a temporary UN commission on Korea was established by the assembly. Once a government was established for a unified Korea, it would form a security force, assume the governmental functions exercised by the occupation forces, and develop the plans necessary for the withdrawal of the occupation forces.

The Soviet Union and North Korea
The North Korean Communists refused to allow the UN commission to hold elections within its borders. Despite the lack of cooperation by the North Koreans, the commission held elections in the south on May 10, 1948. The elections formed the Republic of Korea (ROK) with Syngman Rhee as president. The UN General Assembly twice, in 1948 and 1949, declared that the government of the

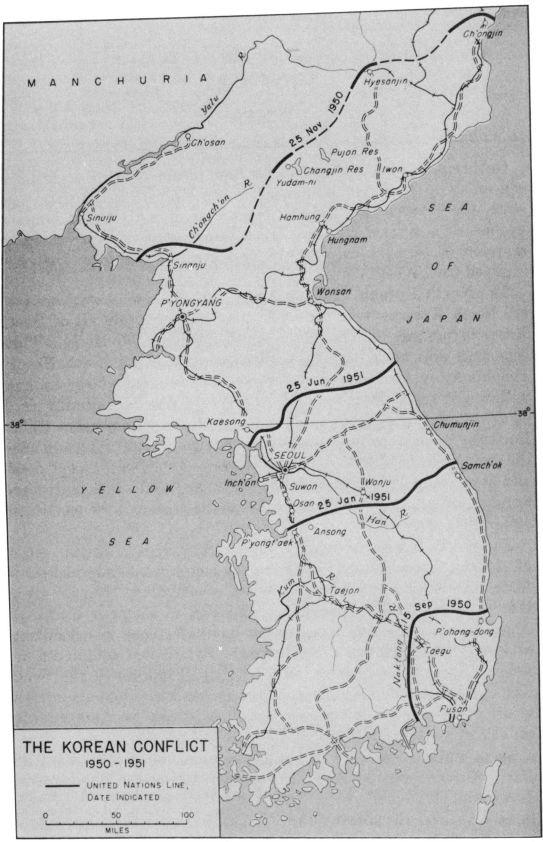

The Korean Conflict 1950–1951 (From ROTCM 145–20: American Military History: 1607–1958. [Washington: HQDA, July 1959])

ROK was the only freely elected and lawful government of Korea. The General Assembly established a UN commission on Korea that was supposed to work for the peaceful unification of the nation.

The Soviet Union refused to take part in the UN activities in Korea. Instead, the Soviets moved to establish a government in North Korea. On May 25, 1948, elections were held for a Supreme People's Assembly, which purported to represent the people of both North and South Korea. The new People's Democratic Republic of Korea was headed by Kim Il-sung, a Russian-trained Communist. On September 20, the Russians announced that they would withdraw all of their troops from Korea by Jan. 1, 1949.

The United States and South Korea

The announcement of Soviet withdrawal was welcomed by U.S. military leaders, who wanted to withdraw American forces from Korea. The 45,000 men in Korea could be used elsewhere in the world. Despite their desire to remove the occupation forces from Korea, there was no desire to abandon the newly formed ROK. A plan was formulated that outlined the potential policy for the United States. The plan, approved by Pres. Harry S Truman on Apr. 8, 1948, outlined a system whereby the United States would train and equip a South Korean security force. In addition, the United States would provide economic assistance to the new nation while trying to persuade its leaders to follow policies that would help to stabilize the new government. The United States would also work to have the UN solve the problems of a divided Korea.

Based upon their perception of the functions to be performed by the ROK military force, the United States worked to train an army of 65,000, a coast guard of 4,000, and a police force of 35,000. Because it was a security force, the army was equipped with small arms, heavy machine guns, and mortars, but no tanks nor artillery. The Koreans believed that they needed a larger force that was more heavily equipped to protect themselves adequately from the North Koreans. Consequently, the Seoul government lobbied for a force consisting of a 100,000-man army, a militia of 50,000, an air force of 3,000, a navy of 10,000, and a police force of 50,000.

Despite U.S. insistence that the South Koreans concentrate on attaining economic stability and not tax its economy with a large military establishment, the South Koreans continued to push for a larger military. At President Rhee's invitation, retired American major general Claire L. Chennault devised a plan for a Korean air force, something the Koreans believed that they needed to insure their independence. Gen. Douglas MacArthur rejected the plan because an air force was not necessary to maintain order. Additionally, MacArthur stated that the establishment of an air force would add credibility to the charges being made by the Communists that the United States was sponsoring an arms race on the Korean peninsula. In the face of U.S. misgivings, the South Koreans activated an air force on Oct. 10, 1949.

As the various South Korean forces reached an effective status, the United States withdrew its occupation forces. By June 29, 1949, the last U.S. units had left Korea, and the next day, MacArthur inactivated the U.S. Army Forces in Korea. Only a force of 500 U.S. military personnel remained in Korea as a part of the U.S. Korean Military Advisory Group (KMAG). With the inactivation of the U.S. Army Forces in Korea, U.S. responsibilities for the defense of South Korea ended.

Although it had withdrawn its military forces, the United States had not abandoned the effort to create a unified, free, and democratic Korea. However, these were political rather than military objectives, and the United States chose to work through the auspices of the UN, which had accepted the idea that Korea should be united and free. Although the UN did not sanction the formation of any particular form of government in Korea, it did advocate free elections to determine the type of government that would be established in the united Korea.

Despite the political nature of U.S. policy toward Korea, there were questions concerning what the reaction of the United States would be if South Korea were attacked by North Korea. On Jan. 12, 1950, Sec. of State Dean Acheson delivered a speech at the Washington Press Club that outlined U.S. defense policy in the Pacific. Acheson stated that America's defensive perimeter in the Pacific ran from the Aleutians to Japan, to the Ryukyus and then to the Philippines. U.S. military forces would unilaterally defend this perimeter. Any attack outside the perimeter would be defended by the people initially attacked and then by the nations of the world acting under the provisions of the UN charter. Acheson's pronouncement seemed to indicate that two areas—Korea and Formosa—fell outside the area the United States was prepared to defend against aggression. This apparent omission seemed to convey the wrong message to the Communists. Although Acheson mentioned that the nations of the world, acting under the UN charter, would defend any nation that was the victim of aggression, the fact that the Soviet Union could veto any action that might be taken by the UN Security Council meant that the UN was unlikely to be able to take any action that might halt aggression.

Policy of NSC-68/2

In an examination of U.S. plans and objectives conducted in response to the detonation of the Soviet atomic bomb, the U.S. National Security Council (NSC) paper numbered NSC-68 was produced by representatives from the State Department planning staff, the JCS, and the Office of the Secretary of Defense. The overall assessment contained in NSC-68 was to drive the foreign and defense policy of the United States for at least the next three decades. NSC-68 viewed the Soviet leadership as intent upon retaining absolute power in all those areas under its control, upon wanting to dominate the Eurasian landmass, and upon subverting and destroying its main adversary, the United States. Soviet possession of the atomic bomb, along with its conventional forces, which were far larger than needed in peacetime, made the Soviet Union a formidable power in the international arena.

The JCS estimated that if Soviet forces were sent to war in 1950, they could easily conquer Western Europe, move into the oil-rich regions of the Middle East, and consolidate their holdings in the Far East. In addition, these forces could strike the United Kingdom through the air, launch both sea and air attacks in the Atlantic and Pacific Oceans, and perhaps even use atomic weapons on selected strategic targets.

The report maintained that the United States had to maintain a strong international community and contain the Soviet system within its existing boundaries by using all means short of war. NSC-68 argued that the United States had to maintain a strong military establishment that could guarantee national security and make containment a viable policy. If the United States was unable to insure that containment was viable, the policy would be reduced to one of bluff.

The report advocated that the United States work to build up the economic, political, and military strength of the Free World. This buildup should include conventional forces in sufficient strength to support foreign commitments on the part of the United States. NSC-68 argued that, above all, the buildup of U.S. military strength had to be completed while the United States still possessed its atomic deterrent.

Although NSC-68 had not been approved when the Korean War began, the report delineated the guidelines that would come to dominate American policy. The United States had clearly indicated in the period following World War II that its national security views had expanded greatly.

INITIATION OF WAR

The North Korean government was primarily a creation of the Russians. Many Koreans had sought refuge in the Soviet Union during the Japanese occupation of their homeland. Very early during the Soviet occupation, a cadre of Communist-indoctrinated Koreans were sent back to Korea. The North Korean army was formed around a nucleus of two divisions composed of Korean exiles and refugees who had served with the Russians during World War II. In 1949 and 1950, three divisions of Koreans who had served with the Chinese Communist Forces (CCF) joined the North Korean forces. By June 25, 1950, the North Korean People's Army (NKPA) consisted of approximately 100,000 troops. The troops served in three infantry divi-

sions, three border brigades, and an armored brigade. The North Koreans also had a small air force that was equipped with 132 combat aircraft as well as additional support aircraft. The combat aircraft were based at two airfields near Pyongyang and one at Yampo.

Although the actions and motives of the Communists were shrouded in secrecy, KMAG monitored the activities in an effort to learn what was being planned. In May, KMAG could confirm that the North Koreans had six regular divisions near the 38th parallel. It also believed, but could not confirm, that seven new divisions were being formed from the constabulary force and new recruits in the area of the Manchurian border. Apprehensions concerning the possibility of military action on the part of the North Koreans increased as the Chinese Communists appeared to be nearing a successful conclusion of their operations against the Nationalists in China. Despite the indications that the North Koreans were building up their forces along the 38th parallel, the intelligence agencies could not agree upon when an attack would be made against the South Korean government.

North Korea Invades South Korea
On Sunday, June 25, 1950, units of the NKPA pushed south across the 38th parallel. The North Koreans quickly defeated the South Korean forces aligned along the parallel and continued their push south. The main North Korean force drove toward the South Korean capital of Seoul, located 35 miles below the 38th parallel on the west coast. Smaller forces advanced down the center of the peninsula and the east coast.

The South Korean troops, surprised by the attack, withdrew in disorder and confusion in the face of the North Korean advance. Those troops driven out of Seoul were forced to abandon much of their equipment, except for small arms, when the bridges across the Han River were destroyed before they could cross. After reaching Seoul, the North Koreans momentarily halted their advance in order to consolidate their gains and regroup their forces.

Because of the time difference between Korea and Washington, news of the North Korean attack arrived late on the night of June 24. On June 25, the UN Security Council adopted a resolution demanding the withdrawal of North Korean forces. On the night of June 25, President Truman, independent of the actions being taken by the Security Council, ordered General MacArthur to furnish ROK forces with equipment and ammunition. MacArthur was also to make certain that Americans were evacuated from Korea.

U.S. and UN Command Structure
The planners at MacArthur's Far East Command were to determine the best way to assist the South Koreans. In addition, Truman ordered the ships of the U.S. 7th Fleet from the Philippines and Ryukyu Islands to Japan. On

June 26, the president gave MacArthur permission to provide support to the South Koreans by employing air and naval strikes against North Korean positions below the 38th parallel. At the same time, in an effort to prevent the conflict from expanding, Truman redirected the bulk of the ships of the 7th Fleet to Taiwan. By placing the fleet's ships between the Chinese Communists on the mainland and the Nationalist Chinese on Taiwan, the United States hoped to prevent the two groups from attacking each other while the nations of the world were watching events in Korea.

On June 30, Truman gave MacArthur permission to use all forces available to him to assist the South Koreans. The forces immediately available to MacArthur in Japan were the 1st Cavalry Division and the 7th, 24th, and 25th infantry divisions, which were part of the 8th Army. In addition, the 29th Regimental Combat Team was stationed on Okinawa. The postwar demobilization had adversely affected the combat readiness of all of the units, which were understrength and short of support elements. There was a severe lack of some essential items, ammunition in particular, as well as tanks and effective antitank weapons. By any method of evaluation, MacArthur's ground forces were hardly prepared to go into combat. The Far East Air Force, MacArthur's air arm, was not prepared for offensive action since it was primarily intended to be an air defense force. The U.S. naval forces available to MacArthur—five combat ships and a small amphibious force—were part of Naval Forces, Far East.

Once the UN adopted the resolution declaring its intention to resist the Communist attack upon South Korea, a new series of problems, both political and military, surfaced. The UN possessed no military staff that could conduct military operations and no police force that could enforce its resolution if the North Koreans decided to ignore the request to withdraw from the South. On July 7, 1950, the UN Security Council adopted a resolution that established a unified command under the president of the United States. The resolution requested that the president appoint a commander of the UN forces. The United States was also the executive agent for all matters dealing with the conflict in Korea. On Jan. 3, 1950, the Soviet Union had begun a boycott of all UN organizations and committees on which Nationalist China participated. The Soviet action was in reaction to the refusal of the UN to replace the Nationalist Chinese representatives with the representatives from Communist China. On February 14, Moscow signed a 30-year treaty of friendship, alliance, and mutual assistance with Communist China. As a result of the boycott, the Soviet representative was not present in the UN Security Council to veto the resolution that authorized military action against the North Koreans.

On July 8, President Truman named MacArthur "commander of the military forces assisting the Republic of Korea which are placed under the unified command of the United States by members of the United Nations." MacArthur was already Supreme Commander Allied Powers (SCAP) for the occupation of Japan; commander in chief, Far East (CinCFE); and commanding general, U.S. Army Forces, Far East. On July 24, MacArthur established the United Nations Command (UNC) and assumed all of the responsibilities of commander in chief, UNC (CinCUNC).

The establishment of the UNC recognized the fact that other nations had joined the fight to repel aggression in Korea. In fact, the command lacked any real significance because General MacArthur simply assumed another title to accompany his title of CinCFE. MacArthur designated his headquarters as General Headquarters, UNC. He did not report directly to the UN; he reported to President Truman through the JCS. Orders were issued to MacArthur by the JCS, after being coordinated with the U.S. Department of State and approved by the president. All of the military units supplied by other members of the UN were attached for operational control to the appropriate U.S. military organizations. This arrangement seemed to be entirely appropriate since the United States was furnishing most of the military forces.

Within a short time, planners in the United States became aware of some of the problems associated with being the primary UN agent. Initially, the only guidance forthcoming from the UN was the June 27 resolution, which had recommended that the members furnish forces in sufficient numbers to repel the invasion of South Korea and to restore peace and security within the region. Interpretation of this resolution was open to question by the military planners. Specifically, did the resolution mean that UN forces could enter North Korean territory or were they only to restore the 38th parallel as the international boundary?

The U.S. State Department very quickly distinguished between UN military and political objectives and those of the United States. On June 30, 1950, the State Department told MacArthur to make it clear that the U.S. military effort was intended solely to restore the Republic of Korea territory to its June 25 status. The lack of a clear-cut policy had little impact on the planning of ground operations during the summer of 1950, since the UN ground forces were being driven steadily southward.

International Considerations

However, the overall policy of the UNC was not determined solely by the United States. Any policy formulated concerning the military or political situation in Korea had to meet the approval of those UN members that were furnishing troops to the war effort. The overall consensus was that the conflict could not be allowed to extend beyond the borders of Korea. During the early stages of the war, the concern about extending the conflict beyond Korea was directed at the employment of UN air power.

On June 30, MacArthur instructed Gen. George E. Stratemeyer, commander of the Far East Air Force, to be certain that the borders of Manchuria and the Soviet Union were not violated during air operations in North Korea. Thus, the sanctity of the border of Manchuria and the Soviet Union was established during the first month of combat and continued for the duration of the war.

Another problem was the policy of indiscriminate bombing of targets in North Korea. Following World War II, the U.S. Air Force had been criticized severely for what some considered to be inhumane mass bombings. Asian Americans had argued that during World War II, U.S. bombing operations had been different in Europe than they had been in Asia. They contended that far more care was taken in Europe to avoid heavy civilian casualties and mass destruction of nonmilitary targets. Truman pledged to the UN that bombing would not be indiscriminate and that care would be exercised to avoid civilian casualties. Consequently, General Stratemeyer received directions on June 30 to make certain that the Far East Air Force attacked only "purely military targets." The intention was that every effort would be made to minimize civilian casualties during military operations, especially during air attacks. On more than one occasion, air operations against North Korean targets were canceled by officials in Washington because they feared that civilian casualties would be high.

The UN policies concerning Korea, originally contained in the June 27 resolution of the UN Security Council, had been vague but they had been sufficient at the beginning of the conflict. However, as the military and political situation changed during the war, the lack of a formal organization capable of giving continuous guidance caused serious problems for the UNC. The problem of agreement among the members of the Security Council was difficult, but when the Soviet delegate returned to the council in August, any action on the part of the council was impossible because of the Soviet veto power. Consequently, questions of policy had to be taken to the UN General Assembly, where they would be subjected to lengthy debate and discussion before being approved or defeated.

In addition to the problem of obtaining guidance from the United Nations, there was the added problem of obtaining the approval of the nations that contributed forces to the UN war effort. This approval was pursued through diplomatic channels that were as slow as debate in the General Assembly. Consequently, requests from CinCUNC concerning issues that were known to be politically sensitive were relayed from Japan to Washington and then to the capitals of the other participating nations for discussion and disposition. In a war with rapidly changing military situations, the delays in resolving the numerous questions concerning policy created serious problems.

Geographical Factors

Two factors that played an important role in the battle for Korea were the physical geography of the peninsula and its climate. The Korean peninsula is bounded on the north by the Yalu and Tumen rivers, which separate Korea from Manchuria and Siberia; on the south by the Korea Strait; on the east by the Sea of Japan; and on the west by the Yellow Sea and Korea Bay. The Korean peninsula has an area of approximately 85,000 square miles, and its maximum extent is about 575 miles long. From Seoul south, the peninsula is about 150 miles wide. The peninsula is covered with mountains and gorges, deep ravines, and narrow valleys. Other features include mud flats, marshes, and rice paddies. The mountains in the north rise to 9,000 feet. From the east coast, the North and South Taebank ranges rise to 5,000–6,000 feet. The peninsula's rivers are channeled by the mountains.

The few good roads were on the peninsula's west coast, connecting the cities of Pusan, Taegu, Seoul, Kaesong, Pyongyang, and Sinuiju. In addition to the roads, the Japanese had constructed a railroad network of more than 3,500 miles of standard-gauge rail lines. The main line began at Pusan and ran north to Raegu, Tarejon, Seoul, and Pyongyang and then crossed the Yalu at Sinuiju.

Spur lines left the main line and ran to the southwest coast and returned to the east along the coast at Pusan. Two other lines ran across the peninsula from Seoul and Pyongyang to the cities of Wonson and Hungnam. Another line ran down the east coast from the Soviet port of Vladivostok to Sanchok. Both the rail lines and roads followed

American infantrymen patrol through marshland in Korea.
(National Archives)

the rivers and valleys. The nature of the terrain meant that operations off the established roads and railways would be extremely difficult, especially for mechanized forces.

The availability of harbor facilities also influenced military operations. Pusan, located at the southeastern end of the peninsula, possessed the best port in the country. The west coast had extremely high tides; for example, Inchon, Seoul's port, had nearly 30-foot tides and a small tidal basin that could only accommodate small ships. Other west coast ports at Kunsan, Yosu, Mokpo, and Chinnampo were primarily fishing ports and offered little or no support for large-scale shipping. On the northeast coast, only the ports of Wonson and Hungnam had facilities capable of supporting military operations.

The Japanese had constructed a number of airfields in Korea, but only two in South Korea could handle high-performance aircraft. These two fields, Kimpo and Suwon, had been improved during the American occupation. The other airfields were not suitable for U.S. air operations without considerable modification.

The Korean climate was usually hot and humid during the summer months and cold and dry during the winter. Heavy rains, accompanied by cloud cover and haze, were usual during the summer months. Temperatures during the winter were bitterly cold, especially in the northern regions and the higher altitudes.

One area of constant confusion for non-Koreans was the bewildering similarity in place names. Pyongyang was the North Korean capital; Pyonggang was the location of an airfield near the 38th parallel; and Pyongyong was a town on the railroad north of Pusan. One airfield on the south-eastern coast of Korea was known as Geijitsu Bay, Yon gil-wan, Pohang-dong, Pohangwan, or Pohong.

Status of the U.S. Military

In the years immediately preceding the North Korean invasion of South Korea, the expenditures by the United States on its military establishment had been small. The United States had a public debt of $247 billion that President Truman was determined to pay off. Consequently, when Congress appropriated extra funds for the military in the fiscal year 1948–49, Truman refused to spend the additional money, and he resisted requests for higher defense budgets in 1949–50 and 1950–51. As a result of budget restrictions and public attitudes, overall U.S. troop levels were low. During 1947, Truman had seriously considered allowing the draft to expire. However, following the problems in Czechoslovakia and Berlin in 1948, he requested a two-year extension of the Selective Service Act. The new law made males 19–25 years old eligible for 21 months of military service. The law also limited the size of the military establishment to 2,000,000. Truman's efforts to provide for universal military training (UMT) failed to gain any significant popular support, and he dropped the plan.

Although the strength of the military establishment was about 1,460,000 in 1950, it was not a combat-ready organization. Nine of its 10 divisions were understrength and lacked sufficient equipment to outfit them even if the manpower could be found to bring them up to authorized strength. Much of the administration's reluctance to build up the military was the result of a fear that the Soviets

U.S. troops were frequently unprepared for Korea's harsh winter conditions. (National Archives)

might view it as a serious challenge. In addition, most people in the United States believed that the monopoly the nation held on the atom bomb would offset any disadvantage caused by the lack of a large military force. Even the end of the atomic monopoly in August 1949 did not immediately change U.S. attitudes.

The military establishment that would direct the war in Korea was much different from the one that had directed World War II. It had been reorganized by the National Security Act of 1947 and the act's 1949 amendment. The secretary of defense headed the organization and was the principal assistant to the president on all matters relating to the Department of Defense. The secretary of defense's most important power was his control of the department's budget. The primary reason for the 1949 amendment was to enhance the secretary's powers by eliminating the provision that any powers not specifically given to the secretary were to be retained by the service secretaries. In addition, the service secretaries lost their status as cabinet members and their places on the NSC.

Despite the fact that the secretary of defense exercised "direction, authority and control" over the Departments of the Army, Navy, and Air Force, his authority was limited by the fact that each of the three departments was to be administered by its own secretary. The secretary of defense could not change the roles of the military forces under the various departments without congressional approval. He was also prohibited from hindering the function of the departments by controlling their personnel or the expenditure of funds.

The National Security Act of 1947 had created three new organizations: the NSC, the National Security Resources Board (NSRB), and the Central Intelligence Agency (CIA). The NSC consisted in 1950 of the secretary of state, the secretary of defense, the vice president, and the chairman of the NSRB. The NSRB was established to advise the president on ways to coordinate the military, industrial, and civilian sectors of U.S. society in time of war. The NSRB included the heads of those departments and agencies designated by the president. The CIA was founded to coordinate U.S. intelligence efforts.

JULY–DECEMBER 1950

When North Korea launched its attack on South Korea on June 25, 1950, the stage for war was irrevocably set. Just six days later, U.S. ground combat troops arrived in Korea, but the North Koreans had already established a footing.

North Korean Advances

By the time MacArthur received permission to assist the South Koreans, the North Koreans had crossed the Han River south of Seoul and were continuing their rapid advance. By July 3, 1950, they had captured Kimpo Airfield and the port of Inchon. Faced with the realization that his forces were not prepared for combat and confronted with the speed of the North Koreans' advance against the disorganized South Korean resistance, Macarthur faced a difficult decision. If he waited until he could commit his forces en masse, the South Koreans might be forced to surrender. However, if MacArthur committed his forces piecemeal, he faced the possibility that they might be defeated along with the South Koreans.

MacArthur decided that committing his troops piecemeal in order to stem the North Korean advance and provide a show of strength and support for the South Koreans was worth the risk. The question of where to commit the first troops was readily apparent. The North Korean advance was down the peninsula from Seoul to the port of Pusan, so a defensible position was picked on the road above Pusan.

On July 5, two rifle companies moved into a position across the main road near Osan. At about 8:00 A.M., the North Korean forces moving down the road engaged the small U.S. force. Despite initial success, the U.S. force—named Task Force Smith—quickly expended its antitank artillery ammunition and found that its rocket launchers and recoilless rifles were ineffective against the Soviet T-34 tanks with which the North Koreans were equipped. The task force could not receive any air support because of the weather, and communications among the various parts of the force broke down and prevented any coordinated defensive effort. By early afternoon, the North Koreans had turned both flanks of the task force and forced the Americans into a disorganized retreat.

On three more occasions, MacArthur committed small forces in an effort to delay the relentless advance of the North Koreans. Although the forces involved were all larger than Task Force Smith, the end results were the same. Each time, the North Koreans pinned the blocking force with strong frontal assaults, while they turned both flanks of the defenders. By July 13, the North Koreans had forced the defenders back to Taejon, some 60 miles below Osan. Lt. Gen. Walton H. Walker was in command of the 8th Army, which consisted of all U.S. ground forces in Korea. At the request of the South Korean government, he also commanded the ROK Army. Walker established his headquarters at Taegu on the same day that the 24th Infantry Division moved into its defensive positions at Taejon.

While the forces in Korea were buying time, MacArthur was gathering forces in Japan. He directed that the 7th Infantry Division be cannibalized in order to bring the 1st Cavalry and 25th Infantry divisions up to combat strength. Once officials in Japan were satisfied with the status of the two divisions, they were moved to Korea. The move was completed by July 18, in time to participate in the battle for Taejon. However, the 24th Division lost the city on July 20. The North Koreans managed to surround the city with two divisions. While the 24th Division was able to escape the trap, its commander, Maj. Gen. William F. Dean, was not so fortunate. He was captured and would spend the next three years in a prisoner-of-war camp.

Following the capture of Taejon, the North Koreans resumed their push toward the south coast with one division. The second division continued toward Taegu. Other North Korean units complemented the main drive. It was evident that the units were moving in such a way that they would eventually join forces at the port city of Pusan.

The only factors working in favor of the U.S. and South Korean forces were the ever-lengthening North Korean supply lines, the establishment of U.S. air superiority, and the imposition of a UN naval blockade of Korea after North Korean naval forces had been destroyed. Despite the arrival of the 29th Regimental Combat Team and the success of the naval and air operations, the North Koreans continued to force the defenders south toward Pusan.

Battle for Pusan

General Walker ordered his forces to make a stand on a line north of Pusan. This line, known as the Pusan perimeter, was approximately 140 miles long. The Pusan perimeter stretched in an arc from the Korea Strait to the Sea of Japan. Along this arc, Walker spread his forces in a thin line and used his interior lines of communications to bolster those areas where North Korean pressure was the greatest.

The North Korean force rose to 13 infantry divisions and 1 armored division. Many of the men in these divisions were new recruits, and they failed to match the ability of the men lost during the advance south. The North Koreans also failed to utilize adequately their superior numbers by launching numerous attacks along the Pusan perimeter rather than directing a massive attack against the lightly held line.

Walker was able to use his interior lines to defeat the attacks thrown against his perimeter. While the UN line units bought time, the strength of the force within the perimeter continued to grow as new units were rushed to Korea from around the world. By September, Walker had received 500 medium tanks and the 5th Regimental Combat Team had arrived from Hawaii, the 2nd Infantry Division and 1st Provisional Marine Brigade from the United States, and a British infantry brigade from Hong Kong. The 8th Army was slowly gaining sufficient strength to take the offensive.

Inchon Landing

While the 8th Army was steadily increasing in strength on the peninsula, General MacArthur was working on a plan to put the UN forces on an offensive footing. As the North

Koreans pushed south, they lengthened their lines of communications and severely taxed the peninsula's rail and highway system. MacArthur, veteran of the numerous amphibious landings and the island-hopping campaign of World War II, could see the possibility of landing a force behind the main North Korean force. Such a landing would cut the lines of communications and trap the North Koreans between the landing force and the 8th Army. The only escape route that would be open for the North Koreans would be through the mountains in the interior. In addition, a successful landing behind the North Koreans would provide a tremendous psychological lift to the UN forces, especially if the landing force was able to capture Seoul.

While UNC planners in Japan rushed reinforcements to the 8th Army, they also worked to build a force that would possess sufficient strength to make the proposed amphibious landing. The X Corps was created with Maj. Gen. Edmond M. Almond, MacArthur's chief of staff, as the commander. The 7th Division was rebuilt with replacement troops from the United States and a large number of South Korean recruits. The rebuilding of the 7th Division was a part of an experiment, known as the Korean Augmentation to the U.S. Army, whereby South Korean troops were interspersed with predominately U.S. units. The planners also had the recently arrived 1st Marine Division to add to the invasion force, which would be a separate command, not a part of the 8th Army.

The site selected for the landing was Inchon. However, the landing site presented the planners with numerous serious problems and offered the very real possibility that the entire effort might end in disaster. The first problem was the fact that Inchon had tides that might range as much as 30 feet. Additionally, the approach to Inchon was through a very narrow channel that presented a serious threat to the ships carrying the landing force. Those in the landing force, once ashore, would be required to scale high sea walls to attain their first objective. Then they would have to fight their way through a built-up area. Perhaps the most serious problem was the fact that MacArthur would be committing his only large reserve force to make the landing. If the invasion met heavy resistance and suffered heavy casualties, there was no large pool of replacements to be sent to reinforce X Corps. In the worst case, the force might be defeated, and a withdrawal back through Inchon would be extremely difficult. Also, the defeat of the landing force would place the 8th Army in an even more precarious position, because there would be no reinforcements available to bolster the defenses of the Pusan perimeter.

There was no possibility of any large-scale reinforcements reaching Korea if the Inchon landing failed and heavy casualties were suffered. On Sept. 1, 1950, four National Guard divisions had been federalized. However, none of the units were ready to take an active role in combat operations. The same problem existed for the ready reserve and the draftees who were rapidly filling the ranks of the regular army. After weighing the pros and cons, MacArthur gave orders to launch the invasion.

On September 15, the invasion force launched its amphibious assault against Inchon. The anticipated problems never materialized: the tides were judged correctly, the ships negotiated the narrow channel, the forces managed to scale the sea walls, and enemy resistance was light. MacArthur had gambled and won. His bold stroke had placed a powerful blocking force behind a large enemy force. Within two weeks, X Corps had fought its way to Seoul and placed itself firmly on the main lines of communications for the North Korean forces that were still threatening the 8th Army within the Pusan perimeter. On September 29, MacArthur returned possession of Seoul to President Rhee.

UN Successes

While X Corps was battling its way to Seoul, General Walker launched an attack in an effort to break out from the Pusan perimeter. During September 16–23, Walker's advance was slow; however, when it became apparent to the North Koreans that they were caught between the 8th Army and X Corps, their will to fight broke. Once the resistance crumbled, the 8th Army moved north rapidly in pursuit of the fleeing North Koreans. On September 26, elements of the two UN forces met.

Perhaps 30,000 North Koreans managed to escape north of the 38th parallel. Several thousand others sought refuge in the mountains south of the parallel and continued to fight as guerrillas. However, the end result of the Inchon landing and the breakout from Pusan was to eliminate the NKPA as an effective fighting force in South Korea.

OCTOBER–DECEMBER 1950

The liberation of South Korea presented the UN members, especially the United States, with an interesting problem. The UN had called for the reestablishment of the old border and a halt to the aggression against South Korea. That goal had been achieved. The United States had also stated that it did not wish to expand the war by taking any action that might prompt the Chinese or Soviets to enter the conflict. Also, the restoration of the old border was fully consistent with the stated policy of containment.

If there were valid reasons for not crossing the 38th parallel, there were also valid reasons for continuing the advance into the northern part of the peninsula. The 30,000 North Koreans who had escaped the envelopment in the south, combined with another 30,000 troops in training camps, represented a formidable military force. In fact,

South Korea would be in the same situation as before the invasion on June 25. A military victory over the North Koreans would also achieve the longstanding goal of unifying all of Korea. The major reason for not crossing the parallel was that both the Chinese Communists and the Soviets had issued warnings about the consequences of an invasion of North Korea.

Invasion of North Korea

Despite the warnings, President Truman issued permission on September 27 for MacArthur to cross the border in pursuit of the NKPA. The only condition imposed by Truman was that no Chinese nor Soviet troops were to have entered Korea or that there had been no announcement that they intended to intervene. Once the UN forces neared the Yalu River (the border with Manchuria) and the Tumen River (the border with the Soviet Union), MacArthur was to use South Korean troops. Ten days after Truman issued permission for MacArthur to cross the 38th parallel, the UN General Assembly passed a resolution calling for peace and security throughout Korea, which seemed to approve the action taken by Truman.

On October 1, two corps of ROK troops crossed the 38th parallel and started to move against objectives to the north. On October 9, after the passage of the UN resolution, General Walker pushed his I Corps across the parallel. Operating against only slight resistance, the three corps pushed north. On October 19, I Corps cleared the North Korean capital of Pyongyang. By October 24, the U.S. corps was within 50 miles of Manchuria. The ROK I Corps and ROK II Corps also moved close to North Korea's northern border. Truman and MacArthur held a conference on Wake Island on October 19. After assurances by MacArthur that the Chinese threats to enter the conflict were only a bluff, Truman authorized MacArthur to continue his advance.

Chinese Intervention

With winter rapidly approaching, MacArthur ordered his commanders to move as swiftly as possible toward the northern border. On both coasts, the UN forces moved steadily, but elsewhere the forces met strong resistance. On October 26, the UNC discovered that the units facing the strong resistance were opposed by Chinese troops. Throughout the last days of October, more Chinese troops appeared at the front lines to stiffen the resistance to the advance of the UN forces. Once an advance was slowed or halted, the Chinese broke contact.

Initially, it was believed by UNC intelligence officers that only a few Chinese had joined the North Korean forces. By the end of the first week in November, estimates placed the strength of the Chinese presence at five divisions. MacArthur was certain that there was no large Chinese commitment. Intelligence evaluations were unable to determine if large numbers of Chinese troops had crossed into Korea. The general conclusion was that the Chinese would engage only in defensive operations designed to keep the UN forces away from the northern border of Korea.

Consequently, the UN forces resumed their advance on November 11 when the X Corps started north. On November 24, Walker's 8th Army moved forward, and part of the U.S. 7th Division reached the Yalu River. On November 25, the entire nature of the Korean War changed.

During the night, strong Chinese forces attacked the center and right of the 8th Army. On November 27, more powerful attacks by the Chinese overran the units on the left flank of X Corps. By November 28, the UN positions had begun to disintegrate under the massive attacks. Finally, with the large-scale engagement of the Chinese, it was possible for the UNC to estimate the strength of the Chinese elements in Korea. A force of 200,000 members of the Chinese XIII Army Group had entered Korea in late October and now faced the 8th Army. In November, China's IX Army Group had entered Korea. By the time the Chinese launched their attack on November 25, there were more than 300,000 Chinese troops in Korea, a total of 30 divisions, plus artillery and cavalry units.

UN Withdrawal

When faced with this massive new force, MacArthur ordered Walker to take whatever actions were necessary to prevent the 8th Army from being totally enveloped by the Chinese. X Corps was ordered to pull back to the port of Hungnam. UN forces quickly began to feel the full impact of Chinese intervention. The enemy ground forces were making steady gains, and enemy aircraft were fighting to gain air superiority. The first MiG-15s that appeared in Korea quickly proved to be far superior to the piston-driven aircraft available to the UN forces.

During the withdrawal of the 8th Army, the Chinese caught and mauled the U.S. 2d Division. The UN troops continued to withdraw each time the Chinese made contact. By December 15, the UN forces were back at the 38th parallel, where they worked to establish a defensive line across the Korean peninsula.

South of the Chosin Reservoir, the 1st Marine Division consolidated its position and prepared to withdraw to Hungnam. The temperatures had dropped below zero, and the marine position would forever be known as "Frozen Chosin." Quickly the Communists, eight divisions strong, surrounded the marines. Marine major general Oliver Smith explained to his surrounded troops that they were not retreating, they were "attacking in another direction." For 13 days, the men of the 1st Marine Division, resupplied by the Far East Air Force, "attacked in another direction." On December 9, elements of the 3d Division met the advance guard of the marines outside of the Hungnam

perimeter. The 1st Marine Division, saved to be evacuated with the rest of X Corps, had added another exploit to the proud history of the Marine Corps.

In late November and December, planning for the withdrawal of X Corps from North Korea had begun. After a November 28 meeting in Tokyo, General Almond ordered his forces to withdraw to Hungnam. By the time the marine and army units managed to withdraw from the Chosin Reservoir area to Hungnam, most of the other units of X Corps had reached the area. The withdrawal of such a large force required a monumental logistical effort. Almond estimated that 400,000 tons of matériel would have to be moved. To accomplish this feat, 75 cargo ships, 15 troopships, and 40 LSTs (landing ships, tank) would be needed. In addition, 500 tons of men and equipment would have to be airlifted each day between December 14 and 18. On December 24, the 3d Division, supported by massive naval gunfire and marine and navy aircraft flying close air-support missions, became the last UN units to leave Hungnam. No serviceable equipment was left behind to be used by the enemy, and all personnel were evacuated. In all, 193 shiploads of men and matériel were moved out of Hungnam. A total of 105,000 soldiers, 98,000 Korean civilians, 17,500 vehicles, and 350,000 tons of cargo were evacuated from the beachhead. In addition to the matériel moved by sealift, 3,600 soldiers, 200 vehicles, and 1,300 tons of cargo were evacuated by the Far East Air Force.

On December 11, when Almond began to withdraw his forces from Hungnam, the Chinese showed little inclination to interfere with the effort, and the last of the troops left on Christmas Eve. The force sailed for Pusan, where it would be incorporated into the 8th Army as its strategic reserve. The day before the evacuation from Hungnam was completed, General Walker was killed in an automobile accident. Lt. Gen. Matthew B. Ridgway was rushed to Korea from Washington to assume command of the 8th Army.

U.S. Strategic Issues

Immediately following notification that the Chinese had attacked the UN forces, President Truman had called a meeting of the NSC. Gen. Omar N. Bradley, chairman of the JCS, reported that while the attack was serious, it was not as serious as the press reports indicated. One of the major concerns of the JCS was that MacArthur's forces would be attacked from airfields in Manchuria, but it advised against allowing the UNC air forces to attack the fields.

Sec. of Defense George C. Marshall counseled that neither the United States nor the UN should become engaged in a war with China. Marshall's view was supported by the service secretaries and the JCS. One of the overriding considerations was that if the United States became involved in a general war with China, it would not be able to continue to build up its forces in Europe. This was extremely important to the NSC, since the overall aim of U.S. policy since 1947 had been containing the Soviet Union within its borders. The NSC also believed that it was entirely possible that if the United States took action against China, a traditional area of special Soviet interest, the United States might become involved in a larger war. The NSC members were well aware that the United States might not be able to win a war against the combined opposition of China and the Soviet Union.

The NSC was in total agreement that the intervention in the Korean War by the Chinese meant that the United States should exert every effort to strengthen its military forces by acquiring additional men and war materials. President Truman agreed with the recommendations of the NSC and also prepared to send a supplemental budget to Congress that would pay for the extra costs of the expanded military effort.

General MacArthur felt that the UN forces should be allowed to strike at China. His willingness to attack the Yalu installations in November had aroused the fears of U.S. allies in Europe. This European concern about U.S. policy in Korea was a product of the situation in post-World War II Europe. The North Atlantic Treaty Organization (NATO) had been formed to protect the member nations against aggression by any other nation, or group of nations. The action of the United States and the UN in facing the aggression of the North Koreans had convinced the NATO members that the United States would fulfill its NATO obligations. Although NATO had been in existence for a year and a half, its military forces were not prepared to engage in major military operations. If the nations of Western Europe had been attacked in the fall of 1950 by the Eastern European nations, they might well have suffered the same fate as South Korea, especially without U.S. aid.

The prospect that the Korean War might expand into a war with Communist China was unsettling to NATO members. If the United States became engaged in a war with China, support of NATO would be diminished. If Russia should attack Western Europe, there would be virtually nothing to stop the destruction of the Western nations.

JANUARY–MAY 1951

At the time he arrived in Korea, General Ridgway hoped to hold a position along the 38th parallel. However, his inspection of his forces and reports from his subordinate commanders revealed that the 8th Army's fighting spirit had been seriously damaged by the massive Chinese attacks and by the constant U.S. withdrawals. In addition, its defensive positions were thinly held and could not withstand a concerted effort to breach the line. Intelligence reports indicated that the Chinese XIII Army Group was

gathering for an attack on Seoul while at least 12 North Korean divisions were assembling for an attack in the center of the peninsula.

Ridgway believed that the only way to maintain the defensive line was to rebuild the 8th Army's morale and commit reserve forces to the battle line. He ordered the 2d Division into the central portion of the line and directed General Almond to speed the refitting of X Corps so it could be returned to the front. Ridgway also ordered the preparation of defensive positions above Seoul.

The Chinese launched an attack on New Year's Eve 1950, directing their assault toward Seoul. After initial holding operations, the 8th Army was forced to withdraw slowly south into Seoul. On Jan. 4, 1951, the last UN troops left Seoul, destroying the bridges across the Han River as they retreated.

The Chinese forces did not push south of Seoul after the 8th Army. By mid-January, the Communist offensive had ground to a stop all across the peninsula. Intelligence reports and reconnaissance operations revealed that the main forces had withdrawn to refit, leaving only screening units to maintain contact with the UN troops. The North Koreans and Chinese found themselves the victims of a logistical system that prevented them from sustaining major operations for an extended period because it could not replace lost men and equipment. Ridgway decided to exploit this disadvantage by inflicting maximum casualties on the Communist forces.

Ridgway became convinced that the UN forces could maintain their position on the Korean peninsula. General MacArthur, on the other hand, informed Washington that the Chinese were capable of driving the UN forces out of Korea unless he received substantial reinforcements.

Global Strategy

Other international concerns on the part of planners in Washington precluded sending large-scale reinforcements to Korea. Washington leaders feared that the war in Korea was just a part of a Russian effort to start a worldwide conflict. The concern was sufficiently great to cause President Truman to declare a state of national emergency on December 16. In addition, four National Guard divisions were brought into federal service in order to provide added strength for the general reserve forces. The JCS directed MacArthur to keep the UNC in Korea if at all possible— if not possible, he was to evacuate the peninsula.

MacArthur still believed that an attack on China was the appropriate method to relieve the pressure on the UN forces. He advocated a blockade of the Chinese mainland and the destruction of Chinese industrial capacity through the use of air and naval forces. In addition, he proposed bolstering UN forces in Korea with Chinese Nationalist forces while other Nationalist forces made diversionary attacks against the mainland.

His desire to attack China could have been implemented in a number of ways. The most readily available means were direct naval and air attacks. These actions were also the most likely to start a full-scale war. Virtually all of the nations allied with the United States were opposed to a direct attack on China. Because China had no large industrial centers, the most advantageous targets were military and air bases, railroad facilities, and shipping installations. However, the bombing of these targets raised the specter of indiscriminate bombings on the part of the UN because there would be no way to avoid extensive civilian casualties. U.S. planners believed that if China were attacked, it would call upon the Soviet Union for assistance.

Although the UNC and MacArthur talked about the sanctuary that the Chinese forces enjoyed, they did not mention that the UN forces also enjoyed a sanctuary in Japan, from which a large portion of the UN air and naval operations were launched. It was entirely possible that if the UN forces bombed Manchuria, the Chinese might attempt to bomb Japan. The question of whether or not they possessed the capability of bombing Japan was academic. It was feared that if the Chinese requested help from the Soviets, they would quickly be supplied with the capability.

Truman was at a loss to understand why MacArthur, an experienced soldier and a longtime expert on Asia, could not see the fallacies inherent in his proposal. The use of Nationalist Chinese troops against the mainland certainly would be an overt act of war. The bombing of Chinese cities would produce a public outcry and steel the resolve of the Chinese people. MacArthur's belief that the bombing of a few cities would cut off the flow of supplies was clearly wrong. The next logical step would be to try to cut off the supplies reaching the war zone from the Soviet Union by bombing the Soviet city of Vladivostok. It was obvious to Truman that MacArthur was willing to start a general war, a step that Truman was not willing to take.

The final part of MacArthur's plan, the blockade of the Chinese coast, could not be undertaken without British approval. That approval was unlikely to be given because of Britain's substantial trade with China through Hong Kong.

The JCS did not believe that air and naval attacks against Chinese targets outside Korea would ever be authorized until China attacked U.S. targets outside Korea. The JCS also doubted that the Nationalist Chinese forces would be useful in the war in Korea. In light of all of these considerations, the JCS advised MacArthur to defend his positions in Korea and inflict the most damage possible on the opposing forces.

MacArthur's Autonomous Actions

On Jan. 25, 1951, Ridgway began an offensive. The operations were characterized by a methodical advance up the peninsula, with each objective secured before moving on to the next. By the middle of March, the UN forces had once again captured Seoul; by March 21, they had reached the 38th parallel. While the UN forces were gaining ground in Korea, the international situation was changing.

Most of the members of the UN coalition, including the United States, had reached the conclusion that the restoration of the 38th parallel was an acceptable result of the war. On March 20, the JCS notified MacArthur that Truman was going to announce a willingness to negotiate with the North Koreans and the Chinese. The statement was to be made before the UN forces would be allowed to advance beyond the 38th parallel.

However, before Truman could make his announcement, MacArthur issued a statement of his own in which he indicated that if the UN decided to expand the conflict to North Korea's coastal areas and interior bases, the Communist Chinese were at risk of being defeated militarily. Undercut, Truman withheld his peace initiative and decided instead to let the military situation in Korea dictate policy for the immediate future.

On April 5, Rep. Joseph W. Martin read to Congress a letter from MacArthur that stated that he believed the opening of a second front by using Nationalist Chinese forces against mainland China was justified. In his letter to Martin, MacArthur made his famous pronouncement that there was "no substitute for victory."

With his actions in March and April, General MacArthur had overstepped the bounds of professional military conduct. He had openly disagreed with and even challenged the direction of national policy. In addition, his conduct was insubordinate: President Truman had issued a directive requiring that all pronouncements on national policy be cleared with Washington.

Relief of MacArthur

The relief of General MacArthur followed five days of meetings between Truman and his military and civilian advisers. On April 6, Truman met with special assistant Averell Harriman, Secretary of State Acheson, Secretary of Defense Marshall, and JCS chairman General Bradley. All agreed, for various reasons, that MacArthur should be removed from command. Bradley wanted to confer with Gen. Lawton J. Collins, army chief of staff, before making his final recommendation. Acheson also believed that MacArthur should be relieved, but only after a unanimous vote by the JCS. Although Marshall felt that MacArthur should be relieved, he warned that it might be difficult to get military appropriations through Congress after taking such a step.

On April 8, Bradley met with General Collins, air force chief of staff Gen. Hoyt S. Vandenberg, and chief of naval operations Adm. Forrest P. Sherman to discuss the situation. All of the Joint Chiefs agreed that MacArthur should be relieved. After reaching their decision, they conferred briefly with Defense Secretary Marshall, who did not reveal his feelings on the situation. One thought that must

General Ridgway (right), *MacArthur's successor as commander, meets with South Korean president Syngman Rhee and U.S. commanders.* (National Archives)

have occurred to Marshall was the potential public reaction to his participation in the action to remove MacArthur. Marshall, although not on active military duty while secretary of state (1947–49), was the only general senior to MacArthur, and he feared that the removal of the almost legendary UN commander might be interpreted by many as a move on his part to remove a competitor.

On April 9, President Truman again met with his advisers. Upon being informed of the unanimous decision of the JCS, he announced that he would relieve MacArthur of his commands. On April 11, the president recalled MacArthur and appointed Ridgway as his replacement. Despite an outpouring of public support for MacArthur, the decision of Truman, as commander in chief, to relieve the general was gradually, although grudgingly, accepted by the American people.

Chinese Spring Offensive

Upon his appointment to command the UN forces, Ridgway turned over command of the 8th Army to Lt. Gen. James A. Van Fleet. On April 22, the Communists hurled

21 Chinese and 9 North Korean divisions at the UN forces. The major effort was in the west in the direction of Seoul, while there were lesser attacks in the east. This was the beginning of the first phase of the Communist spring offensive.

During the fight, Britain's 29th Brigade and a battalion of the Gloucestershire Regiment were cut off when the ROK division on their flank withdrew in the face of the initial assaults. The British troops held their position under tremendous pressure. Just before they were overrun, they attacked the Communists. In the confusion that followed the attack, only 40 British soldiers managed to escape— the rest were either captured or killed. By April 30, the Communist attack had lost its momentum. They broke contact and retired beyond the range of the UN artillery. During the offensive, Communist losses were at least 70,000, while the 8th Army lost about 7,000.

On May 14, the Communists launched the second phase of their offensive. More than 20 divisions attacked the right elements of X Corps in the eastern sector of the front. Van Fleet had expected an attack in this sector and had placed his reserves in positions to support the front-line troops. The U.S. 2d Division and 1st Marine Division counterattacked and blunted the Communist attack. The initial Communist attacks were by small units at night. The intent was to infiltrate and confuse the UN forces and then exploit any advantage that they might gain. During daylight hours, when UN artillery and close-air support missions were effective, the Communists took refuge in prepared bunkers and caves. This was to be the pattern of attack by the Communist forces throughout the remainder of the war. Communist losses during the seven days of the second phase were approximately 90,000. The Chinese and North Koreans found that they had overextended themselves; their supplies were exhausted, and their lines of communications were under continuous UN air attack.

On May 22, Van Fleet ordered his forces to assume the offensive. Just as the attack was gaining momentum all along the front, Van Fleet was ordered to halt his advance. He requested permission to follow the retiring enemy forces, but the JCS refused to allow the continuation of the offensive. The United States was concerned about Soviet threats and by the alarm that the threats had caused among the UN allies. After halting, the UN forces worked to consolidate their position across the entire peninsula. While UN units improved their positions, the Communists were constructing defensive positions to the north.

PEACE NEGOTIATIONS

On June 23, the Soviet UN ambassador, Yakov A. Malik, proposed a cease-fire. This proposal confirmed the extensive damage that had been inflicted on the Communist forces. An estimated 200,000 men had been lost, along with large quantities of equipment. In addition, the Communists had been unsuccessful in building air bases in the south that would have enabled them to provide more air cover for their ground forces.

Delegates from both sides met at Kaesong, a small village in North Korean-controlled territory, during July and August. Little was accomplished, and there were constant clashes between large patrols all along the front. The Communists were able to refit their troops during the lull in the fighting. They were also able to use the negotiations as a propaganda vehicle.

Panmunjom Talks
When the negotiations broke down in late August, Van Fleet ordered his troops to resume offensive operations on a limited basis. By mid-November, the attacks had been effective enough to cause the Communists to ask for a resumption of armistice talks. On November 12, the two sides met at Panmunjom, a small village in no man's land.

With the resumption of negotiations, Ridgway ordered the UN forces to begin an active defense.

The negotiations continued throughout 1952. While the negotiators argued over all types of issues at Panmunjom, minor fighting continued along the front. In May 1952, Gen. Mark W. Clark replaced Ridgway, who had been ordered to command the NATO forces. Throughout the negotiations, the Communists continued to build up their forces by replacing lost personnel and replenishing their supplies and equipment. By the end of 1952, there were approximately 800,000 Communist ground troops in Korea. They had been supplied with new equipment, including improved Soviet artillery and antiaircraft guns.

One of the major sticking points in the negotiations was the disposition of the prisoners of war (POWs) held by the UN forces. Approximately 171,000 Communists had been captured by the UN forces; more than 20,000 of them were Chinese. The Communists demanded the return of all prisoners, but at least 50,000 of the Communists did not want to return home.

The Communists claimed in 1951 that they held 65,000 prisoners. UN figures showed that perhaps as many as 92,000 troops had fallen into Communist hands. Of this number, 10,000 were Americans, 80,000 Koreans, and 2,000 from other UN participants. However, at Panmunjom, the Communists admitted holding only 11,500 prisoners. It is impossible to determine exactly how many prisoners died in Communist hands, but it was a large proportion of those captured.

In October 1952, the negotiations again broke off, and the war became an issue in the U.S. presidential campaign. In November, the American people, tired of the struggle, elected Republican Dwight D. Eisenhower, who had promised to bring the conflict to an honorable conclusion. As Eisenhower began his presidency, combat in Korea continued with a series of attacks and counterattacks.

On Mar. 28, 1953, Premier Kim Il Sung of North Korea and Gen. Peng Teh-huai, commander of the Chinese volunteers, informed General Clark that they were willing to take part in an exchange of sick and wounded POWs. The Communists seemed to have been prompted to resume negotiations because of the unrest in the Communist world caused by the death of Soviet leader Joseph Stalin on March 5. In April, 5,800 Communists were exchanged for 149 Americans, 471 ROK soldiers and 64 UN prisoners. South Korean president Syngman Rhee, however, initially refused to consider any permanent settlement that would leave Korea divided. Throughout June, the North Korean and Chinese forces launched numerous attacks, primarily against ROK units. The attacks were apparently designed to cause the United States to exert pressure on the South Korean government to make concessions. The attacks accomplished little because the Communists were unable to

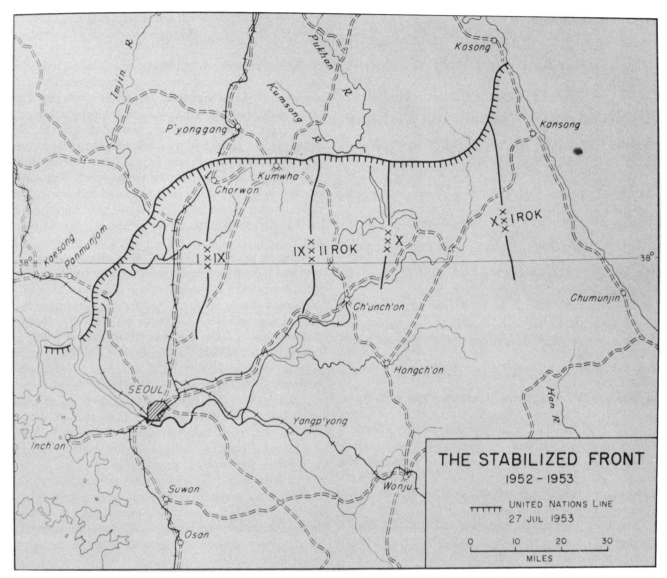

The Stabilized Front: 1952–1953 (From ROTCM 145–20: American Military History: 1607–1958. [Washington: HQDA, July 1959])

exploit their successes. On July 20, negotiations resumed after the UN gave the Communists assurances that the ROK would not be allowed to block progress in the talks. The United States also promised to provide South Korea with economic and military support. At 10:00 A.M. on July 27, the military armistice was signed at Panmunjom. All fighting stopped 12 hours later.

RESULTS OF THE WAR

When the final casualty figures for the 37 months of combat were totaled, the UN forces had lost 118,515 men killed and 264,591 wounded. Among these, the United States had losses of 33,629 killed, 103,284 wounded, and

5,178 missing, while the South Koreans, whose losses can only be estimated, lost about 70,000 killed, 150,000 wounded, and 80,000 captured. The enemy casualties, including prisoners, were estimated to exceed 1,500,000, of which almost two-thirds were Chinese. Approximately 3,000,000 South Korean civilians were killed during the war.

Military Lessons

The Korean War produced a number of positive results for the U.S. defense establishment. Following the successful conclusion of World War II, the powerful U.S. military organization 11that had been quickly demobilized, and then the forces that remained had been allowed to decline in effec-

The exchange of sick and wounded prisoners of war in April 1953 came in the midst of negotiations to end the Korean War. (National Archives)

tiveness. With the outbreak of the Korean War, the necessity to rebuild and revitalize the U.S. military establishment became readily apparent. The resultant inability of the United States to defeat the North Koreans and their Chinese allies was a valuable lesson for both the military and the civilian leadership of the nation. It was clear that the military had to be in a constant state of readiness in order to deal with military challenges.

Following the armistice, there was no large-scale demobilization of the military forces. Such a policy had been implemented after each of the world wars, had worked to the detriment of the military, and had seriously threatened U.S. security. Congress would continue to appropriate the funds necessary to keep a force in the field that was capable of effective military operations in pursuit of the nation's strategic interests. The war also gave the United States military and political leaders a valuable experience in fighting a limited war. The lack of clear and definite military objectives severely complicated the task of the military planners.

The same types of problems that faced military planners also faced the industrial planners. When the Korean War began, the U.S. economy was still in the process of returning to a peacetime footing following World War II. Industry was reluctant to make the expensive conversion back to wartime production, because there was no way of knowing how long war production would be needed. In addition, the consumption of capital goods by the civilian population was high, and industry did not want to disrupt normal production. As a result, it took nearly two years

to get new products into combat use. However, civilian production was hardly affected by the necessity to produce war matériel.

The Korean War proved the importance of air power as an essential ingredient for successful combat operations. It also confirmed that air power alone cannot provide adequate ground reconnaissance, nor can it bring about a successful conclusion of a ground war. Although the UN forces quickly gained and were able to maintain air superiority, the North Koreans and Chinese were able to adjust their tactics to meet the constant threat presented by superior air power. The Communists moved and attacked at night, and during the daylight hours sought refuge in the natural cover offered by the terrain and in prepared positions.

Although the Soviet-produced MiG-15 was superior to both the U.S. F-84 and in some respects the F-85 jets, the training and competence of the UN pilots, primarily Americans, made up for any differences in equipment. Even though the UN pilots were not allowed to pursue the Communists across the Yalu River, they were able to prevent the establishment of bases south of the river. In air-to-air combat, at least 1,108 Communist planes were destroyed, including 838 MiG-15s. The UN forces probably destroyed another 177 aircraft and damaged an additional 1,027. The Communists shot down 114 UN aircraft in air-to-air combat. The vast majority of the 1,213 aircraft lost by the UN forces were lost to ground fire while providing close air support to ground troops.

One innovation that demonstrated its potential on the battlefields of Korea was the helicopter. Although the small helicopters available were primarily for reconnaissance, evacuation, and rescue work during the war, they clearly demonstrated their value as a mobile means of communications and transportation.

The war also confirmed the value of naval domination of the sea lanes. Almost as soon as the war began, the 7th Fleet clamped a right blockade on the Korean coast. Without this blockade, the Communists would have been able to resupply their forces without depending on the overland routes. If it had been possible to stop the overland flow of supplies as effectively as those that moved by sea, the war undoubtedly would have been much more difficult for the Communists to prosecute. In addition, the U.S. Navy supplied valuable fire support to the ground forces operating along the coast, and marine and navy aviators furnished close air support to ground operations.

Another valuable lesson learned by the U.S. military planners was the requirement that they relearn the value of "fire and maneuver" on foot. The UN ground forces found themselves tied to the roads because they were dependent upon the support offered by their tanks and artillery, as well as their logistical support system. The North Korean and Chinese troops were lightly equipped and used move-

The death of Soviet leader Joseph Stalin in March 1953 prompted the Communists to agree first to an exchange of prisoners, with the armistice coming three months later. (National Archives)

ment, surprise, and concealment in the rugged terrain to overcome their lack of firepower. They employed night movement and hid during daylight hours when they were highly susceptible to attacks by UN aircraft and artillery.

The Chinese and North Koreans employed essentially the same tactics throughout the conflict. They used frontal attacks, which were, in fact, holding actions, while attempting to envelop or infiltrate the enemy's position. At no time during the war were the UN forces able to employ their massive firepower to its full effect.

The overall strength of U.S. forces at the beginning of the Korean War had been 1,460,000. Of this number, approximately 20 percent, or 280,000, had been stationed outside the United States. By the time the war ended, of the 3,555,000 U.S. forces, 27 percent, or 963,000, were stationed outside the United States. Following the war, of the U.S. troops outside the United States, the greatest number were stationed in Germany, Japan, and Korea.

Although the Korean War was fought with conventional forces and although the forces being sent to Europe to bolster the NATO defenses consisted of army divisions and tactical air force units, the long-range plan to base U.S. defense policy on the use of air power and nuclear weapons received a boost during the war. The advances in technology that had begun during World War II continued during the Korean War. The ability to produce weapons and other equipment that would substitute technology for manpower struck a responsive chord with the American public. The demand for more advanced weapons and the potential for foreign military sales served to produce an expanded peacetime military-industrial establishment.

International Implications

The Korean War was a major test of the concept that had prompted the formation of the United Nations. UN members united in an effort to ensure the security of the nations

The Korean War was extensively covered by the media, including CBS television's Edward R. Murrow (right center), *shown interviewing troops for "See It Now."* (CBS)

from aggression by their neighbors. Although the United States and South Korea furnished the vast majority of the forces that opposed the aggression of the North Koreans and their Chinese allies, 16 other member nations participated in the war. Great Britain contributed a brigade of troops along with one aircraft carrier, two cruisers, and eight destroyers. Canada furnished a brigade of infantry, an artillery group, and one armored battalion. Australia sent two infantry battalions, one fighter squadron, and one transport squadron, as well as one aircraft carrier, two destroyers, and one frigate. New Zealand sent one artillery group and two frigates. Turkey, like Britain, sent a brigade of infantry. Thailand furnished a regimental combat team, while Ethiopia and Belgium each sent an infantry battalion. Colombia supplied an infantry battalion and a frigate. The Netherlands provided one infantry battalion and a destroyer, while the Union of South Africa dispatched a fighter squadron. Greece provided an infantry battalion and a transport squadron. Denmark, India, Italy, Norway, and Sweden each provided noncombatant units, such as hospital forces or field ambulance units.

On the international scene, both the United States and the UN emerged from the Korean War with greatly enhanced standings among most of the nations of the world, at least those not allied with the Soviet Union. Both the United States and the UN had honored their commitments to oppose aggression in the world community. Action had been taken and resources committed to guarantee the continued existence of South Korea. The swift action to oppose North Korea's invasion of South Korea gave credibility to the promises the United States had made to its allies to assist them if they were attacked. The UN gained credibility as a world body able to take positive action, something its predecessor, the League of Nations, had been unable to do in the 1920s and 1930s. The Korean War had served notice that aggression would not be tolerated by the nations of the world.

4

Vietnam—From Discord to War: 1954–1964

The military involvement of the United States' struggle to control Vietnam began during World War II and ended with the U.S. withdrawal from South Vietnam in 1975. Initially, in the 1940s, Vietnamese Communists and the Americans found themselves on the same side, resisting Japanese aggression and opposing colonialism. However, with the beginning of the Cold War, Washington's attitude changed. U.S. leaders regarded French colonialism as a lesser evil than Communism in Southeast Asia. The United States supported the failed French attempt to hold North Vietnam in the early 1950s and began an extensive aid program to the newly created Republic of South Vietnam after the French defeat and exodus. After 10 years of this effort, at the end of 1964, U.S. policies appeared doomed.

BACKGROUND: 1954–1960

After the French defeat in 1954, the Geneva Conference that year ended French colonialism in Southeast Asia. The terms reached at the conference established a demilitarized zone between the two Vietnams, called for supervised elections in 1956, and established a period of repatriation. As the provisions of these so-called Geneva Accords went into effect, hundreds of thousands of Vietnamese began choosing on which side of the line to stand.

Taking advantage of the opportunity to repatriate (a provision of the Geneva Accords), almost 900,000 Vietnamese living in North Vietnam decided to accept transportation from the U.S. Navy and flee to the uncertainty and confusion of South Vietnam. Only about 10 per-

cent of that number opted to go north, choosing to live under Ho Chi Minh's new Communist government. In contrast to the unorganized flood of refugees from the North, the displacing Southerners proceeded in an orderly oxcart caravan to the port of Vung Tau, where they embarked on Soviet and Polish ships bound for Haiphong. There would have been a few more choosing the trip north except for instructions from the Viet Minh, as Communist supporters were called. Roughly 10,000 Viet Minh and their families were told to stay in the South and conceal their sympathies. These "stay-behinds" were mainly political cadre. Weapons were buried in graveyards, and a recruiting campaign started; each stay-behind was expected to bring in three new adherents to the Communist cause. Those who went north were largely military cadremen.

While the exodus from the South was composed of loyal followers of Ho Chi Minh, the refugees leaving the North were largely in three categories, each of which had somewhat different motivations and sympathies. There were about 200,000 Vietnamese associated with the French colonial army, including soldiers, officers, or families of either who preferred to avoid control by their former enemies. Roman Catholics comprised the second and largest category. They were people fearing the well-known antipathy of Communist governments toward religion of any sort. Finally, there were the Buddhists, who chose to go to the South for much the same reason as the Catholics. Although the Buddhists were a smaller group than the Catholics, the Buddhists were potentially very troublesome since many of the monks traveling south were members of the Buddhist intellectual movement, a faction long noted for antigovernment political activism.

Asia and the Pacific (Facts On File, Inc.)

The flood of people moving to the South were destined to exchange one authoritarian government for another, and the exodus was even greater than the number transported by the U.S. Navy. About 100,000 provided their own transportation to escape the Viet Minh. Thus, a million Vietnamese were moving to the Republic of Vietnam, a new state with a relatively unknown head of government.

The Vietnamese emperor, Bao Dai, selected Ngo Ninh Diem as the prime minister largely because it was assumed that Diem had the unqualified backing of the U.S. government. With the prospect of a 1956 election mandated by the Geneva Accords, however, some Americans believed Diem to be the wrong man for the job. In late 1954, Leo Cherne, an officer of the U.S. Central Intelligence Agency

(CIA), reported that the chaos in South Vietnam would probably be too much for Diem to control and that authoritarian methods could probably be expected. Diem had a reputation for being a recluse, and as a Catholic, he belonged to a religious minority associated with French colonialism. Cherne predicted that freedom had little chance in South Vietnam. The CIA officer's vision proved rather accurate, but an even more brutal form of authoritarian government was unfolding in North Vietnam.

North Vietnamese Programs

The 1954 ranks of the refugees fleeing North Vietnam might have been even more numerous had Viet Minh authorities not obstructed the flight of many. Yet the desire to go south grew during the next year. Shortly after attaining power, the Communists fully implemented a land redistribution scheme, a program that had begun several years earlier in Viet Minh-controlled areas.

Wealthier peasant farmers were often denounced and executed after mock trials, their lands being divided among Communist supporters. Failure of a fellow villager (or on occasion, even family members) to denounce one of these landowners led to even more executions, unwilling "witnesses" being put to death. Estimates vary, but as many as 100,000 Northern landowners and farmers may have been killed during this reign of horror. In 1956, the terrorized peasants of Nghe An Province revolted. Hanoi sent in the 325th Division, and perhaps another 1,000 peasants were slaughtered. Finally, Ho Chi Minh and Vo Nguyen Giap admitted the government's errors and ended the brutal program.

South Vietnamese Programs

The bloody land-reform program in the North stood in stark contrast to the redistribution program in the South. Although Diem's methods were not without error and corruption, they generally worked. Wealthy landowners were required to sell property in excess of 245 acres to the government. Poorer farmers then had the opportunity to buy this land with low-interest, government-sponsored loans. Diem received a considerable amount of admiration for this program.

But Diem feared the ballot box and made the United States a companion to his fear. In 1955, both the U.S. and South Vietnamese governments disputed the need for the 1956 election mandated in the Geneva Accords. Saigon and Washington claimed that since neither the U.S. government nor the South Vietnamese government agreed to the Geneva Accords, neither was bound by the treaty's provisions. In the United States, such sentiment had wide-

In 1948, Vietnamese citizens celebrate their independence from France, but they remained within the French Union and became an associated state of the union in 1949. (Library of Congress)

Ho Chi Minh denounced the new government at a Saigon confer-ence in 1948; by 1950, he had declared his Communist-backed government—the Democratic Republic of Vietnam—in Hanoi to be the only government of the Vietnamese people. (National Archives)

believe that the decision to deny the vote had been a great and tragic mistake. The decision cost the Eisenhower administration some desired support from U.S. allies in Europe. Both Britain and France, signatories to the Geneva Agreements, advocated an election. When the United States seemed to withdraw from its own democratic principles in rejecting the Indochina plebiscite, a gap occurred in Western unity.

Peoples of Southeast Asia

Discounting Burma and Malaya, there were roughly 74,000,000 people in continental Southeast Asia. After the Vietnamese repatriation, there were about 18,000,000 citizens of North Vietnam and perhaps 15,000,000 in South Vietnam. There were about 3,000,000 people residing in Laos and 6,000,000 in Cambodia. Thailand had a population of some 32,000,000.

While the North and South Vietnamese shared the same cultural origins, there were distinct differences. Several centuries of separation and little communication between the two societies had resulted in different accents in the spoken word. Some linguists maintain that there are enough differences in the way the two societies speak that there are two distinct dialects. Both dress and diet were

French troops, members of the elite French Foreign Legion, search the Red River delta for Viet Minh forces, shortly before the French defeat at Dien Bien Phu in 1954. (National Archives)

spread support. The prominent Democratic senator John F. Kennedy, for example, firmly rejected the idea of mandated elections. The government in Hanoi had concealed the peasant revolt, so the full impact of the bloodletting and dissension in the North was not known to either the U.S. government or to Diem. Then, too, the Communist party in the South fell on hard times. From 1954 to 1956, many members defected or were captured or killed by Diem's security service, the dreaded Cong An. So, in a fair Northern election, Ho Chi Minh might not have done well in 1956. In addition, the election called for by the agreements specified observation by an international commission.

Diem, on the other hand, might have been able to gather considerable support in the South during that year. Diem's CIA adviser at the time, Edward Lansdale, who was quite knowledgeable about Third World elections, later came to unquestionably different and so were the lifestyles. The Southerner was more of an individual and more devoted to pleasure and a relaxed pace of life. By comparison, the Northerner was considered to be energetic, businesslike, and willing to submit to authority and teamwork in achieving goals. These differences might stem from the extensive Northern system of corvée labor, essential for the construction of dikes in the highly flood-prone Red River delta. Further, the northern reaches of Vietnam were more densely populated and accustomed to regulation. Of most importance in military and political affairs, Southerners, being less inhibited and more individualistic, tolerated a wide variety of separate religious, political, professional, and fraternal organizations.

It would have been difficult to find a nation with less unity than the Republic of South Vietnam. Most of the population lived in 2,500 rural villages, settlements normally composed of a cluster of hamlets in one geographic area. About 8 percent of the people were Roman Catholics and tended to group together in tight-knit communities. Another 8 percent belonged to the militant and well-armed Hoa Hao, a Nationalist religious sect that mainly lived in the Mekong Delta. The Hoa Hao shared the Catholics' loathing for Vietnamese Communists. About 6 percent of Southerners were Chinese; some were Communists, but the vast majority were apolitical businessmen. Another 5 percent of the population adhered to the Cao Dai religious sect, a group that largely inhabited Tay Ninh Province, just north of Saigon. Like the Hoa Hao, the Cao Dai were armed and generally hostile to the Viet Minh. About 4 percent of the population could be described as practicing, rather than casual, Buddhists. This group was normally passive and rarely given to strong political sentiments (unless aroused by some of the activist monks).

The Montagnards, primitive tribesmen who accounted for perhaps 6 to 8 percent of the population, lived along the Annamite mountain chain and in the high plateau area of the country. For the most part, the 20 or so hill tribes rejected the Viet Minh because most of the Communists were Vietnamese and the Montagnards had fought a centuries-old battle against the "lowlanders." Two prominent political parties, the Dai Viet and VNQDD, constituted about 4 percent of the population. The largest identifiable segment of South Vietnam's population, apolitical peasants, accounted for about one-third of the country's citizens.

With another 6 percent of the population occupying military and government positions, it would seem the Viet Minh were living in a sea of hostility because there were so many anticommunist groups. After all, the Viet Minh stay-behinds accounted for less than 1 percent of the population. But, anticommunism did not necessarily translate into unity. Many of these sects and political groups were pitted against one another, and knowledge of this internal

A Rhade tribe member works at processing harvested rice; the Rhade are Montagnards, highlanders who were among the first to oppose the Viet Minh, mainly because of their tradition of rejecting the lowlanders. (National Archives)

discord probably explained CIA officer Cherne's dismal forecast for Diem's fortunes. Being anticommunist did not necessarily mean being pro-Diem. So, the new prime minister found himself engaged in a series of plots, playing one group against another in order to attain and keep power. It was an unlikely policy to unify the country.

Despite the demonstrated strength of Communism in some quarters of Southeast Asia, the vast majority of the population was either anticommunist, anti-Vietnamese, or both. In general terms, fewer than 19,000,000 North Vietnamese and adherents of Communism were opposed by about 55,000,000 people in South Vietnam, Thailand, Laos, and Cambodia. The line drawn at Geneva by President Eisenhower and British prime minister Winston Churchill largely reflected that division.

The line selected by the Eisenhower administration in Southeast Asia not only reflected existing sociopolitical factors, it corresponded to geostrategic realities. Without having the narrow passes along the Annamite Mountains fully in hand, the North Vietnamese would be restricted to the short border with South Vietnam in order to move overland and influence events to the South. The "corridor of conquest" was squarely blocked by a potential defensive barrier. While it was unlikely to make the small nation of Laos a formidable opponent to contest Hanoi, Thailand, the strongest anticommunist nation in the area, was likely to respond to a troubled or violated Laos. The Eisenhower administration selected Thailand to be its "bastion" against Communism. If Hanoi did try to move south, Laos would become the battleground. The strategy was well-founded on military geography and existing sociopolitical sentiment. It envisioned a three-to-one advantage for anticommunist forces. Eisenhower told the U.S. Congress that if there must be war in Asia, "let it be Asians against Asians." The Thai-American strategy was designed to facilitate that policy.

U.S. Aid

In order to survive the threat posed by Hanoi, the new government of South Vietnam asked for substantial U.S. aid, more than Washington was willing to supply. Diem's generals calculated the need for a 270,000–man army, but the United States initially agreed to support a force of only 90,000. Hanoi had powerful radio transmitters constantly beaming propaganda broadcasts southward while Saigon's request for similar apparatus languished within the U.S. foreign assistance bureaucracy. Diem asked U.S. officials for a radio intercept and code-breaking capability to learn what Ho Chi Minh's government was telling its agents in the South, but the Americans refused to entrust Saigon with such skills and equipment.

The United States did send advisers to Diem's government, men who found themselves working in an atmosphere of distrust. The South Vietnamese organization to resist the Communists was, in many respects, a mirror image of Marxist revolutionary warfare forces. The Communist village militia, or guerrilla force, was countered by Saigon's Self Defense Corps, armed peasants who were formed into village platoons and who reported to Diem's appointed district chiefs. Communist regional forces were to be opposed by the Civil Guard, company-size elements whose commanders reported to Saigon's province chiefs. The Americans discovered that the Self Defense Corps and Civil Guard hierarchies were completely separate from the South Vietnamese army. There was no unity of command. They also found that Diem desired the separation of these armed forces so he could pit one element against the other in times of political turmoil.

Early Conflict

A 20-year Southeast Asian armed conflict began shaping up in late 1958 and finally broke out in 1959. At the outset, there was a loose coalition composed of the United States, Thailand, Cambodia, Laos, and South Vietnam. On the other side, there was the Democratic Republic of Vietnam, outnumbered, but unified and led by Ho Chi Minh. Hanoi made the best use of its rapid decision-making process and astute political calculations. The Northerners remained true to the Communist party goal of 1930: unified Marxist rule over all of Indochina. The decision cycle used by the Communist leaders normally consisted of a probe, a period of waiting to gauge the reaction, consideration and decision by the party's Central Committee (a gathering of the party faithful where functionaries were properly oriented on the decision and the forthcoming

task), and, finally, the campaign. Most of these activities could be accomplished in secret, so Hanoi's adversaries were usually a year or more behind on what the North Vietnamese had decided.

On the ground, where action was seen and reported, Hanoi's various moves fit a pattern. Normally, there was a Communist limited attack and then a pause. A counterattack, delivered in response to the Communists' first attack, was usually met with a partial Communist withdrawal, and then the whole process would repeat itself. At the end of the cycle, Hanoi and its followers held more than they had at the beginning, and the territory gained was used as a base for the next phase.

The ability to use the eastern part of Laos was essential for Hanoi's overland support of the growing insurgency in South Vietnam. That insurgency was initially directed by Le Duan, the Communist leader in the South. On his return to Hanoi, Le Duan proposed a comprehensive plan to defeat the Diem government. The plan, which acknowledged the weakness of the Communist party in the South and advocated a major effort, was accepted and implemented from 1956. Hanoi's efforts were dependent on an indigenous armed force, and in 1957, Unit 250 was therefore created, an element that was to consist of 37 armed companies spread throughout South Vietnam. Almost wholly composed of Southerners, these forces—as well as a number of Communist-controlled political organizations—were to become known by the short title "Viet Cong."

As the North Vietnamese Army (NVA) was in the process of gaining control of eastern Laos, the Viet Cong were well into a campaign of violence designed to intimidate Diem's appointed officials in the Southern countryside. In 1958, 193 Southern officials were assassinated, and by the early months of 1959, the rate of assassination was at 20 officials per month. Those officials and schoolteachers who were judged to be honest or popular were highest on the Communists' assassination list. In terms proportional to 1959, those killings would represent the equivalent of 50 U.S. senators, congressmen, governors, or mayors being murdered every week. The Viet Cong campaign was not restricted to Vietnamese citizens. Two U.S. Army advisers were killed at Bien Hoa in July 1959.

Communist Strategy

Hanoi's gains during 1959 were the result of years of work, brutal but effective techniques, and a superb organization. The large-scale assassination campaign was designed to separate the South Vietnamese government from its people. A district chief, for example, had to surround himself and his family with bodyguards and restrict his travel in order to survive the Viet Cong terror offensive. As a result, the government began losing contact with its people. Tax collection and recruiting for the armed forces began to decline. On the other hand, Viet Cong recruiting and tax collection began to increase.

Some of the Communist recruiting was accomplished among Diem's government officials, army officers, and those South Vietnamese who held important positions. This effort, a campaign of subversion, complemented the terror campaign by keeping Hanoi well-informed, providing opportunities to undermine Diem's anticommunist policies, and presenting the Viet Cong as a legitimate and deserving Southern political movement. For instance, one of Diem's closest advisers on rural security affairs from 1959, Lt. Col. Albert Pham Ngoc Thao, an officer who was one of Diem's trusted province chiefs, worked for the Communist cause in secret. Additionally, one of Saigon's communications officers, a captain, was found passing communications codes to Hanoi. Since few Western news bureaus in Saigon employed reporters who spoke Vietnamese, the Communists targeted these offices for agent placement in hopes of putting a slant on the news that would be favorable to Hanoi's cause.

Terrorism and subversion were not the only problems about which Laos, Cambodia, and South Vietnam had to worry. From 1954, General Giap steadily improved his regular army, supervised a comprehensive, nationwide conscription program, and organized a large, 110,000-man military reserve structure. At the start of war, the North Vietnamese regular army had a strength of 277,000. Since 125,000 male citizens of the North reached military age every year, Giap could fill his ranks even if a mandatory term of enlistment was pegged at 24 or 30 months. By maintaining such a large military structure, Hanoi was forcing its neighbors to invest in a similar regular army structure organized to counter a possible invasion by Giap's forces.

Hanoi established a number of headquarters and units, each with regional and functional interests, to support and direct the terror and subversion campaigns in South Vietnam and the military operations in Laos. For example, the North Vietnamese 603d Battalion, composed largely of Southerners, operated 10 junks equipped with radios and machine guns. These craft and their crews transported men and military equipment from North to South Vietnam on a weekly basis. A similar unit of 8 junks supported the infiltration requirements of intelligence agents and party organizers. Since Diem's navy had only about 20 ships to police the 1,200-mile coastline and since there were approximately 10,000 similar fishing junks legitimately operating off the shores of South Vietnam, it was not surprising that the illegal transits were rarely interrupted. While these maritime organizations accounted for an important part of the equipment sent to the South, they only transported about one percent of the men being sent there. Almost all of the infiltrators sent south traveled overland and were directed by Group 559, which was responsible

for the operation and maintenance of what would become known as the Ho Chi Minh Trail. Cadred by repatriated Southerners assigned to the North Vietnamese 301st Division, Group 559 was established in May 1959 with an initial strength of about 300. The group's tasks included the selection of safe routes and rest stations along the route from North to South. The rest stations were about one day's march apart, located near a water supply, and occasionally stocked with supplies of rice. Group 559 sent its first infiltration element southward in August 1959, transporting weapons. In November, a 28-man infiltration party went south, carrying 60-pound packs containing gold, weapons, food, and medicine. The goal of these infiltration parties of soldiers was "to unleash a military attack in order to liberate the South and reunify the fatherland."

After establishing an organizational structure to support the military overthrow of South Vietnam, the North Vietnamese leadership added to it. The National Liberation Front (NLF) was, perhaps, the strangest of all broad-front political movements. These organizations are almost always formed by the unification of several diverse political groups that temporarily cast aside differences to work for a common goal. When the NLF was formally established in December 1960, there were no diverse political organizations seeking to unify and overthrow the Diem government. There was only a paper structure that was designed in Hanoi. But, there were diligent members of the Communist party who began establishing political organizations. Altogether, about 20 religious, ethnic, and professional political groups were created. Then, Hanoi's agents began recruiting to fill their ranks. Many Southerners, failing to see that the NLF was a Communist organization dominated by the government in Hanoi, joined because of dissatisfaction with Diem, not because they supported the cause of Ho Chi Minh.

Preliminary Skirmishes

Hanoi's use of force in 1959 was not entirely unexpected, yet defense preparations were inadequate. In South Vietnam, American reluctance to support a large standing army under Diem was swept away with the escalation of violence. Efforts to defend the country's villages from Viet Cong incursions were initiated, and a project to support insurgency in North Vietnam was begun.

The overall U.S. war plan for Southeast Asia, called Operation Plan (OPLAN) 32, envisioned a period of subversion and guerrilla warfare, a North Vietnamese invasion, and finally, the involvement of Chinese forces. The Eisenhower administration's governing philosophy was the maximum use of local resources as opposed to an immediate commitment of U.S. armed forces. With the growth of Giap's forces to the north, and with Washington's policies in view, the senior U.S. military officer in Saigon, Lt. Gen. Samuel T. Williams, proposed American financial and logistical support for the Army of the Republic of Vietnam (ARVN). Williams's request was approved, resulting in a program to establish seven South Vietnamese divisions, about half the North Vietnamese number. A substantial contingent of U.S. advisers was considered necessary for each Vietnamese division, and the targeted U.S. advisory strength in South Vietnam was increased to 685. For coastal defense, U.S. naval advisers supported the creation of a South Vietnamese navy "junk fleet" consisting of 80 intercept craft that had the outward appearance of local fishing craft.

Both Diem and his U.S. advisers knew the country could not long sustain the massive loss of officials in the countryside in an unchecked Communist terror campaign. During the late 1950s, South Vietnam had enjoyed considerable economic success and saw its food production grow by an average of 7 percent per year as North Vietnam's dropped by 10 percent. Even though the North had a larger population, Saigon boasted a bigger gross national product. These gains could be easily lost unless the growing war in the rural districts was stemmed. The CIA, which often handled antisubversion projects, and Diem's officials agreed on several programs designed to secure the country's villages and save Saigon's economy from Hanoi's terror campaign.

Hamlet Programs

An effort to secure South Vietnam's 2,500 villages, the "Fortified Hamlet Program," was launched in 1959. This program supplemented an earlier population-control scheme, called the Civil Action Program, that depended on six-man teams sent by the government to live in villages, teaching and assisting the peasants in the areas of health, agriculture, education, and self-help projects. The chief problem with the Civil Action Program was that the teams were not large enough to defend themselves and usually became victims of the Viet Cong assassination program. The idea for the Fortified Hamlet Program was to remove peasants from areas that were becoming heavily influenced by the Communists, create new villages, surround each village with a defensive barrier, arm the villagers, and encourage them to resist the appeals or demands of the Viet Cong.

Later in 1959, the project was overshadowded by the "Agroville Program." This scheme was a bit grander and involved existing villages as well as resettlement efforts. It included economic development, propaganda, and intelligence measures. By 1960, the U.S. Agency for International Development (AID) was designing a special village radio so that settlements involved in the program could immediately communicate with the district headquarters, report Viet Cong activities, and request military assistance if necessary. Between March and September 1960, 15 Agrovilles were created, mainly in the southern part of the

country. The overall village defense program, supported by the CIA rather than by U.S. military advisers, was seen by Diem as a way to increase his political hold on the country. For that reason, he kept this structure out of the hands of his own military forces, giving him one more armed organization to counter others in the event of serious opposition to his control.

THE KENNEDY POLICY

President Eisenhower could claim some, but not complete, success for his policies in Southeast Asia. Communist infiltration of South Vietnam from North Vietnam had taken place; about 5,000 Vietnamese Communists had traveled through the high passes along the Annamite mountain chain, over the Laos border and eventually into South Vietnam. But Diem's army was being greatly strengthened, and a program to secure South Vietnam's countryside was unfolding. Another effort, a coastal defense program, was underway.

The Eisenhower administration had failed to bring about an international coalition that worked in concert to defeat Ho Chi Minh's designs. Yet, while SEATO (Southeast Asia Treaty Organization) did not function as had been hoped, there was a regional unity of effort. Certainly, the Laotian and South Vietnamese governments were vigorously contesting Laotian and Vietnamese Communists. Essentially, four Southeast Asian governments, backed by the United States and representing about 55,000,000 people, were in direct opposition to roughly 19,000,000 North Vietnamese and indigenous Communists. Asians were fighting Asians.

While the United States was prominently involved in assisting the four states in opposition to Ho Chi Minh, American armed forces were not committed to the fight. Field decisions were being made by indigenous commanders, not by American officers, and there were few American troops in combat zones. Every precaution had been made to avoid risk to U.S. prestige in the region.

As president-elect John Kennedy prepared himself for his new duties, he had a long conversation with Eisenhower about Southeast Asia. The talk almost wholly centered on Laos, South Vietnam being barely mentioned. To Eisenhower, Laos was the key. By keeping the war in Laos, the nations of South Vietnam, Cambodia, and Thailand were automatically provided some protection. The North Vietnamese had to get through Laos to get at the governments in Saigon and Phnom Penh. Violation of Laotian soil triggered a response by Thailand, the nation that represented the region's largest population bloc and controlled the area's most modern army. Laos was a true buffer state. Eisenhower told Kennedy that it was imperative that Laos not fall to the Communists.

At a press conference early in his administration, President Kennedy, as advised by outgoing President Eisenhower, discusses restricting the war in Laos as the key to victory in Vietnam. (National Archives)

Status of Laos

In the early days of his presidency, Kennedy suffered two painful reversals. At the Battle of Nam Tha in Laos, North Vietnamese and Communist Lao troops routed a number of Royal Lao battalions, forcing them to flee all the way to the Thai border. Additionally, the Bay of Pigs fiasco (April 1961) in Cuba cast doubt on the young president's judgment and competence. Kennedy then set out to change policies in Southeast Asia. He negotiated a U.S. withdrawal from Laos and decided to make a firm stand in South Vietnam, saying there had to be some compensation

for the Cuban and Laotian defeats. One of Kennedy's close advisers claimed that the national security apparatus in Washington had to have a reason for abandoning the Thais and Laotians and that a staunch defense of South Vietnam seemed to satisfy this need. Kennedy told a reporter that the United States had to make its power appear credible and that South Vietnam looked like the place to demonstrate American strength and resolve.

The agreement on Laos, titled "Declaration of the Neutrality of Laos," was actually a treaty disguised as a joint statement. Eisenhower warned against the arrangement.

Kennedy's negotiator, W. Averell Harriman, gained President Diem's support only by stating that the Russians would keep the North Vietnamese in line and then threatening to end aid to Saigon if Diem did not stop his resistance to the agreements. The document was signed on July 23, 1962, and was never submitted to the U.S. Congress because the administration regarded it as an "executive agreement."

The agreement required all foreign forces to withdraw from Laos, an arrangement that would have damaged Hanoi's chances for achieving its goals. The North Vietnamese could not bring in enough troops and supplies to South Vietnam without using Laos and could not support Communist forces in Cambodia. Kennedy had been told by the senior U.S. military officer in Laos, Maj. Gen. Andrew J. Boyle, that if the Laotians were left to themselves, the Royal Lao Army could eventually handle the indigenous Communists, the Pathet Lao. The North Vietnamese, however, never intended to comply with the document's provisions. In October 1962, when the agreement went into effect, the U.S. government was informed by Georgi Pushkin, the Soviet deputy foreign minister, that the North Vietnamese would not withdraw its forces. At that time, there were an estimated 10,000 North Vietnamese troops in Laos. The agreement required all foreign troops to withdraw through internationally controlled checkpoints. All of the more than 800 U.S. military personnel in Laos passed through the designated points, but only 40 North Vietnamese did so. President Kennedy assured President Diem that "Lao territory will not be used for military or subversive interference in the affairs of other countries."

Counterinsurgency: 1961–1962

In response to Kennedy's request for new measures to assist South Vietnam, the U.S. military held to a view that events in that country were highly contingent on events elsewhere, particularly in Laos. It was noted that an estimated 6,000 infiltrators had made their way through Laos to South Vietnam during 1961. These newly arrived soldiers and the weapons they transported, plus an aggressive recruiting program, increased the armed ranks of the Viet Cong from about 5,500 to 25,000 during that year. In Washington, the concern was slighted in favor of any idea or scheme that held promise of defeating Communist subversion within South Vietnam. The Kennedy administration was determined to find solutions to Communist-supported "wars of national liberation," and the conflict in South Vietnam would be the testing ground. That nation was beginning to experience a flood of U.S. "experts," a multitude of programs, and a sharply increased military assistance program. It was a marked change from the Eisenhower policies. For example, in 1961, there were only about 1,500 Americans in South Vietnam, about half of them engaged in economic assistance projects, activities

that absorbed 30 percent of the U.S. aid budget for the country. All of that was destined to be changed.

The U.S. Army was the only organ of the U.S. government that had published counterguerrilla doctrine, and President Kennedy called for and read the manual. The small book envisioned U.S. forces conducting operations against guerrillas, the existence of U.S. military government on the battlefield, and a European scenario. The doctrine was built around three main principles: denial of external support to the guerrillas, isolation of guerrillas from the civilian population, and destruction of the guerrilla forces through aggressive, offensive operations. Kennedy expressed his displeasure to the army chief of staff, and the manual was revised. The new doctrine added some imperatives: the need for intelligence and an emphasis on economic assistance to the nation undergoing guerrilla attack in order to undercut the appeal of the guerrilla.

Beyond the matériel problems of supporting ARVN, the Americans found counterguerrilla operations frustrating and good Vietnamese military leaders in short supply. A central problem and constant dilemma was whether to use the ARVN to protect the villages or to search out Viet Cong concentrations in the jungle, swamps, and mountains. It seemed that every time the army campaigned in remote regions, more of the population areas were lost to Communist control. Whenever South Vietnamese units were stationed near communities, company- and battalion-size Viet Cong units conducted some devastating raid. To the U.S. advisers, the South Vietnamese officers appeared to be reluctant to conduct night operations, feared risking small-unit patrols, did not supervise closely, and ignored training. The U.S. military leadership in Saigon also came to believe that its own advisory detachments often lost all objectivity and unknowingly engaged in inaccurate reporting. Initially, a new U.S. adviser was highly critical of what he saw. As time went on, however, the adviser usually saw wisdom in some Vietnamese practices, began to identify with his assigned Vietnamese unit, and became overly proud of its efforts.

In the fall of 1961, the Kennedy administration took a direct hand in the war. In order to assist the South Vietnamese navy in intercepting North Vietnamese maritime supply operations, U.S. Sec. of Defense Robert S. McNamara authorized joint, U.S.-South Vietnamese navy patrols south of the 17th parallel. Noting that it took 18–24 months to train a Vietnamese pilot, the expansion of the South Vietnamese air force was augmented with an infusion of U.S. crews and airplanes. American "air commandos" began arriving in Vietnam, along with their defoliant spray aircraft, bombers, and transport planes. U.S. Air Force personnel were tasked to conduct close air support, bombing and strafing missions, and supply flights as long as they had a South Vietnamese in the aircraft. U.S. combat missions began on Jan. 13, 1962. The U.S. Army had

Sec. of Defense Robert McNamara and Chairman of the Joint Chiefs of Staff Gen. Lyman Lemnitzer observe U.S. military advisers during a fact-finding tour of Vietnam for President Kennedy in 1962. (National Archives)

already added a part of its air arm to the war. In December 1961, 32 H-21 helicopters and 400 men of the 57th and 8th transportation companies had arrived in Vietnam. Less than two weeks later, the U.S. crews of these helicopters were flying 1,000 South Vietnamese troops into a skirmish

In 1961, the arrival of helicopters and more personnel in Vietnam signaled that the United States was becoming directly involved in the war; these "flying banana" helicopters support a 1964 jungle attack on the Viet Cong. (National Archives)

with the Viet Cong just west of Saigon. Together with a decision to extend U.S. Army advisers down to battalion level, the Kennedy administration had decided to involve the United States directly in a Vietnamese war. It was now a combined, American-South Vietnamese armed conflict.

North Vietnamese Command Structure

The U.S. and South Vietnamese command and control structures were vastly more complicated than the one they opposed. In late 1960 and early 1961, Hanoi's leaders appointed several high-ranking party officials to control the war effort in South Vietnam, at least the region south of the old territory of Annam. Communist efforts in the northern provinces of South Vietnam were commanded directly from North Vietnam. Viet Cong activities in the largest part of South Vietnam were directed by the newly created Central Office for South Vietnam (COSVN).

Below COSVN there were intermediate headquarters for areas covering five to seven provinces. However, these intermediate headquarters were little more than relay stations. The next two levels of control were province and district, which largely, but not always, reflected the geographic and administrative borders recognized by the Diem government. The Viet Cong chain of authority then went to the village and finally to the smallest unit, the cell of three to seven people. The Communist organizational structure was a simple pyramid, a top-to-bottom hierarchy of authority founded on geography.

U.S. Command Structure

The U.S. control structure was indeed more complicated. So as to emphasize the newfound importance of South Vietnam, the Kennedy administration in February 1962 created a wholly new headquarters in Saigon, the Military Assistance Command Vietnam (MACV). The new headquarters did not replace the military advisory group, but was placed above it. MACV not only commanded the U.S. military advisers, it also controlled U.S. Army helicopter and U.S. Air Force air commando units in the country. A full general, Paul D. Harkins, was placed in command of MACV.

The biggest single restriction on U.S. military authority in Vietnam stemmed from President Diem's peculiarities. Diem insisted on controlling even the moderate-size military operations of his subordinates. He also kept organs of his government divided so that he could maintain control. No fewer than seven different intelligence organizations with overlapping responsibilities operated out of the office of the president. Thus, both the U.S. and the South Vietnamese generals looked to Diem for decisions. The American counterpart to the South Vietnamese president was the U.S. ambassador, not the MACV commander. In some ways, the new U.S. command was more symbolic than substantive.

South Vietnam's Villages

The centerpiece of President Kennedy's drive to counter Communist wars of national liberation was, perhaps, the new system to win the villages of South Vietnam over to government control. Much of the success or failure of counterinsurgency was riding on a U.S.-supported Vietnamese effort, the Strategic Hamlet Program. This program, like its many predecessors, had population control as its chief objective. The CIA-supported Civil Action Program of the mid-1950s was defeated because the six-man team was simply too small to survive Viet Cong attack. It was mishandled by Diem's government and only received scant support from U.S. intelligence. The Fortified Hamlet Program of 1959 was actually a resettlement scheme that was resisted by the peasantry. The large-scale Agroville Program, begun in the same year, failed because it required too much construction, was too labor intensive, and needed too many security forces. Only 23 Agrovilles had been created, mostly in the border regions of southern South Vietnam. By 1961, new ideas and new programs were necessary because the Diem government controlled only about 40 percent of South Vietnam's rural villages, with the others either under Viet Cong influence or being contested.

The chief tool used by the Communists to gain control of South Vietnam's villages was the agitation and propaganda team. Composed of perhaps 10 members, the team's normal method of operation would be to meet with a party

A North Vietnamese propaganda poster, later found in Hanoi, depicts the glories in store for those youth who choose to take the Ho Chi Minh trail to fight with the Communists. (W. L. Boddin)

A North Vietnamese postage stamp glorifies the taking of American prisoners of war between 1964 and 1967. (National Archives)

member or sympathizer from a village in the afternoon. During the evening, the team would come into the village, weapons prominently displayed, but not in a threatening manner. They would ask the villagers to assemble and then lead them in singing some well-known Vietnamese songs. An entertaining skit—one with a heavy political overtone—would then be performed by the team. There would then be a speech extolling the need to resist the Diem regime. The villagers would then be divided into groups for discussions led by appropriate team members. The team would conclude the evening with a long skit and depart amid the villagers' applause. Later, after several such visits, taxation and conscription of the youth would begin, and one more South Vietnamese settlement would have fallen into the hands of the Viet Cong.

All of Saigon's rural population control schemes (locally known as "pacification" programs) had some characteris-

tics common—in fact, almost identical—to the previous program except for a name change. According to a program's plan, the Communist agitation and propaganda teams would be resisted by an armed village defense element; some programs envisioned the villagers themselves being armed, while others relied on a government-trained team that lived in or near the village. There was usually an agricultural facet of the program involving the distribution of rice seedlings and fertilizer, the teaching of modern animal husbandry techniques, and the provision of vegetable and fruit seeds. Normally, there was some sort of program involving self-help construction projects for clean water, improved sanitation, and household electricity. The self-help agricultural projects and the companion educational and medical programs were pushed forward in order to provide a better life for the peasant, hopefully forming a bond between the peasant and the government in Saigon. There was always a propaganda aspect, often concealed in an entertainment program that was usually designed to counter the Communist campaign. Normally, there was also an associated political program aimed at undercutting the appeal of Communism. Pacification was a "zero-sum game": when the ruralists added to their own strength, they detracted from the Viet Cong strength.

Strategic Hamlet Program

In 1961, President Diem's brother, Ngo Dinh Nhu, decided that the South Vietnamese army was ill suited to manage an effective rural population control campaign. Considering the growing size of the NVA, he believed South Vietnam's army was overly committed to counterguerrilla operations. Studying the previous French and Vietnamese programs as well as similar foreign projects, Nhu initiated the Strategic Hamlet Program.

Using a trained cadre called the Republican Youth, he established several criteria for a hamlet to qualify as a "strategic hamlet." The Viet Cong agent, taxation, and conscription system (infrastructure) within the hamlet had to be neutralized. The villagers had to be organized for self-defense. Physical barriers had to be constructed around the village, and concealed, underground shelters had to be dug to hide weapons and provide safe places for the women and children in times of attack by the Viet Cong. A communications system had to exist for contact with the district headquarters. The people of the hamlet had to elect a council, a body that could answer to the government. Once these criteria were met, the village would be given about $600 for a self-help project.

The Strategic Hamlet Program was primarily designed for the ethnic South Vietnamese rural community. A number of U.S. government elements—the CIA, AID, and the U.S. Information Agency (USIA)—became heavily involved in assisting Nhu and his officers.

As part of the pacification program in South Vietnam, MEDCAP (Medicad Community Action Program) doctors "made the rounds" of villages, in an effort to give any medical treatment that was necessary. (U.S. Army)

The Strategic Hamlet Program was based on the "oil spot" theory, which held that if one village were brought into the system, neighboring ones could be persuaded as well and the region of government control would expand like an oil spot, soon covering the map. By the end of 1962, 3,200 of the estimated 11,800 South Vietnamese hamlets had been brought into the program, and some could see this effort freeing ARVN for more offensive operations against the Communists. However, there was much pressure for positive reporting, both from Washington and Saigon, so the statistics could not be entirely trusted. Diem's brother, Nhu, realized that reporting was too optimistic and told the U.S. ambassador that only about 30 percent of the strategic hamlets were truly secure, but even that represented progress. The supply of village radios was running far behind the need, but U.S. intercepts of Viet Cong communications clearly indicated serious concern among the Communist leadership over the South

Vietnamese government's population control programs. Additionally, the progress was being noted in Hanoi, with Ho Chi Minh quoted as saying that "1962 was Diem's year."

Field Operations: 1962

The Communist leadership would have been less concerned if its opponents' population control programs were the only problem to face. In early 1962, most of the more than 40 South Vietnamese provinces contained a full-time, full-strength Viet Cong battalion. Also, each district was likely to contain a Viet Cong company that conducted operations about once a month. These forces could have easily swept aside the lightly armed static defense element charged with protecting strategic hamlets. The problem for Communist leaders was that they could not always count on getting their forces to these government-controlled villages without being engaged by South Vietnam's army, which was rapidly becoming mechanized. A number of bloody clashes resulted in heavy Viet Cong casualties. When Viet Cong leaders learned that their radio communications were being monitored by Diem's forces, they began changing codes daily and instituted an expanded courier system. To the veterans of the Viet Minh, this war was not like the one they fought against the French.

With massive infusions of U.S. equipment, advisers, and funds, ARVN was building rapidly. In early 1962, the NVA had reached a strength of 280,000. ARVN was going beyond that strength, but the two forces were not comparable since the vast majority of South Vietnamese troops were still tied down protecting the country's population, its industry, and its transportation network. Yet, more offensive operations were being conducted against the NVA because the growing numbers of U.S. helicopter units permitted quick strikes and raids into areas previously dominated by the Viet Cong. U.S. Marine Corps helicopter units had joined those of the U.S. Army, and U.S.-supported heliborne operations were becoming so common that the Americans put in a special helicopter unit whose primary mission was to evacuate U.S. casualties.

Most of these helicopter operations were relatively small affairs, but some were large-scale and involved several battalions. In March 1962, one of these larger actions was conducted in the Mekong Delta region in An Xuyen Province. An ARVN infantry battalion and ranger company, plus a Vietnamese Marine Corps (VNMC) battalion, were directed to trap a Viet Cong force of about 200 men against a riverbank. The operation involved 14 U.S. Army H-21 helicopters and their crews, 5 Vietnamese Air Force (VNAF) AD-6 aircraft, and 3 amphibious craft of the Vietnamese Navy (VNN). Using four different helicopter landing zones and a simultaneous river assault, the operation netted 38 Viet Cong killed, but large numbers of the Communists were seen escaping. Regarded as a moderate success, the lesson seemed to be that once contact was made, ARVN and VNMC leaders had to exercise vigorous leadership to close any gaps. Additionally, the operation had been a complicated one, as all such simultaneous trapping operations are.

In November, in northern South Vietnam, a heliborne operation against a jungle area long held by Communist forces was conducted, this time by an ARVN ranger company and a U.S. Special Forces unit commanding a Montagnard strike force company. The VNAF contributed 10 of its helicopters, the U.S. Army supplying 13. Despite a deceptive parachute drop using dummies, the Viet Cong appeared to be ready for the rangers and helicopters when they arrived. Two helicopters were immediately shot down. Suddenly, the weather closed in, causing delays in reinforcement by heliborne troops. After two hours, flights were once more resumed, but two more helicopters were hit. The rangers lost 11 killed, and there were 21

As U.S. equipment arrived in Vietnam, U.S. advisers trained ARVN (Army of the Republic of Vietnam) troops in their use. Here, an ARVN soldier is instructed on making a fast exit from a helicopter at the scene of battle. (Library of Congress)

wounded, including 2 Americans. There were 53 Viet Cong bodies found, including that of a battalion commander, and 8 Viet Cong were captured. In this northern region, helicopter operations could be chancy, and it seemed as if the Viet Cong were beginning to adjust to these air assault tactics.

At the end of 1962, the Diem government and the Kennedy administration had reason for optimism. Counterinsurgency doctrine required the isolation of guerrilla forces from the civilian population, a goal that the Strategic Hamlet Program was beginning to achieve. The doctrine also called for aggressive offensive operations to hunt down and destroy guerrilla units. There were now some 300 U.S.-operated helicopters and combat aircraft in the country, and more were on the way. ARVN was becoming more enthusiastic about attacking the Viet Cong and was learning to use both the helicopters and the new mechanized vehicles. Additionally, ARVN had grown, from 300,000 to 385,000 during 1962. Finally, there was a hopeful trend in captured enemy documents, which from the summer on revealed that the Viet Cong had increasing recruitment and morale problems.

There were costs for this progress, however, and all trends were not positive. When the Kennedy administration took office, U.S. military strength in Vietnam was at about 900. At the end of 1962, there were more than 11,000 U.S. servicemen in the country. No longer restricted to training and advising, more Americans joined into the fight each day. By the end of 1962, 27 had been killed, 65 had been wounded, 5 were Viet Cong prisoners, and 1 was missing. South Vietnam was experiencing 2,000 violent deaths per week: Viet Cong, government troops and officials, peasants, and, now, Americans.

DOUBT AND DECISION: 1963

Some of the U.S. and South Vietnamese optimism of late 1962 was dashed in the first few days of 1963 when the Viet Cong won the significant Battle of Ap Bac in the Mekong Delta region over elements of the ARVN 7th Division. Attempting to mask his defeat, the ARVN division commander lied to General Harkins, and Harkins, in turn, tried to tell the press of a government victory. The American reporters knew better and now had proof that the U.S. military high command in Saigon was being misinformed by ARVN leaders in the delta. The incident caused distrust between senior U.S. military officers and American journalists. More than that, the battle gave the Viet Cong leadership confidence that they could fight successfully against an important part of U.S. counterinsurgency techniques, a type of fighting the Communists labeled as "special war." This newfound confidence stemmed from the fact that a reinforced Viet Cong battalion handily defeated a larger South Vietnamese army force, one well-equipped and well-supported by U.S.-flown helicopters and Vietnamese-manned mechanized vehicles and combat aircraft.

Urban Unrest

In late spring 1963, U.S. reporters shifted their attention from the battlefield to the cities. It began in Hue when nine protesters were killed by Diem's troops at a demonstration staged by Buddhist priests and laymen. During the next seven months, world television viewers saw continuing scenes of public violence from the streets of Vietnam. The growing control that the Saigon government was achieving over the country was being purchased at a price. The people increasingly resented Diem's methods, particularly those of the security service, the attempts to control education and thought, and the arrogance of corrupt officials.

Each of South Vietnam's provinces had upward of 100 agents from the Cong An, Diem's security service. These agents habitually used torture to extract confessions and accusations from their prisoners. One province chief estimated that about 10 percent of the Cong An's members were corrupt, usually extorting payments from businessmen and merchants by threats of reporting them as Communists. The Cong An had been successful in catching and eliminating many Viet Cong, but it had also engendered widespread hatred throughout the country.

The Buddhists were particularly upset with Diem's government because it was increasingly gaining control over information, education, and communications. Nhu, Diem's powerful brother, headed the Can Lo party, whose members dominated nearly all public positions. Loyalty to Diem was the first—and occasionally only—criterion for selection by the party, and thus some loyal, but corrupt and arrogant, officials were occupying important positions. Nhu was also spreading a vague philosophy, "personalism," a French Catholic concept that purportedly elevated the idea of human dignity as opposed to materialism. Nhu advertised the movement as an antidote to Communism. Others saw it as a "brainwashing" technique aimed at supplanting Buddhism and gathering more power for the Ngo family. Some of the nation's Buddhists complained that Catholics and adherents to French philosophy were receiving preferential treatment by the government.

It was probably inevitable that a period of civil unrest would arrive in South Vietnam. While victory over the Viet Cong had not been achieved, most believed the war was finally being won and attention naturally settled on what kind of South Vietnam would emerge in the aftermath. No one wanted a continuation of the sacrifices, midnight arrests, and police state methods that had been endured for so long. Few wanted the Buddhists handled in the callous and foolish way the Diem loyalists chose. After the incident in Hue, Buddhist leaders mounted demonstration after demonstration, seven monks dousing themselves with gasoline and burning themselves to death at various times for the benefit of television cameras and the growing sympathy of an international audience. Diem, his brother, and his brother's wife, Madame Nhu, labeled the Buddhists as Communists and sent troops to raid pagodas. The raids were staged in such a way that the army or police and not the Diem hierarchy might be blamed. This, of course, enraged a number of Vietnamese generals, and they made certain the U.S. Embassy knew the actual facts. Most of all, the antics of the Diem regime during the summer of 1963 became particularly galling to the Kennedy administration.

U.S. Policy and Diem

President Kennedy began acting against President Diem in the late summer. In August, the U.S. ambassador in Saigon, Henry Cabot Lodge, was instructed to make Diem and his brother change their policies or face a withdrawal of U.S. support. Lodge was told, however, that support would not be withdrawn from ARVN. Additionally, Lodge was instructed not to obstruct a military coup d'etat and was informed that the United States would recognize a Diem-deposing anticommunist government.

As the plot to eliminate the Diem regime was working its way through offices in Washington and Saigon, another group of U.S. envoys were sent to South Vietnam. Led by Marine Corps major general Victor Krulak and State Department representative Joseph Mendenhall, the group returned to the United States and reported to President Kennedy on the military and political situation in Vietnam. Mendenhall was darkly pessimistic. Kennedy was told that Diem was losing his political base of support. The Buddhist demonstrations and the brutal reaction of Diem's operatives had alienated much of the country's population. Krulak, however, was quite optimistic, assuring Kennedy that the Viet Cong were at long last being defeated.

There were several reasons for Krulak's upbeat report to Kennedy. ARVN troops were now killing several Viet Cong for every loss in their own ranks. More weapons were being taken from the Communists than the South Vietnamese government was losing. Some U.S. observers were reporting 75 percent of the population as being under South Vietnamese government control. Others stated that Viet Cong strength had suffered a 30 percent reduction between January and August 1963. A new identification card program was being hotly contested by the Viet Cong, but more than 80 percent of South Vietnam's citizens were now registered. In April, the South Vietnamese government had initiated the "Chieu Hoi" program, an amnesty project that had brought in about 14,000 Viet Cong defectors and 3,800 ARVN deserters. Also, the infiltration problem from North Vietnam was being addressed. Some U.S. and South Vietnamese Special Forces detachments were being moved to South Vietnam's frontiers, becoming border surveillance forces with the mission of intercepting intruders. There were some negative aspects, but the Krulak report was confirmed by a similar one from Secretary of Defense McNamara and Gen. Maxwell D. Taylor.

In the fall of 1963, Kennedy was not the only leader sending survey teams and receiving reports from South Vietnam. The Central Committee of the Communist party in Hanoi dispatched a team of experts at about the same time Kennedy was awaiting the reports from Mendenhall and Krulak. The Communist team chief, Col. Bui Tin, an experienced combat veteran of the Indochina War, told the North Vietnamese leaders that the Viet Cong were losing the war and were beyond recovery. The colonel recommended the use of NVA combat units. To his surprise, he found the decision-makers in Hanoi had already made preparations for the deployment of regular army units to the South.

In the fall of 1963, U.S. and North Vietnamese leaders both came to doubt their own policies and strategies. Both leadership groups were forced into making new decisions. President Kennedy faced an increasingly hostile press that criticized U.S. efforts in South Vietnam. The reporters were having a field day with the Saigon regime's foolish handling of Buddhist protesters, and Kennedy distanced himself from the man he had so often praised in the past, Ngo Dinh Diem. Finally, despite General Harkins's warning that no Southern general was capable of leading the nation, Kennedy gave the signal to Saigon's military lead-

Gen. Paul Harkins (right) *escorts Sec. of Defense Robert McNamara* (left) *and Gen. Maxwell D. Taylor* (center) *on a fact-finding tour to Vietnam in September 1963; they confirmed Maj. Gen. Victor Krulak's optimistic report.* (National Archives)

ers to oust Diem. Kennedy did not, however, want to abandon the military effort against the Communists.

The military effort was working, and Hanoi was considering a wholly new approach to its quest for the control of Indochina. Ho Chi Minh and his advisers made their decision some time during the fall. In December, at the Ninth Plenum of the Central Committee, Truong Chin, an expert on revolutionary warfare doctrine, announced that the time had come for a "combined general offensive." He claimed that Communist military forces in South Vietnam needed reinforcement and that North Vietnam had to play a bigger role in order to change the balance of forces. U.S. leaders were ignorant of Hanoi's decision to enter the war.

Diem's Overthrow

Acting in collusion with the Kennedy administration, the South Vietnamese military leadership moved against Diem on Nov. 2, 1963. U.S. military and CIA leaders had been opposed to the coup d'etat, so knowledge of the plan was largely restricted to U.S. political appointees and a small number of South Vietnamese generals. Diem and his brother Nhu were murdered (November 2) when U.S. officials informed the coup leaders no aircraft belonging to the United States was available to take the brothers out of the country.

No longer considered to be an effective leader for South Vietnam, President Diem, shown here at a 1961 meeting with U.S. vice president Lyndon Johnson, was murdered by his own officers (with U.S. acquiescence) in November 1963. (Library of Congress)

A group of American officials was hastily assembled to review Saigon's situation in late November, only to be temporarily interrupted by the news of President Kennedy's assassination (November 22). The views of the group were fundamentally optimistic. Everyone knew the Strategic Hamlet Program was being pushed ahead too rapidly, particularly in the Mekong Delta. There, it was believed only 30 percent of the hamlets reported to meet the criteria of security were actually secure. Elsewhere, that figure was estimated at roughly 60 percent. However, it was believed that almost 80 percent of South Vietnam's rural population was in some stage of being brought into the government's fold and out of the Viet Cong's reach. As a result of this review, a National Security Council memorandum envisioned a secure South Vietnam and the withdrawal of some U.S. troops in 1964; most of the rest would withdraw in 1965.

There were, however, a number of factors that argued against this rosy picture. As the Americans were deliberating Saigon's situation, South Vietnam's new leaders were dismantling the Republican Youth organization. Considered to be "brainwashed" by Nhu, the youth group formed the backbone for the Strategic Hamlet Program (now renamed the New Life Hamlet Program) and supplied the cadre for each hamlet. Additionally, the Cong An security service was being dismembered. This action was particularly damaging to the government in Saigon since it had just been learned that high-level, sensitive conversations among South Vietnamese officials were being quoted verbatim in Viet Cong documents. In the past, the Cong An had been moderately effective in catching Communist penetration agents within the South Vietnamese government.

But now, there seemed to be little chance of capturing or eliminating Hanoi's agents. The Diem regime's programs and some of its institutions were being wrecked, not reformed.

Another factor that argued against a secure Vietnam after a U.S. withdrawal was the growing dependence of the South Vietnamese on the Americans. Saigon was partially depending on the U.S. Navy for coastal surveillance, and the U.S. Air Force was flying a significant percentage of all combat and transport sorties. The U.S. Army was in the same posture. While there were about 2,900 army advisers in the field, there were 3,700 army personnel involved in aviation activities, and the South Vietnamese were redesigning their tactics to accommodate the new air assault techniques and the growing use of close-support aircraft.

Ho Chi Minh, of course, had every intention of carrying on the war, but 1963 had not been a good year for Hanoi. Viet Cong strength had fallen. Curiously, one of the reasons for the decline in Communist ranks in the South was the Buddhist opposition to Diem. Some Southerners joined the Viet Cong because of their hatred for Diem. In 1963, however, the Buddhist movement offered an alternative political effort to oppose Diem and attracted some who might otherwise have opted for the Communists. Also, the NLF was still primarily a political movement. It was estimated that the Communists were devoting only 10 percent of their time to military activities, a situation that was already changing.

Astutely sensing the lack of direction and planning in Saigon, the Viet Cong immediately launched a determined effort to regain the military initiative after Diem's assassination. Within five days, Viet Cong-initiated incidents of violence rose 50 percent. Within two weeks, the incident rate reached 1,000 per week. Infiltration along the Ho Chi Minh Trail from the North had decreased, from about 13,000 in 1962 to 8,000 in 1963, but that was because Hanoi was running out of Southerners to send back to South Vietnam and had not yet begun sending its own army units. To the Americans and South Vietnamese, seaborne infiltration appeared to have decreased, but that was because their naval forces had failed to intercept any of the eight trips south during the year by North Vietnam's 125th Sea Transportation unit.

When Kennedy became president in 1961, North Vietnam was being opposed by the 55,000,000 people of Thailand, Cambodia, Laos, and South Vietnam, with the primary battlefield in Laos. By the end of 1963, the main battlefield was in South Vietnam, where fewer than 16,000,000 Vietnamese and 16,000 Americans would attempt to defend against Hanoi's 19,000,000 people and about 200,000 Southern Communists and sympathizers. Three years before, the energies of the United States were directed at orchestrating the resources of a subcontinent against Hanoi's leadership, an effort that was restricted to U.S. advice and aid. Now, growing numbers of Americans were fighting in a part of the subcontinent. They were attempting to defend an enclave.

ESCALATION OF WAR: 1964

During the first few weeks of 1964, perceptions of the future among national leaders involved in the struggle for Southeast Asia varied widely. Most had seen the fortunes of the South Vietnamese, Communist-led NLF decline during 1963. For a few of Pres. Lyndon B. Johnson's advisers, there were visions of peace, and it appeared the planned withdrawal of U.S. units could begin. Saigon had an improved political climate, Diem's death having dampened Buddhist demonstrations. However, Saigon's new

leaders, some of their American advisers, and a few key U.S. officials were not optimistic. The surge in Viet Cong-initiated violence following Diem's assassination had not ended, and there was a lack either of firm leadership or of discipline in the ranks of the South Vietnamese generals.

In Hanoi, leaders did not have to guess. They knew the future would bring a wholly new era of combat, not peace. The Viet Cong reverses suffered in 1963 would be more than compensated for by the introduction of North Vietnamese regular units. Col. Dong Si Nguyen had been appointed to begin the engineering task of transforming the Ho Chi Minh Trail from a series of Laotian footpaths, with an occasional stretch of road, into a number of concealed north-south routes through both Laos and Cambodia, many of which would handle truck traffic.

Americans were trying hard to discover North Vietnamese intentions, and the U.S. Navy was supplying some

On the battlefield, South Vietnamese troops unload ammunition from a helicopter in 1964. (National Archives)

information. U.S. warships, usually destroyers, had electronic vans temporarily fixed to their decks and conducted extended cruises, just within international waters and off the coasts of Communist nations. While collecting electronic intelligence was the primary object of these sorties, another goal was serving "as a minor Cold War irritant" to adversaries of the United States. Such cruises had been conducted off North Korea, North Vietnam, and China. China had protested the cruises, but none of these countries had taken any action against the U.S. warships.

At the same time, the South Vietnamese were making some minor coastal raids along the North Vietnamese beaches, actions that were designed to retaliate for North Vietnamese direction and assistance to Communist activities in the South. These raids accomplished little; many were aborted due to the lack of intelligence about Hanoi's coastal defenses and the growing North Vietnamese fleet of fast patrol and patrol torpedo craft. By July 1964, the North Vietnamese navy had more than 30 high-speed coastal craft, variously armed with 37-millimeter weapons, torpedoes, and heavy machine guns. In order to avoid confusion, MACV and U.S. Navy officials decided to keep the American intelligence-collection cruises and South Vietnamese raids separate.

Gulf of Tonkin

On July 31, after a failed landing attempt by South Vietnamese commandos in two locations along the North Vietnamese coast, a U.S. Navy intelligence-collection mission was begun by the *Maddox,* which was in radio contact with a National Security Agency station. That station gained knowledge of North Vietnamese orders for an attack on the destroyer during the early morning hours of August 2 and informed the skipper of the *Maddox,* Capt. John J. Herrick. An assault by five North Vietnamese patrol and patrol torpedo craft led by Capt. Le Du Khoai came in the late afternoon, in the Gulf of Tonkin, 25 miles off the North Vietnamese coast. The *Maddox* managed to dodge the torpedoes, kill the commander of an attacking boat, drive off the assault, and call in air support from the aircraft carrier *Ticonderoga.* Captain Khoai lost one of his fleeing boats when it was hit by U.S. aircraft fire. The confrontation was over in about 30 minutes.

Shortly after the attack, President Johnson met with his advisers. Partly, the cruise of the *Maddox* was meant to convey America's strength and resolve. The ship's presence off North Vietnam was to have been a reminder, a "minor irritant." This element of the mission was meant to cause Ho Chi Minh and his subordinates to modify their behavior, reduce their aggressiveness, and consider the consequences of further support for the Viet Cong. Yet, for the first time in reaction to these coastal cruises, a Communist nation had resorted to armed attack in international waters. Johnson, after consulting with his advisers,

decided not to react aggressively. After all, the attack could have been the result of a low-level, hasty decision that did not have the approval of North Vietnam's leaders. Explicit and detailed instructions were dispatched from Secretary of Defense McNamara's office in Washington. The cruise was to be continued, but it would be reinforced.

The continuation on August 4 of the *Maddox* mission, augmented by the destroyer *Turner Joy,* was almost a carbon copy of the August 2 experience, except the North Vietnamese, still under Captain Khoai, chose to attack at night and the engagement lasted longer, about four hours. This attack occurred farther away from the North Vietnamese coast. Understandably, darkness added to the confusion, but two more Communist patrol boats were probably lost, and the Americans once again escaped harm.

With little doubt as to the intent of North Vietnam's leaders, Johnson ordered a reprisal air strike against North Vietnamese naval and fuel-storage facilities. On August 5, the carriers *Ticonderoga* and *Constellation* launched aircraft. By evening, the fuel facility at Vinh was in flames, 7 North Vietnamese patrol boats had been destroyed, and 10 were severely damaged. However, 2 U.S. naval aircraft were shot down, with one pilot killed and the other captured.

The actions in the Gulf of Tonkin resulted in changes, but not those hoped for in Washington. Ho Chi Minh and his lieutenants did not moderate their behavior. The South Vietnamese coastal raids, U.S. Navy intelligence-collection activity, or a combination of both had resulted in increased North Vietnamese aggressiveness. China quickly came to Hanoi's aid, sending 30 high-performance aircraft to North Vietnam's Phuc Yen airfield. Soon, substantial numbers of new radar emissions were detected in North Vietnam, and the number of antiaircraft artillery pieces there were doubled from about 700 to 1,400. The U.S. Congress provided Johnson with more legal authority to contest Hanoi. The Gulf of Tonkin Resolution authorized Johnson to use whatever force necessary to protect U.S. allies in Southeast Asia.

Pacification Campaign of 1964

At MACV headquarters in Saigon, Harkins was being replaced by Gen. William C. Westmoreland. Having a reputation as a superb combat leader and trainer, Westmoreland had progressed in an unconventional way in the army. He had begun his career in artillery, but changed his specialty to infantry. He had largely avoided normal military schooling, attending Harvard Business School rather than one of the war colleges. He was going to be a different commander from General Harkins, and what Westmoreland saw in South Vietnam on his arrival in January 1964 convinced him to be far less optimistic than his predecessor.

The U.S. government had formally stated a policy objective for its efforts in South Vietnam: "an independent, non-Communist South Vietnam." To the new MACV commander, it was a goal that seemed to be growing less attainable each day as the weak government in Saigon became increasingly dependent on U.S. aid and assistance. In March, about 40 percent of the countryside was controlled by the Viet Cong, forces that were becoming armed with heavy weapons, recoilless rifles, mortars, and rocket-propelled grenades. There was chaos in the government, more than 80 percent of the province chiefs were new, and most of the major military organizations had changed commanders since Diem's overthrow. The strength of the South Vietnamese army was actually dropping because of high desertion rates. Finally, the country's economy was weakening, rice production having dropped some 17 percent from the benchmark year of 1958.

Part of the reason for South Vietnam's problems centered on the continued instability of the government in Saigon. Throughout 1964, there were numerous attempts by one faction of generals to oust another group. In such an atmosphere of turmoil, government ministries could not concentrate on the rural pacification program or on the various U.S.-supported economic development projects. Some of the instability and dissension among South Vietnamese senior officers was undoubtedly caused by Communist agents. For instance, Col. Pham Ngoc Thao, the Viet Cong penetration agent who had gained the trust of the Ngo family, had been able to survive Diem's overthrow and be appointed to an important psychological warfare position in Saigon. The colonel spent most of his time, however, in furthering the causes of several succeeding groups of Vietnamese generals trying to gain power in Saigon, adding to the instability.

Another part of Saigon's 1964 woes involved a growing number of military reverses. Toward midyear, battalion-size encounters between Viet Cong and ARVN forces were occurring weekly, and, increasingly, the South Vietnamese army was being ambushed, surprised, or bested on the battlefield. These setbacks can also be attributed in part to Communist agents; for example, a high-ranking intelligence staff officer of Saigon's joint general staff during this period, Col. Vo Bac Trinh, was also a North Vietnamese agent. The military reverses can also be attributed in part to the inability of the South Vietnamese government. As the generals positioned themselves in Saigon's power game, personal loyalty had more merit than combat proficiency.

As Westmoreland traveled throughout Vietnam, he gradually devised a strategy to achieve "an independent, noncommunist South Vietnam." Advising his Vietnamese counterparts, Westmoreland advocated using more of the U.S. Special Forces units in a border surveillance role, disrupting or at least giving warning of infiltration groups coming from North Vietnam. Inside the borders, Communist main force units would be subjected to "search and

destroy" operations by the 192,000-man South Vietnamese army. These forces, composed of 9 divisions, a marine brigade, an airborne brigade, and 4 ranger battalions, would require the majority of the support provided by the air arm, South Vietnam's 190 combat aircraft and the more than 300 U.S. piloted planes and helicopters.

After successful search and destroy operations, an inhabited region of the country, now free of Viet Cong regulars, would be exposed to "clearing operations." These efforts were to be conducted by a mixture of regular and paramilitary Vietnamese units. The latter were primarily the nation's 476 Civil Guard companies (now being renamed "Regional Force" companies). Clearing operations were to eliminate the local Viet Cong guerrilla forces. At that point, "securing operations" could be conducted. This was to be done primarily by the 2,050 Self Defense Corps (now being renamed "Popular Force") platoons and the National Police. The object of the securing operations was to eliminate the Viet Cong political, tax, and agent structure, an organization that the CIA was now calling the "VCI" (Viet Cong infrastructure).

South Vietnamese Initiatives

The most difficult part of the overall strategy was perhaps the last phase: securing operations. The government had to install its New Life Hamlet system in order to eliminate completely the VCI and establish the security that would prevent Viet Cong control from returning. Westmoreland supported South Vietnamese and CIA efforts to rebuild the pacification program, particularly the new ideas and tech-

The U.S. military continued to advise the South Vietnamese on training troops; here, a South Vietnamese officer shows his U.S. counterpart the techniques that are being carried out at a training camp. (National Archives)

niques being used by Maj. Nguyen Be, an imaginative officer in northern South Vietnam.

Be discovered that although the New Life Hamlet militia forces were receiving substantial instruction in securing their villages, the Viet Cong were either not rooted out of the communities or returned shortly after government forces left. Working with the CIA, he developed "People's Action Teams," 40-man units that roamed Quang Ngai Province, talking to villagers and determining the peasantry's grievances against both the South Vietnamese government and the Viet Cong. The teams had the aid of an intelligence network that consisted of two to four agents per village, each with two to four informants. The teams reported their findings and ruthlessly tracked down and eliminated members of the Viet Cong infrastructure.

In a period of about five months, three People's Action Teams under Major Be's direction killed 150 Viet Cong, captured 200 others, and themselves suffered 6 killed and 20 wounded. These results were in dramatic contrast to what was happening in the rest of the country, and the CIA began persuading South Vietnamese officials to supplement the New Life Hamlet program with the major's techniques. Subsequently, it was decided to recruit and train two separate elements: a "census grievance team" to determine peasant attitudes and derive confidential information and a "provincial reconnaissance unit" to track down and eliminate the VCI.

By early summer, Westmoreland knew that the pacification program had to succeed if South Vietnam were going to survive. As a matter of priority, he wanted the program to be pursued aggressively in the six heavily populated provinces surrounding Saigon. He believed that Communist progress was so steady that there was a danger of the capital being strangled, separated from the rest of the country. The operation was named Hop Tac, a Vietnamese term meaning "cooperation." To Westmoreland, Hop Tac was an apt name because there would have to be much cooperation if the plan were to succeed. Not only were numerous South Vietnamese government ministries and combat units involved, there were also five to six U.S. government bureaus and agencies with which to coordinate. When Westmoreland asked the American ambassador for authority to coordinate the U.S. side of Hop Tac, he received agreement that such centralization was necessary, but Westmoreland was never given control over CIA, USIA, AID, or other U.S. organizations involved in the operation. Unfortunately, each of these bureaucracies had its own ideas about how to proceed.

Westmoreland's Concerns

Westmoreland's frustrations with the U.S. bureaucracy and its numerous overseas agencies were outstripped by his anguish with his South Vietnamese military counter-

parts. Hop Tac was failing, partly because the South Vietnamese generals were so involved in palace intrigue that they could not seem to focus on the Viet Cong. Pacification throughout the country was also failing, in part because South Vietnamese units engaged in search and destroy operations were consistently defeated by Viet Cong units. Also, there was no reason in many places to advance to clearing efforts since Communist main force battalions were increasingly unchallenged in populated areas. These setbacks were taking place in the midst of a growing number of U.S. casualties. By late October, U.S. combat deaths in South Vietnam totaled 97 for the year 1964, twice the American deaths there in all of 1963.

Westmoreland found intolerable the selfish squabbling of South Vietnamese generals in the midst of an increasingly desperate military situation and mounting American deaths. On October 31, he wrote to his superior, Ambassador Maxwell Taylor. Westmoreland said the government of South Vietnam was corrupt, ill-motivated, and losing the war. Westmoreland recommended that the United States no longer give Saigon's leaders a "blank check" and instead begin withholding aid until the South Vietnamese generals improved their performances. Westmoreland also took note of a growing problem: the steady increase in South Vietnam of troops, supplies, and weapons from North Vietnam.

Westmoreland favored establishing a blocking force along Route 9, from the South Vietnamese coast, through Laos to the Thai border. It would require a corps-sized force—Americans and Asians—and it would demand the deployment of troops along a 200-mile line. However, such an operation would require far less than the continued and failing attempt to seal the 1,200-mile western border of South Vietnam. Westmoreland's plea received little more attention than his earlier recommendation to unify the U.S. pacification efforts.

Main Force Campaign of 1964

Even though substantial numbers of North Vietnamese regular units had not arrived on the Southern battlefields by late summer 1964, combat between Viet Cong main force battalions and those of the South Vietnamese army had become quite common. Col. Dong Si Nguyen's engineering efforts in Laos had resulted in a number of truck-capable roads and stocked way stations, but the task had taken some nine months. In November, MACV knew of three North Vietnamese regiments traveling south through Laos: the 101st, the 95th, and the 32d.

The U.S. command, however, did not know that control of Communist military efforts in South Vietnam had been turned over to Northern generals. Southerners—Nguyen Van Linh and his military deputy, Tran Van Tra—had controlled Viet Cong efforts under Hanoi's direction until

1964. In mid-1964, Nguyen Van Linh became the deputy to Gen. Nguyen Chi Than, who had been sent from the North. Additionally, Gen. Tran Do, a group of Northern staff officers, and communications elements had arrived in the South. Their purpose was to provide the skill and expertise that Hanoi believed the Southerners lacked.

There was every reason to believe the Communists in South Vietnam might not need help. Viet Cong strength had almost doubled in 1964, reaching 170,000 despite the fact that 20,000 had been killed or captured and another 17,000 had defected under the Chieu Hoi program. The Viet Cong had managed to add 6 battalions to its main forces, which now totaled 46 battalions. Some of these Viet Cong battalions were being grouped into regiments. Further, these units increasingly were being armed with the AK-47 assault rifle, an automatic weapon that permitted the Communists to "outgun" their ARVN adversaries, soldiers largely equipped with outmoded American semi-automatic small arms.

Toward the end of 1964, Southern Communist main force units initiated several operations that decimated a number of ARVN combat formations. In November, just north of Saigon in Binh Dinh Province, two Viet Cong regiments descended on a number of widely dispersed ARVN units in the midst of clearing operations in support of the Hop Tac pacification program. Most of the government forces were badly defeated. In December, 40 miles east of Saigon, two Southern Communist regiments, organizations destined to be grouped into the Viet Cong 9th Division, were receiving a seaborne shipment of heavy weapons and managed to overrun a New Life Hamlet project, the settlement of Binh Gia. When ARVN units began to pour into the coastal area, a series of daylight battles that lasted almost a month resulted. In the end, two ARVN ranger battalions and one South Vietnamese marine battalion had been destroyed. To the north, the 1st and 2d Viet Cong regiments in Quang Ngai Province defeated several ARVN battalions.

These battles clearly indicated that the South Vietnamese government could not expand and possibly could not even hold the countryside it controlled. Pacification could not proceed because ARVN units could not afford to disperse their formations to conduct effective counterguerrilla operations. Survival dictated consolidation in the face of formidable Viet Cong dispositions. These late 1964 battles were also costly in terms of U.S. casualties. By December, American combat deaths for the year totaled 112. The Viet Cong had shot down 63 helicopters during the year, and there were 5 Americans missing in action. As bad as the existing "main force" war appeared to those in Saigon and Washington, the future looked even worse. Intelligence reports showed that North Vietnamese regular units were due to arrive in South Vietnam. The new year would see ARVN pitted against both Southern and Northern regulars.

Transforming the War

To the casual or distant observer, the conflict in South Vietnam was becoming a conventional contest between regular forces. A closer inspection yielded quite another characterization, because all the indicators of political and guerrilla activity were up. For example, the use of mines and booby-traps in populated regions, always an indicator of guerrilla activity, was rising. In 1962, a year regarded by some as a "guerrilla warfare" year, there were about 22 mining and booby-trap incidents per month. In 1964, the rate rose to more than 90 incidents per month. Additionally, it was estimated that the Viet Cong held about 44,000 propaganda and organizational meetings in South Vietnam during 1962. These meetings were aimed largely at exhorting peasants to join guerrilla units and contribute money and labor to the guerrillas. The meetings were not an activity normal to or associated with conventional, main force operations. In 1964, the number of Viet Cong-sponsored meetings rose to about 2,000,000. There were other indicators that showed dramatic growth in guerrilla and political activity as well.

The guerrilla forces could not win the war by themselves, however, so main force units, the regulars, were being nurtured and augmented by Communist leaders. Guerrilla activity usually provoked the opposing conventional forces into dispersion to conduct effective counterguerrilla operations. Those conventional forces were then vulnerable to being destroyed by the Communist main force units. The Communist main force units either destroyed the South Vietnamese conventional forces or kept them concentrated so that the guerrillas could survive and thrive. The doctrine of Mao Zedong, China's Communist leader, envisioned a complementary relationship between the guerrilla and regular forces: both must exist, and both must continue to grow throughout a war. But for Hanoi, there were not enough regular Communist forces in the South to ensure victory, hence, the deployment of regular units from the North.

The introduction of Northern regulars transformed the war. To outward appearances, an armed, ideological argument among Southern factions became more of a war between the North and South. A simple explanation for this shift could be that a civil war had been changed into an invasion by an external intruder. The leaders in Hanoi had been aware of this possible interpretation and realized that international opinion would condemn the invasion. Therefore, shortly after the decision was made to send Northern troops south, a series of spectacular incidents against the U.S. Armed Forces began. These incidents were staged in such a way that the attention of the international media

During the late summer of 1964, President Johnson and his staff, supported by Congress and the majority of the American people, met in Texas to begin plans for full-scale war in Vietnam. (Lyndon Baines Johnson Library)

focused on the presence of U.S. soldiers, airmen, and sailors in South Vietnam. The objective was to make the Americans the intruders in the eyes of the world.

In February 1964, the U.S. advisory compound in Kontum was attacked and a bomb in the Kinh Do Theater in Saigon killed 3 Americans and wounded 50. In May, a U.S. helicopter transport vessel, the *Card,* was sunk. In November, a dramatic mortar attack on the Bien Hoa air base killed 4 Americans and destroyed five B-57 bombers. Near the end of the year, a bomb placed in the Brinks Hotel in Saigon killed 2 U.S. servicemen and wounded 38 others. These events successfully directed the focus of the international print and broadcast media on the U.S. military and naval personnel in South Vietnam, now numbering more than 23,000.

The last two incidents were particularly galling to U.S. authorities, and there were calls to respond in the same way that occurred after the incident in the Gulf of Tonkin: air attacks on North Vietnam. President Johnson did not approve these recommendations for reprisal. The Americans seemed to be mired in the same situation that the French had faced 20 years earlier. As 1965 began, the arguments for a greater, deeper U.S. involvement grew more persuasive.

5

Vietnam—A Decade of American Commitment: 1965–1975

Having become deeply involved by the end of 1964 in assisting the Republic of South Vietnam in its fight against Communist forces, the United States reached a point where it would either have to abandon its failing ally or become even more committed to the conflict. In early 1965, the Lyndon B. Johnson administration set out to save its ally by employing U.S. ground forces in the South and conducting an on-again, off-again limited bombing campaign in North Vietnam. After building a logistical infrastructure, U.S. operations in South Vietnam began to show promise in 1966; in 1967, Gen. William C. Westmoreland, commander of the U.S. Military Assistance Command Vietnam (MACV), projected victory and an eventual U.S. withdrawal. The restricted bombing campaign, however, did not appear to be successful; more and more North Vietnamese troops continued to march southward. Additionally, the war became extremely controversial within the United States. In early 1968, Communist forces managed a massive attack throughout South Vietnam—the Tet Offensive. This offensive seemed to refute Washington's optimistic appraisals and provided fuel to President Johnson's critics. Johnson decided to withdraw U.S. forces and reach a negotiated settlement with North Vietnam.

From the beginning of 1969, Johnson's successor, Richard M. Nixon, continued the withdrawal of U.S. forces and the diplomacy but also directed continued and even expanded fighting as South Vietnam bolstered its armed forces. By the end of 1972, U.S. forces were largely out of South Vietnam, and a peace agreement was signed in early 1973. The South Vietnamese were unable to stand

on their own, and their government fell under a massive North Vietnamese invasion in the spring of 1975.

AMERICANS TAKE CHARGE: 1965

North Vietnam's 1964 campaign against U.S. military personnel in South Vietnam succeeded in drawing attention away from its own large-scale infiltration of forces southward. Although the U.S. air strike on North Vietnam after the Gulf of Tonkin incident did not seem to faze North Vietnamese leader Ho Chi Minh and his followers, a Feb. 7, 1965, attack on Americans at the U.S. military facilities in Pleiku gave reason for another air reprisal. The North Vietnamese transportation center of Dong Hoi was struck by U.S. aircraft while South Vietnamese aircraft hit the headquarters of an antiaircraft unit at Vinh Linh. A Viet Cong response came on February 10 when 23 Americans were killed during an attack on a U.S. compound at Qui Nhon. Another American reprisal air raid was ordered, and soon after, the United States initiated a sustained and graduated bombing campaign on North Vietnam. An "air war" had begun.

The incident at Qui Nhon and a further deterioration in the effectiveness of the Army of the Republic of Vietnam (ARVN) readily demonstrated an inability to protect U.S. facilities and service personnel. The bombing campaign in both Laos and North Vietnam had added some U.S. resources to the vulnerable bases in South Vietnam. Additionally, due to the buildup of forces in North Vietnam following the Gulf of Tonkin incident, there were growing

As the United States became fully committed to eradicating Communism in South Vietnam, special training programs were set up, such as this at Fort Benning, Georgia, for instruction in the Viet Cong's style of guerrilla fighting. (U.S. Army)

numbers of high-performance aircraft being assembled at Communist air bases surrounding Hanoi. There was no assurance that the North Vietnamese could not deliver an effective air attack on some of the South Vietnamese air bases. President Johnson approved the deployment of a U.S. Marine Corps air defense unit and a two-battalion air base defense force to the northern part of South Vietnam.

U.S. Policy

In March 1965, Johnson began additional moves. He believed that South Vietnam might fall and that there would be a divisive debate in the United States over the loss, a blow to U.S. credibility, a continuation of Communist advances, and a later struggle by the United States to regain its position of strength in world affairs. To Johnson, the question was not whether but how the U.S. Armed Forces should attempt to preserve South Vietnam. Despite opposing advice by a number of prominent Americans, the president sent Army Chief of Staff Gen. Harold K. Johnson to South Vietnam. The general asked Westmoreland and his staff, "What do you need to win the war?" On his return, General Johnson stated that South Vietnam would probably fall in six months unless drastic actions were taken. He said that three divisions were immediately required to prevent Saigon's defeat and a total of seven to turn the situation in Saigon's favor. General Johnson said that an international force to block North Vietnamese infiltration down the Ho Chi Minh Trail to South Vietnam was needed, a force that would stretch from the coast of South Vietnam through Laos and to the west bank of the Mekong River. Additionally, the president was advised that the effort to preserve South Vietnam might require 500,000 troops and five years.

During the spring and summer of 1965, the United States began to deploy combat forces to South Vietnam. General Johnson's assessment, however, was only partially used by the Johnson administration. The Laotian blocking force, for example, was rejected. As U.S. combat forces arrived in South Vietnam and began to struggle with logistical problems, it became apparent that there were differing views as to who would be in charge. Westmoreland had proposed a combined command, a command and control arrangement that would unify all of the ground and air organizations fighting the Communists in South Vietnam. South Vietnam rejected the idea at the time, and its new military junta leaders, Gens. Nguyen Cao Ky and Nguyen Van Thieu, opposed the concept. To the Vietnamese, Westmoreland's idea smacked of colonialism. Then, too, South Korea had been persuaded to offer troops, and it wanted to exert its own sovereignty. South Korean forces in South Vietnam would not be subordinate to the Americans. Small contingents were eventually sent by other nations, and they generally followed the Korean model. Thus, there would be several armies and air forces in South Vietnam and no single commander. Additionally, Westmoreland did not control the air war, U.S. efforts in Laos, or U.S. support to the pacification campaign in South Vietnam. Further, the general did not agree with some of the goals Washington established. Bombing efforts in North Vietnam and Laos were controlled by the secretary of defense in Washington. Westmoreland was only a "deputy for military affairs" to the U.S. ambassador in South Vietnam.

During June 1965, Washington's strategic goal of a free and independent South Vietnam was expanded to include

On a fact-finding mission with U.S. Sec. of Defense Robert McNamara in 1965, Henry Cabot Lodge (left), *who had resigned as U.S. ambassador to Vietnam in June 1964 but returned to the position in July 1965, greets Maj. Gen. Nguyen Van Thieu.* (National Archives)

proving to the Viet Cong and North Vietnam that they could not win in South Vietnam. Curtailing Hanoi's efforts in the South was to be achieved by the bombing campaign. The air war's objectives were (1) to reduce the flow or increase the cost of infiltration of men and supplies from North to South Vietnam, (2) to make it clear to the North Vietnamese leadership that continued aggression in South Vietnam would have a heavy price, and (3) to raise the morale of the people of South Vietnam.

Westmoreland immediately argued with Washington's concepts by saying that bombing was unlikely to alter North Vietnamese intentions, at least for the next six months. Two weeks later, in mid-July, the general told Sec. of Defense Robert S. McNamara that since the Communists only offered battle when it was favorable to them, they were in large measure controlling their own logistical requirements. It was estimated that 14 tons per day satisfied the nonfood Communist supply needs. Food was mostly coming from the extensive Viet Cong rice tax system within South Vietnam. McNamara was told that there was less than a 40-percent chance of intercepting a North Vietnamese wooden-hull supply craft at sea. And, despite several months of bombing in North Vietnam and Laos, there was no indication of declining North Vietnamese willpower or of Communist supply shortages in South Vietnam. Westmoreland's preferred method of dealing with the North's support and infiltration was the oft-recommended blocking force along Route 9, a concept opposed in Washington.

Campaign for the Central Highlands

One of the U.S. divisions en route to Vietnam was an entirely new type of organization, an airmobile division. Using ideas developed in Vietnam and the results of extensive testing in the United States, an entire division equipped with 470 aircraft, mostly helicopters, was available for combat in 1965. The 1st Cavalry Division (Airmobile) was employed in the Central Highlands, an area considered important to Hanoi, to search out and destroy North Vietnamese and Viet Cong main force units. Hanoi was making the same sort of decisions. North Vietnamese general Nguyen Chi Than directed a major campaign in Pleiku Province during late 1965 and early 1966. The operation would involve three of the five North Vietnamese regiments now entering South Vietnam. These organizations were to be commanded by Brig. Gen. Chu Huy Man, whose troops were to inflict maximum casualties on the Americans and South Vietnamese and seize both Pleiku and Kontum cities. Chu Huy Man's concept was first to eliminate the two U.S. Special Forces bases that marked the western limit of Saigon's control in the Central Highlands.

Beginning in late summer 1965, the North Vietnamese tried and failed to destroy the Special Forces camps and

began a retreat toward Cambodia. The 1st Cavalry Division's artillery had gotten into the fight at one of the camps, Ple Me, and the division began pursuit. In the early fall, the 1st Cavalry moved battalions by helicopter 22 times and displaced artillery batteries by the same means 66 times, sometimes as far as 75 miles. Likely spots for an infantry company or battalion assault would often be determined by small scout helicopters, infantry platoons, and gunships that ranged well in advance of the primary employment area. The Battle of Ia Drang, as it became known, proved the concept of air assault, but it also proved that the new form of warfare could be costly. Several hundred Americans were killed in clashes throughout the Central Highlands. The North Vietnamese forces were decimated.

Both sides drew lessons from the campaign. Most U.S. military authorities cited the great success of the new air cavalry units. They also noted that Communist forces were learning to cope with the huge volume of U.S. firepower by practicing "hugging tactics": once contact was made, the North Vietnamese and Viet Cong were moving as close as possible to the Americans, avoiding much of the artillery fire and bombing that they knew would be coming. The Communists also quickly learned the American dependence on artillery support. If Communist forces were about 8 miles from a U.S. artillery unit, they knew that it was unlikely that they would encounter a U.S. infantry force. The Northerners also relearned an old lesson: when there is pressure on main force units, have guerrilla forces elsewhere create diversions, and visa versa. U.S. logisticians found that supporting this type of operation was costly; the 1st Cavalry consumed 144 tons of supplies per day during the campaign, or 10 times the entire nonfood supply for Viet Cong and North Vietnamese forces coming out of North Vietnam.

Another U.S. combat technique, B-52 strikes, also showed some promise in destroying Communist forces. Each of the giant bombers delivered 51 750-pound bombs with great accuracy. The bombs were dropped from 30,000 feet, an altitude at which the planes could not be heard or readily seen. In a flight of three closely grouped aircraft, a few square miles of jungle could be devastated. The first such raid, conducted in June 1965 north of Saigon, hit the target, a concentrated Viet Cong unit, causing immense destruction and high casualties. Initially, the Communists were able to find out about the raids because flight plans were coordinated in advance with international air traffic control authorities. The United States changed these procedures, but the Soviets soon began basing their intelligence ships off B-52 bases and warned the Vietnamese Communist forces when the bombers took off. The U.S. Air Force modified the aircraft, achieving even greater bombloads and a more lethal mix of bomb types. Communist forces used more dispersion, used more under-

The U.S. 1st Cavalry Division (Airmobile), a new type of division built around helicopters and other aircraft, was deployed to Vietnam in 1965. Here, pilots of the 1st Cavalry land their helicopters carrying ground troops. (U.S. Army)

ground facilities, and moved more often. The B-52 became a feared weapon, but not a decisive one.

The Air War

By the end of 1965, some were calling the bombing campaign in North Vietnam and Laos a failure. Despite the fact that the campaign saw an average of 200 sorties per week, traffic southward through North Vietnam and Laos was increasing, not decreasing. The morale of the South Vietnamese may have been lifted in the first few months of the year, but as time wore on, news of the air raids to the north became commonplace and unremarkable. It was also obvious that North Vietnamese willpower to continue the war had not been diminished. In fact, some believed that the bombing campaign had actually increased Northern resolve.

The air campaign was certainly expensive, which may have been the primary reason for the growing controversy over its prosecution. The introduction of Soviet SA-2 antiaircraft missiles in the North contributed to increasing numbers of downed U.S. aircraft. The missile crews, some of which were Russian, brought down 1 plane per 18 missile firings; but of greater importance, the mere existence of the missiles forced U.S. pilots to fly at low altitudes, making them vulnerable to the guns of other Communist antiaircraft units. Dodging missile and the more conventional antiaircraft threats placed U.S. pilots at risk to being

brought down by the rising numbers of Communist air interceptors. Although the MiG fighter planes were often on the losing side of these occasional duels, their pilots did manage to score a number of victories during the year. U.S. air losses in the Northern air campaign amounted to 171 aircraft in 1965, and McNamara's analysts argued that the effort was not cost-effective. They calculated it was costing $460,000,000 to inflict only $70,000,000 worth of damage on North Vietnam.

The American airmen—from both the navy and the air force—argued that the unusual restrictions placed on U.S. aircraft caused high losses and inefficient operations. They cited the fact that the Defense Department's rules and tight control of all air operations prohibited the logical exploitation of air attack. For example, once a bridge had been destroyed, on-scene air commanders had no authority to conduct follow-up strikes on the resulting backup of road traffic. Such an attack had to be considered carefully and approved in Washington. They complained of the inability to strike population centers when such areas were used to shield truck convoys during daylight hours. The air forces also argued that the prohibition on dropping mines in the approaches to Haiphong's harbor allowed an uninterrupted flow of Soviet military equipment into North Vietnam. Most of all, they protested the stop-start nature of the air war. The campaign had not been continuous. For example, there had been an order to cease operations for six days in

May, time supposedly used to entice Ho Chi Minh into negotiations to end the war. The Northerners had used the pause in air attacks to effect repairs, move supplies at a greater rate, and enhance defenses. All these arguments were to no avail. Another pause in air operations came during the last week of 1965.

A New War

The focus of the war shifted dramatically during the years 1964 and 1965. By the end of this period, attention was centered on 12 regiments of the North Vietnamese Army (NVA) in the South, the 650 U.S. high-performance aircraft based in Southeast Asia, 3 U.S. aircraft carriers just offshore, and the divisions and brigades of the U.S. Army and Marine Corps pouring into South Vietnam. Now, there were more than 178,000 U.S. soldiers, sailors, airmen, and marines in South Vietnam.

The North Vietnamese were now in complete control of the Southern Communists. Unlike Washington, Hanoi unified its command in the South and placed a general, not an ambassador, in charge of all its efforts there. Meanwhile, North Vietnam itself was becoming a large air defense zone, bristling with antiaircraft guns, interceptors, missiles, and electronic warning and guidance gear. Hanoi's soldiers and suppliers had only to contend with U.S. aircraft along the Ho Chi Minh Trail. The Northern units and their supplies were well into South Vietnam before they were significantly impeded. The Northern units, however, had a different character from that of the Viet Cong. The latter largely lived off the people in the South, and it was rare that the Southern Communists were surprised by their opponents. The Northern units depended on their bases in Laos and Cambodia, and they were not as well-informed as their Southern comrades. And, the initial per-

Helicopters, essential to the topography and the war strategy in Vietnam, were used by the 1st Cavalry Division (Airmobile) and other units to bring troops into and out of combat areas or from base to base quickly. (U.S. Army)

Artillery support, such as this 155-millimeter howitzer, was very important to air strikes; however, the Communist forces soon developed techniques, such as grouping together as close as possible to the Americans, to avoid being hit. (U.S. Army)

formance of the Northerners had been wanting. The U.S. bombing pause and negotiations offer in December 1965 had not been in place long when Hanoi replied. Ho Chi Minh stated he would not accept an offer of talks and denied the existence of North Vietnamese units in South Vietnam. In rejecting the U.S. offer, Ho Chi Minh surely knew that the bombing of his country would recommence and that his people would suffer more. But, he also knew that more than 1,600 Americans had already perished in the war and that the number would climb.

ALLIED OFFENSIVE: 1966–1967

During 1966 and early 1967, logistical constraints often determined the location and intensity of fighting, both for the Communists and their opponents. As time wore on, each side became more capable of conducting operations at almost any location or time of day. Sharp and bloody clashes occurred all over Vietnam. In the North, the war was characterized by a technological race between the Soviet-supported Vietnamese air defense system and the U.S. airmen. Technology was also important, albeit to a lesser extent, in the South, where the Americans used any device or technique to find and engage an elusive enemy. However, the major characterization of the war came to be an agonizing sameness. Battles raged, air raids were staged, but no dramatic change occurred. During these two bloody and frustrating years, final resolution seemed remote, but U.S. forces were gradually gaining the upper hand.

Main Force War in the South

The year 1966 opened with another large-scale effort by the 1st Cavalry Division, this time augmented with a South Korean battalion and several battalions from the South Vietnamese airborne brigade. By March, Binh Dinh Province was considerably less beset by Communist forces due to Operation Masher/White Wing. The cost involved 245 Americans killed in action: of the Communists, more than 1,200 died and about 500 surrendered. From May until the end of the year, the division and the newly arrived U.S. 4th Infantry Division returned to Pleiku Province, conducting Operation Paul Revere, which resulted in another 2,300 Communist dead. The year also saw Operation Birmingham, an effort by the 1st Infantry Division in a remote, uninhabited region that had long been the lair of Viet Cong main force units. The division failed to trap any Viet Cong force of significant size, but South Vietnamese Communists units there had to flee into Cambodia, abandoning many of their supplies. In late 1966, a large-scale operation was initiated just north of Saigon. Operation Attleboro resulted in serious losses for the Communists but was also costly to the Americans. During this fight, U.S. and South Vietnamese forces lost about 100 men, while the Communists lost at least 1,100.

Later, elements of the 4th Division operated in northern South Vietnam, conducting Operations Sam Houston and Francis Marion. Two brigades of the division managed to kill 1,900 enemy soldiers in the High Plateau provinces of Pleiku and Darlac, while U.S. dead totaled 355. To the south, U.S. forces launched another large-scale offensive that rivaled Operation Attleboro. In January 1967, Operation Cedar Falls, an intense effort to clean out a troublesome region called the "Iron Triangle," involved not only the 1st and 25th infantry divisions, but the 11th Armored Cavalry Regiment and 173d Airborne Brigade as well. The Viet Cong lost 720 soldiers, while the Americans lost one-tenth that number and seized enough hidden rice to feed 10,000 men for a year. During February–May 1967, the heavily wooded region of Tay Ninh Province, usually called "War Zone C," was attacked by the 25th Division augmented by the 11th Armored Cavalry Regiment, the 196th Light Infantry Brigade, and the 173d Airborne Brigade. Conducted over the same areas as the 1st Division's Birmingham effort of 1966, the 1967 operation was a bit more productive for the Americans. Enemy losses were counted at more than 2,700 killed.

By 1967, the U.S. 9th Infantry Division began operations. Initially restricted to dry ground just east and south of Saigon, the unit gradually received all of its equipment

Bombing raids into North Vietnam, as pointed out by Sec. of Defense Robert McNamara to journalists in April 1965, frustrated American pilots who felt that they were too restricted by the Department of Defense's policies. (National Archives)

Landing craft deposit marines near the shores of Da Nang, a seaport in South Vietnam that served as a major supply area for the allied forces during the Vietnam War. (U.S. Navy)

and began the difficult task of engaging Viet Cong main force and guerrilla units in the canals, rivers, and swampy areas of the Mekong Delta. The division's operations south of Saigon accounted for some 1,000 Viet Cong deaths in 1967. These operations are only a few of the U.S. efforts and were almost wholly targeted at Communist main force elements. Meanwhile, South Vietnamese forces were engaged in a number of actions, mostly within populated regions and mostly against Communist guerrilla formations.

Logistical Factors

Both sides had to tailor tactical and strategic goals to logistical capabilities. For the allied side, General Westmoreland gained approval of several aims for 1966. The continued loss of rural population to Communist control was to be stopped and turned around. It was hoped that the South Vietnamese government could raise its control of the nation's people from 50 percent to 60 percent. Another aim was to increase the mileage of secure national roadways from 30 percent to 50 percent. A third goal involved reducing the numbers of undisturbed Communist base areas by a factor of 30 percent. Finally, it was agreed that aggressive combat operations would be used to halt the growth in Communist main force troops. In essence, the last goal required the allies to kill or capture as many

troops as North Vietnam sent down the Ho Chi Minh Trail, plus those additional numbers of regulars recruited, trained, and fielded by South Vietnamese Communists. In sum, the allies were committed to a strategy of attrition against their enemies.

General Than, Westmoreland's opponent in most of South Vietnam, did not have to coordinate strategic aims among allies and a myriad of government agencies as did Westmoreland. Throughout 1966 and the first half of 1967, the North Vietnamese commander directed offensive operations conducted by Northern regulars, Viet Cong main force units, and Southern guerrilla forces. His aims were to defeat the allies' regulars, destroy Saigon's forces, and undermine the South Vietnamese government. By early 1967, the Communists had 280,000 troops operating in South Vietnam, 50,000 of them Northerners. Despite a steady flow of units and replacements streaming southward from North Vietnam, the Communist commander had to modify his instructions in the summer of 1967. He began pulling his regular forces out of South Vietnam and into the protected sanctuaries of Cambodia and Laos. Communist regular forces had been so damaged by the Americans, South Vietnamese, Koreans, Australians, New Zealanders, and others (altogether 1,173,800 soldiers) that their survival could no longer be assured if they remained within

South Vietnam. The strategy of attrition was working—at least in South Vietnam.

Allied success was largely due to a growing ability to support simultaneous, division-size operations at almost any time and place within the country, an ability that only came to fruition in the summer of 1967. It had taken almost two years to attain such a logistical structure. North Vietnamese logisticians faced some of the same problems as their U.S. counterparts. While Americans were building port facilities and fuel storage tanks and opening or improving roads, Hanoi's forces were improving the Ho Chi Minh Trail, stocking forward depots, arranging for the use of Cambodia's port of Sihanoukville (Kompong Som) and finding ways to replace porters with trucks. On the trail south, the Northerners' hard work paid off. Whereas an infiltration group took 3–4 weeks to come from North Vietnam to South Vietnam in 1964, the trip was being accomplished in only 11 days in 1967.

The "Other War"

By late 1966, yet one more change in the pacification program began to take shape. Partially based on Maj. Nguyen Be's Quang Ngai experiment and partially based on the previous Agroville, Strategic Hamlet, and New Life Hamlet programs, the Revolutionary Development Program was conducted by 59-member revolutionary development teams. Composed of a 34-member security and military training element, as well as education, land reform, construction, communications, agriculture, and census-grievance sections, the teams were to remain in their assigned

A captured North Vietnamese soldier, no more than 15 years old, receives medical treatment from his captors in July 1966. (National Archives)

villages until the Viet Cong infrastructure was rooted out, a self-defense capability attained, and a National Police section installed. Of great importance, Westmoreland's recommendation that U.S. support to the program be placed under U.S. military supervision was finally approved in 1967.

Much of the 1967 success in pacification can be laid to effective allied operations against Communist regulars, General Than's decision to reduce the exposure of his

A rifle company of the 1st Cavalry Division crosses a rice paddy in Binh Dinh Province while searching for Viet Cong; by early 1966, many of the Communists had been routed at Binh Dinh. (National Archives)

The main duty of the 9th Infantry Division was to clear the Mekong Delta area of Viet Cong. Here, a marine unit wades through the delta's swamps on a search-and-clear mission in 1967. (U.S. Navy)

main force units in South Vietnam, and the resulting allied concentration on local guerrilla units. By mid-1967, under great pressure from ARVN and allied forces, the desertion rate for South Vietnamese Communist units was doubling every six months. In addition, the Central Intelligence Agency and its Vietnamese counterpart organizations had developed a working intelligence system that was targeted on the rural Communist guerrilla infrastructure. Initially called the Intelligence Collection and Exploitation Program, the system combined the techniques of penetration, interrogation, and courier and communications intercept to identify the clandestine Communist organization in the countryside. South Vietnamese intelligence-action teams called provincial reconnaissance units then captured or eliminated Viet Cong infrastructure members. The system, later known as the Phoenix Program, was to become highly controversial, but in 1967, there was little question as to its growing effectiveness.

Air Operations and Negotiations

Gradually, U.S. air operations became more extensive. During 1966 and 1967, the Laos panhandle was being subjected to about 200 air interdiction sorties per 24-hour period, mostly at night. Per day, about 80 North Vietnamese trucks on the Ho Chi Minh Trail complex were targeted by U.S. aircrews. Initially, American airmen estimated that they were successful in destroying only 15–18 percent of the trucks, but results were improving through the use of sensors.

In 1966, U.S. air attacks on North Vietnam dramatically increased, but so did the cost. Whereas there had been

55,000 sorties flown over the North in 1965, some 148,000 were executed in 1966. Bombs delivered grew from 3,000 tons to 128,000 tons. The Johnson administration gradually removed some restrictions, allowing pilots to strike more targets. In June 1966, for example, seven of North Vietnam's nine fuel storage facilities were destroyed. By the end of the year, American airmen calculated that they had destroyed 9,500 ships or boats, 4,100 trucks, and 2,000 rail stock items. However, while there had been 171 U.S. aircraft lost in 1965, the total for 1966 amounted to 318. And, Hanoi was holding a growing number of captured U.S. airmen. Further, the North Vietnamese were becoming masters at making repairs.

The high cost of the bombing campaign was due not only to the increasing number of sorties, but to an improved North Vietnamese air defense system. The Northerners were now operating 7,000 antiaircraft guns and had about 100 SAM-2s (surface-to-air missiles/Model 2) ready to launch at all times. Almost 1,200 of the missiles had been fired in 1966, but they had brought down only 31 U.S. aircraft. As in 1965, the real accomplishment of the missile crews was to force the airmen down into the effective ranges of the antiaircraft guns. Hanoi also had a growing air interceptor fleet, about 65 high-performance aircraft. Of these planes, 28 had been brought down by the Americans, but they were soon replaced. Like the missiles, North Vietnamese aircraft provided one more threat for the attackers to consider, one more factor that could spoil a bomb run or force an evading U.S. pilot into a strong air defense sector. However, U.S. Air Force and Navy pilots greatly improved their records in avoiding the

SAM-2s during 1967. The 1967 figure was 1 plane downed for every 57 missile firings.

Between the beginning of the Northern air campaign and the end of 1967, there had been eight bombing halts to facilitate negotiations, but no talks developed. The U.S. position was that when North Vietnam ended its military operations and support for subversion in other countries, all foreign forces could be withdrawn from Indochina. The bombing campaign might have made Hanoi less agreeable to the talks. Most U.S. officials believed that North Vietnamese leaders would not negotiate while bombing continued, but if the government in Hanoi agreed to talks during a bombing halt, then the Communists might be seen as negotiating under fear of future attacks. There was reason for some Americans to share the opinion of South Vietnam's Nguyen Cao Ky, who contended that the bombing of the North simply hardened the will of Hanoi's leaders.

U.S. Air Force captain Wilmer N. Grubb was among the downed and captured U.S. airmen in early 1966. He is given first-aid treatment for his injuries while he is heavily guarded. (U.S. Air Force)

U.S. Media and Public Attitudes

Long after U.S. forces left Indochina, a debate raged over the role of the U.S. media in the conflict's outcome. Some claimed that the print and broadcast reporters and their editors turned Americans against the rightful cause of the United States. Others said the media merely reflected U.S. public sentiments. Whatever the case, most commentators agree that 1967 was a turning point in the collective attitude of the U.S. media toward the war. President Johnson's approval rating with the public dropped to 40 percent in late 1967, down from 80 percent in 1965. That decline was thought to be related at least in part to the editorial shift of *Time* and *Life* magazines. They had long supported U.S. policy in Asia, but in 1967, the editorial thrust of both magazines began questioning and then turning against the American war effort.

Johnson was well aware of the growing unpopularity of his administration and its policies in Southeast Asia. In late 1967, he acted. Organizing a media offensive, Johnson brought General Westmoreland home for a visit and arranged for the MACV commander to address a joint session of Congress as well as the National Press Club. Westmoreland reported on progress against the Communists and stated that the Viet Cong and North Vietnamese could no longer conduct major unit operations close to South Vietnam's cities. Westmoreland refused to be enticed into a prediction of when the war would end, but he did claim that it would be possible to begin bringing some U.S. troops home within two years. Generally, Westmoreland was optimistic about the future.

At the end of 1967, Westmoreland could point to a good record against Communist main force units, but that claim was a bit hollow. Aggressive offensive operations had largely run North Vietnamese and Viet Cong regulars out of lower South Vietnam. Communist main force units operating in these areas could only remain for brief periods before returning to their sanctuaries. General Than's record in his "big unit war" was a record of consistent failure. One of Westmoreland's 1966 goals had been to eliminate more Communist troops than the North Vietnamese and Viet Cong could replace. It was estimated that during a month, the Viet Cong could recruit about 3,500 troops and the North Vietnamese could send about 7,000 troops down the Ho Chi Minh Trail. During 1966, the allies accounted for 8,400 Communist losses per month, failing to meet the goal. In the summer of 1967, however, monthly Communist losses rose to 12,700 and stayed at a high level. Westmoreland's aim had been achieved. Much of the Communist loss came from a rising number of Viet Cong defections (1,700 per month in 1966, 3,200 per month in 1967). In Southern main force units, losses were being replaced with recently arrived Northern soldiers. Communist guerrilla and regional forces were in rapid decline, but that did not mean the regulars were being seri-

In early 1967, a U.S. Navy amphibious assault craft brings navy combat beachmaster troops ashore south of Chu Lai, while a guard boat watches small craft in the area. (U.S. Navy)

ously diminished because they were often safely located in a Laotian or Cambodian sanctuary.

Westmoreland also achieved his pacification goals. The trends of 1965 had been reversed. A captured Viet Cong document lamented the fact that more than 1,000,000 South Vietnamese villagers (U.S. estimates were at 800,000) had been taken from Communist control and brought under South Vietnamese government control during the last half of 1966. Additionally, about 60 percent of South Vietnam's roadways and waterways were now open, up from about 30 percent during late 1965. The "other war" was being won by the allies.

TET OFFENSIVE: 1968

The year 1968 was a year of change and surprise. It was the year in which the war in Southeast Asia was reshaped. In South Vietnam, an all-out and costly Communist offensive marked a new phase of the war. The causes of the Tet Offensive in January are relatively easy to identify and understand. The effects were less than predictable and remain somewhat debatable. For the allies, it has been described as an "intelligence failure." On the other side, a rift was created between Communists in South Vietnam and those from North Vietnam. The object of the attack,

the fractious and weak society of South Vietnam, showed unanticipated signs of strength and unity. U.S. military forces were finally able to locate their enemies and emerged from battle with clear-cut tactical victories only to be told that the United States had suffered a "psychological defeat."

Hanoi's Strategy

The change in Hanoi's approach to the war and the origins of the Tet Offensive of 1968 can be traced to May 1967, when Ho Chi Minh convened the North Vietnamese Politburo, the Communist party's political bureau. Considering the actual military and political situation in the South, the deliberations could not have included many optimistic projections. The meeting resulted in a change of strategy made known to the party's Central Committee in June 1967. There was to be a "spontaneous uprising in order to win a decisive victory in the shortest possible time." Ho Chi Minh and his lieutenants had opted for the element of Politburo member Truong Chinh's doctrine that called for the all-out offensive—a sudden, simultaneous attack by main force units, guerrillas, and even the people themselves. It was fully expected that the people of South Vietnam would rise up and overthrow the government in Saigon. It was expected that the regulars would lure the allies to South Vietnam's borders, defeat them, and then link up with local forces and guerrilla units, which would be overcoming the South Vietnamese army.

Setting the Bait

Although the Communist general offensive and uprising of 1968 was approached in a different way in each major region of South Vietnam, there were similarities. Along border regions, Communist main force units selected isolated, remote outposts to attack, hoping to draw large contingents of allied forces into areas that were distant from their supply bases. The selected South Vietnamese outposts were Khe Sanh in the north, Dak To in the middle of the country, and Loc Ninh in the south. These places were close to the Communists' protected sanctuaries and well-stocked supply depots in Cambodia, North Vietnam, or Laos. Both Dak To and Loc Ninh were assaulted in late 1967. Khe Sanh, quite close to North Vietnam, was not attacked until January 1968.

The attack on Loc Ninh opened in the early hours of Sunday morning, Oct. 29, 1967. For several days and nights, Communist soldiers threw themselves at a small Vietnamese outpost to no avail. All told, 15 South Vietnamese soldiers and 10 Americans lost their lives during the battle. Radio Hanoi claimed a great victory at Loc Ninh and stated that an entire American battalion had been destroyed. During their retreat, the Communists left hundreds of bodies behind.

About two weeks after the Battle of Loc Ninh, the Battle of Dak To was reaching its culmination. The North Vietnamese began mortar attacks on the Special Forces camp. On November 13, a full-scale battle developed be-

As was often the case in the Vietnam War, ground fighting involved dense foliage, even in the highlands. Here, marines engage the North Vietnamese in a firefight at a secondary tree line. (U.S. Marines)

tween the U.S. 2d Battalion, 503rd Airborne Infantry, and the North Vietnamese 3d Battalion, 174th Infantry. This fight, conducted on a steep mountain slope, was often hand to hand, precluding the effective use of U.S. firepower. The Americans finally prevailed, but the campaign continued, scattered over a 190-square-mile area. During this wide-ranging battle, U.S. and ARVN casualties were far higher than at Loc Ninh, with 289 Americans and 73 South Vietnamese killed. The North Vietnamese also left more dead behind than they had at Loc Ninh, about 1,400.

By December 1967, the North Vietnamese plan to draw the allied forces away from the populated areas had largely failed because most South Vietnamese and U.S. units had returned to their normal operational patterns after Loc Ninh and Dak To. Further north, however, the situation was different. General Westmoreland received increasing indications that the U.S. Marine Corps base at Khe Sanh would be attacked by Hanoi's regulars. North Vietnamese attacks on marine positions along the demilitarized zone (DMZ) were nothing new. In September 1967, the base at Con Tien had been subjected to 3,000 rounds of artillery and rocket fire in nine days. After Westmoreland directed a massive use of B-52 strikes around that base, the shelling stopped. This time, however, road cuts isolating Khe Sanh, radio transmission patterns, and North Vietnamese troop dispositions pointed to a focus on that base and a possible ground assault.

An elaborate plan to defend Khe Sanh began to be implemented. The base and some outlying hills were reinforced by U.S. marine and South Vietnamese forces to about regimental level, or 6,000 troops. Artillery was added, both at Khe Sanh and at several other bases within mutually supporting range. Westmoreland diverted acoustic and seismic sensors from their intended employment along the DMZ to a distribution that surrounded the marine position. A massive air support scheme was designed that included air resupply, an unprecedented level of B-52 strikes, and enormous numbers of close-air support sorties.

The attack on Khe Sanh began on January 21. After a considerable amount of Communist shelling by both 122-millimeter rockets and 152-millimeter artillery, the marine ammunition depot at Khe Sanh was struck and blew up. About 90 percent of the available ammunition supply for the base was destroyed, and a frantic air resupply effort had to be implemented. North Vietnamese antiaircraft gunners became more proficient, and a number of U.S. aircraft were damaged or destroyed.

Attack on Saigon

Although there were many attacks throughout South Vietnam during the Tet Offensive, the Saigon region was Hanoi's main target. There was a false perception in Hanoi that the Communist party was actually in secret control of South Vietnam's population centers. Tran Bach Dang, first secretary of the Communist party in Saigon, had been trying to recruit for the uprising since he received his orders in October 1967. In the end, it was decided to get help from outside the city, bringing a combination of local and main force units into the city's center to seize major targets. Of the city's inhabitants who were to participate in the coming battle, almost all fought against the Communists, not for them.

Like most of the major planning decisions of the offensive, the timing of the attack was chosen in Hanoi. So as to surprise the allies and South Vietnamese, countrywide assaults were to begin during the Tet holidays, a period when a cease-fire (supposedly acknowledged by both sides) was in effect. To Americans, thc Victnamese celebrations at Tet is akin to having all major holidays rolled into one. Tet is a patriotic, religious, and calendar event, but its most important feature is that it is a period of homecoming, the annual family gathering. Although the celebration usually lasts for about a week, two days are more important than the others, and in 1968 those days were January 29 and 30. On January 21, the leaders in Hanoi decided that the offensive should be launched at midnight, January 29–30.

Suspecting something was afoot, Lt. Gen. Frederick Weyand, the U.S. field commander in the Saigon area, positioned 27 U.S. maneuver battalions within a 30-mile radius of the capital. U.S. unit commanders were contacted. No mechanized infantry or armored cavalry squadron could be committed to battle without Weyand's permission. If there was to be a major offensive around Saigon, the first U.S. response would be with armor forces, units that could move rapidly at night, that had excellent communications and firepower, and that could roll over and crush most resistance.

The attack began in a ragged fashion. Hanoi ordered a 24-hour delay in the attack, but units in northern South Vietnam did not obey the order and assaulted a day too early. Some of the Communist attack forces made their way past allied guard posts and reached their designated objectives. For the most part, the North Vietnamese and Viet Cong soldiers that arrived at their destinations died there. Despite numerous failures, the attackers caused havoc in many places for 24–48 hours, and in a few cases, confused, house-to-house fighting lasted for weeks. Many of the attack elements failed to reach their objectives because they were intercepted by allied units, their guides failed to materialize, or their arms and supply caches had disappeared. There was no uprising by the people of South Vietnam. But, there was a general, countrywide offensive.

Hours after the attack began in the Saigon area, General Weyand unleashed his armor forces. He knew most of these enemy formations were in open terrain, between the defenses of Saigon and the loose ring of U.S. bases sur-

rounding the city. By 5:00 A.M. on January 31, more than 500 U.S. armored vehicles were rapidly moving toward South Vietnam's most vital area. With headlights on and at breakneck speed, the Americans were quickly approaching the rear of a number of Communist regular units. In a way, the Viet Cong and North Vietnamese had managed to get themselves surrounded, with well-armed and well-supplied defenders to the front and U.S. armor units closing in on their rear.

All during January 31, North Vietnamese and Viet Cong forces in and around Saigon were decimated. It was like no fight either side had experienced. The unique character was due to Communist orders that demanded their soldiers hold ground in open areas and to unusual allied advantages: the near proximity of reinforcements, supplies, and firepower; good road nets; and short distances between battlefields. Although air operations at both Tan San Nhut and Bien Hoa were temporarily suspended, they soon recommenced. In large part, Communist main force units had been prevented from joining guerrilla and local forces.

However, the fighting was not over in the Saigon area. Most elements of the attacking forces began to disintegrate after the first 48 hours. Some attempted to infiltrate out of the populated areas; others simply tried to hold out, but many units became trapped and fought with desperation and courage. Cholon, the Chinese suburb of Saigon, became the cul-de-sac where slow and costly operations were required to eliminate each island of resistance. Fighting in Cholon lasted for weeks.

On February 2, with few objectives accomplished and no uprising among the people, the Central Office for South Vietnam (COSVN) acknowledged the offensive to be a failure. Several senior Viet Cong and North Vietnamese officers surrendered. Lt. Col. Tam Ha, commander of the Communist 9th Division's supporting artillery, gave himself up, and Col. Tran Van Dac, the regional political officer, defected. The Communist 9th and 5th divisions were all but destroyed.

Other Tet Attacks

It was much the same in the rest of the country. Within three days, January 30 to February 1, Communist forces attacked 5 of the 6 autonomous cities and 36 of the 44 provincial capitals, but only 64 of the 242 district capitals, which were small towns and in some cases little more than villages. The primary target was unquestionably urban South Vietnam, where the Saigon regime had military strength and popular support, but in cases where ARVN needed help, the United States readily supplied it.

U.S. television and print journalists initially focused on the U.S. Embassy in Saigon to the exclusion of almost everything else. The speedy clearing of most South Vietnamese towns and cities by ARVN and the swift mauling of North Vietnamese regular units by U.S. armor forces

CBS news correspondent Walter Cronkite, in battle dress with microphone in hand, conducts an interview with a marine officer during the battle for Hue. (National Archives)

around Saigon went largely unreported to the public in the United States. The media did, however, report on the protracted and bloody fighting in the city of Hue.

The battle in Hue shaped up at the same time as the one in Saigon, but Communist forces in Hue were far more successful than they were in South Vietnam's capital. In Hue, U.S. marines and ARVN held a few spots while the two North Vietnamese regiments and their Viet Cong allies held the bulk of the city. Not until February 10 did the marines and South Vietnamese manage to take the offensive, and Hue was not cleared until February 24. The Communist invaders killed 3,000 civilians, foreigners, and Vietnamese officials in the city. Some of them had been buried alive. It was estimated that more than 5,000 Communist troops had been killed during the fight. About 40 percent of the city was damaged or destroyed, creating 116,000 refugees. South Vietnamese army casualties included 384 killed, while Marine Corps killed in action amounted to 147.

The marine base at Khe Sanh had not been attacked during the first days of the Tet Offensive; in fact, three of the

nine North Vietnamese regiments initially reported around the Khe Sanh area had been identified in the Hue region during the early part of the attack there. Before the end of the fighting in South Vietnam's cities, Gen. Vo Nguyen Giap recommended his costly attempt to destroy the Khe Sanh garrison. In late February, shelling of the base reached more than 1,300 rounds daily. The Northerners began digging siege trenches, but eventually gave up the task under withering U.S. bombing. Labor on the siege works stopped March 10, at a time when General Westmoreland reported only about 6,000–8,000 North Vietnamese troops around the marine base. On April 1, the 1st Cavalry Division and a marine column effected a linkup—the base at Khe Sanh had been relieved.

While there were some relatively minor "second wave" and "third wave" attacks later in the year, the Communist general offensive ended with the North Vietnamese withdrawal from Khe Sanh. It would be some time before Hanoi could launch an offensive of the magnitude seen in January and February 1968. Of the 84,000 attackers, MACV believed that roughly 45,000 perished. Overall, the massive offensive had been directed at urban South Vietnam. If the object was to break the will of the people of the republic and their government, the great general offensive of 1968 had most assuredly failed.

Aftermath of Tet

In South Vietnam, the Tet Offensive ignited some long hidden sparks of patriotism. With their enemies in the streets, many Southerners chose to fight rather than stand apart from the war and simply watch the Americans and the Northerners fight. In the first 90 days after the beginning of the offensive, almost 15,000 ARVN deserters returned to the army. Between February and September, 240,000 people volunteered for military service. Proportionally, it was as if 15,000,000 Americans had swamped U.S. military recruiting offices.

The Viet Cong movement was transformed. Some of the veteran Southern Communists bitterly remarked that their ranks were so thin that they had become only an auxiliary for the NVA. In 1967, the guerrilla units had largely ceased direct battles in favor of sniper attacks and assassination. Now, even those capabilities seemed to be lost. While almost all of South Vietnam's cities and towns experienced difficulty in throwing the invaders out, few of the government-controlled villages fell or were even penetrated. About two-thirds of the country's villages were characterized as "relatively secure" in January 1968. By

March, that figure had only dropped to 60 percent, and there was every indication that an immediate improvement was in sight.

Rural communities began asking the government for weapons. A people's Self Defense Force was created, and thousands of carbines were transferred from the Regional Forces (RF) and the Popular Forces (PF) to peasants as M-16s were given to the RF and PF. President Thieu enthusiastically supported the program, saying that since the election process had taken hold, the government's authority rested on the people in any event. In September, the Accelerated Pacification Program was initiated, and by the end of 1968, an unprecedented 76 percent of South Vietnam's rural villages were considered to be in the "relatively secure" status.

Perhaps the most astonishing aspect of the Tet Offensive's aftermath concerned American, rather than Vietnamese, actions and attitudes. In the face of clear indications of Communist withdrawal after a bloody defeat, President Johnson, with the counsel of a number of advisers, began seeking a way out of the war. Those in the United States who had been advocating a U.S. withdrawal were now joined by more voices. Public confidence in U.S. military policies in Vietnam began a rapid decline: by the end of March 1968, there was a 20-percent drop—from 74 to 54 percent. By then, American combat deaths in the war had topped 20,000. The death rate, at an aver-

After conferring with the commander of the U.S. Military Assistance Command Vietnam (MACV), Gen. Creighton Abrams, at the White House on Oct. 28, 1968, President Johnson called for a complete halt to bombing in North Vietnam. (National Archives)

age of about 780 per month during 1967, had grown to 2,000 per month in February 1968. The war was now costing the American taxpayers $30 billion per year. The air war was going badly. The U.S. Air Force kill ratio (North Vietnamese aircraft shot down versus U.S. aircraft lost) in air-to-air combat was one-to-one, the worst in the history of U.S. aerial warfare.

On March 10, a news story indicated that General Westmoreland was asking for 200,000 more men in Vietnam. The story was only partially true. Gen. Earle G. Wheeler, chairman of the Joint Chiefs of Staff, had persuaded the MACV commander to request more troops so that President Johnson's military advisers could have sound grounds to recommend a call-up of reserves. The U.S. military posture worldwide was becoming weak because of the need for replacements in Vietnam. But by the time the story was printed, Westmoreland's request (which had not asked for the entire 200,000—many were to be held in the United States as a reserve) had already been denied. There would be no large-scale mustering of reserves in the United States. Nevertheless, the damage was done. Those politicians who opposed Johnson were now in full bay. In mid-March, a national public opinion poll indicated that almost 70 percent of the American people favored a phased withdrawal of U.S. Armed Forces from Vietnam.

At the end of March, President Johnson began a process designed eventually to take the United States out of the war. He did grant some reinforcements to Westmoreland, with U.S. troop strength in Vietnam reaching more than 536,000 by the end of the year. Johnson also authorized a call-up of a few reservists and National Guardsmen. His prime objective, however, was to accelerate efforts to reach a negotiated settlement. To facilitate Hanoi's acceptance, Johnson initiated the seventh bombing halt, prohibiting U.S. air attacks north of the 20th parallel within North Vietnam. Johnson also announced that he would not seek reelection. (Years later, Johnson said his decisions were based on events in the United States, not on those in Southeast Asia.)

It took some time before the Communists realized they had gained the upper hand. The purpose of the general offensive had been to spur uprisings, and it was almost immediately known that Hanoi's decision had been, in the words of one high-ranking Viet Cong official, "a grievous miscalculation." In Hanoi, Truong Chinh, author of the general uprising doctrine, stated that the Tet Offensive had failed and that there must be a return to guerrilla warfare and political action. Lt. Col. Phan Viet Dung, commander of the Viet Cong 165th Regiment, defected, characterizing North Vietnam's strategy as "bankrupt." It was not long, though, before the North Vietnamese propaganda organ began a steady stream of broadcasts and publications claiming that the original plan had been targeted on weakening U.S. willpower.

A WIDER WAR: 1969–1970

During 1969 and 1970, the number of participants in Southeast Asia's war grew, and the conflict's battlegrounds were extended. The growth was achieved despite reductions in Soviet and U.S. involvement; thus the war gained an even greater Asian character. In the South, as Communist main force units recovered and recuperated from the Tet Offensive, the allies were able to concentrate on rooting out the Viet Cong infrastructure and assisting the South Vietnamese government in strengthening its institutions, particularly the ARVN. The Nixon administration, which had come into office in January 1969, tried a number of initiatives to further U.S. aims in Southeast Asia, efforts that had been shunned by previous administrations as entailing too much risk. U.S. policy centered on a gradual but steady withdrawal of American combat forces and on limiting resources used to defeat the Communists. The war's character was also changed by a growing reliance on diplomacy, attempts to resolve Southeast Asian political differences through negotiations. In some respects, the war in Southeast Asia started to resemble the latter phases of the Korean War, 20 years earlier. Combat operations and campaigns began to be conducted in coordination with specific diplomatic initiatives and periods of activity or impasse at the bargaining table.

The war, however, also reflected some of the same characteristics that had shaped it a decade earlier, in 1959–60. In spite of Ho Chi Minh's death in 1969, the Communist leaders in Hanoi remained dedicated to their goal: a Marxist Indochina. A slightly diminished Soviet role was more than compensated for by growth in Chinese involvement. The 1960s had begun with Western concerns over the forced imposition of Communist rule in Southeast Asia and ended with those concerns still firmly in place.

New Policies

The Nixon administration's new policies for Southeast Asia were grouped under an umbrella term, the "two track" approach. On one track, military operations and military assistance to U.S. allies in the region would be used as a stick against North Vietnam. On the other track, diplomatic initiatives would be used as a carrot in convincing Hanoi's leaders of the mutual benefits of a negotiated and peaceful resolution of the conflict. All of this was to be done while withdrawing U.S. troops. The first increment of the withdrawal was announced on June 8, 1969, and involved 25,000 of the 538,000 U.S. military in South Vietnam.

In diplomatic negotiations, sensing that the United States was leaving the area in any event, the government in North Vietnam took an aggressive and uncompromising stance at the peace talks. During 1968 and most of 1969, the Northerners refused to allow South Vietnam to partici-pate in the discussions. In May 1969, Hanoi's envoys took the position that the only way to end the war was for the United States to withdraw its forces and dissolve the gov-ernment of South Vietnam. Also in May, the United States proposed a simultaneous withdrawal of U.S. and North Vietnamese troops together with internationally supervised elections in South Vietnam, elections with the participation of the Viet Cong's National Liberation Front (NLF). At that point, the talks reached an impasse. It became increas-ingly evident that the Communists would not risk a plebi-scite and were simply waiting for the U.S. Armed Forces to leave the region. In October 1969, they reversed course, welcoming the Southerners, but only on the condition that the NFL, the Viet Cong's political arm, would receive an equal status at the talks, sitting opposite the representatives of the elected government in Saigon.

Militarily, the Northerners were now increasingly aided by China. In the latter part of 1968, the government in Beijing maintained 80,000–100,000 troops in North Viet-nam, some manning air defense systems. China was pro-viding upward of $750,000,000 of aid per month to Hanoi, supplying 15 percent of the Northerners' rice and 25 per-cent of their consumer goods. By 1969, Chinese support was about twice that of the Soviet Union.

In 1969, Hanoi initiated a new campaign against U.S. units and installations. It began on February 22 with more than 500 attacks throughout the country, but it proved too costly for the Communists to sustain. More than 1,100 Americans were killed in three weeks, but about the same number of Viet Cong defected within a single week. In April, instructions were modified. Communist military forces were to be preserved and were not to be risked in major offensives. Attacks using mortars and rockets were to be emphasized. However, U.S. countermortar and counterrocket defenses produced casualties, and Viet Cong defections continued to mount. By July, more Communist soldiers—over 20,000—had given themselves up during 1969 than during all of 1968. COSVN changed course again, ordering sniper attacks. The idea was to employ only the highly trained, the dedicated, and the elite forces to conduct raids. Sappers used stealth to emplace explo-sives and then escaped. It seemed a good way to keep the pressure on the Americans and on the pacification program while preserving strength. But by October, COSVN de-clared this campaign a failure as well and announced yet another approach, a return to guerrilla warfare.

Revolutionary Development Program

In 1970, 95 percent of the South Vietnamese villages and hamlets elected their own officials. The improved security in the countryside removed many restrictions on the trans-portation network. Hundreds of miles of roads, long closed

because of danger from the Viet Cong, were reopened to traffic by the end of 1970. At long last, after a decade, it was possible to drive from the DMZ to the Mekong Delta in comparative safety. Land reform and improved trans-portation promoted agricultural progress. The country, about 80-percent self-sufficient in rice production in 1968, reached 98-percent self-sufficiency in 1970. Finally, in June 1970, revolutionary development officials reported that more than 90 percent of the hamlets were "relatively secure" or better and that only 1.4 percent of them were under undisputed Communist control. For Saigon, the campaign for the peasants, "the other war," was going very well.

Vietnamization

The Revolutionary Development Program was succeeding, and, to some, that meant that victory over the Communists was at hand. Communist main forces still existed, how-ever, with about 12 divisions located in Cambodia and Laos and just above the DMZ. If the Americans continued their withdrawal and if South Vietnam were to survive, it had to have a well-led army of sufficient size, strength, and competence to counter and block these Communist di-visions. Thus, the awkward term "Vietnamization" was created and much used in 1969–70. The competence of ARVN, however, was a serious impediment to achieving South Vietnamese military self-sufficiency.

Decline in American Performance

During 1969–70, there was an increased amount of drug use, disciplinary problems, and mutinous behavior among U.S. soldiers, sailors, air force personnel, and marines. By 1969, the use of marijuana in all types of U.S. units was widespread. In marine and army units, disciplinary cases rose about 13 percent from 1968 to 1969. In 1969, there were 126 cases of soldiers trying to kill their officers or noncommissioned officers, incidents that resulted in 37 deaths. Cases of insubordination rose from 94 to 128 in the same period. In 1969, there were 8,400 drug-related arrests, a number that climbed to more than 11,000 in 1970, a year that saw a 30-percent growth in insubordina-tion and mutiny. These problems escalated during a period of declining U.S. troops strength: 474,000 at the end of 1969; 335,800 at the end of 1970.

The incident known as the My Lai massacre took place at My Lai, Quang Ngai Province, in March 1968. It oc-curred shortly after the Tet Offensive but was not fully discovered until later; it crystallized for many the problems associated with the American presence in South Vietnam. The village chief of Son My reported on March 22 that U.S. forces had massacred 570 civilians (men, women, and children) in several hamlets, including My Lai. South Vietnamese officials referred the report to the Americal Division, and the commander of the 11th Brigade conducted an investigation of the activities of his subordinate, Lt. Col. Frank Barker. Barker had commanded a three-company task force in and around the village during March 16–18. The brigade commander's report was a whitewash, indicating that only 20 civilians had been killed in a "cross fire" between U.S. and Viet Cong troops. Although the actual number of civilians killed during this operation remains unknown, there is no doubt that a deliberate massacre occurred. U.S. Army officials in Washington did not become aware of the event until a year later when a former soldier wrote a lengthy letter to them, describing the action. An investigation was launched, and all during 1970 and 1971, the American people were inundated with atrocity stories, most of them true, about the village of Son My. The trial of lower-ranking officers and the dismissal

of charges against higher-ranking Americal Division officers further inflamed the growing ranks of military critics and war protesters in the United States.

Cambodia

By 1969, U.S. successes against Communist forces in South Vietnam as well as the specter of a U.S. withdrawal caused growing concern in nearby Cambodia among Prince Sihanouk, the country's leader, and his supporters. Cambodia's previous inclination to side with the Communists in a logistical support role seemed inappropriate and perhaps even dangerous. With North Vietnamese regular forces on Cambodian territory, Sihanouk wanted to change course. His senior military commander, Gen. Lon Nol, was dispatched to Hanoi in May to protest the occupation

Antiwar protests, such as this one at the Pentagon in 1967, continued throughout the Vietnam War, including a huge demonstration in Washington, D.C., in 1970 against U.S. involvement in Cambodia. (National Archives)

of eastern Cambodia by an estimated 40,000 North Vietnamese troops.

Initially, the North Vietnamese tried to negotiate with Sihanouk in order to preserve North Vietnam's sanctuaries and logistical arrangements. In December 1969, the North Vietnamese encouraged Pol Pot, leader of a group of Cambodian Communists, the Khmer Rouge, to remain underground, not resist Sihanouk, and await a Communist victory in South Vietnam before attempting to defeat Sihanouk's government. However, as Lon Nol's soldiers began searching out Cambodian Communists, survival for the 800 party members and 4,000 armed Khmer Rouge often hinged on their ability to fight.

The complete break between the Communists and the Cambodian government came in March 1970 with the ouster of the mercurial Sihanouk by Lon Nol. The first U.S. moves were to aid Lon Nol by providing a shipment of arms on April 15 and rescuing some surrounded and overmatched Cambodian units in the eastern regions with an airlift. During April, both the Americans and the South Vietnamese considered ways to help Lon Nol. The Americans began supplying the Cambodian army, and South Vietnam's President Thieu authorized limited incursions into Cambodian territory just west of Saigon in mid-April, so as to put ARVN units in the North Vietnamese rear.

As the days went by, it became obvious that the North Vietnamese might destroy Lon Nol's army and that more substantial allied assistance was immediately needed to prevent a Communist conquest of Cambodia. In late April, President Nixon approved a plan to send U.S. infantry, armor, and air cavalry units into a section of Cambodia thought to hold COSVN headquarters and some large Communist supply depots. On May 1, the large-scale allied offensive began with a massive B-52 strike on the suspected location of the Communist headquarters. A dramatic announcement of the operation was made by Nixon to a nationwide television audience as the assault was in progress.

The allied campaign into Cambodia lasted for two months and was only partially successful. COSVN headquarters had been moved far to the west almost five weeks before the operation, so the North Vietnamese command and control apparatus remained intact. Then, too, the Northerners avoided pitched battles, so none of their combat units were wholly destroyed. North Vietnamese fortunes suffered a severe logistical blow, however, as the Americans captured or destroyed huge stocks of weapons and supplies.

President Nixon's decision on Cambodia enraged many opponents of U.S. policy in Southeast Asia. Demonstrations were so violent on 21 college campuses in the United States that National Guard troops had to be called out to restore or maintain order, six students at Kent State University losing their lives in the process. On May 8,

100,000 people assembled in Washington, D.C., to protest Nixon's actions. Nixon was now in a bitter and acrimonious domestic political struggle because of the conflict in Southeast Asia.

The war in Cambodia spread rapidly. While there had been only about 40 allied combat air sorties in the country during 1969, there were more than 25,000 such sorties during 1970. The speedy expansion of Lon Nol's army was almost matched by the growth in the ranks of Pol Pot's Khmer Rouge. Hanoi sent southward several thousand members of the Khmer Rouge who had been trained in North Vietnam. The Vietnamese-indoctrinated Cambodians were used as cadre for Pol Pot's army. By late 1970, there were about 15,000 well-armed Khmer Rouge in 25 main force battalions and 60,000 rural Communist guerrillas. China agreed to support an ultimate Khmer Rouge force of three divisions, or 50,000 regulars. Although most of the sizable battles in Cambodia were still fought by the 40,000 North Vietnamese regulars, the Khmer Communists were quickly attaining enough strength to stand on their own.

U.S. WITHDRAWAL: 1971–1973

At the beginning of 1971, there were 200,000 fewer U.S. service personnel in South Vietnam than at the beginning of 1970. From New Year's Day 1971 until late January 1973, the prime feature of the war in Southeast Asia was an unremitting effort by both sides to gain a military position that supported the best possible negotiating stance at the peace talks. Taking territory from an opponent, for example, was believed to compel that opponent to accede to bargaining table demands by reason of the opponent's fear that even more territory might be taken if a settlement were not reached. The same logic applied to the U.S. bombing campaign in North Vietnam. It was assumed that the more bombs dropped and targets struck, the more likely Hanoi would be to yield and to end its quest to bring all Indochina under its control.

Laos: Lam Son 179

Gen. Creighton Abrams, the MACV commander, had been considering a dramatic operation into the Laos panhandle area for some time. The plan's objectives included the destruction of North Vietnamese logistical and troop support bases in southern Laos and the defeat of North Vietnamese forces there. When Abrams proposed the plan to his superiors in Washington, in December 1970, he described it as primarily a South Vietnamese effort; in fact, a Vietnamese title—Lam Son 719—was chosen as its code name. President Nixon approved the plan on December 23. It was a risky plan that pitted about 17,000 ARVN

South Vietnamese troops pose with a Soviet-made antiaircraft gun, captured during their U.S.-backed invasion of Laos in early 1971. (National Archives)

troops against 22,000 North Vietnamese Communist forces that could be rapidly reinforced to two times that number. Also, the backbone of the attacking forces, ARVN airborne and marine units, had yet to conduct divisional-sized operations.

During the night of Jan. 29–30, 1971, U.S. engineers began opening Route 9 from the Vietnamese seacoast to the Laotian border. With headlights on, bulldozers, trucks, and scoop loaders moved westward along a badly damaged road that had been seldom used since 1968. Elements of the 101st Airborne Division began an attack into the A Shau Valley, partly as a diversion to the forthcoming main thrust into Laos by the South Vietnamese rangers and paratroopers and members of the 1st ARVN Division. Saigon's forces were headed toward the central part of the Laos panhandle. An operation that had been advocated and considered essential by many U.S. leaders since 1964 was finally underway, but it was only a temporary incursion.

Initially, the South Vietnamese met with success. But by early March, the North Vietnamese began reinforcing. By March 10, there were an estimated 40,000 North Vietnamese troops in the region and more coming. Faced with this information, President Thieu decided to withdraw his forces much earlier than planned. The withdrawal began in an orderly fashion, but as North Vietnamese pressure mounted, the operation dissolved into an ignoble rout. As the last Southern combat forces escaped from Laos on March 25, U.S. reporters watched South Vietnamese soldiers clinging to the skids of American helicopters, a clear indication of defeat and desperation.

Although the campaign in Laos lasted less than 60 days, the losses were high on both sides. The Americans lost 8 fighter bombers, 215 killed, 38 missing, and more than 1,000 wounded. All told, U.S. and South Vietnamese helicopter losses amounted to 103 aircraft, and there were more than 600 damaged. More than 1,500 South Vietnamese troops died in Laos, and almost 690 were reported missing. Altogether, there were about 8,000 South Vietnamese casualties, roughly 45 percent of the attacking force. The Southerners left 54 of their tanks and 87 of their M-113 vehicles behind, either destroyed or abandoned. The allies claimed that they had destroyed or captured 106 North Vietnamese tanks, 7,000 weapons, and about 2,000 other vehicles. They also estimated that more than 19,000 Communist soldiers were killed during Lam Son 719.

Easter Offensive

In Hanoi, shortly after the South Vietnamese had withdrawn from Laos in the spring of 1971, the Politburo reached a decision to win "a decisive victory in 1972." The resulting offensive was fundamentally a straightforward invasion staged by North Vietnamese mechanized forces. Although many local-force Communist battalions and regional regiments took part in the attack, the major thrusts were carried out by 11 North Vietnamese divisions. There was no effort at a general uprising as there had been in 1968 and practically no coordination between the Northern regulars and the Communist guerrilla forces based in South Vietnam.

On Mar. 30, 1972, a North Vietnamese armor and infantry attack, heavily supported by large-caliber artillery, rolled across the DMZ between North and South Vietnam and began crushing a newly created ARVN unit, the 3d Infantry Division. This was the Communist main attack and involved five divisions, the 304th, 320B, 325C, 308th, and 324B. Three days later and 60 miles north of Saigon, the North Vietnamese 5th, 7th, and 9th divisions attacked out of Cambodia and surrounded An Loc, a small settlement town along Route 13. The final major thrust came in mid-April. It was directed at the city of Kontum in the Central Highlands and at several settlements along the north-south coastal road, Route 1. The North Vietnamese 2d and 320th divisions took on Kontum and settlements along Route 14, while the Communist 3d Division came out of the hills to sever Route 1 along the coast. The offensive was meant to whipsaw the Southerners, initially pulling Saigon's reserves to the north, then to the south, and finally cutting the country in half with the three-division attack along both Routes 14 and 1 in the center of South Vietnam.

By mid-May, the Northern offensive was bogged down and being destroyed by incessant U.S. bombing and naval gunfire support. Unable to conquer quickly Hue, Kontum, and An Loc, the Communists closed on these towns in tight perimeters for sieges. That loss of momentum allowed reinforcement of the defending garrisons. The U.S. Air Force and Navy were pounding exposed Northern units, some 2,724 sorties of B-52 bombers alone being flown against the Communists in South Vietnam from March 30 to June 30. At the height of the fighting around An Loc, a daily average of 185 fighter-bomber sorties and 11 B-52 sorties were used around the small defensive perimeter. In the North, U.S. Navy gunfire was available and was being used on the Communists at the rate of 7,000–10,000 rounds per day.

In June, at the close of the offensive, both sides were disappointed with the results. This time, the Northerners conducted 90 percent of the combat and lost upward of 100,000 dead, about 450 tanks, and large numbers of trucks and artillery pieces. The Communists clung to some remote areas of South Vietnam but had given up all hopes of taking An Loc and Kontum and found themselves in a hopeless defense of Quang Tri City. Hanoi would have no "decisive victory in 1972." However, the Northerners had used only about 20 percent of their available military forces in South Vietnam.

The allies' experience with the offensive was bittersweet. They had not only halted the invasion in its tracks, they had largely thrown the invaders out of the country. ARVN combat units, however, understrength at the beginning of the attack, were now seriously weakened. In addition, the 1972 defense of the country was only possible by virtue of U.S. firepower, demonstrating that the Southerners still needed the Americans to succeed.

Operation Linebacker

The Nixon administration's response to the Easter Offensive included a resumption of the bombing campaign in North Vietnam above the 20th parallel. The new air campaign, called Linebacker, was primarily an interdiction effort, but one without some of the previous restrictions to which U.S. airmen were accustomed. The 30-nautical-mile safety zone around Hanoi and along the Chinese border was largely removed, as was Haiphong's 10-mile safety radius. Most important, the ban on mining North Vietnam's ports was cast aside. On May 9, the date of Nixon's announcement, nine U.S. Navy aircraft effectively sealed North Vietnam's major ports with air-delivered mines. A mostly unfettered air interdiction campaign began.

The bombing of North Vietnam was canceled in October when the Northerners indicated a willingness to resume negotiations. When this willingness proved to be a ploy, President Nixon ordered a resumption of the bombing on December 18. The operation, called Linebacker II, was aimed at bringing Hanoi's negotiators to the bargaining table. This time, the bombing went on day and night and featured a continuous use of B-52s.

The Communists soon agreed to come back to the negotiating table, and Linebacker II was hailed by U.S. diplomats, administration officials, and air force officials to be a huge success, and there was a genuine outpouring of relief in the United States—relief founded on an expectation that Americans were finally going to withdraw completely from Southeast Asia. About 40 percent of North Vietnam's rail yards and 80 percent of Hanoi's large-scale electrical facilities had been destroyed during Linebacker II. Only one of the three targeted bridges was destroyed, however, and damage to the North Vietnamese airfields was characterized as "temporary." This level of damage cost the Americans 15 B-52 bombers, 14 fighter bombers or other aircraft, 11 airmen killed, and 45 new U.S. prisoners of war.

Peace Agreement

The "Agreement on Ending the War and Restoring the Peace in Vietnam" was signed on Jan. 27, 1973, and went into effect on January 29. The arrangement provided for a cease-fire, for withdrawal of allied troops from the South, and for future elections in South Vietnam to resolve political disputes. The agreement did not, however, require North Vietnam to withdraw its troops from the South, an omission to which President Thieu strenuously objected. Thieu's concurrence with the agreement was gained only after President Nixon threatened to cut off aid to South Vietnam. Nixon then promised Thieu that the United States would "react vigorously to violations of the Agreement."

HANOI'S SUCCESS: 1973–1975

During the period 1973–75, North Vietnam's leaders were able to achieve most, but not all, of the goals set by the Indochinese Communist party in 1930 to bring all of Vietnam, Cambodia, and Laos under the control of a Marxist government. Hanoi's success was due to a number of factors, including the weakness of the U.S. presidency, a global economic jolt that spurred rapid and damaging inflation within those economies dependent on U.S. aid, and the corrupt and incompetent leadership that seemed to permeate the Royal Lao, Cambodian, and South Vietnamese armies. But there were other factors contributing to this success. The North Vietnamese triumph of 1975 was also due to skilled military and political leadership and to a substantial recovery of the indigenous Communist rural political and military structure in South Vietnam.

One of the provisions of the peace agreement was withdrawal of all U.S. forces from South Vietnam. Shown are U.S. Marines lining up to board their transport ship during the first phase of withdrawal. (National Archives)

Plan for Conquest

Gen. Tran Van Tra, the COSVN military commander of Nam Bo (all of South Vietnam below the Central Highlands province of Darlac), had been working since the failed Communist Easter Offensive of 1972 on a new plan for the conquest of South Vietnam. Tra was convinced that the time was ripe for a major offensive against Saigon. He had been rebuilding the Communist infrastructure and using his regular forces to keep ARVN units concentrated. A Southerner, General Tra did not believe in winning solely by the use of regular forces, as Hanoi had directed in 1972, or solely by the use of guerrilla forces, as Hanoi had directed in 1968. Tra believed victory would come with an orchestrated employment of both guerrillas and regulars.

By mid-1974, Tra and his subordinates at COSVN headquarters saw an end to the war in Vietnam. Their analysis of their own strength and the opposition that Thieu could muster yielded a prediction of final victory in 1975 or in 1976 at the latest. In September 1974, without Hanoi's knowledge, Tra and his staff drew up a plan that took account of the lessons learned from both the Tet and Easter offensives. Planned and projected guerrilla forces were adequate, but the planners needed more regular units to ensure success. Tra calculated that with three divisions added to his own strength, it would be entirely possible to conquer South Vietnam in 1975.

There were a variety of reasons for Tra's assessment, some derived from Communist strengths and some derived from the weaknesses of South Vietnam. Tra could count on a substantially improved NVA operating in South Vietnam. Two weeks after signing the cease-fire agreement in early 1973, Hanoi began a massive buildup of forces in the South. Northern tanks in South Vietnam increased from 100 to about 500; heavy artillery was doubled; and 13 new antiaircraft artillery regiments were added. During the first year of the agreement, Hanoi added about 75,000 troops to its forces in the South, constructed all-weather roads to reach and supply them, and refurbished and extended its fuel pipeline from North Vietnam through Laos and into eastern Cambodia. By 1975, the NVA would reach its greatest strength to date, 25 divisions. In the South, the Communist cadre strength in the villages and towns had grown to 40,000–50,000 members, an enrollment that not only recovered the lost numbers of the 1960s, but exceeded those figures by about 20 percent. Then, too, Tra knew that Communist regulars and guerrilla forces had never effectively coordinated their actions in a major offensive. Against an enemy grown weaker in comparison to his forces, General Tra now had reason to feel confident.

The ARVN was weaker in comparison to its adversary—for both old and new reasons. Of course, the departure of the U.S. units placed the South Vietnamese in a new and unwelcome situation: they had to face the Communists alone. The U.S. exodus also left vacant a number of sprawling bases, large installations that had specifically been sited so as to provide a loose protective perimeter around South Vietnam's population centers. All of that was now gone, but the Americans had left a legacy, a reliance on mechanized warfare that South Vietnam could ill afford in the economic and political situation of the early 1970s.

A Middle East economic problem and a U.S. domestic political problem had severe effects on the South Vietnamese government. The Arab oil embargo of 1973 increased the price of petroleum products 400 percent in two years. With severe inflation, previously appropriated U.S. aid bought far less. Meanwhile, President Nixon's resignation had weakened the presidency, and his successor, Gerald R. Ford, could not persuade Congress to support South Vietnam adequately. Aid was provided in monthly increments at an annual rate of about $400,000,000, approximately 30 percent of what had been considered essential.

Hard economic times brought on a wave of corruption in Saigon. A South Vietnamese Senate committee investigating the rapid rise in the price of fertilizer discovered that it was being hoarded and then resold to peasants at twice the import price. About 60 businessmen and 10 province chiefs were involved in the lucrative scheme. At the same time, an internal ARVN report revealed widespread corruption in the army's leadership. President Thieu dismissed 2 division commanders for selling rice to the Communists, and 377 colonels and majors were relieved for dishonest practices. A highly respected South Vietnamese officer, Col. Nguyen Van Ngan, reported to Thieu that only about one-third of the 60 generals and 200 top-ranking colonels were honest. Public interest groups were formed and soon an anticorruption league was organized, protesting the performance of the Thieu government. The people of South Vietnam began turning against their government.

To some degree, the uninspiring leadership displayed by these South Vietnamese military and government officials was the product of a well-orchestrated and enduring Communist program. Since the very beginning of the war in 1959, the Viet Cong had averaged about 350 assassinations per year. District and province chiefs, who were usually but not always military officers, were the prime targets of the campaign. Naturally, ineffective and corrupt officers and officials were not chosen for elimination because they inadvertently and unwittingly were aiding the Communist cause. So, over the course of 14 years, some of the most effective and honest of Saigon's leaders had been systematically killed, leaving the incompetent and corrupt to remain and perhaps rise to the top.

General Tra was ordered to Hanoi for a conference in October 1974 and, after some argument, won Politburo backing. A Northerner, Gen. Van Tien Dung, was selected to execute the Ho Chi Minh Campaign, the plan to destroy the Saigon regime.

Fall of Cambodia

On the first hour of the new year, 1975, Pol Pot and his forces began an all-out offensive to conquer Cambodia. During that first week, Lon Nol lost about 600 killed and 1,600 wounded among the defenders of the capital city of Phonm Penh, which was being reinforced from those outlying enclaves that were under little or no pressure. President Ford asked Congress for additional funds for Lon Nol's underequipped army, but U.S. legislators refused to bring the matter to a vote. At the end of January, Cambodian losses were reported at 1,645 killed and 5,765 wounded on the Phnom Penh perimeter alone.

In early April, U.S. citizens in Cambodia began to be evacuated to Thailand. On April 12, the final evacuation of the U.S. Embassy began, using Marine Corps helicopters. The Khmer Rouge took control of Phnom Penh on April 17, beginning a regime of astounding brutality.

FALL OF SOUTH VIETNAM: 1975

During February 1975, ARVN intelligence officers in Saigon had received a Communist defector, an agent report, and a document, all three of which pointed to a major attack in March on Ban Me Thout, the capital of Darlac Province in the Central Highlands. President Thieu and his generals knew that the Central Highlands had always been of special interest to Hanoi because the region's geographic position meant that whoever controlled it could split the country in half. Dividing South Vietnam in the middle would prevent northern ARVN units from reinforcing southern ones and vice versa. Additionally, the Communists would then be able to hold one half while they massed forces on the other, ultimately defeating Saigon's army in detail.

Ban Me Thout was attacked on March 10 after it had been effectively isolated by roadblocks to the east and north. Resistance collapsed, and more Communist units sped through the province, heading north and east, the latter thrusts toward the coast. At about the same time, North Vietnamese armor and infantry columns began a massive attack in the northern part of South Vietnam. Thieu began withdrawing his forces toward the south. Soon, a race southward was taking place.

General Dung was able to make a quick advance because he did not have to secure his rear. The secret to Dung's speed was in General Tra's planning and the way in which Communist guerrilla and local forces were used during the Ho Chi Minh Offensive. As North Vietnamese armor columns moved past them, guerrilla and local force

Refugees from South Vietnam crowd their small boats around the USS Durham, *part of the U.S. naval fleet participating in the evacuation of Saigon in 1975.* (National Archives)

units attacked the South Vietnamese PF and RF. In some cases, these Communist light elements seized a number of towns and important government-held pockets such as the Qui Nhon, Phuoc Ly, and Phuoc Hai peninsulas. Communist local forces provided garrisons for towns in the rear of the advancing regular forces and ensured that vital lines of supply were open. In many instances, guerrilla units seized transportation and supplies, sending fuel, food, and ammunition forward to the lead elements of the attacking forces. They also took charge of the many prisoners that fell into the hands of the regulars.

As the dimensions of the debacle in the north became evident, Thieu looked to the United States for the support and assistance he had been promised. Thieu was not asking for U.S. troops but for the fuel, ammunition, and spare parts necessary to conduct a defense of southern South Vietnam. Additionally, he needed B-52 strikes against Communist troop concentrations. Thieu was informed that nothing could be done before Congress returned in mid-April, by which time the Battle of Saigon began shaping up. The massive assault by Northern armor units could not be seriously resisted by the three understrength ARVN units just north of Saigon.

The U.S. evacuation of Saigon quickly became a shambles. Many people in the city were identified with the U.S. government and its politics and would be prime candidates for a Communist prison or execution if the capital fell. Ambassador Graham Martin, however, refused to press for a mass exodus of the embassy and the large numbers who were in jeopardy because he clung to the hopeless thought that there would be a last-minute understanding among the Communists, the United States, and the Thieu govern-

ment. So, in the early morning of April 30, the Communists were coming into the city while more than 2,000 desperate Americans, other foreigners, and Vietnamese were fighting their way to the U.S. Embassy, trying to escape by helicopter to a U.S. naval fleet standing off the coast. The day before, about 7,000 people had been evacuated, but the helicopter crews had been flying nonstop for many hours and there were simply too many people trying to get out of Saigon.

When the U.S. evacuation of Saigon was finally terminated, many were left behind, still waiting at the embassy. A group of South Vietnamese firemen were among those abandoned. They had been promised evacuation by the fleeing Americans if they would control the crowds attempting to storm the helicopters. The Vietnamese firemen performed their task of keeping order as they said they would. The Americans, however, left without them.

War's End

The long war in Vietnam was over. In May 1975, a few days after the fall of Saigon, Pathet Lao soldiers ended the charade of feigned cooperation with Laotian neutralists and rightists by forcing the government to resign and by jailing Royal Lao Army leaders. Since North Vietnamese "advisers" were in every Pathet Lao unit, Laos was now under the effective control of Hanoi. But the Politburo did not dismantle its army and settle down to the business of peace. The Communists' large and successful People's Army of Vietnam remained at a strength of 600,000, the fourth largest army in the world. Four years later, in 1979, that army overran Cambodia. The goal set in 1930 had finally been achieved.

6

The Era of Flexible Response: 1961–Present

"Let every nation know, whether it wishes us well or ill, that we shall pay any price, bear any burden, meet any hardship, support any friend, oppose any foe to assure the survival and success of liberty." Pres. John F. Kennedy sounded this clarion call during his inaugural address in January 1961. In the 1990s, after the U.S. experience in Vietnam, the message appears unduly overconfident; the commitment contained within, unwise and overextended. As the Vietnam War painfully taught the American people, the United States cannot be the policeman of the world: the price *can* be too high; the burdens, too heavy; the hardships, too severe. The war also revealed that not all challenges from the revolutionary left threaten the vital national interests of the United States, thus requiring a response in kind. The American people, for better or worse, do not appear to be prepared to make the kind of broad, open-ended commitment to world order that Kennedy envisioned.

Yet, when Kennedy made his stirring pledge, his words did not seem unrealistic or rash. In fact, they eloquently phrased what the American people had come to accept as the country's solemn obligation as the leader of the "Free World"'s struggle against international Communism. The appeal reiterated the commitment made by Kennedy's two predecessors, Harry S Truman and Dwight D. Eisenhower, during the first 15 years of the Cold War. As with his predecessors, Kennedy believed in the global dimension of the struggle against Communism, as outlined, for example, in the National Security Council document NSC-68. But Truman and Eisenhower had recognized the limitations on U.S. power. An effective strategy for waging cold war had to balance aims and resources, and the United States, they believed, did not have the resources to fight Communism everywhere while maintaining a viable economy at home. Except for the Korean War years, Truman had been every bit the fiscal conservative that Eisenhower would be in the effort to provide a sound defense while trying to balance the budget.

Kennedy did not accept this view. The United States could have both guns and butter; it could fight Communism virtually anywhere in the world without disrupting the domestic economy—in fact, Cold War expenditures could help stimulate economic growth. An effective foreign policy, therefore, was less a question of resources, which Kennedy's advisers said were plentiful, than of the will to employ them. The Eisenhower administration, Kennedy had charged during the 1960 presidential campaign, had at times been reckless, as when it brought the country to the brink of war over the islands of Quemoy and Matsu off the coast of China, but more often it had been complacent, as when it failed to take vigorous action to prevent Cuban leader Fidel Castro from establishing a Communist foothold in the Western Hemisphere. Throughout the presidential debates, Kennedy took every opportunity to convince voters that he would be tougher on Communism than his opponent, Vice Pres. Richard M. Nixon, a man who had made his political career by denouncing Communists at home and abroad. Kennedy promised an activist foreign policy that would accommodate change and diversity in the world, while offering a range of options between nuclear war and quiescence in dealing with the Communist threat.

FLEXIBLE RESPONSE

In the realm of national security, this new U.S. policy translated into the strategy of "flexible response." Kennedy accepted the conventional (if erroneous) wisdom regarding Eisenhower's "New Look," namely that it left the United States few choices between nuclear brinkmanship or humiliation in dealing with Communist aggression. Nuclear war was unthinkable, while inaction created the perception of weakness. Perceptions, Kennedy believed, were often more important than reality. It benefited the United States little to be the greatest military power in the world if allies and adversaries believed that, for fear of escalation to nuclear war, the country would not use that power. Flexible response would restore credibility to U.S. policy by providing the president with the capability to act across the spectrum of conflict without resorting to nuclear brinksmanship in all but the most extreme cases.

Flexible response entailed a strategy of "symmetrical" containment in which the United States would respond to aggression at the place and time of its occurrence with forces tailored to defeat the threat on its own terms. If the Soviet Union rattled its rockets in a crisis, the United States would rattle its own, thereby deterring the Kremlin from rash action. If a Communist country employed conventional forces to achieve its objectives, the United States would respond with enough conventional force to make the aggressor back down. If an adversary resorted to insurgency, or guerrilla warfare, the United States would respond with counterinsurgency. In each case, the United States would beat the Communists at their own game.

The implementation of flexible response required a military buildup on a scale not seen since the Korean War. During the 1960 presidential campaign, Kennedy had claimed that a "missile gap" existed in favor of the Soviet Union and that the U.S. arsenal of strategic nuclear weapons had to be increased so as to deter nuclear blackmail by the Soviet Union. The missile gap was in fact an illusion, but in this one area, flexible response and the New Look coincided. Kennedy implemented programs begun under Eisenhower to replace the antiquated liquid-fuel, vulnerable Atlas intercontinental ballistic missile (ICBM) with the solid-fuel, silo-based Minuteman ICBM and to launch a fleet of submarines carrying Polaris missiles. Combined with the intercontinental bombers of the Strategic Air Command, these assets formed the triad on which U.S. nuclear strategy would rest for the duration of the Cold War. By the end of 1968, the United States had deployed 54 Titan liquid-fuel ICBMs, 1,000 Minuteman ICBMs, 41 Polaris submarines, and 650 B-52 intercontinental bombers.

At the other end of the conflict spectrum, Kennedy advocated a dramatic expansion of U.S. capability to conduct unconventional warfare. Long before entering the White House, he had expressed fears about Communists seizing control of anticolonial and other revolutionary movements in the Third World, as well as exploiting Third World nationalism to further their own universalist designs. These fears were reinforced just two weeks before his inauguration when Soviet premier Nikita Khrushchev proclaimed Communist support for "wars of national liberation" in Asia, Africa, and Latin America. Kennedy intended to counter Khrushchev's threat by adopting a more flexible policy toward Third World nations, by accepting the position of nonaligned nations that sought to remain neutral in the East-West conflict, and by working with left-of-center governments, as long as they were not Communist-oriented. If pro-West or certain nonaligned countries became targets of Communist aggression through guerrilla warfare, Kennedy would respond with economic aid and, where necessary, with military assistance in the form of counterinsurgency programs.

To give the United States a counterinsurgency capability, Kennedy expanded the U.S. Special Forces, especially the army's Green Berets, and changed their mission from one of preparing for partisan warfare behind Soviet lines in the event of a European war to one of training the military forces of threatened Third World nations to fight Communist guerrillas. The army, traditionally suspicious of elite units within its ranks, reluctantly accepted the mission of devising counterinsurgency doctrine. By the early 1960s, Special Forces teams were active in Latin America and Southeast Asia, the two areas most afflicted with unconventional warfare.

The B-52 bomber saw service throughout the Cold War and beyond—advanced versions were flown in Operation Desert Storm in 1991; this B-52H Stratofortress drops Mark 82 500-pound high-drag bombs. (U.S. Air Force)

Should nuclear deterrence and unconventional methods fail to halt Communist expansion, Kennedy could look to conventional forces to do the job. As president, he began the buildup of U.S. conventional forces and set in place the means to deploy them. The army, which had been cut to the bone during the Eisenhower years, was the principal beneficiary of this program, expanding from 11 to 16 divisions. Several of these divisions would be based in the United States. To allow them to deploy rapidly overseas in the event of an emergency, the U.S. Strike Command was established in 1962 with operational control over two army corps and the air force's Tactical Air Command. U.S. Navy and Marine Corps units also remained available for deployment in a crisis. As with the nuclear triad, the range of conventional and unconventional, or special operations, forces set in place during the Kennedy administration would remain the basis for military strategy below the nuclear threshold for the duration of the Cold War.

The military buildup under Kennedy was managed by Sec. of Defense Robert S. McNamara (a former president of Ford Motor Company) and by a group of civilians known as the "whiz kids" that McNamara brought into the Department of Defense. McNamara introduced systems analysis into the budgetary process, cutting programs that were wasteful or did not contribute to the overall defense strategy. Career officers in the Pentagon who watched the demise of many sacred cows found McNamara abrupt and abrasive and complained that sound military judgments were being overridden by civilian amateurs. Despite these complaints, President Kennedy and his successor, Lyndon B. Johnson, both supported the defense secretary, who served until 1967, when his increasing doubts over the course of the war in Vietnam caused him to resign.

DANGEROUS YEARS

The Kennedy years witnessed the last of the perennial superpower confrontations that had characterized the Cold War since its inception. The most dangerous confrontation came during the week of the Cuban Missile Crisis in October 1962, when the United States and the Soviet Union stood poised to launch nuclear weapons at each other. Yet, if the missile crisis was the darkest hour of the Cold War, the crises that preceded it also caused a nervous world to hold its breath.

Bay of Pigs
On New Year's Day 1959, the revolutionary forces that had been fighting the corrupt dictatorship of Fulgencio Batista in Cuba entered the capital city of Havana. The "maximum leader" of that revolution was Fidel Castro, a lawyer and longtime political activist. As Castro consolidated his

power, the Eisenhower administration adopted a wait-and-see posture. There was some optimism at first that the United States and the Castro regime might establish friendly relations. During his days as a guerrilla fighter, Castro had stated emphatically that he was not a Communist.

By the end of Castro's first year in power, President Eisenhower had concluded otherwise. The Cuban leader's anti-American rhetoric, his calls for revolution throughout Latin America, and his overtures to the Soviet Union convinced key U.S. officials that Cuba under Castro was a threat to U.S. national security. Only 90 miles from the U.S. coast, the island presented a potential military base for the Soviet Union in the Western Hemisphere. Also, Castro's open support for revolutions in Latin America was having a destabilizing effect in what U.S. policymakers considered a U.S. sphere of influence in the Cold War. Given these considerations, Eisenhower, in the spring of 1960, instructed the Central Intelligence Agency (CIA) to plan the overthrow of the Cuban leader.

President Kennedy inherited this plan, which called for a brigade of Cuban exiles, trained by the CIA in Central America, to invade Cuba. The underlying premise of the plan was that the invasion would set off a popular uprising against Castro's tyranny. If the uprising failed to materialize, the invasion force could take to the mountains of Cuba and begin a campaign of guerrilla warfare. The CIA's plan underwent several changes during its development, but when it was presented to Kennedy, the president, on the advice of the CIA and the Joint Chiefs of Staff (JCS), approved its implementation. As he did so, he made clear to the CIA that he would not involve the U.S. military in the operation under any circumstances.

The invasion was scheduled for Apr. 17, 1961. Two days before, CIA aircraft were scheduled to bomb the Cuban air force, but the first of these strikes failed to accomplish its mission. Thus, when the Cuban brigade began its amphibious assault at the Bay of Pigs, Castro's small air force wreaked havoc upon the invaders and their ships. Within two days, most of the 1,400-man brigade had been killed or captured. The survivors blamed Kennedy for not committing U.S. forces to the fight. The president, while taking public responsibility for the failed invasion, blamed the CIA for the debacle. Whoever was at fault, there was no doubt that the new president had been humiliated at the Bay of Pigs. The ramifications of that humiliation would be widespread.

Laos
The Bay of Pigs experience had one salutary effect, according to Kennedy. The president conceded that he came away from the fiasco more cautious about the use of military power to resolve Cold War crises. This caution was

first tested in Indochina, where Laos, ostensibly neutral since the 1954 Geneva Conference, was in the midst of a three-sided civil war in which the Soviets backed the leftist faction, while the United States backed the right. When Kennedy took office, the right wing in Laos was on the verge of defeat. The president's initial reaction was to send 500 U.S. marines to Thailand and to move the 7th Fleet closer to Indochina. The stage was set for U.S. intervention. Kennedy's military advisers advocated such a course and insisted that the president give them authority in advance to use tactical nuclear weapons if necessary.

Kennedy seemed prepared to follow this advice until the Bay of Pigs caused a change of heart. From that point on, he heeded those advisers who favored a negotiated settlement. Kennedy raised the issue with Khrushchev when the two met in Vienna, Austria, in the summer of 1961. The Soviet leader had his own reasons for supporting a negotiated settlement and proved receptive to Kennedy's approach. A year later, a fragile peace reinforcing the neutrality of Laos was successfully negotiated.

Berlin Crisis

Progress on Laos was about the only good news to emerge from the Kennedy-Khrushchev meeting in Vienna. Khrushchev was not impressed with Kennedy's youth or his failure to take decisive action at the Bay of Pigs. By all accounts, the Soviet leader tried to intimidate Kennedy, particularly on the still festering issue of Berlin. There was nothing subtle in Khrushchev's approach, which amounted to an ultimatum. The Soviet Union, he told Kennedy, intended to sign a separate peace treaty with East Germany by the end of the year. Such a treaty would violate World War II agreements concerning the West's access rights to Berlin, a city well inside East Germany. It might also threaten the West's right to stay in Berlin.

Kennedy told Khrushchev in strong terms that the United States would honor its commitments in Berlin. But the president reportedly came away from the meeting visibly shaken after the Soviet leader responded that for the United States to do so would mean war. When Khrushchev had shown Kennedy his Lenin Peace Medal, the president cracked, "I hope you keep it." In private, Kennedy acknowledged, "It's going to be a long winter."

Once home, Kennedy went on television to warn Americans about the impending crisis. He asked for an increase in the draft and called up some reserve and National Guard units. He also requested an additional $3.2 billion for defense spending and recommended enhanced civil defense in the United States through a program to build fallout shelters. In Berlin, tensions mounted in early August 1961, as U.S. and Soviet tanks stood virtually muzzle to muzzle across the boundary dividing West Berlin from East Berlin.

Then, on August 13, the East Germans began building a brick wall surrounded by barbed wire. The Berlin Wall would effectively seal off the eastern, or Soviet, portion of Berlin from the rest of the city and stop the flood of refugees crossing daily into the Western zone. The world waited to see if the United States would move militarily to tear down the wall, but Kennedy had no intention of doing so. He correctly regarded the wall as a symbolic defeat for the Soviet Union; more important, with the wall in place, Khrushchev began backing away from the issue of a separate peace treaty. With the end of the 1961 crisis, Berlin ceased to be a Cold War flash point. In the summer of 1963, Kennedy traveled to West Berlin and, from a platform in the shadow of the wall, declared his solidarity with the city's inhabitants when he shouted, "*Ich bin ein Berliner.*" The crowd of thousands roared their approval at the intended sentiment, fully aware, however, that the president had just proclaimed himself a "jelly doughnut."

NATO

Kennedy's acceptance of the Berlin Wall and his stated willingness to negotiate over Berlin upset Charles de Gaulle, the imperious president of France, and increased de Gaulle's determination to follow an independent course in Europe. In fact, de Gaulle's frustrations were but an extreme example of the restiveness within the North Atlantic Treaty Organization (NATO) itself. Many of the alliance's members were tired of being treated by the United States as junior partners. More unsettling were certain military questions raised by de Gaulle, but shared by all. Given the Soviet nuclear capability, could the United States really be counted upon to defend Europe if the outcome were likely to be a nuclear exchange that would atomize much of the U.S. homeland? Also, given the commitments of the alliance system, would the European allies be expected to support the United States in a crisis over some issue of little concern to Europe, if such support meant risking a Soviet nuclear strike against the Continent? De Gaulle's pessimistic answers to these questions led him to start a program to acquire for France an independent nuclear capability. In time, he would also remove France from the military activities of NATO.

The British also posed a problem for NATO. Great Britain had developed nuclear warheads but relied on U.S. missiles to mount them. When Secretary of Defense McNamara canceled in 1962 a deal to provide the British government with a number of Skybolt missiles, British prime minister Harold Macmillan found himself in the midst of a domestic crisis. To help Macmillan at home, Kennedy traveled to Bermuda in December 1961 to meet with the British leader. To compensate for the loss of the

French president Charles de Gaulle, greeting followers in Rheims in 1958, worried that the North Atlantic Treaty Organization would fail the European nations if it meant that the superpowers were heading toward nuclear war. (French Embassy Press and Information Division)

Skybolts, Kennedy offered Great Britain Polaris missiles and proposed the creation of an all-NATO nuclear, or multilateral, force (MLF). The MLF offer allayed the immediate crisis within NATO, but problems of national sovereignty and other complex issues doomed the project. In the meantime, European allies continued to express reservations about NATO's ambiguities, and the United States continued to voice its frustrations that its European allies were not contributing their full share to the force structure and other military aspects of the alliance. These problems would plague NATO for the duration of the Cold War.

Missiles in Cuba

A year after the Berlin Crisis, Kennedy would face his greatest challenge as president. On Oct. 14, 1962, a U-2 reconnaissance flight over Cuba revealed the existence of Soviet medium-range missiles capable of launching nuclear warheads on two-thirds of the United States. Kennedy was on record as saying the introduction of offensive strategic weapons onto the island would not be tolerated by the United States. When informed of the missiles, the president called together his top advisers to discuss in secret what to do about them. The Cuban Missile Crisis, which brought the world "just inches away from a nuclear holocaust," was underway.

Kennedy did not want to go public with the information until he had decided what response to make. For a week, his advisers deliberated. They discussed Khrushchev's motives for taking such a risk, but reached no consensus. Nor was there consensus on the threat the missiles posed to the United States. Some advisers argued that a missile fired from Cuba was no more dangerous than one fired from the Soviet Union. Others argued that, by placing missiles within minutes of their U.S. targets, the Soviets had altered the strategic balance of power. Still others maintained that, although the balance of power had not been altered in fact, other nations would perceive a change adverse to the United States and that the perception alone could give the Soviets a significant advantage in future Cold War crises. During this debate, a consensus did emerge on one point: the missiles had to be removed.

The question then focused on the most effective way to achieve this objective. The JCS and some civilian advisers argued strongly for an air strike to destroy the missiles before they became operational and for an invasion to settle the Cuban problem once and for all. In line with this advice, Kennedy authorized intensified planning for military action. Contingency plans were updated and the designated military units mobilized. Command-and-control and logistical problems complicated both the planning process

and the deployment of units to bases within striking distance of Cuba. Even so, a formidable invasion force was assembled and awaited orders.

As discussions continued among Kennedy's advisers, the president began to favor a course of action that would delay a direct military confrontation, thus giving the Soviet leaders additional time to reconsider their position and, it was hoped, seek a face-saving way to end the crisis. The recommendation he finally accepted was for a blockade, or "quarantine," of Cuba by the U.S. Navy. The blockade would not get rid of the missiles already on the island, but it would prevent additional missiles from reaching Cuba and, more important, would convince the Kremlin of U.S. resolve.

Kennedy announced the presence of the missiles in Cuba and the decision to quarantine the island in a somber speech to the American people and the world on Monday,

Reconnaissance photographs revealed Soviet missile sites in Cuba, 90 miles off the coast of the United States, and precipitated a Cold War crisis between the two superpowers. (U.S. Air Force)

October 22. The blockade would go into effect on Wednesday. In the most frightening sentence of his address, he warned the Soviets that a missile launched from Cuba against any target in the Western Hemisphere would be regarded as an attack by the Soviet Union on the United States, requiring a full retaliatory response.

The United States and the Soviet Union were now on a nuclear collision course. On Wednesday, the day the blockade went into effect, Soviet ships sailing for Cuba stopped in midcourse, thus providing a temporary respite. By the weekend, however, hostilities seemed inevitable. Work continued on the missile sites in Cuba, as Khrushchev demanded and Kennedy rejected a deal whereby the Soviet Union would remove the missiles in Cuba if the United States removed its Jupiter missiles from Turkey. On Saturday, a U-2 flying over Cuba was shot down by a Soviet ground-to-air missile. This was the darkest day of the crisis.

As the world awaited the anticipated military action against Cuba, behind-the-scenes diplomacy averted a cataclysmic showdown. Through unofficial channels, Khrushchev offered to remove the missiles in return for a U.S. pledge not to invade Cuba. The president, for his part, had his brother, Atty. Gen. Robert F. Kennedy, privately approach the Soviet ambassador Friday night to convey two messages: one was an ultimatum to remove the missiles from Cuba within 24 hours; the other was an unpublicized promise that the United States would remove its Jupiter missiles from Turkey at some unspecified point in the future. On Sunday morning, the world learned that Khrushchev had agreed to remove the missiles in return for the noninvasion pledge. For all practical purposes, the crisis was over.

As the two superpowers stepped away from the brink of nuclear war, Kennedy was praised for his judicious handling of the crisis. In fact, the Cuban Missile Crisis would become a textbook example of crisis management. The principal lesson learned was not to back an adversary into a corner but to allow him sufficient time and room to maneuver to find a face-saving way to back down. The lesson was and is valid, but in retrospect many analysts came to believe that, in light of both Kennedy's and Khrushchev's determinations to avoid war, the possibility of a nuclear exchange during the crisis was greatly exaggerated. Recent evidence suggests, however, that the threat was very real indeed. Unknown to the Kennedy administration, the Soviets had ground-to-ground tactical nuclear weapons in Cuba. In the event of an invasion, the Soviet commanders on the scene had authority to employ these weapons. Had they done so, the loss of large numbers of U.S. troops would have compelled the president to respond in kind, perhaps even with a nuclear strike on the Soviet Union. Also unknown, the Soviets had 43,000 troops in Cuba (four times the estimates of U.S. intelligence). Many of these soldiers would have died in a U.S. air strike on the missile sites, thus forcing Khrushchev to retaliate. Officials of the Kennedy administration who were involved in the crisis concede that they now realize even more than at the time just how close the world came in October 1962 to a nuclear holocaust.

The missile crisis had a sobering effect on the behavior of the two superpowers. In the aftermath, both sides moved to sign a Nuclear Test Ban Treaty, prohibiting the testing of nuclear devices above ground. Also, in an attempt to facilitate communications in a future crisis, a "hotline" teletype machine was installed, linking the White House in Washington, D.C., with the Kremlin in Moscow. There would be fewer superpower crises in the future, and when they did occur, as during the 1967 and 1973 Arab-Israeli wars and after the United States mined Haiphong harbor during the Vietnam War, they were quickly defused. On a less positive note, the Soviet Union vowed that it would never again suffer such a humiliation as it had in Cuba. The result was an acceleration in the Kremlin's massive buildup of strategic weapons in an effort to close the enormous advantage held in that area by the United States. Future presidents would have to deal with a Soviet Union bristling with several thousand nuclear warheads (compared to the several hundred it possessed at the time of the missile crisis) and the means for delivering them.

JOHNSON IN THE WHITE HOUSE

On Nov. 22, 1963, 13 months to the day after Kennedy had revealed to the world the presence of Soviet missiles in Cuba, he was assassinated in Dallas, Texas. Vice Pres. Lyndon B. Johnson of Texas took the oath of office as president that afternoon. Johnson shared Kennedy's fundamental Cold War views and inherited his predecessor's Cold War burdens. Although superpower tensions diminished considerably after the missile crisis, U.S. and Soviet interests continued to work at cross purposes throughout the world. Within the year, the unpredictable, but at times conciliatory Khrushchev would be ousted from power; the new Soviet leadership presented a more businesslike, but no less determined, face to the West. Also in 1964, the People's Republic of China, which the United States still refused to recognize, tested its first nuclear device. Communist-controlled guerrilla forces continued their revolutionary warfare throughout Latin America and Southeast Asia, with the United States continuing to provide the threatened countries with training and aid for counterinsurgency programs. Johnson's concern about Communist takeovers in Indochina, especially a victory in South Vietnam, would lead him to commit U.S. combat troops to the war that ultimately engulfed his administration. The Mid-

Sen. Barry Goldwater, Republican candidate for president in 1964, ran on a platform of an all-out war effort to end the war in Vietnam against President Johnson's seemingly more peacelike policies. (Office of Senator Goldwater)

dle East remained a tinderbox, as no resolution to Arab-Israeli antagonism seemed likely. Finally, the problems within NATO and the European community in general continued to vex U.S. policymakers.

In the interval between Kennedy's assassination and the presidential election of 1964, the only foreign policy crisis challenging Johnson was the war in Vietnam. The Gulf of Tonkin incident and the congressional resolution that followed gave Johnson the authority he sought to act in Southeast Asia, but during the election campaign he pledged not to send U.S. troops to fight in a foreign war. The promise helped to contrast his concerns for peace with the presumably more warlike mentality of his opponent, Sen. Barry Goldwater of Arizona, a conservative Republican whom Johnson repeatedly branded as trigger-happy. Johnson won the election in a landslide, making him president in his own right and clearing the way for an escalation of U.S. involvement in Vietnam.

The increasing demands of the Vietnam War made it difficult for Johnson to sustain major efforts to resolve other festering foreign policy problems. The result was that his administration tended to manage international crises on an ad hoc basis with only slight acknowledgement of their deeper roots, their context, and their long-term implications.

Congo Rescue Mission

Aside from Indochina, Johnson's first major crisis requiring the use of U.S. military forces occurred in the republic of the Congo (now Zaire). Since gaining its independence in 1960, the country had experienced little but civil strife and disorder. In the fall of 1964, while Johnson was campaigning for the presidency, headlines from the Congo followed the vicissitudes of the Simba revolt against the government. In August 1964, the rebels captured the city of Stanleyville, where they took 1,600 European hostages. They threatened to kill the hostages if government forces tried to retake the city.

Because U.S. citizens were also in danger, the U.S. military began planning a rescue mission. In the ensuing weeks, however, what was originally envisioned as a joint U.S. military operation was transformed into a combined operation in which the United States would provide the airlift and Belgium the paracommandos. Code-named "Dragon Rouge," the hostage rescue mission began on November 24. After CIA-piloted B-26 bombers hit the Stanleyville airport, five U.S. C-130 transports carrying 340 Belgian troops launched an assault to seize the airfield. The air assault was timed to coincide with the arrival in Stanleyville of forces composed of Belgian and U.S. officers, a CIA element, and Congolese army troops.

Upon hearing that they were about to be attacked, the Simbas assembled 250 hostages and began shooting them. The arrival of the rescue force stopped the massacre, but not before 18 hostages died and another 40 were wounded. Once the city was secured, the Belgian paracommandos launched another rescue operation toward a town several hundred miles away. The Dragon Rouge operations were hailed as successful, despite the death of many hostages and the continuation of the Simba revolt. Many more Europeans and Congolese would die before the fighting in the Congo ran its course.

Dominican Republic

Several months after the Congo rescue mission, Johnson confronted another crisis, this time in Latin America, where, the president pledged, the United States would not tolerate further Communist expansion. Simply put, there would be "no more Cubas" in the hemisphere. In April 1965, that policy was put to the test in the Dominican Republic, a country occupying the eastern two-thirds of the island of Hispaniola. Since the early 1930s, the Dominican Republic had been ruled by strongman Rafael Leonidas Trujillo Molina. After the dictator was assassinated in May 1961, the Kennedy administration, through a show of military force and the threat of armed intervention, forced the removal of the Trujillo family from Dominican politics. Kennedy could not, however, impose a stable democracy on the country. A democratically elected president was overthrown by the Dominican military in

September 1963 after serving less than one year in office. A governing triumverate soon came to power and was recognized by the United States in December.

In April 1965, a successful armed revolt against the head of the triumverate quickly escalated into a civil war when conservative "Loyalists" in the military attacked the rebels just after they had formed a "Constitutionalist" left-of-center government. At first it appeared that the Loyalists would easily defeat the rebels, a prospect welcomed by the U.S. Embassy in Santo Domingo, the capital and scene of most of the fighting. Embassy officials reported that radicals were taking over the rebel movement and that the country stood on the brink of a Communist takeover. When, to the surprise of all, rebel forces turned back a Loyalist offensive, the embassy recommended U.S. intervention.

President Johnson first ordered U.S. marines into the Dominican Republic to evacuate U.S. citizens. The next day, he sent in more marines and ordered the deployment of the army's XVIII Airborne Corps from Fort Bragg, North Carolina. On May 2, he spoke to justify the intervention on the grounds that he was preventing the spread of Communism in the Western Hemisphere. At the height of the troop buildup, U.S. forces in the Dominican Republic numbered 24,000.

The marines and paratroopers managed within a few days and with little fighting to separate the warring parties. In the process, U.S. forces confined the bulk of the rebels to a small sector of the capital. Johnson proclaimed U.S. neutrality in the conflict, but for reporters on the scene, it was obvious that U.S. troops, on orders from the commander in chief, were supporting the Loyalist junta. Not until mid-May did the United States take a truly neutral position, imposing peace talks on both sides. By then, combat for U.S. troops consisted primarily of nightly engagements with rebel snipers. When the marines and paratroopers were not fighting, they engaged in a variety of humanitarian aid and civil affairs activities designed to stabilize the situation so as to facilitate a political solution to the crisis.

The Organization of American States (OAS), after much arm-twisting from the Johnson administration, endorsed the U.S. intervention and approved the unique step of creating an Inter-American Peace Force (IAPF). Under the command of a Brazilian general, who arrived in the Dominican Republic in late May, the IAPF included military units and token police forces from six Latin American countries. The commander of U.S. troops in the Dominican Republic, after having his objections overridden by the Pentagon and State Department, reluctantly placed his forces under the operational command of the Brazilian officer.

Once negotiations bore fruit, the principal mission of the IAPF was to protect a newly formed provisional government from armed critics on the right and left. Not until June 1966 did the situation stabilize to the point that democratic elections could be held. On September 21, the last U.S. troops left the country. As a stability operation, the intervention had been a success, but one for which Johnson paid a high price at home and abroad. Latin Americans denounced his decision to intervene unilaterally as a violation of the OAS Charter. Domestic critics questioned the degree of Communist involvement in what had begun as a popular revolt. They also charged, with some good reason, that the president had not been completely honest with the American people in explaining the reasons for the intervention or in describing the activities of U.S. forces once they were deployed. The "credibility gap" that would haunt Johnson during the Vietnam War had its origins in the Dominican Republic.

War in the Middle East

The Dominican intervention was barely underway when Johnson began the escalation of U.S. involvement in Vietnam. For the rest of his term, he would remain preoccupied with that war. The world outside of Indochina, however, could not be put on hold, and other crises would demand his attention. One of these was the 1967 Arab-Israeli War, called the Seven-Day War. Gamal Abdel Nasser, president of Egypt, espoused a brand of radical Arab nationalism but showed little inclination to get into a war with Israel as a demonstration of his sincerity. A radical new government in Syria, however, was goading Nasser toward action. Nasser's response was to demand that the United Nations (UN) Peacekeeping Force in the Sinai, which had served as a buffer between Egypt and Israel since the 1956 hostilities, withdraw. To Nasser's apparent surprise, the UN secretary-general agreed to these demands. Forced to follow up on this "triumph," Nasser closed the Gulf of Aqaba to Israel, thus cutting Israel's lifeline to the Red Sea. When international diplomacy failed to resolve the crisis, war became virtually inevitable. On June 5, Israel launched preemptive strikes against Egypt, Syria, and Jordan. Within days, Israeli troops had occupied the Sinai, the West Bank section of Jordan, and Syria's Golan Heights.

Three days later, while fighting on the Golan Heights continued, Israeli aircraft and torpedo boats attacked a U.S. intelligence-gathering communications ship, the *Liberty,* operating in the Mediterranean Sea near the battle area. When the attack was over, 34 U.S. servicemen were dead, another 171 wounded. Officially, the deadly incident was described as an "accident," even though Israeli planes had overflown and inspected the *Liberty* at least 13 times in the 16 hours preceding the attack. The Israeli government immediately proffered its apologies and offered to pay damages. The White House and Pentagon managed to keep investigation of the affair to a minimum. The exact reasons for the Israeli attack are still not clear. What is clear is that the attack, in the words of former secretary of state Dean Rusk, "was and remains a genuine outrage."

By June 9, the day following the attack on the *Liberty,* Jordan and Egypt had accepted international appeals for a cease-fire; neither country was in any condition to continue the war. Fighting raged, however, on the Golan Heights. The next morning, Johnson received a message from Soviet premier Aleksei Kosygin. Unless the Israelis halted all operations within a matter of hours, Kosygin warned, the Soviet Union would take "necessary actions, including military," to impose peace. Johnson had his Russian specialists go over the message several times to confirm that it, in fact, represented a Soviet threat. Once it was established that it did, the president ordered the U.S. 6th Fleet in the Mediterranean Sea to sail to within 50 miles of Syria. Johnson knew that Soviet intelligence would pick up the movement immediately and interpret it as a sign of the intention of the United States to prevent any great power from intervening in the conflict. The atmosphere in the White House remained tense until a second message from Kosygin arrived, this one making no reference to Soviet intervention. The superpower confrontation, which had lasted only a matter of hours, was over.

That neither superpower viewed the Middle East crisis as an impediment to improving bilateral relations was con-firmed when Kosygin arrived in the United States later in June for a cordial summit conference with Johnson. The talks demonstrated that relations between the United States and the Soviet Union, although adversarial, coud be conducted in a businesslike way, despite occasional saber rattling. This impression was sustained even after the Soviet Union intervened in Czechoslovakia in 1968 to suppress the movement in that country to promote freedom by breaking away from the Soviet bloc. The United States denounced the intervention but, as in the case of East Germany in 1953 and Hungary in 1956, ruled out the use of force in the Soviet sphere of influence. The most serious impact of the Soviet invasion on relations with the United States was the indefinite postponement of the strategic arms limitations talks to which both sides had assented.

Pueblo Affair

While Johnson dealt with crises in the Middle East and the continuing war in Vietnam, the United States and North Korea engaged in what one U.S. officer called the "Second Korean Conflict," a series of minor engagements along the demilitarized zone between North and South Korea. This conflict was clearly overshadowed by Vietnam until Jan. 23, 1968, when North Korean patrol boats seized the *Pueblo,* an electronic surveillance ship operating in international waters off the North Korean coast. North Koreans

Soviet premier Aleksei Kosygin (left) *attended a special emergency session of the United Nations in 1967 after the Arab-Israeli Seven-Day War, which was marked by near-Soviet interference.* (United Nations)

boarded the vessel, killing 1 American and taking 82 captives. Also seized in the attack was sensitive intelligence equipment. The ship was taken to the port of Wonsan. While it was en route to Wonsan, the United States launched fighter aircraft from Okinawa, but these were ordered to turn back after nightfall.

Johnson assembled his advisers to consider the U.S. response to this act of piracy. Both civilian and military officials urged a strong military response, lest the incident set an unacceptable precedent. The war in Vietnam, however, had siphoned off much of the capability of the United States to retaliate against North Korea with anything but nuclear weapons, which Johnson wisely refused to authorize. Also, a military response was almost certain to put the crew of the *Pueblo* in jeopardy. The beginning of the Tet Offensive in Vietnam one week after the incident made a military response against North Korea even less likely.

The *Pueblo* affair illuminated how the Vietnam War had virtually rendered the United States unable to act decisively when its interests were challenged elsewhere. Johnson tried to put the best face he could on a national humiliation, but his assurances that the captured crewmen were not being mistreated turned out to be grossly inaccurate. After extensive talks with North Korean representatives and the signing of a "confession" by U.S. negotiators, the crew was released in December 1968. By that time, Johnson was a lame-duck president. He had announced in March his intention not to seek another term. In November, former vice president Nixon had won the presidential election, ending eight years of Democratic occupancy of the White House.

RISE AND FALL OF DÉTENTE

Nixon entered the White House in January 1969 having pledged to end the Vietnam War on honorable terms. Fulfilling that commitment would take his entire first term. In the meantime, the war continued its brutal course, while protesters at home continued to demonstrate. Nixon, however, would not let the war detract him from the broader issues of international affairs. Together with Henry Kissinger, his national security adviser, who would later become secretary of state, the incoming president was determined to formulate a more cohesive foreign policy suitable to significant changes that had taken place in the international system since the first, more strident phases of the Cold War.

Vietnam had by 1969 revealed the limits of U.S. power, thus prompting a reassessment of U.S. globalism as practiced to varying degrees by Presidents Truman, Eisenhower, Kennedy, and Johnson. In short, it was not in the interests of the United States to play the role of world policeman. In what became known as the Nixon Doctrine, the president began to reduce U.S. commitments abroad. He promised to honor U.S. treaty obligations, to shield other nations from Soviet nuclear blackmail, and to provide economic and military assistance, but not necessarily U.S. troops, to countries threatened by nonnuclear forms of Communist aggression. What the United States would do if economic and military assistance were insufficient to save these countries was left deliberately vague. As the Nixon administration's active support for a violent coup d'etat against a popularly elected Marxist government in Chile demonstrated in 1973, there were still limits to what U.S. foreign policymakers would tolerate before they reacted as part of the ongoing effort to contain Communist expansion.

As with Kennedy and Johnson, Nixon also had to come to terms with Europe and Japan, whose increasing economic competitiveness and political determination to follow more independent courses in world affairs strained relations with the United States. Nixon's policies in dealing with the allies failed to alleviate those points of friction, but this caused less consternation than anticipated in the White House. For, above all else, the Nixon-Kissinger grand design for a new approach to foreign affairs rested not on better relations with the friends of the United States but on a restructured relationship with its adversaries.

What Nixon and Kissinger sought was a more stable world order based on the principle of equilibrium and legitimacy. Both believed that the Communist threat should not be allowed to determine U.S. interests. Rather, what constituted a threat should be defined in terms of a new conception of U.S. interests derived less from ideological and more from geopolitical considerations. Stability required some form of agreement among the superpowers on the nature of their interaction and on what were permissible methods and aims of foreign policy. A modified relationship between the United States and the Soviet Union would provide the centerpiece of this new arrangement. An integral part of the equilibrium, though, called for taking advantage of the Sino-Soviet split, apparent to the West since the early 1960s, by revising U.S. policy toward the People's Republic of China. Closer U.S.-Chinese relations, Nixon and Kissinger believed, would provide leverage with the Soviet Union in the quest for a more stable world.

In short, the Nixon-Kissinger grand design called for normalizing U.S. relations with China and pursuing détente with the Soviet Union. Regarding the former, Nixon began a series of conciliatory gestures toward the Chinese leadership on the mainland in late 1969. In April 1971, the Chinese invited a U.S. table tennis team to Beijing. Two months later, Kissinger made a secret trip to China, during which he discussed Vietnam and other pressing issues. This set the stage for President Nixon's surprise announcement that he would visit the People's Republic of China in February 1972. The visit produced no breakthroughs on outstanding issues, but the process of normalization was underway. From that point on, Soviet foreign policy would have to take into account the state of U.S. relations with the hostile giant to Russia's east.

Principles of Détente

In pursuing détente—an easing of tensions—with the Soviet Union, the Nixon administration sought to work out rules of mutual conduct that would minimize the danger of accidental war and make the Soviet Union realize that it was in the mutual interest of both countries to seek a more stable world. A combination of incentives and pressures would be used to compel Soviet leaders to cooperate in this endeavor. At the same time, the administration would make it clear that it did not endorse the Soviet system, that it did recognize fundamental political and ideological differences between the two countries, and that it was opposed to any attempt by the Soviet Union to gain a position of global or regional predominance, or to use détente as a cover under which existing conflicts could be exacerbated.

Productive negotiations between the two countries were essential to the success of détente. During Nixon's first term in the White House, negotiations seemed to bear fruit. An agreement was reached on Berlin, in which the Soviets recognized Western rights in the divided city. Other accords involved cooperative ventures on several nonmilitary projects, such as health and science; an understanding to curtail the risk of incidents at sea; and pledges to behave responsibly in world affairs.

SALT

The principal détente agreement, signed at a summit conference in Moscow in May 1972, came out of the Strategic Arms Limitations Treaty (SALT) talks, which President Johnson had postponed after the Soviet invasion of Czechoslovakia in 1968. The talks (SALT I) had finally opened in November 1969, with both sides agreeing in principle that the objective of any arms agreement would be mutual deterrence. Each country, by maintaining a strategic force capable of obliterating the other country, would know that launching a first strike would be tantamount to national suicide. In this context of Mutual Assured Destruction (MAD), the United States changed its Cold War policy from one of seeking nuclear superiority over the Soviet Union to one of settling for a nuclear force "sufficient" to ensure deterrence. The United States, in effect, conceded the status of nuclear "parity" to the Soviet Union.

What the size and nature of each side's strategic force should be posed complex technical questions that seemed at times to defy answers. For example, Soviet ICBMs had greater thrusts than their U.S. counterparts and, thus, could carry larger warheads. The United States, for its part, was rearming many of its missiles with multiple warheads, a technology that the Soviets had not yet mastered. Also, most of the Soviet strategic capability rested with land-based missiles, whereas the United States had its more balanced triad of ICBMs, submarine-launched missiles, and strategic bombers.

At times, an agreement appeared unattainable, but both sides made concessions so that before Nixon left the Moscow summit, he and Soviet premier Leonid Brezhnev could sign two arms limitations accords. One limited the number of antiballistic missile (ABM) launch sites each side could construct. The logic behind the accord was simple: an extensive system of ABMs would endanger mutual deterrence since the country with such a system in place could launch a first strike in the expectation of surviving

The United States and the Soviet Union finally came to an agreement of sorts—labeled détente—at the SALT I conference when President Nixon and Soviet premier Leonid Brezhnev signed an arms limitation accord in 1972. (Soviet Embassy)

retaliation by destroying the incoming missiles of its victim.

The second accord to come out of SALT I placed a five-year ceiling on the number of nuclear weapons launchers each side could deploy. To compensate for the U.S. advantage in multiple warheads, the Soviets were allowed more land-based launchers (1,618 ICBMs to 1,054 for the United States). The agreement also covered the number of missile-launching submarines each country could have. It did not cover qualitative improvements that either could make in its strategic arsenal. The accord was termed the "Interim Agreement," in that it would serve as the basis for negotiations on a formal treaty in the next round of arms limitation talks, SALT II.

Crises in the Middle East

To the extent that détente lowered Cold War tensions, it enjoyed popular support during Nixon's first term. But the president and Kissinger were not entirely satisfied with the new dispensation. For one thing, the Soviet Union's defi-

In 1970, the United States was ready to intervene in Jordan when Palestinian guerrillas, with the aid of Syrian troops, sought to depose King Hussein (above). (Consulate of Jordan)

nition of détente did not coincide exactly with that of the United States. This was especially the case in regard to competition in the Third World, which the Soviets continued to accept as legitimate so long as it did not escalate into a superpower confrontation. To the Nixon administration, however, the existence of the competition always carried with it that risk, as was revealed in two crises that erupted in the volatile Middle East, an area in which U.S. and Soviet vital interests overlapped.

If Vietnam was Nixon's most constant foreign policy worry, the Middle East was his most dangerous. Japan and Western Europe relied heavily on Mideast oil, and the United States had to make sure the oil fields did not fall into unfriendly hands. The Arab-Israeli conflict was no nearer solution, as Arab nations vowed to avenge the humiliation of 1967. The longstanding issue of Arab nationalism was complicated by the emergence of radical guerrilla/terrorist groups that threatened pro-Western governments in Jordan, Lebanon, and Saudi Arabia.

In September 1970, Palestinian guerrillas in Jordan began a campaign of terrorism and military activity to depose Jordan's King Hussein and to use Jordanian territory to launch attacks on Israel. Hussein committed his army to expel the guerrillas, prompting Syria to send tank columns into Jordan to help the Palestinians. Privately, President Nixon told advisers that the United States might have to intervene militarily to save Hussein. To back up his words, he beefed up the U.S. 6th Fleet in the Mediterranean and placed U.S. troops in West Germany on alert. The administration also promised to protect Israel (which was poised to intervene against the Palestinians) from Egyptian and Soviet counteractions. Finally, the White House put pressure on the Kremlin to convince its Syrian client to pull its forces out of Jordan.

Nixon was engaging in brinkmanship, and the stakes were high. Fortunately, before the crisis could escalate into a superpower confrontation, Hussein's army reversed the situation on the battlefield and won a convincing victory. The Syrians pulled back across the border, and the Palestinian guerrillas were expelled from Jordan (from where they gravitated to Lebanon).

Yom Kippur War

In 1971, negotiations to resolve the Arab-Israeli conflict got underway, but the failure to reach a settlement caused Anwar Sadat, who had become president of Egypt in 1970 after Nasser's death, to conclude that only another war would force Israel and the United States to make concessions. In late November 1972, Sadat asked the Soviet Union for more arms to support a war, but Brezhnev turned him down. Sadat thereupon expelled Soviet military advisers from his country. Once Brezhnev realized that Sadat could not be restrained, Soviet weapons, including

U.S. Sec. of Defense James Schlesinger used the threat of nuclear force to persuade the Soviets to back off during the Arab-Israeli Yom Kippur War in 1973. (Department of Defense)

ground-to-ground Scud missiles, began arriving in Egypt.

In 1973, on October 6 (the date of the Jewish holy day of Yom Kippur), Egypt and Syria launched a surprise attack on Israel. The so-called Yom Kippur War had started. Egyptian forces managed to penetrate Israeli defenses along the Suez Canal, while Syrian tank columns poured into the Golan Heights. The sophisticated weaponry available to Egypt and Syria prevented Israel from reversing the situation quickly. Instead, both fronts became littered with burnt-out tanks and human remains. At first, the Nixon administration balked at Israeli requests for additional arms, but when the president learned that the Soviets were stepping up arms shipments to Egypt and Syria and that Brezhnev had placed Soviet airborne units in Eastern Europe on alert, he ordered a massive airlift of war matériel to the beleaguered Jewish nation. The results were immediate. Israeli troops punched across the Suez Canal and threatened to surround the Egyptian 3d Army. On the Syrian front, Israeli forces prepared to march on Damascus.

At this turning point in the war, all sides heeded the call for a cease-fire. But continued Israeli movements on the West Bank of the Suez brought a thinly veiled ultimatum from Brezhnev to Nixon. In a letter to Nixon, the Soviet leader raised the serious possibility of Soviet military intervention in the war. Wallowing in the domestic mire of the Watergate crisis, Nixon left it to Kissinger and Sec. of Defense James Schlesinger to formulate the U.S. response. Both agreed that the only way to dissuade the Soviet Union from acting unilaterally was to place U.S. nuclear forces on alert, a move Soviet intelligence would pick up immediately. Another consideration in their decision was the report that the Soviet Union was shipping atomic warheads to Egypt.

News of the superpower confrontation set off a brief "war scare," but after about 12 hours of high tension, the Soviets indicated publicly that they had no intention of intervening in the conflict. News that the cease-fire had finally taken hold also helped defuse the situation. The crisis passed, but not before demonstrating the limits of détente. With the war over, Kissinger undertook several rounds of shuttle diplomacy in the Middle East to separate the warring parties and to set the stage for a general peace conference. He was more successful in attaining the first objective than the second, although the agreements he negotiated convinced Arab leaders to lift the oil embargo they had enacted during the war.

Decline of Détente

Within a year after the October war, Nixon, who had won reelection in 1972 by a landslide, was forced to resign the presidency over the Watergate affair. His successor, Gerald Ford, pressed forward with Nixon's foreign policy agenda, retaining Kissinger as secretary of state. One item near the top of the agenda was to get stalled talks on SALT II moving again.

The negotiations had bogged down over new technological developments. The Soviets, who continued to enjoy an advantage in missile throw weight, now had MIRVs (multiple independently targetable reentry vehicles) to place atop their huge ICBMs. They also had a new Backfire bomber that the Americans maintained had a strategic capability. From its perspective, the Kremlin was concerned about U.S. forward-based aircraft capable of delivering nuclear weapons on Soviet targets and about the U.S. development of long-range cruise missiles. When Ford met Brezhnev in Vladivostok in November 1974, the best the two leaders could do was defer the difficult issues for further negotiation, reach a basis of understanding for guidelines for those talks, and agree in principle on the total number of MIRV launchers each country could have. When negotiations resumed in early 1975, little progress was made toward a final accord.

The disappointing results of SALT reflected a broader deterioration in U.S.-Soviet relations during the mid-1970s. From the U.S. perspective, the Soviet Union was intensifying world tensions, especially around the Horn of Africa. When Ford ran for the presidency in 1976, so changed was the mood of the country that he felt compelled to omit any reference to détente in his foreign policy statements.

LOW-INTENSITY CONFLICT

Ford had been the first president since Truman not to have to deal with Vietnam as a major foreign policy issue. Nixon had finally extricated the United States from the war in 1973. Almost two decades would pass before the United States would become involved in another large-scale war. In the interim, the U.S. military shifted the emphasis of its doctrine, force structure, and training back to a European scenario and the possibility of war with the Soviet Union. The Pentagon considered such a war highly unlikely, but prudence (and, perhaps, a determination never again to become involved in a Vietnam-like war) dictated this reorientation. When U.S. military force was employed during the remainder of the Cold War, it was in what became known as low-intensity conflict, or "LIC."

A comprehensive, satisfactory definition of LIC does not exist. The most recent U.S. Army field manual on the subject, however, defines it in general terms as "a politico-military confrontation between contending states or groups below conventional war and above the routine, peaceful competition among states." The operational categories of LIC include insurgency/counterinsurgency, combatting terrorism, peacekeeping operations, and peacetime contingency operations. The U.S. military had performed these kinds of missions throughout its history; "low-intensity conflict," in some respects, was simply a more sophisticated term for what once had been called simply "small wars."

Mayaguez Incident

The first significant example of LIC after Vietnam occurred in May 1975. On May 12, Cambodian gunboats of the Communist Khmer Rouge seized the American crew of a commercial ship, the *Mayaguez*. When word reached Washington about the seizure, President Ford called a

U.S. Marines board the Mayaguez *only to find the ship deserted. This commercial ship, with its American crew, had been captured by Cambodia's Khmer Rouge Communists.* (U.S. Navy)

meeting of the National Security Council, at which it was determined that the United States had to take action. The president, it was agreed, could not allow the "Vietnam Syndrome"—a reluctance on the part of the American people to employ force in the wake of the Vietnam War—to dictate policies that would render the country impotent in defense of its interests abroad. With this in mind, Ford ordered warships carrying U.S. marines into the waters off Cambodia.

On May 13, reconnaissance planes sighted the *Mayaguez* near the Cambodian island of Koh Tang. Intelligence reports, which later proved erroneous, indicated the crew had been transferred to the island. On the basis of this information, U.S. commanders in the area prepared plans to retake the ship and rescue the crew. During these preparations, a helicopter carrying 18 security policemen slated to take part in the mission crashed, killing all aboard.

Military operations were scheduled to begin before dawn on May 15. By that time, the Khmer Rouge who had seized the *Mayaguez* had already been ordered to release the crew. This information had not reached Washington when Ford ordered the rescue plan to be executed. Soon thereafter, a marine company boarded the *Mayaguez*, only to find the ship deserted. Nearby, a force from Marine Battalion Landing Team 2/9, in a joint operation with the air force, which provided helicopter crews and air cover, began an assault on Koh Tang. The marines encountered up to 200 well-armed and entrenched Khmer Rouge troops. Sixteen marines died when their helicopter was hit by a rocket-propelled grenade. The battle for the island was fierce, with both sides suffering heavy casualties. As the fighting raged, Ford received word that the *Mayaguez* crew had been released. From that point on, the military's priority was to rescue the marines on Koh Tang. By evening, the operation was over. A total of 18 marines had been killed, while 50 others were wounded or missing. Ford had demonstrated U.S. resolve in the aftermath of Vietnam, but at a very high cost in men and matériel.

Carter Presidency

In January 1977, Jimmy Carter became the first Democratic president since Johnson. The new president expressed a desire to reorient U.S. foreign policy from East-West Cold War issues to a North-South dialogue between industrial and Third World countries. Among Carter's achievements were the Panama Canal Treaties, which would turn the canal over to Panama and remove U.S. bases from the country by the year 2000, and the Camp David Accords, in which the president played a critical role in epochal peace negotiations between Israel and Egypt. Yet, however lofty his intentions, Carter could not break out of the Cold War mold, not with a strategic arms

Pres. Jimmy Carter's hopes that the signing and ratification of the arms limitations SALT II treaty would abate the Cold War were dashed by the Soviet invasion of Afghanistan in 1979. (The White House)

agreement with the Soviet Union still pending and not with continued Soviet adventurism in the Horn of Africa and, through Cuban proxies, in Angola.

On the first issue, there had been little progress on SALT II since the Ford-Brezhnev Vladivostok agreement. Carter attempted to break the impasse essentially by putting forward new proposals for sweeping cuts in strategic offensive weapons, but the Soviets rejected the offer. Negotiations continued, however, and finally produced an accord. On June 18, 1979, Carter and Brezhnev signed the second Strategic Arms Limitation Treaty (SALT II). The agreement called for a slight reduction in delivery systems, set limits on the number of MIRVs that missiles could carry, and placed a ceiling on throw weight. By an executive agreement, both leaders pledged to put SALT II into effect immediately while awaiting ratification.

Carter referred the treaty to the U.S. Senate on June 22, precipitating a stormy debate. Opponents argued that the agreement conceded to the Soviet Union a substantial lead in megatonnage, did nothing to curb the first-strike threat of the Soviets' large and increasingly accurate SS-18 ICBMs, and relied solely on Soviet promises to place restrictions on the Backfire bomber. Besides having differing opinions over the merits of the treaty, many Americans urged that its ratification be linked to better behavior by the Soviet Union internationally. The linkage argument gained support after the Soviet invasion of Afghanistan began in December 1979. Carter responded by putting SALT II on hold and declaring that any attempt by the Soviets to gain control of the Persian Gulf would be resisted by the United States, with military force if necessary. To back up this Carter Doctrine, the president called for increased defense spending, which had fallen off during the Nixon-

Shortly after helicopters, involved in the 1980 rescue mission in Iran, lifted off from the deck of the USS Nimitz, *the mission was aborted because of a freak dust storm and mechanical difficulties.* (U.S. Navy)

Ford years, and enacted measures designed to improve the nation's capability "to deploy U.S. military forces rapidly to distant areas."

Hostages in Iran

As Carter dealt with SALT II and the Soviet invasion of Afghanistan, he was also confronted with the crisis for which his presidency would be most remembered: the prolonged detainment of American hostages in Iran. The roots of the crisis could be traced back at least to the U.S.-instigated coup in 1953, which returned the Shah of Iran to his throne. U.S. support for the increasingly unstable and dictatorial ruler came back to haunt the United States after the Shah's government fell in early 1979 and radical Islamic fundamentalists seized power. In November, militant Iranian students overran the grounds of the U.S. Embassy in Teheran, taking hostage the embassy staff. Carter's efforts to negotiate the release of the hostages failed, after which he authorized a military rescue mission.

Special operations personnel from a newly formed counterterrorist unit would conduct the mission. The first phase of the plan called for six C-130 transports carrying troops and fuel to rendezvous with eight helicopters from U.S. carriers. The rendezvous point, deep inside Iran, was designated Desert One. From there, the helicopters would take the troops under cover of darkness to a second rendezvous point outside Teheran. An assault on the embassy and the rescue of the hostages would take place the following night.

Execution of the plan never got beyond the first phase. On Apr. 24, 1980, a dust storm forced two of the eight helicopters to turn back en route to Desert One. Of the six that arrived, one experienced a hydraulic problem. With only five helicopters left, the commander at the scene felt he had no choice but to abort the mission. As the troops and aircrews prepared to evacuate the area, a helicopter collided with a C-130, setting off an explosion in which eight servicemen were killed.

Subsequent investigations raised numerous reasons for the failure of the mission, including an inflexible plan, excessive operational security, and a lack of experience in joint special operations. Carter's presidency never recovered from the psychological impact of the hostage crisis, which contributed to his loss to Ronald Reagan in the 1980 presidential elections. (The hostages were freed immediately after Reagan took the oath of office, in January 1981, a final Iranian insult to Carter.) For the U.S. military, the tragic lessons of Desert One triggered efforts to improve the equipment, joint training, force structure, and range of U.S. special operations forces (SOF).

Reagan-Bush Years

Reagan represented the conservative wing of the Republican party. On Cold War issues, he reemphasized ideology as a critical factor in U.S.-Soviet relations, called for a defense buildup that well exceeded Carter's, and vowed, in general, to stand up to Communist aggression. On a practical level, this meant shelving ratification of SALT II (although he continued to abide by it after it expired in 1985). In place of SALT, the United States and the Soviet Union began Strategic Arms Reduction Talks (START) in 1982. Agreement proved elusive, as Soviet negotiators objected to U.S. sea-launched cruise missiles, the placement of U.S. intermediate-range missiles in Europe, and the Reagan administration's plan to develop a Strategic Defense Initiative (or "Star Wars") system that, if brought to fruition, could destroy incoming Soviet ICBMs. U.S. negotiators sought, but failed to obtain, Soviet concessions on their large land-based ICBMs.

Although both countries signed an accord in December 1987 to remove intermediate-range missiles from Western and Eastern Europe, they reached no agreement on strategic weapons until changes within the Soviet Union, followed ultimately by its disintegration, changed the international situation and opened the door to the START I treaty of 1991, which called for the reduction of strategic offensive weapons by 30 percent over seven years. In January 1993, Reagan's successor, Pres. George Bush, and Russian president Boris Yeltsin met in Moscow and signed a START II treaty, which would reduce strategic weapons to one-third their existing strength. Doubts about the efficacy of the accords were raised, however, when some former Soviet republics with nuclear weapons refused to recognize START I.

Against the background of strategic arms talks, the Reagan administration's hard-line foreign policy was most pronounced within the Western Hemisphere, where the president pledged to stop Communist expansion. In Central America, Reagan stepped up U.S. military assistance to the government of El Salvador in its struggle against Marxist-led guerrillas, supplied, in part, by neighboring Nicaragua. Nicaragua had already "gone Communist" with the success in 1979 of a popular revolution dominated by the Sandinistas, a Marxist-led guerrilla movement with an organized political base. To oppose the Sandinista government, the Reagan administration gradually came to support and then orchestrate a counterrevolutionary movement, the Contras. These anticommunist policies continued into Reagan's second term, but abated somewhat in response to congressional opposition, to a scandal over the means of providing weapons to the Contras, and to hopeful political changes taking place inside the Soviet Union. U.S. assistance did not directly produce the desired results in either country, but it did shape events in ways that both helped and hindered the attainment of a fragile peace in the region by the early 1990s.

Grenada

For the Reagan administration, there was a smaller, but highly dangerous link in the Soviet-Cuban-Nicaraguan chain that threatened stability and noncommunist governments throughout Latin America. The threat came from the Marxist New Jewel government on the island of Grenada

Army rangers disembark from helicopters at Point Salines Airfield, Grenada; the U.S. government believed that this runway would be used by Grenada's Communist government to threaten the interests of the United States. (U.S. Air Force)

Although Operation Urgent Fury, the invasion of Grenada, was beset with logistical and leadership problems, the mission's objectives were achieved; marines (above) *take a break from patrolling.* (U.S. Navy)

in the eastern Caribbean. In the spring of 1983, Reagan specifically warned the American people that Grenada was continuing construction on a "commercial" runway that could be used by military aircraft for purposes of subversion and aggression. In October, internecine strife within the revolutionary government of the island led to a violent coup d'etat in which an even more radical faction of the New Jewel movement seized power after executing the prime minister, several of his followers, and numerous protesters. The bloodshed and instability, when combined with the presence of U.S. medical students on the island who the administration alleged were now in danger, gave Reagan the pretext for direct action. First planned as a mission to evacuate the U.S. students, the U.S. invasion of Grenada that began on Oct. 25, 1983, had as one additional objective the overthrow of the island's government.

The final operations plan gave each service a role in the action. The navy would direct the invasion and provide naval support, while the air force would provide transport. Marines would land near Pearls Airport and secure the northern half of the small island. Army rangers would seize the controversial runway at Salines on the southwest tip of the island. From this base, U.S. forces would move overland to reach the students. Any resistance from the People's Revolutionary Army (PRA) of Grenada or from Cuban forces on the island was to be overcome. Meanwhile, SOF units would conduct operations around St. George's, a few miles from Salines. The 82d Airborne Division would provide follow-on forces to conduct stability operations once the combat objectives had been achieved. The Organization of Eastern Caribbean States would also provide troops to help stabilize the country.

Operation Urgent Fury, as the invasion was codenamed, achieved all its objectives, but not before encountering numerous problems. The invasion was to begin before dawn, but delays forced rangers to begin the attack on the runway at Salines during twilight. The runway itself contained many obstacles, which caused part of the force to delay its landing even further, leaving those already on the ground to face stiff resistance from the PRA and Cubans. The students were located at three sites, but because of insufficient intelligence data, the U.S. forces knew of only one location. (The students at that site, once they were "rescued," told the troops about the other two sites.) When the 82d arrived later that day, the fighting was still going on. The division's subsequent efforts to secure the southern half of the island were complicated by problems in communication with other services, a friendly-fire incident, and a chain of command that left questions as to who was in charge of the invading force once it was on the island. Eighteen U.S. soldiers were killed in the fighting, but that number could have easily been higher had the PRA been a more disciplined force. In retrospect, Urgent Fury is seen as a military success best known for the lessons it provided on how *not* to conduct a contingency operation. One product of the invasion, the Goldwater-Nichols Act of 1986, sought to improve the U.S. capability to conduct joint, or multiservice, operations.

Lebanon

The invasion of Grenada took place just two days after the U.S. Marine Corps barracks in Beirut, Lebanon, had been blown to rubble, killing 218 marines, 18 sailors, and 3 soldiers. The marines were in Beirut as part of a trinational force deployed to maintain the peace and help restore stability to civil-war-torn Lebanon.

The causes of the war were very complex. The political, religious, and ethnic divisions that rocked Lebanon in 1958, when President Eisenhower sent U.S. troops into the country, were still present. Fueling the volatile mix was the arrival of guerrillas of the Palestinian Liberation Organization (PLO) who had been forced out of Jordan in 1970. The outbreak of civil war in 1975 was followed by Syrian intervention. In 1982, Israel intervened to clear hostile forces out of southern Lebanon, then moved north to Beirut. As the Israelis inflicted enormous damage on the PLO in the capital city, the United States, by request, stepped in to help arrange a cease-fire and the evacuation of PLO fighters. U.S. marines participated in the evacuation. When the new Lebanese president was assassinated, various factions asked that the marines stay on as a part of a peacekeeping force that included French and Italian troops as well. For a year, the marines mounted patrols in their sector of Beirut and, in general, made their presence known as a neutral, stabilizing force.

As peacekeepers, the marines operated under strict rules

The 1983 bombing of the U.S. Embassy in Beirut, Lebanon, by Muslim terrorists changed the nature of the peacekeeping mission of marines stationed there. (U.S. Navy)

of engagement that defined when, why, and how they could employ their weapons. These rules continued in effect, even after events demonstrated that certain Muslim factions did not regard the United States or the marines as neutral. The bombing of the U.S. Embassy in Beirut on Apr. 18, 1983, was but one sign of the increased danger to Americans in the city. In July, renewed fighting in the civil war witnessed the first rocket attack against marine positions. A month later, Israel pulled its troops out of the area, and the Lebanese army (which the marines had helped to train) and Christian militiamen prepared to fight Muslim opponents. Caught in the line of fire, the marines were drawn into the war, even though their mission remained the same (peacekeeping) and few changes were made in the rules of engagement. Thus, when a driver pulled his TNT-laden truck into the marine compound on October 23, the guards did not even have ammunition in their weapons. By the time they had inserted ammunition, it was too late.

Given the dangers of a wider conflict inherent in the situation in Lebanon, there was little the United States could do in retaliation for the tragedy. No longer able to perform a peacekeeping role, the marines were pulled out of the country. The whole experience provided a lesson in the dangers a peacekeeping force can encounter when there is no general agreement that the force should be there in the first place, or when that agreement breaks down, as it did in Lebanon. For the marines, the bombing of their barracks in Beirut left an indelible imprint regarding the vagaries of low-intensity conflict and a commitment that such a tragedy will never be repeated.

The internecine struggle in Lebanon continued after the departure of the marines, and U.S. citizens continued to be targets of radical groups seeking revenge or hostages. Unlike Carter, however, Reagan did not let the hostages in Lebanon become the overriding issue of his presidency. His second term ended in January 1989, when he was succeeded by Vice President Bush.

Operation Just Cause

As with every president, Bush inherited a world in turmoil, but one in which the Cold War was about to come to an end. An indication of this changing world could be seen in Bush's use of military power. When he first employed U.S. forces in substantial numbers, it was to rid Panama of a dictator, an issue that had virtually nothing to do with Communism nor East-West balance-of-power calculations.

Gen. Manuel Antonio Noriega, the commander of the Panamanian Defense Force (PDF) and the power behind the civilian government in Panama, had at one time been an intelligence asset for the U.S. government. In 1987, however, he became an embarrassment to the United States when an officer he relieved charged the general with

U.S. troops and tanks secure a road in Arrijan, Panama, during Operation Just Cause, the invasion of Panama designed to protect U.S. interests there and to capture the elusive Gen. Manuel Noriega, wanted in the United States for drug charges. (U.S. Marines)

murder, corruption, and drug trafficking. The charges set off an internal political crisis in Panama, which expanded into a U.S.-Panamanian crisis when two federal grand juries in Florida indicted Noriega on drug charges in 1988. Noriega retaliated by stepping up his anti-American rhetoric and PDF harassment of U.S. service personnel based in Panama. Attempts by the Reagan administration to negotiate Noriega's removal from power had failed, and in May 1989, the general voided democratic elections that favored opposition candidates. In response to the ensuing violence, President Bush sent additional U.S. forces into the country to protect U.S. lives and property. When the PDF shot and killed a U.S. marine on Dec. 16, 1989, Bush ordered the military to execute a contingency plan for the invasion of Panama. Operation Just Cause began in the early morning hours of December 20 with U.S. attacks on PDF installations throughout the Panama Canal area and Panama City.

The invasion was the largest military operation since Vietnam. As in Grenada, every service participated, although most missions were assigned to army units. The plan had evolved over the two-year crisis, thus giving the forces involved time to coordinate and rehearse their missions. The combat operations went very well, as PDF resistance was overcome in the first day or two of fighting. Noriega, whose capture was one of the objectives of the operation, proved elusive, however. U.S. forces could not pin down his whereabouts until Christmas Eve, when he entered the nunciature in Panama City. As U.S. military commanders tried to negotiate his surrender, the 27,000 U.S. service personnel in Panama began the task of restoring the country and helping a democratic government consolidate its authority. On Jan. 4, 1990, Noriega surrendered and was turned over to U.S. Drug Enforcement Agency officers. He was flown to Miami, where two years later he stood trial and was found guilty of the

U.S. government drug-enforcement officers guard captured Panamanian general Manuel Noriega on the airplane that will fly him to the United States to face trial on drug charges. (U.S. Air Force)

charges brought against him. A total of 23 U.S. servicemen and several hundred Panamanian citizens died during the fighting.

Unlike Grenada, Operation Just Cause offered the military several lessons on how to conduct a joint contingency operation. The army especially trumpeted the rapid projection of U.S. power overseas as the kind of mission it could perform in a post-Cold War environment. As President Bush repeatedly told the American public, even with the Cold War coming to an end, the world was still a very dangerous place. Later in 1990, Iraqi dictator Saddam Hussein proved him right by invading Kuwait. Bush vowed that that act of aggression would not stand. The resulting war in the desert dwarfed the triumph of U.S. arms in Operation Just Cause.

7

The Gulf War: 1990–1991

For virtually the first time in American history, the armed forces of the United States were prepared to make a rapid transition from peace to war when Iraq invaded Kuwait on Aug. 2, 1990. A decade of generous defense budgets had produced the most sophisticated arsenal in U.S. history; public approval of operations in Grenada and Panama had raised military morale to a post-Vietnam War high; and the military services had developed the capability and willingness to conduct complex joint operations. The high state of U.S. military readiness contributed to Pres. George Bush's decisions to issue an ultimatum to the government of Iraq to leave Kuwait, because he had confidence he could back up words with action. Iraq chose to defy the ultimatum, but that defiance crumbled under the awesome forces unleashed by the armed forces of the United States and its allies.

ORIGINS OF THE WAR

On Aug. 2, 1990, Iraq surprised the world by invading its smaller neighbor, Kuwait. The Iraqi army, the fourth largest ground force in the world at the time, had been assembling along the border with Kuwait for some time, but Pres. Saddam Hussein of Iraq had repeatedly given assurances that he had no intentions of launching an attack. Reaction to the surprise invasion was swift. In New York City, the United Nations (UN) Security Council condemned the invasion, and in Washington, D.C., President Bush signed executive orders freezing Iraqi and Kuwaiti assets in the United States and halting all trade with Iraq.

Although condemnations of Iraq's aggression came from national leaders around the world, the invasion forces occupied Kuwait so quickly that it was a *fait accompli*. Spearheaded by three divisions of Iraq's Republican Guard

(Saddam Hussein's elite armored forces), the attack came without warning; in less than a week, Kuwait was under the complete control of the Iraqi occupation forces. The attack was so swift that the Kuwaiti military had virtually no chance to organize any defense, although some elements fought isolated small-unit actions before being forced south into Saudi Arabia.

As Iraq consolidated its gains in Kuwait, there was widespread fear that the attack would continue south into Saudi Arabia. While there was considerable sympathy in the world over the fate of Kuwait—a small, independent country swallowed up by a larger, more powerful neighbor—the threat to Saudi Arabia posed a greater problem. The area around the Persian Gulf contains more than half of the world's known oil reserves, and the bulk of them are under Saudi Arabia. If Saddam Hussein's aggression were allowed to stand, he would directly control the flow of oil from Iraq and Kuwait, and even without any further invasion, he was in an excellent position to intimidate Saudi Arabia and thus influence a major portion of the world's oil supply. The leading industrialized countries of the world, for whom oil is lifeblood, simply could not allow that to happen.

THEATER OF OPERATIONS

For centuries, the Persian Gulf has been a center of conflict. In recent years, oil has been the focal point of global attention in the area, but well before oil became the essential fuel of the industrial nations, the Persian Gulf was the stage for disputes over control of the oldest trade routes in the world. The focus of the Gulf War was the tiny country of Kuwait, but the conflict eventually involved a vast area of air, land, and sea in the Middle East.

Pres. George Bush's threat of war if Iraq refused to leave Kuwait was backed up by trained forces, a sophisticated arsenal, and the support of the American people. (David Valdez/The White House)

Kuwait is a small, arid country about the same size as the state of Hawaii. Its only resource is oil, and it relies on petroleum and petroleum products for 90 percent of its considerable income. Virtually everything the country needs to exist must be imported. Roughly triangular in shape, on the east it has a fairly long coastline on the Persian Gulf, and it borders Iraq on the northwest and Saudi Arabia on the southwest. Neither of the land boundaries offer any natural obstacles to invasion.

Iraq was a functioning country long before the discovery of oil. It is almost self-sufficient in agriculture, and its growing industrial capability makes it much more economically viable than Kuwait. Iraq has had border disputes with many of its neighbors, including an inconclusive eight-year war (1980–88) with Iran and a brief occupation of Kuwait in 1973. There has been a longstanding dispute between Iraq and Kuwait over the Rumaila oil field, which straddles their common border, and Iraq has long coveted the Warba and Bubiyan islands, which belong to Kuwait but which pose a potential threat to direct access between the Persian Gulf and the port of Umm Qasr, Iraq's only oil-shipping facility.

Iraq, centrally located in the Middle East, shares long borders with Iran on the east, Saudi Arabia on the south, and Syria on the west and a short border with Turkey on the north. Two very short borders with Kuwait on the southeast and Jordan on the west figured prominently in the Gulf War, the former being violated by Iraq to start the war and the latter serving as virtually the only access to Iraq during the UN embargo. Iraq's short coastline along the northernmost extremity of the Persian Gulf gives it access to the world's sea lanes.

U.S. Involvement

Middle East oil production was essential to the world's industrialized countries, so anything that threatened its availability became a U.S. concern. Pres. Jimmy Carter formally expressed the vital interest of the United States in the region in 1979. At that time, the concern was that Soviet expansion into the area could influence the oil-rich Persian Gulf states and thereby exert control over the highly industrialized West. One of the direct consequences of the Carter declaration was the establishment of the Rapid Deployment Joint Task Force (RDF) in the United States. Because none of the countries in the area would allow permanent basing of U.S. forces, the RDF was designed to be a planning staff. With headquarters in Florida, its mission was to be prepared to control any U.S. forces that might be needed in the Persian Gulf area. In 1983, under the administration of Pres. Ronald Reagan, the RDF was reorganized into a unified command and designated the Central Command (CENTCOM). CENTCOM was the headquarters that planned and fought the Gulf War.

U.S. military interest in the Middle East predated the RDF, however. In 1953, the United States had been instrumental in reestablishing in power the Shah of Iran and for 25 years supported him as a shield against possible Soviet expansion into the area. During that period, Iraq, a primitive military dictatorship, figured very little in U.S. foreign policy. But that changed when the Ayatollah Khomeini's revolution overthrew the Shah of Iran and established a fundamentalist Islamic government that branded the United States as the "Great Satan." In reaction to the fear of Islamic fundamentalism spreading throughout the Middle East, President Carter turned to Iraq, a secular state headed by Saddam Hussein, as a possible balance to Iran's aspirations.

United States and Iraq

In September 1980, Iraq invaded Iran over a border dispute. During the eight-year Iran-Iraq War, the United States, although publicly neutral, supported Iraq as the lesser of two evils. As the war wore on, the United States became more involved. In 1986, Iraq became the beneficiary of U.S. intelligence information on Iranian troop movements, and when Iran threatened the supply of oil from Iraq in 1987 by attacking tankers in the Persian Gulf, the United States responded by arranging for a number of Kuwaiti ships to fly U.S. flags. The reflagging arrangements made the ships eligible for American protection, and CENTCOM, the descendant of the RDF, deployed a forward headquarters to the Gulf to control the convoy operations. During that period of tension, Iraq, then a U.S. ally, attacked the *Stark,* a U.S. Navy frigate, with an Exocet missile, killing 37 U.S. sailors and severely damaging the ship. Iraq apologized for what it termed an accident and eventually paid the U.S. government $27,000,000 for death benefits and repairs. In view of the Iranian threat to Persian Gulf shipping, the incident was soon officially forgotten, and U.S. support continued for Iraq.

During the 1980s, the United States supported Iraq with trade and credit guarantees, in addition to assisting with the war. The two countries seemed to be comfortable with their relationship. Even Iraq's use of poison gas against the Kurds in 1988 drew only a mild reaction from the U.S. government. In spite of the continuing involvement with Iraq, however, the United States learned very little about Saddam Hussein, partly because of the closed nature of his police state and partly because primary U.S. interests at the time were elsewhere.

While President Reagan worked toward better relations with the Soviet Union, U.S. relations with Iraq received little attention. Ironically, while the lack of attention to Iraq may have contributed to the world being surprised at the invasion of Kuwait, the improved relations with the Soviets made possible the coalition that eventually forced Iraq out of Kuwait.

The Iraqi invasion of Kuwait and its subsequent threat to Saudi Arabia posed a potential threat to U.S. interests in the region that could not be ignored. In spite of the longstanding relationship with Iraq, the United States lost no time in determining where the vital U.S. interests lay. Not only had Saudi Arabia been a longtime friend of the United States, but the oil reserves under the Saudi sands could not be allowed to fall under Saddam Hussein's control. The deployment of substantial forces to the Persian Gulf during the reflagging operations had set a precedent for U.S. forces in the region, although very little of that deployment had involved land bases. Maintaining naval forces in international waters is one thing; gaining access for land-based air forces and ground forces, however, is quite different. Although the United States quickly voiced opposition to the Iraqi invasion of Kuwait, it needed land bases for substantial air and ground forces if there were to be a credible military option with which to threaten Saddam Hussein.

Climate for the Coalition
The United States was the major force in developing and maintaining the UN coalition that opposed Iraq. The cooling of east-west tensions and the recent good U.S.-Soviet relations contributed significantly to the coalition's success. For virtually the first time since 1945, when they had been allies in World War II, the United States and the Soviet Union were on the same side in a major international crisis. The reduced tensions allowed the United States and its European allies to deploy significant forces into the Middle East with little fear of the Soviet Union taking advantage of the situation.

Navy Task Force 155 is shown in the Red Sea during Operation Desert Storm. Task forces can be deployed on short notice. (Department of Defense)

President Bush and Sec. of State James Baker were very active in personal diplomacy, forging a spirit of cooperation among a disparate group of nations. The United States eventually made the largest military contribution to the coalition because it had the greatest capability. It did so, however, with the understanding that a significant portion of the cost of that contribution would be borne by other coalition members.

Major Participants

Iraq, the aggressor, had virtually no allies after the invasion of Kuwait but was not completely without support. On the one hand, Saddam Hussein attracted a group of countries that were predisposed to support almost any action that opposed the United States; on the other hand, he appealed to Arabs who saw the troubles of the Middle East as being the fault of continued U.S. support of Israel. The former group included Cuba, Yemen, and Libya. The appeal to Arabs was that siding with the UN coalition equated to being allied with Israel. It was a strong appeal that made the U.S. diplomatic effort to keep Israel out of the war a key element for the coalition's success. Both of these attractions to Saddam Hussein affected Jordan.

Jordan, sharing a border of about 100 miles with Iraq, was caught in the middle of the Gulf War. Nominally a pro-Western country, it had become closely allied with Iraq during the Iran-Iraq War. Since most of the inhabitants of Jordan are Palestinians who support any action that poses a threat to Israel, there was great popular support for Iraq. Although Jordan supported Iraq, it was an unhappy ally at best. While Jordan was a trading partner of Iraq, it also looked to Kuwait and Saudi Arabia for financial aid. Jordan was in a no-win situation if there were a war, and its ruler King Hussein (no relation to the Iraqi president) worked very hard to find a negotiated settlement to the crisis. For its part, Iraq was particularly anxious to maintain Jordanian support since it provided a way around the UN economic blockade.

The UN coalition that formed against Iraq was led by the United States in both its diplomatic and military actions. There were two general levels of support for the coalition. The coalition's strongest supporters were those who contributed military forces and wanted to remove Saddam Hussein and Iraq as a military threat to the area, but there were other members of the coalition, particularly China and the Soviet Union, who supported the restoration of Kuwait but had reservations about sanctioning the use of force. Between these two groups, however, the coalition had the support of virtually the entire world.

Coalition Roles

Saudi Arabia and other Arab states in the region hosted the UN military buildup, providing port facilities, airfields, and staging areas for ground forces. Military forces came from 30 different countries, while another 18 provided economic, humanitarian, or other assistance. The U.S. contribution was by far the largest in terms of forces and equipment, but some of the costs were shared by other members of the coalition.

Although the United States provided most of the coalition's armed forces, it did not exercise command over all of them. CENTCOM was the planning headquarters and coordinated the activities of the armed forces, but many coalition members would not allow their forces to be under the direct command of a U.S. headquarters. The Arab forces, for example, fought under a Joint Forces Command that operated closely with CENTCOM, and the European participants initially attempted to organize a command under the Western European Union. In the end, however, the British example and tradition of cooperation prevailed.

Nations that contribute forces to coalition military operations traditionally do not like to place their forces under the command of another country, but cooperation is generally the rule, not the exception. In the Gulf War, President Bush and his very personal brand of diplomacy—which appealed directly to his counterparts in the coalition—probably had much to do with the success of coalition command cooperation.

Israeli Position

Israel presented the coalition with a problem. Any participation by Israeli forces in the war could have torn the coalition apart. As members of the coalition, Arab countries could oppose Iraqi action, but had Israel been a member of the coalition it is probable that Iraq would have been able to convince a number of Arab states that fighting alongside Israel was intolerable, thereby driving a wedge deep into the coalition.

During the war, Iraq did try to lure Israel into active participation, while the United States worked to keep Israel neutral. Even though Israel prides itself on its military prowess, its restraint in military action during the Gulf War turned out to be a major factor in the coalition's success.

War Goals

Iraq sought to annex Kuwait as Iraq's 19th province. The use of force to accomplish that goal would also demonstrate Saddam Hussein's military power to the other Arab states in the area. Failing that, Iraq apparently set about to loot as much money and goods from Kuwait as possible, although the escape of the Kuwaiti ruling family to establish a government in exile in Saudi Arabia enabled Kuwait to transfer much of the country's financial assets away from Iraqi control. Whether Saddam Hussein had any grand designs about continuing the invasion south into Saudi Arabia is problematic. At the time, it was widely believed that an invasion of Saudi territory was a distinct possibility, and Bush used that belief to help foster support for the UN coalition.

Sec. of Defense Richard Cheney (center) *and Chairman of the Joint Chiefs of Staff Colin Powell* (back right) *arrive in Saudi Arabia during Operation Desert Shield to discuss military intervention against Iraq.* (U.S. Air Force)

With the benefit of hindsight, however, it is not clear that Saddam Hussein had any intent to move into Saudi Arabia. The invasion, brief and successful though it was, took its toll on Iraqi forces. The week or so of resistance put up by the Kuwaitis provided enough time for the first U.S. forces to arrive in Saudi Arabia and for the Saudis to begin their defensive preparations. Any further move into Saudi Arabia would have required additional Iraqi forces to move into Kuwait, which would have given additional time for defensive preparations. If Saddam Hussein had any designs on Saudi Arabia, they proved unrealistic within days of the invasion. The Iraqis simply went into a defensive posture, hunkering down to take whatever the coalition could throw at them.

The UN's stated goal was to get Iraq out of Kuwait and reinstate the legitimate Kuwaiti government. U.S. goals coincided with UN goals as far as they went, but the United States also apparently wanted to depose Pres. Saddam Hussein and destroy the capability of the Iraqi military to dominate the area. Although there was considerable international support for the use of economic sanctions to force Iraq out of Kuwait, support for the use of force was less widespread. Eventually, the strongest supporters of the coalition were able to gain a UN Security Council reso-

lution that approved the use "of all necessary means" to remove Iraqi forces from Iraq.

As it turned out, the UN goal was only a partial solution to the problem, but it was the only realistic solution. The UN tends to search for compromise in order to avoid the destruction of member states, so it was not willing to advocate the removal of Saddam Hussein, a legitimate, if not universally palatable, leader, from power. In this case, proposing the destruction of Iraq could have destroyed the coalition, since China or the Soviet Union, both of which had reservations about the use of force, could have vetoed any Security Council resolutions that included that goal. While the UN coalition attained its stated goal of restoring the government of Kuwait, that goal did not completely resolve the issue.

CRISIS DEVELOPMENT

U.S. opposition to the invasion of Kuwait proceeded on a number of fronts simultaneously. While diplomatic efforts moved forward to resolve the crisis peacefully, military planning began in anticipation that only force would ultimately drive Iraq out of Kuwait. The vast distances be-

U.S. soldiers of the 24th Infantry Division ready a defensive position in Saudi Arabia by filling sandbags to create a bunker in the desert. (Department of Defense)

tween the United States and other coalition countries meant that military preparations had to begin early and proceed rapidly. Within hours of the invasion, the UN passed a resolution demanding Iraqi withdrawal from Kuwait. On August 6, only four days after the invasion began, the UN announced worldwide economic sanctions against Iraq. Under President Bush's leadership, U.S. diplomatic efforts began to build a realistic coalition that could stand up to Iraq's aggression. In addition to the Western nations that had an interest in the oil, the coalition had to include Arab countries and the Soviet Union and be endorsed under the auspices of the UN, so it would not appear to be yet another attempt at American or European interference in the area. In Moscow, Secretary of State Baker and Soviet foreign minister Eduard A. Shevardnadze demonstrated the change in Soviet-American relations by issuing a joint statement calling for an arms embargo against Iraq. That kind of cooperation between the two superpowers demonstrated how badly Saddam Hussein had miscalculated the world situation. He needed Soviet assistance to maintain his armed forces, but Shevard-

nadze had promised Baker that there would be no resupplying of Iraq.

While the diplomatic process of building a viable coalition was going on in the UN, the United States also used diplomatic action to gain access to bases in Saudi Arabia and other Gulf states for air and ground forces. The Arab states in the region were reluctant to allow entrance to U.S. forces because of the close U.S. relationship with Israel and because of cultural differences. When Saudi Arabia agreed to allow access to U.S. armed forces, it was with two stipulations: that they would depart immediately after they were no longer needed and that the United States would not begin a war without Saudi approval. Diplomatic efforts were also necessary to arrange with other countries, such as Turkey, for permission to use U.S. forces based there against Iraq should that prove necessary.

Desert Shield Begins

The same day that the UN authorized economic sanctions against Iraq, Saudi Arabia requested assistance from the

United States for defense against a possible Iraqi invasion. Approval of this request by Bush put into motion a number of U.S. actions that had been waiting for the Saudi request. Although Bush had ordered U.S. naval forces into the area the day after the invasion, the movement of ground-based air and land forces could not begin until they had a place to go. On August 7, Operation Desert Shield began. The purpose of Desert Shield was to deploy enough U.S. armed force to deter further Iraqi aggression and to defend Saudi Arabia, no small task.

Sufficient sea, air, and land forces had to be moved into the area to pose a credible threat to deter Iraq from moving into Saudi Arabia. Although the U.S. Navy had eight ships in the Persian Gulf in August, they were not enough to pose a realistic threat directly to Iraq, but they would be needed to enforce the UN economic sanctions. U.S. naval forces from the Mediterranean and Indian oceans were initially deployed into the Middle East to interdict shipping to and from Iraq.

Although the enforcement of the embargo was not considered an act of war, the memory of the attack against the *Stark* in 1987 kept ships' crews alert. The enforcement of the embargo eventually involved ships from many navies, but the overall coordination effort was the responsibility of the U.S. Navy. The first interceptions were made on August 17; between then and the Iraqi acceptance of the cease-fire in April 1991, almost 7,000 ships were intercepted.

While the navy prepared to enforce the embargo, the air force and army began their deployments. The first U.S. Air Force tactical fighters arrived in the theater on August 8, and the lead elements from the U.S. Army were on the ground on August 9. During August, the United States initiated a number of actions that demonstrated just how seriously it took Operation Desert Shield; President Bush activated the ships of the Ready Reserve Fleet and the aircraft participating in the Civil Reserve Air Fleet and called up National Guard and reserve forces.

Getting forces to the Middle East was only part of the massive logistical undertaking of Desert Shield. Bases for air and ground forces were developed in the desert, and thousands of tons of equipment and supplies were shipped from the United States. The extreme temperatures and the desert terrain meant that troops had to be acclimatized and issued hot-weather uniforms, while vehicles and equipment required appropriate camouflage paint. All of this took time. Bush used the time to continue efforts to build international support for the use of force against Iraq. Saddam Hussein, for his part, apparently did not understand that it would take considerable time for a credible force to be assembled against him and let his only real opportunity to intimidate Saudi Arabia or any of the Gulf states pass by, watching the U.S. and coalition forces assemble against him.

By September, the coalition had enough firepower on the ground to deter any further invasion by Iraq, although the liberation of Kuwait by force was not yet an option. With the crisis stabilized by the military buildup, diplomacy took center stage in the crisis while negotiators searched for a peaceful solution.

U.S. WAR ORGANIZATION

In 1990, U.S. military forces, although on a peacetime footing, were organized to facilitate a rapid transition to war. The president, as commander in chief of the armed forces, has the authority to deploy those forces virtually anywhere in the world in time of crisis. In recognition of the worldwide national interests of the United States, the Joint Chiefs of Staff (JCS) developed in 1947 the Unified Command Plan (UCP), which provided for the command and control of U.S. military forces around the world. This plan, modified periodically as required by changes in U.S. interests globally, divided the world into areas in which a single commander in chief, or CinC, commanded all U.S. forces.

In 1990, the Middle East was in the U.S. CENTCOM area of responsibility. The headquarters for CENTCOM were in Florida, although during the Kuwaiti tanker reflagging, a forward headquarters had controlled the operations from a command ship in the Persian Gulf. Like other unified commands, CENTCOM had few forces permanently assigned in peacetime. The UCP was designed so forces could be tailored for a specific crisis and then assigned to the CinC.

U.S. Command Structure

When Iraq invaded Kuwait, Gen. H. Norman Schwarzkopf, an army officer, was the CinC in CENTCOM. As the CinC of a unified command, Schwarzkopf reported directly to the secretary of defense and the president, not to the chief of staff of the army. Known collectively as the National Command Authority (NCA), the secretary of defense and the president passed their instructions to the CinCs through the chairman of the JCS. At the time of the Iraqi invasion, the chairman was another army officer, Gen. Colin Powell.

Although the UCP with its CinCs had been in existence since 1947, a significant piece of legislation passed in 1987 had made some far-reaching changes in how the NCA, the chairman of the JCS, the uniformed heads of the services (who also serve on the JCS), and the CinCs dealt with one another. The Goldwater-Nichols Act of 1987 made the chairman of the JCS the senior military officer rather than simply the representative of the JCS, and it clearly established that the chain of command for the unified command CinCs went from the president and

Gen. H. Norman Schwarzkopf (third from left), *commander in chief of U.S. Central Command in Saudi Arabia, was highly visible during Operation Desert Shield as he visited with troops from other countries.* (U.S. Army)

the secretary of defense, through the chairman of the JCS, to the CinC. The chairman relayed directions and orders from the president and the secretary of defense, he did not initiate them. The service chiefs were not involved in the development of plans and operations in the theater of operations; that was the responsibility of the CinC and his staff, not the service staffs in Washington.

The first real test of the command arrangements under Goldwater-Nichols came in 1989 when Bush ordered U.S. forces into Panama to remove dictator Manuel Noriega from power. The command system worked then, so when Bush ordered U.S. forces into the Persian Gulf area, he was comfortable with leaving the planning and conduct of operations in the theater to the CENTCOM CinC, General Schwarzkopf.

Functions of the Military Service

Although U.S. war-fighting doctrine calls for the use of joint forces—forces drawn from all the services fighting together under a single commander—there is inevitably some disagreement among the services about how this works. The service rivalry comes about in large part because while the Department of Defense is apparently logically organized into three separate services for air, sea, and land operations, in reality the services are more complex than that.

The navy, clearly the service responsible for sea operations, also has a considerable land force in the Marine Corps and a large air force on its aircraft carrier fleet. Both the marines and naval air have the capability to project combat power a considerable distance inland, where they must work with the army and the air force. The marines also have their own air force, designed to work closely with marine ground forces. The air force, responsible for air operations including strategic bombing, tactical support of land operations, and air transportation, provides the army with close air support but is also capable of accomplishing strategic missions by itself. The army operates on land but relies on the air force and navy to get it to the theater of operations and support it there, and the army has significant air power in its large fleet of helicopters. Coordination of the services varied capabilities toward attaining a specific strategic goal in the theater of operations is the CinC's responsibility.

At the time of the Gulf War, U.S. military doctrine called for a CinC to have a number of component commanders. Doctrinally, there were to be three or four component commanders: one each for air, land, and sea forces, and one for special operations forces when required, although each CinC was free to organize his command as he saw fit. In the Kuwaiti theater of operations General Schwarzkopf had an air component commander, a naval component commander, and a special operations, component commander, but he did not have an overall commander of the land component, designating instead an army component commander and a marine component commander for the two major elements of U.S. ground forces.

CENTCOM Cooperation

When all the services work together in a joint operation such as the Gulf War, frictions inevitably occur. For example, although a CinC, like Schwarzkopf, can establish an air component under the command of an air force general, the navy and the marines may be reluctant to give up complete control of their air power. The navy is sensitive to the requirement to protect its ships at sea and wants to retain control of the air power it needs to do that, and the marines have designed their doctrine so that they have close air support readily available and are reluctant to lose control of that essential asset. Both the marines and the army would prefer to fight under control of their own generals, so naming a single land-component commander can be a sore point since one or the other of those services will not have one of its officers in command. Although these factors, and others, had an effect on operations during the Gulf War, the services did exhibit a high degree of cooperation with one another, demonstrating that in spite of long-standing rivalries, they are capable of conducting effective joint operations.

By the time the war was over, each of the U.S. services had made significant contributions to the success of the Gulf War. The navy protected the sea lanes, enforced the UN embargo, and contributed to the air campaign; the air force put the initial combat power on the ground in Saudi Arabia and planned, coordinated, and participated in the coalition air campaign; the army put the first light land forces in Saudi Arabia, which, along with marines aboard

Sec. of Defense Richard Cheney (left) *introduces Chairman of the Joint Chiefs of Staff Colin Powell, the senior U.S. military officer, at a press conference.* (U.S. Navy)

navy ships offshore, deterred further Iraqi aggression. The army eventually built up a powerful armored force for the land campaign, and the marines provided forces on land for the attack into Kuwait and forces afloat that kept a considerable Iraqi force tied down on the beaches.

INITIAL BUILDUP OF FORCES

In U.S. military doctrine, "joint operations" consist of forces from U.S. services working together, while "combined operations" involve a combination of U.S. and allied forces. Although the United States worked very closely with forces indigenous to the region and with forces sent into the region by other countries, only the U.S. joint forces were actually under the command of CENTCOM. The coalition's combined operations depended on cooperation of forces, not command.

The first goal in Operation Desert Shield was a show of resolve that would present a credible force to oppose further Iraqi aggression into Saudi Arabia. Military planning, therefore, initially consisted of simply getting enough military power into the theater of operations.

Naval Forces

The first forces the United States called on were the naval assets already in the area. The navy had eight ships in the Persian Gulf in early August, and they became the nucleus around which naval power assembled. By late fall, the navy had four carrier battle groups in the theater, each battle group consisting of an aircraft carrier with about 74 airplanes, at least 1 guided missile cruiser, 3–5 destroyers or frigates, and 1 or 2 support ships. There were also two surface action groups, each with a battleship, a missile cruiser, and a few destroyers or frigates. The surface action groups were designed to project firepower inland with the 16-inch guns and Tomahawk cruise missiles carried on the battleships. In addition to the surface forces, the navy usually had in the area between 6 and 8 nuclear submarines, which were also capable of launching Tomahawk missiles.

Air Forces

While the navy was able to begin assembling combat power in the theater almost immediately after President Bush decided to take military action, the air force had to wait for Saudi Arabia to decide whether it would permit a military buildup on its territory. The request for assistance came from the Saudi government on August 6; on August 8, the lead elements of the air force's 1st Tactical Fighter Wing arrived in the theater. By September 2, the air force had some 400 combat and 200 support aircraft available in the theater. These included a wide variety of aircraft required to conduct effective air operations, including

The aircraft carrier USS Saratoga, *underway with planes on its flight deck during Operation Desert Storm, was the nucleus of one of the battle groups, Task Force 155, deployed to the Persian Gulf.* (Department of Defense)

fighter, attack, bomber, surveillance and control, reconnaissance, electronic, tanker, and transport planes.

As the air component commander, Lt. Gen. Charles Horner of the air force began planning the air campaign.

Aircraft sent to Saudi Arabia included this F-114A Tomcat fighter plane, which is shown flying over burning Kuwaiti oil wells after Operation Desert Storm. (Department of Defense)

The capabilities of each of the different types of aircraft had to be integrated into the plan. Not only did he have to plan for the use of U.S. Air Force aircraft, but also those of the U.S. Navy and Marine Corps and aircraft from the 11 other countries that eventually took part in the air war.

Ground Forces

The potential threat facing Saudi Arabia when it requested assistance on August 6 was a land invasion from Iraq's army in Kuwait, so it was imperative that the United States deploy ground forces to deter that threat. Those forces, however, had to come from the United States. While the army and the marines both maintain forces available for rapid deployment by air, they are not equipped to face armored forces such as those in the Iraqi army. The land forces that could be immediately airlifted could demonstrate resolve on the part of the United States, but time was needed to build up enough force to have a chance of actually stopping Iraq if there really were an invasion of

Saudi Arabia. The heavy armored forces necessary to counter the Iraqi army had to come by ship. It took time to gather the shipping, move the forces from bases to ports, and make the trip from the United States to the Persian Gulf.

There had been some planning and preparation by CENTCOM in the years leading to the Gulf War, which paid off in the first weeks of Desert Shield. One of the ways a light ground force deploying by air can have an increased capability to fight is by the use of prepositioned stocks of weapons, equipment, and supplies. Although countries in the area would not allow CENTCOM to preposition anything on land, ships loaded with weapons, equipment, and supplies for army and marine forces had been based for some time in Diego Garcia, a small island in the Indian Ocean. By mid-August, both the army and the marines had moved their prepositioned ships to Saudi ports to support the first U.S. land forces arriving by air. At the same time, fast sealift ships were entering U.S. ports to begin moving the army's heavy armored forces to the theater. The end of August saw the 7th Marine Expeditionary Brigade and the army's 82d Airborne Division in the theater and ready to fight. Additional marine expeditionary brigades, which would eventually comprise the I Marine Expedition Force (I MEF), and three more army divisions, which would be organized for combat under the headquarters of the XVIII Airborne Corps, were on their way to the theater. The first phase of Desert Shield was completed by October, with adequate combat power in place to defend Saudi Arabia against almost anything that Iraq might attempt.

SECOND-PHASE BUILDUP

As it became apparent that Iraq had no intention of moving out of Kuwait of its own volition, the buildup of opposing military forces in the area continued. The coalition elected to develop an offensive capability that could be used for forcing Iraq to comply with UN demands to withdraw from Kuwait. As the size of the coalition force to oppose Saddam Hussein mounted, he increased the size of his army in Kuwait. At the end of October, there were 210,000 U.S. and 65,000 coalition troops in the theater. During the coalition buildup, however, Iraq had maintained a numerical advantage by increasing its forces in Kuwait from 100,000 to 430,000. At the time, it did not appear that there would be a voluntary Iraqi withdrawal in the near future, and the economic sanctions against Iraq did not seem to be having any immediate effect.

In late October, President Bush sent Sec. of Defense Richard Cheney and Chairman of the JCS General Powell to find out what General Schwarzkopf would need to transform his defensive force into one with the capability to

U.S. infantry troops construct a camouflage net shelter for their M-2 Bradley fighting vehicle during Operation Desert Shield; some heavy armored equipment had been prepositioned on an Indian Ocean island for rapid deployment. (U.S. Army)

remove the Iraqi army from Kuwait by force. An offensive force meant thinking in larger terms, and Schwarzkopf did. He recommended doubling the number of U.S. forces by mid-January 1991. Cheney and Powell took the proposal to Bush, who approved the increased force and issued the orders to implement it on November 8. The diplomatic efforts to avoid war continued, and the United States pushed for a UN resolution that would authorize the use of force against Iraq. By the beginning of November, there had been 11 anti-Iraq resolutions, none of which had seemed to sway Saddam Hussein.

On the domestic front, Bush and his advisers were working hard to maintain public support for the deployment and for possible war. Mindful of the lessons of Vietnam, where a long, apparently aimless conflict had finally brought widespread public dissent, Bush wanted to be sure he had the support of the American population if he ordered the country to war. Part of this campaign for public support was to compare Saddam Hussein to Adolf Hitler, making sure there was a clearly defined and thoroughly repulsive opponent, which would justify U.S. participation in a war.

Diplomatic Efforts

U.S. diplomatic efforts in November concentrated on persuading members of the UN Security Council that a resolution authorizing force against Iraq was necessary. Those efforts paid off on November 29, when the Security Council voted 12-2 to authorize the use of force to expel Iraq from Kuwait. With Cuba and Yemen casting no votes and China dissenting, the resolution set a deadline of Jan. 15, 1991, for Saddam Hussein to remove his forces from Kuwait.

Not coincidentally, mid-January was also the time by which the United States anticipated completing the second phase of the ground force buildup in Saudi Arabia. President Bush, ever mindful of the necessity to work as hard for peace as for war, surprised the country and the world on the day after the UN vote by announcing that he would "go the extra mile for peace." He invited the Iraqi foreign minister to Washington and offered to send Secretary of State Baker to Baghdad. The offer, he made clear, was not to make concessions, but to insure that Saddam Hussein understood the seriousness of the U.S. commitment in the Middle East. Tariq Aziz, the Iraqi foreign minister, and Baker did meet in Geneva, Switzerland, on January 9 for six and a half hours, but the meeting ended with the situation essentially unchanged.

President Bush got his final assurance of domestic support on January 12, when both houses of Congress voted to support the use of force if it became necessary. Although the House vote was overwhelming, the Senate gave it only a five-vote margin. With all the international and domestic support he could muster behind him, Bush signed a National Security directive that would send U.S. forces into battle on Jan. 15, 1991.

Additional U.S. Forces

While Bush developed public support for the use of force, the services worked to insure that the necessary combat power would be in place when it was needed. The navy deployed two more carrier battle groups, the marines sent the II Marine Expeditionary Force (II MEF), and the army moved three heavy divisions into the theater of operations. Two of the army's divisions came from its forward deployed forces in Germany, a clear indication of the change in the relations between the United States and the Soviet Union. Only a year earlier, it would have been highly unlikely that there would have been any serious thought of taking that much combat power out of the North Atlantic Treaty Organization (NATO). Saddam Hussein seriously misread the international situation if he was counting on support from the Soviet Union.

EVE OF WAR

In January 1991, as Iraq continued to defy the wishes of the UN, Saddam Hussein, on paper at least, commanded an impressive force. His army totaled 1,200,000 men with 5,500 tanks. It was an experienced army, having fought for eight years in the Iran-Iraq War.

The heart of the army was the Republican Guard, a force originally organized as the personal bodyguard for Saddam Hussein. The guard consisted of seven divisions, all well-equipped by Iraqi standards. Three divisions of the guard had led the invasion of Kuwait, but by January, they

had been withdrawn and replaced with regular infantry divisions. The Republican Guard returned to Iraq to form a highly mobile reserve for the defense of Kuwait. Although it is difficult to know with any precision, on the eve of the war, Iraq was thought to have had 530,000 troops in Kuwait armed with about 4,300 tanks, 2,700 armored fighting vehicles, and 3,000 pieces of artillery, all of which, if properly deployed, could present a formidable defense.

The doctrine under which Iraq fought its war with Iran was apparently the basis on which it prepared its defense of Kuwait. This doctrine emphasized positional warfare with attacks taking place only under highly controlled situations. Defensive positions were built around fortified triangular clusters held by infantry troops. The Republican Guard, which had increased in number since the Iran-Iraq War, received the best equipment and the best troops. While concentrating superior matériel and talented manpower in the Republican Guard made it a potentially powerful force, this policy tended to weaken the rest of the army by leaving it with fewer highly motivated troops and inferior leadership.

Iraqi Military

Iraq's military strength was centered in its army, but it also had a small navy of 43 ships and boats, which posed at least a coastal threat to the coalition naval forces working in the Persian Gulf. The Iraqi air force, like the army, looked good on paper. It was the sixth largest in the world, and its newest combat aircraft (received from its benefactor the Soviet Union) were rated as among the best in the world.

Based on experience gained in the Iran-Iraq War, Iraqi aircraft were kept in hardened revetments, which made them difficult, if not impossible, to destroy on the ground. It remains difficult to determine just how many of the 700 aircraft in the Iraqi air force were actually operational in January, but the embargo may have begun to take its toll on spare parts.

Coalition Forces and Plans

As the UN deadline approached, the forces of the coalition arrayed against Iraq had become quite impressive. In terms of naval and air power, the numbers were overwhelming, while on land they were at least approaching parity. Naval forces from 17 nations together deployed more than 170 ships in the Persian Gulf and the Red Sea. The U.S. Navy had 6 aircraft carriers and 2 battleships in the theater; these could hit targets in Kuwait and Iraq with aircraft and missiles. Coalition air forces consisted of more than 2,200 combat aircraft. Ground forces in the coalition, assembled from some 30 different countries, amounted to 450,000 troops armed with more than 3,000 tanks.

Once the deadline had passed, the coalition forces planned an extensive air campaign to wear down forward-deployed Iraqi forces in Kuwait, to destroy infrastructure in Iraq, and to destroy Iraq's capability to manufacture or deliver chemical, biological, or nuclear weapons of mass destruction. A land campaign was planned to insure that Iraqi land forces would be forced from Kuwait if they were not induced to do so by air power. At sea, naval forces protected the military buildup from interference, enforced economic sanctions, prepared to join the land-based air forces in the air campaign, and established an amphibious landing force that could be used in the land campaign.

AIR CAMPAIGN

When Jan. 15, 1991, the UN-mandated deadline, came and went with no sign of an Iraqi withdrawal from Kuwait, Operation Desert Shield became Operation Desert Storm, and the coalition opened offensive operations early in the morning of January 16 with an air campaign unprecedented in history. The plan was to take advantage of the one area where the coalition had a clear superiority over Iraq—air power. Coordinated by Lieutenant General Horner, a comprehensive air campaign began, applying aerial firepower throughout Kuwait and Iraq.

Initial Operations

Initially, the air campaign concentrated on gaining control of the air for the coalition forces. Once the coalition had control of the airspace over Iraq and Kuwait, the air campaign had a number of strategic objectives: elimination of Iraq's ability to strike Israel and Saudi Arabia with long-range missiles, elimination of Iraq's capability to produce biological and nuclear weapons, and destruction of Saddam Hussein's ability to control his forces. There was also some hope that the disruption caused by the air attacks would lead to the overthrow of Saddam Hussein.

While the initial phase of the Gulf War is generally referred to as the air campaign, it was not exclusively a U.S. Air Force operation. The U.S. Navy and Marine Corps contributed hundreds of high-performance aircraft to the campaign, and the navy launched numerous Tomahawk cruise missiles from its ships in the Persian Gulf and Red Sea to hit strategic targets in Iraq and Kuwait. Even ground forces were instrumental in the success of the air campaign. It has been reported that in the opening minutes of the campaign, a U.S. Army special operations team destroyed Iraqi radar, allowing coalition aircraft to slip into Iraqi air space undetected.

While it may never be known exactly how the coalition forces actually began the air war, it is apparent that the first wave caught Iraq unawares. Stealth and surprise marked the opening attacks, which hit high-value targets, blinding the Iraqis' integrated air defense system and disrupting their communications. Once that happened, the rest of the attacking aircraft could enter Iraqi air space. High-priority targets were anything that would minimize coalition casualties including known Scud (Iraq's long-range surface-to-surface missile) launch sites, Iraqi Air Force facilities, and surface-to-air missile (SAM) sites. The almost complete surprise attained by the first wave of the air campaign was apparent in that the attackers suffered no losses. Even though there were some coalition losses later in the day, the overall result on the air campaign's first day was fewer aircraft lost than would be expected in a training exercise of the same magnitude.

Success and Problems

The air war continued uninterrupted for five weeks, with virtually no resistance from Iraq. The number of combat missions flown by coalition air forces exceeded 88,000, with losses of only 22 U.S. and 9 other coalition aircraft. While the aerial bombardment was successful in wearing down the Iraqi army, cutting off basic utility services to the civilian population of Iraq, and eliminating Saddam Hussein's ability to communicate directly with his armed forces, there were two areas of frustration for the coalition forces: the Iraqi air force's refusal to fight and the Scud missile.

The coalition had expected the Iraqi air force to launch its fighters and interceptors early in the air war, at which point they could have been destroyed in the air by coalition aircraft. Instead, Iraq kept its aircraft on the ground in hardened revetments, which caused the coalition two problems: it was unknown whether the Iraqi planes had been destroyed, and because of this uncertainty, the coalition had to provide fighter escorts for the bombing strikes and maintain fighter patrols along the Saudi borders and over the navy's carriers in the Red Sea and Persian Gulf. The Iraqi air force did react when the coalition began using laser-guided 2,000-pound bombs that could be guided directly into the aircraft shelters, but the reaction was to send planes into Iran, rather than fight the coalition forces. Whether the flights to Iran were a sign of panic or part of a plan to use the planes later, it forced the coalition to continue its fighter escorts and patrols just in case the planes returned to the war from Iran.

The second frustration, the Scud missile, gained greater international attention and posed a greater overall threat to the coalition's war effort. The coalition had so much air power that the fighter patrols were more an inconvenience than anything else, but with the Scud, Iraq had the potential to fragment the coalition. Scud was a NATO code word for a Soviet-designed missile that Iraq had modified for use in the Iran-Iraq War by increasing the range so it could reach Teheran. Although the increased range allowed it to be used against Israel and Saudi Arabia, the modifications reduced the size of the warhead and the missile's accuracy.

Iraq launched its first Scud attack on the second night of the war, sending eight missiles into Israel with the hope of inducing that country to enter the war. The fact that the war was receiving worldwide television coverage meant that the Scud attacks could be seen live and thus increased their emotional impact. The West feared that if Israel joined into active hostilities against Iraq, the coalition's Arab members would refuse to fight alongside the forces of their longtime enemy, thereby destroying the fragile alliance. The United States exerted diplomatic pressure to keep Israel on the sidelines and also provided a timely solution to the Scud problem.

Before the war, the Scud was considered by many to be militarily insignificant because it was inaccurate and carried a relatively small warhead. The coalition also anticipated that it would be a rather simple task to eliminate the fixed Scud launch sites and apparently discounted mobile launchers as little or no threat. However, the mobile

launchers proved virtually impossible to locate. The Iraqi crews proved to be quite adept at setting up the launchers, firing a missile, and evacuating the launch site before it could be located and attacked by coalition air forces. While the Iraqis could launch Scuds almost at will (although they were pretty much limited to night firings because of the coalition's dominance of the air), the coalition was able to deflect most of them with the U.S. air defense missile system, the Patriot. The Patriot was a system that almost did not make it to the war. Plagued by problems during its development, the first antiballistic Patriot missile was delivered to the U.S. Army only in September 1990. Fortunately, Patriot proved more than a match for the Scud, intercepting virtually every one Iraq launched into Israel and Saudi Arabia, although the coalition's largest single loss of life was due to a Scud that made it through the Patriot radar system and killed 28 Americans late in the war.

A Patriot missile launcher, ready to knock down incoming SCUD missiles fired by the Iraqis, sits on the Saudi Arabian desert during Operation Desert Storm. (U.S. Army)

Among the coalition forces gathered in Saudi Arabia during Operation Desert Shield was the Egyptian II Corps, of which this ranger battalion, standing at attention, is part. (U.S. Air Force)

The remarkable success of the air campaign was a clear victory for the investment in technology the United States had made in the decades preceding the war. It was also the culmination of a longstanding U.S. belief that destroying an enemy by using massive firepower is preferable to expending lives. The coalition air campaign had a number of strategic objectives, but one of its primary goals was to prepare for the ground campaign that would eventually be required for the final punch if the Iraqi army refused to leave Kuwait.

THE GROUND CAMPAIGN

Coalition planning for military options, going from simply a defense against further Iraqi aggression to preparing an offensive that would force Iraq to relinquish its hold on Kuwait, evolved as Iraq simply stayed in Kuwait and built

up defenses. Prudent planning required an increase in land forces in anticipation of a ground campaign, and the recent changes in superpower relations provided a strategic situation that allowed U.S. ground forces to be withdrawn from Europe.

The coalition ground forces that forced Iraq out of Kuwait were as diverse as the air forces that conducted the air campaign, with some differences. The air forces shared some common operational experience. The non-U.S. air power came in approximately equal parts from NATO countries, where they had been working closely with U.S. airmen for more than 40 years, and from members of the Gulf Cooperation Council, which had trained closely with the U.S. Air Force. The universal language of aviation is English, which alleviated potential communications problems. Also, the air campaign was planned and coordinated by the U.S. Air Force, which operates according to a doctrine of centralized direction but decentralized execution, which gave each participating air force some flexibility in how it flew its assigned missions. The ground forces did not fit together quite so neatly.

In organizing the ground forces for combat, General Schwarzkopf did not attempt to put them all under a single commander. The result was an organization that relied more on cooperation than direct lines of command for much of its success. The largest contingent of land forces was from the U.S. Army and Marine Corps. The army forces were organized into Army Forces Central (ARCENT), with two major subordinate commands, XVIII Airborne Corps and VII Corps. The marine forces ashore were under the control of Marine Forces Central (MARCENT), while the marine forces afloat in the Persian Gulf remained under the control of Naval Forces Central (NAVCENT). The American special operations forces, which included troops from all the services, were organized into the Special Operations Command Central (SOCCENT).

Significant land forces came from other coalition partners. The French and British forces were organized to fight under the tactical control of ARCENT, but they remained under national command. The French forces, a light division, fought with XVIII Airborne Corps; the British forces, an armored division, operated with VII Corps. The other coalition ground forces were organized into the Arab-Islamic Joint Forces Command (JFC), which had two subordinate commands, JFC North and JFC East. The Egyptian II Corps, the third largest contingent of coalition ground forces (only the Saudi and U.S. forces being greater), were under the tactical control of the JFC but remained under national command.

The success of the ground offensive depended in large part on the air campaign reducing the effectiveness of the Iraqi army forces defending the Kuwaiti border and of the Republican Guard, the mobile armored reserve held in Iraq. One of the first things the coalition air offensive did was to blind the Iraqi high command. By keeping the Iraqi air force out of the air, it became virtually impossible for Saddam Hussein to conduct aerial reconnaissance to find out what the coalition ground forces were doing. A need for information may have been what prompted the Iraqi army in Kuwait to initiate offensive action along the border.

Battle for Khafji

At the end of January, Iraq launched a sizeable attack toward the Saudi town of Khafji in what became the first significant ground action of the Gulf War. Late on January 29, attacking with three brigades of tanks and armored infantry, the Iraqi army moved out of its defensive positions in Kuwait toward Khafji, a fairly large Saudi town that had been evacuated some months previously. The coalition's defensive line in the area was lightly held by Saudi forces

north of the town and by some small U.S. marine reconnaissance units in the town itself. The Iraqi forces moved easily through the outposts and quickly occupied the town. They were, however, prevented from reinforcing their initial successes as the coalition forces reacted with attacks on the Iraqi follow-on forces, and the marine reconnaissance elements in Khafji held their positions, directing air strikes on the Iraqis occupying the town. Iraqi success was short-lived. The Saudis, embarrassed by the Iraq attack, launched a counterattack on January 30 and recaptured Khafji with fierce fighting the next day.

Khafji was significant for two reasons: it provided the coalition with its first chance to see how the Iraqis would react to U.S.-style mobile warfare, and it illustrated the confusion that accompanies ground combat, as seven American marines were killed by "friendly fire" when a U.S. attack aircraft mistook their vehicles for Iraqi. The battle was the first and last Iraqi attack of any significance against coalition forces before the coalition's ground campaign started.

Their analysis of the Iraqi performance at Khafji encouraged coalition planners; they had every reason to believe that the Iraqis would not be able to stand up to the fast-paced offensive the coalition had on the drawing boards. Inspections of Iraqi's equipment showed it to be in poor condition; the Iraqis' performance under fire demonstrated that they could not conduct a combined arms attack; and the troops surrendering en masse when confronted by coalition forces indicated a lack of will on the part of the Iraqi soldiers. These were signs that the highly touted Iraqi army was not going to be able to live up to its reputation. The friendly-fire incident, however, was less encouraging. In this first sizeable engagement, U.S. forces had become confused and fired on each other. With forces from many armies armed with a wide variety of equipment poised to go into combat together, planners and commanders had to be concerned that this would not be the last problem of mistaken identity.

Preparations for the Ground Campaign

By the time of the Khafji attack, the coalition air campaign had all but blinded the Iraqi command. With no aerial reconnaissance, no access to satellite intelligence, and no capability for effective ground probes, Saddam Hussein could only guess what Schwarzkopf had in mind for the ground campaign.

The coalition's ground campaign began on February 24, but only after a series of air, sea, and land operations set the stage. As the date—known as "G-Day"—for the ground campaign approached, the air campaign shifted its emphasis to the Revolutionary Guard and the Iraqi army forces in Kuwait. Air strikes concentrated on knocking out bridges over the Euphrates River, which would impede both reinforcements from Iraq and retreat from Kuwait.

The II MEF aboard ships in the Persian Gulf conducted repeated rehearsals for an amphibious assault along the Kuwaiti coastline, and in the final hours before G-Day, the U.S. Navy moved its battleships *Missouri* and *Wisconsin* into position to shell the beaches.

Preparations for the amphibious assault were all part of a deception plan that kept six Iraqi divisions occupied along the Kuwaiti coast, effectively removing them from the actual battle. In a complementary operation, U.S. marines ashore conducted a series of feints that simulated a division getting ready to breach the defensive line where it met the coast. In reality, when the I MEF actually attacked on February 24, it was 100 miles west of where the phantom division had conducted its diversion.

In preparing his defenses in Kuwait, Saddam Hussein had obviously been impressed by the amphibious capability of the U.S. Navy and Marine Corps and the possibility of a major ground attack up the coastal highway that led from Saudi Arabia directly up the coast to Kuwait City, and he deployed his forces to meet that threat. What he did not see, however, was the possibility of an attack through the desert west of Kuwait. As early as October, CENTCOM planners had been looking at the open flank on the west, so when asked what he needed, General Schwarzkopf knew that he wanted the highly mobile armored forces the army kept in readiness for combat in Europe.

For some time, the army had been preparing its NATO-committed forces to fight the Soviets in Europe with its "AirLand Battle," a doctrine that emphasized attacking an enemy deep in its rear to disrupt force on the front lines. The doctrine depended on coordination between air and ground forces, hence the name AirLand Battle, and had been developed jointly by the army and the air forces. Once they knew that the additional forces were on the way, theater planners began developing the ground campaign. Until the air campaign could effectively blind Iraq, however, coalition armies stayed in their assembly areas south of Kuwait to bolster Iraqi perceptions of an amphibious assault out of the Persian Gulf in conjunction with a frontal attack directly into their defensive lines.

The ground campaign plan called for the army's XVIII Airborne Corps to be on the left flank of the coalition forces. The corps was a mix of units, each with specific capabilities that would allow the corps to move into Iraq on the far west and then strike deep into the country to cut the Iraqi army in Kuwait off from any support or reinforcements from the north. The corps consisted of the 24th Infantry Division, a mechanized force equipped with tanks and infantry fighting vehicles; the 101st Airborne Division, an air assault force armed with Apache helicopter gunships and airmobile infantry carried in hundreds of helicopters; the 82d Airborne Division, a light infantry force; and the 3d Armored Cavalry Regiment, a reconnaissance force.

Members of the 3d Armored Cavalry Regiment test an Abrams battle tank on the sands of the Saudi Arabian desert during Operation Desert Shield. (U.S. Army)

The French 6th Light Armored Division covered the left flank of the XVIII Airborne Corps as it swept through Iraq.

The center of the coalition force was occupied by the formidable VII Corps, which had four U.S. divisions (1st Infantry, 1st Armored, 3d Armored, and 1st Cavalry), all equipped with M-1 Abrams tanks and Bradley infantry fighting vehicles developed for rapid cross-country operations; the British 1st Armored Division, the "Desert Rats" famed for their World War II exploits in North Africa; and the U.S. 2d Armored Cavalry Regiment. The mission of the corps was to move north into Iraq after the coalition's left and right flanks had been secured, make a sharp turn to the right, and push into Kuwait from the west to attack Iraqi army units and the Republican Guard in northern Kuwait.

The right of the coalition offensive, which would breach the Iraqi defensive lines into Kuwait, consisted of the JFC and the I MEF. The marines, with the "Tiger Brigade" of the army's 2d Armored Division attached, were in the center, with the JFC North on their right and the JFC East on their left.

First-Day Operations

The ground campaign lasted only four days and, like the air campaign, was far more successful and suffered fewer coalition casualties than anyone dared predict prior to the war. The ground assault opened with the far right of the coalition line attacking at 4:00 A.M. on Sunday, February 24. These initial attacks were as distant as possible from the planned main attack to keep the Iraqis believing that they had to maintain their strength on the coast of Kuwait. The defenses were, as predicted, well-developed, but Iraqi resistance was surprisingly light. Iraqi units simply collapsed in front of the coalition advance, and by Monday, the swelling numbers of Iraqi prisoners were slowing the coalition advance as much as the defenders were. The marines could have been in Kuwait City by Tuesday, but the decision had been made earlier to leave the liberation of the capital city to Arab forces in the JFC. On February 27, the Kuwaiti 35th Brigade entered the city. By then, it was simply a matter of mopping up large numbers of disorganized Iraqi soldiers in and around the city.

Prior to beginning the ground attack, but after the Iraqis had been blinded, the XVIII Airborne had moved 500 miles west in 12 days to establish a forward logistics base and staging area for the offensive. While the JFC and the marines were beginning their assaults on February 24, the French 6th Light Armored Division, reinforced with a brigade of the 82d Airborne Division riding in trucks, began its move into Iraq to cover the left flank of the coalition as it prepared to advance into the desert. At the same time, the French moved forward on the left flank of the XVIII Airborne Corps, and the 24th Infantry Division (Mechanized) moved forward on the right flank. A heavily armored force oddly out of place in an airborne corps, the 24th Infantry was exactly the right force to take on the Republican Guard north of Kuwait. With the French covering them on the left and the 24th Division on the right, the 101st Airborne Division, in the center of the corps with its massive airlift capability, moved rapidly north to seize an abandoned airfield at Al Ubayyid in the Iraqi desert in order to establish a forward supply base. The only combat of the first day of the ground campaign in the west came when the assault forces of the 101st Airborne surprised and captured 500 Iraqis at Al Ubayyid.

Coalition Advances

The second day in the west saw the French 6th Division racing forward to attain all assigned objectives within 36 hours of the beginning of the campaign, the 24th Division making good time with little enemy contact, and the 101st Airborne struggling against bad weather to build up its advance base so it could continue the offensive. By the third day, the French had secured the left flank and were actively patrolling with little or no interference from the Iraqis. The 101st had its forward supply base in full operation and moved to its final objective, An Nasiriyah, where it cut off the Iraqi retreat route across the Euphrates River. By Wednesday, February 27, while Kuwaiti forces were entering Kuwait City, the 24th Infantry Division slammed into elements of the Republican Guard north of Kuwait, and while the Guard put up a better fight than other Iraqi units, it still was no contest. The 24th Division ended its advance in the Iraqi city of Basra, plugging the last escape route from Kuwait.

While the JFC and the marines tied up the Iraqis on the right in Kuwait, and XVIII Airborne Corps surprised them on the left in the west, VII Corps advanced in the middle with more than 2,000 armored vehicles to seek out and destroy the Republican Guard. The corps, originally scheduled to begin its attack after dark on February 24, moved its assault time up to early afternoon as a result of the excellent progress of the JFC and the marines in the east. Within hours, the corps had achieved a clean breakthrough, and the offensive moved rapidly north as planned. By nightfall on February 25, the corps was turning east to move into Kuwait. Having pivoted in a right turn, the corps advanced east on a north-south front into Kuwait, overrunning everything in its path. On February 26, the corps began to meet elements of the Republican Guard that fled before them. By February 27, with the 24th Infantry Division blocking the escape routes at Basra, the Republican Guard was caught. The premier division of

During Operation Desert Storm, some of the wounded were transported by helicopter to a fleet hospital in Bahrain, which was part of the coalition. (U.S. Navy)

the Guard, the Hammurabi Division, an armored force, prepared to fight a delaying action while the remainder of the Guard escaped. In the ensuing day-long battle, U.S. Army tanks destroyed the Hammurabi Division; the low visibility caused by a combination of poor weather and smoke from oil wells set ablaze by fleeing Iraqi forces gave the advantage to the U.S. forces. With their thermal sights, the U.S. Abrams tanks could penetrate the rain and smoke while the Iraqis, with no such devices, were almost literally fighting blind.

The coalition ground campaign was a three-pronged offensive, each with a specific mission that contributed to the success of the other. It was a bold plan that, given the disparate forces executing it, could have easily gone awry. While it did not run with the computer precision of the air campaign, the ground offensive succeeded like no other ground campaign in the history of warfare. But for one side to be so successful, it is likely to have confronted a foe of unusual incompetence. In spite of the many predictions of their prowess, the Iraqis turned out to be amazingly inept in virtually all phases of the Gulf War.

IRAQI REACTION

Immediately after his successful August invasion of Kuwait, Saddam Hussein's reaction to the international response of disapproval was mainly bluster. He apparently thought that after a brief period of criticism the Iraqi occupation of Kuwait would be accepted by the international community. His miscalculation, however, was twofold: he did not recognize that the Soviet Union's situation had changed to the point where it could not support the invasion, and he failed to predict the intensity of the U.S. response. The loss of active support by the Soviet Union—Iraq's primary arms supplier and its only real candidate to veto the UN Security Council's resolutions against the invasion—coupled with President Bush's tireless efforts to develop the opposing coalition and to commit U.S. military forces to the area, meant that it was really only a matter of time before Saddam Hussein's army was forced out of Kuwait. The real surprise of the Gulf War was that the cost to the United States and the other coalition members in terms of lives was so small.

Although one of the rallying cries for the coalition was prevention of a further invasion of Saudi Arabia, in retrospect it may be that Iraq had no intention of going any further than Kuwait. If there were further invasion plans, they would have had to depend at least in some part on continued Soviet support. Like all modern military forces, Iraq's army and air force required a reliable supply of spare parts and technical support to keep them operational. This kind of support was available to Iraq in quantity only from the Soviet Union. Even the relatively unopposed in-

vasion by Iraq's best ground forces, the Republican Guard, took its toll on equipment that had to be evacuated to Iraq for refurbishment. Continuing the invasion into Saudi Arabia was not possible immediately, and by the time Iraq could have been ready, it was apparent that the world was clearly opposed to the actions already taken.

The early decision to go on the defensive in Kuwait indicates that Saddam Hussein either had no real intentions of moving into Saudi Arabia or did not understand that it would take time for the coalition to build a defensive force there. He did have a small window of opportunity in which he could have made a limited excursion into Saudi Arabia, which he might have been able to parlay into a bargain with the Saudis to stop the coalition buildup. Because he did not take advantage of the necessarily slow buildup of coalition forces, he gave up the military initiative and went into a passive, positional defensive, offering not the slightest challenge to the buildup going on against him. In the initial period of the concentration of coalition forces in Saudi Arabia and the surrounding area, Iraq could have

A U.S. soldier guards a desert post following the withdrawal of the Iraqi army from Kuwait. He is holding an M-152A rifle on which an M-203 grenade launcher is mounted. The grenades are in pockets on his vest. (U.S. Navy)

inflicted at least some damage and casualties, which might have given the participating nations pause to consider the implications of a war.

Even after the air campaign began, the Iraqi response was almost nonexistent. One reason, of course, is that the initial coalition attacks were extraordinarily successful, but there was also a clear decision by Iraq to keep its planes on the ground. If there was any real plan behind holding the Iraqi air force out of the war, this plan had no significant effect on the war, although it did require the coalition forces to keep part of its air power available to counter possible Iraqi strikes.

Resistance Efforts

The Scud missiles amounted to Iraq's only real response to the coalition. They were used to attack Israel in the hope of enticing that country into combat, an act that could have destroyed the coalition. However, the U.S. Patriot air defense system effectively countered virtually all of the Scud attacks. Although the Scuds did not have the hoped-for effect, they demonstrated the potential of a relatively simple ballistic missile against even the most technologically sophisticated opponent. The mobile Scud launchers proved to be very hard to find, and coalition forces had to devote considerable time and resources in their attempts to eliminate the Scud threat. In the end, they were unable to remove it completely from the battlefield. The Iraqi threat of a Scud attack somewhere in Israel or Saudi Arabia remained viable up until the end of the war.

During the buildup of coalition forces, Saddam Hussein promised that they would be humiliated in the "mother of all battles" when they attacked his forces in Kuwait. At the time, it was not an empty threat. His army had had eight years of experience fighting Iran, and it had grown larger since the end of that war. By the time the coalition attacked on the ground, however, the Iraqi army had been worn down and demoralized by constant air attacks. Saddam Hussein's "mother of all battles" turned out to be not the meat-grinder defense he had anticipated but a sharp-edged offensive that sliced the Iraqi army to pieces in less time than its own invasion of Kuwait had taken in the first place. The swiftness of the ground attack completely degraded the already hard-pressed Iraqi army. The Iraqis offered virtually no resistance, and even when they fought,

After the withdrawal of Iraqi forces, coalition troops, such as those shown above, patrolled Kuwait City in armored personnel carriers equipped with M-2, 50-caliber machine guns. (U.S. Navy)

As Iraqi troops retreated from Kuwait, they left behind their equipment, their booty ransacked during the occupation, and burning Kuwaiti oil wells. (U.S. Air Force)

it was no contest against the coalition forces. The Iraqi army's experience in war, although considerable, was geared to defensive and positional warfare. It was prepared to fight another World War I based on the lessons they learned in the war with Iran, but the coalition armies attacked using the tactics and operations developed from their experience in World War II. The Iraqi army simply could not deal with the rapid war of movement that the coalition forced upon them.

At sea, the 43 ships and boats of the Iraqi navy were sunk or otherwise rendered ineffective during the course of the war. Although they might have had an effect during the buildup by slowing shipping or drawing additional air power away from the air and ground campaigns, they had little or no impact on the results of the Gulf War.

Cease-fire

With the Iraqi acceptance of U.S. terms, President Bush halted the ground attack on February 28 with a cease-fire at 8:00 A.M., just 100 hours after it began. The ground campaign had ended much sooner than expected. General Schwarzkopf's so-called Hail Mary maneuver around the Iraqi right flank was bold and obviously surprised Iraq. The coalition casualties were amazingly light during both the air and ground campaigns.

Although the Gulf War attained the UN goal of forcing Iraq out of Kuwait, and although the cease-fire terms allowed UN inspection teams into Iraq to seek out weapons of mass destruction, Saddam Hussein remained in power.

At the end of the war, Iraq was no longer the dominant military power in the region, but it had not been rendered impotent. In spite of the overwhelming defeat of his military forces and the obvious widespread destruction of his country by the bombing campaign, Saddam Hussein appeared to have lost little of his prestige within Iraq. Even as the coalition began withdrawing its military forces and

In the aftermath of Operation Desert Storm, Gen. H. Norman Schwarzkopf (right) *personally visited the allied troops that had taken part in the operation; here, he thanks Maj. Gen. Barry McCaffrey of the 24th Infantry Division.* (U.S. Air Force)

Gen. H. Norman Schwarzkopf, on a tour of coalition countries after Operation Desert Storm, arrives at Batteen Air Base in the United Arab Emirates. (U.S. Air Force)

the UN began to impose the cease-fire terms, he began to obstruct inspection teams and ruthlessly to suppress internal uprisings opposing his continued rule.

On the battlefield, the results of the war were clear: the Iraqi military had suffered a shattering defeat. In other areas, however, the results were shades of gray. The Gulf War changed the balance of power in the region, but both Iraq and Kuwait lay in need of massive reconstruction. During its occupation of Kuwait, Iraq had looted the country. Iraqi matériel destroyed on the roads leading from Kuwait City to Iraq included large numbers of stolen civilian vehicles loaded with a wide variety of consumer goods. Kuwaiti oil released into the Persian Gulf and oil fields set afire by Iraq forces caused immense environmental damage and destroyed a considerable amount of oil. The damage to Kuwait's oil production facilities and the damage inflicted on Iraq set back the economy of the entire area. The rebuilding of Iraq and Kuwait would require considerable time and money.

Iraq was bloodied and bowed at the end of the war, but not knocked out. Saddam Hussein retained his Republican Guard relatively intact, and he challenged the UN cease-fire inspection teams at every opportunity. Even though Iraq clearly was the big loser in the Gulf War, Saddam Hussein continued to be in charge of the country. He never admitted defeat and actually acted in some respects as though he had won a victory.

The Gulf War provided a stunning example of the capabilities of modern armed forces, demonstrated that relations among the superpowers had changed for the better, and bolstered UN prestige by providing a forum in which member countries could express their collective outrage at Iraq's aggression. The war did not accomplish the elimination of Saddam Hussein, complete neutralization of Iraq as a threat to the stability of the Middle East, nor the solution to the Israeli-Arab problem.

U.S. MILITARY PERFORMANCE

The armed forces of the United States had been successful because their complex high-technology weapons systems worked, the doctrine of all of the services worked, the leadership at all levels of command was good, and the troops were excellent. Each of the services made an essential contribution to the success of the Gulf War.

The air force provided the first combat power in the area on the ground, and it controlled and supported the air war. The navy protected the essential sea lanes of communications, provided combat power at sea plus air power that extended over land, and had the capability to contribute additional ground power through the marines on ships. The Marine Corps was an essential part of the ground campaign: its forces breached defensive lines in Kuwait, were involved in first ground combat, and provided deception with forces afloat offshore that tied down six Iraqi divisions waiting for an amphibious assault. The army had light forces on the ground early to provide a show of U.S. resolve, provided the heavy armored forces that were decisive in the ground war, and provided logistics support to the U.S. and coalition forces ashore. Each of the services contributed elements of the special operations forces, most of whose contributions remain secret. It is known that they operated throughout the war well inside Iraq and Kuwait, providing indispensable support to the conventional air and ground campaigns.

Ironically, at the end of one of their most stunning successes, the U.S. forces returned home to face one of their largest reductions in force. With the end of the Cold War and the improved relations with the Soviet Union, the general feeling among Americans was that the United States could safely reduce the military establishment that had given it victory in the Gulf War and had contributed greatly to ending the Cold War. While the beginning of the Gulf War found the military forces of the United States better prepared for war than at any time in their history, the end of the war saw the return of the traditional U.S. response of reducing its armed forces in time of peace.

PART II

Biographies

ABRAMS, CREIGHTON WILLIAMS
(1914–1974)

U.S. army commander, Abrams was born in Springfield, Massachusetts. Following graduation from West Point in 1936, his first assignment was to the 7th Cavalry Regiment at Fort Bliss, Texas, where he spent four years as a troop officer in the horse cavalry.

World War II. He volunteered for the newly established Armored Force in 1940 and helped establish the 4th Armored Division. He served with that unit throughout World War II, first as commander of the 37th Tank Battalion, then as a Combat Command commander. Later, Gen. George S. Patton, in whose 3d Army the 4th Armored was usually to be found, said, "I'm supposed to be the best tank commander in the Army, but I have one peer, Abe Abrams. He's the world's champion."

During the war, Abrams won two Distinguished Service Crosses, commanded the tank column that punched through to Bastogne to relieve the encircled 101st Airborne Division during the Battle of the Bulge, led the dash to and across the Rhine, and used up or wore out seven tanks, all of them appropriately named "Thunderbolt."

Career Development. Following World War II, Abrams headed the Tactics Department of the Armor School at Fort Knox, Kentucky, where he was responsible for incorporating into the program of instruction the doctrine and procedures successfully employed by armored forces during World War II. Then he returned to Europe and the Army of Occupation to command in succession the 63d Tank Battalion and the 2d Armored Cavalry Regiment, the showcase regiment of the U.S. Constabulary.

At the end of the Korean War (1953), Abrams was successively chief of staff of three different corps—the I, X, and IX. After next serving as chief of staff at Fort Knox, he became a brigadier general and was given a reserve affairs assignment in the Pentagon. In what many regular officers would consider a career backwater, Abrams became so indispensable that in the General Staff committee on reserve matters, with Chief of Staff Gen. Maxwell Taylor in the chair, far more senior officers deferred offering their opinions until they had heard Abrams's views.

Abrams commanded the 3d Armored Division in Europe during the period of the Berlin Crisis in the early 1960s. He concentrated single-mindedly on readiness, maintenance, and professionalism. Will Lang, who had reported the breakthrough to Bastogne for *Life* magazine, now filed for a *Time* cover story on Abrams that his peers said he was not an army politician, that "his idea of how to get ahead is to do the best possible job on the assignment he has at the moment." Abrams's corps commander called him "the outstanding armor commander of his generation, open, frank, sincere, completely dedicated to the Army and the highest ideals of service."

Civil Rights Crises. Service of a radically different kind was just ahead. Again assigned to Pentagon duty, Abrams was sent as the chief of staff's personal representative to oversee the use of troops at Oxford, Mississippi, when James Meredith was enrolled as the first black to enter the University of Mississippi. This brought Abrams into close contact with both Atty. Gen. Robert F. Kennedy and Pres. John F. Kennedy, who credited Abrams's coolness and presence with averting further violence once troops were committed to take over from hard-pressed U.S. marshals. Subsequently, Abrams was given similar assignments at Birmingham, Alabama, and elsewhere, earning the same kind of confidence for his professional and low-key performance.

Vietnam War. Following command of V Corps in Germany, in 1964, Abrams was promoted to full general and appointed vice chief of staff of the army during the period of the buildup for the war in Vietnam, a task made more difficult by the decision of Pres. Lyndon B. Johnson not to call up the reserves. Abrams served for three years as vice chief under tremendous pressure to meet the ever-growing requirements for army troops, units, and equipment.

Having built the force, Abrams was in 1967 ordered to Vietnam, first as deputy commander for a year, then for four more years as commander, U.S. Military Assistance Command Vietnam. During the first year, he concentrated on improving South Vietnamese forces, then during the fighting of Tet 1968 took command of the crucial battles in the northern provinces. "It was a critical time," recalled a senior officer. "It could have gone down the tube." But "once Abe was up there, you could almost hear the thunder striking against those hills against Phu Bai." South Vietnamese lieutenant general Ngo Quang Truong said that when Abrams arrived on the battlefield, "he was decisive, he gave me confidence." Abrams, said Truong, "was a pure soldier."

As overall commander during 1968–72, Abrams significantly revised the approach to fighting the war, pulling together in "one war" the combat operations, pacification, and upgrading of the Vietnamese forces; simultaneously shifting the measure of merit from "body count" in a war of attrition to population security; and insisting that stringent measures be taken to reduce the harm done to noncombatants by military operations. He worked to put the Vietnamese in a position to defend themselves, while his own army was incrementally sent home before him. A journalist, summing up Abrams's superb performance as commander in Vietnam, described him in memorable terms as a "general who deserves a better war." Abrams also retained a reputation for absolute personal integrity, refusing to issue the optimistic predictions of success that had plagued earlier regimes. Asked what he saw ahead in

Vietnam, his reply was characteristic: "I look for more hard fighting."

Command in Vietnam was, during Abrams's tenure, arguably the most difficult assignment any top American soldier in the field has ever had to face. Not only was the tug of gravity away from the theater of operations and back toward the United States, but a whole host of political and societal problems was having its impact on the American armed forces. A building antiwar movement at home; increases in drug abuse, racial intolerance, and dissent; and the stresses induced by manning a large force by means of an increasingly unpopular draft were all reflected in the forces in the field.

Final Days. In 1972, Abrams came home to become chief of staff of an army desperately in need of leadership and reform. He set about the slow and painful task of restoring the integrity, self-confidence, and self-respect of the force, at the same time faced with the problem of transitioning the army to an all-volunteer environment. Abrams chopped back headquarters staffs (including his own), eliminated unproductive layers, built three additional divisions with no increase in overall strength, and improved the "tooth to tail" ratio, the balance between combat and support forces, something he thought there was plenty of room to do. "In my experience in three wars," he said, "I don't recall that it was ever very crowded at the front." Most of all, he set the example of his own integrity, dedication, and professionalism.

"I cannot emphasize too strongly the critical necessity for candor," Abrams cabled his commanders worldwide. "Tell it like it is." And always there was his dedication to the soldier. "People are not *in* the Army," he would say. "People *are* the Army." And "by people I do not mean personnel," he added. "I mean living, breathing, serving human beings. They are at the heart of our preparedness, and this preparedness—as a nation and as an Army—depends upon the spirit of our soldiers. It is the spirit that gives the Army life. Without it we cannot succeed."

Abrams died two years into his tour as chief of staff. But already he had charted a course that, carried on by others, restored the army to health and competence. The degree to which he succeeded is reflected in the fact that later army leaders attributed to Abrams the initiatives and reforms that led to the victorious army of Operation Desert Storm during the Gulf War of 1990–91.

Abrams's death sent a shock wave through the army. He was one of the most celebrated, admired, beloved, and trusted American soldiers of any rank and any era. He had understood the role of the chief of staff as spiritual leader of the army and had charted a course that was restoring the professionalism and pride in service of that institution.

Sec. of Defense James Schlesinger, eulogizing Abrams as "an authentic national hero," recalled his legendary battlefield exploits, but also that "Abe had those additional dimensions of morality, wit, experience, judgment and serenity that marked him as a superb commander and organizer as well as field soldier."

He was a warm and human personality, one who could laugh and sing and drink and tell stories with the same enthusiasm he brought to the business of being a soldier. As one who served under him in battle put it so well: "He wasn't perfect, but he was special."

Bibliography: Buckley, Kevin, "General Abrams Deserves a Better War," *New York Times Magazine* (Oct. 5, 1969); Flanagan, Edward M., "Abe: His Wit and Wisdom," *Army* (Feb. 1977); Hollis, Harris W., "The Heart and Mind of Creighton Abrams," *Military Review* (Apr. 1985); Sorley, Lewis, *Thunderbolt: General Creighton Abrams and the Army of His Times* (Simon & Schuster, 1992).

Lewis Sorley

ACHESON, DEAN GODDERHAM
(1893–1971)

U.S. secretary of state (1949–53), Acheson was born in Middletown, Connecticut. In 1946, as Pres. Harry S Truman's undersecretary of state, he proposed the international relief action and bilateral arrangements that became the essentials of the European Relief Program, which eventually appropriated $350,000,000 in aid for the war-torn nations of Austria, Greece, Italy, Hungary, and Poland. When Congress initially failed to recognize the need of U.S. relief for these countries, Acheson painted a stark picture of Soviet Communism poised and waiting to intercede in Eastern Europe and the Mediterranean. An advocate of "containment," Acheson quickly became the spokesman and master architect for the Truman Doctrine, which sought to block Communism's expansion in the immediate post-World War II years.

On Oct. 1, 1946, Undersecretary Acheson reasserted the U.S. intention to remain in Korea until that nation was united and free. The following September, the United States notified the Soviet Union of its intention to refer the question of Korean independence to the United Nations. On May 10, 1948, elections were held in U.S.-occupied South Korea and the Republic of Korea was proclaimed at Seoul. On Sept. 9, 1948, a "People's Republic" claiming authority over the entire country was proclaimed in North Korea. On June 25, 1950, North Korea invaded the South and Acheson's containment policy was put to its most severe test.

Despite his key role in the development of the containment policy, Acheson soon became the target of Republican criticism of Truman's foreign policies. His State Department was the primary target of Sen. Joseph R. McCarthy's charges of Communist infiltration of the government during the early 1950s. Nevertheless, Acheson survived these attacks, and over time, his policies became much admired in conservative circles. He later became a defender of U.S. policy in Vietnam. Near the end of his life, Acheson remained a controversial figure as he defended the Southeast Asia policy of Pres. Richard M. Nixon.

Bibliography: Acheson, Dean G., *Present at the Creation: My Years in the State Department* (Norton, 1969).

M. Guy Bishop

ADAMS, PAUL DEWITT (1906–1987)

U.S. army officer, Adams was born in Heflin, Alabama. He graduated from West Point in 1929, but his military career skyrocketed during World War II, which he ended as a temporary brigadier general. Adams again excelled in combat during the difficult attrition warfare of the later Korean War (1951–53), where he commanded two different infantry divisions and was chief of staff of the 8th Army.

In July 1958, as a major general, Adams was ordered to Beirut as commander of U.S. land forces in the Lebanon intervention. His measured response to various provocations prevented any escalation of violence and allowed Lebanon to reestablish a compromise government that endured into the 1970s. After this performance, it was perhaps inevitable that, in 1961, the Kennedy administration chose Adams to be the first commander in chief, Strike Command (CinCStrike). As CinCStrike, he coordinated the U.S. airlift during the first Congo crisis and prepared forces for deployment during the 1962 Cuban Missile Crisis.

Bibliography: Spiller, Roger J., *"Not War, But Like War": The American Intervention in Lebanon* (Greenwood Press, 1981).

Jonathan M. House

ALDRIN, EDWIN EUGENE, JR. (1930–)

U.S. astronaut, "Buzz" Aldrin was born in Montclair, New Jersey. Upon graduating from West Point in 1951, he entered the air force, where he received pilot training. Aldrin flew 66 combat missions in F-86s in Korea, destroying two MIG-15 aircraft. Aldrin served in several other air force units until his selection as a member of the third group of astronauts by NASA in October 1963. On Nov. 11, 1966, he orbited aboard the *Gemini 12* spacecraft, a four-day 59-revolution flight that successfully ended the Gemini program.

Aldrin was chosen as a member of the three-man *Apollo 11* crew that landed on the moon on July 20, 1969, fulfilling the mandate of Pres. John F. Kennedy to land Americans on the moon before the end of the decade. Aldrin and *Apollo 11* commander Neil A. Armstrong spent about 20 hours on the moon before returning to the orbiting *Apollo 11* command module. The spacecraft and the lunar explorers returned to Earth on July 24.

Astronaut Edwin "Buzz" Aldrin made history on July 20, 1969, when he and fellow crewman Neil Armstrong became the first two people to walk on the moon. (NASA)

In 1971, Aldrin returned to the air force. He retired a year later and continued to be an important analyst of the space program.

Bibliography: Aldrin, Edwin E., Jr., with Wayne Warga, *Return to Earth* (Random House, 1973); Compton, W. David, *Where No Man Has Gone Before: A History of Apollo Lunar Exploration Missions* (Nat. Aeronautics & Space Admin., 1989); Murray, Charles, and Catherine Bly Cox, *Apollo: The Race to the Moon* (Simon & Schuster, 1989).

Roger D. Launius

ALMOND, EDWARD ("NED") MALLORY (1892–1979)

U.S. army officer, Almond was born in Luray, Virginia. He graduated from the Virginia Military Institute in 1915 and commanded machine-gun units during World War I, exhibiting both bravery and exhaustive attention to detail.

In September 1942, Almond assumed command of the 92d Infantry Division (Colored). Despite the dedication and bravery of this division, the 92d repeatedly failed both in training and in combat in the Italian theater (1944–45). Almond himself, however, was never held responsible for these failures. Instead, in 1946, Major General Almond was sent to Japan, where he became chief of staff to Gen. Douglas MacArthur in 1949. In August 1950, MacArthur appointed Almond to command X Corps, the U.S. Army-Marine component of the amphibious invasion at Inchon, Korea.

Almond was so dedicated to MacArthur's strategic concept that he rode roughshod over any objections about the difficulties of the Inchon landing. Marine major general Oliver Smith, commander of the 1st Marine Division, clashed repeatedly with Almond during the planning and conduct of the invasion. The matter came to a head on Sept. 23–24, 1950, when stubborn North Korean resistance delayed reoccupation of the capital city of Seoul. General Almond bypassed Smith and adjusted the boundary between the U.S. 1st Marine and 7th Infantry divisions, assigning the latter to clear southeastern Seoul.

Throughout the subsequent withdrawal of X Corps, its invasion of eastern North Korea, and the difficult battles of the Chinese intervention, Almond loyally executed MacArthur's wishes even at the risk of overextending his forces. In addition, his prejudicial treatment of segregated black and Puerto Rican units caused further controversy. Almond managed the difficult evacuation of X Corps from North Korea, but Smith's distrust was only increased by Almond's performance during the withdrawal.

Recommitted in central Korea, X Corps continued to have mixed success in 1951. In particular, Almond pressed northward in Operation Roundup in February, ignoring intelligence warnings that he would be the focus of a major Chinese counterattack. This counterattack destroyed two Korean divisions under Almond's control. After the Korean War, Almond served as commandant of the Army War College in Carlisle, Pennsylvania, from 1951 until 1953. He retired in 1953 with the rank of lieutenant general and worked in the public relations field.

Bibliography: Blair, Clay, *The Forgotten War: America in Korea, 1950–1953* (Random House, 1987); Stanton, Shelby L., *America's Tenth Legion: X Corps in Korea, 1950* (Presidio Press, 1989).

Jonathan M. House

ALVAREZ, EVERETT, JR. (1937–)

U.S. naval officer who became the first U.S. pilot shot down and captured during the Vietnam conflict, Alvarez was born in Salinas, California. On Aug. 5, 1964, he participated in the first air attack on targets inside North Vietnam as retaliation for the Gulf of Tonkin incident. Taking off from the carrier *Constellation* in an A-4 Skyhawk fighter-bomber, Alvarez bombed targets in Hon Gai harbor as part of a raid against four North Vietnamese patrol-boat bases and oil facilities. As he returned to his carrier, Alvarez's plane was hit by enemy flak. Forced to abandon the crippled craft, Alvarez was captured and taken to the infamous "Hanoi Hilton" prison, where he endured loneli-

ness and torture for eight and a half years. After returning home with other prisoners of war in 1973, Alvarez retired from the navy in 1980 with the rank of commander.

Bibliography: Alvarez, Everett, Jr., and Anthony S. Pitch, *Chained Eagle* (Donald I. Fine, 1989); Maitland, Terrence, and Steven Weiss, *The Vietnam Experience: Raising the Stakes* (Boston Pub. Co., 1982); Moss, George Donelson, *Vietnam: An American Ordeal* (Prentice-Hall, 1990).

John F. Wukovits

ANDERSON, GEORGE WHALEN, JR. (1906–)

U.S. naval officer, Anderson was born in Brooklyn, New York. He graduated from Annapolis in 1927 and entered naval aviation three years later. He spent much of World War II in staff and shore billets but had one combat tour on the new carrier *Yorktown*. He attained flag rank in 1954 and subsequently held such posts as commander, Taiwan Patrol Force, and commander, Carrier Division 6. Prior to his appointment as chief of naval operations (CNO) in 1961, Anderson commanded the 6th Fleet. His tenure as CNO was marred by a series of disagreements with Sec. of Defense Robert McNamara over such issues as budgets, McNamara's insistence that a new tactical fighter be developed for use by both the air force and the navy, and the conduct of the blockade of Cuba. Anderson resented what he perceived as political interference in the management of the blockade. He retired in 1963 and became ambassador to Portugal.

Bibliography: Korb, Lawrence, "George Whalen Anderson, Jr.," *The Chiefs of Naval Operations*, ed. by Robert William Love, Jr. (Naval Inst. Press, 1980).

Lloyd J. Graybar

ARNOLD, HENRY HARLEY ("HAP") (1886–1950)

U.S. air force commander, Arnold was born in Gladwyne, Pennsylvania. He graduated from West Point in 1907 and became an army aviator in 1911. Appointed chief of the U.S. Army Air Corps in 1938, he went on to command all U.S. air forces throughout World War II. Arnold's post-World War II active service career was short, only a few months, but he used this critical time to continue the effort to achieve what he had already carefully planned: a strong and independent U.S. Air Force.

Even before the Japanese surrender in September 1945, the Army Air Force began the first steps in dismantling a huge air armada. Comprising 2,500,000 personnel, 243 combat groups, 63,000 aircraft, and hundreds of airfields scattered about the globe, the massive organization was already well on its way to becoming a much smaller, more modernized, and thoroughly independent U.S. armed service. Its chief officer, General Arnold, had laid the groundwork for the postwar era some two years before. He had listened carefully to such scientific personalities as Dr. Theodore von Karman and others about the type of aircraft that would be needed in the coming age. During the war, Arnold had arranged for his promising young officers to rotate through a variety of assignments and combat theaters so as to provide the air force with a substantial pool of experienced, knowledgeable leadership. Arnold had also worked hard at a plan for a postwar U.S. Air Force.

Arnold's plan had begun in a formal form in 1943 and contained some basic principles. He believed a peacetime American air force should be able to protect the country against a massive surprise air attack. It logically followed that such a force would have to be largely professional since it would be engaged in combat from the very outset of hostilities. There could be no dependence on a lengthy mobilization period. There could be no time allocated to manufacture aircraft. U.S. combat airplanes would have to be ready for war at the first moment of hostilities. Additionally, Arnold was skeptical of plans for universal military training (UMT).

The UMT proposal was favored by President Truman's administration. It envisioned each male U.S. citizen being given a brief period of military training upon graduation from high school or upon attaining the age of 18, whichever was later. In order to manage this massive training program, each of the armed services would have to staff numerous training facilities, and these trainers and administrators could not be counted on for combat duties in the first few days of a war. Arnold did not object to his airmen being involved in the UMT program, but he did object to those airmen being counted against his basic numbers to defend the nation against a surprise attack. Eventually, he persuaded the new army chief of staff, Gen. Dwight D. Eisenhower, to support his view. The Army Air Force would consist of an adequate, professional organization that could defeat an enemy air assault on the United States. Air personnel involved in the UMT program would be in addition to those manning the basic defense structure.

Perhaps the most volatile of Arnold's postwar fights involved the issue of defense establishment centralization. The general saw a distinct Army Air Force advantage in a more centralized national defense organization. He believed when all the facts including costs were carefully considered, land-based combat aircraft—as opposed to the more limited and more expensive sea-based aircraft—would be logically favored. Therefore, the concept of an air force would probably flower in a centralized defense establishment and suffer in an arena where each service was allowed to conduct its own planning. These views happened to coincide with those of the army staff, but for different reasons. Thus, as General Arnold began his re-

tirement in early 1946, the organization he had nurtured was generally in league with its parent, the U.S. Army, and opposed to the positions of the U.S. Navy. While the debate has usually been civil and rational, it still exists.

Bibliography: Arnold, H. H., *Global Mission* (Harper & Brothers, 1949); Coffey, Thomas, *Hap: General of the Air Force Henry Arnold* (Viking, 1982); Wolk, Herman S., *Planning and Organizing the Postwar Air Force, 1943–1947* (Office of Air Force History, 1984).

Rod Paschall

BAGLEY, WORTH HARRINGTON (1924–)

U.S. naval officer, Bagley was born in Annapolis, Maryland. He graduated from Annapolis in 1946. He then served aboard destroyers and had further professional schooling. From 1951 to 1953, he was assistant naval attaché in Saigon. He briefly returned to sea before duty in the Bureau of Naval Personnel. After study at the Naval War College, he served at the White House as a naval aide and then as an assistant to the chairman of the Joint Chiefs of Staff. In 1965–66, he was readiness and training officer on the staff of the commander, Cruiser-Destroyer Force, Pacific Fleet. During the Vietnam War, Bagley commanded Cruiser-Destroyer Group, 7th Fleet, directing several operations in Vietnamese waters. Promoted to vice admiral, he served as director, Navy Program Planning, prior to becoming commander, U.S. Naval Forces, in Europe (1973) and then vice chief of naval operations. He retired in 1975.

Bibliography: Martell, Paul, and Grace P. Hayes, eds., *World Military Leaders* (R. R. Bowker, 1974).

Lloyd J. Graybar

BALCHEN, BERNT (1899–1973)

U.S. aviator-explorer and air force officer, Balchen was born in Tveit, Norway, and became a U.S. citizen in 1931, by which date he was well-established as a pioneer in arctic aviation, having worked with the explorers Roald Amundsen and Lincoln Ellsworth. Balchen was chief pilot with Adm. Richard Byrd's 1928–30 Antarctic expedition and on Nov. 29, 1929, piloted the first flight over the South Pole. He joined the U.S. Army Air Force in 1941 and played an active role in Allied operations in the far north, including construction of secret air bases in Greenland and special missions for the Office of Strategic Services in Scandinavia. Following World War II, Balchen headed the Royal Norwegian Airlines and commanded the 10th Air Rescue Squadron in Alaska (1948–50). He piloted the first transpolar flight from Alaska to Norway in 1949 and supervised construction of the U.S. air base at Thule, Greenland, in 1953. Colonel Balchen retired in 1956.

Bibliography: DuPre, Flint O., *U.S. Air Force Biographical Dictionary* (Franklin Watts, 1965); Knight, Clayton, and Robert C. Durham, *Hitch Your Wagon: The Story of Bernt Balchen* (Bell, 1950).

Lt. Col. (Ret.) Charles R. Shrader

BARROW, ROBERT HILLIARD (1922–)

U.S. marine officer, Barrow was born in Baton Rouge, Louisiana. He enlisted in the Marine Corps in 1942. Commissioned a second lieutenant the next year, he served in China operating with guerrilla forces behind the Japanese lines. During the Korean War, Barrow earned a Silver Star as a company commander while participating in the liberation of Seoul and later was awarded the Navy Cross for heroic actions at the Chosin Reservoir. In Vietnam (1964–67), Barrow commanded the 9th Marine Regiment and received the Distinguished Service Cross. Barrow went on to hold numerous commands in the 1970s. He became assistant commandant and was promoted to full general in 1978. In 1979, Pres. Jimmy Carter nominated General Barrow to become the 27th commandant of the Marine Corps, a position he assumed in June 1979 and held until his retirement in July 1983.

Steve R. Waddell

BECKWITH, CHARLIE ALVIN (1929–)

U.S. army officer, Beckwith was born in Atlanta, Georgia. He attended the University of Georgia before entering the army in 1953. Following duty with the 82d Airborne Division (1955–58), he joined the Special Forces in 1958 and served in Laos (1960) as an exchange officer with the British 22d Special Air Service Regiment (1962–63) and with the 7th Special Forces Group at Fort Bragg. He attended the Command and General Staff College (1964–65) and then joined the 5th Special Forces Group in Vietnam in June 1965. There he commanded long-range reconnaissance forces operating with the South Vietnamese Special Forces.

After convalescing from serious wounds received in January 1966, Beckwith ran the Ranger School camp in Florida before returning to Vietnam in 1967 to command the 2d Battalion, 327th Airborne Infantry (101st Airborne Division). He subsequently served in Hawaii (1968–73) and Thailand (1973–74) before returning to Fort Bragg to command the Special Forces School. Beckwith later helped establish the elite counterterrorist unit known as Delta, which he commanded during its formative period. In April 1980, he led the ground element in the disastrous attempt to rescue American hostages held in the U.S. Embassy in Teheran, Iran. Colonel Beckwith retired in 1981.

Bibliography: Beckwith, Charlie A., and Donald Knox, *Delta Force* (Harcourt Brace Jovanovich, 1983).

Lt. Col. (Ret.) Charles R. Shrader

BESSON, FRANK SCHAFFER, JR. (1910–1985)

U.S. army engineering officer, Besson was born in Detroit, Michigan. He graduated from West Point in 1932 and was commissioned in the Corps of Engineers. During World War II, he served as director of the 3d Military Railway Service in the Persian Gulf Command (1943–45). Following service in the Far East Command (1945–48), as assistant chief of transportation (1949–53), and in Supreme Headquarters Allied Powers, Europe (1954–57), he became chief of transportation in 1958. Known for his promotion of containerization and the roll-on/roll-off technique, Besson supported Sec. of Defense Robert S. McNamara's reorganization schemes and thus emerged from the 1961 "massacre" of the technical service chiefs with a fourth star and command of the new Army Materiel Command (1962–69). He chaired the Joint Logistics Review Board in 1969–70 and then retired. He subsequently was a member of the board of Amtrak (1971–77).

Lt. Col. (Ret.) Charles R. Shrader

BOATNER, HAYDON LEMAIRE (1900–1977)

U.S. army officer, Boatner was born in New Orleans, Louisiana. He served in the Marine Corps during World War I. Following the war, he entered the U.S. Military Academy and graduated in 1924. During World War II, he commanded the China Area Command in the China-Burma-India theater. Early in the Korean War, Boatner was deputy commanding general of the 2d Division until the capture of the Koje-do prison camp commander, Brig. Gen. Francis T. Dodd, by the Communist prisoners of war (POWs) and the threat of riots and mass escapes in May 1952. Boatner was placed in charge of the Koje-do POW camp and later the entire Pusan POW command. He restored discipline in the camps, ending Communist plans for a mass breakout. For the remainder of the war, Boatner served as deputy commanding general of the 4th Army. He retired in 1960.

Steve R. Waddell

BORMAN, FRANK (1928–)

U.S. astronaut, Borman was born in Gary, Indiana. He graduated from West Point in 1950 and entered the air force, where he became a fighter pilot. From 1951 to 1956, he was assigned to various fighter squadrons. After completing a master's degree in aeronautical engineering, in 1957 he became an instructor of thermodynamics and fluid mechanics at West Point.

On Sept. 17, 1962, Borman became an astronaut with the National Aeronautics and Space Administration. He commanded the *Gemini 7* mission launched on Dec. 4, 1965, where he participated in the longest space flight to that time—330 hours and 35 minutes—and the first rendezvous of two maneuverable spacecraft. He was also a crew member of the *Apollo 8* mission that flew around the moon in December 1968. In 1975, Borman was appointed president of Eastern Airlines. In 1986, he left Eastern and began private consulting work.

Bibliography: Borman, Frank, with Robert J. Serling, *Countdown: An Autobiography* (Morrow, 1988).

Roger D. Launius

BRADLEY, OMAR NELSON (1893–1981)

U.S. army general of the armies, Bradley was born in Clark, Missouri. A 1915 West Point graduate, he pursued a distinguished military career that earned him acclaimed status as an army commander in the African and European theaters in World War II. Following the war, Bradley held a number of important positions until his retirement from active service in 1953. Although his postwar career was not marked by acrimony and celebrated disputes, it was not without controversy. The general was frequently called on for military advice after 1953 and was involved in a number of public and private enterprises. Of all the World War II U.S. military leaders, Bradley was perhaps the least controversial.

Soon after the guns went silent in Europe and Asia in 1945, Bradley was made veterans administrator, an enormous undertaking since millions of American men and women in uniform were making the transition to private life. Among the criteria for his selection to this important post, his reputation for being approachable, caring, and the World War II American "soldier's general" undoubtedly ranked high. Bradley's tasks included making that transition as quick and efficient as possible while ensuring there was minimal disruption to the U.S. economy, making certain the laws regarding veterans were observed, and seeing after the medical and rehabilitation needs of the thousands of injured and maimed. During his tenure, Bradley set in motion hundreds of veterans hospitals throughout the United States.

On Feb. 7, 1948, Bradley became the chief of staff of the army and soon found himself in the middle of U.S. social crisis. His primary task centered on trying to preserve some U.S. ground combat capability in the midst of a wave of new strategic thinking. Many defense analysts, admirals, and bomber enthusiasts believed the day of foot soldiers, tanks, and artillery was over. Future war would be dominated by atomic bombs, missiles, and high-flying bombers. Bradley and his staff fought a losing battle against this surge, having to watch U.S. conventional warfare capabilities wither away.

Meanwhile, Pres. Harry S Truman, was bent on using the armed services as the social spearhead for racial integration within the United States. As chief of staff, Bradley had to answer to congressional committees concerned with

the armed services, committees often under the control of elderly, tradition-bound Southern senators and representatives. Bradley, in his testimony to Congress, took the view that while racial integration should be pursued as rapidly as possible, the process should not be disruptive to the good order, discipline, and mission accomplishment of the army. Additionally, Bradley argued that while the northern part of the United States was ready for racially integrated units and facilities in the army, the South was not. This, to Bradley, was an important consideration since so many U.S. Army installations were located in the South and Southwest. Truman, on the other hand, was for rapid, universal action. The record is clear that Bradley was not a segregationist, but he was perhaps unknowingly proceeding on a collision course with his civilian political master.

An embarrassing incident occurred in the summer of 1948. When Bradley spoke to a group of instructors at Fort Knox, Kentucky, he made the comment that the army would have to retain segregation as long as the country at large condoned the practice. Bradley was unaware that news reporters were in the audience. Additionally, the chief of staff did not know that the president had just signed Executive Order No. 9981, ordering the desegregation of the U.S. Armed Forces. In the midst of a widely publicized controversy, Bradley found himself supported by those who forcefully argued the army should not be used for social experiments. In reality, the last thing Bradley wanted was a dispute with the president. His remarks were made in ignorance of Truman's intense desires, and the incident has as much to say about the lack of coordination in the Truman administration as it does about bigotry in the highest echelons of the U.S. government. Bradley apologized to the president, and Truman publicly sloughed off the affair. However, at the same time that the president was making light of Bradley's gaff, Truman specifically told the press that the U.S. armed services would become racially integrated institutions. Subsequently, the U.S. Army became a leader in erasing age-old racially based biases, practices of discrimination, and injustice.

Truman nominated Bradley to become the chairman of the Joint Chiefs of Staff on Jan. 16, 1949, the first officer to hold the position after the postwar reorganization of the national defense establishment. During this assignment, Bradley had to deal with the development of a cold-war military strategy that underpinned the U.S. policy of containment. In less than 18 months, that policy was challenged by North Korea's invasion of South Korea. The Joint Chiefs began translating President Truman's directives to save South Korea into concrete plans and orders. In this same post, General Bradley was promoted to five-star rank in September 1950 and presided over the Joint Chiefs of Staff during the president's dismissal of Gen. Douglas MacArthur. Additionally, Bradley passed judgment on the many initiatives to provide the fledgling North

Atlantic Treaty Organization with sound leadership and military strength.

On Aug. 15, 1953, Bradley finished his day-to-day military duties and retired to a life of a sometimes military adviser, sometimes corporate executive, and full-time advocate of benevolent causes, particularly in the service of U.S. soldiers. As late as 1967, he and his wife were visiting with U.S. soldiers in Vietnam combat zones.

Bradley's chief reputation was that of a caring, honest, stabilizing influence in times of crisis. His career has long been a model for army officers to follow in matters of seeing to the needs of soldiers. When he had to be firm or in opposition to others, he did so without passion or heated acrimony. He exhibited wisdom in his professional relations. Few officers could have handled Gen. George S. Patton as well as Bradley did in World War II. Bradley managed to get the best out of the colorful, profane, and energetic American armor leader without yielding to his subordinate's more outlandish behavior or suggestions. The test of rising from being a subordinate of Patton to being his superior was a stern one, and Bradley succeeded magnificently. His image was that of a father figure, a leader of practicality, competence, and common sense, not one of brilliance and dash. As such, the leadership methods of Bradley will ever be linked with the command styles of Gens. Ulysses S. Grant and Zachary Taylor.

Bibliography: Bradley, Omar N., *A Soldier's Story* (Holt, Rinehart & Winston, 1951); Whiting, Charles, *Bradley* (Ballantine Books, 1971).

Col. (Ret.) Rod Paschall

BREWER, MARGARET (1930–)

U.S. marine officer, Brewer was born in Durand, Michigan. She graduated from the University of Michigan in 1952. Commissioned a second lieutenant in the U.S. Marine Corps the same year, she eventually rose to the rank of brigadier general. Brewer held numerous commands in the 1950s and 1960s. After commanding the women's marine companies at Norfolk, Virginia, and Camp Lejeune, North Carolina, from 1955 to 1958, she was the executive and commanding officer of the Woman Officers School (1963–66) and served as deputy director of women marines (1968–71). In February 1973, Colonel Brewer became the seventh and last director of women marines. The Marine Corps disbanded the position in June 1977. On May 11, 1978, Brewer became the first woman general officer in the Marine Corps. She retired in July 1980.

Steve R. Waddell

BROWN, GEORGE SCRATCHLEY (1918–1978)

U.S. air force officer, Brown was born in Montclair, New Jersey. He graduated from West Point in 1941. Assigned to the 8th Air Force in England during World War II,

Brown was awarded the Distinguished Service Cross after his participation in the August 1943 low-level, oil refinery bombing raid on Ploesti, Rumania. When the Korean War broke out, Brown was sent to the Far East as director of operations for the 5th Air Force (1950–53). After the war he was in charge of flight instructors in Arizona (1953–56), and in 1957 he attended the National War College. Brown served as executive officer to the air force chief of staff (1957–59), as assistant to the secretary of defense (1959–63), and, after a tour of duty as commander of the East Air Force Military Air Transport Service (1963–66), as assistant to the Joint Chiefs of Staff (1966–68). He was promoted to the rank of general in 1968.

After the 1968 Tet Offensive in Vietnam, General Brown became the commander of the 7th Air Force and deputy for air operations to the U.S. Military Assistance Command Vietnam (MACV). Serving under the MACV commander, Gen. Creighton Abrams, Brown was closely associated with the bombing operations against North Vietnamese and Khmer Rouge forces in Cambodia. Not only were these missions not publicly acknowledged, air force reports were falsified so as to hide the fact that the United States was engaged in more wide-ranging operations in Southeast Asia than was immediately apparent. Only after the 1970 incursion of U.S. and Vietnamese ground forces into Cambodia did the bombing missions become public knowledge. The earlier secret raids had the tacit approval of authorities in Phnom Penh, but they had not been revealed to the U.S. Congress.

The secret bombing of Cambodia became public in 1973, during Brown's testimony before a Congressional committee hearing on his nomination by Pres. Richard M. Nixon to become air force chief of staff. When asked about the bombing, the general asked the committee to go into a closed hearing and then admitted both to the bombings and to the falsification of records. He told the legislators that B-52 raids had been conducted on Cambodian targets before the 1970 incursion into that country. Later, Brown wrote the committee a letter and recanted some of his testimony. In the letter, Brown equivocated, stating the reports were not false so long as they met "the requirements imposed" and were not intended to deceive those who had a "need to know" about bombing missions over Cambodia. Despite this strange letter, Congress confirmed General Brown as the new air force chief of staff.

In 1974, Brown became the chairman of the Joint Chiefs of Staff. In this capacity, the general became once again involved in the U.S. attempt to save Cambodia, encouraging Congress to authorize more military aid to Gen. Lon Nol's doomed government. Congress failed to provide an adequate response. The same type of congressional attitude affected U.S. assistance to South Vietnam. Brown's efforts on behalf of Pres. Nguyen Van Thieu's government were no more successful than his work for aid to Cambodia, and both South Vietnam and Cambodia fell to Communist control. Brown felt bitter and stated that the United States had failed to replace its allies' lost weapons and to provide Thieu and Lon Nol with sufficient ammunition. Suffering serious illness, Brown retired in 1978 and died in December of that year.

Bibliography: Shawcross, William, *Sideshow: Kissinger, Nixon and the Destruction of Cambodia* (Simon & Schuster, 1979).

Rod Paschall

BROWN, HAROLD (1927–)

U.S. secretary of defense, Brown was born in New York City. He earned a Ph.D in physics from Columbia University in 1949. While working at the Livermore Radiation Laboratory in the 1950s, Brown served on the Polaris Steering Committee, the Conference on Discontinuing Nuclear Tests, and the Air Force Science Advisory Board. He was director of defense research and engineering for the Department of Defense (1961–65). He then served four years as secretary of the air force. In addition to serving as president of the California Institute of Technology in Pasadena, Brown was a delegate to the Strategic Arms Limitations Talks from 1969 to 1977. Jimmy Carter nominated Brown to the post of secretary of defense, a position he held from Jan. 23, 1977, to Jan. 20, 1981.

Steve R. Waddell

BUCHER, LLOYD (1928–)

U.S. navy commander, Bucher was born in Pocatello, Idaho. He received his commission through a reserve officer candidate program at the University of Nebraska and received diverse assignments before being given command of the U.S. intelligence ship the *Pueblo*. On Jan. 23, 1968, as the *Pueblo* gathered intelligence on North Korea from outside the 12-mile international limit, four North Korean patrol boats and two gunboats approached and began to harass the U.S. ship. Bucher turned the *Pueblo* away from the intruders, but a North Korean gunboat fired from 3,000 yards, wounding four *Pueblo* crewmen, one mortally. Bucher, possessing little armament and under orders to avoid dangerous incidents that might spark a war, decided to surrender the ship. His crew burned as many secret documents as possible, but most fell into North Korean hands.

Bucher and his crew of 82 officers and men were imprisoned in North Korea for 11 months. U.S. and North Korean negotiators worked out an agreement that freed the crew on Dec. 22, 1968, in exchange for a false U.S. admission the *Pueblo* had entered North Korean waters.

A naval court of inquiry later recommended Bucher be tried by court-martial, but Sec. of the Navy John Chafee opted instead to take no action. Bucher remained in the navy until 1973. He wrote an autobiography in 1970 called *Bucher: My Story*.

Bibliography: Bucher, Lloyd, *Bucher: My Story* (Doubleday, 1970); ———, "The PUEBLO Incident," *Naval History* (fall 1988); ———, "The PUEBLO Incident: Commander Bucher Replies," *Naval History* (winter 1989).

John F. Wukovits

BURKE, ARLEIGH ALBERT (1901–)

U.S. naval officer, Burke was born in Boulder, Colorado. He graduated from Annapolis in 1923. By 1943, he had been promoted to the rank of captain. Following his extensive combat service in World War II, he became one of the U.S. Navy's prime experts in national security policy. In 1947, Burke was appointed to the General Board, an advisory organ for the secretary of the navy that dealt with policy issues. In this capacity, he authored a highly influential study on the structure, role, and missions of the post-World War II U.S. Navy. Two years later, the rising officer was appointed to head the Organizational Research and Policy Division within the Office of the Chief of Naval Operations. Here, Burke developed the navy's response to proposals to reorganize the nation's defense establishment. Despite the bitter opposition of the navy's top leadership, the National Security Act of 1949 became law and launched a steady march in Washington toward taking power and control away from the country's armed services and vesting the newly created Office of the Secretary of Defense with great authority.

Much of the turmoil within the Pentagon in this period during the late 1940s had to do with two linked episodes, the "Revolt of the Admirals" and the B-36 controversy. The latter dispute pitted the newly formed U.S. Air Force against the U.S. Navy in a wide-ranging debate as to which service would provide the country with a nuclear strike force. The former controversy involved the top uniformed leadership of the navy resisting the Harry S Truman administration's efforts to reduce redundancy within the armed services, create unified organizations, and provide the secretary of defense with power and authority. Burke was in the middle of both disputes, often providing the rationale used by his superiors. His involvement resulted in his removal from promotion eligibility; but Burke's name was restored to the list in 1950, when he was made a rear admiral.

At the outbreak of the Korean War, Burke was sent to the Far East for staff duty. In 1951, he was appointed to the United Nations Truce Negotiating Team. Returning to Washington, he headed the navy's Strategic Plans Division and became deeply involved in restructuring the navy in the early years of the Dwight D. Eisenhower administration.

Later, and once again at sea, Burke commanded the U.S. Navy Destroyer Force of the Atlantic Fleet. In June 1955, he was selected as the new chief of naval operations (CNO) by President Eisenhower. It was a surprising choice since there were 92 admirals who were more senior. This was to be a lengthy assignment. Burke was reappointed twice to the navy's top uniformed post, serving until his retirement in 1961.

As CNO, Burke became deeply involved in modernization efforts. He accelerated the design, development, and construction of nuclear-powered submarines and surface ships. He insisted on creating faster warships and earned the nickname "31-Knot Burke." Additionally, Burke pushed programs designed to give the navy a wide array of guided missile weapons. Then, too, he was instrumental in approving and advocating modernized aircraft projects and new, more capable communications systems. However, the program he may be best remembered for is the Polaris submarine-launched nuclear strike system. This farsighted, novel program seemed to be an engineering impossibility at the time. Additionally, the project was in full swing during a period of great public controversy about the high costs and multiplicity of competing weapons systems. Almost alone among its competitors, the Polaris program was developed within its projected time span and involved an austere overhead budget and staff, and, despite the technical risks, it worked. The Polaris management system became a widely studied example of how things should be done in both the armed services and in U.S. industrial circles.

Although Burke's tenure as CNO was taking place in an era when U.S. political leadership was emphasizing a nuclear response to aggression, he pushed two programs that had little to do with "massive retaliation." Burke steadily searched for young, vigorous officers to take positions of responsibility in a navy that was in constant transition. Essentially, the service was going from guns to missiles and from steam to nuclear power. Burke had little sympathy for the traditionalists. Second, he pressed for a wide spectrum of capabilities. Despite the emphasis on strategic nuclear arms, the admiral was interested in improving and further developing a limited war capability in the navy.

Among Burke's defeats and disappointments, issues involving centralization within the Department of Defense figured most prominently. Included in that list is his unsuccessful campaign against the 1958 amendments to the National Security Act. Another blow came two years later when the navy was forced into the joint targeting process for the nation's strategic nuclear weapons. Additionally, Burke was wholly unsuccessful in resisting Pres. John F. Kennedy's new secretary of defense, Robert McNamara, in imposing a comprehensive and uniform management system for the country's defense establishment. The Planning, Programming and Budgeting System, as it was

known, became a complex, tightly ordered administrative process where all defense expenditures, development programs, plans, and so forth were taken into account and transformed into dollar figures. The new system greatly increased the authority and role of the secretary of defense at the expense of Congress and the armed services.

Bibliography: Davis, Vincent, *The Admirals Lobby* (Univ. of North Carolina Press, 1967); Hewlett, Richard G., and Francis Duncan, *Nuclear Navy, 1946–1962* (Univ. of Chicago Press, 1974); Jones, Ken, and Hubert Kelley, Jr., *Admiral Arleigh (31-Knot) Burke, the Story of a Fighting Sailor* (Chilton, 1962).

Col. (Ret.) Rod Paschall

BUSH, GEORGE HERBERT WALKER
(1924–)
Forty-first president of the United States (1989–93), Bush was born in Milton, Massachusetts, the son of an investment banker who became a U.S. senator. A navy pilot during World War II, he was shot down and narrowly escaped death. Following graduation from Yale University (1948), Bush married and moved to Texas.

Using family financial connections, Bush engaged in petroleum exploration. He ultimately settled in Houston,

Pres. George Bush's decision in 1990 to mobilize troops against Iraqi forces in Kuwait was overwhelmingly supported by the American public. (The White House)

Texas. In 1964, he ran unsuccessfully for the U.S. Senate but came back to win election to the House of Representatives in 1966. After losing another Senate race four years later, Bush served in succession as ambassador to the United Nations (1971–73), chairman of the Republican National Committee (1973–74), U.S. representative to the People's Republic of China (1974), and director of the Central Intelligence Agency (1967–77). In 1980, after losing the Republican presidential nomination to Ronald Reagan, Bush was nominated and elected as vice president.

While vice president (1981–89), Bush apparently had slight impact upon policy matters. His partisan loyalty and boyish enthusiasm led critics to label Bush a "wimp," but they underestimated his ambition and political shrewdness. He wooed Republican conservatives, thus establishing himself as Reagan's heir apparent. In 1988, he defeated Democrat Michael Dukakis to win the presidency.

As president, Bush pursued both détente with the Soviet Union and old-fashioned intervention in the Third World. He ordered an invasion of Panama (1989) and later (1990–91) organized an international coalition and sent 540,000 U.S. troops to liberate Kuwait following its invasion by Iraqi forces in 1990. Bush has been described as the latest "Bull Moose," an elite Easterner, resembling Theodore Roosevelt, who made a career in the West and wielded a big stick in foreign policy.

M. Guy Bishop

BYERS, CLOVIS ETHELBERT
(1899–1973)

U.S. army officer, Byers was born in Columbus, Ohio. He graduated from West Point in 1920, the Command and General Staff School in 1936, and the Army War College in 1940. During World War II, Byers saw action in the Pacific with Gen. Robert L. Eichelberger. Byers served as his chief of staff with the 77th Infantry Division, the I Corps, and finally the 8th Army. He received his own command, the 82d Airborne Division, in 1948. In August 1951, he took command of the X Corps in Korea, where he oversaw the heavy fighting at Bloody Ridge, the Punchbowl, and Heartbreak Ridge. Following a short stint as commander of the XVI Corps in Japan, he served as chief of staff, Allied Forces, Southern Europe, from 1952 to 1954. Byers retired in 1959 with the rank of lieutenant general.

Steve R. Waddell

CARAWAY, PAUL WYATT (1905–1985)

U.S. army commander, Caraway was born in Jonesboro, Arkansas. After graduating from West Point in 1929, he earned a law degree before beginning troop duty. During World War II, in 1942, he joined the strategy section of the War Department General Staff's Operations Division.

Caraway left Washington in 1944 to become the deputy chief of staff of the China theater, and he remained in China after the war to head the Chungking Liaison Group. He achieved the rank of brigadier general in 1945. While he commanded a regiment after returning from China, Caraway continued to be an important staff officer. He became a major general in 1951. In 1953, he served in the Office of the Assistant Chief of Staff for Operations, and in 1958, he became a member of the Joint Chiefs of Staff's influential Joint Strategic Survey Committee. In 1961, he again left Washington for the Far East, this time as U.S. high commissioner and commanding general, U.S. Army, Ryukyu Islands. Caraway retired in 1964 with the rank of lieutenant general.

Richard F. Kehrberg

CARLUCCI, FRANK CHARLES, III
(1930–   )

U.S. secretary of defense, Carlucci was born in Scranton, Pennsylvania. For several years, he was a foreign service officer in such posts as Johannesberg, Kinshasa, and Rio de Janeiro and later became U.S. ambassador to Portugal. Carlucci was best known for a succession of Washington bureaucratic posts, including director of the Office of Economic Opportunity (1970), associate and deputy director of the Office of Management and Budget (1971–72), and undersecretary of Health, Education, and Welfare (1972–74). He was later deputy director of central intelligence (1978–81) and deputy secretary of defense (1981–83). Returning to government in 1986, he became national security adviser to Pres. Ronald Reagan, who subsequently appointed him secretary of defense (1987–89), during which time he supervised a buildup of U.S. military capability.

Lewis Sorley

CARNEY, ROBERT BOSTWICK
(1895–1990)

U.S. naval officer, Carney was born in Vallejo, California. He graduated from Annapolis in 1916. During both world wars he had extensive experience at sea. He was promoted to rear admiral in 1943 and spent the remainder of the World War II as chief of staff to Adm. William Halsey. After the war, Carney served as deputy chief naval officer (logistics) and held several major commands including that of Allied Forces, Southern Europe. In 1953, during Harry S Truman's presidency, he was named chief of naval operations. While he supported Pres. Dwight D. Eisenhower's "New Look" defense policy, which stressed nuclear capability, Carney insisted that the navy's mobility could provide a key element in U.S. defense. Embarrassed by the publication of his remarks that the United States should bomb mainland China in the event the Chinese attacked the Nationalist-held island of Quemoy, the Eisenhower administration did not offer Carney reappointment. He retired in 1955.

Bibliography: Shratz, Paul R., "Robert Bostwick Carney," *The Chiefs of Naval Operations,* ed. by Robert William Love, Jr. (Naval Inst. Press, 1980).

Lloyd J. Graybar

CARTER, JAMES EARL, JR. (1924–   )
Thirty-ninth president of the United States (1977–81), Carter was born in Plains, Georgia. He graduated from Annapolis in 1946. His naval career ended in 1953 when his father died and it became necessary for him to return home to Plains and the family farm. He started several successful businesses of his own. Carter made a bid for a state senate seat in 1962 and served in the Georgia legislature from 1963 until 1967. Unsuccessful in the 1966 elections for the governorship, he won in 1970. During his one term as governor (1971–75), he pared down and reorga-

President Carter's dedication to the cause of Middle East peace was rewarded by the historic 1978 summit talks between Israel's Menachem Begin and Egypt's Anwar Sadat. (The White House)

nized state government and adhered to zero-based budgeting.

As president, he inherited a nation still divided by the social turmoil of the 1960s and disillusioned by the cynical political practices of the Nixon White House. While Carter seemed initially to be a breath of fresh air, his Democratic victory proved an historical anomaly in a period of Republican domination of the presidency.

Carter had been a modest success as Georgia governor prior to seeking the White House. His efforts at governmental reorganization and aggressive attempts to end racial discrimination gained Carter a strong regional reputation, but knowledgeable political observers were stunned by his announcement in December 1975 that he would seek the presidency. But they underestimated Carter's appeal. Disgusted by the corruption of Watergate, voters were drawn to Carter's soft-spoken style and apparent integrity. He narrowly defeated incumbent Gerald R. Ford with 50.1 percent of the vote.

In 1978, President Carter pushed through the Panama Canal Treaty and brokered a peace agreement between Israel's Menachem Begin and Egypt's Anwar Sadat. But failures in domestic and foreign policy overshadowed these accomplishments. Carter was dogged by events beyond his control, particularly the Iran hostage crisis. When an attempt to rescue Americans held in Iran failed (1980), his political future was further damaged. Later that year, he lost the presidency to an overwhelming defeat by Republican candidate Ronald Reagan.

M. Guy Bishop

CATES, CLIFTON BLEDSOE (1893–1970)
U.S. marine commander, Cates was born in Tiptonville, Tennessee. He graduated from the University of Tennessee with a law degree in 1916. He joined the Marine Corps Reserve as a second lieutenant and fought with the 6th Marines in the Aisne-Marne and Meuse-Argonne campaigns and the St.-Mihiel Offensive during World War I. For the next 20 years, Cates held a variety of assignments, including two tours of foreign duty in Shanghai (1929–32, 1937–38). By 1940, he had been promoted to colonel. A regimental commander with the 1st Marine Division in the Solomon Islands' Guadalcanal campaign in 1942, he was promoted to brigadier general in 1943 and major general in 1944. He commanded the 4th Marines during the final Pacific battles of World War II.

After the war, Cates became commanding general of the marine barracks at Quantico (1946–47). In 1948, he was promoted to general and then served as commandant of the Marine Corps (1948–51). As commandant, Cates was committed to maintaining the end-of-war strength of the Marine Corps, even as the Marine Corps' budget was cut. He advocated that the Marine Corps be no smaller than 2 divisions of 6-battalion landing teams each, with 2 air wings of 12 squadrons each. He also urged that a place be made on the Joint Chiefs of Staff (JCS) for the commandant of the Marine Corps.

When war in Korea broke out in 1950, General Cates informed the JCS that he could have a full division of marines ready in a few weeks should the United States commit ground troops to the war effort. The 1st Marines landed at Inchon in September 1950 and fought through the rest of the war.

When his term as commandant of the corps was up at the end of 1951, the heavily-decorated Cates voluntarily reverted to the rank of lieutenant general and commanded the Marine Corps schools at Quantico. He retired from the Marine Corps in 1954.

Leo J. Daugherty III

CHAPMAN, LEONARD FIELDING, JR. (1913–)

U.S. marine commander, Chapman was born in Key West, Florida. An R.O.T.C. (Reserve Officers Training Corps) graduate of the University of Florida in 1931, he resigned his army commission in 1935 to accept one as a second lieutenant in the Marine Corps. He fought in the Pacific during World War II, ending the war as a lieutenant colonel.

After World War II, Chapman served in staff positions in Washington, D.C. (1946–49). Reassigned to Quantico, Virginia, in 1949, he coordinated the reserve artillery training unit there and then commanded the supporting arms groups at the corps' development center. He was promoted to colonel in 1950.

Chapman was assigned to the 3d Marine Division in 1952. He then held commands in Japan until 1956, when he became commander of the Marine Corps Institute. He was promoted to brigadier general in 1958 and was assigned to Camp Lejeune, North Carolina, where he served as commanding general of force troops, Fleet Marine Force, Atlantic, until 1961, the year he was raised to major general. After several years as assistant chief of staff, he was promoted to chief of staff and lieutenant general in 1964. Appointed assistant commandant of the Marine Corps in 1967, he became commandant in 1968.

As Chapman entered the top office, the North Vietnamese Tet Offensive had begun in full force. Chapman argued against pooling all air assets in South Vietnam under the army, contending that if the marines lost their control aircraft to a single manager, the army might lose its helicopters to air force control. He dealt with the problems of race relations and discipline, many a result of the Vietnam War, by implementing procedures for quick administrative dismissal of such malcontents. Chapman was able to bring the marine forces back from Vietnam with their pride in-

Richard Cheney, secretary of defense (1989–93), oversaw Operation Desert Shield/Desert Storm in 1991 and the deployment of troops to facilitate the distribution of relief supplies in war-ravaged Somalia at the end of 1992. (U.S. Navy)

tact, urging a return to the traditional marine role as that of an amphibious force in constant readiness. Chapman retired in 1971, at the end of his tenure as commandant.

Leo J. Daugherty III

CHENEY, RICHARD BRUCE (1941–)

U.S. political figure and secretary of defense (1989–93), Cheney was born in Lincoln, Nebraska. He was a White House staff assistant for Pres. Richard M. Nixon and chief of staff for Pres. Gerald R. Ford. Elected to Congress as a Republican representative from Wyoming in 1978, Cheney served in the House of Representatives until 1989. He supported Pres. Ronald Reagan's economic and foreign policies throughout the 1980s. Pres. George Bush appointed Cheney secretary of defense in March 1989. In this capacity, he oversaw the successful Desert Shield and Desert Storm operations to expel Iraqi military forces from Kuwait in 1990–91 and subsequently dealt with the military implications of the collapse of the Soviet Union and its satellites.

Steve R. Waddell

CHURCH, JOHN HUSTON (1892–1953)

U.S. army officer, Church was born in Glen Iron, Pennsylvania. He served in France during World War I. Assigned to the 45th and 84th infantry divisions in World War II, he fought in North Africa, in Italy at Salerno and Anzio, in southern France, and in the Netherlands. Despite poor health, Church gained assignment to the Far East Command in 1949. As commander of ADCOM, the Advance Command and Liaison Group in Korea, he controlled the U.S. Korean Military Advisory Group (KMAG) and South Korean forces after the North Korean invasion of June 1950. Assuming command of the 24th Division, Church earned the dubious distinction of being the oldest division commander in Korea. Church left Korea in January 1951 to command the Infantry Center at Fort Benning, Georgia. He retired the following year.

Maj. James Sanders Day

CLARK, MARK WAYNE (1896–1984)

U.S. army commander, Clark was born in Madison Barracks near Watertown, New York. He graduated from West Point in 1917 and was commissioned in the infantry. He served with the American Expeditionary Force during World War I in France's Vosges Mountains and with the army of occupation in Coblenz, Germany. He returned to the United States in 1919 and was promoted to captain. During the interwar period, Clark held a variety of assignments and attended the army's Command and General Staff School and the Army War College. He reached the rank of a lieutenant colonel in 1940.

As part of the staff of general headquarters and as a temporary major general at the beginning of the U.S. involvement in World War II, Clark took part in the planning of training maneuvers in Louisiana in 1942. Later that year, he was appointed chief of staff of the army's ground forces and took up command first from an office in the Pentagon and then from a London office. He implemented a rigorous training schedule, preparing his men for the eventual onslaught of Hitler's forces. Promoted to the permanent rank of lieutenant general, he took command of the 5th Army and conducted that army's campaign in Italy, from the landing at Salerno and the seizure of Naples to the drive for Rome and the landings at Anzio (1943–44). Considered one of the most difficult campaigns of the war, it prepared the U.S. Army for the war in Korea in 1950 and illustrated the value of small-unit operations.

At the conclusion of the war, Clark's army occupied southern Austria in order to forestall Soviet absorption, and he served as military governor there until 1947. Upon his return to the United States, he became commanding general of the 6th Army, which was headquartered at the Presidio. In 1949, Clark was appointed chief of the army's field forces at Fort Monroe, Virginia. During the first stages of the Korean War, he trained U.S. troops, implementing, as usual, a rigorous training schedule and, for realism, using live ammunition in his exercises. Always a champion of infantrymen and small-unit tactics, Clark saw in the Korean War a vindication of their necessity.

Although Clark was considering retirement, he remained on active duty at the request of Pres. Harry S Truman. When Clark was called upon to succeed Gen. Matthew Ridgway as commander in chief, United Nations Command, in Korea in 1952–53, Clark guided the allied forces and successfully negotiated the armistice with the Communist forces in July 1953. He also assisted in the revitalization and retraining of the South Korean army and placated South Korean president Syngman Rhee's doubts about signing the armistice. Clark assured Rhee that the United States would sign a mutual security pact between the two countries as well as provide long-term economic and military assistance that included a U.S. pledge to expand and improve the South Korean military forces.

Clark retired in late 1953, deeply resentful that an armistice had been signed without victory in Korea and that he was the first U.S. Army commander in history to have signed such an armistice. In *From the Danube to the Yalu* (1954), he expressed his opinion that the United Nations forces should have fought until North Korea was defeated; he even went so far as to say that he favored dropping the atomic bomb on the North Korean and Chinese forces. He maintained until his death in 1984 that the Americans had lacked the will to win in Korea and that he was the victim of this lack of will.

From 1954 until 1965, Clark served as president of The Citadel, a military college in Charleston, South Carolina. He was appointed to the American Battle Monuments Commission in December 1969 and shortly thereafter became its chairman. Clark's pre-Korean War memoir, *Calculated Risk*, was published in 1950.

Leo J. Daugherty III

CLAY, LUCIUS DUBIGNON (1897–1978)

U.S. army officer and administrator, Clay was born in Marietta, Georgia, the sixth and youngest child of Georgia senator Alexander Stephens Clay and a direct descendant of statesman Henry Clay. He graduated from West Point in 1918, where he was a fine student but constantly in trouble for poor conduct, and was assigned to the Corps of Engineers, where he remained a first lieutenant without distinction for the next 17 years.

Clay, promoted to the rank of captain in 1933, got a chance to shine during Pres. Franklin D. Roosevelt's New Deal, serving as an engineer on several Works Progress Administration and Civilian Conservation Corps projects. He was also brought to Washington, where he was the Corps of Engineers chief liaison with Congress (1933–37).

Following this assignment, Clay spent the years just before World War II in a variety of high-priority jobs, notably in the Philippines as Gen. Douglas MacArthur's chief engineer and later as engineer in charge of the Denison Dam construction project on the Red River in Texas. From there, he was assigned as assistant administrator of the Civil Aeronautics Authority, responsible for the Defense Airport Program to improve or construct nearly 500 airfields in the United States.

World War II. With the coming of World War II, Clay's career advancement accelerated. His first wartime post was in Brazil where he oversaw the construction of air bases used to support the South Atlantic route to North Africa. In March 1942, just promoted temporarily to brigadier general, Clay became assistant chief of staff for materials within the Services of Supply. He later became chief of this unit, and with it assumed responsibility for the details of army war production from procurement to delivery.

Clay stayed in this job for about two years, but after the Normandy landings in June 1944, Supreme Allied Commander Gen. Dwight D. Eisenhower asked for his help in handling the logistics of his force as it began to move inland. Clay went to France and organized the port of Cherbourg as the principal gateway to Europe. His efforts facilitated the flow of supplies to troops on the battlefield in numbers 10–20 times greater than during the first part of June 1944. In December 1944 Clay was called back to Washington and appointed as deputy to James F. Byrnes of the War Mobilization and Reconversion Administration. Clay was not happy in this position, but he remained until March 1945 when Byrnes allowed him to take an assignment as Eisenhower's deputy for military government in occupied Germany.

Postwar Experience. He later held the same position for Gen. Joseph T. McNarney, Eisenhower's successor. In that position, Clay held overall responsibility for the management of Germany: food, housing, currency, industry, government, refugees, de-Nazification, and so forth. In addition, Clay was responsible for the transfer of troops in Europe, either sending them back to the United States or to the Pacific. Promoted to the permanent rank of brigadier general in 1946, in March 1947, Clay succeeded McNarney as military governor and theater commander. This was a unique accession for an engineer, since the theater commander was a combat leader, and the appointment demonstrated how effective he had been in governing Germany. He attained the rank of major general in 1948.

Clay's leadership in Germany was based on two fundamental priorities. First, he believed that the role of the United States in Germany was to assist it with recovery from the war, not to treat it as a conquered province. His efforts were aimed at fostering an eventual civilian takeover of the occupation and the creation of a viable German state. Second, while the U.S. Army held primacy in Germany, he wanted to keep it out of civilian affairs as much as possible. The creation of a heritage of separation of civil and military action he believed was important for a revived Germany.

Berlin Blockade and Airlift. The most serious crisis Clay faced as military governor of Germany was the Soviet attempt to blockade jointly occupied Berlin in 1948–49. On June 24, 1948, the Soviets cut off all supply of food and electricity to Berlin, in an attempt to gain control of the city. Clay immediately anticipated using aircraft to overcome the blockade, and he organized what became the massive effort known as the Berlin Airlift. On June 26, he began the first airlift flights, using C-47s.

Clay directed his air commander to create a permanent airlift structure to ensure that West Berlin did not fall to the Soviets. By the time of the negotiated settlement to the blockade on May 12, 1949, the airlift had succeeded in delivering more than 2,325,000 tons of supplies to Berlin in 15 months.

Later Career. On May 15, 1949, Clay left Germany and retired from the army with the rank of full general. He became chief executive officer of the Continental Can Company (1950–62) and then served as a senior partner with the investment banking firm of Lehman Brothers (1963–73). He was also politically active, using his contacts with Eisenhower to persuade him to seek the presidency on the Republican ticket in 1952 and serving as Pres. John F. Kennedy's personal envoy to Berlin during the 1961 Berlin Wall crisis.

Bibliography: Clay, Lucius D., *Decision in Germany* (Doubleday, 1950); Coles, Harry L., and Albert K. Weinberg, *Civil Affairs: Soldiers Become Governors* (Center of Military History, U.S. Army, 1964); Gimbel, John, *The American Occupation of Germany: Politics and the Military, 1945–1949* (Stanford Univ. Press, 1968); Shlaim, Avi, *The United States and the Berlin Blockade, 1948–1949: A Study in Crisis Decision-Making* (Univ. of California Press, 1983); Smith, Jean Edward, ed., *The Papers of General Lucius D. Clay: Germany, 1945–1949* (Indiana Univ. Press, 1974).

Roger D. Launius

CLIFFORD, CLARK McADAMS (1906–   )

U.S. presidential adviser and secretary of defense, Clifford was born in Fort Scott, Kansas. He was commissioned as a reserve naval officer in 1944 and served as a staff assistant to Pres. Harry S Truman (1946–53). For many years thereafter, as a Washington attorney, he was consulted by successive Democratic administrations on defense and foreign policy, as well as political, matters. His most significant role was a brief stint as secretary of defense for Pres. Lyndon B. Johnson in 1968–69. Johnson expected strong support for his Vietnam War policies from Clifford, who instead—according to his own autobiographical account—worked actively to undermine the existing policy and to force Johnson to withdraw U.S. forces from Vietnam.

Clifford's tenure ended with the inauguration of Pres. Richard Nixon. In the early 1990s, Clifford's reputation was tarnished by his implication in a banking scandal.

Bibliography: Clifford, Clark, *Counsel to the President: A Memoir* (Random House, 1991).

Lewis Sorley

COLLINS, JOSEPH LAWTON (1896–1987)

U.S. army chief of staff, "Lightning Joe" Collins was born in New Orleans, Louisiana. He graduated from West Point in 1917, and, after being sent to various posts in the United States, served with the German occupation forces (1919–21). He was promoted to the rank of captain in 1919. The years between 1921 and 1941 were spent at numerous army schools as a student and instructor with a brief stint (1933–36), after his promotion to captain in 1932, with military intelligence in the Philippines. Made a temporary brigadier general in 1941, Collins became chief of staff of the 7th Corps (1941) and then commanding general of the 25th Division. In 1942, he took the 25th to Guadalcanal where he was heavily decorated for his leadership in the battle to rid the island of the Japanese. Back in England with the 7th Corps in 1943, he led them through the 1944 Normandy invasions, across France, into Belgium, and, in the south, to the Elbe River to meet the Russian army. He was promoted to lieutenant general in 1945. In late 1945, he began an extended tenure in Washington, serving within the U.S. Army's top leadership. Initially, he was appointed to become the army's spokesman to the press and the manager of army information programs. His duties at this juncture involved the difficult change from a conscript to a volunteer force and the emotionally charged issue of balancing the desires of combat veterans to return to civilian life against the nation's new found military occupation duties. In 1947, he began successive appointments as deputy and then vice chief of staff within Headquarters, Department of the Army. During 1948, he was promoted to full general. In these positions, Collins faced such major issues as trying to salvage some U.S. ground combat capability while the nation rushed to disarm, developing new strategies at the dawn of the Cold War, and integrating the U.S. armed services. The latter movement was strongly pushed by Pres. Harry S Truman and bitterly resisted by some Southern Congressmen. In the end, the army led the nation's federal institutions in racial integration.

In August 1949, Collins was elevated to the position of chief of staff of the army. During the next four years, he administered the country's primary ground force through a period that included the Korean War, the military buildup of the North Atlantic Treaty Organization (NATO) and the growing involvement of the United States in Southeast Asia. Collins's Korean War duties often involved dealing with Gen. Douglas MacArthur, his former World War II superior. When the Joint Chiefs of Staff (JCS) learned of a dramatic amphibious operation about to unfold in Korea while United Nations (UN) forces were struggling to maintain a foothold on the Pusan perimeter, Collins was dispatched to MacArthur's headquarters to learn of the specific details. Although there were serious objections from naval and Marine Corps officers to MacArthur's daring plan for the Inchon invasion, Collins apparently came to approve of it. Returning to Washington, he persuaded the Joint Chiefs to send a message to MacArthur with a JCS seal of approval, an act that was not considered necessary. Additionally, Collins briefed President Truman on the plan, a briefing that won the commander in chief's enthusiasm. Soon, however, with the Chinese intervention in the war, Collins had to endure the painful tasks associated with MacArthur's relief and replacement.

Since Collins had become knowledgeable with NATO affairs in supplying much of the organization's combat and logistical ground forces, Pres. Dwight D. Eisenhower asked the general to go to Europe after his second term as chief of staff ended. Appointed as the U.S. representative on NATO's Military Committee and Standing Group, Collins was deeply involved in the defense of Western Europe from late 1953 until late 1954.

In October 1954, he was given a new mission, in Vietnam. In 1950, during the Indochina War, Collins had recommended that the United States should be prepared to enter the fight as long as other UN forces participated and as long as U.S. involvement did not degrade U.S. capabilities to wage general war. When Eisenhower gave the general ambassadorial rank and a mission to determine the size and scope of U.S. assistance to the newly formed Republic of South Vietnam, Collins's enthusiasm for U.S. resistance to Communism in this corner of the world began to cool. Mostly, his wariness about a Vietnam adventure for the United States centered on the lack of sound leadership in South Vietnam. Occasionally, Collins noted a bit of optimism about South Vietnam's Pres. Ngo Dinh Diem. But on the whole, he was doubtful about Diem's chances to rally South Vietnam against a growing menace in North Vietnam and doubtful also about Diem's ability to defeat a number of internal threats, including the Communists. Collins believed that Diem's brother, Nhu, and Nhu's wife were bad influences. He reported that his own advice to Diem was rarely heeded. In April 1955, during a personal session with President Eisenhower, General Collins flatly stated there was no good solution in South Vietnam as long as Diem remained in power. When Collins left South Vietnam in 1955, Diem was still in power, and the United States was committed to a perilous course.

Retired from active service in 1956, Collins became vice chairman for international operations for the Charles Pfizer Company. At the same time, Collins became the director of the President's Committee for Hungarian Refu-

During this 1951 visit to Hanoi, U.S. Army chief of staff Gen. Joseph L. Collins favored U.S. military involvement in Indochina, but by 1955, he had serious doubts about such a commitment. (National Archives)

gee Relief shortly after the Soviet Union had brutally put down the 1956 Hungarian uprising. He subsequently served as chairman of other public service organizations. In 1969, he published a highly readable and informative account of the Korean War from the perspective of the JCS. Ten years later, he produced an autobiography, *Lightning Joe*.

Collins's public service was characterized by sound judgment. Unlike so many who were heavily influenced by their experience in Europe or others who saw the world from the perspective of Asia, Collins's firsthand knowledge included both regions during and after World War II. In retrospect, the judgments of Collins deserved close attention.

Bibliography: Collins, J. Lawton, *Lightning Joe, An Autobiography* (Louisiana State Univ. Press, 1979); ———, *War in Peacetime, The History and Lessons of Korea* (Houghton Mifflin, 1969); Spector, Ronald H., *The U.S. Army in Vietnam: Advice and Support: The Early Years, 1941–1960* (Center of Military History, U.S. Army, 1983).

Col. (Ret.) Rod Paschall

CRAIG, EDWARD ARTHUR (1896–)

U.S. marine officer, Craig was born in Danbury, Connecticut. He was commissioned a marine second lieutenant in 1917. He later served as a captain in Nicaragua. During World War II, he was executive officer, then commander, of the 9th Marine Regiment, followed by assignment as operations officer of the V Amphibious Corps. He was promoted to brigadier general in 1947.

In Korea from 1950, he commanded the 1st Provisional Marine Brigade, then became assistant division commander of the 1st Marine Division. Under Craig's leadership, the Marine Brigade fought in the Pusan perimeter with the élan that has always been the hallmark of the U.S. Marine Corps. After the war, Craig went on to become a lieutenant general before his retirement in 1951.

Bibliography: Davis, Burke, *Marine! The Life of Chesty Puller* (Bantam Books, 1962); Montrose, Lynn, and Nicholas A. Canzona, *U.S. Marine Operations in Korea 1950–1953; Vol. 1: The Pusan Perimeter* (U.S. Marine Corps Hdqrs., 1954).

Brig. Gen. PNG (Ret.) Uzal W. Ent

CROWE, WILLIAM JAMES, JR. (1925–)

Chairman of the U.S. Joint Chiefs of Staff (1985–89), Crowe was born in La Grange, Kentucky. In 1943, after one year at the University of Oklahoma, he enrolled at the Naval Academy. Three years later, he captained the academy's debate squad, which captured the intercollegiate championship. After his graduation in 1946, Crowe received air indoctrination training at Jacksonville, Florida, then attended the Submarine School in New London, Connecticut, in preparation for duty on the submarine *Flying Fish*. In 1951, he joined the staff of Commander Submarine Force, U.S. Atlantic Fleet; qualified for command of submarines in 1954; then held his only sea command on board the submarine *Trout* (1960–62). In the meantime, Crowe furthered his education, even taking a leave from the navy to obtain a master's degree in education from Stanford University in 1956. Nine years later, Crowe added a Ph.D. in politics from Princeton University.

Crowe became the commander of the 31st Submarine Division in 1966, then headed the East Asia and Pacific Branch at the Office of the Chief of Naval Operations the next year. From 1970 to 1971, Crowe served in Vietnam as senior adviser for Amphibious Task Force 211 and commander of Task Force 210 and advised South Vietnamese river forces.

Promoted to rear admiral in 1974, Crowe spent two years as the director of the East Asia and Pacific Region at the Pentagon before heading a Middle East Force based at Bahrain (1976–77). As vice admiral, he commanded NATO (North Atlantic Treaty Organization) forces in southern Europe for three years, helping to mediate Greek-Turkish disputes during his tenure. Crowe followed that service as commander in chief, Pacific Command, from 1983 to 1985.

Crowe gathered admirers as he rose through the ranks. Sec. of Defense Caspar W. Weinberger liked his negotiating talent, and in April 1984, Crowe impressed Pres. Ronald Reagan and a group of his advisers with his performance in a briefing. On Oct. 1, 1985, Crowe became chairman of the Joint Chiefs of Staff, emphasizing in his swearing-in speech that he would strive for a more harmonious interservice relationship to help eliminate waste. Crowe advised President Reagan in 1987 during talks with the Soviet Union over the Intermediate-range Nuclear Forces Treaty and later urged the president to prepare for a military response after Reagan ordered commercial ships in the Persian Gulf brought under U.S. protection when Iran began harassing such traffic. Crowe, the first chairman not to have served in World War II, was succeeded by Gen. Colin L. Powell in October 1989.

Bibliography: *Current Biography Yearbook, 1988;* "Rear Admiral William J. Crowe, Jr." (Navy Office of Information).

John F. Wukovits

CUSHMAN, JOHN HOLLOWAY (1921–)

U.S. army officer, Cushman was born in Tientsin, China. He graduated from West Point in 1944 as an engineer officer and served in the Pacific during World War II and in the postwar Occupation of Japan. He transferred to the infantry in 1951.

Cushman first served in Vietnam in 1963 as the senior adviser to the 21st ARVN (Army of the Republic of Vietnam) Infantry Division. Later as a brigade commander in 1967, he deployed the 2d Brigade, 101st Airborne Division, to Vietnam. Under his command, his brigade fought in the intense fighting around Hue and Quang Tri during the 1968 Tet Offensive. On a third tour to Vietnam (1970–72), Cushman served as the commanding general, Delta Regional Assistance Command (DRAC). Rising to the rank of lieutenant general, Cushman later commanded the 101st Airborne Division and I Corps in Korea prior to his retirement in 1978.

Bibliography: Pearson, Willard, *The War in the Northern Provinces, 1966–1968* (U.S. Govt. Printing Office, 1975).

Capt. Leslie Howard Belknap

CUSHMAN, ROBERT EVERTON, JR. (1914–1985)

U.S. marine commander, Cushman was born in St. Paul, Minnesota. He graduated from Annapolis in 1935 and prior to World War II served in China. During the war, Cushman was awarded the Navy Cross for valor while serving as the commander of the 2d Battalion, 9th Marine Regiment, in the liberation of Guam. Later, he participated in operations at Bougainville and Iwo Jima.

In June 1967, Lieutenant General Cushman became commander of the 3d Marine Amphibious Force, directing the Vietnam War efforts of U.S. Armed Forces in the northern reaches of South Vietnam. During his command, Cushman had to deal with the Communist attacks on Khe Sanh, the Tet Offensive, and the protracted battle for the city of Hue. During the great majority of Cushman's command, the marines were on the defensive, and he was the object of some criticism because most of his forces were involved in static defense.

On his return to the United States in 1969, General Cushman became deputy director of the Central Intelligence Agency, serving there until 1972. In that year, he was elevated to become the commandant of the Marine Corps. His service as commandant included the difficult drawdown period after the Vietnam War and the costly and futile Marine assault on a well-defended Cambodian island during the *Mayaguez* incident. Cushman retired in 1975.

Bibliography: Nolan, Keith W., *Battle for Hue, Tet 1968* (Dell, 1983); Pisor, Robert, *The End of The Line: The Siege of Khe Sanh* (Ballantine Books, 1982).

Col. (Ret.) Rod Paschall

DAVIS, BENJAMIN OLIVER, JR. (1912–)

First black general in the U.S. Air Force, Davis was born in Washington, D.C., the son of the first black promoted to brigadier general in the U.S. Army. He attended three different colleges before gaining an appointment to West Point, where he became only the fourth black to graduate (1936). For four years, he endured "the Silence" at West Point, demonstrating a determination that would earn him respect throughout his career, as well as forcing changes in the military.

Although interested in flying, Davis was assigned to the infantry at Fort Benning, Georgia, after graduation because the Air Corps was completely segregated. After a year as commander of an all-black service company, he attended the Infantry School (1938), then became a Reserve Officers Training Corps instructor at Tuskegee Institute in Alabama (1938–41), during which time he was promoted to the rank of captain (1940). He then went to Fort Riley to become his father's aide (1941).

In August 1941, he became the class leader of the first 13 Tuskegee Airmen. He and the four others who graduated in March 1942 formed the initial cadre of the 99th Pursuit Squadron—the first black flying unit. As commander, he was promoted to temporary lieutenant colonel and led the unit into combat in North Africa, Sicily, and Italy. Late in 1943, he returned to the United States to take command of the 332d Fighter Group, taking it into combat over southern France and Italy. Having been promoted to colonel in 1944, he once again returned to the United States in 1945, this time to command the 477th Composite Group, which was having racial problems, and in 1946 to command Lockbourne Army Air Base.

Here was where Davis's attitude and ability shone. As an officer and commander, he was held in high regard. He taught his men to deal with discrimination with intelligence and patience, driving them to perform regardless of pressure. Because of his success in solving these types of problems, he was delayed in attending the Air War College until 1949, when a suitable replacement could be found to take over the group with the same drive and concern.

In 1954, he became the air force's first black general officer, received his second star in 1959, and a third in 1965. As a general officer, he served in Korea, Taiwan, West Germany, and the Philippines, and his final tour was as the deputy commander of U.S. Strike Force.

After retiring from active duty as a lieutenant general in 1970, Davis held several key positions as a civil servant. Between 1970 and 1971, he served in Cleveland as the director of public safety, on the President's Commission on Campus Unrest, and then led the "sky marshals" of the Department of Transportation in eliminating skyjacking in the United States. In 1971, he became assistant secretary of transportation. He later served on the Presidential Commission on Military Compensation.

Bibliography: Davis, Benjamin O., Jr., *Benjamin O. Davis, Jr., American* (Smithsonian Inst. Press, 1991);

Gropeman, Alan, "Benjamin O. Davis, Jr.: History on Two Fronts," *Makers of the United States Air Force,* ed. by John L. Frisbee (Office of Air Force History, 1987).

Capt. Michael J. Reed

DEAN, WILLIAM FRISHE (1899–1981)

U.S. army officer, Dean was born in Carlyle, Illinois. After graduating from the University of California at Berkeley, he joined the regular army as an infantry officer in 1923. He graduated from the Command and General Staff School in 1940 and attended the Army War College. At the outset of World War II, Dean served on the War Department Staff, rapidly rising in rank. He became an assistant division commander of the 44th Infantry Division, a unit that entered France in the summer of 1944. In December 1944, Dean took command of the division, a position he held until the end of the war.

Following World War II, Dean became the military governor of South Korea (1947–48). When U.S. occupation forces withdrew from that nation, he once again became a division commander in 1949, first with the 7th Infantry Division and later with the 24th Division in Japan. A few days after the North Korean invasion of South Korea in 1950, Dean was ordered to move his command to Korea as the lead element of the 8th Army. Sending a task force (Task Force Smith) forward, Dean arrived on the rapidly changing battlefield on July 3, 1950. The initial American ground defense was crumbling before large tank-led columns of North Korean troops. The South Korean army was largely destroyed, and morale among Dean's badly outnumbered and often outflanked Americans was vanishing. The division's task soon became simply to delay the onrushing Communist forces long enough for other U.S. units to arrive. Out of communications with his forward units and needing to set an example for his retreating soldiers, Major General Dean moved to the critical point on the battlefield, Taejon. He rallied his troops and began using a rocket launcher to demonstrate its effectiveness against the Communist T-34 tanks.

Dean fell into enemy hands. Unaware that Taejon was quickly being outflanked, Dean had lingered too long and found himself belatedly trying to lead his men out of a closing trap. Many escaped, but Dean's aid to the wounded cost him time. Briefly losing his way, the general became separated from his men. He wandered about, trying to find allied lines for 36 days but was finally captured. Suffering brutal treatment at the hand of his captors, Dean bore up under the pressure.

At war's end in 1953, Dean returned to the United States a hero. He came in for some criticism when he advocated clemency for U.S. prisoners who had cooperated with their captors. Dean took more than his share of the blame for the defeat of his division and readily admitted to some tactical mistakes. He served as deputy commander of the 6th Army from 1953, and retired in 1955.

Bibliography: Appleman, Roy E., *The United States Army in the Korean War: South to the Naktong, North to the Yalu* (U.S. Govt. Printing Office, 1961); Dean, William F., and William L. Worden, *General Dean's Story* (Viking, 1954).

Col. (Ret.) Rod Paschall

DECKER, GEORGE HENRY (1902–1980)

U.S. army officer, Decker was born in Catskill, New York. He graduated from Lafayette College in 1924 and was commissioned in the infantry in the same year. Prior to World War II, he served at a number of posts throughout the United States and graduated from the Command and General Staff School at Fort Leavenworth in 1937.

At the outset of World War II, Decker was in Washington, as a lieutenant colonel assigned to the Office of the Assistant Chief of Staff for Supply. In October 1942, he left Washington to join the 3d Army but was subsequently sent to the Southwest Pacific theater of operations. There, he became the 6th Army chief of staff, participating in campaigns from New Guinea to the Philippines. During the war, he advanced in rank to the temporary grade of major general.

By 1948, Decker was commanding the 5th Infantry Division at Fort Jackson, South Carolina. During the Korean War, he was assigned to staff duties in Washington, becoming the army's comptroller in 1952. By 1954, Decker was in Germany, as the new VII Corps commander. Subsequently, he was named to command the 8th Army in Korea.

Returning to Washington in 1959, General Decker became the army chief of staff in 1960. His tenure included the initial difficulties involved in acrimonious disputes over the reorganization of the army's logistical structure, a program that had heavy influence from the new secretary of defense, Robert McNamara. Additionally, Decker oversaw plans for the reorganization of the army's combat divisions before his retirement in 1962.

Bibliography: Bell, William G., *Commanding Generals and Chiefs of Staff, 1775–1987* (Center of Military History, U.S. Army, 1987).

Col. (Ret.) Rod Paschall

DENFELD, LOUIS EMIL (1891–1972)

U.S. naval officer, Denfeld was born in Westboro, Massachusetts. He graduated from Annapolis in 1912 and saw duty in a Queenstown, Ireland-based destroyer during World War I. Denfeld attained flag rank during World War II, serving as assistant chief of the Bureau of Personnel before commanding a battleship division during the Okinawa Campaign. In early 1947, he took command of the

Pacific Fleet and in December succeeded Fleet Adm. Chester Nimitz as chief of naval operations.

Denfeld took office at a time when the navy was under the pressures imposed by postwar demobilization and drastic cuts in defense spending. Although his experience was as a surface officer, Denfeld made an effective presentation of the navy's case that carriers were a flexible and essential weapons system and gained approval for construction of a 65,000-ton super-carrier. Denfeld's position, however, became even more difficult when Louis Johnson replaced James Forrestal as secretary of defense in early 1949. Johnson cancelled funding for the super-carrier while supporting the air force's call for additional strategic bomber groups. Navy secretary John Sullivan resigned in protest, but Denfeld tried his best to represent the navy. Johnson remained adamant that there would be no super-carrier and trimmed the navy's budget in other areas. Matters erupted into the news, however, and Denfeld decided to speak out at hearings before the House Armed Services Committee without first informing the secretary of the navy. New secretary Francis Matthews now demanded and got Denfeld's relief. Denfeld rejected the fleet command that was offered him instead and in retirement took his case to the popular press.

Bibliography: Coletta, Paolo E., *The Chiefs of Naval Operations,* ed. by Robert William Love, Jr. (Naval Inst. Press, 1980).

Lloyd J. Graybar

DEPUY, WILLIAM EUGENE (1919–1992)

U.S. army officer, DePuy was born in Jamestown, North Dakota. As a young officer in World War II, he advanced to command of the 1st Battalion, 357th Infantry, in the 90th Infantry Division during the fighting in Europe. During the Vietnam War, DePuy commanded the 1st Infantry Division, then had a major impact on army management and structure as assistant vice chief of staff (1969–73). When the Training and Doctrine Command was established in 1973, DePuy was assigned as its first commanding general. Under his leadership, both missions prospered, with "AirLand Battle" doctrine and innovative force-on-force training being developed. DePuy's influence continued long after his retirement as these achievements were demonstrated in the 1991 Gulf War.

Bibliography: DePuy, William E., *Changing an Army: An Oral History* (U.S. Army Military History Inst., 1988); Herbert, Paul H., *Deciding What Has to Be Done: General William E. DePuy and the 1978 Edition of FM 100-5, Operations* (U.S. Army Command and General Staff College, 1988).

Lewis Sorley

DIEM, NGO DINH (1901–1963)

President of South Vietnam (1954–63), Diem was born in Quang Binh, Annam, a Catholic of noble birth. He was captured by Ho Chi Minh in 1945 but escaped and fled into exile. In 1954, Diem returned to head a U.S.-backed government in South Vietnam. He established an autocratic regime staffed by family and friends. His advancement of Catholics offended the Buddhist majority, and furthermore he did not fulfill his promise of land reform nor curb growing Viet Cong infiltration. Diem's imprisonment and execution of hundreds of South Vietnamese Buddhists on charges of Communist fraternization persuaded the United States to withdraw its support. This precipitated a coup d'état, during which Diem was assassinated (Nov. 2, 1963).

Russell A. Hart

DUERK, ALENE BERTHA (1920–   )

First woman in the U.S. Navy to be promoted to rear admiral (lower half), Duerk was born in Defiance, Ohio. She was commissioned in the Nurse Corps in January 1943 and received a regular navy commission in 1953. During World War II, she served as a ward nurse at naval hospitals. At war's end, Duerk left the service and obtained her bachelor's degree. Early in the Korean War, she was recalled on active duty to serve at the Naval Hospital Corps School, Portsmouth, Virginia, 1951–56, and subsequently served in a variety of posts in the United States and overseas. Selected as director of the Navy Nurse Corps in 1970, Duerk intensified nurse specialist and technical training, improved housing and uniforms, and opened professional education and assignment opportunities for navy nurses. In July 1971, she received her promotion to rear admiral. After retirement in 1975, she remained a member of the Navy Nurse Corps Association as well as other professional nursing associations.

Bibliography: "Rear Admiral Alene B. Duerk, Nurse Corps, United States Navy" (Navy Office of Information, Bureau of Naval Personnel, July 1972).

Col. (Ret.) Bettie J. Morden

DULLES, ALLEN WELSH (1893–1969)

U.S. diplomat and director of the Central Intelligence Agency (CIA), Dulles was born in Watertown, New York. After receiving bachelor's and master's degrees from Princeton University and a law degree from George Washington University, he went on to serve in a number of posts in the diplomatic service. He was a member of the U.S. delegation to the Versaille Peace Conference in 1918–19. Dulles's first intelligence-related post was as a top official of the Office of Strategic Service in World War II, in which he oversaw all espionage activities against Germany.

After a two-year stint (1951–53) as deputy director of the newly formed CIA, Dulles in 1953 was appointed the organization's director, a post he held until 1961. An avid proponent of maximum secrecy in intelligence matters,

Dulles oversaw a number of successful CIA operations, including the overthrow of left-wing governments in Iran in 1953 and Guatemala in 1955. During Dulles's tenure, the CIA made great technological strides in intelligence gathering, including the development of the U-2 spy plane. According to a 1975 Senate select committee report, Dulles authorized a plan to assassinate Congolese premier Patrice Lumumba, although the assassination was not carried out.

Dulles helped to plan the failed Bay of Pigs invasion, and it was he, along with Richard Bissell, who briefed Pres. John F. Kennedy on the Cuban exile force and obtained the new president's go-ahead for the invasion. Dulles thought of the Cold War as largely a struggle between the forces of good and evil—an outlook shared by his brother, Pres. Dwight D. Eisenhower's secretary of state John Foster Dulles—and he frequently justified the clandestine adventures of the CIA on that basis.

Bibliography: Ranelagh, John, *The Agency: The Rise and Decline of the CIA* (Simon & Schuster, 1987).

James A. Warren

DULLES, JOHN FOSTER (1888–1959)

U.S. secretary of state (1953–59), Dulles was born in Washington, D.C., the grandson of Sec. of State John Foster and nephew of Sec. of State Robert Lansing. Prior to entering government service, he practiced international law and rose to be a senior partner in the prestigious Wall Street law firm of Sullivan and Cromwell. Until 1919, he was a Wilsonian Democrat, but he and the president parted ways when Wilson pushed for "peaceful change" following the Treaty of Versailles.

During World War II, Dulles emerged as a leading spokesman for the foreign policy views of the eastern wing of the Republican party. By the late 1940s, he was acting as a Republican adviser to the Harry S Truman administration. However, by 1952, partisanship and policy differences led Dulles to become an outspoken critic of Truman's foreign policy. His well-publicized 1952 article in *Life* magazine condemned Truman's and Sec. of State Dean Acheson's containment policy.

During the 1952 presidential campaign, Dulles stridently called for a rollback of Soviet territorial gains in Eastern Europe as well as support for Chiang Kai-shek in Taiwan. The bold, foreign policy views of Dulles led president-elect Dwight D. Eisenhower to mark him for the secretary of state post. In this capacity, Dulles was often seen as a stern Presbyterian moralist whose speeches condemned Communism and threatened massive retaliation. For many historians, he became the model of the "cold warrior," a vigorous anticommunist whose rhetoric only fanned the flames of U.S.-Soviet animosity. Dulles was long regarded as the sole architect of U.S. foreign policy during the Eisenhower years. However, recently declassified documents

John Foster Dulles, secretary of state to President Eisenhower, was an outspoken anticommunist whose sentiments did little to quell Cold War animosities. (National Archives)

reveal that President Eisenhower was an activist in shaping foreign policy and that he participated in a collaborative effort with Dulles.

M. Guy Bishop

EBERSTADT, FERDINAND (1890–1969)

U.S. defense adviser, Eberstadt was born in New York City. He graduated from Princeton University in 1913 and Columbia University law school in 1917. Following World War I service in France, he became an investment banker. During World War II, he served as chairman of the Army-Navy Munitions Board (1942) and as vice chairman of the War Production Board (1942–43). In 1945, Eberstadt prepared a report for Sec. of the Navy James Forrestal on the question of the unification of the armed forces. Eberstadt recommended three coordinate services rather than one unified defense organization. His report became the basis for the National Security Act of 1947. He later chaired the Committee on National Security Organization of the first Hoover Commission and recommended important changes in the financial management of the Department of Defense.

Bibliography: Hewes, James E., *From Root to McNamara: Army Organization and Administration, 1900–1963* (Center of Military History, U.S. Army, 1975); Weigley, Russell F., *History of the United States Army* (Macmillan, 1967).

Lt. Col. (Ret.) Charles R. Shrader

EISENHOWER, DWIGHT DAVID ("IKE") (1890–1969)

U.S. five-star general; commander of Supreme Headquarters, Allied Expeditionary Force, in World War II; and 34th president of the United States (1953–61), Eisenhower was born in Denison, Texas. He graduated from West Point in 1915 and was commissioned a second lieutenant of infantry. He did not serve overseas in World War I and during the interwar period had both staff and school assignments.

Promoted in September 1941 to brigadier general, Eisenhower became deputy chief of the War Plans Division for the Pacific and Far East, working closely with the chief of staff, Gen. George C. Marshall. Promoted to major general, Eisenhower became head of the Operations Division of the War Department, the military's worldwide command post. These assignments clearly qualified Eisen-

Gen. Dwight D. Eisenhower, a national icon since World War II, rode his popularity all the way to the White House, becoming in 1953 the first Republican inaugurated since 1929. (U.S. Military Academy)

hower to become commander of the European Theater of Operations to prepare in England for the invasion of the Continent.

Although Eisenhower and Marshall favored a prompt invasion of France, their strategy was not supported by the British, who urged instead an Allied invasion of North Africa. Having gained the confidence of British political and military leaders, Eisenhower was selected to command Operation Torch, which led to the defeat of the Axis in North Africa by May 1943. Eisenhower then took command in the Mediterranean and oversaw the invasion of Sicily and the Italian mainland later in 1943. Eisenhower's selection in December to command Operation Overlord, the invasion of France, confirmed his rise to preeminence among World War II commanders.

Ordering the invasion was probably the single most important decision of Eisenhower's military career. A storm in the English Channel delayed the invasion and posed concern for Eisenhower, who made the decision to carry out the successful D-Day invasions of Normandy, France, on June 6, 1944.

After a hard campaign in France, Eisenhower's forces crossed the Rhine River in March 1945. Germany was defeated, and Eisenhower's mission was accomplished with Germany's surrender on May 7, 1945.

Postwar Career. World War II had made Eisenhower (promoted in December 1944 to the rank of General of the Army) a popular international celebrity. After the war, he served as chief of staff and retired from the army to become president of Columbia University. He returned to active duty in 1950 as the first commander of the North Atlantic Treaty Organization (NATO) military forces.

Sought by both political parties to run for president, Eisenhower accepted the Republican nomination in 1952 and was elected president in November. He served two terms, during which he worked to keep the nation at peace while encouraging economic development and limiting government spending.

Eisenhower forced severe spending cuts on the military services in his desire for a balanced budget. He stressed reliance on nuclear weapons to deter Soviet aggression. His famous farewell address warned the United States about the growing power of the military-industrial complex. He died in Washington, D.C., on Mar. 28, 1969.

Eisenhower was the outstanding general of World War II. His efforts were critical to the forging of the military alliance that defeated Germany. Soldier and statesman, Eisenhower always placed duty above personal ambition.

Bibliography: Ambrose, Stephen E., *The Supreme Commander: The War Years of Dwight D. Eisenhower* (Doubleday, 1970); Eisenhower, David, *Eisenhower At War 1943–1945* (Random House, 1986); Eisenhower, Dwight D., *Crusade in Europe* (Doubleday, 1948).

Robert H. Berlin

ENTHOVEN, ALAIN CHARLES (1930–)

U.S. defense analyst, Enthoven was born in Seattle, Washington. He was a Phi Beta Kappa economist educated at Stanford University and the Massachusetts Institute of Technology and at Oxford as a Rhodes scholar. In 1960, he went from the Rand Corporation to the Department of Defense, soon advancing to deputy comptroller and subsequently to the key position of assistant secretary of defense for systems analysis (1965–69). Enthoven became one of the most controversial figures in a turbulent Defense Department, lauded by Sec. of Defense Robert S. McNamara and others for bringing a systematic, logical, and accountable process to the analysis of defense issues, but resented by many senior military officers for using the techniques of systems analysis to override professional military judgment. As the Vietnam War continued without resolution, these tensions became increasingly aggravated. Enthoven left government service at the end of the Lyndon B. Johnson administration (1969) and thereafter devoted himself to teaching, writing, and business.

Bibliography: Enthoven, Alain C., and K. Wayne Smith, *How Much Is Enough? Shaping the Defense Program, 1961–1969* (Harper & Row, 1971).

Lewis Sorley

EVEREST, FRANK KENDALL, JR. (1920–)

U.S. air force officer and test pilot, Everest was born in Fairmont, West Virginia. He attended West Virginia University for the sole purpose of passing the entrance exams to enter the Air Corps' flying cadet program when World War II broke out. After completing training, he flew P-40s in Africa and Italy before going to China in 1944. There, he was shot down and became a prisoner of war, released at war's end.

After the war, Colonel Everest became a test pilot, first at Wright Field, and then at Edwards Air Force Base. He was qualified in more than 100 different aircraft and was the first pilot to break the sound barrier in a turbojet-powered aircraft in level flight. He led the testing programs for the X-1 and X-2, as well as for the Century-series fighters. Everest's autobiography, *The Fastest Man Alive,* was published in 1958.

Capt. Michael J. Reed

FORD, GERALD RUDOLPH (1913–)

Thirty-eighth president of the United States (1974–77), Ford was born Leslie King, Jr., in Omaha, Nebraska, and assumed his stepfather's name at age two. He graduated from Yale Law School in 1941 and served in the navy throughout World War II. After the war, he became a leader of the Republican party, serving in the House of Representatives from 1949 until 1973. At that time Pres. Richard M. Nixon chose Ford to be vice president, follow-

Pres. Gerald R. Ford, who took office when President Nixon resigned in 1974, ordered the evacuation of Americans and Vietnamese sympathizers from Saigon in early 1975, as the city fell to the North Vietnamese. (Library of Congress)

ing the resignation of Spiro T. Agnew. Upon the resignation of Nixon himself in August 1974, Ford acceded to the presidency. Ford had no clear-cut political agenda, seeking only to end the "long political nightmare" provoked by the Watergate scandal that had led to Nixon's forced departure. As president, Ford presided over the evacuation of U.S. personnel from Vietnam beginning in April 1975. Because he was linked to this withdrawal, Ford was destined to have no notable strength in foreign affairs. In the 1976 presidential election, he lost to Democrat Jimmy Carter.

M. Guy Bishop

FORRESTAL, JAMES VINCENT
(1892–1949)
U.S. secretary of defense (1947–49), Forrestal was born in Beacon, New York. A navy veteran of World War I, he became a Wall Street financier and then played a key role in the navy's buildup in World War II as undersecretary (1940–44) and secretary (1945–47) of the navy. For-

restal was against what he considered excessive demobilization after the war, supported universal military training, and, although personally opposed the merger of the armed forces, supported President Truman's creation of the Department of Defense.

Selected as the first secretary of defense, Forrestal worked hard to increase cooperation among the service branches and to formulate a comprehensive strategy to oppose Soviet expansion in Europe and Asia. He was criticized for his supposed opposition to Israel and lack of control of the air force and resigned in March 1949. Hospitalized for depression, he committed suicide later in the year.

Stephen Robinson

FREEMAN, PAUL LAMAR, JR.
(1907–1988)
U.S. army commander, Freeman was born in the Philippines. He graduated from West Point in 1929 and was commissioned a second lieutenant in the infantry. He served in China with the 15th Infantry Regiment (1933–36), then returned to that country three years later as a language student and intelligence officer. Soon after World War II began, he became Gen. Joseph Stilwell's G-4 (Logistics) and later organized the commando team known as Merrill's Marauders. In mid-1943, Freeman became a member of the Army War Plans Division until late 1944, when he was appointed chief of staff of the 77th Division. Later, Freeman became G-3 (Operations and Training) of the 6th Army and I Corps.

During the Korean War, he commanded the 23d Infantry Regiment with singular distinction. After that war, Freeman's assignments included commander, 2d Infantry Division (1955–56); deputy commander in chief, U.S. Army in Europe and Central Army Group (1962–65); and commanding general, Continental Army Command (1966–67). Freeman retired as a full general in 1967.

Bibliography: Blair, Clay, *The Forgotten War* (Time Books, 1987).

Brig. Gen. PNG (Ret.) Uzal W. Ent

GALVIN, JOHN ROGERS (1929–   )
U.S. army officer and historian, Galvin was born in Wakefield, Massachusetts. He graduated from West Point in 1954 as an infantry officer. He served in Central America and in Vietnam. In 1962, Galvin became an English teacher at West Point. After battalion, brigade, and division commands, he commanded the VII Corps in Stuttgart, West Germany, during 1983–85. After commanding Southern Command in Latin America, he returned to Europe in 1987 as the Supreme Allied Commander, Europe, the senior army commander in the North Atlantic Treaty

Organization. Seen by many in the military as an intellectual, Galvin published several books, including three on the American Revolution and one on the development of air mobile warfare.

Maj. George B. Eaton

GATES, THOMAS SOVEREIGN, JR.
(1906–1983)
U.S. secretary of the navy and of defense, Gates was born in Philadelphia and became a prominent investment banker. He saw combat as a naval reserve officer in World War II. Gates was named undersecretary of the navy in 1953 and was appointed secretary the following year. As a peacetime secretary, Gates inevitably presided over a shrinking of the navy. His incumbency, however, was also noted for technological advances, particularly in the construction of several nuclear submarines and the nuclear-powered cruiser *Long Beach,* as well as in antisubmarine capabilities. Gates also tried to make the navy more appealing as a career for able officers and enlisted men. In 1959, he left the navy department to become deputy secretary of defense and then secretary of defense. He resigned in 1961 and reentered banking. In 1976–77, Gates headed the U.S. liaison office in China.

Bibliography: Wadleigh, John R., "Thomas Sovereign Gates, Jr.," *American Secretaries of the Navy, 1913–1972,* ed. by Paolo Coletta (Naval Inst. Press, 1980).

Lloyd J. Graybar

GAVIN, JAMES MAURICE (1907–   )
U.S. army officer and presidential adviser, Gavin was born in Brooklyn, New York. He graduated from West Point in 1929 and was commissioned a second lieutenant of infantry. One of the pioneers of the U.S. Army airborne branch, he commanded the 505th Airborne Infantry Regiment (82d Airborne Division) in 1942. His regiment participated in an ineffective airdrop during the Sicilian Campaign, when 80 percent of his men were dropped up to 65 miles from their designated zones.

In December 1943, Gavin was named assistant division commander of the 82d. Subsequently, at the age of 37, he was given command of the division and led it as a brigadier general during the Allied Market-Garden operation. In 1944, he was promoted to major general and led his division at the Battle of the Bulge. He won numerous awards for heroism during the war, including two Distinguished Service Crosses and two Silver Stars.

After the war, Gavin served with the Joint Chiefs of Staff (1949–51) as chief of staff, Allied Forces, Southern Europe (1951–52), then as commander of the U.S. VII Corps in Europe (1952–54). Returning to the United States, he became army deputy for research and develop-

ment. In that position, he was regarded by some as being more interested in initiating projects than in following through on them. Others thought that he was unable to make recommendations about development. He retired as a lieutenant general in 1958.

When John F. Kennedy was campaigning for president of the United States, Gavin was called upon for advice. He subsequently served as ambassador to France (1961–62) before becoming chairman of the board for the Arthur D. Little Company. Early in the Vietnam War, Gavin argued for a strategy limiting U.S. involvement to the protection of a few key bases such as Da Nang and Cam Ranh Bay, halting the bombing of North Vietnam, and negotiating a solution through the United Nations or a Geneva conference (the so-called enclave strategy).

Bibliography: Ryan, Cornelius, *A Bridge Too Far* (Simon & Schuster, 1974); Taylor, John M., *General Maxwell Taylor: The Sword and the Pen* (Doubleday Dell, 1989); Weigley, Russell F., *Eisenhower's Lieutenants* (Indiana Univ. Press, 1981).

Brig. Gen. PNG (Ret.) Uzal W. Ent

GAY, HOBART RAYMOND (1894–1983)
U.S. army officer, Gay was born in Rockport, Illinois. Graduating from Knox College in 1917, he commanded cavalry patrols along the Mexican border during World War I. Blinded in one eye while playing polo, he transferred to the Quartermaster Corps until 1941. After returning to the cavalry in World War II, "Hap" Gay became chief of staff to Gen. George S. Patton, who described him as "the bravest man I ever knew."

Gay commanded the 1st Cavalry Division during the Korean War, fighting in the Pusan perimeter and at Unsan. After rotating to the United States, he commanded VI and III Corps and served as commanding general of the 5th Army in Chicago. Gay retired on Aug. 31, 1955, and assumed duties as superintendent of New Mexico Military Institute.

Maj. James Sanders Day

GLENN, JOHN HERSCHEL, JR. (1921–   )
U.S. astronaut and politician, Glenn was born in Cambridge, Ohio. He entered the Marine Corps in 1943 and flew as a fighter pilot in World War II and the Korean War. After serving as a flight instructor and test pilot, he was chosen as one of the original astronauts in 1959. In 1962, he became the first American to orbit the earth, circling the globe three times in *Friendship 7,* and immediately achieved enormous fame. He retired from the military in late 1964 with the intention of entering politics, but it was not until his third campaign that he won election to the Senate in 1974 as a Democrat. In the Senate he worked for nuclear testing and arms control. He failed to

On Feb. 20, 1962, U.S. astronaut John Glenn, piloting the space capsule Friendship 7, *became the first American to orbit the earth.* (NASA)

win the Democratic presidential nomination in 1984 and was subsequently reelected to the Senate in 1986 and 1992.

Stephen Robinson

GOODPASTER, ANDREW JACKSON
(1915–   )

U.S. army commander, Goodpaster was born in Granite City, Illinois. He graduated second in the West Point Class of 1939 and was commissioned in the Corps of Engineers. During World War II, he commanded the 48th Engineer Combat Battalion in Italy, earning the Distinguished Service Cross for heroism, along with the Silver Star and two Purple Hearts. Following three years on the Army General Staff, he earned multiple graduate degrees, including a doctorate, at Princeton University.

With Eisenhower.   A four-year assignment (1950–54) as a staff officer at SHAPE (Supreme Headquarters Allied Powers, Europe), the NATO (North Atlantic Treaty Organization) military command, began for Goodpaster a long association with Gen. Dwight D. Eisenhower, who served as the first NATO commander. When Eisenhower was president, Goodpaster had an extended assignment to the White House, serving as staff secretary in 1954–61, during which time he advanced to brigadier general.

Increased Responsibility.   Following his White House service, Goodpaster went to Europe to command the 8th Infantry Division, was for four years assistant to the chairman of the Joint Chiefs of Staff (JCS), and then became director of the joint staff for a year. Next, he was commandant of the National War College (1967–68).

Vietnam and Beyond.   In the summer of 1968, when Gen. Creighton Abrams took command of U.S. forces in Vietnam, Goodpaster was promoted to full general and was sent to be his deputy. During the year of that assignment, he also had extensive duties in Washington, drawing on his experience with Eisenhower in helping the new Richard M. Nixon administration develop its National Security Council arrangements.

Ahead was the crowning assignment of Goodpaster's career: Supreme Allied Commander, Europe, heading the NATO military establishment where he had served under Eisenhower. Goodpaster took command in July 1969, commencing a five-year stint during very challenging times for the alliance. Many of the European members were hostile to U.S. involvement in Vietnam, and it fell to Goodpaster to ensure that this attitude did not adversely affect NATO cooperation.

Goodpaster also faced continuing efforts by certain U.S. politicians for force reductions in the U.S. troop contribution to NATO; during the years immediately preceding his tenure, the force had been cut back substantially. Rebuilding the readiness of the U.S. forces, adversely affected by the personnel and supply demands of the war in Vietnam, was also a major concern. Goodpaster concentrated on maintaining the alliance's viability in the face of an era of East-West détente, recurring Middle East crises, and MBFR (Mutual and Balanced Force Reduction) and SALT (Strategic Arms Limitation Treaty) negotiations. His most important contribution, however, was probably as a strategist, for under him NATO devised ways of implementing flexible response.

Further Service.   Goodpaster retired from his NATO post in 1974, but only three years later, in the wake of a major cheating scandal at the Military Academy, he was called back to active duty for a four-year assignment as its superintendent, his wisdom and reputation for integrity commending him as the ideal man to right the damage at West Point. Later, he served for five years as chairman of the American Battle Monuments Commission, and for many years at the head of the Atlantic Council of the United States.

Bibliography: Sorley, Lewis, "Goodpaster: Maintaining Deterrence during Détente," *Generals in International Politics: NATO's Supreme Allied Commander, Europe,* ed. by Robert S. Jordan (Univ. Press of Kentucky, 1987).

Lewis Sorley

GRAVELY, SAMUEL LEE, JR. (1922–)

U.S. naval officer, Gravely was born in Richmond, Virginia. His career spanned two eras: when the navy was segregated and when it was desegregated but not without various types of discrimination. A student at Virginia Union University when the United States entered World War II, Gravely, a black, enlisted in the U.S. Naval Reserve in September 1942. His recruit training was segregated, and his first assignment prior to being accepted for officer training in the V-12 program was to janitorial work. In 1944, he was commissioned an ensign in the reserves and assigned to Great Lakes to train black recruits. In May 1945, Gravely first went to sea in a subchaser whose function was to train black personnel for sea duty. Gravely was the first black officer on board. He was released from active duty in April 1946 and recalled three years later when the navy, now desegregating, was recruiting black personnel. He was assigned to recruiting duty in Washington, D.C. He then undertook further training in communications prior to assignment as radio officer for the battleship *Iowa* and then for the heavy cruiser *Toledo*. Both ships operated in the Korean War zone.

Soon after his detachment from the *Toledo*, Gravely was transferred from the naval reserve to the regular navy and moved steadily ahead in his career while establishing many firsts. He became the first black officer to command a warship and then a warship in combat; he was also the first black line officer to reach the rank of captain and to attain flag rank. Gravely was selected for rear admiral in 1971 and for vice admiral five years later. As a flag officer, his commands included Cruiser-Destroyer Group Two, the 11th Naval District, 3d Fleet, and the Defense Communications Agency. He retired in 1980.

Bibliography: "Guardian of the Pacific," *Ebony* (Sept. 1977); "Proud New 'Victory' for Navy Destroyer," *Ebony* (July 1966).

Lloyd J. Graybar

GREENE, WALLACE MARTIN, JR. (1907–)

U.S. Marine Corps commandant, Green was born in Waterbury, Vermont. He received his Marine Corps commission in 1930. He helped plan the 1944 Marshall Island assault during World War II, then served as assistant chief of staff, Fleet Marine Force, Pacific Command (1948–50). After graduating from the Naval War College in 1953, Greene rose through various posts to become Marine Corps chief of staff in the early 1960s, working with Commandant Gen. David M. Shoup to implement changes aimed at improving corps readiness. Pres. John F. Kennedy named Greene commandant in 1963 during the early phases of U.S. involvement in Vietnam, and Greene subsequently pushed for an increased role for the marines in Vietnam. He retired in 1968.

Bibliography: Moskin, J. Robert, *The United States Marine Corps Story* (McGraw-Hill, 1977); Sheehan, Neil, *A Bright Shining Lie* (Random House, 1988).

John F. Wukovits

GRUENTHER, ALFRED MAXIMILIAN (1899–1983)

U.S. army staff officer, Gruenther was born in Platte Center, Nebraska. He graduated fourth in his class from West Point in 1919 and was commissioned a second lieutenant of field artillery. In 1941–42, as a brigadier general, he was chief of staff of the 3d Army in the United States. In August 1942, Gruenther was assigned as Gen. Dwight D. Eisenhower's deputy chief of staff in London. When Eisenhower went to North Africa, Gruenther went with him in the same role.

In January, at Gen. Mark Clark's request, he became chief of staff of Clark's 5th Army in the Mediterranean. Gruenther was promoted to major general in 1943. Gen. Omar Bradley regarded him as a superb staff officer, writing that his plan for Salerno was "flawless." When, in November 1944, Clark was elevated to command the 15th Army Group in Italy, Gruenther went along as his chief of staff.

In 1945, he was appointed deputy commanding general, U.S. Forces in Austria. Returning to the United States, he became director of the Joint Chiefs of Staff (1947–49). He was promoted to lieutenant general in 1949 and was assigned as army deputy chief of staff for plans (1949–50).

Between 1950 and 1953, Gruenther served as chief of staff, Supreme Headquarters Allied Powers, Europe (SHAPE). He was promoted to general in 1951. His last assignment was as Supreme Allied Commander, Europe, a position he held from 1953 to 1956. He retired with a physical disability. He never commanded troops in combat, but his career as a highly successful staff officer bears out Bradley's assessment of him.

From 1957 to 1965, Gruenther served as president of the American Red Cross. He was also director of several corporations. His military awards included the Legion of Merit, two Distinguished Service Medals, and the Bronze Star.

Bibliography: Bradley, Omar N., *A General's Life* (Simon & Schuster, 1983); Fisher, Ernest F., Jr., *The United States Army in World War II. The Mediterranean Theater of Operations. Casino to the Alps* (Center of Military History, U.S. Army, 1977).

Brig. Gen., PNG (Ret.) Uzal W. Ent

HAIG, ALEXANDER MEIGS (1924–)

U.S. army commander and statesman, Haig was born in Bala-Cynwyd, Pennsylvania. After a year at Notre Dame University, he received an appointment to West Point, where he was commissioned a second lieutenant in the

Alexander Haig, a former NATO commander and four-star general, resigned as Pres. Ronald Reagan's secretary of state amid conflicts with other cabinet members. (U.S. Military Academy)

cavalry in 1947. After further schooling, he was posted to Japan, where he soon joined the staff of Gen. Douglas MacArthur. On the outbreak of the Korean War, Haig accompanied MacArthur's staff ashore immediately after the Inchon landing on Sept. 15, 1950, and was then attached to X Corps.

In 1951, Haig was transferred to Fort Knox, where he underwent the army's advanced officers course before being assigned to West Point as an instructor in tactics. From 1956 until 1966, he held a succession of line, staff, and school assignments in Europe and the United States.

Promoted to lieutenant colonel, he reported to the U.S. 1st Infantry Division in South Vietnam in 1966 and became a brigade commander. In 1967, he returned to the United States to become regimental commander and deputy commandant at West Point.

Selected to serve on the National Security Council in 1968 as a military adviser, Brigadier General Haig assisted President Nixon's national security adviser, Henry Kissinger. Haig's function was to act as chief of staff and advise Kissinger on military issues and policy. Haig played a key part in the negotiations that eventually led to the Paris Peace Accords in 1973. During the last year of the Nixon administration, Haig, then a four star general,

was appointed White House chief of staff. When Nixon resigned in 1974 due to the Watergate scandal, Haig returned to the army and was soon appointed Supreme Allied Commander, Europe (SACEur) and was also placed in command of all North Atlantic Treaty Organization (NATO) forces. During his tenure as SACEur, Haig was particularly focused on the modernization of the Western military in the face of the Soviet nuclear threat that had emerged in the late 1960s. He therefore devoted his energies to the creation of a tried-and-tested NATO fighting unit, one whose strategic emphasis was readiness.

After his term as SACEur expired, Haig retired from the army in 1979. In 1980, he was appointed secretary of state by Pres. Ronald Reagan. While secretary, he successfully outlined a policy of confronting Soviet support of the so-called wars of national liberation that began to threaten the Western Hemisphere, particularly in Nicaragua and El Salvador. Haig supported Great Britain during the Falklands War in 1982 and the Israeli invasion of Lebanon in 1982. Clashing with Sec. of Defense Caspar W. Weinberger and Reagan's national security adviser, William P. Clark, Haig resigned in June 1982. In 1988, he was briefly a Republican candidate for the presidency.

Bibliography: *Haig, Jr., Alexander M., General, United States Army* (Center of Military History, U.S. Army, 1973); Morris, Roger, *HAIG! The General's Progress* (Playboy Press, 1982); Westmoreland, William C., *A Soldier Reports* (Doubleday, 1976).

Leo J. Daughtery III

HARKINS, PAUL DONAL (1904–1984)

U.S. army commander, Harkins was born in Boston, Massachusetts. He graduated from West Point in 1929 and served in Gen. George Patton's 3d Army during World War II. In the last weeks of the Korean War in 1953, General Harkins became the chief of staff of the 8th Army. In 1962, he was named as the first commander of the U.S. Military Assistance Command in Vietnam. In Saigon, he carried out the dictates of the John F. Kennedy administration, policies that entailed a steady buildup of both U.S. advisory and combat elements in South Vietnam. In early 1963, Harkins misinformed several U.S. reporters after the costly Battle of Ap Bac. He had accepted a South Vietnamese report as being accurate and repeated it to reporters who were knowledgeable about the actual events. The incident was the beginning of a long era of distrust between the U.S. headquarters in Saigon and the U.S. news media. Harkins was opposed to the Kennedy administration's efforts to oust South Vietnam's Pres. Ngo Dinh Diem by violence and fell out of favor with Kennedy's appointed officials. In July 1964, Harkins was replaced by his deputy, Gen. William C. Westmoreland. Harkins retired later that year.

Bibliography: Halberstam, David, *The Best and the Brightest* (Random House, 1972); Karnow, Stanley, *Vietnam: A History* (Viking, 1983).

Col. (Ret.) Rod Paschall

HARRISON, WILLIAM KELLY, JR.
(1895–1987)

U.S. army officer, Harrison was born in Washington, D.C. He graduated from West Point in 1917 and during World War II, having been promoted to the rank of brigadier general in 1942, worked in the War Plans Division of the War Department's General Staff and served with the 30th Infantry Division in Europe. After occupation duty in

Gen. Paul Harkins, the first commander of the U.S. Military Assistance Command Vietnam, was appointed in 1962 by Pres. John F. Kennedy and replaced in 1964 after disputes with the White House. (National Archives)

Japan, he became deputy commander of the U.S. 8th Army in Korea. In January 1952, Gen. Matthew Ridgway appointed now Lieutenant General Harrison to the United Nations (UN) delegation to the Panmunjom armistice negotiations. Replacing Adm. C. Turner Joy as the senior UN delegate in May 1952, he struggled with one unresolved issue—voluntary repatriation of prisoners of war—until the end of the war in July 1953. Harrison retired in February 1957.

Bibliography: Lockerbie, D. Bruce, *A Man Under Orders: Lieutenant General William K. Harrison, Jr.* (Harper & Row, 1979).

Maj. James Sanders Day

HAYS, ANNA MAE McCABE (1920–   )

U.S. army officer, the first woman in the U.S. armed services to attain general officer rank, Hays was born in Buffalo, New York. She was commissioned as a nurse in 1942 and served in the China-Burma-India theater throughout World War II. Hays served in various supervisory roles in the United States (1945–50), at the 4th Field Hospital in Korea (1950–51), and at Tokyo Army Hospital (1952). While assigned to Washington, D.C., at Walter Reed General Hospital (1953–60), she served as private nurse for Pres. Dwight D. Eisenhower during a serious illness. She returned to Korea as chief nurse of the 11th Evacuation Hospital (1960–62).

After a brief tour at Walter Reed in 1963, Hays served as assistant chief of the Army Nurse Corps and in 1967 was appointed chief of the Army Nurse Corps. Throughout the Vietnam War, she guided a major recruitment effort that doubled the size of the corps, notably improved patient care throughout army hospitals, and obtained additional educational opportunities for nurses. Hays was promoted to brigadier general in 1970 and retired in 1971. An active member of numerous professional nursing and military-affiliated associations and boards, Hays' post-retirement contributions earned her many honors from both civilian and military organizations.

Bibliography: Shields, Elizabeth A., *Highlights in the History of the Army Nurse Corps* (Center of Military History, U.S. Army, 1981).

Col. (Ret.) Bettie J. Morden

HEINTGES, JOHN ARNOLD (1912–   )

U.S. army commander, Heintges was born in Coblenz, Germany. He graduated from West Point in 1936 and was commissioned a second lieutenant in the infantry. In 1943, he was ordered to North Africa with the 3d Infantry Division. During World War II, he served as battalion and regimental commander with the 3d Infantry Division in the battles of Tunisia, Sicily, Italy, France, and Germany. His regiment, the famous U.S. 7th Infantry, had the distinction of capturing Adolf Hitler's last stronghold—in and around Berchtesgaden, Germany, on May 4, 1945.

Heintges became an associate professor of foreign language at Heidelburg University (1946–51) in Germany. After completing airborne school in the United States, he went back to Europe to implement the German army training plan. After two years as deputy commander of Fort Dix, New Jersey, he served in the U.S. Army Element Pacific Command in Laos (1958–61) during the guerrilla insurgency. He held other command and staff positions at the Pentagon (1961–63); Fort Carson, Colorado (1963–64); Fort Benning, Georgia (1964–65); and I Corps in Korea (1965) before being appointed deputy commander, United Military Assistance Command, Vietnam (1965–67). Heintges retired as a lieutenant general in 1971.

Byron Hayes

HEISER, JOSEPH MILLER, JR. (1914–)

U.S. army commander, Heiser was born in Charleston, South Carolina. He attended Providence College (1932–34) and The Citadel (1939–41). During World War II, he served in a logistics capacity, supporting troops during the Normandy invasion and the liberation of northern Europe. During the Korean War, Heiser served at the Pusan Base Command and in the 7th Infantry Division.

In August 1968, he became the commanding general, 1st Logistical Command, U.S. Army, Vietnam. Under his command, the "Logistical Offensive" improved the flow of supplies to the troops in the field, resulting in increased efficiency and improved readiness rates. He returned to the United States in 1969 and became deputy chief of staff for logistics. Heiser retired in 1973.

Bibliography: Heiser, Joseph M., Jr., *A Soldier Supporting Soldiers* (Center of Military History, U.S. Army, 1991).

David Friend

HERSHEY, LEWIS BLAIN (1893–1977)

U.S. director of the military draft, Hershey was born near Angola, Indiana. He served in France during World War I as a captain. After graduating from the Command and General Staff School in 1932 and from the Army War College in 1934, he became the secretary and executive officer of the Joint Army and Navy Selective Service Committee, which formulated the plans for national conscription. Out of this emerged the Selective Training and Service Act of 1940. Hershey was named deputy director of the new Selective Service System in October 1940, then became its director the next year. He held this position for most of the next 30 years, overseeing almost 4,000 draft boards during U.S. engagement in World War II, Korea, and Vietnam. In World War II alone, 13,000,000 men were drafted, and Hershey established a deferment system and alternative duty plan for conscientious objectors. By the

1960s, the popular deferment plan had to be curtailed because of the increased demands of the Vietnam conflict, an action that struck at the American middle classes who had benefited from the deferments. War protestors descended on Hershey, whose name quickly became synonymous with the unpopular war. In February 1970, Pres. Richard M. Nixon promoted Hershey to four-star general and named him adviser on manpower, effectively removing him from the Selective Service. Hershey retired from military duty in March 1973.

Bibliography: Davis, James W., Jr., and Kenneth M. Dolbeare, *Little Group of Neighbors: The Selective Service System* (Markham, 1968); Gerhardt, James M., *The Draft and Public Policy* (Ohio State Univ. Press, 1971).

John F. Wukovits

HITCH, CHARLES JOHNSTON (1910–)

U.S. economist and defense adviser, Hitch was born in Boonville, Missouri. He graduated from the University of Arizona in 1931 and later studied at Harvard and Oxford. An economist, he served during World War II on the War Production Board and with other government agencies, including the Office of Strategic Services (1943–45). Hitch was an official of the RAND Corporation when selected as assistant secretary of defense (comptroller) in 1961. He was instrumental in promoting the increased use of computers, cost-effectiveness analysis, and other quantitative methods in the Department of Defense. The Planning-Programming-Budgeting system with functionally oriented "program packages" was largely Hitch's creation. He left the Department of Defense in 1965 and subsequently served as an administrator and professor of economics at the University of California, Berkeley, of which he was president 1968–75.

Bibliography: Hewes, James E., Jr., *From Root to McNamara: Army Organization and Administration, 1900–1963* (Center of Military History, U.S. Army, 1975); Weigley, Russell F., *The American Way of War: A History of United States Military Strategy and Policy* (Macmillan, 1973).

Lt. Col. (Ret.) Charles R. Shrader

HOGABOOM, ROBERT EDWARD (1902–1967)

U.S. marine officer, Hogaboom was born in Meridian, Mississippi. He graduated from Annapolis in 1925 and was commissioned in the Marine Corps. During World War II, he served with the 5th Amphibious Corps, participating in operations at the Aleutian Islands, Makin, Kwajalein, Saipan, Tinian, Guam, and Iwo Jima. By the end of the war, he was 3d Marine Division chief of staff.

Following the war, Hogaboom returned to Quantico (1946–49), served at the National War College (1949–51), was marine liaison officer in the Office of the Chief of

Naval Operations (1951–52), and was assistant commander of the 2d Marine Division (1952–53). He retired as a lieutenant general in 1959, while serving as Marine Corps chief of staff.

Bibliography: Millett, Allan R., *Semper Fidelis: The History of the United States Marine Corps* (Macmillan, 1991).

David Friend

HOISINGTON, ELIZABETH PASCHAL (1918–)

U.S. army officer, the first U.S. Women's Army Corps officer to attain the rank of brigadier general, Hoisington was born in Newton, Kansas, the daughter of an army officer. In 1942, she enlisted in the Women's Army Auxiliary Corps—named the Women's Army Corps (WAC) in 1943—and was commissioned in 1943. During World War II, she served primarily in WAC command duties in the United States and overseas.

Released from active duty in 1946, Hoisington was recalled in 1948, was commissioned in the regular army, and served in Tokyo until 1950. She commanded the WAC unit at Fort Monroe, Virginia, during 1950–51 and served three years in the Office of the Director of WAC at the Pentagon (1951–54). She held personnel officer positions worldwide between 1954 and 1964. She was then commander of the WAC Center and commandant of the WAC school at Fort McClellan, Alabama (1964–66).

Hoisington served as director of WAC from 1966 until her retirement in 1971. She led the corps throughout the Vietnam War—increasing the size of the corps while retaining high enlistment and retention standards. She improved WAC housing and uniforms as well as the training and assignment opportunities for enlisted women and officers. In a joint ceremony on June 11, 1970, both Hoisington and Anna Mae Hays, chief of the Army Nurse Corps, were promoted to brigadier general. Hoisington retired in 1971. In retirement, she served on the Army-Air Force Mutual Aid Association, the WAC Foundation, and other civic organizations.

Bibliography: Morden, Bettie J., *The Women's Army Corps 1945–1978* (Center of Military History, U.S. Army, 1990).

Col. (Ret.) Bettie J. Morden

HOLM, JEANNE MARJORIE (1921–)

First woman to attain the rank of brigadier general and major general in the U.S. Air Force, Holm was born in Portland, Oregon. She enlisted (1942) in the Women's Army Auxiliary Corps—named the Women's Army Corps (WAC) in 1943—and was commissioned in 1943. During World War II, she served in command positions primarily at the Third WAC Training Center, Fort Oglethorpe, Georgia. At war's end, she left the service but returned on active duty in 1948 during the Berlin Crisis. She transferred from the army to the air force in 1949.

Holm served in air force war plans and manpower positions in Germany, Italy, and the United States until 1962, when she was assigned as congressional staff officer for Headquarters, U.S. Air Force. She was the first woman to attend the Air Force Air Command and Staff College. Appointed director of Women in the Air Force (WAF), Holm opened new career opportunities for women to include combat support jobs. She doubled WAF strength and on July 16, 1971, was promoted to brigadier general. Upon leaving the WAF directorship in 1973, she was appointed director of the secretary of the air force's personnel council and was promoted to major general on June 1.

She retired in 1975 and subsequently served as special assistant to the president during the Gerald R. Ford administration, as a member of the Defense Advisory Committee on Women in the Services (1977–80), and as consultant on military women to the undersecretary of the air force (1978–80). She wrote *Women in the Military: An Unfinished Revolution* in 1982.

Col. (Ret.) Bettie J. Morden

IGNATIUS, PAUL ROBERT (1920–)

U.S. secretary of the navy, Ignatius was born in Los Angeles, California. He was commissioned in the navy during World War II and served on board the USS *Manila* until 1944. He remained in the naval reserve until December 1955. Ignatius trained at Harvard Business School and in 1960 was appointed assistant secretary of the army for installations and logistics. By 1965, he had been promoted to assistant secretary of Defense, supervising the shipment of reinforcements to Indochina. In September 1967, Pres. Lyndon B. Johnson appointed him secretary of the navy, a post he held until January 1969. His short tenure was characterized by the maintenance of maximum military effectiveness and the promotion of a mixed modern fleet at the least cost.

Russell A. Hart

JABARA, JAMES (1923–1966)

First U.S. jet air ace, Jabara was born in Muskogee, Oklahoma. After shooting down 9 enemy planes in World War II, he served with the 4th Fighter Wing in Korea. Jabara became that war's initial ace on May 20, 1951, when, from his F-86 Sabre jet, he shot down 2 enemy jets to raise his total to 6. Sent home to the United States at the expiration of his combat tour, he rejoined the 4th Fighter Wing in January 1953 and became the second-leading U.S. ace by tallying 15 kills, 1 behind Captain J. D. McConnell, Jr. Promoted to colonel, Jabara commanded a stateside fighter group during the Vietnam conflict. He died on Nov. 19, 1966, two days after suffering extensive head injuries in a Florida car accident.

Bibliography: Walker, Bryce, *Fighting Jets* (Time-Life Books, 1983).

John F. Wukovits

JAMES, DANIEL, JR. (1920–1978)

First black to achieve a four-star rank in the U.S. armed services, James was born in Pensacola, Florida. He graduated from Tuskegee Institute in 1942. Having learned to fly in the Civilian Pilot Training Program at Tuskegee, he entered the Aviation Cadet Program in January 1943, was commissioned in the Army Air Corps in July 1943, and served in various training assignments during the remainder of World War II. During the Korean War, James flew 101 combat fighter missions. He then served in various command and staff positions until being assigned to the 8th Tactical Fighter Wing in Thailand in 1966. As the deputy wing commander for operations and later as vice wing Commander, he flew 78 combat missions into North Vietnam and led the mission that recorded the highest total kill (seven MiG-21s) of any mission during the Vietnam War. James subsequently served in command positions in Florida and Libya before being named deputy assistant secretary of defense (public affairs) in 1970. He remained in that position until September 1974 when he became vice commander of the Military Airlift Command. On Sept. 1, 1975, he was promoted to general and was assigned to command the North American Air Defense Command. Gen. "Chappie" James died shortly after his retirement in February 1978.

Bibliography: Guimond, Gary, "The Power of Excellence," *Airman* (June 1970); McGovern, James R., *Black Eagle: General Daniel "Chappie" James, Jr.* (Univ. of Alabama Press, 1985); Phelps, J. Alfred, *Chappie—American's First Black Four-Star General: The Life and Times of Daniel James, Jr.* (Presidio Press, 1991); *Washington Post* (Jan. 23, 1978); *Webster's American Military Biographies* (Merriam, 1978).

Lt. Col. (Ret.) Charles R. Shrader

JOHNSON, HAROLD KEITH (1912–1983)

U.S. army officer and chief of staff, Johnson was born in Bowesville, North Dakota. He graduated from West Point in 1933 and was commissioned in the infantry. During World War II, he was captured in the Philippines by the Japanese, endured the Bataan Death March, and spent three years as a prisoner of war. He made up for the time lost while a prisoner of war through incredible application and ability. This included heroic action during the Korean War in battalion and regimental command, including of the 8th Cavalry, service that earned him the Distinguished Service Cross and other decorations.

After three years (1960–63) as commandant of the army's Command and General Staff College, Johnson became deputy chief of staff for operations and plans on the army staff. A year later, he was advanced to full general and was appointed army chief of staff (1964–68).

His service in this top army leadership post–coincided with the period of the buildup for the war in Vietnam, a task made far more difficult by Pres. Lyndon B. Johnson's refusal to call up reserve forces. All contingency plans had contemplated a reserve mobilization for any conflict of such magnitude, and, instead, the army was forced to expand its ranks and build new outfits almost entirely by means of new accessions, progressively eroding the experience and maturity levels of the force in the process. Chief of Staff Johnson, widely admired as a man of unassailable integrity and total dedication, worked tirelessly to maintain readiness and professional standards during these very difficult times. He also directed an objective, and critical, study of how the war in Vietnam was being conducted. Later, when his vice chief of staff Gen. Creighton Abrams took command in Vietnam, this study significantly influenced changes in the battlefield tactics and integration of elements of the U.S. effort.

Bibliography: Johnson, Harold K., *Challenge: Compendium of Army Accomplishment: A Report by the Chief of Staff: July 1964–April 1968* (Dept. of the Army, July 1, 1968).

Lewis Sorley

JOHNSON, LOUIS ARTHUR (1891–1956)

U.S. lawyer and secretary of defense, Johnson was born in Roanoke, Virginia. He graduated from the University of Virginia with a law degree in 1912 and began his law practice in Clarksburg, West Virginia; at the same time, he served as a state legislature representative. He served in World War I (1917–18), after which he resumed his law practice and became active in Democratic politics. He was assistant secretary of war (1937–40). During World War II, Johnson held a variety of posts, beginning with his appointment as Pres. Franklin D. Roosevelt's personal representative to India. Pres. Harry S Truman appointed him secretary of defense in 1949.

Johnson's task as secretary of defense was to preside over the continuing demobilization of the armed forces and to reorganize them in line with the National Security Act of 1947. In order to make budget cuts ordered by President Truman, Johnson favored a closer unification of the armed forces. He advocated putting naval aviation and the Marine Corps under the army, thus stripping the navy of all duties except for the protection of sea lines of communication and engaging in antisubmarine warfare.

While both Truman's and Johnson's policies were intended to reduce costs, they came at an inopportune time in U.S. relations with the Soviet Union. While they were making cuts in the budget, foreign policy planners were advocating massive rearmament, maintaining that U.S. forces stronger than those proposed by Johnson were required to deter Soviet aggression. Despite this and other warnings, the president and secretary of defense were not thinking in terms of foreign affairs, but of domestic realities. In order to balance the budget, Truman was steadily decreasing defense outlays as the Soviets were exploding their first atomic bomb (1949) and the North Koreans were preparing to invade South Korea (1950).

Johnson became so intent on unification of the armed services and decreasing the defense budget that even President Truman became concerned with his erratic behavior. Under pressure from the president and from bitter armed forces officers, Johnson resigned his post in August 1950.

Leo J. Daugherty III

JOHNSON, LYNDON BAINES (1908–1973)

The 36th president of the United States (1963–69), whose term was marked by increasing U.S. involvement in the Vietnam War, Johnson was born near Johnson City, Texas. Elected to the House of Representatives as a Democrat in 1937 and reelected until he successfully ran for the Senate in 1948, Johnson became a master of the political process and was elected Democratic leader in the Senate in 1953. He was chosen to be John F. Kennedy's vice-presidential running mate in 1960 because of his political

Upon assuming the presidency in 1963, Lyndon B. Johnson attempted to continue the Southeast Asian policy of "flexible response" that had been initiated by his assassinated predecessor, John F. Kennedy. (The White House)

skills and his influence in the South. Johnson succeeded to the presidency with Kennedy's assassination in November 1963.

Successful in having major bills adopted, such as the 1964 civil rights legislation, Johnson was elected president in 1964, overwhelming Republican Barry Goldwater. During 1964, Johnson had expanded the U.S. military presence in South Vietnam by more than 50 percent, to 25,000 troops, and they played an increasing part in the war. In 1965, U.S. air forces began bombing North Vietnam, and the number of troops jumped to nearly 200,000, a figure that multiplied to more than 350,000 in 1966 and nearly 500,000 by 1968. Johnson came under increasing domestic pressure as troop commitments soared, casualties and prisoners of war mounted, and the U.S. economy showed signs of strain. Despite the massive U.S. involvement in Vietnam, the Communists were not defeated and remained viable, as the Tet Offensive of 1968 demonstrated. In March 1968, Johnson announced that he would not seek reelection and that the bombing of North Vietnam would stop. At the same time, the first peace negotiations with North Vietnam started. His influence among Democrats slid, and after the victory of Republican Richard Nixon in the 1968 elections, Johnson retired to his ranch in Texas.

Bibliography: Johnson, Lyndon B., *The Vantage Point* (Holt, 1971); Schandler, Herbert, *The Unmaking of the President: Lyndon Johnson and Vietnam* (Princeton Univ. Press, 1977).

Stephen Robinson

JOY, C(HARLES) TURNER (1895–1956)

U.S. naval officer, Joy was born in St. Louis, Missouri. He graduated from Annapolis in 1916 and during World War I served on the USS *Pennsylvania*, the flagship for the commander in chief of the Atlantic Fleet. After the war, Joy attended the University of Michigan, graduating in 1923 with a master's degree in ordnance engineering. In 1937, he returned to the Naval Academy, where he served as executive officer and then head of the Department of Ordnance and Gunnery.

In June 1940, Joy left Annapolis to serve as executive officer and operations officer aboard the USS *Indianapolis*. In the early stages of World War II, he served on the USS *Lexington* in the Pacific at Bougainville, Salamau, and Lae. Commanding the USS *Louisville* from September 1942 through June 1943, Joy participated in the fight for Guadalcanal and in the Aleutian Islands Campaign. Transferring to Washington, D.C., he served several months in the Navy Department before returning to the Pacific theater. He spent the final year of the war as commander of Cruiser Division 6, Pacific Fleet, participating in the campaigns for Saipan, the Philippine Sea, Guam, the Philippines, Taiwan, Iwo Jima, and Okinawa. War's end found

Joy in California training an amphibious group for the assault on Japan.

After the war, Joy spent six months in command of Task Forces 73 and 74. In China, he led the Yangtze Patrol Force in clearing mines from the river before assuming command of the Naval Proving Ground in Dahlgren, Virginia. Promoted to vice admiral in August 1949, Joy took command of U.S. Naval Forces, Far East. In 1950, after the outbreak of the Korean War, he directed a naval blockade of North Korea while also providing protection to the Nationalist Chinese contingent on Taiwan. He commanded the naval forces during amphibious landings at Inchon and Wonsan and by November commanded a fleet of more than 400 ships representing 9 nations.

Appointed by Gen. Matthew B. Ridgway as chief delegate to the United Nations Command Delegation in Korea, Joy opened negotiations with the Communists on July 10, 1951. Quickly recognizing that concessions constituted perceived weakness, Joy noted that "nothing is so persuasive to Communists as force." His efforts gained results in establishing an agenda, drawing a demarcation line along the main battle line, creating a Neutral Nations Supervisory Commission (NNSC) to monitor armistice agreements, and providing for settlement of political issues after the cease-fire. Before his departure from Korea in May 1952, Joy presented a package proposal to the Communists in an attempt to resolve three outstanding issues: the reconstruction of North Korean airfields, the Soviet Union's status with regard to the NNSC, and the voluntary repatriation of prisoners of war.

Joy returned to the United States to become the 37th superintendent of the Naval Academy (1952–54). He retired two years later.

Bibliography: Goodman, Allan E., ed., *Negotiating While Fighting: The Diary of Admiral C. Turner Joy at the Korean Armistice Conference* (Hoover Inst. Press, 1978); Joy, C. Turner, *How Communists Negotiate* (Macmillan, 1955).

Maj. James Sanders Day

KELLEY, PAUL XAVIER (1929–)

U.S. marine officer, Kelly was born in Boston, Massachusetts. He graduated from Villanova University and was commissioned a second lieutenant in the marines in 1950. He was promoted to captain in 1953 and major in 1958 after various assignments at sea, in the Pacific area, and at marine training schools in the United States. He commanded the Marine Corps Barracks at Newport, Rhode Island (1964–65), and the 2d Battalion, 4th Marines, in Vietnam (1965–66). He was promoted to lieutenant colonel in 1966. Reassigned to Vietnam in 1970, Kelley served as aide to Gen. Lewis Walt and, in 1971, commanded the 1st Marines. He was promoted to brigadier general in 1975

and soon after became a major general. As assistant commandant of the Marine Corps, he was promoted to general and in 1983 became the corps' commandant. He continued the modernization programs established by his predecessors and stressed the necessity of proper leadership at all levels. Kelley retired in 1987.

Leo J. Daugherty III

KENNEDY, JOHN FITZGERALD
(1917–1963)
Thirty-fifth president of the United States (1961–63), Kennedy was born in Brookline, Massachusetts. He graduated from Harvard University in 1940 and served with distinction as a naval officer in World War II. After representing Massachusetts in the U.S. House of Representatives (1947–53) and the U.S. Senate (1953–60), in 1960, he became the youngest man elected to the U.S. presidency.

Kennedy's White House years left two distinct legacies to U.S. politics. The first was his mission for a "New Frontier," which embodied his highly inspiring rhetoric, his youthfulness, and his lofty dreams for the country. Through programs such as the Peace Corps, the Alliance for Progress, and the promise of sending a man to the

In April 1961, Pres. John F. Kennedy accepted "sole responsibility" for the failure of anti-Castro forces (trained by the U.S. Central Intelligence Agency) to invade Cuba at the Bay of Pigs. (Library of Congress)

moon, Kennedy helped push forward social and political reform and the advance of U.S. technology.

The second Kennedy legacy, and arguably the more controversial, was his attempt to confront the spread of Soviet Communism. Kennedy's ill-conceived effort to topple Fidel Castro's regime in Cuba, resulting in the Bay of Pigs fiasco (April 1961), triggered a chain of events that heightened U.S.-Soviet tensions and placed the world on the brink of war. Also, his continuation of the U.S. commitment to the unpopular government of Pres. Ngo Dinh Diem in South Vietnam furthered the escalation of the U.S. presence in Southeast Asia.

While motorcading through Dallas, Texas, on Nov. 22, 1963, President Kennedy was assassinated. Vice Pres. Lyndon B. Johnson thus succeeded to the presidency, inheriting the politically volatile situation in Vietnam.

M. Guy Bishop

KERWIN, WALTER THOMAS, JR.
(1917–   )

U.S. army commander, Kerwin was born in West Chester, Pennsylvania, and graduated from West Point in 1939. Commissioned in the artillery, he rose rapidly through the ranks while serving with the 3d Infantry Division in Europe during World War II. Following the war, he served in a variety of assignments leading to his promotion to brigadier general in 1961. He later commanded the 3d Armored Division in Germany (1965–66).

After a brief tour in the Pentagon, Major General Kerwin became chief of staff, U.S. Military Assistance Command Vietnam (MACV) in May 1967. While serving as Gen. William C. Westmoreland's chief of staff, he coordinated the MACV staff efforts throughout a period of extensive U.S. air and ground operations, including the 1968 Tet Offensive. In August 1968, Kerwin was promoted to lieutenant general and assumed command of II Field Force, which was responsible for the III Corps area and later the IV Corps area.

He commanded II Field Force until April 1969 when he returned to the Pentagon. Upon his promotion to general in February 1973, Kerwin commanded Continental Army Command. He was selected as the vice chief of staff of the army in 1974 and served in that position until his retirement in 1978.

Bibliography: Clarke, Jeffrey J., *Advice and Support: The Final Years, 1965–1973* (U.S. Govt. Printing Office, 1988); Westmoreland, William C., *A Soldier Reports* (Doubleday, 1976).

Capt. Leslie Howard Belknap

KIDD, ISAAC CAMPBELL, JR. (1919–   )

U.S. naval officer, Kidd was born in Cleveland, Ohio. He graduated from Annapolis in 1941, less than two weeks after his father, an admiral, had died aboard the *Arizona* at Pearl Harbor. Kidd's first sea duty was as gunnery officer on a destroyer in the North Atlantic. He also served in the Pacific. After staff assignments, he returned to sea in 1951–52 as gunnery officer of the heavy cruiser *Salem*. His first command was of the new destroyer *Barry* (1956–58), after which he spent two years on the staff of the commander in chief, Pacific. Subsequent assignments included study at the National War College, command of Destroyer Squadron 18 (the navy's first all-guided-missile destroyer group), and a four-year tour as senior aide to the chief of naval operations. In this capacity, Kidd helped plan U.S. deployment during the blockade of Cuba.

Promoted to rear admiral in 1965, Kidd served in succession as commander, Cruiser-Destroyer Force, Atlantic Fleet; commander, 1st Fleet; and commander, 6th Fleet. Extremely knowledgeable in electronics, he developed fleet exercises while commanding the 1st Fleet that enhanced the electronics capabilities of ships being readied for combat off Vietnam. As an admiral, Kidd's first assignment was as head of the Naval Material Command (1971–75). On one occasion, the forceful, outgoing Kidd wore the uniform of a Soviet officer when speaking before the San Diego Navy League. His purpose was to emphasize his concern that the United States needed to work to maintain naval supremacy. During his tenure at the giant Naval Material Command, major controversies about cost overruns brought Kidd to the attention of the media. He concluded his naval career as commander, Atlantic Fleet (1975–78).

Bibliography: Hume, Britt, "Admiral Kidd vs. Mister Rule," *New York Times Magazine* (Mar. 25, 1973).

Lloyd J. Graybar

KIMBALL, DAN ABLE (1896–1970)

U.S. secretary of the navy, Kimball was born in St. Louis, Missouri. He entered government service from the business world, where he had been a vice president with the General Tire and Rubber Company and general manager of its subsidiary, Aerojet Engineering Corporation. In 1949, he was appointed assistant secretary of the navy for air but soon became undersecretary and then, in 1951, secretary of the navy. Kimball gave the Navy Department a needed period of strong and effective leadership, calling attention to the need for large carriers of the Forrestal class and nuclear submarines to follow the *Nautilus,* which was under construction. He enhanced antisubmarine capabilities as well as air-defense missiles to replace conventional antiaircraft weaponry. Kimball returned to business in 1953.

Bibliography: Bauer, K. Jack, *American Secretaries of the Navy; Vol. 2: 1913–1972,* ed. by Paolo Coletta (Naval Inst. Press, 1980).

Lloyd J. Graybar

KINNARD, HARRY WILLIAM OSBORNE, JR. (1915–   )

U.S. army commander, Kinnard was born in Dallas, Texas. He joined the infantry after graduating from West Point in 1939 and served with distinction in the 101st Airborne Division during World War II. Kinnard held a number of command and staff positions during the 1950s, including a tour as executive to the secretary of the army. In 1963, he took command of the 11th Air Assault Division. Over the next two years, the division was involved in a series of tests to evaluate the concept of using helicopters to move troops into combat. With the success of these tests and increasing U.S. involvement in Vietnam, the army moved Kinnard and his division there in 1965. While en route to Southeast Asia, however, the army redesignated the division the 1st Cavalry Division (Airmobile).

Within a month of arriving in South Vietnam, the 1st Cavalry moved to block a North Vietnamese invasion of the Ia Drang Valley. Over the thick jungle, Kinnard maneuvered his heliborne troops, who surprised, and, after heavy fighting, defeated the North Vietnamese. The fighting in the Ia Drang Valley was the first major battle between the U.S. and North Vietnamese forces and dashed the North's hopes of defeating South Vietnam before the United States could decisively intervene. Moreover, the battle also seemed to validate the airmobile concept. Kinnard returned to the United States in 1966 and headed the Army Combat Development Command before retiring in 1969.

Bibliography: Stanton, Shelby, *Anatomy of a Division: The 1st Cav in Vietnam* (Presidio, 1987).

Richard F. Kehrberg

KISSINGER, HENRY ALFRED (1923–   )

U.S. national security adviser and secretary of state, Kissinger was born in Fürth, Germany, and came to the United States in 1938, escaping Nazism. As a professor of government at Harvard University during the 1950s and 1960s, he emerged as an expert on foreign affairs. While Pres. Richard M. Nixon's national security adviser (1969–73) and later as secretary of state (1973–77), he concentrated power in the White House. Kissinger sidestepped the professional U.S. foreign service by conducting personal, secret negotiations with North Vietnam, the Soviet Union, and China. He engineered a short-lived era of détente with the Soviet Union and thawed previously strained relations with the People's Republic of China. In 1973, Kissinger received the Nobel Peace Prize for his role in negotiations leading to the Paris Peace Accords that ended U.S. military action in Vietnam.

His reputation began to fade in 1973 along with that of the Nixon administration in the aftermath of Watergate. Congressional investigations discovered that Kissinger had

Henry Kissinger, national security adviser (1969–73) under Pres. Richard Nixon and secretary of state (1973–77) under Presidents Nixon and Gerald Ford, received the Nobel Peace Prize for his part in the peace accords that put an end to U.S. fighting in Vietnam. (National Archives)

ordered the Federal Bureau of Investigation to tap the telephones of subordinates on the National Security Council. His part in helping destabilize the Chilean government of Socialist Salvador Allende also came to light at this time. Secretary of State Kissinger proved a great liability to Gerald Ford during the 1976 presidential campaign. By 1977, when President Jimmy Carter took office, Kissinger left the government. In 1980, he won the American Book Award for *White House Years* (1979).

M. Guy Bishop

KRULAK, VICTOR HAROLD (1913–   )

U.S. marine commander, Krulak was born in Denver, Colorado. He graduated from Annapolis in 1934 and served in World War II, where he won a Navy Cross. He helped plan Gen. Douglas MacArthur's daring 1950 Inchon landing in Korea. By 1962, Krulak's innovative views on military strategy lifted him to the post of special adviser to the

Joint Chiefs of Staff for counterinsurgency warfare, where for two years he contributed to the formation of U.S. policy in Vietnam. In March 1964, he was promoted to commander of the Fleet Marine Force, where he strongly advocated the use of helicopters (vertical envelopment) to deploy marines and supported pacification of Vietnam rather than a bloody war of attrition. After being bypassed for the post of commandant in 1968, Krulak retired to write for newspapers.

Bibliography: Krulak, Victor H., *First to Fight: An Inside View of the U.S. Marine Corps* (Naval Inst. Press, 1984); Sheehan, Neil, *A Bright Shining Lie* (Random House, 1988).

John F. Wukovits

KY, NGUYEN CAO (1930–)

South Vietnamese military leader and premier. He was born in Son Tay, French Indochina, and trained at a French military academy, eventually becoming a pilot. By the mid-1950s he was an influential South Vietnamese aviation officer, opposing North Vietnam and its Viet Cong sympathizers in the south. He was made a general and commander of the air force after the overthrow of the Diem regime in 1963 and made the air force the elite arm of South Vietnam's forces. The flamboyant Ky continued to lead the air force while assuming greater power in South Vietnam's government, reaching the status of premier in 1965. In the 1967 election, he was chosen as vice president, giving way to his rival, Nguyen Van Thieu, as president. Deciding not to challenge Thieu for the presidency in 1971, Ky resumed his former rank of air marshal and remained influential. When the South Vietnamese government collapsed in 1975, Ky fled the country, eventually settling in the United States.

Bibliography: Ky, Nguyen Cao, *Twenty Years and Twenty Days* (Stein & Day, 1976).

Stephen Robinson

LAIRD, MELVIN ROBERT (1922–)

U.S. secretary of defense, Laird was born in Omaha, Nebraska. He served in the U.S. House of Representatives (from Wisconsin) for nine terms (1952–69) before becoming Pres. Richard M. Nixon's defense secretary in January 1969. During his four years in the Department of Defense, Laird pressed hard for continuation and acceleration of the U.S. withdrawal from Vietnam—implementing what he called the "Vietnamization" effort—a position that often put him at odds with certain other senior administration officials. By the time he left office, however, the redeployment he had desired was complete. In 1973, Laird moved to the White House as a policy adviser to Nixon. A year later, he returned to private life, beginning a long association as an adviser to the Reader's Digest Association.

Lewis Sorely

LAVELLE, JOHN DANIEL (1916–1979)

U.S. air force commander, Lavelle was born in Cleveland, Ohio. He graduated from John Carroll University in 1938, enlisted as an aviation cadet in the Army Air Corps in 1939, and qualified as an aviator and was commissioned in 1940. His World War II service was with the 412th Fighter Squadron in the European theater.

Development. As an air force officer following the war, Lavelle served in staff assignments in Japan and, during the Korean War, commanded a supply depot at Tachikawa (1951–52). Later, he commanded McGuire Air Force Base (1952–53), served on the Air Staff as deputy director of requirements (1957–58), and was deputy chief of staff for operations at the 4th Allied Tactical Air Force in Europe (1962–64). Following further Pentagon duty, he took command of the 17th Air Force at Ramstein Air Base, Germany, in 1966.

Vietnam War. In July 1971, Lavelle was promoted to full general and given command of the 7th Air Force. Very early on, he became greatly concerned for the safety of his pilots, who were required to operate under very complex and restrictive rules of engagement during missions over

As Pres. Richard Nixon's secretary of defense (1969–73), Melvin Laird pushed for an agenda of "Vietnamization," which boosted an expeditious withdrawal of U.S. troops from Vietnam. (U.S. Army)

North Vietnam. Essentially, these rules permitted them to strike enemy targets only in what were termed "protective reaction" strikes, and these had to be triggered by prior hostile acts on the enemy's part.

In what came to be known as the "Lavelle case," Lavelle was charged with having directed—in violation of these rules of engagement—that preplanned strikes be conducted against certain especially dangerous targets in the off-limits areas. Although this apparently involved only a small number of cases, it nevertheless constituted serious disobedience of orders. The matter was exacerbated by the fact that in the absence of actual hostile actions that would have justified reactive strikes, returning aircrews were fabricating such actions. It was this practice that led eventually to discovery of the problem when a young airman, involved in the debriefing of those aircrews, reported the deceptive practices to his senator.

Lavelle maintained that the enemy, knowing of the restrictions imposed on U.S. air missions, had begun to employ a wide-area radar network that was constantly in use to alert the enemy's more localized target acquisition radars and the related missile sites. The local radars produced signatures that could be read by aircraft being "bathed" by them, warning of impending attack. But the larger-area radar provided no such warning; use of it for the preliminary stages of target acquisition permitted the local radars to flick on at the last moment, followed almost immediately by delivery of their antiaircraft missiles, leaving the aircrews little or no reaction time and greatly increasing the danger.

Lavelle also maintained that, given this use of the wide-area radars, there was *always* an enemy reaction—that this use of radar in itself constituted a reaction—and thus the protective reaction strikes he ordered were legitimate under the existing rules of engagement. However, the communication of this interpretation to his aircrews was evidently not always clear. But, for whatever reason, aircrews returning from preplanned strikes began to submit false reports of enemy reaction in the form of missiles fired or some other act.

When these matters were first rumored back in Washington, the air force chief of staff, Gen. John D. Ryan, sent an investigating party to Vietnam. It came back and told him there was no problem. Soon thereafter, Lavelle sent an urgent message requesting a change in the rules of engagement. The Joint Chiefs of Staff supported this request, but it was not approved.

When more evidence came in relating to Lavelle, General Ryan went out himself to look into the case. Lavelle denied doing anything wrong. Then, when the senatorial inquiry came up, the case blew wide open. This time, the air force inspector general went personally to Vietnam. When his report was submitted, Ryan sent for Lavelle, relieved him of his command, and recommended he be retired as a major general, a rank two grades below that he had just held.

Congressional hearings were generated by the Lavelle case. One issue was whether anyone senior to Lavelle was aware of and had approved the preplanned strikes. Gen. Creighton Abrams, then commanding in Vietnam, stated for the record that he had been debriefed by the air force inspector general. "I knew then," he said, "and not before then, that some air strikes had struck in North Vietnam which exceeded the authorities granted this command."

Outcome. In September 1972, the Senate Armed Services Committee held hearings to decide at what grade General Lavelle should be retired. Its decision hinged on resolution of the issue of his alleged disobedience to orders. A total of about seven hours over two days were devoted to grilling Lavelle. When it was over, Lavelle was retired as a major general.

Bibliography: *Nomination of John D. Lavelle for Appointment as Lieutenant General on Retired List of U.S. Air Force* (hearings, 92d Congress, 2d Session; U.S. Govt. Printing Office, 1972).

Lewis Sorley

LeMAY, CURTIS EMERSON (1906–1990)

U.S. air force commander, LeMay was born in Columbus, Ohio. He studied civil engineering and completed the Reserve Officers Training Corps program at Ohio State University, but before graduation, he left school and entered the National Guard with the goal of securing flight training. LeMay was eventually successful and received his pilot's wings on Oct. 12, 1929. He then joined the 27th Pursuit Squadron at Selfridge Field, Michigan.

At Selfridge, he completed his college degree and participated in the controversial military airmail operation of 1934. Not long thereafter, he was transferred to Hawaii where he conducted a navigation school to train flight crews for long-range over-water missions. In this process, LeMay became convinced that strategic bombing was the decisive mission of the army air forces, capable of defeating an enemy without aid from other ground and sea forces.

To help test his ideas, LeMay secured a transfer in 1936 to the 305th Bombardment Group at Langley Field, Virginia, where he worked on aerial navigation techniques and operational tactics. The next year, he participated in an exercise demonstrating the capability of bombers to find and destroy ships at sea. He capped his prewar experience with a tour at the Air Corps Tactical School at Maxwell Field, Alabama, where his faith in strategic bombardment was reinforced.

World War II. By the time the United States entered World War II (1941), LeMay was a promising young major in command of a bomber squadron at Westover Field, Massachusetts. In May 1942, as a new lieutenant colonel,

In 1961, former commander of the Strategic Air Command (1948–57) Curtis E. LeMay (right) *was sworn in as chief of staff of the U.S. Air Force.* (U.S. Air Force)

he was given command of the 305th Bomb Group, which he took to England later that year. He immediately took issue with the tactics employed in the strategic bombing campaign, arguing that evasive maneuvering on the bomb run damaged the bombardier's accuracy and contributed little to the safety of the aircraft. He proved his point both theoretically and by leading raids that successfully employed his tactics.

In June 1943, he was named commander of the 3d Bombardment Division. While in this position, he planned and led the first shuttle bombing raid on Regensburg, Germany, landing in North Africa. In August 1944, LeMay, promoted to major general, was transferred to the China-Burma-India theater to command the 20th Bomber Command. In January 1945, he was sent to head the 21st Bomber Command at Guam, where in March 1945 he conducted four destructive firebombing raids on Japanese cities. Forces under LeMay's command dropped the atomic bombs on Hiroshima and Nagasaki on August 6 and 9, 1945.

Immediate Postwar Career. After the war, LeMay was sent to the United States and made head of Air Staff research and development activities. On Oct. 1, 1947, he was assigned as commander of the U.S. Air Forces in Europe (USAFE), which had important responsibilities for aerial defense against the Soviet Union.

In June 1948, the Soviets blockaded Berlin, and the military governor immediately anticipated using aircraft to overcome the Berlin Blockade. He directed LeMay to organize the C-47 transports in theater into a massive airlift. LeMay began the first airlift flights using 102 C-37s on June 26, 1948. LeMay created a permanent airlift structure to ensure that West Berlin did not fall to the Soviets, and a year later, the crisis was successfully ended.

Strategic Air Command. The Berlin Blockade had uncovered serious weaknesses in the ability of the newly created Strategic Air Command (SAC—the organization charged with conducting strategic bombing) to execute its mission of deterrence. LeMay was brought back to the United States in October 1948 to command SAC. With a broad mandate to resolve the command's inadequacies, he embarked on a program of intense training, alerts, and realistic exercises. He also became, in 1951, the youngest four-star general in air force history.

LeMay was by all accounts a harsh and domineering commander, shoving aside any who opposed his plans, but he got results. He fully understood that the nation's first line of defense—indeed in many respects it was the only line of defense—was the nuclear deterrent that SAC was charged with maintaining. The command, he knew, had to be prepared to carry out effectively its nuclear mission at any time for the deterrent to have any viability. He therefore refined the procedures for strategic bombardment, both with intercontinental ballistic missiles (ICBMs) and manned bombers, and made them increasingly more effective. The preparedness of SAC to execute its mission was legendary and set standards of excellence still idealized within the U.S. Air Force.

LeMay also campaigned for, and obtained, much additional personnel and aircraft. The B-29s he inherited when he took over SAC were not adequate, as service in the Korean War between 1950 and 1953 showed, and he worked toward the acquisition of heavy bombers with a global reach. While commanding SAC, LeMay secured the first jet bombers (B-47s and B-52s) and tankers (KC-135s), as well as supporting the beginnings of the air force's ballistic missile program. At the same time, he increased the SAC infrastructure to support the impressive strategic bombardment capability he was building within SAC.

Air Force Chief of Staff. After commanding SAC until 1957, LeMay became air force vice chief of staff under Gen. Thomas White. In 1961, LeMay began his tenure as air force chief of staff. A strong leader and proponent of the doctrine of strategic deterrence through nuclear weapons, he was a counterpoint to the flexible response strategies supported by Sec. of Defense Robert S. McNamara. The two frequently clashed over approaches to defense issues. For instance, during the October 1962 Cuban Missile Crisis, LeMay strongly urged the use of military force, but McNamara argued for the less threatening quarantine of the island. When the United States found itself being drawn ever more tightly into the conflict in Vietnam, LeMay suported the expansion of strategic bombing against North Vietnam to cripple its will to fight. Again, he lost that argument.

Later Career. With disagreements over fundamental defense decisions abounding, LeMay retired as chief of staff on Feb. 1, 1965. He became an executive for an electronics manufacturing firm and dabbled in conservative politics. He expressed concern about the future of the United States, chastising the counterculture of the 1960s and condemning the "Great Society" of Pres. Lyndon B. Johnson as a drift toward socialism.

With the goal of stemming this trend, he agreed to run as vice president during George Wallace's third-party bid for the presidency in 1968. The American Independent party was one of the most successful third-party efforts in U.S. history. The Wallace/LeMay team received 13 percent of the popular vote and collected 46 electoral votes.

LeMay later regretted having participated in this political contest. Although he agreed with many of the conservative political ideas of Wallace, who had made his name as an antiintegration governor of Alabama, LeMay recognized that he was not a politician and should have stayed outside that arena.

Bibliography: Coffey, Thomas M., *Iron Eagle: The Turbulent Life of General Curtis LeMay* (Crown, 1986); LeMay, Curtis E., "U.S. Air Leadership in World War II," *Air Power and Warfare* (Office of Air Force History, 1979); LeMay, Curtis E., with MacKinley Kantor, *Mission with LeMay* (Doubleday, 1965).

Roger D. Launius

LEMNITZER, LYMAN LOUIS (1899–1988)
U.S. army officer and diplomat, Lemnitzer was born in Honesdale, Pennsylvania. He graduated from West Point in 1920 and was commissioned in the coastal artillery. He graduated from the Coastal Artillery School at Fort Monroe, Virginia, in 1921. During 1926–30 and 1934–35, he served as an instructor at the Military Academy. He completed postgraduate studies at the Command and General Staff School in 1936 and at the Army War College in 1940. From 1941 to 1942, he was assigned to the General Staff Corps, War Planning Division, and was in charge of secret missions connected with the invasion of North Africa. He served as commanding general of the 34th Anti-Aircraft Brigade in the Tunisian and Sicilian campaigns. He then took part in the secret negotiations that led to the surrender of the German armies in Italy and South Austria in May 1945.

From November 1945 to August 1947, Lemnitzer was army member of the Strategic Survey Committee of the Joint Chiefs of Staff and then deputy commandant of the National War College until October 1949. He directed the Office of Military Assistance in the Department of Defense

in 1950 before undergoing paratroop training, at age 51, and taking command of the 11th Airborne Division in December 1950 at Fort Campbell, Kentucky.

He went to Korea in November 1951 to command the 7th Infantry Division and the next year was promoted to lieutenant general and named deputy chief of staff, army planning and research. He returned to Asia in March 1955 as commander of the 8th Army and in June became commander of the Far East Command, of the United Nations Command. In July 1957, he returned to the United States as army vice chief of staff, succeeding Gen. Maxwell D. Taylor as chief of staff in July 1959 until September 1960, when he was appointed chairman of the Joint Chiefs of Staff. He was identified with the alleged disastrous Bay of Pigs operation of April 1961. In November 1962, he became commander of U.S. forces in Europe, and in January 1963 Supreme Allied Commander, Europe (SACEur). Lemnitzer retired from the military in July 1969.

Russell A. Hart

LITZENBERG, HOMER LAURENCE (1903–1963)
U.S. marine officer, Litzenberg was born in Steelton, Pennsylvania. He enlisted in the Marine Corps in 1925 and, after various tours of duty, served on expeditionary duty in Nicaragua (1928–29). Through the 1930s, he was an instructor/inspector, an aide to the governor of Guam, and in the War Plans section of naval operations. He entered World War II as a major, saw service in Europe and the Pacific, and emerged from the war a colonel. He commanded the 6th Marines (1947–50) and in 1950 took the 7th Marines to Korea, where his troops participated at Inchon and the push north to and beyond the 38th parallel. In less than three weeks, Litzenberg's marines fought their way through several enemy divisions.

Upon his return to the United States, he served as the legal and legislative counsel to the commandant of the marines until 1952. He was assistant commander of the 3d Marine Division (1953–54); inspector general of the Marine Corps (1954–55); commanding general, Parris Island, South Carolina (1955–57); and a member of the Korean Armistice Commission (1957–59). He retired in 1959.

Leo J. Daugherty III

LOVETT, ROBERT ABERCROMBIE (1895–1986)
U.S. secretary of defense, Lovett was born in Huntsville, Texas. He left Yale University in 1917 to organize Yale pilots for service in World War I, during which he commanded the first U.S. Naval Air Squadron. An eminently successful postwar investment banker, Lovett entered government service during World War II, when he was assistant secretary of war for air (1941–45), responsible for the massive buildup of the Army Air Force. This assignment

put him in close touch with Gen. George C. Marshall, and, when Marshall became secretary of state, Lovett served with him as undersecretary (1947–49). When Marshall moved to the Department of Defense, Lovett accompanied and then succeeded him, serving as deputy secretary of defense in 1950–51 and as secretary of defense during 1951–53, his Pentagon service spanning the period of the Korean War. Lovett was subsequently awarded the Presidential Medal of Freedom; after his death, a Lovett Chair of Military History was established in his honor at Yale University.

Lewis Sorley

LYNCH, JAMES HENRY (1914–   )

U.S. army officer, Lynch was born in Washington, D.C. He graduated from West Point in 1938, then served a number of years at Fort Benning, Georgia. During the Korean War, he commanded the 3d Battalion, 7th Cavalry Regiment, 1st Cavalry Division. His battalion spearheaded the division's breakout from the Pusan perimeter. Later, he served in the G-3 Section of I Corps. Subsequent assignments included Fort Benning; the Personnel Section, Department of the Army; deputy chief of staff for reserve components; J-1 (Personnel), Headquarters, European Command; assistant division commander, 24th Infantry Division; assistant deputy chief of staff, unit training and readiness, Headquarters, Continental Army Command. Lynch retired as a brigadier general in 1968.

Bibliography: Blair, Clay, *The Forgotten War* (Random House, 1987).

Brig. Gen. PNG (Ret.) Uzal W. Ent

MacARTHUR, DOUGLAS (1880–1964)

U.S. army commander, MacArthur was born in Little Rock, Arkansas, son of the renowned Gen. Arthur MacArthur. He graduated from West Point, first in the Class of 1903. He served on the War Department General Staff (1913–17) before seeing action in World War I, during which time he led troops into several significant battles and earned two Distinguished Service Crosses and seven Silver Stars. After the war, he became superintendent of West Point (1919–22) and attained the rank of major general (1925). MacArthur was army chief of staff (1930–35) before his retirement in 1937. During World War II, he was recalled to active duty as lieutenant general in command of all U.S. forces in the Far East (1941) and then as the Allied Supreme Commander in the Southwest Pacific (1942).

Occupation of Japan. In the late summer of 1945, MacArthur, with a small contingent of U.S. soldiers, moved into a still well-armed Japan to supervise the dramatic and emotional surrender ceremonies ending World War II. The documents were signed under 16-inch naval guns on board a U.S. battleship in Tokyo Bay. With the

General of the Army Douglas MacArthur (center), *commander in chief, U.S. Forces, Korea, visits Inchon in September 1950, accompanied by Vice Adm. Arthur Struble* (left) *and Gen. Oliver Smith* (right). (U.S. Army)

best view of the scene, above all the ranking officers, sat row on row of ordinary U.S. sailors, a fitting tribute to their predecessors who had died at Pearl Harbor four years before. Standing behind the general was the frail and weak Gen. Jonathan Wainwright, fresh from a Japanese prison camp. Having made the strength and pain of the United States vividly evident, MacArthur signed the document ending a world war and rose to make an eloquent, brief plea for world peace.

Charged with the difficult and complex task of removing centuries-old militarism from Japanese culture and instituting democratic procedures, MacArthur began a career as a military governor in a foreign land. To his credit, U.S. Occupation authorities managed to bring about giant strides in women's rights and nurtured a labor movement. MacArthur was less successful in creating a Western-style commercial and industrial system independent of government planning. However, the Japanese largely accepted a form of representative government with recognized individual rights in which most issues were publicly debated and brought to a vote. Japan thus joined the ranks of democratic nations.

The most far-reaching of MacArthur's reforms centered on Japanese militarism. The nation not only abandoned military solutions for foreign problems, it relegated the formerly revered and respected profession of arms to the status of a common trade. Japan created a true Self Defense Force, one wholly devoted to protection of the homeland, an organization that could not realistically be regarded as a threat to Japan's neighbors. Much to his credit, MacArthur conducted his duties in Japan in such a way that U.S. insistence on fundamental societal change was neither resented nor shunned by the bulk of the Japanese people.

Korean War. At the outbreak of the Korean War in June 1950, MacArthur began his last call to arms. As his United Nations (UN) forces were driven back to a small corner of the Korean peninsula by the onrushing North Korean Communist troops, he formulated a dramatic and daring envelopment of his enemies. Using his great skill and understanding of amphibious warfare, the general directed a landing on the western coast of Korea, deep in the rear of the Communist invaders. The move was viewed with some suspicion in Washington. The selected landing point, the port of Inchon, had great tide variations and was only marginally developed. Through force of personality and determination and using his considerable reputation to advantage, MacArthur sold his plan and got a good portion of the resources he demanded. The Inchon landing was a great success. It isolated the North Korean armies, severed their lines of communication, and placed the Communists between two UN attacking forces. The North Korean units rapidly disintegrated, and it looked as if the UN would be able to halt future aggression.

Seeking and gaining permission to advance into North Korea, MacArthur raced both winter and retreating enemy forces in a rushed attempt to conquer the entire country. Splitting his forces on either side of an extensive mountain range, he urged his commanders forward. In some ways, the general's technique was much like the World War II experience where he placed his 8th Army and 6th Army commanders in competition rather than in an environment of coordination and mutual support. By the beginning of a period of intense cold in November 1950 and with increasing indications China might be entering the war, MacArthur simply continued the march of his divided command. Soon, his lightly clad troops were far from their supply bases, exposed to both a harsh climate and a powerful adversary. His actions indicated that he believed that the Chinese would probably not attack, but if they did, they would be no match for the Americans. Regrettably, MacArthur was wrong on both counts.

The massive and well-executed Chinese offensive overpowered MacArthur's troops and forced them into a bloody and ignoble withdrawal down the Korean peninsula. Early in 1951, UN forces, largely U.S. and South Korean, managed to bring the Communists to a halt and even produced a limited offensive back toward the north. Nonetheless, MacArthur's reputation was in decline, and

he realized that his fate as a commander was, as in World War II, to be in the secondary theater. Despite the desperate fight in Korea, the United States was sending more troops and matériel to Europe than to Asia. When he made a number of injudicious policy statements that reached the public ear, Pres. Harry S Truman relieved MacArthur of his command and directed him to return to the United States.

Last Years. On reaching the United States, MacArthur was greeted as a hero. His dismissal had created a public uproar. Delivering a memorable speech to the Congress, he found himself the object of political overtures to become a presidential candidate in the 1952 elections. At first, he was a serious contender. Americans were concerned about the seeming inability of their nation to defeat the forces of relatively primitive Asian societies. Many looked to MacArthur to reclaim military laurels for the United States and put a simple and forceful end to the Cold War. As the summer of 1951 wore on, however, there were steadily decreasing crowds at his speeches. Sensing his own lack of a formidable following, MacArthur turned away from politics and settled down to a life of honorary appointments, leisure, and writing in New York City. On occasion, he would visit West Point and recall more glorious days to cadets at the academy. His memoirs, *Reminiscences,* a somewhat self-congratulatory book, was published in 1964, the year of his death.

A complex figure in American history, MacArthur achieved a number of solid achievements and committed some noticeable blunders in a long career. His tenure as superintendent at West Point vastly modernized the Military Academy. Some of the success enjoyed by the U.S. Army during World War II is due to the sound leadership that that organization enjoyed at mid-level commands, a tribute to both MacArthur and West Point. His military feats during World War II were considered by many to be perhaps the best performance of any general on either side. In the Korean War, the Inchon landing will long be remembered as an outstanding example of intelligent daring. When it came to the integration of air, naval, and land forces in a broad-scale campaign, MacArthur had few peers. On the debit side, the faulty defense of the Philippines in 1941–42 and the rush to the Yalu 10 years later cloud an otherwise bright image. Both episodes smack of carelessness, possibly even arrogance. Then, too, MacArthur's example in Korea will stand out as the type of behavior to avoid in the crucial relationship between U.S. soldiers and their civilian superiors. However, MacArthur's reform of Japanese society and his impact on that nation's structure will likely overshadow all of his other achievements. Few American military figures have engendered such loyalty among subordinates and contemporaries, and few have fostered such derision.

Bibliography: James, Clayton D., *The Years of MacArthur,* 2 vols. (Houghton Mifflin, 1970–1975); MacArthur, Douglas, *Reminiscences* (McGraw-Hill, 1964); Manchester, William, *American Caesar* (Little Brown, 1978); Willoughby, Charles A., ed., *Reports of General MacArthur,* 4 vols. (Dept. of the Army, 1966).

Col. (Ret.) Rod Paschall

McCAIN, JOHN SIDNEY, JR. (1911–1981)

U.S. naval officer, McCain was born in Council Bluffs, Iowa. He graduated from Annapolis in 1931 and served on a battleship before spending almost 20 years as a submariner. While commanding the USS *Gunnel* from its commissioning in 1942 to 1944, he and his crew engaged in combat from the coast of North Africa, where they took photos of the beach before the invasion there, to the Pacific, where the *Gunnel* sank Japanese shipping including a destroyer, for which McCain was awarded the Silver Star.

In addition to extensive command at sea, McCain served as a legislative liaison for the secretary of the navy, as chief of information for the Department of the Navy, and with a U.S. delegation to the Military Staff Committee of the United Nations. In 1965, Admiral McCain was the senior officer in the region when U.S. troops moved into the Dominican Republic. From 1967 to 1968, he was the commander in chief, U.S. Naval Forces, Europe, before becoming commander in chief, Pacific, a position he held from 1968 to 1972 and from which he advocated the bombing of Haiphong and North Vietnam. He retired from the navy in 1972. McCain was the first full U.S. admiral who was the son of a full admiral. He was also the father of a U.S. senator who was a naval aviator and prisoner of war in North Vietnam.

Col. (Ret.) Henry G. Gole

McDONALD, DAVID LAMAR (1906–)

U.S. naval officer, McDonald was born in Maysville, Georgia. He graduated from Annapolis in 1928 and soon entered naval aviation. During World War II, he had duty with the Naval Operation Training Command, after which he went to sea as executive officer of the carrier *Essex.* Gaining flag rank in 1955, McDonald then headed the Air Warfare Division in the Office of the Chief of Naval Operations, served as deputy assistant chief of staff at NATO (North Atlantic Treaty Organization) headquarters, and commanded the 6th Fleet.

In 1963, McDonald became chief of naval operations (CNO). He was able to gain authorization for the construction of nuclear-powered attack carriers but was less successful in getting escorts for the 15 carrier groups he wanted. He was in office until 1967 but had relatively little to do with naval operations off Vietnam, since by then the CNO had lost most of his authority over operational matters.

Bibliography: Kennedy, Floyd D., Jr., *The Chiefs of Naval Operations,* ed. by Robert William Love, Jr. (Naval Inst. Press, 1980).

Lloyd J. Graybar

McELROY, NEIL HOSLER (1904–1972)

U.S. secretary of defense, McElroy was born in Berea, Ohio. He was a prominent businessman at the time Pres. Dwight D. Eisenhower appointed him defense secretary in 1957. McElroy joined the cabinet days after the Soviet Union launched *Sputnik I,* the world's first satellite, an event that raised the "missile gap" issue that would figure prominently in the 1960 presidential campaign. He initiated countering the Soviet intercontinental ballistic missile (ICBM) threat by forward deploying U.S. intermediate range ballistic missiles (IRBMs). He was also a strong advocate of military assistance but resisted pressures to increase the defense budget. McElroy influenced the Reorganization Act of 1958 that strengthened the Department of Defense and the Joint Chiefs of Staff at the expense of the individual military services.

Col. (Ret.) Henry G. Gole

McGARR, LIONEL CHARLES (1904–)

U.S. army officer, McGarr was born in Yuma, Arizona. He graduated from West Point in 1928 and led an infantry regiment and served the assistant division commander of the 3d Infantry Division during World War II. Transferred to Korea in 1952, he briefly acted as the head of the United Nations Prisoner of War Command before taking over the 7th Infantry Division. In 1960, McGarr became the head of the Military Assistance Advisory Group Vietnam (MAAG-Vietnam). During his tenure, the MAAG-Vietnam expanded, and the U.S. Army became increasingly aware of the political dimensions of Viet Cong operations, although its countermeasures continued to rely on conventional antiguerrilla tactics and techniques. Moreover, it was during this period that U.S. advisers became more involved in assisting South Vietnamese units in the field. In 1962, as a result of his seven combat wounds from two wars, McGarr retired for disability.

Bibliography: Spector, Ronald H., *Advice and Support: The Early Years, 1945–1960* (Center of Military History, U.S. Army, 1983).

Richard F. Kehrberg

McKEE, FRAN (1926–)

First woman line officer to obtain flag rank in the U.S. Navy, McKee was born in Florence, Alabama. She was commissioned in 1950 and served throughout the Korean War in the Office of the Chief of Naval Research, Washington, D.C. After the war, she was assigned to recruiting duties in Boston (1954–57), to Morocco (1957–58), and to the Naval Women Officers School (1965–67), where she was officer in charge. In 1970, she and another WAVES (Women Accepted for Volunteer Emergency Service) officer were the first women to attend the regular course at the Naval War College, after which she was assigned to the Bureau of Naval Personnel in Washington. From 1973 to 1976, McKee commanded the Naval Security Group Activity at Fort Meade, Maryland—the first woman to head an activity of the Naval Security Group Command.

After promotion to rear admiral in 1976, she directed the Naval Education Division at Pensacola, Florida. Two years later, she became assistant chief of naval personnel for human resources management, at the Bureau of Naval Personnel. After a reorganization of that bureau, she served as director of human resource management in the Office of the Chief of Naval Operations. She retired in 1981.

Col. (Ret.) Bettie J. Morden

McNAMARA, ROBERT STRANGE
(1916–   )

U.S. secretary of defense (1961–68), McNamara was born in San Francisco. He earned a degree in economics from the University of California at Berkeley (1937) and a master's in business from Harvard (1939), after which he worked briefly as an accountant before returning to Harvard as an assistant professor of business.

McNamara was at first rejected for World War II service due to poor eyesight, so he taught statistical analysis to Army Air Force officers at Harvard. His classes were such a huge success that he received a commission in the army, where he applied business management techniques to military logistics problems. During the war, McNamara helped coordinate production, training, and supply for both the B-17 and B-29 bomber programs, determined ways to assess damage inflicted by the B-29s, and traveled to India and China to develop methods to increase the volume of supplies flowing over the Himalayan Mountains from Burma to China.

McNamara spent the next 14 years amassing an incredible reputation in the business world. Nicknamed the "Human Computer" for his amazing ability to comprehend and analyze enormous amounts of data, McNamara and nine other former Army Air Corps officers formed a consulting firm after the war. These "whiz kids" were quickly hired by Henry Ford II for his financially plagued automobile company, and McNamara remained to work for Ford. Between 1949 and 1957, McNamara rose to company vice president. When Ford Motor Company suffered a serious setback with the Edsel automobile, McNamara helped return it to profitability with new models. Following record

sales, he was elected president of the company in 1960, the first president from outside the Ford family.

He remained as president for less than a year, however, as he was selected as secretary of defense by Pres. John F. Kennedy, who had promised in his 1960 campaign that he would bring to Washington the best talent he could find. Kennedy believed that the vast Pentagon needed efficiency and reform, areas in which McNamara had earned his stellar reputation. Disdaining popularity and ignoring military traditions and politics, McNamara speedily instituted changes to bring the Pentagon under civilian control. He brought in his team of whiz kids to apply systems analysis to Pentagon operations, centralized control over programs such as intelligence and supply, reorganized budget procedures for greater efficiency, eliminated wasteful military bases and programs, and strove for improved interservice harmony. Although his changes angered some military officials and members of Congress, McNamara brought much-needed reform to the Defense Department and the Pentagon.

During the Kennedy presidency (1961–63), McNamara also instituted programs to increase the military's ability to respond to a wide range of situations. Kennedy had criticized former president Dwight D. Eisenhower for allowing U.S. conventional capability to wither while enlarging the nuclear arsenal, so McNamara developed a "flexible response" capability that could react to any military situation from guerrilla warfare to nuclear threat and that included the ability to airlift U.S. troops to any spot in the world in a relatively short time. These changes paid dividends in October 1962 when U.S. forces efficiently responded during the Cuban Missile Crisis.

Vietnam War Role. The expanding conflict in Southeast Asia occupied most of McNamara's energy as secretary of defense. In the fall of 1963, he visited South Vietnam with Gen. Maxwell Taylor and concluded that any U.S. military role would end by 1965. As Viet Cong forces rolled to a disturbing string of successes, however, he began to doubt his conclusion. In August 1964, after North Vietnamese gunboats attacked two U.S. destroyers in the Gulf of Tonkin, McNamara urged Congress to grant Pres. Lyndon B. Johnson what amounted to a free hand with the Gulf of Tonkin Resolution. Retaliatory air strikes against North Vietnam began.

McNamara urged an increased U.S. role in South Vietnam through much of 1965 and became known as one of the conflict's firmest advocates. After renewed Viet Cong attacks on U.S. bases in February, the air war intensified, and four months later, McNamara approved Gen. William C. Westmoreland's request for 185,000 troops by year's end. McNamara also supported a reserve call-up and tax increase to pay for the war's cost, but both measures were rejected by Johnson as politically unwise. He pushed for construction of a 25-mile electronic barrier across the de-

Sec. of Defense (1961–68) Robert S. McNamara's early advocacy of a strong U.S. presence in the Vietnam War had diminished greatly by late 1966, when peace seemed unlikely. (International Bank for Reconstruction and Development)

militarized zone that would alert U.S. forces of any infiltration by North Vietnamese forces, but "McNamara's Wall," as journalists labeled it, was never implemented. The secretary believed in 1965 that a gradual escalation of the war would force North Vietnam to agree to an independent South Vietnam, and he continued to support the air war against the North, although he kept it more limited than the Joint Chiefs wanted.

Near the end of 1965, McNamara urged President Johnson to order a bombing halt in hopes of bringing North Vietnam to the peace table. When the December cessation failed to work, Johnson had justification to renew the bombing on a more vigorous scale, which he did in January 1966. Although McNamara remained optimistic about eventual victory, he told reporters, "It will be a long war."

As 1966 dragged on, McNamara began doubting the war. Despite vigorous bombing and greater numbers of U.S. troops, enemy supplies and men continued to pour into South Vietnam, and he was amazed at the enemy's willingness to absorb casualties. According to the calculations of his experts, by now the enemy should have been brought to the peace table. Some of his critics maintained that McNamara handled the war as another business and never fully comprehended the human element in conflict— that emotion and battle for one's own land can overturn carefully prepared agendas. In addition, corruption in the South Vietnamese government and its failure to implement substantive democratic changes angered McNamara. After a visit to South Vietnam in October 1966, McNamara began privately expressing his doubts about the conflict.

These doubts became public in 1967. Instead of victory or a more stable South Vietnamese government, McNamara saw only a growing list of U.S. casualties. Supporters of the war attacked McNamara for not giving the military a freer hand, while antiwar protestors castigated him for his role. As his doubts grew, so did his willingness to recommend a change in the war effort. During the summer of 1967, McNamara helped draft the San Antonio Formula, a peace proposal that asked North Vietnam to enter into negotiations in exchange for an end to U.S. bombing of the North. The proposal was rejected by the North Vietnamese in October. The next month, McNamara wrote a memorandum to Johnson recommending a freeze in troop levels, a halt in the bombing, and the gradual handing over of responsibility for the ground war to the South Vietnamese, but the president angrily disdained the advice. In fact, Johnson was extremely upset that brilliant advisers, including McNamara, were advocating the opposite of what they had earlier proposed—now that more than 500,000 U.S. troops had been sent to South Vietnam and more than 30,000 had lost their lives. Believing his secretary of defense had strayed too far from his administration's position, in November 1967, Johnson asked McNamara to resign.

Later Career. From 1968 to 1982, McNamara worked as president of the International Bank for Reconstruction and Development. More commonly known as the World Bank, the bank attempts to aid developing nations by asking advanced countries to help with loans and technological assistance. Formerly occupied as a secretary in time of war, McNamara ended his public career striving for peace.

Bibliography: Davidson, Phillip B., *Vietnam at War* (Presidio, 1988); Halberstam, David, *The Best and the Brightest* (Random House, 1972); Roherty, James M., *Decisions of Robert S. McNamara* (Univ. of Miami Press, 1970); Sheehan, Neil, *A Bright Shining Lie* (Random House, 1988); Trewhitt, Henry L., *McNamara* (Harper & Row, 1971).

John F. Wukovits

McNARNEY, JOSEPH TAGGART
(1893–1972)

U.S. army and air force officer, McNarney was born in Emporium, Pennsylvania. He graduated from West Point in 1915. Trained as a pilot, he served in France during World War I. McNarney then graduated from the Command and General Staff School in 1926 and the Army War College in 1930. During World War II, he served on the Roberts Commission investigating the Pearl Harbor attack and in March 1942 became army deputy chief of staff. From October 1944 through the end of the war, McNarney served in the Mediterranean theater, eventually becoming the Supreme Allied Command there. In November 1945, he succeeded Gen. George Patton as commander of all U.S. forces in Europe and served as military governor of the U.S. occupation zone. He transferred to the newly created air force in September 1947 and commanded the Air Material Command at Wright-Patterson Air Force Base. McNarney retired in 1952.

Steve R. Waddell

MARSH, JOHN OTHO, JR. (1926–)

U.S. army officer and defense adviser, Marsh was born in Winchester, Virginia. He received an army commission in 1945 and after service with occupation forces in Germany, attended law school at Washington and Lee University, graduating in 1951. Marsh set up a law practice in Virginia, and later served in the U.S. House of Representatives (1963–71), after which he returned to law practice, this time in Washington, D.C.

In March 1973, Marsh was appointed assistant secretary of defense for legislative affairs. In January 1974, he was appointed Vice Pres. Gerald R. Ford's assistant for national security affairs. From August 1974 to January 1977, he was President Ford's counselor. He again returned to private law practice until January 1981, when he was sworn in as secretary of the army. Marsh was the longest serving individual to hold that position to date, holding the office until August 1989, when he was succeeded by Michael P. W. Stone.

Bibliography: Bell, William G., *Secretaries of War and Secretaries of the Army, Portraits & Biographical Sketches* (Center of Military History, 1982).

David Friend

MARSHALL, GEORGE CATLETT (1880–1959)

U.S. army officer and statesman, Marshall was born in Uniontown, Pennsylvania. He graduated from the Virginia Military Institute in 1901 and received a commission in the army the following year. During his early career, he impressed his superiors with his knowledge of military tactics. In World War I he held increasingly responsible staff positions, followed by staff and command assignments during the interwar years.

He was promoted to brigadier general in 1936, and in 1938, he was detailed to the General Staff as chief of the War Plans Division. He served as chief of staff with the rank of general (1939–45) throughout World War II and emerged as the war's principal strategist. In opposition to Churchill's plan to enter Germany via the Balkan states,

As chief of staff of the U.S. Army (1939–45), Gen. George Marshall was responsible for the training, supplying, and deployment of U.S. troops during World War II. (Library of Congress)

Marshall insisted on an entry from the west. His plan, not Churchill's, was accepted. Due primarily to Marshall's pressure and determination, the Allies eventually launched Operation Roundup, creating a Second Front in 1943. In 1944, Roosevelt appointed Marshall General of the Army, which entitled him to the rank of five-star general and which was a clear indication of the success of his position. Following the war, Churchill proclaimed Marshall "the true organizer of victory" for his work as a planner and strategist.

Postwar Career. Almost a prophet of the cold war to come, Marshall, realizing the potential risk for Soviet opportunism in the postwar world, insisted, unsuccessfully, that the Soviet Union's help was not needed in the Pacific theater. Nevertheless, the U.S.S.R. belatedly declared war on Japan, which ultimately led to the Soviet influence in Southeast Asia that Marshall had anticipated.

Following Marshall's retirement from the army (November 1945), Pres. Harry S Truman dispatched him on a mission to China. After Japan had been driven from the region, civil war erupted between Chinese Communists led by Mao Zedong and Nationalists under Chiang Kai-shek. U.S. Marines and General Marshall were dispatched to the area in hopes of ensuring the peace, but the mission failed. Truman later named Marshall secretary of state (1947–49), and as such, Marshall attended a conference in Moscow with his British, French, and Soviet counterparts. They tried futilely to draw up treaties with Germany and Austria. After seeing firsthand the impending economic collapse of Europe and sensing the Soviet Union's intent to step in and benefit from the resulting turmoil, Marshall returned determined to seek a solution to Europe's problems.

In a commencement address at Harvard University on June 5, 1947, Marshall announced his plan. Officially known as the European Recovery Program, but commonly referred to as the Marshall Plan, it proposed sending more than $13 billion in aid to assist the economic recovery of postwar Europe. The Marshall Plan successfully sparked economic recovery in Western Europe, thus blocking any Soviet penetration from Eastern Europe. Ironically, in 1952, Senators McCarthy and Jenner would damn Marshall and other leading officials for the loss of China and North Korea to the Communists.

The American public perceived the Marshall Plan as a generous subvention to war-ravaged Europe. The Soviets, however, viewed the plan in a much different light. They saw it as an attempt to interfere in the internal affairs of other states. Ultimately, the Soviet Union prevented Poland and Czechoslovakia from participating. The Marshall Plan, according to late-20th-century revisionist historians, allowed the United States to remake the European economy in the image of the American economy, thereby providing a more congenial environment for U.S. investment.

Marshall resigned as secretary of state early in 1949 due to health problems. But when North Korean forces invaded South Korea on June 25, 1950, Truman urged Marshall to become secretary of defense. While the defense of South Korea was carried out under the auspices of the United Nations (UN), ultimately 1,800,000 U.S. troops served in Korea. During the one year he agreed to stay in the post, the aging Marshall augmented army strength, secured increased UN aid, and bolstered the North Atlantic Treaty Organization (NATO), which he had helped to develop in 1948 as a response to imminent cold war.

Marshall retired for the last time in September 1951, after nearly 50 years of military and civilian public service. Strictly nonpartisan, he remained stridently opposed to politics to the point of never voting. For his efforts toward European political and economic reconstruction after World War II, Marshall received the Nobel Peace Prize in 1953.

Bibliography: Bland, Larry I., ed., *The Papers of George Catlett Marshall* (Johns Hopkins Univ. Press, 1981); Mosley, Leonard, *Marshall: Hero for Our Times* (Hearst, 1982); Pogue, Forrest C., *George C. Marshall,* 4 vols. (Viking, 1963–87).

M. Guy Bishop

MATTHEWS, FRANCIS PATRICK (1887–1952)

U.S. secretary of the navy, Matthews was born in Albion, Nebraska. He was a prominent Omaha businessman and attorney with no military experience but was named secretary of the navy in 1949 to replace Sec. John Sullivan, who had resigned in protest over the cancellation of the navy's first 65,000-ton super-carrier. Matthew's admitted ignorance of naval affairs gained him the nickname of "the rowboat secretary" but did nothing to ease the concerns in the Office of Naval Operations and the major fleet commands over budget austerity in general and the status of naval aviation in particular. These worries culminated in the so-called Revolt of the Admirals. Thereafter, his incumbency was eased by the November 1949 appointment of the adroit Forrest Sherman as chief of naval operations and by the Korean War (1950–53), which helped make funds available for new construction. Matthews resigned in 1951.

Bibliography: Coletta, Paolo, "Francis P. Matthews," *American Secretaries of the Navy; Vol. 2: 1913–1972* (Naval Inst. Press, 1980).

Lloyd J. Graybar

MEDINA, ERNEST (1936–)

U.S. army officer, Medina was born in Springer, New Mexico. He entered the army as a private in 1956 and was commissioned a second lieutenant in 1964. Three years later, a captain, he went to Vietnam where he earned a Bronze Star and a Silver Star for bravery and leadership.

On Mar. 10, 1970, Medina was charged with murder and manslaughter for his apparent role in the March 1968 My Lai massacre, when U.S. troops slaughtered more than 150 innocent civilians in a Vietnamese hamlet. Medina was not present at the site, but he reported to headquarters a body count of 90 Viet Cong soldiers dead. After an investigation of the affair, a jury of five officers acquitted him on Sept. 22, 1970. Medina resigned his commission the next year.

Bibliography: Hersh, Seymour, *My Lai 4* (Harper & Row, 1970); Karnow, Stanley, *Vietnam: A History* (Penguin, 1983).

Johh F. Wukovits

MELOY, GUY STANLEY, JR. (1903–1968)

U.S. army commander, Meloy was born in Lanham, Maryland. He graduated from West Point in 1927. He served as chief of staff of the 103d Infantry Division during World War II and commanded the 19th Regiment, 24th Infantry Division, during the early stages of the Korean War. Wounded on July 16, 1950, in the battle for the Kum River line, Meloy returned to the United States, where he served as chief of information, Department of the Army, and as Commandant of the Infantry School at Fort Benning, Georgia. In subsequent assignments, he commanded the 1st Infantry Division, U.S. 4th Army, and VII Corps. Meloy returned to Korea in July 1961 as commander in chief, United Nations Command; commander,

U.S. Forces Korea; and commanding general, U.S. 8th Army. He was promoted to brigadier general in 1951 and retired in 1963 as a full general.

Maj. James Sanders Day

MEYER, EDWARD CHARLES (1928–)

U.S. army officer and chief of staff, Meyer was born in St. Mary's, Pennsylvania. He served as an infantry officer in the Korean War after graduating from West Point in 1951. In 1965, he accompanied the 1st Cavalry Division to Vietnam and served two tours (1965–66; 1969–70) with it there. After several important posts, including deputy chief of staff for operations, he reached the rank of full general. Pres. Jimmy Carter appointed Meyer chief of staff of the army in 1979.

Meyer took charge of the army as it began to emerge from its post-Vietnam doldrums. He was instrumental in establishing an army-wide modernization program that emphasized quality, both in manpower and equipment, over quantity. One element of this program was the revitalization of the army school system, especially at the War College level. Another component was a new "unit-manning system" designed to reduce personnel turbulence and thereby increase unit cohesion and combat readiness. Furthermore, Meyer emphasized the need to update the army's equipment and to develop long-term plans in that area.

In addition to the modernization program, he helped fashion the army's portion of the new Rapid Deployment Joint Task Force (RDF). Created in part as a response to the Iranian revolution and the Soviet invasion of Afghanistan, the RDF was designed to deliver U.S. military power rapidly into the Middle East. The RDF, however, was still largely in its formative stages when Meyer's tour as chief of staff expired in 1983, and he retired.

Richard F. Kehrberg

MOORER, THOMAS HINMAN (1912–)

U.S. naval commander, Moorer was born in Mount Willing, Alabama. He graduated from Annapolis in 1933. A naval aviator in Hawaii during the December 1941 Japanese attack, Moorer was shot down two months later north of Australia but was rescued. Moorer rose quickly during the postwar period, attaining the position of commander of the 7th Fleet in 1962. In this position, in charge of U.S. naval operations in the western Pacific, Admiral Moorer became privy to the John F. Kennedy administration's program to increase the U.S. commitment to South Vietnam. In August 1964, a little more than a month prior to the Gulf of Tonkin incident, Moorer was again advanced, this time to be commander in chief of the Pacific Fleet, a position he held until March 1965. During the first week of August 1964, Moorer was involved in trying to determine what happened to the Navy ships *Maddox* and *Turner Joy*.

On orders from the commander in chief of the Pacific Command, Adm. U. S. Grant Sharp, Moorer had dispatched first the destroyer *Maddox* and then both the *Maddox* and the *Turner Joy* on two electronic intelligence collection missions just off the North Vietnamese coast. The missions were to be conducted within international waters. The *Maddox* reported being attacked by North Vietnamese torpedo boats on the first sortie, defended itself, and withdrew. Other than a diplomatic protest, the United States took no reprisal action. Two days later, both destroyers returned and reported another attack. At the time, President Johnson was running for election and was facing charges from opponent Sen. Barry Goldwater that the United States was meekly yielding to Communist aggression. When the Johnson administration decided on a reprisal air raid on North Vietnam in response to the second attack, the suggestion of domestic politics influencing combat operations began to spread. Later, that suggestion became a major issue in most of the histories of the Vietnam War, because in obtaining legislative support for a reprisal, Johnson asked for and received congressional approval to take what action was necessary against North Vietnam. The Gulf of Tonkin Resolution became the U.S. authority to wage war, and Moorer's analysis of what happened to the *Maddox* and *Turner Joy* probably influenced Washington decision-makers.

Although enemies of Johnson's Vietnam War policies long claimed there was no second North Vietnamese attack on the two U.S. destroyers, Moorer believed there was. At the time, radio intercepts of North Vietnamese naval communications could not be released to the public. However, in 1986, the navy published its official history of the event, and in that volume, it appears that Moorer was correct. The record indicates that there were probably not as many torpedoes fired at the U.S. destroyers as initially claimed, but North Vietnamese communications clearly point to an assault on the U.S. warships during the second mission off Hanoi's coastline.

From the summer of 1964 until March 1965, when he was named commander in chief of the Atlantic Command, Moorer directed much of his attention to U.S. logistical activities in Southeast Asia. He believed the United States would be drawn into major combat operations against the Vietnamese Communists and sought to prepare bases and facilities to support those operations. He pushed for major naval and air facilities at Da Nang and Cam Ranh Bay, South Vietnam, and pressed for a sizable air base at Chu Lai, all of which were eventually built.

In August 1967, Moorer became chief of naval operations, and in July 1970, he was selected to be the chairman of the Joint Chiefs of Staff. In this latter position, he finally received the go-ahead to do what the navy and air force had long advocated: a substantially unrestricted bombing campaign of North Vietnam together with the mining of Haiphong harbor. The decision was made in December 1972 after yet one more frustrating and failed U.S. attempt to negotiate with Hanoi. Soon after this operation (Linebacker II) was launched, the agreement with the North Vietnamese government and South Vietnamese Communist representatives was signed.

Admiral Moorer retired from active duty in July 1974. Reflecting on the Vietnam War, he believed the U.S. mistake had been the attempt to resist Hanoi's designs within the territory of South Vietnam, rather than taking the war to the North from the very start.

Bibliography: Kissinger, Henry, *White House Years* (Little, Brown, 1979); Marolda, Edward J., and Oscar P. Fitzgerald, *The United States Navy and the Vietnam Conflict, Vol. 2: From Military Assistance to Combat, 1959–1965* (Naval Hist. Center, 1986).

Col. (Ret.) Rod Paschall

NIMITZ, CHESTER WILLIAM
(1885–1966)
U.S. naval commander, Nimitz was born in Fredericksburg, Texas. He graduated from Annapolis in 1905 and was commissioned an ensign in the U.S. Navy. He was promoted to commander (1921), captain (1927), rear admiral (1938), and admiral (1941). He served, among other duties, as chief of staff to the commander of the U.S. Atlantic Submarine Fleet (1917–18), chief of the Bureau of Navigation (1939), and commander in chief, Pacific Fleet (1941–45). After brilliantly planning and executing the navy's strategic Central Pacific island "leapfrogging" drive toward Japan during World War II, he represented the navy in signing the surrender.

After the war, Nimitz became chief of naval operations (1945–47), lobbying Congress to retain the nation's naval strength and enthusiastically overseeing research and development for the creation of a nuclear navy. During his tenure, he was responsible for appointing a special board of submarine officers to study the ramifications of a nuclear navy. An ardent opponent of defense unification, he succeeded in retaining the navy's air arm and fought for the retention of the Marine Corps.

Nimitz retired in 1947 but retained a deep interest in national security affairs and continued to advocate the necessity of maintaining a large navy. He was often consulted by the secretary of the navy and the president on naval affairs.

Leo J. Daugherty III

NITZE, PAUL HENRY (1907–)
U.S. defense official, Nitze was born in Amherst, Massachusetts. He graduated from Harvard University in 1928 and became successful in investment banking. In 1940, he entered government service, where for 50 years, under ad-

ministrations of both political parties, he was involved at high levels in defense and foreign policy.

Nitze began as an aide to Undersec. of the Navy James V. Forrestal in 1940. During 1944–46, he was vice chairman of the U.S. Strategic Bombing Survey. His posts in the Department of State (1946–53) included director of the policy planning staff, during which he drafted the celebrated NSC-68, the basic document for U.S. Cold War strategy. In the Department of Defense, Nitze held the posts of assistant secretary of defense for international security affairs (1960–63), secretary of the navy (1963–67), and deputy secretary of defense (1967–69).

During 1969–74, he was a member of the delegation conducting Strategic Arms Limitation Talks (SALT I) with the Soviet Union. In 1981–84, with the rank of ambassador, he headed the U.S. delegation to the Intermediate-Range Nuclear Forces Negotiations with the Soviets. During 1984–89, he was special adviser to the president and the secretary of state for arms control matters.

Nitze was a cofounder of Johns Hopkins University's School for Advanced International Studies, subsequently named for him as the Nitze School. In 1985, Pres. Ronald Reagan awarded him the Medal of Freedom, the nation's highest civilian decoration.

Bibliography: Nitze, Paul H., *From Hiroshima to Glasnost: At the Center of Decision—A Memoir* (Grove Weidenfeld, 1989); Talbott, Strobe, *The Master of the Game: Paul Nitze and the Nuclear Peace* (Knopf, 1988).

Lewis Sorley

NIXON, RICHARD MILHOUS (1913–1994)
The 37th president of the United States (1969–74), under whom U.S. involvement in the Vietnam War ended, was born in Yorba Linda, California. After becoming a lawyer and serving in World War II, he was elected as a Republican to the House of Representatives in 1950 and then became vice president (1953–61) under Dwight D. Eisenhower. He lost the presidential election of 1960 to John F. Kennedy but beat Hubert Humphrey in 1968.

Nixon took office in 1969 at the height of domestic opposition to the Vietnam War and at the beginning stages of peace negotiations with North Vietnam. His Nixon Doctrine, which permitted military aid but no troops to countries in Asia opposing Communism, was a response to antiwar critics. Nixon's Vietnam War policies included gradual withdrawal of U.S. troops (from more than 550,000 in 1969 to fewer than 50,000 in 1972), increased bombing of North Vietnam, incursions into Communist sanctuaries in Cambodia and Laos, and accelerated "Vietnamization" of the war. Nixon and national security advisor Henry Kissinger defused international support of North Vietnam, particularly through U.S. recognition of China, and pursued peace negotiations, which led to a cease-fire in 1973. Nixon had been overwhelmingly reelected in

When Richard Nixon became president in 1969, he inherited a most unpopular war in Vietnam. His intensive bombing campaigns fueled the antiwar fervor at home but also helped to force Hanoi to the peace table. (Library of Congress)

1972, but the scandal of the Watergate Affair forced him to resign in 1974. He subsequently devoted his time to defending his tenure as president and writing.

Bibliography: Ambrose, Stephen B., *Nixon: The Triumph of a Politician: 1962–1972* (Simon & Schuster, 1989), Nixon, Richard M., *RN: The Memoirs of Richard Nixon* (Grosset, 1978).

Stephen Robinson

NORSTAD, LAURIS (1907–1988)

U.S. air force officer, Norstad was born in Minneapolis, Minnesota. He graduated from West Point in 1930 and entered the Air Corps the next year. After pilot training, he was assigned to the 18th Pursuit Group in Hawaii, of which he assumed command in 1933. He served in several other pursuit and bomb groups until the outbreak of World War II.

In February 1942, Norstad became a member of the advisory council to Gen. Henry "Hap" Arnold, along with future generals Laurence Kuter and C. P. Cabell. They mapped out plans for conducting an air offensive in Europe. In July 1942, Norstad was promoted to colonel and sent to the 12th Air Force in Algiers as assistant chief of staff for operations. He served in the North African and Mediterranean theaters of operations until August 1944, when he was named chief of staff for the 20th Air Force.

At the end of the war, Norstad was called to Washington and served in several key positions. In October 1950, he became commander in chief of the U.S. Air Force in Europe. In 1953, he was named air deputy to the Supreme Allied Commander, Europe, and head of the U.S. European Command. He held that position until his retirement on Jan. 2, 1963. Norstad later became chief executive officer of the Owens-Corning Fiberglass Company (1967–72).

Bibliography: DuPre, Flint O., *U.S. Air Force Biographical Dictionary* (Franklin Watts, 1965); *New York Times* (Sept. 14, 1988).

Roger D. Launius

O'DANIEL, JOHN WILSON (1894–1975)

U.S. army officer, known as "Iron Mike," O'Daniel was born in Newark, Delaware. He enlisted in the army in 1916 and was commissioned during World War I. During World War II, he commanded the 3d Infantry Division in Europe. In 1951, he went to Korea, where he led the I Corps until 1952, when he became a lieutenant general and commander of the U.S. Army, Pacific. In 1954, O'Daniel arrived in South Vietnam to head the Military Assistance Advisory Group (MAAG) there. The small advisory group worked to create a new South Vietnamese army with an eye on the experience of Korea. Therefore, MAAG fashioned a conventional army designed to repel a cross-border attack from the North. This new force was just emerging, however, when O'Daniel retired in 1955. After retirement, he became a founding member of the pro-South Vietnamese lobbying organization, the American Friends of Vietnam.

Bibliography: Spector, Ronald H., *Advice and Support: The Early Years, 1945–1960* (Center of Military History, U.S. Army, 1983).

Richard F. Kehrberg

O'DONNELL, EMMETT, JR. (1906–1971)

U.S. air force officer, O'Donnell was born in Brooklyn, New York. He graduated from West Point in 1928. After flight training, he was assigned to the First Pursuit Group in 1930. O'Donnell subsequently switched to bombers and was commanding a squadron of B-17s in the Philippines when war began. He later served in Java and India. From 1944, O'Donnell, then a brigadier general, commanded a wing of B-29s based in the Marianas. He then became deputy chief of the Air Matériel Command's engineering division, after which he was air force director of information. In 1948, he was named to command the 15th Air Force. He was promoted to the rank of lieutenant general in 1953. O'Donnell later served successively as commander, Far East Air Force Bomber Command (1950–51); deputy chief of staff for personnel (1953–59); and commander in chief, Pacific Air Forces (1959–63). He retired in 1963 as a full general and became president of the United Service Organizations.

Bibliography: *Current Biography* (1948).

Lloyd J. Graybar

OLDS, ROBIN (1922–)

U.S. air force officer, Olds was born in Honolulu, Hawaii. He joined the Army Air Force after graduating from West Point in 1943. After serving in Europe during World War II, he held a number of command and staff positions before taking over the 8th Tactical Fighter Wing in Thailand in 1966 during the Vietnam War. The following year, Olds helped plan Operation Bolo to protect a new wave of air force Rolling Thunder bombing attacks from North Vietnamese fighters. What appeared to be normal bombing runs drew the North Vietnamese pilots into the air, and then Olds's fighters pounced on them. In 12 minutes, the 8th Tactical Fighter Wing shot down seven MiG fighter planes, with Olds personally downing two of them. After flying more than 100 missions over North Vietnam, he returned to the United States in 1967 to become commandant of cadets at the Air Force Academy and then director of Aerospace Safety. Olds retired in 1973 as a brigadier general.

Richard F. Kehrberg

PACE, FRANK, JR. (1912–1988)

U.S. army secretary (1950–53), Pace was born in Little Rock, Arkansas. He held various government posts between 1946 and 1982. During the Korean War, as secretary of the army, he took action to expand it and rapidly reinforced the Far East. When United Nations forces first counterattacked the Chinese, he cautioned against crossing the 38th parallel, except to gain favorable defense terrain. Pres. Harry S Truman intended Pace to inform Gen. Douglas MacArthur of his relief from command, but the message did not reach the secretary in time.

After the war, Pace became chief executive officer of General Dynamics Corporation (1953–63). He founded and chaired the International Executive Service Corps (1964–1982) and the National Executive Service Corps (1977–88). He was also chairman of the Public Broadcasting Corporation (1968–72).

Bibliography: Schnabel, James F., *United States Army in the Korean War, Policy and Direction: The First Year* (U.S. Govt. Printing Office, 1972).

Brig. Gen. PNG (Ret.) Uzal W. Ent

PALMER, BRUCE, JR. (1913–)

U.S. army commander, Palmer was born in Austin, Texas. He graduated from West Point in 1936 and was commis-

sioned in the cavalry. In World War II, he was chief of staff of the 6th Infantry Division during fighting in the Southwest Pacific, where he won a Silver Star and other decorations.

As a brigadier general, Palmer was deputy commandant of the Army War College (1959–61) and then assistant division commander of the 82d Airborne Division (1961–62). Promoted again, he was chief of staff of the 8th Army in Korea (1962–63); then, as a lieutenant general, he became the army's deputy chief of staff for operations and plans (1963–65).

While on the Pentagon assignment, Palmer was given a demanding special mission: command of U.S. forces intervening in the Dominican Republic. In April 1965, he led a combined army and marine force directed to prevent a Communist takeover of that small Caribbean nation. Palmer was simultaneously given command of XVIII Airborne Corps. Remaining until September 1966, the U.S. forces made possible a peaceful resolution of the conflict.

Palmer left command of the corps in 1967 and went to South Vietnam. In a year there, he was commanding general of II Field Force and then deputy commanding general of U.S. Army, Vietnam. During 1968–72, he was back in Washington and was promoted to full general as the army's vice chief of staff, including a period of several months as acting chief of staff in 1972. During his final years of active service, Palmer was commander in chief, U.S. Readiness Command. In retirement, he was executive director of the Defense Manpower Commission (1946–76) and a member of the Senior Review Panel at the Central Intelligence Agency (1978–84).

Bibliography: Palmer, Bruce, Jr., *Intervention in the Caribbean: The Dominican Crisis of 1965* (Univ. Press of Kentucky, 1989); ———, *The 25-Year War: America's Military Role in Vietnam* (Univ. Press of Kentucky, 1984).

Lewis Sorley

PARTRIDGE, EARLE EVERARD (1900–1990)

U.S. air force commander, Partridge was born in Winchendon, Massachusetts. He graduated from West Point in 1924 and quickly distinguished himself in the Air Service. In 1940 and 1941, he helped establish flying schools in the southeastern United States. In June 1944, he succeeded Curtis LeMay as commander of the 3d Bombardment Division.

Perhaps his greatest contributions to air power occurred while he was the senior air officer in Korea (1950–51), where he pioneered combat tactics and doctrine for jet aircraft, a method for rapidly moving fighter units, and efficient jet maintenance. General Partridge's career also included a tour as air force deputy chief of staff (1953–55) before becoming commander in chief of the North

American Air Defense Command (NORAD) in 1955. He retired as a general in 1959.

Bibliography: *Generals of the Army and the Air Force* (Dunleavy, 1954).

Capt. Philip A. Bossert, Jr.

PATE, RANDOLPH McCALL (1898–1960)

U.S. marine officer, Pate was born in Port Royal, South Carolina. After a year of enlisted service in the army in 1918, he entered the Virginia Military Institute, graduating in 1921. During World War II, he was at Guadalcanal and Iwo Jima. After the war, he was named director of the Division of Reserve, Marine Corps Headquarters (1946); to the Navy Department General Board (1947); chief of staff of Marine Corps Schools (1948); and director of the Marine Corps Educational Center (1950).

Pate commanded the 1st Marine Division in Korea (June 1953–May 1954) and in July 1955 was appointed assistant commandant and chief of staff of the Marine Corps. He was promoted to lieutenant general in 1956 and served as commandant of the corps until 1960.

Bibliography: Millett, Allan R., *Semper Fidelis: The History of the United States Marine Corps* (Macmillan, 1991).

David Friend

PATTERSON, ROBERT PORTER (1891–1952)

U.S. secretary of war, Patterson was born in Glen Falls, New York. He interrupted a law practice to serve in the infantry during World War I. After a decade as a federal judge, he accepted appointment as assistant secretary of war and then undersecretary in 1940. Much of Patterson's work had to do with speeding economic mobilization. In addition, he represented the War Department on other agencies such as the War Production Board and the Committee for Congested Production Areas. In September 1945, Patterson replaced Henry Stimson as secretary of war. As such, he focused on the problems of postwar demobilization and retrenchment. During his tenure, he also supported the establishment of a North Atlantic alliance and unification of the armed services. Patterson returned to the practice of law in 1947.

Lloyd J. Graybar

PEERS, WILLIAM RAYMOND (1914–1984)

U.S. army commander, Peers was born in Stuart, Iowa. He attended the University of California at Los Angeles (1933–37) and was commissioned through the Reserve Officers Training Corps. During World War II, Peers advanced rapidly to full colonel and command of the Office of Strategic Services Detachment 101, a guerrilla unit operating on the India-Burma border. By the time of the

Vietnam War, Peers was a major general who, in 1967, took command of the 4th Infantry Division in the Vietnam highlands. Subsequently promoted to lieutenant general, he commanded I Field Force Vietnam, and then was posted to the Pentagon. There he took on the difficult and thankless task of heading an inquiry into the 1968 massacre committed by American soldiers at the South Vietnamese village of My Lai. Peers conducted a thorough and honest investigation (1969–70), establishing beyond question the facts of the incident and those responsible for committing it and for attempting to cover it up. Then, following a stint as deputy commanding general of the 8th Army in Korea (1971–73), he retired.

Bibliography: Department of the Army, *Report of the Department of the Army Review of the Preliminary Investigations into the My Lai Incident* (Free Press, 1978); Peers, William R., and Dean Brelis, *Behind the Burma Road: The Story of America's Most Successful Guerrilla Force* (Little, Brown, 1963); Peers, William R., *The My Lai Inquiry* (Norton, 1979).

Lewis Sorley

POWELL, COLIN LUTHER (1937–)

Chairman of the Joint Chiefs of Staff (1989–93), Powell was born in New York City, the son of Jamaican immigrants. He attended City College of New York, where he enrolled in the Reserve Officers Training Corps program and graduated in 1958 as cadet colonel, the highest rank available to students. After graduation, Powell was commissioned a second lieutenant in the army and four years later was sent to Vietnam.

During his first tour of duty (December 1962–November 1963), Powell sustained a serious foot injury but returned to the field, where he won a Bronze Star.

Returning to the United States, Powell entered the Army Command and General Staff College at Fort Leavenworth, Kansas, graduating second in a class of 1,244. He then served a second tour in Vietnam (June 1968–July 1969), mostly as a battalion executive officer and division operations officer. After being injured in a helicopter crash-landing, Powell pulled others from the burning wreckage, an action for which he received the Soldiers Medal.

After earning a master's degree in business administration from George Washington University in 1971, Powell won a coveted White House Fellowship over 1,500 other applicants. For the next year, he worked as assistant to the deputy director of the Office of Management and Budget (OMB), Frank C. Carlucci. Both Carlucci and OMB director Caspar W. Weinberger were impressed with Powell's work.

Following a stint as battalion commander in Korea and as commander of the 2d Brigade, 101st Airborne Division, at Fort Campbell, Kentucky, Powell held a series of posts both in Washington and as a commander. By July 1983,

Gen. Colin Powell, chairman of the Joint Chiefs of Staff (1989–93), oversaw U.S. military activity in Operation Desert Storm, which drove Iraqi forces from Kuwait. (U.S. Army)

he had risen to major general and was named military assistant to Weinberger, then the secretary of defense. Over the next three years, Powell developed a reputation in political circles as a man who could work smoothly with diverse groups and get them to work together. He even emerged with his reputation untarnished during the Iran-Contra arms deal, where U.S. missiles were to be sent to Iran in exchange for a hostage release. Powell opposed the exchange but checked his dissent when it became an order from the president. He then wrote a memo to National Security Council (NSC) chairman Rear Adm. John M. Poindexter reminding him of the legal necessity to inform Congress about the deal, advice that Poindexter ignored. Powell, however, won praise for his honesty.

In June 1986, Powell became commander of the V Corps in Frankfurt, Germany, but the post was to be short-lived. Within six months, Carlucci, who had succeeded Poindexter as national security adviser, asked Powell to be his deputy. Initially reluctant, Powell accepted the position in January 1987. With orders to "clean up" the national security staff, Powell quickly established clear lines of authority for members of the staff and ensured that everyone had a chance to be heard in determining policy. These moves helped restore the staff's credibility and morale.

Powell's diplomacy was also evident during the 1987 meetings between U.S. and Soviet negotiators who successfully crafted an intermediate-range nuclear forces arms control treaty. Powell impressed everyone with his self-control during these crucial days, and Carlucci stated that Powell's arguments were "always so reasoned that by and large he carries the day." On Nov. 5, 1987, Reagan named Powell to succeed Carlucci as chairman of the NSC, a position he held until January 1989.

Powell, now a four-star general, in 1989 took the reins of the army's largest single command: Forces Command, based at Fort McPherson in Atlanta and charged with defense of the continental United States and Alaska. Later that same year, however, Pres. George Bush named him as chairman of the Joint Chiefs of Staff, a post he assumed in October. Powell, the youngest officer and the first black to hold the position, ably combined his military skills with his knowledge of foreign affairs and diplomatic talents honed by his years in Washington. He needed all the ability he could muster, for he quickly was embroiled in military actions. An abortive coup against Panamanian leader Gen. Manuel Noriega occurred on Powell's first night as chairman. And within the next two months, U.S. pilots had to be dispatched to the Philippines to help put down a rebellion, troops had to be sent into San Salvador to rescue Green Berets trapped in a hotel, and a large U.S. military force invaded Panama.

These events would precede a much greater task: overseeing U.S. troops sent to Saudi Arabia to check Iraqi president Saddam Hussein in 1990–91 (Operation Desert Storm). Powell believed in first establishing clear goals and instructions for the military before placing them in the field, then following that with whatever force is needed to achieve those goals as quickly as possible. Thus, he pushed for a large consignment of men, women, and supplies for the Persian Gulf region, action that paid dividends when allied forces routed the Iraqi army. His appointment as chairman was extended for a second term in 1991, and at the end of 1992 he oversaw the U.S. relief mission to Somalia. He retired in 1993.

Bibliography: Booker, Simeon, "Black General at the Summit of U.S. Power," *Ebony* Magazine (July 1988); Means, Howard, *Colin Powell* (Fine, 1992); Rowan, Carl T., "Called to Service: The Colin Powell Story," *Reader's Digest* (Dec. 1989).

John F. Wukovits

PULLER, LEWIS BURWELL (1898–1971)

U.S. marine officer, "Chesty" Puller was born in West Point, Virginia. He attended Virginia Military Institute in Richmond for the 1917–18 academic year and then enlisted in the Marine Corps in 1918. After graduation from the Marine Corps officers selection course at Quantico,

Virginia, he was commissioned a second lieutenant in the Marine Corps Reserve in 1919.

Early Assignments. Puller served (1920–24) in the Haitian Garde, a U.S.-trained and -staffed native constabulary that had been established in revolution-torn Haiti. When he returned to the United States in 1924, he reenlisted in the Marine Corps as a sergeant and was soon promoted to the rank of second lieutenant; after a brief time at U.S. bases, he was posted to the marine barracks at Pearl Harbor, Hawaii. From there, Puller became part of an expeditionary brigade to Nicaragua, where U.S. interests were being threatened by violence. The marines were ordered to establish the Nicaraguan Garde, a native constabulary. Puller served as a captain in the Garde until 1933, except for a brief respite in 1931 to study at the Infantry School at Fort Benning, Georgia. It was in Nicaragua that he earned the first two of five Navy Crosses and where he gained the respect of his men for leading them into battle.

In 1933, Puller was assigned to Peking, China, where he commanded the "Horse Marines." Then, as a major, he led a marine detachment on duty aboard the *Augusta,* part of the Asiatic Fleet, until 1936. After teaching basic training for new marine second lieutenants at the Philadelphia navy yard (1936–39), he was assigned to Shanghai, where he gained fame when he drove Japanese troops from the American quarter.

World War II. In 1941, as commanding officer of the 1st Battalion, 7th Marines, he sailed with them in 1942 to the Pacific. Now a lieutenant colonel, he distinguished himself at the Battle of Gaudalcanal (third Navy Cross) by standing off a Japanese division with half of a battalion, on New Britain Island (fourth Navy Cross) by leading two stalled battalions under fire to victory, and at the Battle of Peleliu, one of the bloodiest marine battles of World War II. He returned to the United States in November 1944 to become the executive officer of the Infantry Training Regiment at Camp Lejeune, North Carolina. After World War II, Colonel Puller became director of the 8th Marine Corps Reserve District at New Orleans, Louisiana, in 1946. Despite his annoyance at not being given a regimental command, he did an outstanding job and was responsible for doubling the number of men in the reserve and for building it into a viable fighting unit. In 1948, he was reassigned to command the marine barracks at Pearl Harbor.

Korean War. In 1950, after the Korean War began, Puller was assigned to take command of the 1st Marine Regiment, the same unit that he had led in the Pacific during World War II. Puller went into action in Korea with his 1st Marines during the Inchon landing and led them on the advance to retake Seoul, the South Korean capital. As the marines neared Seoul, North Korean resistance became more intense, forcing Puller's men to begin a savage house-to-house firefight with the enemy. All the while, Puller stayed at the front, encouraging his men forward. Even though it was a very intense, demanding, and costly operation, the drive toward and the capture of Seoul helped to speed the advance toward the 38th parallel, the dividing line between South and North Korea.

As the 1st Marine Division pressed its attack against the remnants of the enemy, Puller's men fought a series of battalion-level actions against both the North Koreans and the Communist Chinese. Forced to deploy along the western side of the Chosin Reservoir, the 1st Regiment was left exposed at Koto-ri. With some support from Britain's Royal Marines, Puller's force absorbed the brunt of the Chinese attack, but managed to blunt the offensive, enabling the 5th and 7th marines to break out of the trap and fight their way toward Hungnam. Puller's forces were the last to leave Koto-ri. Acting as the rear guard for the 5th and 7th marines, they marched out on foot, Puller leading the way. For his heroic action during the bitter fighting to break out of the Chinese trap at Chosin Reservoir, Puller received his fifth Navy Cross.

While in Korea, Puller was promoted to brigadier general and was named assistant commander of the 1st Marine Division. In May 1951, he returned to the United States; in January 1952, he assumed command of the 3d Marine Division at Camp Pendleton, California. In June of that year, his assignment was to take charge of troop training at Coronado, California. Puller was promoted to the rank of lieutenant general in September 1953, and assumed command of the 2d Marine Division at Camp Lejeune in July 1954. He suffered a mild stroke in January 1955, was briefly appointed deputy commander at Lejeune, and then was retired in August of that year.

Legacy. Chesty Puller was the most highly decorated marine in history. An outstanding combat officer, he was eminently regarded as a leader, and he did much to bring marine training up to maximum efficiency. His emphasis on leadership qualities in both his commissioned and noncommissioned officers was demonstrated in their effectiveness on and off the battlefield. He believed strongly that the only objective of military training is success in battle and that the most important element in military training is discipline.

Bibliography: Davis, Burke, *Marine! The Life of Lt. Gen. Lewis B. Puller* (Little, Brown, 1962); Debs, Robert, Jr., *Victory at High Tide* (1968; reprint Nautical and Aviation, 1979).

Leo J. Daugherty III

RADFORD, ARTHUR WILLIAM
(1896–1973)

U.S. naval officer, Radford was born in Chicago. After graduating from Annapolis in 1916, he spent two years at sea aboard the battleship *South Carolina.* Following staff assignments with surface forces, he was accepted for flight training and qualified for carrier landings on the *Langley* in 1923. He then served in the aviation complement of the battleship *Colorado,* at the Naval Air Station in San Diego, and with an aerial survey party in Alaska before joining the *Saratoga* as flight deck officer in 1929.

Over the next decade, Radford, who received promotions to commander in 1936 and to captain in 1941, had a variety of duties in naval aviation: flag secretary to commander, Aircraft, Battle Force; personnel officer in the Bureau of Aeronautics; navigator of the seaplane tender *Wright;* tactical officer on the staff of commander, Aircraft, Battle Force; and executive officer of the *Yorktown.* Radford then commanded the Naval Operating Base, Trinidad.

World War II. Just before the outbreak of war in 1941, Radford was named head of the Aviation Training Division of the Bureau of Aeronautics. Radford's goal was to expand the number of young men entering flight training without compromising the quality of aviation personnel. To accomplish this, he took the initiative in forging an agreement between the navy and the army air corps to drop the educational requirement for acceptance into pilot training from two years of college to a high school diploma. To compensate, Radford succeeded in establishing at several universities preflight schools that provided a demanding 12-week curriculum. He also sought to expand the navy's aviation program by requesting the enlistment of women as naval reservists to handle such duties as operating flight simulators.

Although he had never commanded a ship, one of only a handful of flag officers in the 20th century to bypass this rite of passage, Radford was promoted to rear admiral in 1943 and ordered to the Pacific to command a carrier division, which he led in a raid on Tarawa. Next he commanded Task Group 50.2 in Operation Galvanic, the seizure of the Gilbert Islands. While in this post, he set up one of the earliest night-fighting units to operate in the Pacific. Radford then served as chief of staff to commander, Air Force, Pacific Fleet, after which he reported to Washington as assistant deputy chief of naval operations (air). In 1945, he returned to sea to command various carrier task groups in operations in the western Pacific.

Unification Controversies. Recalled to Washington shortly after the end of the war, Radford was one of three flag officers assigned to revise the navy's Basic Post War Plan Number 1, a document prescribing what forces to retain in the much-reduced peacetime navy. Radford was then directed by Sec. of the Navy James Forrestal to organize a committee to study the problems involved in the anticipated unification of the armed services. The group was named SCOROR (Secretary's Committee of Research on Reorganization). While Radford preferred to see the air force remain part of the army rather than be established as

an independent and co-equal branch of the armed services, as was likely to happen, he was undoubtedly more interested in retaining for the navy its own air organization that included both carrier air groups and land-based aviation that facilitated such navy operations as reconnaissance and antisubmarine patrol. Senior air force officers held much different views on these matters and believed that the navy should be divested of its land-based air units and perhaps of its carriers, which in their view no longer had a useful function to perform. While occupied with SCOROR, Radford also served as deputy chief of naval operations (air).

In 1947, Radford was named to command the 2d Fleet in the Atlantic. This assignment was followed by a tour as vice chief of naval operations and then in April 1949 an appointment as commander in chief, Pacific (CinCPac).

For much of the summer and fall of 1949, however, Radford's attention was divided between the Pacific and Washington, where unification and related budgetary disputes led to the "Revolt of the Admirals." His unparalleled knowledge of naval aviation and prior work with SCOROR made him the navy's de facto leader in many issues related to unification. Although the Department of Defense had been established in 1947, conflict still ensued among the three services, primarily between the navy and the air force, over budgetary and other matters. The navy especially believed that to modernize its aviation establishment, crucial to the navy's mission, it needed a large flush-decked carrier of some 60,000 tons displacement designed specifically to operate larger, longer-range planes than had previously operated from aircraft carriers in squadron strength. These planes would be capable of delivering nuclear weapons to targets inside the Soviet Union.

No carrier designed during World War II, even the Midway class, was as suitable for such operations as the new super-carrier would be. Such a ship, the *United States,* was authorized while Forrestal was serving as secretary of defense, but to the dismay of navy officers, his successor, Louis Johnson, ordered construction stopped in April 1949. At the same time, however, the air force was seeking to acquire more B-36 bombers, claimed by air force officers to be far superior to the B-29 (which had delivered the atom bombs dropped on Hiroshima and Nagasaki) and invulnerable to interception by enemy fighters.

Hearings over these and related issues were held before the House Armed Services Committee in the summer and fall of 1949. Radford was recalled to Washington as a technical consultant and while there also coached many of the navy's other witnesses in their presentations. In his own testimony in October, he argued that the B-36 was not the invulnerable plane its partisans declared, that its performance fell short of claims, and that to rely on this one weapon would risk the nation's security. The theory that victory in the next war could be gained quickly and cheaply by relying on a nuclear onslaught was fallacious. Carrier aviation was essential in the balanced military force that the nation needed to maintain, he asserted.

Korea and Vietnam. During much of the four years Radford was CinCPac, the Korean War was in progress. As CinCPac, Radford had no direct responsibility for the prosecution of the Korean War, for the naval forces committed there fell under the purview of commander in chief, Far East (CinCFE). Yet, Radford was kept familiar with the situation in Korea and made several visits during the war. Many facilities in Radford's far-flung command were used to support the war logistically. In other ways, Radford was much involved with Far Eastern affairs. In 1951, for instance, defense of the Ryukyus, Taiwan, and the Philippines was transferred to his jurisdiction from that of CinCFE. Thus directly concerned with the defense of the Far East and Southeast Asia, Radford pushed for and got the development of large naval facilities, including a naval air station, at Subic Bay in the Philippines.

In August 1953, he was confirmed as chairman of the Joint Chiefs of Staff to serve under Pres. Dwight D. Eisenhower. By this time, the defense budget had grown considerably since the B-36 hearings four years before, but with the Korean War over, some retrenchment was inevitable. The cuts were disguised under the name "New Look," a term attributed to Radford. Once more, the concept of balanced forces was deemphasized in favor of the ostensible simplicity and supposed economies of nuclear weaponry. Great reliance upon nuclear weapons also had a certain political appeal at this time, given the nation's frustrations with limited warfare in Korea. Radford, who had opposed just such thinking four years before, had modified his views and believed in the New Look. Complaints from the armed forces about budget cutbacks were again forthcoming. This time, the army appeared most resentful, and Radford, who as chairman of the Joint Chiefs did not wish to be perceived as a partisan of the navy's interests, enjoyed a cordial relationship with President Eisenhower and ready access to him.

During his tenure, Radford was greatly concerned about the situation in Indochina, where he regarded French military efforts against the Vietminh as doctrinally flawed. A believer in the domino theory, Radford made clear in his memoirs that he thought the Truman administration had not done enough to oppose Communism in China or in Korea and that he would have liked to see the West take a stronger stand against Communism in Indochina; if the French could not do it, then the United States and associated nations should. If allies could not be found to join the United States in intervening in the Vietnamese conflict of the early 1950s, as Eisenhower wished, Radford was willing to see the United States act unilaterally. Although, U.S. policy in Indochina was not all he wanted, Radford presented his views within channels and remained an in-

fluential and respected voice within the Eisenhower administration. He retired in 1957.

Summary. Radford had spent almost his entire career closely associated with naval aviation. He was too junior in rank to make a great name for himself at sea during World War II, but he nevertheless left his imprint on the war effort both in the enormous expansion of naval aviation training he helped bring about and in his innovative leadership at sea. A forceful personality and a master of bureaucratic politics, Radford was thereafter at or near the center of many of the policy decisions that shaped U.S. military history in the period after World War II: in the unification disputes, in the B-36 hearings, and in the development of U.S. military capability and policy during the Korean War and when conflict in Vietnam was becoming of much concern to U.S. policymakers.

Bibliography: Davis, Vincent, *The Admirals Lobby* (Univ. of North Carolina Press, 1952); Jurika, Stephen, ed., *From Pearl Harbor to Vietnam: The Memoirs of Admiral Arthur W. Radford* (Hoover Inst. Press, 1980); Palmer, Michael A., *Origins of the Maritime Strategy: American Naval Strategy in the First Postwar Decade* (Naval Hist. Center, 1988); Potter, E. B., *Admiral Arleigh Burke: A Biography* (Random House, 1990).

Lloyd J. Graybar

RAYE, MARTHA (1916–)

U.S. entertainer, Raye was born Margaret Reed in Butte, Montana, and joined her family's vaudeville act when she was three. She studied nursing during the Depression but by 1936 was winning recognition in films and radio as a comedienne and singer. During World War II, she worked as a nurse and did several USO (United Service Organizations) tours, playing herself in the film *Four Jills in a Jeep,* based on a North African tour Raye and three other actresses had made. She also did USO shows during the Korean War and during the Vietnam War put on hundreds of shows in remote areas of South Vietnam, where the troops affectionately referred to her as "Boondock Maggie." When casualties were being treated, she also pitched in to work as a nurse. She won numerous awards for her efforts in morale building and was commissioned a lieutenant colonel in the Army Nurses Corps Reserve.

Bibliography: Parish, James Robert, *The Slapstick Queens* (A. S. Barnes, 1973).

Lloyd J. Graybar

REAGAN, RONALD WILSON (1911–)

Fortieth president of the United States (1981–89), Reagan was born in Tampico, Illinois. He worked briefly as a radio broadcaster, then went to California where he quickly established himself as an actor in motion pictures. During the 1930s and 1940s, he was a staunch Democrat who four times voted for Franklin D. Roosevelt. He eventually

Republican Ronald Reagan, the 40th U.S. president (1981–89), promoted the largest military buildup in U.S. history. (The White House)

changed his political views, left the Democratic party, and became a conservative Republican. As such, Reagan was elected governor of California (1967–75) and ultimately U.S. president. Initially, he supported the largest military buildup in U.S. history while denouncing the Soviet Union as the "evil empire." From 1985, relations with the Soviet Union warmed as Reagan and Soviet leader Mikhail Gorbachev met to improve international relations. A treaty eliminating intermediate-range missiles was signed in 1987. Reagan's administration intervened briefly in the Lebanese civil war (1982), invaded the island nation of Granada (1983), bombed Libya, and sponsored the rightist Nicaraguan Contras; the Iran-Contra scandal erupted in 1986 when it was discovered that, against the resolutions of Congress, members of the administration secretly had sold arms to Iran and had used the profits to aid the Nicaraguan guerrillas. Reagan left office as the most popular president since Dwight D. Eisenhower.

M. Guy Bishop

RESOR, STANLEY ROGERS (1917–   )

U.S. secretary of the army, Resor was born in New York City. He served in Europe with the 10th Armored Division during World War II. An attorney in New York City, he was named Pres. Lyndon B. Johnson's undersecretary of the army in February 1965 and secretary in June. During his tenure, Resor had major responsibility for the buildup in troop strength for the Vietnam War. Resor backed Sec. of Defense Robert McNamara's efforts to create a well-trained reserve force drawn from both National Guard and army reserve units while disbanding many low-priority reserve units. A Republican, he continued in office under the Richard M. Nixon administration. Resor resigned in 1971 but returned to government service in 1973 to represent the United States in Vienna in negotiations on Mutual and Balanced Force Reductions in Central Europe. From 1978 to 1980, he served as undersecretary of defense for policy.

Lloyd J. Graybar

RHEE, SYNGMAN (1875–1965)

First president of the Republic of Korea (1948–60), Rhee was born in Hwanghae Province (now the North Korean provinces of Hwanghae-namdo and Hwanghae-pukto). He was sentenced to life imprisonment in 1897 for involvement in independence movements but regained his freedom in 1904 as the result of general amnesty for political prisoners. He then traveled to the United States, graduating from Princeton University with a doctorate in theology in 1910, the first Korean to earn a doctorate from an American university. He returned to Korea and, in protest to Japan's seizure of control there, resumed his revolutionary activities. In exile in Hawaii, he became the first president of the Provisional Korean Republic (1919–41). After the Allied defeat of Japan in 1945, he returned to Korea a national hero. In 1948, the strongly anticommunist Rhee was elected president of the newly formed Republic of Korea (South Korea). During the Korean War, he welcomed United Nations aid to oppose North Korea's invasion in 1950 and later opposed the truce talks and agreement to end hostilities because he still wanted to unite the two countries. A student revolt in 1960 forced the increasingly distrusted and autocratic Rhee to resign and flee to Hawaii, where he remained until his death.

Bibliography: Allen, Richard C., *Korea's Syngman Rhee: An Unauthorized Portrait* (Tuttle, 1960); Oliver, Robert T., *Syngman Rhee and American Involvement in Korea, 1942–1960: A Personal Narrative* (Panmun Book Co., 1978; ———, *Syngman Rhee: the Man Behind the Myth* (Dodd, Mead, 1954).

Maj. James Sanders Day

RICHARDSON, ELLIOT LEE (1920–   )

U.S. statesman, Richardson was born in Boston, Massachusetts. He graduated from Harvard Law School in 1947. Pres. Richard M. Nixon appointed him undersecretary of state (1969–70), secretary of health and welfare (1970–73), and secretary of defense (1973). As defense secretary,

Richardson was expected to slash the Pentagon bureaucracy and play a secondary role to Henry Kissinger as foreign policy adviser. After 91 days in office, Richardson was appointed attorney general during the preliminaries of the Watergate scandal, which forced his resignation. In 1974, he was appointed ambassador to Great Britain and later joined Pres. Gerald R. Ford's cabinet as secretary of commerce (1975–77).

Russell A. Hart

RICKOVER, HYMAN GEORGE
(1900–1986)
U.S. naval engineer and administrator, Rickover was born in the Russian part of what is now Poland. His family, along with thousands of other Jews, immigrated to the United States and eventually, in 1910, settled in Chicago. Rickover graduated from Annapolis in 1922.

Early Career. After accepting his commission, Rickover was assigned to the Destroyer *La Vallette*. Within a short time, he transferred to the battleship *Nevada,* where he continued to study engineering and mathematics, subjects for which he earned honors. In the late 1920s, he received a master's degree in electrical engineering from Columbia University and then went to submarine school, where he became a convert to the merits of the "silent service."

In 1937, he was reassigned as commander of the *Finch,* an old minesweeper used to tow gunnery targets. He was so dissatisfied with this assignment that he requested shore duty as an electrical engineer. This proved to be a significant move for Rickover, as throughout World War II he headed the Electrical Section of the Bureau of Ships, directing improvements in the design and implementation of electrical systems. His work led directly to assignment in 1946 as head of a team to explore the use of nuclear energy for use on ships. This effort set the stage for the rest of Rickover's career.

Nuclear Navy. Beginning in 1947, Rickover started a crusade to build ships with nuclear reactors for propulsion. From a position as director of the Nuclear Power Branch of the Bureau of Ships, he was persistent. In August 1950, he persuaded Pres. Harry S Truman to approve the construction of the first nuclear-powered submarine, the *Nautilus,* launched in 1954.

Rickover continued to expand his nuclear base of power within the navy. Land-based nuclear power stations that he championed as well as nuclear vessels appeared. He was also instrumental in expanding the curriculum at the Naval Academy and at other service schools to emphasize the skills necessary to serve in the nuclear navy. As time progressed, Rickover, who had never served in combat or commanded anything more important than a target towing barge, assumed more power within the navy, to the extent that he personally chose commanders of nuclear vessels.

When Rickover reached mandatory retirement age in the early 1960s, the navy retained him for another 20 years as the director of the Division of Nuclear Reactors. In 1982, Sec. of the Navy John Lehman finally forced Rickover into retirement.

Bibliography: David, Heather M., *Admiral Rickover and the Nuclear Navy* (Putnam's, 1970); Lewis, Eugene, "Hyman G. Rickover," *Leadership and Innovation: A Biographical Perspective on Entrepreneurs in Government,* ed. by Jameson W. Doig and Erwin C. Hargrove (Johns Hopkins Univ. Press, 1987); Rickover, Hyman G., *Education and Freedom* (Dutton, 1959).

Roger D. Launius

RIDGWAY, MATTHEW BUNKER
(1895–1993)
U.S. army commander, Ridgway was born in Fort Monroe, Virginia. He graduated in 1917 from West Point, where he served on the faculty for six years following World War I. During World War II, he commanded an infantry division that, under his direction, became one of the army's first airborne units. World War II's end found Ridgway in the Philippines. As commander of the Luzon Area Command, he coordinated all airborne operations and was preparing the XVIII Airborne Corps for the invasion of Japan.

The postwar world would provide even greater opportunities for him, however. Ridway served briefly as commander of the Mediterranean theater of operations and as deputy supreme allied commander, Mediterranean. In January 1946, he became the senior U.S. Army member of the United Nations (UN) Military Staff Committee. Appointed by Gen. Dwight D. Eisenhower, Ridgway also served as chairman of the Inter-American Defense Board. In this dual capacity, he developed the concept of an international police force, an armed force controlled by the UN Security Council. In addition, he standardized the organization, training, and equipment for the Western allies. In 1948, Ridgway took command of the Caribbean Defense Command and the Panama Canal Department. He directed this joint field command until his appointment as deputy chief of staff for administration and training in August 1949. While in this position, he championed the development of the 3.5-inch bazooka, airdrop capability for heavier weapons and vehicles, and the 105-millimeter recoilless cannon.

Korean War. Upon Lt. Gen. Walton Walker's death on Dec. 23, 1950, Ridgway transferred to Korea, where he assumed command of the U.S. 8th Army. Faced with the onslaught of Chinese Communist forces, Ridgway sought to remedy the proliferation of "bugout fever," the tendency for precipitous retreat among front-line U.S. units. With only three of seven divisions intact, he countermanded Walker's original directive to hold at all costs.

Rather, he ordered a delaying action. Seeking to inflict maximum damage on the enemy, Ridgway inspired his charges with the motto, "Find them! Fix them! Fight them! Finish them!" He replaced tired commanders and moved the 8th Army command post forward.

Ridgway increased infantry patrolling and enhanced the use of high ground. Emphasizing good fighting positions, he heightened security and flank protection. He stressed cover and concealment and conducted more nighttime operations. To improve morale, he increased the supply of hot rations, mail, and gloves. Daring to counterattack in January 1951, Ridgway began to reverse the momentum of the war. Personally ordering the defense of Chip'yongni in February, he drove the 8th Army northward, forcing the Chinese forces to withdraw. After recapturing the city of Seoul in March, Ridgway advanced to the 38th parallel, tailoring unit dispositions to defensible terrain. Ridgway, through inspired leadership, transformed the 8th Army in two months and created a formidable fighting force. Author S. L. A. Marshall argues that this transition represents "the most dramatic American command achievement of this century."

When Pres. Harry S Truman relieved Gen. Douglas MacArthur of all command authority on Apr. 11, 1951, Ridgway assumed responsibilities as commander, UN Command; commander in chief, Far East Command; and Supreme Commander for Allied Powers. In this multiple capacity, he directed UN military operations and supervised the negotiations effort.

Post-Korean War. When General Eisenhower resigned to run for president in 1952, Ridgway received the appointment as Supreme Allied Commander, Europe. During his one-year tenure, he increased the NATO (North Atlantic Treaty Organization) defense force from 12 to nearly 80 active and reserve divisions along a 4,000-mile front. Furthermore, he advocated the defense of all of Europe, not just readily defensible areas.

Leaving Europe in August 1953, Ridgway became chief of staff of the army. During his tour in Washington, he defended the army against numerous attacks. He opposed President Eisenhower's "New Look," arguing against the "more bang for a buck" approach. He also fought budget cuts and personnel reductions, arguing that total reliance on nuclear weapons spelled disaster. Promoting a multidimensional force capable of fighting a nuclear war as well as limited, guerrilla wars, Ridgway set the stage for John F. Kennedy's "flexible response" strategy. In addition to his opposition to "massive retaliation," Ridgway defended Sec. of the Army Robert Stevens and the entire officer corps against Sen. Joseph McCarthy's accusations of support for Communism.

Ridgway considered his most important contribution as chief of staff to be his advice concerning U.S. involvement in French Indochina in 1954. The Ridgway Report enumerated myriad difficulties inherent in waging war in mainland Asia. He argued that the jungle environment would negate the advantages of mobile, mechanized warfare. Moreover, ground forces required roads, harbors, docks, communication facilities, staging areas, and warehouses. After his retirement in 1955, Ridgway, in conjunction with the army's Gen. James M. Gavin and U.S. Marine Corps commandant David M. Shoup, continued to advocate moderation in Southeast Asia. As a member of Pres. Lyndon B. Johnson's senior advisory group—the "Wise Men"—Ridgway supported a negotiated settlement based on the improbability of victory.

In addition to his military accomplishments, Ridgway served as director of Colt Industries and as chairman of the board of trustees of the Mellon Institute of Industrial Research. His general observations based on military and civilian service include the following: (1) the United States must recognize the limitations of its national power; (2) war must be waged judiciously, and the cause must be right; (3) "total war" is an antiquated concept; (4) the use of nuclear weapons is immoral due to its international impact; (5) correctly forecasting and planning for the next war is paramount; (6) vital national interests should drive policy, and military objectives should be subordinate to both; (7) civilian control of the military is "fundamental and unchallengeable;" (8) civil-military relations must depend on mutual trust and forthright discussion; and (9) policy must adhere to morality.

Bibliography: Alberts, Robert C., "Profile of a Soldier: Matthew B. Ridgway," *American Heritage* (Feb. 1976); Appleman, Roy E., *Ridgway Duels for Korea* (Texas A&M Univ. Press, 1990); Ridgway, Matthew B., *The Korean War: How We Met the Challenge* (Doubleday, 1967); ———, *Soldier: The Memoirs of Matthew B. Ridgway* (Harper, 1956).

Maj. James Sanders Day

RIVERS, L(UCIUS) MENDEL (1905–1970)

U.S. congressman, Rivers was born in Gumville, South Carolina. In 1940, he began a 30-year career representing South Carolina in the U.S. House of Representatives. Congressman Rivers was a strong Democratic supporter of the U.S. armed forces. During both the Korean and Vietnam conflicts, he called for an all-out war effort to achieve complete and rapid victory. Rivers became chairman of the House Armed Services Committee in 1965 and used the position to manage the military as much as possible. His influence on military affairs was reflected by the Pentagon's decisions to locate numerous military installations in his district. Rivers wanted the best of everything, from weapons to pay, for U.S. uniformed personnel, and his efforts often put him in conflict with Sec. of Defense Robert McNamara.

Steve R. Waddell

ROGERS, BERNARD WILLIAM (1921–)

U.S. army officer, Rogers was born in Fairview, Kansas. He graduated from West Point in 1943 and, after a tour of duty as a platoon leader, taught economics and served as aide to Gen. Maxwell Taylor at West Point (1944–46). Promoted to captain in 1946, Rogers served on the staff of Gen. Mark Clark in Austria (1946–47). After studying in England on a Rhodes scholarship (1947–50), he was promoted to major (1951), served in Korea (1952), and was executive officer to the commander in chief of the Far East Command (1953–54). A lieutenant colonel by 1953, he attended the Command and General Staff College (1954–55).

After a variety of assignments, including staff officer and executive officer to the army chief of staff (1956–59), battalion commander in Germany (1960–61), executive officer to the chairman of the Joint Chiefs of Staff (1962–66), and assistant commander of the 1st Infantry Division (1966–67) in Vietnam, Rogers became commandant of cadets at West Point (1967–70). Promoted to brigadier general in 1967, he attained the rank of major general in 1970. After holding several executive positions in the Department of the Army, he became a full general (1974) and commanding general of Army Forces Command at Fort McPherson, Georgia (1974–76). Rogers was army chief of staff (1976–79) before he was appointed Supreme Allied Commander, Europe (SACEur) of NATO (North Atlantic Treaty Organization), a position he held from 1979 until 1987, when he retired.

Leo J. Daugherty III

ROSSON, WILLIAM BRADFORD (1918–)

U.S. army officer, Rosson was born in Des Moines, Iowa. He graduated from the University of Oregon and was commissioned a second lieutenant of the infantry in June 1940. He fought in 10 campaigns with the 3d Infantry Division in North Africa, Sicily, Italy, France, and Germany. He then commanded the 30th Infantry Regiment during the German occupation. He had normal command and staff assignments that included early involvement in Southeast Asia with the U.S. Military Advisory Group during the French-Viet Minh struggle in the 1950s. Rosson was the commanding general of Task Force Oregon in the Republic of Vietnam; commanding general, I Field Force; and commanding general, Provisional Corps Vietnam. He spent a short time as director, Policy and Plans Directorate, Joint Chiefs of Staff, before becoming the deputy commander of the U.S. Military Assistance Command Vietnam. He retired as a full general in August 1975.

Byron Hayes

RUMSFELD, DONALD HENRY (1932–)

U.S. statesman, Rumsfeld was born in Evanston, Illinois. He was a naval aviator and flight instructor (1954–57) be-

fore becoming an administrative assistant to Congressmen (1957–59). As a Republican from Illinois, he served in Congress (1963–69) until he was tapped by Pres. Richard M. Nixon to head the Office of Economic Opportunity (OEO; 1969–70). In late 1970, he left the OEO and became a full-time member of the White House staff (1970–73) under Presidents Nixon and Gerald Ford. He served as U.S. ambassador and permanent representative to the North Atlantic Treaty Organization (1973–74). In 1975, Rumsfeld replaced James Schlesinger as secretary of defense, supporting a strong military and "parallel policies of deterrence and détente." Although Rumsfeld successfully steered the defense budget through Congress, no substantial changes in defense policy materialized during his term (1975–77) in office. Rumsfeld became special envoy to the Middle East under Pres. Ronald Reagan during 1983–84.

Russell A. Hart

RUSK, (DAVID) DEAN (1909–)

U.S. secretary of state, Rusk was born in Cherokee County, Georgia. He left a career in higher education to serve in the army during World War II. He saw extensive duty in the China-Burma-India theater on the staff of Gen. Joseph Stilwell. Upon his demobilization as a colonel in 1946, Rusk briefly served as special assistant to the secretary of war and then joined the State Department in 1947 as director of the Office of Special Political Affairs, which dealt with a wide variety of issues that came before the United Nations, including the Palestinian question and nu-

Sec. of State Dean Rusk (left), *meeting with Sen. J. William Fulbright in mid-1961, had the difficult task of handling U.S. relations with South Vietnam throughout the Kennedy and Johnson administrations (1961–69).* (National Archives)

clear controls. In March 1950, Rusk was named assistant secretary of state for Far Eastern Affairs. From this post, he exerted much influence on Korean War policy. He left the State Department in 1952 to become president of the Rockefeller Foundation. He was appointed secretary of state by Pres. John F. Kennedy in 1961 and continued to serve until 1969, throughout the Lyndon B. Johnson administration. As secretary of state, Rusk ably handled the Cuban Missile Crisis in 1962 and the tenuous nature of U.S. relations with Laos, which was enmeshed in civil war, during the 1960s. His expertise came to the fore, however, during the Vietnam War when he played a key role in the diplomacy that initiated early peace talks in 1968. Upon retirement in 1969, he returned to his home state to teach at the University of Georgia.

Bibliography: Cohen, Warren I., *Dean Rusk* (Cooper Square Publishers, 1980).

Lloyd J. Graybar

SCHLESINGER, JAMES RODNEY
(1929–)

U.S. government official, Schlesinger was born in New York, New York. An economics professor at the University of Virginia who had published *The Political Economy of National Security* (1960), he first entered government service as assistant director of the Bureau of the Budget in 1969 in the Nixon administration. With a reputation as efficient and forthright, he was appointed to increasingly responsible positions, including chairman of the Atomic Energy Commission (1971–73) and director of the Central Intelligence Agency (1973), before becoming secretary of defense (1973–75) as the Vietnam War wound down. As secretary he fought against Department of Defense budget cuts, sought a balance of conventional and nuclear forces, and opposed President Ford's détente policy toward the Soviet Union. The latter stance led to Schlesinger's dismissal in 1975. Under President Carter, Schlesinger was the first secretary of energy (1977–79).

Stephen Robinson

SCHWARZKOPF, H. NORMAN (1934–)

U.S. army commander, Schwarzkopf was born in Trenton, New Jersey, the son of a professional army officer. As a youngster, he lived abroad for several years, including a period in Iran, where his father headed an American mission.

Early Service. Graduating from West point in 1956, he was commissioned in the infantry. Early assignments began with the 101st Airborne Division at Fort Campbell, Kentucky (1957–59). Next came the Berlin Brigade (1959–61), during which he also served as an aide-de-camp, then graduate schooling at the University of Southern California (1964) preparatory to an assignment teaching mechanics at West Point (1964–65). One year into

In July 1973, James Schlesinger replaced Elliot Richardson to become the fifth and final U.S. secretary of defense to serve during the Vietnam War. (Department of State)

what was normally a three-year tour, he arranged for an interruption in the faculty duty so he could serve in Vietnam (1965–66).

Vietnam War. Schwarzkopf arrived in Vietnam in the summer of 1965 and was assigned as an adviser to the South Vietnamese Airborne Brigade. During the one-year tour, he earned two Silver Stars, a Purple Heart, and a number of other decorations. Then, after returning to West Point to complete his faculty assignment (1966–68) and an additional year as a student at the Army Command and General Staff College, he was back in Vietnam in 1969, this time as executive officer to the chief of staff of U.S. Army, Vietnam. In a few months, he managed to be reassigned from that desk job to take command of the 1st Battalion, 6th Infantry, a part of the Americal Division stationed in the northern coastal region near Chu Lai. While leading his battalion in 1970 during the difficult period of the progressive U.S. withdrawal from Vietnam, he earned another Silver Star and another Purple Heart, along with the Legion of Merit and many other decorations.

Career Progression. In the immediate post-Vietnam years, Schwarzkopf served as a Washington staff officer; graduated from the Army War College; worked as military assistant to a Pentagon civilian official; was deputy com-

Gen. H. Norman Schwarzkopf, conferring with XVIII Airborne commander Lt. Gen. Gary Luck, became an international hero as commander of all U.S. and non-Arab allied forces in Operation Desert Storm. (U.S. Air Force)

mander of the 172d Infantry Brigade at Fort Richardson, Alaska (1974–76); and commanded a brigade of the 9th Infantry Division at Fort Lewis, Washington (1976–78).

Promoted to brigadier general, Schwarzkopf next served on the staff (1978–80) at Pacific Command Headquarters in Hawaii, then became assistant division commander of the 8th Infantry Division in Germany (1980–82). Another promotion led to a Pentagon tour as director of military personnel management (1982–83), then to division command at the head of the 24th Infantry Division (Mechanized) at Fort Stewart, Georgia (1983–85).

Grenada. While leading the 24th Division, Schwarzkopf received a special assignment in 1983 that involved the island nation of Grenada, where a military junta had seized control of the government. The United States had decided to intervene militarily, and Schwarzkopf was sent as an adviser on the use of ground forces to Vice Adm. Joseph Metcalf, commander of the operation. The short campaign got off to a bad start, with much confusion and lack of coordination. Before long, Metcalf appointed Schwarzkopf as his deputy commander to help improve organization. Afterward, Schwarzkopf was uncompromising in his evaluation. Although the mission had eventually been accomplished, he wrote, "we had lost more lives than we needed to, and the brief war had revealed a lot of shortcomings—an abysmal lack of accurate intelligence, major deficiencies in communications, flareups of interservice rivalry, interference by higher headquarters in battlefield decisions, our alienation of the press, and more." It was an educational experience for him.

Road to the Gulf War. After two years commanding the division and a year as the army's assistant deputy chief

of staff for operations and plans in the Pentagon, Schwarzkopf received a promotion to lieutenant general and command of I Corps at Fort Lewis. A year later, he was back in the Pentagon, this time as the deputy chief of staff of operations and plans. One year later (1988), promoted to full general, he took command of the U.S. Central Command (CENTCOM), headquartered at MacDill Air Force Base, Florida.

Persian Gulf War. When, in August 1990, Iraqi forces sent by Saddam Hussein invaded neighboring Kuwait, and it appeared that Saudi Arabia might be next, the United States reacted quickly by sending military forces. Soon, an international coalition, acting under a United Nations mandate, was in the field, with the U.S. contingent numbering some 550,000.

While the strategic and tactical aspects of the campaign were impressive, the logistical achievements were even more so. A successful mobilization of reserve forces, movement of heavy forces from the United States and Europe, and positioning of the matériel needed to receive and sustain them constituted one of the most extensive and impressive military deployments in history.

Schwarzkopf was in overall command of U.S. and non-Arab allied forces, while Saudi Prince Khalid led the Arab elements. Together they built first a credible defense, then an offensive capability that in Operation Desert Storm drove Iraqi forces from Kuwait and inflicted such damage on them, and on facilities in Iraq for manufacturing weapons of mass destruction, that Iraq's aggressive capabilities were largely destroyed.

In a celebrated end-of-the-war briefing seen live on worldwide television, Schwarzkopf described the operation as having culminated in a massive left hook executed by an armored corps that, following a month of devastating pounding of the enemy by coalition air elements, slammed into the flank of the Republican Guard and quickly and definitively ended Iraqi aggression.

Soon after overseeing redeployment of the U.S. forces, Schwarzkopf retired from military service, receiving numerous honors from his own and other governments, including an honorary knighthood bestowed by Great Britain. He turned then to publishing his memoirs, *It Doesn't Take a Hero* (1992), and to an extensive worldwide lecture program.

Bibliography: Bryan, C. D. B., *Friendly Fire* (Bantam Books, 1977); Cohen, Roger, and Claudio Gatti, *In the Eye of the Storm: The Life of General H. Norman Schwarzkopf* (Farrar, Straus & Giroux, 1991); Schwarzkopf, H. Norman, *It Doesn't Take a Hero* (Bantam Books, 1992).

Lewis Sorley

SEAMAN, JONATHAN OWEN (1911–1986)

U.S. army commander, Seaman was born in Manila, the

Philippines. He graduated from West Point in 1934 and was commissioned in the field artillery. He served in both the Pacific and European theaters during World War II. Seaman was promoted to brigadier general in 1961 and assumed command of the 1st Infantry Division in 1964. Major General Seaman deployed the 1st Infantry Division to Vietnam in late 1965. He served as its commanding general until March 1966 when he assumed command of II Field Force and was promoted to lieutenant general. The II Field Force units under Seaman conducted numerous major combat operations, such as Cedar Falls. Following his assignment in Vietnam, he commanded the 1st U.S. Army until his retirement in 1971.

Bibliography: Rogers, Bernard, *Cedar Falls-Junction City: A Turning Point* (U.S. Govt. Printing Office, 1974).

Capt. Leslie Howard Belknap

SHARP, ULYSSES SIMPSON (1906–)

U.S. naval commander, Sharp was born in Chinook, Montana. He graduated from Annapolis in 1927 and served as a line officer. During World War II, he commanded the minesweeper *Hogan* and the destroyer *Boyd*. After the war, the bright and popular officer rose steadily in rank and responsibilities in a series of command and staff assignments. At the outset of the Kennedy administration's difficulties over foreign policy, Sharp was serving as the deputy chief of naval operations for plans and policy. In this position, one he had held since 1960, he oversaw U.S. naval deployments and missions worldwide and was privy to much debate that was taking place within the Joint Chiefs of Staff (JCS). During this Pentagon assignment he saw the results of the Bay of Pigs fiasco in 1961 and the weakening of the U.S. position in Asia when Laos fell under Communist control.

In September 1963, Sharp relieved Adm. John H. Sides as commander in chief, Pacific Fleet, an office in direct command of all U.S. naval forces in the Pacific region. Shortly after the November 1963 assassinations of President Kennedy and South Vietnam's Pres. Ngo Dinh Diem, the White House issued a national security action memorandum that reaffirmed U.S. policy in South Vietnam and portrayed a relatively optimistic picture of improving security throughout the country. However, in December, Secretary of Defense McNamara's on-scene evaluation indicated a decline in South Vietnamese government fortunes and an alarming growth in the power and presence of Communist forces. Subsequently, both Sharp and McNamara became increasingly absorbed in Southeast Asian affairs, often in disagreement.

In June 1964, Sharp was elevated to the position of commander in chief of the Pacific Command, directly responsible for all U.S. forces—air, land, and naval—throughout the Pacific region. McNamara's observations six months before had proved accurate, and Sharp had to

contend with an apparently failing U.S. military aid and assistance program in South Vietnam. Communist gains were continuing, and there was increasing evidence of extensive North Vietnamese support for their comrades in the South. Sharp, however, discovered that his actual authority over U.S. forces and U.S. military and naval personnel in South Vietnam was quite limited because national security officials in Washington applied themselves directly to foreign problems, circumventing the regional unified commands, and the U.S. ambassador was usually the senior U.S. representative, with authority over U.S. military personnel. Therefore, in some instances, Sharp found himself on the sidelines, watching the secretary of defense delivering decisions directly to U.S. leaders in Saigon or finding that his Pacific Command subordinates in South Vietnam had been given some important instructions by the U.S. ambassador.

Vietnam War. Soon after assuming his new command, Sharp became directly involved in Southeast Asian affairs along the coasts of North Vietnam. In early July, he recommended an intelligence-gathering mission along the North Vietnamese coastline. Such voyages had been staged along the coasts of China and North Korea for years without incident. Since the courses of these U.S. warships were wholly in international waters, there was nothing particularly provocative in the procedure. Washington approved his recommendation, and the *Maddox* was sent on patrol to the Gulf of Tonkin. When the *Maddox* was attacked by North Vietnamese torpedo boats on August 2 in international waters, a formal protest to Hanoi was filed by the U.S. Department of State. No military reprisals were made, but Sharp proposed that the cruise be completed, this time with two destroyers, and that two aircraft carriers be stationed nearby. Again, the admiral's recommendation was approved, and the mission was resumed immediately.

On August 4, the *Turner Joy* and the *Maddox* reported being attacked. Sharp immediately recommended a punitive air strike against North Vietnam. Within hours, he was told to plan such an attack. As his staff worked out target lists and bombloads, Sharp conferred with Secretary of Defense McNamara and the chairman of the JCS, General Wheeler, reporting his understanding of what had occurred in the Tonkin Gulf. On August 5, the U.S. air strikes were launched. The fuel-storage facility at Vinh and a number of North Vietnamese patrol boats were destroyed. Two U.S. Navy aircraft were lost in the action. On the same day, Pres. Lyndon B. Johnson asked for congressional support for his decisions, and Congress passed the Gulf of Tonkin Resolution, authorizing the president to "take all necessary measures" to repel armed attacks and to forestall further aggression.

In February 1965, an attack on U.S. personnel and aircraft in South Vietnam resulted in the president's approval of more bombing of the North and a "graduated reprisal" campaign. Sharp watched these events unfold and then communicated his own thoughts to the JCS. Although the admiral agreed with the need for the air campaign, he urged a more ambitious aim, an aim of relentless pressure on Hanoi to convince the Northerners of the prohibitive costs of their activities. It was the opening rift between Sharp and the authorities in Washington.

As the start-stop, hesitant, and restricted U.S. bombing campaign of North Vietnam developed, Sharp continued to express his disagreement with the nature of the effort. Although he wholeheartedly agreed with the idea of making Hanoi pay for its transgressions in Laos and South Vietnam, he objected to the lack of freedom U.S. military leaders had in selecting targets. He protested the frequent pauses in the campaign, pauses that supposedly allowed Hanoi to respond to diplomatic initiatives. Sharp argued that the Northerners simply used the pauses to replenish their stocks in the South and to repair damaged bridges, railways, and roads. He disagreed with the geographical limits placed on the pilots. Sharp believed the off-limits circle around Hanoi was too large and cited evidence that the Communists were taking advantage of the space, placing airfields, supply dumps, and military installations within the safety zone. He had similar objections about the wide off-limits area along the Chinese border. Sharp continually pressed for the mining of the port of Haiphong, the major entry point for Soviet bloc military supplies and protested that U.S. targets were too restricted.

Sharp continued his barrage of carping messages to Washington for the next three and a half years while consistently supporting the requests of Gen. William C. Westmoreland in dealing with the ground war in South Vietnam. But Sharp's only real authority had to do with the character of the air campaign against North Vietnam. Retiring from active duty in mid-1968, Sharp wrote of his frustrating experiences in *Strategy for Defeat*, published in 1978. For Sharp, the last 10 years of his career were often marred by his lack of influence on the Washington policymakers, but his writings and steadfast battle to remove limits on the air campaign have survived beyond the Vietnam War.

Bibliography: Nichols, John B., *On Yankee Station: The Naval Air War Over Vietnam* (U.S. Naval Inst. Press, 1987); Sharp, U. S. Grant, *Strategy for Defeat: Vietnam in Retrospect* (Presidio, 1978).

Col. (Ret.) Rod Paschall

SHEPHERD, LEMUEL CORNICK, JR.
(1896–1990)

U.S. marine officer, Shepherd was born in Norfolk, Virginia. He graduated from Virginia Military Institute in 1917, was commissioned a lieutenant in the Marine Corps, and fought in World War I, after which he was promoted to captain. In the interwar years, his assignments included tours of duty in Brazil, China, and Haiti. During World War II, Shepherd was attached to the 1st Marine Division, commanded the 1st Provisional Marine Brigade, and commanded the 6th Marine Division, first as a brigadier general (1943) and then as a major general (1944). He served as assistant commandant and chief of staff at headquarters, Marine Corps (1947–48); commandant of Marine Corps schools, Quantico, Virginia (1948–1950); and commanding general, Fleet Marine Force, Pacific (1950–52), during the Korean War. He commanded the 1st Marine Division at Inchon and assisted in the evacuation during the retreat from the Chosin Reservoir.

In 1952, Shepherd became the 20th commandant of the Marine Corps, a post in which he served until 1955, shortly before his retirement in early 1956. During his tenure as commandant, he was responsible for the establishment of the Marine Corps Cold Weather Warfare School and the Marine Corps Combined Arms and Desert Warfare Center. He was also the first commandant to become a member of the Joint Chiefs of Staff.

Leo J. Daugherty III

SHERMAN, FORREST PERCIVAL
(1896–1951)

U.S. naval officer, Sherman was born in Merrimack, New Hampshire. He graduated from Annapolis in 1918 and saw service at sea in both world wars. Sherman, who had been in naval aviation since the early 1920s, was best known, however, for his intellectual and organizational abilities and spent much of World War II as the Pacific Fleet's top planner.

Postwar Planning. In December 1945, Sherman was named Deputy Chief of Naval Operations (Operations). Together with air force major general Lauris Norstad and presidential adviser Clark Clifford, Sherman helped iron out the basics of the plan to unify the U.S. armed services that became law in 1947. Thought by some fellow officers to have compromised the navy's best interests in his advocacy of unification, Sherman believed that the navy's future position in the defense establishment rested on its ability to develop a nuclear capability. He assiduously promoted efforts to develop the new AJ-1 bomber, which would be capable of delivering atom bombs from carriers. He was also much involved in preparing early plans for possible war with the Soviet Union. Sherman helped persuade Pres. Harry S Truman that emphasis needed to be placed on the defense of the eastern Mediterranean in order to ensure the flow of Middle East oil to the West.

Appropriately, Sherman's next assignment was as commander, U.S. Naval Forces, Mediterranean. The backbone of these forces was the 6th Fleet. Although he initially planned to testify before the House Armed Services Committee during the so-called Revolt of the Admirals, Sherman eventually restricted his comments to a written statement saying that he supported Chief of Naval Operations (CNO) Louis Denfeld's advocacy of naval preparedness before the committee but he disagreed with some aspects of Denfeld's testimony. When Denfeld was not reappointed as CNO in 1949 because of his role in this revolt, Sherman was offered and accepted the position.

Chief of Naval Operations. Each of the navy's platform communities, as well as the marines, regarded Sherman with some suspicion, but he soon revealed himself to be an effective spokesman for the navy. He saved some of the navy's more able younger officers, especially the much admired Capt. Arleigh Burke, from reprisals for their parts in the revolt and managed to circumvent the secretary of defense's desire to mothball the navy's only active battleship, the *Missouri.* Sherman also succeeded in keeping seven fleet carriers at sea and even gained sufficient funds to begin development of the *Nautilus,* the first nuclear-powered submarine. Construction of a super-carrier that had been canceled the previous year was now authorized. When the outbreak of the Korean War made even more funds available, Sherman was quick to order preparation of a comprehensive plan for long-range expansion of the fleet.

While questions concerning the Korean War and Far Eastern affairs absorbed much of Sherman's time, he also believed the United States must be willing to base ground forces in Europe as well as to commit strong naval and air forces to NATO (North Atlantic Treaty Organization). Although he did not yet advocate NATO membership for Spain, he believed that the United States needed to acquire bases there in order to have an effective defense of southern Europe and the Mediterranean. He died in Naples, Italy, while on an exhausting trip to discuss defense matters in Spain and other European nations.

Bibliography: Palmer, Michael A., *Origins of the Maritime Strategy: American Naval Strategy in the First Postwar Decade* (Naval Hist. Center, 1988); Reynolds, Clark G., "Forrest Percival Sherman," *The Chiefs of Naval Operations,* ed. by Robert William Love, Jr. (Naval Inst. Press, 1980).

Lloyd J. Graybar

SHOUP, DAVID MONROE (1904–1983)

U.S. marine commander, Shoup was born in Battle Ground, Indiana. He received his marine commission in 1926. His World War II duty was distinguished by numerous acts of heroism. After observing Allied Pacific operations at New Georgia in 1943, during which he earned the Purple Heart, Shoup was awarded the Medal of Honor for rallying his forces against heavy enemy fire at Betio, Tarawa (Nov. 20–23, 1943).

After the war, Shoup held a series of posts in which he honed his command skills and solidified his reputation as a blunt-speaking leader who emphasized discipline. "I can be tough when it is required and compassionate when that is required," he stated, and his career bore that out. After commanding the Marine Basic School at Quantico for two years, Shoup became fiscal director of the Marine Corps in 1953. Promoted to major general in 1955, he assumed the post of inspector general in 1956 before taking over command of the 1st Marine Division in 1957 and command of the 3d Marine Division in 1958. In November 1959, Shoup was promoted to lieutenant general and elevated to marine chief of staff.

It was as inspector general that Shoup found himself immersed in a heated controversy that threatened to divide the Marine Corps. On Apr. 8, 1956, six recruits drowned during a night march at Parris Island, South Carolina. As Congress had already begun investigating earlier accusations of recruit abuse by marine drill instructors, Commandant Gen. Randolph McCall Pate quickly announced he would revamp the recruit training system and eliminate overzealous drill instructors, news that angered corps traditionalists who saw nothing wrong with marine training. The drill instructor in charge of the six drowned recruits was found guilty of negligent homicide and drinking on duty, reduced to private, and given three months' confinement. Pate named Shoup inspector general with orders to reform recruit training. Although investigation uncovered some instances of abusive training, which Shoup promised would no longer be tolerated, he declared that the training system "which has served us so well for so many years" was generally sound and would be continued. However, the controversy dragged on for two years, harming corps unity and bruising its reputation.

On Aug. 8, 1959, Pres. Dwight D. Eisenhower bypassed nine senior officers and selected Shoup to succeed General Pate as commandant of the Marine Corps. Eisenhower wanted a leader unencumbered with marine biases who could work with other branches of government, and he was attracted by Shoup's bluntness and independent thinking. Shoup assumed the top marine post on Jan. 1, 1960, at which time he also became a full general.

Shoup remained as commandant when John F. Kennedy succeeded Eisenhower as president. In fact, the young president so liked Shoup's honesty and incisive comments that the marine general became the sole holdover from Eisenhower's Joint Chiefs of Staff. Since Kennedy had run, in part, on American unpreparedness for conventional warfare and wanted more flexible options other than a nuclear strike capability, Shoup received great support from the new administration to make needed changes in the corps.

A five-year program to increase the corps' ability to respond quickly in a crisis assumed increased importance. Shoup stripped marines from support groups to put more units in the field; and he reorganized every facet of the corps, from headquarters to squads, to increase readiness.

He also centralized control by appointing deputy chiefs of staff to oversee crucial programs such as air, planning, and research; and he transformed the Marine Corps Reserve from a training pool for replacements into its own complete division, thereby increasing reserve morale. Shoup also helped implement the strategy of vertical envelopment, which altered the longstanding corps reliance on amphibious operations by calling for increased use of helicopters to lift marines to combat areas. Simultaneously, Shoup emphasized improved training for the corps, better supply management to eliminate waste, and heightened physical fitness while abolishing those marine traditions he considered superfluous, such as swagger sticks, gun salutes, and other officer amenities. Although his moves ruffled feathers, Shoup's inherent decency and his status as a Medal of Honor winner blunted major attacks on him, and the corps' superb showing during the October 1962 Cuban Missile Crisis further answered critics.

Congress, however, would be another matter. In 1961, a group of senators led by Strom Thurmond charged that the Marine Corps was not receiving sufficient indoctrination about its main enemy, Communism. Shoup's quick reply that the corps' strength came from superb training and conditioning and that it needed no political indoctrination to sharpen its readiness defused the criticism.

Shoup stepped down as commandant and retired from the marines in 1964. He became an early critic of U.S. involvement in Vietnam, arguing that U.S. safety and freedom was unrelated to Southeast Asia and stating that the war could not be won without major assaults on North Vietnam.

Bibliography: Acker, Dudley, Jr., *The World According to Shoup* (Northern Arizona Univ. Press, 1985); Clifford, Kenneth J., *Progress and Purpose: A Developmental History of the U.S. Marine Corps, 1900–1970* (Marine Hist. Div., 1973); Millett, Allan R., *The History of the United States Marine Corps* (Free Press, 1980); Parker, William D., *A Concise History of the United States Marine Corps, 1775–1969* (Marine Hist. Div., 1970).

John F. Wukovits

SMITH, OLIVER PRINCE (1893–1977)

U.S. marine officer, Smith was born in Menard, Texas. He graduated from the University of California at Berkeley in 1916 and was commissioned a 2d lieutenant in the Marine Corps in 1917. After tours of duty including Guam (1917–19) and Haiti (1928–31), he returned to the United States and entered the U.S. Army's infantry officers course (1931–32) and the Marine Corps schools at Quantico, Virginia, where he served as an instructor.

During World War II, Smith worked in the marine headquarters plans and policies office (1942–44) and then commanded the 5th Marine Regiment at Peleliu in late 1944;

he was also marine deputy chief of staff to the 10th Army on Okinawa. In July 1945, he returned to the United States to become the commandant of Marine Corps schools and later commanding general, Marine Barracks, Quantico, Virginia. In October 1945, he became assistant commandant of the Marine Corps.

Named commanding general of the 1st Marine Division in 1950, he was deployed to Korea, where his division took part in the landings at Inchon. Fighting their way to Seoul, the marines secured the city after bitter house-to-house fighting and then advanced toward the 38th parallel and on to the Chinese border. When the Chinese launched their first counterattack, the 1st Division bore the brunt as it attempted to fight its way out of a carefully laid trap. As the front around them collapsed, Smith's marines fought perhaps one of the most famous retreats in U.S. military history. Fighting back to the port of Hungnam, Smith's resistance assisted in the stabilization of the United Nations forces' position and enabled the 1st Marines to withdraw with all of its casualties for safe evacuation.

When he returned to the United States in 1951, Smith became commanding general at Camp Pendleton, California. In 1953, he was appointed commanding general, Fleet Marine Force, Atlantic. After several more tours of duty, Smith retired in 1977. He possessed one of the best tactical minds in the U.S. Marine Corps.

Leo J. Daugherty III

SPAATZ, CARL ANDREW (1891–1974)

U.S. air force officer, Spaatz was born in Boyerstown, Pennsylvania. He graduated from West Point in 1914. He served in a series of military posts with the Army Air Corps through the 1930s, in each position earning distinction. In the process, he also became an air power zealot, vocally supporting air supremacy as the means to obliterate the will of the enemy to wage war. For his strident efforts, Spaatz was much disliked by more traditionally minded officers, probably contributing to his long stint, 15 years, with the rank of major. By the beginning of World War II, however, he was a brigadier general.

The coming of war in Europe in 1939 brought an opportunity not present previously for airmen such as Spaatz to prove their air-power ideas. In May 1942, he got the opportunity to command the newly created 8th Air Force in England and set about the systematic destruction of enemy-held strategic targets in Europe. A few months later, Spaatz became Allied air forces commander under Dwight D. Eisenhower for Operation Torch, the invasion of North Africa. He remained in the Mediterranean theater of operations until early 1944, when he returned to Great Britain to command the newly established U.S. Strategic Forces in Europe, which coordinated all air operations for the invasion of the continent. In 1945, he was promoted to general.

In June 1945, a month after the surrender of Germany, Spaatz was sent to Guam to command the U.S. Strategic Forces in the Far East. There he presided over the efforts of Maj. Gens. Curtis E. LeMay and Nathan F. Twining in the strategic bombardment of Japan. The 509th Composite Wing, under his suzerainty, dropped nuclear weapons on Hiroshima and Nagasaki in August 1945.

Following the war, Spaatz served in senior posts within the Army Air Forces. In 1947, Spaatz succeeded Gen. Henry H. "Hap" Arnold as head of the newly independent U.S. Air Force. As air force chief of staff, Spaatz continued to advocate the importance of air power in the defense of the United States and was a disciple of the principle of nuclear deterrence. He served only a short time, however, retiring in 1948. Spaatz then served in a variety of aeronautics positions, including head of the Civil Air Patrol.

Bibliography: Copp, DeWitt S., *A Few Great Captains: The Men and Events that Shaped the Development of U.S. Air Power* (Doubleday, 1980); Mets, David R., *Master of Air Power: Carl A. Spaatz* (Presidio, 1988); Zuckerman, Sir Solly, *From Apes to Warlords* (Hamish Hamilton, 1978).

Roger D. Launius

STARRY, DONN ALBERT (1925–)

U.S. army officer, Starry was born in New York City. He served as an enlisted soldier in World War II before entering West Point in 1944. He was commissioned an armor officer upon graduation in 1948. Starry served in a variety of command and staff assignments prior to his two assignments to Vietnam. In his second tour, he commanded the 11th Armored Cavalry Regiment during the 1970 Cambodian incursion, Operation Toan Thang 43. Later in the 1970s, he commanded the Armor School, V Corps, in Europe, and subsequently was put in charge of Training and Doctrine Command. Throughout this period, he was instrumental in the development of the "air-land battle" doctrine. A full general, Starry later served as the commander of Readiness Command until his retirement in 1983.

Bibliography: Starry, Donn A., *Mounted Combat in Vietnam* (U.S. Govt. Printing Office, 1978).

Capt. Leslie Howard Belknap

STENNIS, JOHN CORNELIUS (1901–)

U.S. senator and Armed Services Committee chair, Stennis was born in Kemper County, Mississippi. A conservative Democrat, he served in the U.S. House of Representatives (1929–31) and the U.S. Senate (1947–89). In the early 1960s, Stennis headed the Senate Preparedness Subcommittee and worked diligently for a first-rate defense. Once Pres. Lyndon B. Johnson committed U.S.

troops to South Vietnam in 1965, Stennis became one of the strongest supporters of the military effort in Vietnam. Among the most influential members of the Armed Services Committee, he was appointed its chairman in 1969. Stennis and the military officer corps conflicted on certain issues, particularly on Stennis's desire to limit the number of admirals and generals to 1,200 rather than the 1,600 the Pentagon desired. Officers complained that the "Stennis Ceiling" limited promotions.

Steve R. Waddell

STRATEMEYER, GEORGE EDWARD (1890–1969)

U.S. army officer, Stratemeyer was born in Cincinnati, Ohio. He graduated from West Point in 1915. During World War II, he served successively as chief of the Air Staff, commander of Army Air Forces in the China-Burma-India theater (coincident with command of the Eastern Air Command, a joint U.S.-British air organization) and commander of Army Air Forces in China. Between 1946 and 1949, he led the Air Defense Command. In April 1949, Stratemeyer became commander of the Far East Air Force.

When the United States entered the Korean War in June 1950, Stratemeyer juggled his meager forces so as to attack the North Koreans with maximum air power while maintaining the air defense of the entire Far East Command. On July 8, he organized a bomber command, and on July 22, he formed a Target Selection Committee of army, navy, and air force representatives.

He astutely and adroitly directed the combined U.S. and United Nations (UN) air forces to support the UN war effort. His command successfully faced Chinese intervention and maintained air supremacy over Korea.

On May 20, 1951, Stratemeyer's tenure as commander was cut short by a massive heart attack. A lieutenant general, he retired with a physical disability the following year.

Bibliography: Futrell, Robert F., *The United States Air Force in Korea 1950–1953*, rev. ed. (Office of Air Force History, 1983); *The Official Guide to the Army Air Forces* (Pocket Books, 1944).

Brig. Gen. PNG (Ret.) Uzal W. Ent

STRUBLE, ARTHUR DEWEY (1894–1983)

U.S. naval officer, Struble was born in Portland, Oregon. He graduated from Annapolis in 1915 and saw service in a Queenstown, Australia-based destroyer during World War I. After a short tour as executive officer of the battleship *Arizona* in 1940–41, he was promoted to captain and received command of the light cruiser *Trenton*. Struble was promoted to rear admiral in 1942 and served as chief of staff to the commander of the Western Naval Task

Force during the Normandy landings. He then commanded an amphibious group of the 7th Fleet in several operations in the Philippines. In 1946, Struble became amphibious commander, Pacific Fleet. After a tour as deputy chief of naval operations, during which he was promoted to vice admiral, he was appointed commander of the 7th Fleet in May 1950. As such, he had overall command of the amphibious operations at Inchon and Wonsan during the Korean War. In 1951–52, Struble commanded the 1st Fleet. He then had shore duty and retired in 1956 as a full admiral.

Bibliography: Reynolds, Clark, *Famous American Admirals* (Van Nostrand-Reinhold, 1978).

Lloyd J. Graybar

SULLIVAN, JOHN LAWRENCE (1899–)

U.S. secretary of the navy, Sullivan was born in Manchester, New Hampshire. His tenure as navy secretary (Sept. 18, 1947–May 24, 1949) was marked by a series of momentous global events: the Soviets blockaded Berlin, the North Atlantic Treaty Organization was established, the Communists won in China, and the Truman Doctrine and the Marshall Plan marked the early Cold War years. The new Department of Defense tested its relations with the services in the midst of a struggle for roles and missions in the postwar world. The Air Force demanded ascendancy as the strategic deliverer of atomic, then nuclear, weapons. Service acrimony, particularly "the Revolt of the Admirals," resulted in Sullivan's resignation when Sec. of Defense Louis A. Johnson cancelled the construction of the supercarrier *United States*.

Bibliography: Coletta, Paolo E., *American Secretaries of the Navy; Vol. 2: 1913–1972* (Naval Inst. Press, 1980).

Col. (Ret.) Henry G. Gole

SYMINGTON, (WILLIAM) STUART
(1901–1988)

U.S. senator and air force secretary, Symington was born in Amherst, Massachusetts. He was educated at Yale University and in the 1920s and 1930s worked as an executive for several radio and steel companies. He moved to St. Louis, Missouri, in 1938 and became president of the Emerson Electric Manufacturing Company.

In 1945, Symington began working with the war demobilization effort, and in 1946–47 was assistant secretary of war for air. When the Department of Defense was established in 1947, he became the first secretary of the air force (1947–50). He then served in Washington as a Missouri senator (1953–77). Throughout his senatorial career, Symington was a knowledgeable leader in international and defense affairs, as well as an able counselor to several Democratic presidents. He himself ran unsuccessfully for the Democratic presidential nomination in 1960.

Bibliography: Martin, Ralph, and Edward Plaut, *Front Runner, Dark Horse* (Doubleday, 1960); Wellman, Paul, *Stuart Symington: Portrait of a Man with the Mission* (Doubleday, 1960).

Roger D. Launius

TAYLOR, MAXWELL DAVENPORT
(1901–1987)

U.S. army commander, Taylor was born in Keytesville, Missouri. He graduated from West Point in 1922. He was commissioned in the engineers and was posted to the Engineer School at Fort Belvoir, Virginia, before being assigned to the 3d Engineers in Hawaii.

Early Career. Because of his interest in technology, Taylor transferred to the Field Artillery in 1926. After completing his duty in Hawaii, he spent five years at West Point teaching Spanish, then French. In 1933, he was sent to the two-year course at the Command and General Staff College at Fort Leavenworth, Kansas. After graduation, Taylor was assigned to Tokyo as an assistant military attaché and language student. In two years, he became fluent in Japanese.

He accepted an assignment in late 1937 as translator and assistant to Col. Joseph W. Stilwell. Returning to Washington in 1939, Captain Taylor attended the National War College at Fort McNair, Washington, D.C. Upon graduation in 1940, he was assigned to command the 12th Field Artillery Battalion at Fort Sam Houston, Texas. Within a year, he was appointed to the personal staff of Gen. George C. Marshall, army chief of staff. Marshall profoundly influenced Taylor.

World War II. Early in World War II, Taylor was appointed chief of staff of the new 82d Airborne Division (Maj. Gen. Matthew Ridgway commanding) at Fort Bragg, North Carolina. Taylor, himself, made only a few parachute jumps in his military career; he viewed the parachute strictly as a means to get to battle, to be used only when a better vehicle was not available.

Soon he was made commander of the division's artillery and promoted to brigadier general. The division's assistant division commander was lost in an abortive airdrop in Sicily on July 9, 1943, and Taylor was appointed to replace him. On September 7, Taylor and air force intelligence officer Col. William T. Gardiner secretly entered Rome, then deep in enemy territory. They were to assess the capability of the nearby Italian army formations to support Operation Giant II (a projected airborne assault by the 82d designed to free Rome). After meeting with the Italian army's leadership, Taylor and Gardiner concluded that the Italian army was incapable of rendering the desired aid. Their radio report to Gen. Dwight D. Eisenhower caused the airborne attack to be canceled just as the first trooper-laden aircraft were taking off on the mission.

A few days later, Taylor was appointed to the Allied Control Commission, which dealt with the Italian government. Soon relieved of this assignment, he rejoined the 82d in England. In March 1944, he took command of the 101st Airborne Division.

Taylor had a penchant for attention to detail and realistic training. He solved the problem of locating equipment dropped at night by using luminous cord. To help distinguish friend from enemy he used toy metal "crickets" that gave out a loud chirp when squeezed.

Taylor led the 101st in its airdrop during the Normandy invasion and in Operation Market-Garden. He was then ordered home for discussions concerning the future structure and equipment of airborne divisions. As a result, he was absent when the 101st went to Bastogne (Battle of the Bulge). He rejoined it there on Dec. 27, 1944.

Taylor was not universally liked, but he was respected as a cool professional who seemed to be everywhere at once in a fight. He attacked the enemy as often as possible, but did not lose men for no purpose.

Postwar Assignments. In September 1945, Taylor was appointed superintendent of West Point. He stressed physical fitness and liberalized the science-heavy curriculum by introducing language as an elective and by adding Russian history, U.S. diplomatic history, and international economics. He also improved the English Department. To the extreme distress of the Academic Board, he introduced the study of military leadership, assigning it to the Tactical Department.

In 1949, he was assigned to Germany as chief of staff, European Command. In September, he was made U.S. commander, Berlin, a post he held until 1951, when he was promoted to lieutenant general and became army assistant chief of staff for operations and training and, in August, deputy chief of staff for both operations and administration.

On Feb. 11, 1953, Taylor became commander of the 8th Army in Korea and field commander of United Nations Forces, Korea. He spent most of his time dealing with the stubbornness of South Korean president Syngman Rhee, who resisted armistice arrangements. In 1953, Taylor was promoted to full general. The following year, he was appointed commanding general, Army Forces Far East, then commander in chief, Far East Command, in 1955.

On June 30, he was elevated to chief of staff of the army. During his tenure, the army was reduced from 18 to 16 divisions and his vision of a reorganized division with five maneuver elements (instead of three) failed to take hold, but he kept the army in the tactical missile field and frustrated even further cuts in army personnel.

Taylor retired in 1959 and wrote *The Uncertain Trumpet* (1960), a book condemning the Eisenhower administration's strategy of "massive retaliation" (based on the use of nuclear weapons) and espousing, instead, an approach

of "flexible response." This strategy was based on a diversified military force capable of meeting a range of challenges—from the conventional to the nuclear. While writing this book, he was the chairman of the board of the Mexican Light and Power Company and was living in Mexico City.

In 1960, he returned to the United States and accepted a five-year contract as president of the Lincoln Center for the Performing Arts. In 1961, the new U.S. president, John F. Kennedy, asked him to investigate the Bay of Pigs fiasco. He stayed on as military representative of the president. On Oct. 7, 1962, he became chairman of the Joint Chiefs of Staff, holding this post until his retirement in 1964.

Vietnam War. Early in the U.S. involvement in Vietnam, Taylor believed in "gradualism"—attempting to obtain U.S. objectives in Vietnam at the outset without major military involvement and then with minimal forces. He later changed this view in *Swords and Plowshares* (1972), his memoirs. He wrote that gradualism "violated the military principals of surprise and mass as means to gain prompt success."

At the beginning of the Cuban Missile Crisis, he advocated air strikes in conjunction with a naval blockade. The United States was on the point of invading Cuba when the Soviet Union finally agreed to withdraw the missiles.

In 1964, Taylor was appointed ambassador to South Vietnam. In his year as ambassador, he worked hard, but in vain, to convince South Vietnamese generals that they had to establish a real civilian government, not a facade. Returning from Saigon in August 1965, he was retained by Pres. Lyndon Johnson as a special consultant.

Taylor's memoirs disclosed that he believed that the news media misled the people of the United States, preventing American success in Vietnam. In retirement, among other endeavors, Taylor was president of the Institute for Defense Analysis (1966–69) and president of the Foreign Intelligence Advisory Board (1965–70). About 1975, he contracted a form of Lou Gerhig's disease (amyotrophic lateral sclerosis), a debilitating condition that eventually claimed his power of speech.

Bibliography: Bradley, Omar N., and Clay Blair, *A General's Life* (Simon & Schuster, 1983); Taylor, John M., *General Maxwell Taylor* (Doubleday Dell, 1989); Taylor, Maxwell D., *Swords and Plowshares* (Norton, 1972); ———, *The Uncertain Trumpet* (Harper, 1960).

Brig. Gen. PNG (Ret.) Uzal W. Ent

THIEU, NGUYEN VAN (1923–)

South Vietnamese military officer and president (1967–75), Thieu was born near Phan Rang, later in South Vietnam. Trained in military schools in French Indochina, he fought against the Viet Minh (1949–54) and held important commands after South Vietnam became independent in 1954. As a division commander, Thieu played a key role in the overthrow of the Diem regime in 1963, rose in rank to major general during the ensuing political instability, and headed the National Leadership Committee that took power in 1965. Thieu, who had received advanced training in the United States, had the confidence of many American officials and consolidated his power in South Vietnam while pursuing the war against the Communists. He outmaneuvered Nguyen Cao Ky for the presidential nomination in 1967 and won the presidency in both the 1967 and 1971 elections. Thieu opposed the 1973 Vietnam peace agreement but was forced to accept it under U.S. pressure. In 1975, as North Vietnamese forces closed in on Saigon, Thieu resigned and fled the country.

Stephen Robinson

THURMAN, MAXWELL R. (1931–)

U.S. army commander, Thurman was born in High Point, North Carolina. He was educated at North Carolina State University, through which he was commissioned in 1953 from the Reserve Officers Training Corps. In the post-Vietnam era, he had enormous influence on the army's course and character, especially as commander of the Army Recruiting Command (1979–81) at a time when recruiting sufficient qualified soldiers was the key element in assuring success of an all-volunteer army. His influence continued as the army's deputy chief of staff for personnel (1981–83) and, promoted to full general, as army vice chief of staff (1983–87) and then commanding general, U.S. Army Training and Doctrine Command from 1987. On the point of retirement, Thurman was at the last moment asked to undertake another assignment when the Bush administration decided to appoint a new commander in Panama. He thus served as commander in chief, U.S. Southern Command, at the time of Operation Just Cause, the 1989 U.S. intervention in Panama.

Lewis Sorley

TOMPKINS, RATHVON McCLURE (1912–)

U.S. marine officer, Tompkins was born in Boulder, Colorado. He graduated from the University of Colorado in 1935 and joined the Marine Corps Reserve that same year. After completing the reserve officers class at Quantico in 1939, he was assigned to the 2d Marine Brigade. During World War II, Major Tompkins saw much action with the 2d Marine Division (1942–44) in the Pacific, from which he returned wounded and with the rank of lieutenant colonel.

Following the war, he served in numerous staff, teaching, and joint assignments. In 1967, Major General Tompkins was commander of the 3d Marine Division and directed the successful defense of Khe Sanh (Jan. 21–Apr. 7, 1968) during the Vietnam War.

Bibliography: Millett, Allan R., *Semper Fidelis: The History of the United Marine Corps* (Macmillan, 1991).

David Friend

TRUDEAU, ARTHUR GILBERT (1902–1991)

U.S. army officer, Trudeau born in Middlebury, Vermont. He graduated from West Point in 1924 and was commissioned in the Corps of Engineers. During a long and colorful career, he commanded the 1st Constabulary Brigade in occupied Germany (1948–50), the 1st Cavalry Division in Japan (1952–53), and the 7th Infantry Division in combat in Korea (1953), earning two Silver Stars and other decorations. Returning to Pentagon duty, he was army assistant chief of staff for intelligence (1953–55). During 1956–58, Trudeau returned to Korea to command I Corps, then concluded his career as army chief of research and development (1958–62).

Bibliography: Trudeau, Arthur G., *Engineer Memoirs* (Office of the Chief of Engineers, 1988).

Lewis Sorley

TRUMAN, HARRY S (1884–1972)

Thirty-third president of the United States (1945–53), Truman was born in Lamar, Missouri. Just one month after becoming Pres. Franklin D. Roosevelt's fourth-term vice president, Truman succeeded to the presidency upon Roosevelt's death (Apr. 12, 1945). In World War II, his most dramatic decision was approving the use of the atomic bomb against Japan in August 1945. Earlier in the summer, Truman met with other Allied leaders at the Potsdam Conference, which called for the unconditional surrender of Japan and dealt with European problems in the aftermath of Germany's surrender.

Remembered for his congeniality and outspoken bluntness, Truman hoped to maintain Roosevelt's diverse political coalition. His aggressively liberal domestic program (the Fair Deal) helped him retain the presidency in 1948. Truman's foreign policy was internationalist; he saw the United States as a world leader obligated to spread democracy and capitalism. This stance placed Truman's administration in direct conflict with postwar Soviet expansionism. The Truman Doctrine (which committed U.S. support to Greece, Turkey, and unspecified "other nations"), the Marshall Plan, and the North Atlantic Treaty Organization (NATO)—all vigorously promoted by Truman—were designed to block Soviet incursions into Western Europe. These European programs proved highly successful and established U.S. military policy for the Cold War era. His successors often modified policies to meet changing circumstances, but the policy structure had been developed by Truman in the aftermath of World War II.

Truman's Asian policy led to U.S. involvement in the Korean War (1950–53) after the takeover of China by the

Communists in 1949. Truman reacted quickly to North Korea's invasion of South Korea in June 1950, securing United Nations' support and committing U.S. troops to South Korea's defense. Truman's historic confrontation with Far East commander Gen. Douglas MacArthur led to MacArthur's relief and an affirmation of the supremacy of civilian authority over the military. The fact that U.S. military intervention had prevented a Communist takeover of a friendly country was often lost in the recriminations that followed the military stalemate in Korea. Truman decided not to run again in 1952, and Dwight D. Eisenhower led the Republican ticket to victory.

Bibliography: Donovan, Robert J., *Tumultuous Years: The Presidency of Harry S. Truman, 1949–1953* (Norton, 1984; McCullough, David, *Truman* (Simon & Schuster, 1992); Truman, Harry S, *Memoirs,* 2 vols. (Doubleday, 1955, 1956).

M. Guy Bishop

TUNNER, WILLIAM HENRY (1906–   )

U.S. air force officer, Tunner was born in Elizabeth, New Jersey. He graduated from West Point in 1928. He entered the Air Corps and earned his pilot's wings. Early in World War II, he commanded the ferrying division of the Air Transport Command (ATC). As such, he oversaw the operations of the Women's Air Force Service Pilots. In July 1944, Tunner became commanding general of the India-China division of the ATC. He overhauled and greatly improved the efficiency of the air transport effort in the Far East. Supplies carried over the "Hump" (Himalayas) proved invaluable. After the war, Tunner managed the Berlin Airlift (1948–49). He repeated the feat (1950–51) in the Far East during the Korean War. Promoted to lieutenant general in 1953, Tunner retired in 1960 as commander of the Military Air Transport Service.

Steve R. Waddell

TURNER, STANSFIELD (1923–   )

U.S. naval officer, Turner was born in Chicago. He graduated from Annapolis in 1946. After service at sea, he attended Oxford University as a Rhodes scholar in international affairs. In 1953, during the last months of the Korean War, he served on a destroyer in the war zone. He again saw combat when he commanded the guided missile frigate *Horne* in Vietnamese waters. After duty as aide to secretaries of the navy Paul R. Ignatius and John H. Chafee, Turner was promoted to rear admiral. He then commanded a carrier task group in the Mediterranean (1970–71), had a tour as president of the Naval War College, commanded the 2d Fleet and commanded NATO (North Atlantic Treaty Organization) forces in southern Europe. Turner then replaced George Bush as head of the Central Intelligence Agency (CIA). His tenure at the CIA

(1977–81) was marked with controversy, including the Iranian hostage crisis.

Bibliography: Ledeen, Michael, "Tinker, Turner, Sailor, Spy," *New York* (Mar. 3, 1980); Reynolds, Clark G., *Famous American Admirals* (Van Nostrand-Reinhold, 1978).

Lloyd J. Graybar

TWINING, NATHAN FARRAGUT
(1897–1982)

U.S. air force officer and administrator, Twining was born in Monroe, Wisconsin. His first military experience was as a corporal with the Oregon National Guard on the Mexican border during Gen. John J. Pershing's Punitive Expedition against Pancho Villa in 1916. In June 1917, Twining entered West Point, from which he graduated on an accelerated wartime curriculum in November 1918. He then accepted a commission in the infantry.

After a brief tour with the army of occupation in Germany after World War I, Twining attended the Infantry School at Fort Benning. In 1923, he entered the flying school at Brooks Field, Texas. He became a thoroughgoing air power enthusiast over the next several years, and by the beginning of World War II, he and a number of other young officers had won virtual acceptance for the doctrine of air supremacy in the army.

World War II. Just after the U.S. entrance into World War II (December 1941), Twining transferred to the Air Corps Operations Division. From there his career took off. In February 1942, he was named assistant executive to the Army Air Forces chief of staff; in May, he became director of War Organization and Movements. From there he obtained an appointment as chief of staff of Army Air Forces (AAF) in the South Pacific. In the spring of 1943, he was named commander of the 13th Air Force, formed to handle air combat in the Solomon Islands. Twining amassed air forces, navy, and Marine Corps aircraft to destroy more than 700 Japanese aircraft during the second half of 1943, including the complete destruction of enemy air power over Bougainville.

On Jan. 3, 1944, Twining was sent to the Mediterranean theater of operations to assume command of the 15th Air Force. Later that same month, he was given the additional duty of commanding the Mediterranean Strategic Air Forces. In both positions, he oversaw the strategic bombardment of Italy, Austria, and Hungary. Most important, Twining commanded the aerial forces that conducted the disastrous attacks, beginning Apr. 4, 1944, that bombed 11 oil refineries at Ploesti, Rumania, later described by Lt. Gen. Ira Eaker as "the bloodiest single air battleground of the war." These attacks, made by 221 heavy bombers, practically eliminated Germany's principal source of oil.

After the end of the war in Europe, Twining returned briefly to the United States before succeeding Maj. Gen.

Curtis E. LeMay as commander of the 20th Air Force in the Marianas Islands of the Pacific. From that base in August 1945, Twining's bombers conducted brutal firebombing raids against Tokyo, and his 509th Composite Group dropped atomic bombs on Hiroshima and Nagasaki.

Postwar Promotions. With the conclusion of the war in the Pacific, Twining was sent to the United States and given command of the Air Matériel Command. In October 1947, he was assigned as commander in chief of the Alaskan Command, which had important responsibilities for aerial defense against the Soviet Union. He served there for almost two years and then was brought to Washington in May 1950 to serve as deputy chief of staff for personnel.

On Oct. 10, 1950, Twining became air force vice chief of staff and attained the rank of full general. At that time, the *Washington Post* characterized him as "something of an elder statesman in the Air Force despite his relative youth"—he was then 53 years old—because he could handle "tactical support as well as the strategic side of the Air Force job."

In the summer of 1952, Hoyt S. Vandenberg, the air force chief of staff, was hospitalized for an extended period. In his absence, Twining took over management of the air force and did a credible job. When the ailing Vandenberg eventually resigned his post, Twining was named as his permanent replacement, taking office in June 1953 and serving until August 1957.

During that period, he was a strong proponent of the nuclear deterrence strategy and aided the efforts of LeMay and others to make the Strategic Air Command the preeminent military force of the United States. Fielding an ever-more-capable succession of manned bombers during his tenure, Twining believed that "the steadily rising Communist strength in the air makes it increasingly necessary that Air Force personnel be on the alert at all times against sudden and heavy attack." As part of the nuclear deterrent, he presided over the air force's acquisition of the B-52 "Superfortress," as well as the beginnings of the air force's ballistic missile program.

Twining's commitment to the nuclear defense strategy was so strong that he advocated the use of nuclear weapons to relieve the French garrison at Dien Bien Phu, Vietnam, in 1954 before the French withdrew from Indochina. He argued that three tactical nuclear bombs would have allowed the French to win the battle and thereby remain in control in Southeast Asia. The use of nuclear weapons in Indochina, Twining also suggested, would have done more than just allow the French to hang on. It would have demonstrated the resolve of the United States to employ atomic weapons in virtually any combat scenario. Such a demonstration, he believed, would have ensured that the Soviet Union would have treated the possibility of U.S. interventions in other theaters more seriously.

Joint Chiefs of Staff Chairman. Twining's commitment to the nuclear strategy sat well with Pres. Dwight D. Eisenhower, who promoted him to chairman of the Joint Chiefs of Staff (JCS) in August 1957. As chairman, Twining continued to advocate the nuclear deterrent, seeing to fruition the ballistic missile program with the fielding of the first Jupiter and Atlas missiles and the advancing of the readiness of the strategic bomber force. He also supported the development of the first navy nuclear missile program, the Polaris system that could be launched from nuclear submarines.

Later Career. Near the end of the Eisenhower administration, Twining's strategic vision of nuclear deterrence began to be displaced by a more flexible response that saw nuclear warfare as only one type of combat that should be available to the president. The Democratic presidential candidate in 1960, John F. Kennedy, had adopted the latter idea, and his election would ensure that Twining could not serve effectively as chairman of the JCS. That possibility contributed to Twining's decision to retire, effective Sept. 30, 1960, even before the presidential contest had been decided.

Immediately after retirement, Twining was named vice chairman of the board of the publishing firm of Holt, Rinehart & Winston, a position he held until 1967. During much of that time, he worked on an analysis of postwar defense policy, *Neither Liberty Nor Slavery*, published in 1966. In it he traced the development of the nuclear deterrent strategy, offering a rationale for the arming of both bombers and ICBMs (intercontinental ballistic missiles) with nuclear weapons.

Bibliography: DuPre, Flint O., *U.S. Air Force Biographical Dictionary* (Franklin Watts, 1965); Hammond, Paul Y., *Organizing for Defense* (Princeton Univ. Press, 1961); Mrozek, Donald J., "Nathan F. Twining: New Dimensions, a New Look," *Makers of the United States Air Force,* ed. by John L. Frisbee (Office of Air Force History, 1987); Twining, Nathan F., *Neither Liberty Nor Slavery* (Holt, Rinehart & Winston, 1966).

Roger D. Launius

VANCE, CYRUS ROBERTS (1917–)

U.S. attorney and secretary of state, Vance was born in Clarksburg, West Virginia. He was special counsel to the Senate Armed Services Committee, then moved to the Pentagon as general counsel of the Department of Defense (1961–62) under Sec. Robert S. McNamara. He subsequently served as secretary of the army (1962–63) and then as deputy secretary of defense (1964–67) during the period of rapidly increasing U.S. involvement in the Vietnam War. During 1968–69, he was in Paris as a member of the U.S. negotiating team dealing with the North Vietnamese. His career was crowned by appointment as Pres. Jimmy Carter's secretary of state (1977–80), although he resigned in protest to a mission to rescue American hostages in Iran. From 1991, Vance served as a special United Nations envoy to try to resolve the civil war in Bosnia.

Bibliography: McLellan, Davis S., "Cyrus Vance," *American Secretaries of State and Their Diplomacy* (Rowman & Allanheld, 1985); Vance, Cyrus R., *Hard Choices: Critical Years in America's Foreign Policy* (Simon & Schuster, 1983).

Lewis Sorley

VANDENBERG, HOYT SANFORD
(1899–1954)

U.S. air force officer and administrator, Vandenberg was born in Milwaukee, Wisconsin. He graduated from West Point in 1923. He then attended the army flight school at Kelly Field, Texas, from which he entered the army's Aviation Section.

Vandenberg took to flying well, and his first assignment was to the elite 3d Attack Group. There followed a succession of appointments in various aero squadrons that distinguished him as an outstanding pilot and officer. He achieved his first major command in November 1929 when he took over the 6th Pursuit Squadron at Wheeler Field, Hawaii. Several other tours followed in the 1930s, notably attendance at the Air Corps Tactical School in 1935, where he learned the gospel of air superiority, and the Command and General Staff School, where he met Carl A. Spaatz, an individual who became both his friend and benefactor.

World War II. With the coming of World War II, Vandenberg's career took off. He was promoted to colonel in January 1942 and assigned as the Army Air Forces operations and training officer. Later in the year, he went to North Africa as the chief of staff for the 12th Air Force, commanded by Maj. Gen. James H. Doolittle. Vandenberg was very effective in this organization as it achieved air superiority in North Africa and played key roles in the taking of both Sicily and Italy.

Vandenberg stayed with the 12th Air Force until August 1943, when he returned to the United States and was assigned as deputy chief of the Army Air Forces headquarters staff. In the fall of 1943, he was also sent as a member of the U.S. mission to the Soviet Union. There, Vandenberg negotiated for bases used by U.S. bombers as part of the shuttle bombing concept of airplanes flying from England to bomb Germany and landing in the Soviet Union.

Vandenberg longed to get back into the action, however, and secured for himself in March 1944 an appointment as deputy to Britain's testy air vice marshal Sir Trafford Leigh-Mallory, commander of the Allied Expeditionary Air Force, which provided air support for the Normandy invasion. He was Sir Trafford's second for only a short time, as in July, Vandenberg was given command of the 9th Air Force in Europe. In this capacity, his force supported Gen. Omar Bradley's 12th Army Group on its drive across France and into Germany.

Postwar Career. Following the war, Vandenberg, by then a lieutenant general, was sent to the War Department General Staff as G-2 (Intelligence). In June 1946, he was appointed by Pres. Harry S Truman as director of the Central Intelligence Agency.

Vandenberg returned to the Air Force in April 1947 and was quickly tapped by Spaatz as his vice chief of staff of the newly independent U.S. Air Force. He took over as chief of staff when Spaatz retired in April 1948. Vandenberg presided over the air force for more than five years at the beginning of the Cold War. He was responsible for the air force's operations in the Berlin Airlift of 1948–49 and the Korean War of 1950–53.

To a very real extent, Vandenberg was the architect of the independent air force. In addition to major confrontations between the United States and the Soviet Union and the Peoples' Republic of China, Vandenberg was constantly involved in battles with the other services over roles, missions, and resources. Vandenberg built a solid place for the air force in these contests based on the doctrine of strategic deterrence.

Realizing that budgets were going to be slight, Vandenberg advocated "more bang for the buck" with nuclear weapons and structured the air force to achieve primacy in the Cold War era. He was an articulate and determined advocate for the air force who worked with the president and Congress to create an air arm with such tremendous striking power that no nation would dare to attack it. During his administration, the air force made the jump from prop-driven aircraft to the long-range jet bombers carrying atomic bombs. The air force also began the development of nuclear warhead ballistic missiles in earnest and achieved an operational capability with them in the latter 1950s. Near the conclusion of the Korean War, in June 1953, Vandenberg retired from the air force.

Bibliography: Copp, DeWitt S., *A Few Great Captains: The Men and Events that Shaped the Development of U.S. Air Power* (Doubleday, 1980); Meilinger, Philip S., *Hoyt S. Vandenberg: The Life of a General* (Indiana Univ. Press, 1989); Overy, R. J., *The Air War, 1939–1945* (Stein and Day, 1980).

Roger D. Launius

VAN FLEET, JAMES ALWARD
(1892–1992)

U.S. army officer, Van Fleet was born in Coytesville, New Jersey. He graduated from West Point in 1915, with the "class the stars fell on." Commissioned in the infantry, he commanded the 17th Machine-Gun Battalion of the 6th Division in the Meuse-Argonne Offensive in World War I. During the interwar years, Van Fleet served as a Reserve

Officers Training Corps instructor at Kansas State College, South Dakota State College, and the University of Florida. While in Gainesville, he also worked as head football coach. He served with the 42d Infantry in the Panama Canal Zone; the 5th Infantry at Fort Williams, Maine; and the 29th Infantry at Fort Benning, Georgia.

Van Fleet's early career stagnated when Gen. George C. Marshall confused him with an alcoholic officer with a similar name. Nevertheless, World War II found him a colonel in command of the 8th Infantry Regiment, 4th Infantry Division. Van Fleet trained his regiment for three years at various posts throughout the United States in preparation for the invasion of the European continent. On D-Day (June 6, 1944), Van Fleet led his unit ashore as part of 4th Infantry Division's assault on Utah Beach. Advancing from regimental to corps commander in nine months, and to the temporary rank of major general, Van Fleet served in Gen. George S. Patton's 3d Army and commanded III Corps in its drive across Germany.

Van Fleet served in stateside assignments at Fort Polk, Louisiana, and at Governor's Island, New York, before returning to Europe as the deputy chief of staff for the army's European Command. In February 1948, Pres. Harry S Truman appointed him director of the Joint U.S. Military Advisory and Planning Group, and he was promoted to lieutenant general. In this capacity, Van Fleet worked in Greece and Turkey to combat guerrilla insurgents. Because of his success in reorganizing and training Greek forces, he gained appointment to the Greek National Defense Council. In 1950, Van Fleet returned to the United States as commander of Second Army.

With Gen. Douglas MacArthur's relief and Gen. Matthew Ridgway's promotion in the spring of 1951, Van Fleet assumed command of the U.S. Eighth Army in Korea. His outlook differed little for MacArthur's in that he advocated total victory over the Chinese and the military reunification of Korea. His mission read otherwise: "You will direct the efforts of your forces toward inflicting maximum personnel casualties and material losses on hostile forces in Korea, consistent with the maintenance intact of all your major units and the safety of your troops." Consequently, Van Fleet prepared South Korean forces for offensive action while emphasizing the use of firepower in lieu of manpower. Believing that artillery contributed to 90 percent of United Nations Forces' successes, Van Fleet increased ammunition stockpiles to a 45-day supply— "Van Fleet's load." Using artillery and tactical air in support of limited attacks, Van Fleet directed assaults against the Punchbowl, bloody Ridge, and Heartbreak Ridge. He also improved and increased counterbattery, interdiction, and harassing fires. Van Fleet relinquished command of the 8th Army to Gen. Maxwell D. Taylor in February 1953 and retired that spring as a full general.

Maj. James Sanders Day

VINSON, CARL (1883–1981)

U.S. congressman noted for his advocacy of strong national defense, Vinson was born near Milledgeville, Georgia. He was elected to the U.S. House of Representatives from Georgia in 1914, becoming the youngest member in Congress at that time. He gained membership on the House Naval Affairs Committee in his first term and became chairman in 1931. Vinson soon became known for his support of naval preparedness. He received credit for helping to secure enactment of major funding measures in 1934 and 1940. In 1940, he was also identified with support of the Selective Service bill. During World War II, obtaining funds for naval expansion was no problem, but Vinson also backed other, more controversial measures. He sponsored legislation to curb strikes in defense industries and called for a ban on the employment of Communists, members of the German-American Bund, and anyone else suspected of un-American activities in defense industries.

Vinson remained chairman of the Naval Affairs Committee until 1947. From 1949 to 1964, he headed the House Armed Services Committee and continued to champion a strong national defense. Vinson was always known as a stern taskmaster in his chairmanship of a committee. He kept colleagues in line and pretended to forget the names of many generals and admirals who testified before his committee in order to remind them that he—representing Congress—was the boss. Over a 25-year period, he lost only three floor fights on bills reported by his committee. At the time of his retirement in 1964, he had served longer than any previous member of the House. One of a small group of long-serving congressmen from the South who were identified with many defense-related measures, Vinson's particular association with the navy was recognized when a nuclear carrier was named for him.

Lloyd J. Graybar

VUONO, CARL EDWARD (1934–)

U.S. army officer, Vuono was born in Monongahela, Pennsylvania. He graduated from West Point in 1957, attended the Air Defense Artillery School (1962), and was an exchange officer with Britain's 7th Royal Horse Artillery (1964–65). He stayed in Europe (1965–66) with the 7th Corps Artillery, the unit he served with in Vietnam (1966–67). After more schooling, staff positions, and a tour of duty with the 77th Artillery (1970–71), he assisted (1971–72) in the massive reorganization of the army following the Vietnam War. Graduating from the Army War College in 1973, Vuono held a series of staff assignments and commanded the 82d Airborne's artillery unit (1975). Promoted to brigadier general in 1977, he became assistant division commander of the 1st Infantry Division (1977–79) and then of the army's training and doctrine command.

Advanced to major general in 1982, Vuono briefly commanded the 8th Infantry Division in Europe. Head of the Combined Arms Center (1983–85), he became a lieutenant general. After commanding the army's training and doctrine command (1985–87), he was appointed chief of staff of the army, a position he held until his retirement in 1991.

As chief of staff, he envisioned a versatile, deployable, lethal, and expansible army and began the process of reorganization that would make the army a multitheater force, capable of fighting heavy battles as well as of rapid intervention as demonstrated during Operations Just Cause (Panama, 1989) and Desert Storm (Middle East, 1991).

Leo J. Daugherty III

WADE, SIDNEY SCOTT (1909–)

U.S. marine commander, Wade was born in Bloomington, Illinois. He graduated from Annapolis in 1933 and was commissioned in the Marine Corps. He subsequently served at sea, with the 4th Marines in China, with the III Marine Amphibious Corps in the Pacific in World War II, and in command of the 1st Marines in Korea (1951–52). In January 1958, following headquarters assignments in Washington, Wade assumed command of the 2d Provisional Marine Force at Camp Lejeune, North Carolina, and subsequently commanded all marine forces participating in the U.S. intervention in Beirut, Lebanon (July 15–Oct. 4, 1958). He later commanded Camp Lejeune and the Marine Corps Recruit Depot, San Diego. Following high-level positions with the Fleet Marine Force in both the Pacific and Atlantic, Wade was deputy chief of staff, commander in chief, Atlantic. Major General Wade retired in 1967.

Bibliography: Millett, Allan R., *Semper Fidelis: The History of the United States Marine Corps* (Macmillan, 1980); Parker, William D., *A Concise History of the United States Marine Corps, 1775–1969* (Historical Div., U.S. Marine Corps Hdqrs., 1970); Schuon, Karl, *U.S. Marine Corps Biographical Dictionary* (Franklin Watts, 1963).

Lt. Col. (Ret.) Charles R. Shrader

WALKER, WALTON HARRIS (1889–1950)

U.S. army commander, Walker was born in Belton, Texas. He graduated from West Point in 1912. During World War I, he commanded a machine-gun battalion in France. In the early 1930s, he commanded a battalion of the 15th Infantry Regiment in China. During World War II, he commanded XX Corps in Gen. George S. Patton's 3d Army. Patton once wrote that Walker, who was promoted to lieutenant general in 1945, was "a fighter in every sense of the word."

After World War II, he commanded the 5th Army for two years. In 1948, he took command of the 8th Army in Japan. At the beginning of the Korean War in 1950, he was faced with the enormous task of stopping the rapidly advancing North Korean army, while building a force that could eventually take the offensive. During those early days, he tenaciously and ferociously defended the Pusan perimeter, justifying his nickname of "Bulldog." His skillfull formation and defense of the perimeter allowed the time necessary to launch the Inchon landing, leading to the expulsion of the North Korean army from South Korea.

To retain his perimeter, Walker combined an extremely fine sense of timing and a judicious employment of the meager reserves he could gather at any one time. His viewpoint shifted almost constantly as factors changed in the fast-moving, confusing, and swirling struggles. He absolutely refused to give up any part of the perimeter without a bitter fight. Fortunately, he had an uncanny knack of moving reserves to the right place at the correct, decisive time.

Walker's command problems were legion. He had to analyze meticulously every action in progress, or which action was imminent. He had to make tactical decisions promptly, balancing the needs of one part of the perimeter against those of others. He utilized his small reserves and threatened, coerced, and exhorted U.S. and South Korean leaders.

On Dec. 23, 1950, Walker met an untimely death when his jeep was struck by a South Korean army truck. Although his army met defeat when the Chinese intervened in the Korean War, Walker's powerful leadership and extraordinary tactical skill won the critical Pusan perimeter campaign. Had he lost there, the war could have been lost in its first months.

Bibliography: Appleman, Roy E., *The U.S. Army in the Korean War: South to the Naktong, North to the Yalu* (Dept. of the Army, 1961); Blair, Clay, *The Forgotten War* (Times Books, 1987).

Brig. Gen. PNG (Ret.) Uzal W. Ent

WALT, LEWIS WILLIAM (1913–1990)

U.S. marine officer, Walt was born near Harveyville, Kansas. He graduated from Colorado State University and was commissioned a second lieutenant in the U.S. Marine Corps (1936). He then served in Shanghai (1937–39) and Guam (1939–40). During World War II, he fought with the 1st Marines in the Pacific, was wounded twice, and was awarded the Navy Cross twice.

Walt taught at officer's combat school at Quantico, Virginia (1945–47). After several tours of duty with the 1st Marine Division and commanding basic school at Quantico (1952–58), he worked at marine headquarters (1958–59) and attended the National War College (1960–61). He held posts at Camp Lejeune, North Carolina (1962—the same year he was promoted to brigadier general), and at Quantico (1963–65).

Promoted to major general in 1965, Walt was sent to command the 3d Marine Division (1965–68) in Vietnam, where as the senior marine general, he dealt with an ongoing pacification program. Advocating aggressive patrolling, along with effective civic action programs, he was able to reduce substantially the Viet Cong threat to the many villages. He introduced the Combined Action Platoon (CAP), a specially selected and trained marine rifle squad augmented with members of local militias. Made a full general in 1968, Walt served as assistant commandant of the U.S. Marine Corps until his retirement in 1971. Walt wrote *Strange War: Strange Strategy* (1970).

Leo J. Daugherty III

WALTERS, VERNON ANTHONY
(1917–)

U.S. army officer and diplomat, Walters was born in New York City. He enlisted in the army in 1941 and soon proved to possess extraordinary linguistic talents that shaped a singular career. He served in North Africa and Italy during World War II, entering Rome with Gen. Mark Clark, and subsequently as an attaché at several posts, including Rio de Janeiro and Paris. At international conferences all over the world, he served as interpreter for senior officials at the highest levels—Presidents Roosevelt, Truman, Eisenhower, and Nixon among them. Walters retired from the army a lieutenant general in 1976 after four years as deputy director of Central Intelligence. Subsequently appointed ambassador, he was U.S. permanent representative to the United Nations (1985–89) and ambassador to West Germany (1989–91).

Bibliography: Walters, Vernon A., *Silent Missions* (Doubleday, 1978).

Lewis Sorley

WEINBERGER, CASPAR WILLARD
(1917–)

U.S. secretary of defense, Weinberger was born in San Francisco, California. He graduated from Harvard Law School in 1941 and practiced law before enlisting in the army at the outbreak of World War II. He served with the 41st Infantry Division in the Pacific theater before switching over to the Signal Corps, where he served as an intelligence specialist on the staff of Gen. Douglas MacArthur.

After the war, Weinberger again practiced law and then entered politics, serving in the California state legislature (1952–58) and, during the 1960s, on various state committees. After a brief time in 1970 as head of the Federal Trade Commission, he was appointed by Pres. Richard M. Nixon to the new Office of Management and Budget; he became director in 1972. In 1973, he became Nixon's secretary of health, education, and welfare, a post he held until 1975.

Weinberger became best known as the secretary of defense who served through both of Pres. Ronald Reagan's terms (1981–89). Despite being a fiscal conservative, Weinberger managed one of the largest defense buildups in U.S. military history. He instituted a tight fiscal policy at the Pentagon in an effort to eliminate fraud and waste. During his tenure, he resurrected several key weapon systems that had been cut from the defense budget, and he developed the Strategic Defense Initiative, a space-based missile defense shield. Although sometimes accused of interference in U.S. foreign policy, Weinberger was responsible for the restoration of U.S. military power in the face of a strong challenge from the Soviet Union.

Leo J. Daugherty III

WESTMORELAND, WILLIAM CHILDS
(1914–)

U.S. army commander, Westmoreland was born near Spartanburg, South Carolina. He attended The Citadel, South Carolina's military college, for a year, then entered West Point. There, he was chosen first captain of the Class of 1936 and, upon graduation, was commissioned a lieutenant in the field artillery. His first assignment was to Fort Sill, Oklahoma, where he joined the 18th Field Artillery. Three years later, he was sent to Hawaii and the 8th Field Artillery at Schofield Barracks.

World War II. In mid-1941, Westmoreland was brought home to Fort Bragg, North Carolina, for duty with the 9th Infantry Division. The following spring, at the age of 28, he took command of its 34th Field Artillery Battalion, the unit he was destined to lead into combat. Initially, however, his battalion was left behind when the remainder of the division sailed to spearhead Operation Torch, the invasion of North Africa. The 34th caught up two months later, arriving administratively at Casablanca after the landings.

Westmoreland's outfit was in time to take part in the Battle of Kasserine Pass, however, arriving with other elements of the division artillery at a critical juncture and earning a Presidential Unit Citation for helping to stop Field Marshal Erwin Rommel's attacking German forces. Westmoreland subsequently became chief of staff of the 9th Division, then in postwar occupation duty commanded its 60th Infantry Regiment. For wartime duty, he received two Legions of Merit and the Bronze Star.

Career Development. Back in the United States in 1947, he was given command of the 504th Parachute Infantry Regiment in the 82d Airborne Division, his transition from artillery to a succession of line commands. Then, he served for three years as the division's chief of staff. Next, although he had not himself graduated from the institutions, he received successive assignments to the staff and faculty of the Command and General Staff College and the Army War College.

During the static third year of the Korean War, Westmoreland for a year commanded the 187th Regimental

For four critical years (1964–68) of the Vietnam War, Gen. William Westmoreland was commander of U.S. Military Assistance Command Vietnam. (U.S. Army)

Combat Team, another airborne unit, which was at various times during his tenure stationed in Korea and in Japan. He earned another Legion of Merit, along with another Bronze Star, and was promoted to brigadier general.

During the period of 1953–56, Westmoreland served his first Pentagon tours of duty. He began as a deputy assistant chief of staff for personnel, departing after a year for a brief management course at Harvard University. When he returned, he was made secretary of the General Staff under then Army Chief of Staff Gen. Maxwell D. Taylor and was promoted to major general.

During 1958–60, Westmoreland commanded the 101st Airborne Division at Fort Campbell, Kentucky. Next, he served for three years as superintendent of the Military Academy at West Point. Promoted to lieutenant general, Westmoreland returned to Fort Bragg, where he then took command of XVIII Airborne Corps. It proved to be a brief assignment, for after only six months, he was selected to go to Vietnam as deputy to the commander, U.S. Military Assistance Command Vietnam (MACV), Gen. Paul D. Harkins.

Vietnam War. Even as he assumed his new duties as deputy in January 1964, it was anticipated that before long

Westmoreland would move up to the top job, which he did in June 1964, the beginning of a four-year stint as the senior U.S. military officer in Vietnam. He simultaneously was promoted to four-star general.

Soon, escalation of U.S. involvement in the war was underway. The Gulf of Tonkin incident in early August 1964 provided the occasion for Pres. Lyndon B. Johnson to obtain congressional backing for the war by means of a resolution authorizing him to "take all necessary measures" to deal with aggression against South Vietnam. In the continuing absence of a formal declaration of war, the resolution—and periodic appropriations for support of the forces involved—provided the legal basis for continued prosecution of the conflict.

U.S. troop strength in Vietnam rose rapidly and dramatically as well. There had been some 16,000 U.S. personnel serving as advisers in South Vietnam when Westmoreland arrived as deputy. By the time Westmoreland finished his tour of duty four years later, the troop authorization would stand at 549,500, and he was pushing for yet another increment of more than 200,000 additional forces to be deployed.

The first combat forces were introduced in the spring of 1965, and by the end of that year, some 180,000 U.S. military personnel were serving in Vietnam, and Westmoreland had requested a buildup to 443,000 by the end of the following year.

Westmoreland's tactics centered around the "search and destroy" operation, in which large multibattalion forces conducted sweeps in remote areas, seeking to discover enemy forces and bring them to battle. The measure of merit under Westmoreland was the "body count," which accorded with his determination to wage a war of attrition. The essence of this approach was inflicting an unacceptably high level of casualties on the enemy while maintaining friendly casualties at "acceptable" levels. An important component was interdiction of the flow of supplies and replacements from North Vietnam to the battlefield. Theoretically, there would come a "crossover point" at which the enemy could no longer make up his losses, eroding his will to continue to fight and bringing about capitulation. This strategy did not succeed.

At the same time that U.S. forces were attempting to resolve the war by defeating the enemy on the battlefield, there were parallel problems of dealing with entrenched guerrillas in the populated areas and of improving the capabilities of the South Vietnamese armed forces so they could assume greater responsibility for defense of their own country. Under Westmoreland, these programs also languished.

As year after year went by with no end to the war in prospect, domestic opposition to U.S. involvement grew apace. Westmoreland continued to make a series of optimistic public pronouncements, particularly during the latter part of 1967 when, on a visit to the United States, he told audiences he was "absolutely certain that whereas in 1965 the enemy was winning, today he is certainly losing" and that "the enemy's hopes are bankrupt" and "we have reached an important point where the end begins to come into view."

When, at the end of January 1968, the Tet Offensive erupted with enemy attacks at virtually every important point across South Vietnam, including in the heart of Saigon, these prognostications proved to be overly optimistic. Although Westmoreland pointed out, with some justification, that the attacking forces had suffered heavily, the real battle took place in the United States. There, the enemy scored a decisive psychological victory.

When, in the wake of these battles, Westmoreland asked for another 206,000 troops, things began to come apart. Instead of additional troops, there followed a full-scale review and revision of U.S. policy on Vietnam, including the decisions to turn more of the fighting over to the South Vietnamese—dubbed "Vietnamization" of the war—while simultaneously progressively withdrawing U.S. forces. Soon, too, Westmoreland was replaced as commander of MACV and brought home to become army chief of staff.

Final Assignment. During fours years in the army's top uniformed post (1968–72), Westmoreland sought to cope with growing problems of indiscipline, drug abuse, racial disharmony, and internal dissent, at the same time devoting himself extensively to justifying his role in Vietnam and the results he had achieved. "As American commander in Vietnam," he wrote in reflecting on the experience, "I underwent many frustrations, endured much interference, lived with countless irritations, swallowed many disappointments, bore considerable criticism."

Retirement. Following his 1972 retirement from the army, Westmoreland ran an unsuccessful campaign (1974) to become governor of South Carolina. Then, one more celebrated episode brought him back into the public spotlight. It stemmed from the 1982 broadcast of a CBS television documentary entitled "The Uncounted Enemy: A Vietnam Deception." The program focused on enemy order of battle estimates prepared under Westmoreland's command in Vietnam and charged that they had been deliberately understated so as to deceive the president, the Congress, the media, and the public. Westmoreland sued CBS for libel. Eventually, the matter came to trial, but before a legal resolution of the issues had been reached, Westmoreland withdrew his suit in February 1985.

Bibliography: Furgurson, Ernest B., *Westmoreland: The Inevitable General* (Little, Brown, 1968); Palmer, Bruce, Jr., *The 25-Year War* (Univ. Press of Kentucky, 1984); Westmoreland, William C., *Report of the Chief of Staff of the United States Army: 1 July 1968 to 30 June 1972* (Dept. of the Army, 1977); ———, *A Soldier Reports* (Doubleday, 1976); Westmoreland, William C., and

U. S. G. Sharp, *Report on the War in Vietnam* (U.S. Govt. Printing Office, 1969).

Lewis Sorley

WEYAND, FREDERICK CARLTON
(1916–   )

U.S. army commander, Weyand was born in Arbuckle, California. He graduated from the University of California at Berkeley in 1939. He soon entered military service via the Reserve Officers Training Corps and was commissioned in the Coast Artillery Corps. During World War II, he was an intelligence officer in the China-Burma-India theater. After the war, in 1948, Weyand transferred to the infantry.

He took command of the 1st Battalion, 7th Infantry Regiment, in January 1953. When Gen. Matthew B. Ridgway, newly in command of the 8th Army, ordered a general offensive, the 7th Infantry became involved in some of the hardest fighting in the Korean War. Weyand's battalion was awarded a Presidential Unit Citation, and he won a Distinguished Service Cross.

Within the years 1966–73, Weyand had two lengthy tours of duty in South Vietnam, on the first serving as commanding general of the 25th Infantry Division, then of

In Paris from March 1969 to June 1970, Gen. Frederick Weyand served as military adviser to the U.S. team sent to negotiate a peace with the North Vietnamese. (National Archives)

II Field Force. He returned to Washington to be chief, Office of Reserve Components, on the army staff, then was posted to Paris (March 1969–June 1970) as part of the U.S. negotiating team dealing with the North Vietnamese. In 1970, he returned to Vietnam as deputy commander, U.S. Military Assistance Command Vietnam (MACV), under Gen. Creighton Abrams. When in June 1972 Abrams became army chief of staff, Weyand succeeded him as commander, MACV. Soon, the United States had phased its forces out of the war, however, and Weyand took command of U.S. Army, Pacific, in Hawaii.

In 1973, Abrams again sent for Weyand, this time to become his vice chief of staff. When, a year later, Abrams died in office, Weyand succeeded him as chief of staff, a post he held until his retirement as a full general in 1976.

Lewis Sorley

WEYLAND, OTTO PAUL (1902–1979)

U.S. air force commander, Weyland was born in Riverside, California. He graduated from the Air Corps Tactical School and from the Army Command and General Staff School, and by the time of U.S. entry into World War II (1941), Weyland was in command of the 16th Pursuit Group in the Panama Canal Zone. In February 1944, he was given command of the 19th Tactical Air Command, supporting Gen. George S. Patton's 3d Army in Europe. Weyland set up his command post next to Patton's and had his intelligence and operations officers keep in constant contact with their Patton counterparts. As a result, his command set new standards for joint-service teamwork.

In the Korean War, he utilized this tactical experience as vice commander for operations of the Far East Air Force. He briefly returned to the United States as deputy commander, U.S. Air Force Tactical Command. On June 10, 1951, Lieutenant General Weyland took command of the Far East Air Force and led it to the end of the war. He retired as a full general.

Bibliography: Futrell, Robert F., *The United States Air Force in Korea 1950–1953,* rev. ed. (Office of Air Force History, 1983); Weigley, Russell F., *Eisenhower's Lieutenants* (Indiana Univ. Press, 1981).

Brig. Gen. PNG (Ret.) Uzal W. Ent

WHEELER, EARLE GILMORE (1908–1975)

U.S. army officer and chief of staff, Wheeler was born in Washington, D.C. He served for four years in the District of Columbia National Guard before entering West Point. He graduated in 1932 and was commissioned in the infantry, with an initial assignment to the 29th Infantry Regiment at Fort Benning, Georgia (1932–36). In a later assignment, he was with the 15th Infantry in Tientsin,

China (1937–38), and he also taught mathematics at West Point (1940–41).

During World War II, Wheeler was the wartime chief of staff of the 63d Infantry Division in the European theater. During 1951–52, he commanded the 351st Infantry in Trieste. Following a series of staff assignments in the Pentagon and elsewhere, he commanded the 2d Armored Division in 1958–60.

Wheeler became director of the joint staff of the Joint Chiefs of Staff (JCS) in 1960, and in October 1962 army chief of staff. Less than two years later, he was appointed chairman of the JCS, a post he held until 1970. Those were the turbulent years of the U.S. buildup for and involvement in the Vietnam War, and Wheeler was a central figure in those events. He, like other senior military leaders, was dismayed that Pres. Lyndon B. Johnson had refused to call up reserve forces for the war in Vietnam. Wheeler made strenuous efforts to have the decision reversed, but to no avail.

In the wake of the enemy's 1968 Tet Offensive in Vietnam, he made one final attempt. Persuading the field commander, Gen. William C. Westmoreland, to ask for 206,000 more troops, Wheeler told the president it was essential to provide them. That would have necessitated calling up the reserves. The request precipitated a full-scale review of U.S. policy, which led to the decision to withdraw progressively and turn the fighting over to the South Vietnamese. Wheeler's ploy had failed. He retired in 1970 to a farm in West Virginia.

Bibliography: Halberstam, David, *The Best and the Brightest* (Random House, 1972); Davidson, Phillip B., *Vietnam at War: The History 1946–1975* (Presidio, 1988).

Lewis Sorley

WHITE, ISAAC DAVIS (1901–1990)

U.S. army commander, White was born in Peterboro, New Hampshire. He joined the cavalry in 1922 after graduating from Norwich University. During World War II, he served in the 2d Armored Division, advancing from full colonel in 1942 to major general and division commander in January 1945.

He fought in North Africa and Sicily, landed at Normandy (June 1944), and led the division across Germany to the Elbe River. White returned to the United States after the war to head (1946–48) the army's new Ground General School at Fort Riley, Kansas. The school provided general instruction for all new officers and training for army intelligence personnel as well. In 1948, White moved to Germany as commander of the U.S. Constabulary. U.S.-Soviet tensions had increased by the late 1940s, while the constabulary's original internal security mission had disappeared. Therefore, White supervised the constabulary's conversion into a modified armored cavalry division. Subsequently, White was promoted to lieutenant

As chairman of the Joint Chiefs of Staff (1964–70), Earle G. Wheeler (right)—shown with Pres. Richard Nixon (left) and Sec. of Defense Melvin Laird—was the senior U.S. military officer during the crucial years of the Vietnam War. (National Archives)

general (1952) and served as the commander of X Corps in Korea. He then became, after his promotion to full general (1955), commanding general of U.S. Army, Far East (1955–57) and commander in chief of U.S. Army, Pacific (1957–61), retiring after this last assignment.

Richard F. Kehrberg

WHITE, THOMAS DRESSER (1901–1965)

U.S. air force officer, White was born in Walker, Minnesota. After graduating from West Point in 1920, he served in the infantry before entering flight training in 1925. In addition to his combat command of the 7th Air Force in World War II during the Iwo Jima and Okinawa campaigns (1944–45), White showed expertise in dealing with foreign governments. He served as the language officer in the embassy in Peking (1928–31) and was the military air attaché to the Soviet Union, Italy, and Greece prior to World War II. After the war, he served as chief of staff of Far East Air Forces and as commanding general of the 5th Air Force (1951–53). White retired in 1961 as a full general after serving as air force chief of staff (1957–61), where he had directed the growth of American ICBM (intercontinental ballistic missile) capabilities.

Capt. Michael J. Reed

WICKHAM, JOHN ADAMS, JR. (1928–   )

U.S. army officer and chief of staff, Wickham was born in Dobbs Ferry, New York. He joined the infantry after graduating from West Point in 1950. Wounded in action while serving with the 1st Cavalry Division in Vietnam, he subsequently held a series of important posts, including commander of the 8th Army in Korea. In July 1983, Pres.

Ronald Reagan appointed Wickham, a full general, army chief of staff.

Wickham assumed office just as the army was beginning to feel the full weight of the Reagan defense buildup. Increased funding allowed the army to speed up purchases of new equipment, such as the M-1 tank, begun under Wickham's predecessor, Gen. Edward C. Meyer. Furthermore, the number of regular army divisions expanded from 16 to 18, and the number of reserve divisions from 8 to 10. This expansion required a sizable reshuffling of army base and housing arrangements. Notably, Wickham stressed the need to care for military families during these changes.

Another development during Wickham's tenure was the advent of the light division. Based on its experience in the Vietnam War and concerned about Latin American insurgencies, the army designed the light division to fight in rugged terrain with a minimum of heavy equipment and to be easily transportable. U.S. concerns over Latin America also prompted an increase in military assistance to the area. Moreover, during the mid-1980s, army training and maneuvers in the region expanded, most noticeably in Honduras. Wickham retired from the army in 1987.

Richard F. Kehrberg

WILSON, CHARLES ERWIN (1890–1961)

U.S. businessman and secretary of defense (1953–57), Wilson was born in Minerva, Ohio. He worked as an electrical engineer for Westinghouse Electric and Manufacturing Company and then joined General Motors in 1919. He became vice president of General Motors in 1929, a director in 1934, and then its president (1941–53).

In 1953, Wilson was appointed secretary of defense under Pres. Dwight D. Eisenhower. His period in office was plagued by interservice rivalry and bitter defense budget debates. He was a staunch supporter of Eisenhower's defense policy, as shown in the 1953 debate over a $5 billion reduction in the air force budget and the dissension surrounding the defense program of 1955–56. Wilson was a steady advocate of a strong military and treated circumspectly the friendly overtures of peace made by the Soviets at the Geneva Conference (1955). He increased military spending for that year by $285 million and refused to limit defense spending merely to balance the budget.

In 1956, Wilson faced disputes regarding the comparative military powers of the United States and the Soviet Union. To strengthen the much-criticized guided-missile program, he appointed Edgar Murphee as his civilian aide to coordinate the program and to arbitrate interservice arguments regarding the viability of particular weapons in the guided-missile program. Wilson opposed the proposed cessation of both the draft and H-bomb testing as irresponsible.

Russell A. Hart

WRIGHT, WILLIAM HENRY STERLING (1907–   )

U.S. army officer and administrator, Wright was born in Duluth, Minnesota. He graduated from West Point in 1930 and was commissioned in the cavalry. He was a member of the Army Equestrian Team (1937–40) and a tactical officer at West Point (1940–42) before serving as aide-de-camp to the secretary of war (1942–44) and as provost marshal of the U.S. 1st Army in Europe and the Pacific (1944–45). Wright was later chief of the U.S. Korean Military Advisory Group (1948–50) and played a key role in the early days of the Korean War. He subsequently served as deputy director of military assistance in the Office of the Secretary of Defense (1959–61), commanded the 2d Armored Division (1961–63), and was chief of the Office of Reserve Components, Department of the Army (1963–65). Lt. Gen. Wright retired in 1965.

Bibliography: Sawyer, Robert K., *Military Advisors in Korea: KMAG in Peace and War* (Office of the Chief of Military History, U.S. Army, 1962).

Lt. Col. (Ret.) Charles R. Shrader

YARBOROUGH, WILLIAM PELHAM (1912–   )

U.S. army air officer and military adviser, Yarborough was born in Seattle, Washington. He graduated from West Point in 1936 and was commissioned a second lieutenant in the infantry. As a test officer for the Provisional Parachute Group in 1941, he was responsible for designing the paratrooper's boot, uniform, qualification badge, and a number of aerial delivery containers for which he received U.S. patents. He was the airborne adviser for Gen. Mark Clark and, as such, developed the initial plan for the airborne phase of the North African invasion. He commanded the 2d Battalion, 504th and 509th Parachute Infantry Regiment, 82d Airborne Division, during the Sicilian invasion, and on D-Day (June 6, 1944) organized the night-drop zone as part of Darby's Ranger Force. Yarborough was provost marshal U.S. Forces in Austria (1945–47) and organized the Four Power International Patrol. He was deputy chief U.S. Military Advisory and Assistance Group Cambodia and other command and airborne command assignments. He commanded the John F. Kennedy Center for Special Warfare (1961). He was a senior member of the United Nations Command in Korea (1964–66; 1968–69) and was assistant deputy chief of staff Military Operations for Special Operations (1966–68). He retired as a lieutenant general in 1971.

Byron Hayes

YEAGER, CHARLES (CHUCK) ELWOOD (1923–   )

U.S. air force officer and aeronautics specialist, Yeager was born in Myra, West Virginia. He enlisted in the Army

Air Corps shortly before the outbreak of World War II and underwent pilot training in 1942. In 1943, he flew P-39s in Europe, completing 64 combat missions and shooting down 13 enemy planes by the end of the war. After destroying two enemy aircraft in March 1944, Yeager was shot down over German territory but escaped capture by crossing the Pyrenees Mountains into neutral Spain. He then rejoined his unit and flew another 55 missions, shooting down another 11 airplanes.

After the war, Yeager went to Muroc Air Base, California, to work on the X-1 experimental rocket-plane program. On Oct. 14, 1947, he flew the Bell X-1 faster than the speed of sound, becoming the first to break the sound barrier. During the next two years, he flew the X-1 on more than 40 flights, exceeding 1,000 miles per hour and 70,000 feet in altitude. In December 1953, Yeager flew the X-1A at 1,650 miles per hour. The next year, he went to Germany to command a fighter squadron and then went to George Air Force Base, California, in 1957 to head an F-100 squadron. He retired as a brigadier general in 1975, having spent much of his career in fighter test activities. After his retirement, he became a celebrity as a spokesman in commercials for industrial products.

Bibliography: Yeager, Chuck, and Leo Janos, *Yeager: An Autobiography* (Bantam Books, 1985).

Roger D. Launius

ZUMWALT, ELMO RUSSELL, JR.
(1920–   )

U.S. naval commander, Zumwalt was born in San Francisco, California. Upon graduation from Annapolis in 1942, he was assigned to the destroyer *Phelps*. In 1943, he was transferred to the destroyer *Robinson,* where he worked in the ship's combat information center and won a Bronze Star for bravery at Surigao Strait during the crucial Battle of Leyte Gulf. He remained on the *Robinson* until war's end, rising to lieutenant. With cessation of hostilities, Zumwalt commanded 20 men on-board a captured Japanese gunboat, the *Ataka,* and sailed up the Yangtze and Whangpoo rivers in China. His ship became the first unit flying the U.S. flag to enter Shanghai.

After the war, Zumwalt became executive officer on the destroyers *Saufley* and *Zellars,* then served in the Korean War as navigator for the battleship *Wisconsin.* Following a year of classes at the Naval War College, he ran the Shore and Overseas Section of the Bureau of Naval Personnel in Washington, D.C., from 1953 to 1955. In 1959, Commander Zumwalt was selected as the initial commanding officer of the new guided-missile frigate *Dewey.* He then attended the National War College in Washington for 10 months. While at the college, Zumwalt delivered a lecture about the Soviet Union that brought him to the attention of Paul H. Nitze, assistant secretary of defense for

international affairs, who had Zumwalt assigned to his staff. A long friendship developed between the naval officer and politician, and when Nitze became secretary of the navy in 1963, Zumwalt went with him as executive assistant and senior aide. In 1965, Zumwalt was promoted to rear admiral and placed in charge of Cruiser-Destroyer Flotilla Seven. He returned to Washington the next year to head the Systems Analysis Division of the Office of the Chief of Naval Operations.

Vietnam War Era. In September 1968, Zumwalt received his most challenging assignment to date when he became the commander of U.S. naval forces in Vietnam. Promoted to vice admiral, he was responsible for all naval operations in Vietnam. He quickly instituted an enormous operation called SEALORDS (Southeast Asia Lake, Ocean, River, Delta Strategy), to interdict North Vietnamese river and canal supply lines from Cambodia into South Vietnam. Allied units also assaulted Viet Cong strongholds in the Mekong Delta, U Minh Forest, and the Ca Mau Peninsula. SEALORDS successfully reduced the flow of supplies to the Viet Cong and raised navy morale in South Vietnam by finally handing them a recognizable front in which to battle the enemy.

A project that Zumwalt termed "one of my favorite wild ideas"—called Sea Float—placed 11 huge pontoons in the Cua Lon River at Nam Cam, a city that had been largely deserted after the Tet Offensive in early 1968. Zumwalt hoped that, by placing a powerful presence in the area and combining it with medical and economic assistance to the local inhabitants, people would again return to the area. This, too, met with success. Simultaneously, in light of Pres. Richard M. Nixon's wish, Zumwalt gradually brought South Vietnamese forces into his operations, with the goal of eventually handing over control to the South Vietnamese Navy.

In July 1970, Zumwalt, as a full admiral, became the youngest officer to hold the post of chief of naval operations. As he did in Vietnam, Zumwalt wasted little time instituting bold changes. In a series of more than 120 messages known as "Z-grams," Zumwalt attempted to bring the navy more in tune with the changing times. He eased hair styles, relaxed liberty restrictions for ships' crews, established a grievance system for naval personnel, and committed the navy to equal opportunity for minorities and women. Critics, a number from within the navy, lambasted Zumwalt's moves as a desire to gain popularity—and racial disturbances on-board some ships in 1972 fueled their objections—but Zumwalt defended his changes as necessary to make the navy more attractive to modern youth. A second program, designed to eliminate navy dependence on World War II ships, called for the replacing of a number of these older ships with smaller, low-cost ships with specialized capabilities. Zumwalt received more heated criticism on this program, especially in light of the fact that the number of major warships dropped from 769 to 512 during his tenure. Before he could complete his renovations, Zumwalt retired on July 1, 1974.

Later Activities. During retirement, Zumwalt defended his policies in a 1976 book titled *On Watch*. He unsuccessfully ran for a U.S. Senate seat from Virginia in the same year, then worked as a business executive in Milwaukee, Wisconsin. In 1986, he produced a second book, co-authored with his son, Elmo Zumwalt III. Called *My Father, My Son,* the touching book recounted the story of the admiral's son in Vietnam as a naval officer and of his struggle with cancer after the war, a cancer attributed to the son's exposure to Agent Orange, a chemical defoli-ant widely used in Vietnam. Ironically, his own father had ordered its use during his tenure as commander of U.S. naval forces. The son died from the disease shortly after the book's appearance.

Bibliography: Marolda, Edward J., and G. Wesley Pryce, III, *A Short History of the United States Navy and the Southeast Asian Conflict, 1950–1975* (Naval Hist. Center, 1984); Wukovits, John F., "Enemy Supply Lines Assaulted," *Vietnam Magazine* (Apr. 1991); Zumwalt, Elmo R., Jr., *On Watch* (Quadrangle Books, 1976); Zumwalt, Elmo R., Jr., and Elmo Zumwalt III, with John Pekkanen, *My Father, My Son* (Macmillan, 1986).

John F. Wukovits

PART III

Battles and Events

ADMIRALS, REVOLT OF THE
(October 1949)

Name given to a post-World War II protest by high-ranking U.S. naval personnel who questioned the equity of U.S. defense administration decisions in regard to the navy's status among the armed forces. Although the U.S. Navy had emerged from World War II with unprecedented might, its postwar leaders felt anxious about the future. Air force B-29s had delivered the two atom bombs dropped on Japan and remained the only type of plane capable of using this weapon. Demobilization meant that hundreds of ships were scrapped or mothballed. The three services were made independent but supposedly unified under a single secretary of defense by the National Security Act of 1947; in practice, they vied for maximum shares of a shrinking defense budget. In particular, the air force now claimed to be the nation's first line of defense—the traditional mission of the navy—and wanted funds for the B-36, the first intercontinental strategic bomber. In turn, the navy had to establish its capacity to deliver A-bombs; to do so it needed planes capable of handling atom bombs as well as a new 65,000-ton super-carrier able to accommodate the larger, longer-range planes then being developed.

Construction of such a carrier, the *United States*, was approved and the keel laid down, but on Apr. 23, 1949, Sec. of Defense Louis Johnson, who had been in office only a month, cancelled the carrier. The secretary of the navy resigned to be replaced by Francis Matthews, a friend of Johnson. Chief of Naval Operations (CNO) Louis Denfeld remained hopeful, however, of reconciling the differences among the armed services and between the navy and its civilian superiors.

In September, with tensions over funding and other defense issues continuing, a navy captain, John G. Crommelin, Jr., broke regulations and gave to the press a statement critical of Johnson and the Joint Chiefs; he thought the army and air force chiefs were combining to outvote the CNO. Several admirals endorsed Crommelin's contentions, bringing to a head the "Revolt of the Admirals." Some weeks later, in hearings held on "Unification and Strategy" by the House Armed Services Committee, Adm. Arthur Radford, perhaps the navy's most influential aviator and the current commander in chief, Pacific, attacked the B-36 as vulnerable to fighter interception and claimed that a super-carrier and appropriate naval aircraft were needed to provide an alternate weapons system to the giant bomber. Reliance upon it, Radford further argued, reflected the misguided strategy that future wars could be won quickly and cheaply by employing an atomic blitz. Since the secretary of the navy had already referred to the revolt as mere grumbling by malcontents, CNO Denfeld, testifying after Radford, made a forceful presentation of the navy's case for the super-carrier while criticizing De-

partment of Defense procedures that had sanctioned large purchases of the B-36 before the plane had been thoroughly evaluated. Matthews gained permission to transfer Denfeld, who resigned and took his case to the popular press.

The worst was now over. In its final report issued in early 1950, the House Armed Services Committee sought to promote conciliation. Adm. Forrest Sherman, the new CNO, proved more adroit than Denfeld in his handling of matters, and in April 1950, Congress approved construction of a super-carrier that would be named *Forrestal* to honor Johnson's predecessor. The outbreak of war in Korea gave the navy renewed opportunity to demonstrate its vital role in defense and to emphasize the need for more funds for the next generation of ships, not just super-carriers but nuclear-powered submarines and more.

Bibliography: Davis, Vincent, *The Admirals Lobby* (Univ. of North Carolina Press, 1952); Palmer, Michael A., *Origins of the Maritime Strategy: American Naval Strategy in the First Postwar Decade* (Naval Hist. Center, 1988); Potter, E. B., *Admiral Arleigh Burke: A Biography* (Random House, 1990); Reynolds, Clark G., "Forrest Percival Sherman," *The Chiefs of Naval Operations*, ed. by Robert William Love, Jr. (Naval Inst. Press, 1980).

Lloyd J. Graybar

AIR AMERICA

Airline connected with the U.S. government in Southeast Asia during the Cold War, Air America operated transport aircraft and helicopters mostly flown by ex-U.S. military pilots. Air America was a registered U.S. company, one that grew out of the American-owned, Taiwan-based Civil Air Transport. Air America was involved in U.S. intelligence-gathering operations but mostly was used in delivering supplies to U.S.-supported minorities in Southeast Asia. Additionally, organs of the U.S. government, including the military, often contracted with the company for transport services. Air America was equipped with obsolescent military aircraft capable of paradrop and of using short, unimproved airfields. Additionally, the company bought and used a number of civilian-model aircraft and was given some military helicopters. Maintenance personnel and some of the company's crewmen were foreign nationals including Thais and Filipinos. The company's most celebrated operations occurred in Laos.

Bibliography: Robbins, Christopher, *Air America* (Putnam's, 1979).

Col. (Ret.) Rod Paschall

ANZUS TREATY (September 1951)

Mutual defense treaty signed by the United States, Australia, and New Zealand, the first in a series of agreements regarding U.S. national security in the Pacific and part of the final peace conference between the United States and

Japan in San Francisco. Developed during the Korean War, it was designed primarily as a base agreement for dealing with a remilitarized Japan and growing Soviet and Chinese power in the region. The treaty was not binding nor did it provide for an immediate military response in case of attack on one or more signatories. Instead, it created a council of foreign ministers for the implementation of the treaty, and it did foster a mutual sense of unanimity among the three allied nations. Opposition to the treaty came primarily from the U.S. Joint Chiefs of Staff, who preferred an informal set of defensive arrangements and individual treaties.

Leo J. Daugherty III

ARMORED PERSONNEL CARRIERS

Military vehicles initially designed to transport troops in combat and later enhanced for combat roles as well. In order to allow the infantry to keep up with tank units, the U.S. Army introduced the M-75 and M-59 armored personnel carriers (APCs) in the 1950s. Both were full-tracked, fully enclosed armored vehicles. The M-59, however, was lighter, amphibious, and air transportable. The M-113 continued this idea in the 1960s and made extensive use of aluminum armor in order to keep its weight down. These early designs were lightly armed and in-

The aluminum-armor design of this M-113 armored personnel carrier made for a lighter vehicle than previous models. The M-113 gave way to the more heavily armed M-2 in the 1980s. (U.S. Army)

tended mainly to transport troops. In the late 1960s, the army became interested in a vehicle that could both move troops and fight. It was not until the 1980s, however, that the M-2 "Bradley" began replacing the M-113. Fast, protected from both conventional and chemical weapons, and heavily armed with a 25-millimeter cannon and TOW (tube-launched, optically-guided, wire-tracked) antitank missiles, the M-2 provided the infantry with an APC that could not only move them into battle, but also materially aid them once there.

Richard F. Kehrberg

ARMY-McCARTHY HEARINGS (1954)

The televised hearings that began in April 1954 and that became known as the Army-McCarthy hearings were the culmination of Wisconsin Republican Sen. Joseph R. McCarthy's investigation of alleged Communist influences in American life, particularly the federal government. Since 1950, when he announced that he had a list of Communists in the State Department, McCarthy had made headlines and accumulated great power by denouncing and investigating "Communists." He used his chairmanship of the Senate's Permanent Investigating Subcommittee of the Government Operations Committee as a forum for his anti-Communist rhetoric, which became known as McCarthyism.

McCarthy first became embroiled with the army when he investigated in late 1953 and early 1954 the Signal Corps Engineering Laboratory at Fort Monmouth, New Jersey, for Communist influences. Then, a conflict developed between McCarthy and Sec. of the Army Robert Stevens, with McCarthy accusing the army of attempting to force him to end the Fort Monmouth investigation and with the army charging McCarthy of seeking favoritism for a former associate who was an army private. Until this point, most McCarthy targets had avoided standing up to the senator, but army special counsel Joseph Welch, a Boston attorney, was often aggressive in dealing with McCarthy and subcommittee counsel Roy Cohn during the hearings, which started on April 22 and lasted until June 17. McCarthy participated directly in the hearings, rather than as a member of the subcommittee. Public opinion came to support the army's contention that McCarthy had improperly sought favored treatment for G. David Shine, a former associate, and that the allegations of Communist influence at Fort Monmouth were unfounded. Although the subcommittee's final report cleared McCarthy of using "improper influence," his extreme performance during the hearings discredited him. In August 1954, the Senate began an investigation into McCarthy's conduct, and in December the full Senate condemned his behavior at the hearings by a vote of 67–22. Essentially, McCarthyism's power had been broken by the firm stance of the army.

Bibliography: Fried, Richard M., *Nightmare in Red: The McCarthy Era in Perspective* (Oxford Univ. Press, 1990); Griffith, Robert, *The Politics of Fear: Joseph R. McCarthy and the Senate,* 2nd ed. (Univ. of Mass. Press, 1987).

Stephen Robinson

ARMY OF THE REPUBLIC OF VIETNAM

The largest of South Vietnam's armed forces, the Army of the Republic of Vietnam (ARVN) was begun in 1949 as the Vietnamese National Army under French control. It became independent of France on Oct. 26, 1955. For 20 years, the army was constantly engaged in combat. It collapsed before an onslaught of North and South Vietnamese Communist troops in April 1975.

Assisted and advised by U.S. Army personnel from 1955 until 1972, ARVN was plagued by a number of problems. Since it was the primary defense arm for the young republic and since the government continuously faced armed attack, there was never enough time to conduct proper training for either enlisted troops or officers. Second, until 1962, ARVN was competing for resources and authority against other armed South Vietnamese organizations because Prime Minister Ngo Dinh Diem believed he needed to balance power among several forces in order to survive as the country's leader. His suspicions were correct: ARVN officers were usually involved in some plot against their country's leader and continued to be highly political in the years after Diem's assassination (1963). All of this put a premium on political reliability as opposed to competence in battle. Therefore, ARVN's leaders, unlike many of their Communist adversaries, were not the products of a combat merit process. And, the South Vietnamese army was dependent on American material support, support that was withheld from it by U.S. refusal to supply sufficient ammunition, spare parts, and fuel during the 1975 North Vietnamese invasion.

The Army of the Republic of Vietnam, called ARVN, received intensive training from the U.S. Army from 1955 until 1972. (National Archives)

Bibliography: Cao Van Vien and Dong Van Khuyen, *Reflections on the Vietnam War* (U.S. Govt. Printing Office, 1980); Tran Van Don, *Our Endless War* (Presidio, 1978).

Col. (Ret.) Rod Paschall

ARVN (*see* Army of the Republic of Vietnam)

A SHAU VALLEY, BATTLE OF THE
(May 1969)

Fierce fighting that occurred between North Vietnamese Army (NVA) units and 2,800 allied (principally U.S.) troops sent to interdict supply routes through the A Shau Valley, located near the South Vietnam-Laos border. In Operation Apache Snow, allied units were dropped along the border in a heliborne assault on May 10. The next day, they encountered entrenched North Vietnamese forces on Hill 937—called Ap Bia Mountain by the Vietnamese but soon to become known as Hamburger Hill. Bloody fighting to wrest control of the hill from the NVA continued for 10 days until, on May 20, four allied battalions swept to the top. Finding no trace of NVA soldiers, allied forces were soon ordered to abandon the hill for which so much blood had been shed, an action that roused bitter antiwar feelings in the United States.

Bibliography: Page, Tim, and John Pimlott, *Nam: The Vietnam Experience* (Mallard Press, 1988); Pearson, Willard, *The War in the Northern Provinces* (U.S. Govt. Printing Office, 1975).

John F. Wukovits

ATTACK HELICOPTERS

U.S. military aircraft developed during the Vietnam War era. As the U.S. Army began to experiment with the idea of a heliborne division in the early 1960s, it recognized the need to develop "flying artillery" to support the infantry. Rather than build a special machine to fulfill this role, the army decided to mount rocket pods onto its existing utility helicopters. The Vietnam War proved the worth of attack helicopters, but these armed utility machines were vulnerable to ground fire. Therefore, the army began searching for a purpose-built attack helicopter. In 1966, Lockheed received a contract to produce 10 prototype AH-56 "Cheyenne" helicopters. The Cheyenne would not be ready for years, however, so the military turned to Bell's privately developed AH-1G "Cobra" as an interim measure. The first Cobras arrived in Southeast Asia in 1967 and proved to be tough, reliable, and popular with their crews.

High costs and development problems forced the cancellation of the Cheyenne project in 1972, and the Cobra was utilized after the Vietnam War in several updated versions. The army still sought an improved attack helicopter, but it

The first AH-1G Cobra attack helicopters arrived in Vietnam in 1967 and proved so efficient that the U.S. military relied on them for many years. (U.S. Army)

now viewed the new machine primarily as an antitank weapon. After a decade of development, the army received its first AH-64 "Apache" helicopters in 1985. Fast, heavily armored, and equipped with sophisticated targeting and navigation avionics, the Apache's main weapon was the new Hellfire antitank missile. The combination first saw action in the Persian Gulf War in 1991 and proved very effective against Iraqi armored vehicles and bunkers.

Bibliography: Gunston, Bill, *AH-64 Apache* (Osprey, 1986); Zaloga, Steven J., and George J. Balin, *Anti-Tank Helicopters* (Osprey, 1986).

Richard F. Kehrberg

ATTLEBORO, OPERATION
(November 1966)

Allied offensive—conducted just north of Saigon in the fall of 1966 against elements of the Viet Cong 9th Division—that resulted in the largest number of Communist casualties in South Vietnam in the Vietnam War to that date. The operation was begun by a newly arrived U.S. unit, the 196th Light Infantry Brigade. Elements of the brigade discovered a large Communist rice cache and a revealing map detailing a number of Viet Cong installations in the deep jungle areas of War Zone C. The brigade was reinforced by units from the U.S. 25th Infantry Division and began exploiting the intelligence. Heavy contacts with Communist units soon resulted, and U.S. forces throughout the region were funneled into the combat area. Operation Attleboro progressed throughout November 1–25 and resulted in 1,106 Communist deaths and 44 Viet Cong prisoners. The Viet Cong 9th Division was forced to flee to Cambodia. The allies lost 107 men killed in action.

Bibliography: Marshall, S. L. A., *Ambush: The Battle of Dau Tienq* (Battery Press, 1983).

Col. (Ret.) Rod Paschall

BAY OF PIGS INVASION
(April 15–20, 1961)

Failed attempt by anticommunist Cuban exiles and the Central Intelligence Agency (CIA) to overthrow Fidel Castro's regime; one of the greatest U.S. foreign policy failures of the Cold War era. American intelligence reports in 1959–60 revealed sharp increases in the flow of Soviet weaponry into Cuba, and Castro's campaign to nationalize U.S. interests there was an acute embarrassment to the United States. In late 1960, with approval from the Dwight D. Eisenhower administration, the CIA began to train a brigade of Cuban exiles in Florida for an invasion of the island. Their objective, after establishing a beachhead at the Bay of Pigs, was to spark a general uprising against Castro's regime. After receiving an upbeat briefing from Richard Bissell, chief of the CIA's Clandestine Service, recently inaugurated Pres. John F. Kennedy gave the green light for the invasion.

On the morning of April 15, six World War II-vintage U.S. B-26 bombers, flown by Cuban pilots, attacked the Cuban air force on the ground, hoping to diminish Castro's ability to halt the amphibious assault that was to follow at three separate landing points. Members of Brigade 2506 began to disembark from their landing craft at 1:15 A.M., April 17. Unexpected coral reefs slowed the landing, and much of the heavy equipment, including tanks, never got ashore. The landing force, which consisted of some 1,400 men, was rapidly pinned down by heavy artillery fire and strafing from the Cuban air force's T-33 jet trainers. By April 20, the exiles, having expended most of their ammunition and lacking adequate air cover, had been routed. During the invasion, 114 brigade members died; the remainder were taken prisoner. Castro's losses have been estimated at about 1,600 killed in action.

Once it was clear that the attack had been sponsored by the CIA, anti-American demonstrations erupted throughout Latin America. Castro released 1,189 prisoners in December 1962 in exchange for $62,000,000 in food and medicine that had been raised by private sources in the United States.

President Kennedy took full responsibility for the debacle, although recent scholarship suggests that the CIA plan was based on overly optimistic assessments of what the exiles could accomplish. The failure of the raid prompted the retirement of a number of CIA officials, including Bissell and Director Allen Dulles. The invasion marked the end of what historians have called the "golden age of covert action" for the CIA.

Bibliography: Higgins, Turnbull, *The Perfect Failure: Kennedy, Eisenhower and the CIA at the Bay of Pigs* (Norton, 1989).

James A. Warren

BERLIN BLOCKADE AND AIRLIFT
(June 1948–May 1949)

Antagonistic Soviet action and subsequent Allied reaction that arose from the unique situation in Europe at the end of World War II. The victorious Allies divided Germany and Berlin into four zones, one each for France, Great Britain, the United States, and the Soviet Union. As Soviet-American relations deteriorated during 1946 and 1947, jointly occupied Berlin, which was deep inside the Soviet zone, began to be the focus of confrontation between the two ideologies.

In early 1948, the Soviets began to exploit the vulnerability of the other (or Western) Allies' position in Berlin by stopping coal deliveries to the Western-controlled sections of the city. A larger crisis arose in April when the Soviets restricted rail traffic into Berlin in a "mini-blockade" to protest the development of a proposed West German state. The Western Allies responded with what became known as the "little airlift" as local transport aircraft, mostly C-47s, carried enough supplies into Berlin to overcome the short-lived blockade.

Blockade.   When Allied efforts on behalf of the establishment of an independent West Germany did not end during the spring of 1948, the Soviets, on June 24, cut off all supply of food and electricity to Berlin, claiming that it was the result of "technical difficulties."

From the Soviet perspective, the blockade of Berlin represented an opportunity to gain a valuable prize, the city itself, at very little risk. All the alternatives open to the Western Allies appeared inadequate. If they remained in Berlin they would be unable to supply their sectors of the city. If they tried to force a supply convoy through the Soviet occupation zone, war could result. The Russians did not believe the Allies would risk war, and if they did, world opinion would label them responsible for a third world war. Moreover, Soviet officials believed that they had sufficient forces in the area to quickly expel the Allies from Germany if fighting began.

Airlift.   Gen. Lucius D. Clay, American commander in Germany, immediately anticipated using aircraft to overcome any blockade. When the Russians slammed the doors to Berlin, he organized the C-47 transports in theater into a massive airlift. Clay began the first airlift flights using 102 C-47s on June 26. The British also furnished some "Dakota" transports to carry a share of the tonnage. That first day of the airlift, American crews took 80 tons of milk, flour, medicine, and other high-priority cargo to the city on 32 C-47 flights.

Within a month, the airlift was proving successful, but not spectacular. Clay had early estimated that 4,500 tons of supplies would be needed each day to sustain Berlin's inhabitants. At that time, however, Americans were moving about 1,000 tons per day and the British about 750 tons more. To achieve the minimum tonnage necessary, the airlift required an increased rate of delivery. To accomplish this, Clay brought in Brig. Gen. William H. Tunner, an airlift expert of proven ability, to command the operation. Tunner, with the wholehearted support of numerous other military and civilian leaders, expanded the number of bases between which airlift missions flew, swapped out the small C-47s for larger C-54 transports, raised the number of aircraft and personnel assigned to the airlift, streamlined the size and complexity of the airlift support system, and, most important, greatly increased the efficiency of the operation through a number of management innovations.

Tunner emphasized using all 1,440 minutes of the day for the airlift. He envisioned having an airplane land every minute. This was an impossible rate, and he settled for the more practical, but still very efficient, rate of one every three minutes. It "provided the ideal cadence of operations with the control equipment available at the time," and "there was little time wasted sitting at the ends of the runways."

Early in the operation, Britain's Royal Air Force (RAF) permanently attached three representatives to the task force to coordinate the efforts of the two nations. On October 14, the RAF was incorporated more directly into the headquarters when the United States and the United Kingdom created the Combined Airlift Task Force. The two nations merged their efforts and placed them under a single commander, General Tunner, with RAF Air Commodore J. W. F. Merer as his deputy.

All of these diverse elements came together to establish the Berlin Airlift as an operation that could continue indefinitely. Milestones along the way reflected the airlift's success. On July 7, 1948, before the arrival of the C-54s, tonnage exceeded 1,000 tons for one 24-hour period. The airlift set another record of 1,918 tons on July 30. But that record was broken on the following day, and almost every other day until winter set in. The harsh weather did not end the airlift, and by November 5, the total amount delivered had reached 300,000 tons.

The tonnage records climaxed with the "Easter Parade" on Apr. 16, 1949. Wanting to stretch the potential of the airlift force and to send a message to the Soviet Union that the blockade would not succeed, Tunner ordered a maximum effort for 24 hours. His goal was one completed mission for each of the 1,440 minutes of the day. The task force did not reach that goal. It did complete 1,398 missions; deliver 12,941 tons of food, coal, and other supplies; and fly with no accidents or injuries. Col. William Bunker, an army transportation officer, put this effort into

perspective when he told Tunner, "You guys have hauled the equivalent of 600 cars of coal into Berlin today. Have you ever seen a 50-car coal train? Well, you've just equaled 12 of them."

One project, dubbed "Operation Little Vittles," was an especially important contribution to the morale of the airlift. First Lt. Gail S. Halvorsen, an airlift pilot, decided to supplement Berlin's children's meager supply of candy. He dropped three handkerchief "parachutes" with candy from the flare chute in the bottom of his aircraft; thereafter, he made daily drops. At first, Halvorsen was concerned that Tunner might disapprove, but the task force commander immediately grasped the morale benefit of the action for both the aircrews and the Berliners. Tunner institutionalized the "Little Vittles" airdrops by establishing collection points for candy and handkerchiefs and by arranging special flights for Halvorsen to circle the city dropping candy, even to children in the Soviet zone.

Resolution. From the beginning of the airlift, U.S. diplomats worked to resolve the blockade, at first with little success. The Soviets were positive that the airlift would fail, that Berlin would starve or freeze, or both, and that the Western Allies would vacate the city. The airlift's success during the winter of 1948–49, however, began to erode Soviet resolve. After months of negotiation, on May 4, 1949, officials from both sides announced that the blockade would end on May 12. As promised, on that day, the Soviets reopened the rail lines and highways from the West into Berlin. Fearing that the Soviets might reinstate the blockade after the Allies had deactivated the Combined Airlift Task Force, Clay continued the operation through the summer to stockpile a reserve food and coal supply. On July 30, the Allies announced that the airlift would officially end on October 31. The headquarters of the Combined Airlift Task Force was inactivated on Sept. 1, 1949, and completely phased out by the end of October.

In terms of sheer numbers, it would be an understatement to call the Berlin Airlift impressive. It delivered more than 2,325,000 tons of food, fuel, and supplies to Berlin in 15 months and transported 227,655 passengers either into or out of the city aboard 189,963 American and 87,606 British missions. There were 126 U.S. aircraft accidents and 31 fatalities during the airlift.

The Berlin Airlift was significant for many reasons. U.S. allies around the world regarded the airlift as a triumph of will, and it solidified the Western position in the early Cold War era. The size and extent of the airlift, the requirement for close coordination, and the resourcefulness of Allied leadership also impressed the Soviet Union. The airlift affected Air Force doctrine as well, demonstrating that virtually any amount of cargo could be moved anywhere in the world with little concern for geography or weather. It provided valuable experience in operational techniques, air traffic control, and aircraft maintenance and reconditioning. Furthermore, the Berlin Airlift proved for the first time what has been confirmed many times since: airlift is a more flexible tool for executing national policy than either fighter or bomber aircraft.

Bibliography: Collier, Richard, *Bridge Across the Sky: The Berlin Blockade and Airlift, 1948–1949* (McGraw-Hill, 1978); Davison, W. Phillips, *The Berlin Blockade: A Study in Cold War Politics* (Princeton Univ. Press, 1958); Giangreco, D. M., and Robert E. Griffin, *Airbridge to Berlin: The Berlin Crisis of 1948, Its Origin and Aftermath* (Presidio, 1988); Launius, Roger D., and Coy F. Cross, *MAC and the Legacy of the Berlin Airlift* (Office of Military Airlift Command History, 1989); Shlaim, Avi, *The United States and the Berlin Blockade, 1948–1949: A Study in Crisis Decision-Making* (Univ. of California Press, 1983).

Roger D. Launius

BERLIN CRISIS (1961)

Politically sensitive situation in the divided city of Berlin that would characterize the Cold War tensions of the 1960s. Impatient with what he saw as Western foot-dragging on the formal resolution of Berlin's status and embarrassed by the flow of East Berliners to the West, Soviet premier Nikita Khrushchev issued an ultimatum to Pres. John F. Kennedy in Vienna, Austria, in June 1961. Either the Western powers must agree to negotiate an agreement eliminating all foreign troops from the city by Dec. 31, 1961, or all Western access routes to Berlin would be turned over to the East Germans, who were not bound to respect the agreement guaranteeing that such routes would remain open. As a show of Soviet seriousness, Khrushchev, on July 8, 1961, scrapped plans to reduce the size of the Soviet army by 1,500,000 men.

After consulting with his national security staff and elder statesman Dean Acheson, Kennedy decided to hold his ground; there would be no negotiation. In late July, the president, holding that the freedom of West Berlin was essential to "the entire free world" and that withdrawal of Western troops would be the first step toward limiting the freedom of all West Berlin, authorized a dramatic buildup of U.S. forces. He asked Congress for an additional $3.2 billion for military spending, much of which would go for expanding the size of the regular armed forces. The army and Marine Corps were ordered to prepare to deploy an additional six divisions (four army, two marine) to Europe by December 1961. An increase in the number of bombers on ground-alert status was ordered, and 158,000 reservists and National Guardsmen were mobilized. Kennedy also asked for funds for a civil defense program from Congress. The president had two objectives, according to historian Michael Beschloss: "to reduce the chance that Khrushchev could quickly and easily take over the city. The other was to convince him that if the Western position was seriously

challenged, Kennedy might well choose holocaust over humiliation."

The war scare that resulted from the Khrushchev ultimatum subsided somewhat on August 13, when East German security guards in one night constructed a 25-mile-long wall of barbed wire, later replaced with concrete, separating East Berlin from West Berlin, thereby ending the exodus of East Germans to the West. The move drew strong protests from the Western powers, who saw the wall as a flagrant violation of wartime agreements on the German city. Vice Pres. Lyndon B. Johnson was dispatched to Berlin to show American resolve. On the morning of August 20, a 1,500-man combat team from the 18th Infantry Division left its base in Mannheim, heading via convoy to the western section of the city. It arrived without incident. The United States agreed to begin four-power talks on Berlin, and on September 1, Khrushchev withdrew his December 31 deadline. Additional U.S. armored units were sent into West Berlin to signal Western firmness. Although the Soviet Union's longstanding efforts to gain control of all Berlin came to nothing, the Berlin Wall remained in place.

Bibliography: Beschloss, Michael R., *The Crisis Years: Kennedy and Khrushchev 1960–1963* (Harper Collins, 1991).

James A. Warren

BIEN HOA (*see* Tan Son Nhut and Bien Hoa)

BIG SWITCH AND LITTLE SWITCH, OPERATIONS (1953)

Two occasions in 1953 during which Korean War belligerents exchanged prisoners of war (POWs). Operation Little Switch, involving sick and wounded POWs, began on April 20 and continued for two weeks. This brief exchange included 6,670 Communists (5,194 North Koreans, 1,030 Chinese, 446 civilian internees) and 684 United Nations Command (UNC) prisoners.

Operation Big Switch followed the armistice of July 27. From August 5 to September 6, the UNC and the Communists released 75,000 and 12,000 repatriates, respectively. From September 23 through December 23, an additional 628 Communists and 12 UNC prisoners returned to their native countries. The final tally showed 75,823 Communist and 12,773 UNC repatriates; 21,839 Communist and 347 UNC nonrepatriates.

Maj. James Sanders Day

CAM RANH BAY

One of the world's great natural harbors, Cam Ranh Bay in Vietnam has been the scene of considerable military and naval activity during the 20th century. En route to the eastern provinces of Russia, the Imperial Russian Navy briefly anchored and consolidated its forces at Cam Ranh Bay in 1905 just prior to its defeat at the hands of the Japanese fleet during the Russo-Japanese War. During the Vietnam War, Cam Ranh Bay was extensively developed with piers, warehouses, and a large airfield by U.S. forces.

Located a few miles south of the Vietnamese city of Nha Trang in Khanh Hoa Province, Cam Ranh Bay is partially surrounded and protected from the region's occasional typhoons by a chain of hills. The bay's deep water will accommodate almost any merchant or war ship. The bay was recommended for development by U.S. naval authorities in 1964 when it appeared the United States would be enlarging its involvement in South Vietnam's defense. In 1965, the U.S. Army's First Logistical Command established a support unit at Cam Ranh to furnish supplies and services for allied forces. The facility was turned over to South Vietnamese control in 1972.

Bibliography: Dunn, Carrol H., *Base Development, 1965–1970* (U.S. Govt. Printing Office, 1972).

Col. (Ret.) Rod Paschall

CEDAR FALLS, OPERATION
(January 1967)

Multidivision Vietnam War operation launched by U.S. forces to eliminate a major North Vietnamese Army/Vietcong base area, the "Iron Triangle," just northwest of Saigon. In early 1967, Gen. William C. Westmoreland sought to maintain the strategic initiative and ordered Cedar Falls, the largest U.S. ground operation thus far in the war. U.S. units included the entire 1st and 25th infantry divisions, the 173d Airborne Brigade, the 11th Armored Cavalry Regiment, and massive aviation and fire support. This 19-day, "search and destroy" operation physically destroyed most of the enemy base area but failed to engage decisively the North Vietnamese and Vietcong units occupying the Iron Triangle at the onset of the operation.

Bibliography: Palmer, Dave R., *Summons of the Trumpet* (Presidio, 1978); Rogers, Bernard, *Cedar Falls-Junction City: A Turning Point* (U.S. Govt. Printing Office, 1974).

Capt. Leslie Howard Belknap

CENTRAL TREATY ORGANIZATION (CENTO)

International defense group initially formed to oppose the expansion of Soviet influence. It had its origins in the alliance between Iraq and Turkey established by the Baghdad Pact (1955), which Great Britain, Iran, and Pakistan joined later in 1955. The United States agreed to cooperate with CENTO in 1956 but did not become a full member. Iraq withdrew in 1959, and the organization dissolved in 1979. CENTO devoted more attention to regional problems than to developing a comprehensive plan to combat Soviet foreign policy.

Stephen Robinson

CHIP'YONG-NI, BATTLE OF
(February 11–18, 1951)

Korean War engagement that resulted when a Chinese offensive in mid-February 1951 threatened to envelop the U.S. 8th Army via Chip'yong-ni and the Han River valley. The U.S. 23d Regimental Combat Team (RCT)—23d Infantry Regiment, French Battalion, 1st Ranger Company, 37th Field Artillery, a battery each from the 503d Field Artillery and 82d Antiaircraft Artillery, and an engineer company—defended the town.

Supplied by airdrops, the RCT held against repeated company-sized assaults by six Chinese regiments on February 14 and 15. When relieved, the team had lost some 350 men; the Chinese about 5,000. The 23d Regiment's success at Chip'yong-ni marked the beginning of new confidence within the 8th Army.

Bibliography: Blair, Clay, *The Forgotten War* (Times Books, 1987); Mossman, Billy C., *U.S. Army in the Korean War: Ebb and Flow November 1950–July 1951* (Center of Military History, U.S. Army, 1990).

Brig. Gen. PNG (Ret.) Uzal W. Ent

CHOSIN RESERVOIR, BATTLE OF
(November 27–December 11, 1950)

Korean War engagement that, for the U.S. forces involved, proved to be perhaps the most ill-advised, ill-fated operation of the war. When the Chinese intervened in the Korean War in October 1950, the U.S. X Corps and Republic of Korea (ROK) I Corps were scattered on an arc almost 300 miles long in northeastern Korea: the ROK Capital Division at Ch'ongjin on the coast, the ROK 3d Infantry Division at Hapsu, elements of the U.S. 7th Infantry Division near the Yalu River, the U.S. 1st Marine Division south of the Chosin Reservoir, and the U.S. 3d Infantry Division protecting the southwestern and southern flank. Overall, this force was commanded by Maj. Gen. Edward M. Almond.

Task Force MacLean/Faith. On November 27, in spite of intelligence that as many as six Chinese Communist Force (CCF) divisions were nearby, Almond ordered the marines to attack west from Chosin and a two-battalion army task force to advance north along the east shore of the reservoir. (The task force—named "Task Force MacLean" for its leader, Col. Allan D. MacLean—was composed of the 1st Battalion, 32d Infantry, and 3d Battalion, 31st Infantry, supported by artillery and tanks.)

That night, the CCF 79th and 89th divisions struck the U.S. 5th and 7th marine regiments at Yudam-ni while the CCF 59th Division cut the road leading south to Hagaru-ri. The CCF 80th Division attacked Task Force MacLean east of Chosin.

The task force was scattered in two battalion perimeters and a small separate tank company perimeter. The positions were too far apart to support one another. Under heavy pressure, the two battalion perimeters were combined on November 29. The force suffered heavy casualties, MacLean was killed, and Lt. Col. Don Carlos Faith (1st Battalion, 31st Infantry) assumed command of what then became "Task Force Faith." Attempts by the tankers and others to help were thwarted by the enemy. Faith was ordered to fight his way south to the marines at Hagaru-ri. In the effort, Faith was killed, and the task force lost more than 2,000 of its 3,200 men. Only 385 were fit for duty on December 3, after they reached the marine lines. They were added to an army provisional battalion that was attached to the 7th Marine Regiment.

Withdrawal Preparations. While the army task force was slowly being destroyed east of Chosin, the 1st Marine Division had been, since October, waging a bitter, desperate, and bloody struggle west and south of it. On November 29, the 5th Marines held Yudam-ni, while the 7th attacked south to open the road to Hagaru-ri. Elements of the division's 1st Regiment came under heavy attack at Kot'o-ri (11 miles south of Hagaru-ri). A force—consisting of the British 41st (Marine) Commando Battalion, Company B, 31st Infantry, and 30 tanks—set out from Kot'o-ri for Hagaru-ri, but were bloodily repulsed by the CCF.

By December 1, the 5th and 7th marines of Maj. Gen. Oliver P. Smith's 1st Marine Division had battled four miles south of Yudam-ni. The 1st Battalion, 7th Marines, then attacked through the mountains toward Fox Hill (defended by Company F, 7th Marines) and the Toktong Pass, which they reached about noon on December 2. Protected by excellent air support, the two regiments completed their move into Hagaru-ri by 2:00 P.M. on December 4.

The CCF 58th Division had attacked Hagaru-ri on November 30, without success, then left the town alone. The marines used this respite to air-evacuate some 4,300 casualties (and bring in 500 replacements) during the next five days.

Almond suggested to Smith that he destroy equipment to facilitate withdrawal, and Maj. Gen. William H. Tunner, commanding Far East Air Force Combat Cargo Command, offered to airlift up to 10,000 troops out of Hagaru-ri. Smith refused both suggestions, deciding instead to fight his way south, taking most of his equipment.

Withdrawal. The 7th Marines, with the provisional army battalion attached, led the way south to Kot'o-ri. The 5th Marines, 3d Battalion; 1st Marines; and British Commandos defended Hagaru-ri and were the rear guard. Remaining division troops and vehicles were divided and attached to the two regiments. The artillery leapfrogged south in order to provide continuous support, while the artillery at Kot'o-ri added its support. Twenty-four aircraft provided a daytime umbrella, while others searched ridges flanking the road. Other aircraft took over at night.

Intelligence indicated that the CCF 76th and 77th divisions had moved south into the area east of the withdrawal route, relieving the CCF 60th Division, which had apparently moved farther south to block the Funchilin Pass. The CCF 89th Division had apparently moved even farther south, but on the west of the road.

Smith, wishing to move the 1st Battalion, 1st Marines, north from Chinhung-ni to clear the road to Kot'o-ri, asked Almond for a relief force for Chinhung-ni. Task Force Dog (Brig. Gen. A. D. Mead)—consisting of the 3d Battalion, 7th Infantry and the 92d Armored Field Artillery Battalion (Self Propelled), plus engineers, reconnaissance, and other support troops—was given the task.

Three and a half miles south of Kot'o-ri, Smith's column would face a 16-foot chasm in the road, a gap that had to be bridged. After Smith's engineer surveyed the site from the air on December 6, he asked for and received an airdrop of eight 2,500-pound bridge sections at Kot'o-ri.

Also on December 6, Smith's rear guard seized what was known as East Hill, which dominated the withdrawal route. Before 5:00 P.M. that day, the 7th Marines battled its way into Kot'o-ri, supported by aircraft, artillery, and tank fire. The rear guard left Hagaru-ri late on the morning of December 7, after destroying supplies that could not be taken along and entered Kot'o-ri before midnight.

Meantime, Col. Lewis B. Puller, commanding the 1st Marine Regiment at Kot'o-ri, ordered the airstrip there lengthened. Between December 8 and 10, all casualties were airlifted out of his perimeter.

Task Force Dog arrived at Chinhung-ni on December 7, enabling the 1st Battalion, 1st Marines, to attack north the following day. The battalion seized Funchilin Pass a few miles north of Chinhung-ni. At the same time, the 7th Marines cleared the enemy along the road south from Kot'o-ri to within a mile of the road chasm. By noon on December 8, the 7th Marines arrived at this gap. The southern force that day captured dominant Hill 1081 north of the Funchilin Pass. The 7th made contact with them shortly afterward.

A few hours after the road chasm area had been cleared of the enemy, a bridge across the chasm was completed with the air-dropped sections and crossing began at 6:00 P.M. The column reached the Chinhung-ni area by 3:00 A.M. on December 11. At Sudung, south of Chinhung-ni, the Chinese attacked the 1st Marines regimental supply train, but a counterattack cleared the area. By 1:00 P.M. on December 11, the marine column cleared Majon-dong, successfully completing the withdrawal.

On December 15, the 1st Marine Division was shipped to Pusan for redeployment as part of the 8th Army. Between October 26 and December 15, these marines had sustained sobering losses: 718 killed in action or dead of wounds, 192 missing, 3,508 wounded in battle, and 7,313 noncombat (mostly frostbite) casualties. The marines and army had engaged eight CCF divisions, rendering a large part of the CCF 9th Army Group militarily ineffective.

Bibliography: Appleman, Roy E., *East of Chosin* (Texas A&M Univ. Press, 1987); Montross, Lynn, and Nicholas A. Canzona, *U.S. Marine Operations in Korea 1950–1953; Vol. 3: The Chosin Reservoir Campaign* (Historical Div., U.S. Marine Corps Hdqrs., 1957); Mossman, Billy C., *U.S. Army in the Korean War: Ebb and Flow, November 1950–July 1951* (Center of Military History, U.S. Army, 1990).

Brig. Gen. PNG (Ret.) Uzal W. Ent

CIVIL OPERATIONS AND REVOLUTIONARY DEVELOPMENT SUPPORT (CORDS)

U.S. program created in May 1967 by a presidential directive, CORDS was designed to manage more efficiently the pacification program in South Vietnam during the Vietnam War. For the first time, CORDS incorporated all aspects of the pacification efforts under the control of U.S. Military Assistance Command Vietnam (MACV) to include the military services, the Central Intelligence Agency, the State Department, the Agency for International Development, and the U.S. Information Agency. Headed by Robert W. Komer, CORDS was, in the words of historian Guenter Lewy, "a unique experiment in civil-military organization." Holding ambassadorial rank and the title of deputy to the commander of MACV for CORDS, Komer managed the organization and implementation of many initiatives designed to secure the countryside and gain the support of the rural South Vietnamese. CORDS established unified civilian-military advisory teams for all 44 provinces and 250 districts, which no longer answered to the nearest Army of the Republic of Vietnam (ARVN) division advisory teams. Moreover, CORDS under Komer's direction asserted itself in a renewed emphasis on the improvement of the Vietnamese Regional and Popular Forces. Additional areas of emphasis included the strengthening of the South Vietnamese police force, accelerated efforts in the Chieu Hoi program, and the focus on the Phung Hoang (Phoenix Program). At the height of the CORDS' pacification efforts, more than 6,500 military personnel and 1,100 civilians were assigned to CORDS. Although the Viet Cong threat to South Vietnam decreased following the 1968 Tet Offensive, the effectiveness of CORDS is still widely debated among scholars. Clearly, CORDS was an improvement of previous pacification efforts with the elimination of the Viet Cong threat, yet the ultimate goal of winning the peasant's loyalty to the South Vietnamese government was never achieved.

Bibliography: Blaufarb, Douglas, *The Counterinsurgency Era; U.S. Doctrine and Performance* (Macmillian, 1977); Lewy, Geunter, *America in Vietnam* (Oxford, 1978); Tho, Tran Dinh, *Pacification* (U.S. Govt. Printing Office, 1980).

Capt. Leslie Howard Belknap

CIVIL RESERVE AIR FLEET (CRAF)

U.S. civilian air reserve created in 1952 as a means of augmenting the air force's organic airlift resources with commercial airliners. In a crisis, military leaders could activate the CRAF to provide additional airlift for deployment. In the first stage, 45 aircraft from the airlines became available; in later stages, the CRAF had the resources to airlift 95 percent of the passengers and 35 percent of the cargo required in war plans for overseas theaters. The numbers of aircraft participating in the CRAF have varied over the years. Although it had been in operation since 1952, the CRAF was not activated until August 1990 when it was called upon to assist with the deployment of U.S. forces to the Persian Gulf.

Bibliography: Lacombe, Phil, "The Air Force and the Airlines," *Air Force Magazine* (Feb. 1985); Thayer, Frederick C., Jr., *Air Transport Policy and National Security: A Political, Economic, and Military Analysis* (Univ. of North Carolina Press, 1965).

Roger D. Launius

CLAYMORE MINE

An antipersonnel device, the M18A1 "claymore" is a directional, fixed-fragmentation mine. Widely used by U.S. and allied forces in the Vietnam War, the claymore mine delivered hundreds of spherical steel fragments over a 60-degree fan-shaped pattern, 2 meters high and 50 meters wide, at a range of 50 meters. Due to its light weight (3.5 pounds) and lethal effectiveness, the claymore was ideally suited for defensive positions and ambushes against the North Vietnamese and Viet Cong. Normally command-detonated and treated as a weapon as part of a unit fire plan, the claymore was used also in the uncontrolled firing mode as a booby trap.

Bibliography: *Army Field Manual 23–23, Antipersonnel Mine, M18A1* (U.S. Govt. Printing Office, 1966).

Capt. Leslie Howard Belknap

CODE OF CONDUCT

U.S. military policy, designed as an ethical guideline rather than an inflexible law, that set standards, guiding principles, moral obligations, and professional ethics. On Aug. 17, 1955, Pres. Dwight D. Eisenhower signed the six-article Executive Order No. 10631, thereby instituting a new code of conduct for the U.S. Armed Forces. A 10-man Advisory Committee on Prisoners of War appointed by Sec. of Defense Charles E. Wilson developed the code in response to prisoner of war behavior during the Korean War. After the war, 21 U.S. prisoners declined repatriation, and postwar studies estimated that one-third of all

A U.S. infantryman sets a claymore mine, an antipersonnel device used widely by U.S. and allied forces during the Vietnam War. (U.S. Air Force)

U.S. prisoners collaborated in some way. Modified on Nov. 3, 1977, by Executive Order No. 12017, the Code of Conduct applies to all ranks and provides a unified policy for all services.

Bibliography: Biderman, Albert D., *March to Calumny* (Macmillan, 1962); Kinkead, Eugene, *In Every War But One* (Norton, 1959); Rees, David, *Korea: The Limited War* (St. Martin's Press, 1964).

Maj. James Sanders Day

CONSTABULARY, UNITED STATES

Highly mobile U.S. police force created by the U.S. Army to patrol the occupied territories of post-World War II Germany and to allow the demobilization of several divisions. The U.S. Constabulary became active on July 1, 1946. The new force consisted of three brigades of three regiments each. In turn, each of these regiments included three cavalry-type squadrons, a light tank company, and a 30-man horse platoon. The constabulary's mission of provid-

ing internal security rapidly disappeared, however, as the new German police took over. In 1947, the army reduced the force from 30,000 to 20,206 men and reorganized it as a modified armored cavalry division. Three years later, the army activated the U.S. 7th Army in Germany and broke up the constabulary to provide the mechanized cavalry for its corps.

Bibliography: Frederiksen, Oliver J., *The American Military Occupation of Germany, 1945–1953* (Hdqrs., U.S. Army, Europe, 1953).

Richard F. Kehrberg

CON THIEN, BATTLE OF
(August–September 1967)
Series of Vietnam War engagements between the U.S. marines and the North Vietnamese Army at Con Thien, a strategic location with an excellent vantage point two miles south of the demilitarized zone. The North Vietnamese began attacking the marine firebase at Con Thien in August 1967 and were repeatedly repulsed by the marine defenders. The marines prevented the North Vietnamese from surrounding the base and from cutting off Southern supply lines. During this battle, SLAM (seeking, locating, annihilating, monitoring), a new concept in marshaling firepower, came into being.

Leo J. Daugherty III

CORDS (*see* Civil Operations and Revolutionary Development Support)

CROSSROADS, OPERATION (July 1946)
The first postwar test of atom bombs, Operation Crossroads was held in the Pacific Ocean at Bikini Atoll in the Marshall Islands in July 1946. Announced in late 1945, Crossroads was the first—and still just one of a handful—of nuclear tests to be witnessed by media representatives. This openness made Crossroads one of the major ongoing news stories of 1946. Commanded by Vice Adm. William H. P. Blandy, Crossroads was a weapons-effects test in which two atom bombs of the design used on Nagasaki, Japan, were employed against an array of more than 70 target ships anchored in the lagoon of Bikini Atoll. The first test (July 1) was an airburst; the second and more interesting (July 25), an underwater explosion. A third was planned but not held. Much data was obtained, especially on radiation, and the evaluation of it was presented to the Joint Chiefs of Staff in 1947.

Bibliography: Shurcliff, W. A., *Bombs at Bikini: The Official Report of Operation Crossroads* (William H. Wise, 1947).

Lloyd J. Graybar

CRUISE MISSILES
Guided missiles designed to carry warheads at altitudes low enough to elude enemy radar. The first practical cruise

Technological advances since World War II have led to such sophisticated cruise missiles as the BGM-109 Tomahawk, shown here being launched toward an Iraqi target during Operation Desert Storm (1991). (U.S. Navy)

missiles, essentially pilotless aircraft, appeared during World War II. In the 1950s, the United States developed a number of such missiles: the Snark, for intercontinental missions; the Mace and Matador, for intermediate ranges; and the Regulus series, for the U.S. Navy. All of these missiles, however, were extremely vulnerable due to their large size and need to fly at high altitudes. Moreover, their primitive guidance systems made them inaccurate at long ranges. Therefore, ballistic missiles soon replaced them for strategic missions.

During the 1970s, however, advances in jet engine technology and miniaturized electronics permitted a revival of the cruise missile concept. The development of small turbofan engines markedly reduced missile size, and new guidance systems allowed the missiles to strike targets at great distances reliably and to fly to them at low altitudes. In the early 1980s, the United States began deploying both the air-launched cruise missile (ACLM), and the Tomahawk, which had land-launched and sea-launched versions. While the ACLM was armed with a nuclear warhead, some versions of the Tomahawk were equipped

with a conventional one. The reintroduction of cruise missiles touched off a storm of debate both inside and outside the military. Air force and naval aviators worried that the missiles might replace their bombers, while some civilians believed that the missiles threatened to destabilize the U.S.-Soviet nuclear balance.

Bibliography: Betts, Richard K., *Cruise Missiles: Technology, Strategy, Politics* (Brookings Inst., 1981); Werrell, Kenneth P., *The Evolution of the Cruise Missile* (Air Univ. Press, 1985).

Richard F. Kehrberg

CUBAN MISSILE CRISIS (October 1962)
One of the most serious episodes of the Cold War. The discovery by U.S. reconnaissance aircraft on Oct. 14, 1962, of Soviet intermediate-range missile installations under construction in Cuba precipitated the crisis. Soviet planners had reckoned that by placing missiles with a range of 1,100 miles in Cuba, they could offset the overwhelming U.S. advantage in intercontinental ballistic missiles (ICBMs). John F. Kennedy, in his first year as U.S. president and still smarting from the abortive Bay of Pigs fiasco, resolved to take decisive action against what was seen both as a Soviet move into an historically American sphere of influence and as a very real threat to the security of the United States. The resulting standoff brought the world to the brink of nuclear war as the United States and the Soviet Union stood "eyeball to eyeball" waiting for the other to blink.

Background. Pres. Dwight D. Eisenhower and his secretary of state, John Foster Dulles, had adopted the policy of massive retaliation as a cost-effective counter to the growing Soviet nuclear threat of the 1950s. They reasoned that Soviet aggression worldwide could be held in check by the threat of a massive nuclear strike against the Soviet Union. As the decade wore on, the inadequacy of this policy became apparent as growing nuclear arsenals on both sides seemed to suggest that massive retaliation would ultimately result in complete mutual destruction. The resultant stalemate increased the desire of both nations for a summit meeting in an effort to resolve peacefully such issues as the Soviet-supported insurgency in Laos, the continued Allied occupation of Berlin, and a nuclear test ban treaty. Hopes for this summit were dashed when, just days prior to the scheduled opening of the meeting in Paris, a U.S. U-2 reconnaissance aircraft was shot down while overflying the Soviet Union on May 1, 1960.

The U-2 incident highlighted the growing military might of the Soviet Union and hinted at potentially unknown Soviet strengths. The conventional superiority of Soviet forces in Europe was well known, but was felt to be more than offset by U.S. technological superiority in aircraft and missile forces. This supposed U.S. advantage now appeared nullified, and American vulnerability became the issue as the need to close the "missile gap" became a theme of the Democratic party during the 1960 presidential election.

After taking office in January 1961, President Kennedy and his cabinet were eager to begin implementing his new strategic policy of "flexible response." Designed to offer an escalating menu of responses to aggression, Kennedy's plans necessitated large increases in defense spending to provide the wide range of forces necessary to cover the spectrum of possible responses. However, before Kennedy had the opportunity to embark on his own defense initiatives, he was forced to deal with the legacy of the outgoing administration in the form of the Bay of Pigs invasion. Unwilling to appear soft by canceling the CIA-sponsored invasion and in spite of his own doubts, Kennedy reluctantly allowed the invasion to proceed. Ironically, his fail-

ure to commit U.S. forces fully in what amounted to the first test of his new administration made him appear weak and indecisive to Soviet leadership.

Although Kennedy quickly discovered that the "missile gap" was a chimera and that the United States actually enjoyed a numerical advantage in strategic weapons, he and his advisers determined that the United States needed a nuclear striking force as much as four times greater than that of the Soviets. Kennedy was still feeling the effects of his Bay of Pigs humiliation and was concerned that the Soviet preponderance in conventional weaponry in Europe might encourage Soviet aggression against Berlin. Rejecting the advice of his senior military advisers that a smaller advantage over the Soviets would produce the necessary deterrence, Kennedy desired a "counterforce" strategy aimed at totally obliterating the Soviet Union in the

U.S. surveillance flights and photographs (above) revealed the presence of Soviet missiles in Cuba that precipitated the Cuban Missile Crisis, a U.S.-Soviet confrontation, in October 1962. (U.S. Air Force)

wake of a Soviet first strike. His resolve was strengthened during the Vienna summit meeting of June 1961, as the Soviet delegation, headed by Premier Nikita Khrushchev, aggressively announced support for wars of national liberation throughout the world.

Increasing Soviet pressure for an end to the Allied occupation of Berlin continued to strengthen Kennedy's determination to appear strong. Yet, in spite of his declaration of Berlin as a "great testing place of Western courage and will," he did nothing when the Soviets erected the Berlin Wall in August 1961. In Soviet eyes, although Kennedy was clearly increasing U.S. forces, he was apparently loath to use them. Thus, while Khrushchev was aware of the preponderance of U.S. strategic superiority, he believed Kennedy did not have sufficient resolve to interfere with Soviet efforts to mitigate the U.S. advantage by installing intermediate-range missiles in Cuba.

The Showdown. American U-2 reconnaissance aircraft discovered the Soviet missile sites on Oct. 14, 1962. After two days of interpretation and analysis, the photographs were presented to Kennedy as evidence of intermediate-range missile launching pads. The real significance of the newly discovered missiles was that they gave the Soviets a credible first-strike capability. Missiles launched from Cuba could reach any target in the United States and were virtually undetectable. Not only were U.S. strategic defenses oriented away from Cuba, the proximity of the missiles meant that they could strike the U.S. mainland before any warning could be given. Kennedy immediately called an emergency meeting of the National Security Council's executive committee to discuss possible options.

The options presented by the president's advisers included a surgical air strike, an outright invasion of Cuba, a naval blockade, and a trading of the removal of the Soviet missiles in Cuba for the removal of U.S. missiles in Turkey. Kennedy was convinced of the need to take decisive action to force the Soviets to back down, but rejected the air strike option when the U.S. Air Force could not guarantee destruction of all the missiles and suggested that such a strike might involve Russian casualties. Atty. Gen. Robert Kennedy, the president's brother, pointed out that such a strike would invite comparison to Pearl Harbor and might result in a Soviet countermove against Berlin. Likewise, an invasion of Cuba was dismissed because of the expected high level of U.S. casualties and the likelihood of a Soviet response. Not wanting to appear too conciliatory, Kennedy refused to consider any kind of a trade and was left with the option of a naval blockade.

On Monday, Oct. 22, 1962, the president went on national television to announce the impending naval quarantine of Cuba. Aware that a blockade was considered an act of war, Kennedy declared that a picket of U.S. warships would establish a quarantine line at a 500-mile radius from the eastern end of Cuba and would intercept any vessel

capable of carrying missiles. Any vessel refusing to submit to the quarantine force would be sunk. The quarantine was to remain in effect until the Soviets removed the offending missiles. Task Force 136, composed of approximately 180 ships, was set to take position on October 24. The two-day delay was designed to allow room for negotiations since it was known that no Soviet ship was close enough to reach the quarantine line before that time, and Kennedy wanted to avoid backing Khrushchev into a corner.

After two days of standing on the brink of a nuclear war, Khrushchev responded with a letter to Kennedy on October 26, offering to remove the missiles in exchange for a public American promise not to invade Cuba. The next day, while the president was drafting his response, a second, much harsher letter arrived from Khrushchev demanding that the Americans remove the U.S. missiles based in Turkey as a precondition for the removal of the Soviet missiles. President Kennedy viewed the second letter with consternation until convinced by his brother Robert to ignore it and answer the first. The Soviets, just as eager to find a resolution to the crisis as the Americans, accepted Kennedy's pledge to respect Cuba's territorial integrity as sufficient and on October 28 offered the dismantling of the missiles without further mention of the U.S. missiles in Turkey. Although the crisis had been averted, the U.S. quarantine remained in effect as American ships continued to monitor the removal of the Soviet missiles until Nov. 20, 1962.

While President Kennedy's handling of this crisis was applauded by most observers, critics saw it as a dangerous attempt by the administration to prove itself against the Soviets. Most Soviet ships turned back on the first day of the quarantine, and only one ship was actually boarded by U.S. forces, but a single incident of hostile action against a Soviet ship might have been sufficient to trigger a nuclear war. Ultimately, the Cuban Missile Crisis helped to lessen international tensions and led directly to the 1963 Nuclear Test Ban Treaty and the installation of the "hot line" between the White House and the Kremlin.

Bibliography: Abel, Elie, *The Missiles of October: The Story of the Cuban Missile Crisis, 1962* (MacGibbon & Keo, 1966); Chayes, Abram, *The Cuban Missile Crisis: International Crises and the Role of Law* (Oxford Univ. Press, 1974); Detzer, David, *The Brink: Cuban Missile Crisis, 1962* (Crowell, 1979); Dinerstein, Herbert S., *The Making of a Missile Crisis, October 1962* (Johns Hopkins Univ. Press, 1976); LaFaber, Walter, *America, Russia, and the Cold War, 1945–1984* (Knopf, 1985).

Maj. Gilbert B. Diaz

DAK TO, BATTLE OF (November 1967)

Border clash near a U.S. Army Special Forces camp located about 280 miles north of Saigon alongside North Vietnamese supply routes from Cambodia to South Vietnam. Heavy fighting started in the summer of 1967 as the North Vietnamese attacked from concealed positions in mountain caves and tunnel complexes. U.S. troops assaulted the North Vietnamese in November, focusing particularly on Hill 875, 12 miles west of the Special Forces camp. After intense bombing, U.S. soldiers stormed up the hill on November 19. Four days of bitter fighting resulted in North Vietnam abandoning its positions, and on November 23, U.S. units reached the hill's summit. Approximately 1,400 North Vietnamese troops died at Dak To, while 289 American and 49 South Vietnamese soldiers gave their lives.

Bibliography: Karnow, Stanley, *Vietnam: A History* (Penguin, 1983); Maitland, Terrence, and Peter McInerney, *The Vietnam Experience: A Contagion of War* (Boston Pub. Co., 1983).

John F. Wukovits

DELTA FORCE

Name given to a joint U.S.-Vietnamese unit created by the U.S. 5th Special Forces Group based at Nha Trang during the Vietnam War. Officially titled Special Forces Operational Detachment Delta, the unit was primarily used to reinforce remote Special Forces camps undergoing Communist attack. On occasion, Delta performed reconnaissance missions. It was composed of U.S. Special Forces and Vietnamese rangers. Following the war, in the late 1970s, the title of the organization was reused for the newly formed U.S. commando and counterterrorist unit, an organization patterned on the British Special Air Service. Delta Force became publicly known and officially acknowledged after the failure of the U.S. hostage rescue operation in Iran during April 1980. In that episode, the unit, sent to rescue American hostages, was unable to perform its mission because of a series of helicopter and weather-related mishaps.

Bibliography: Beckwith, Charlie A., and Donald Knox, *Delta Force* (Harcourt Brace Jovanovich, 1983).

Col. (Ret.) Rod Paschall

DESERT ONE (April 24–25, 1980)

Code name for the attempted rescue of U.S. hostages in Iran. In response to the seizure of U.S. diplomatic personnel at the American Embassy in Tehran, Iran, on Nov. 4, 1979, and after diplomatic negotiations over their release failed to resolve the issue, Pres. Jimmy Carter decided upon a rescue mission. By April 2, after the so-called Iranian moderates placed new conditions on the release of the U.S. captives, Carter instructed his advisers to complete tentative plans for a hostage-rescue mission.

Even while the diplomatic maneuvering was reaching its climax, the Pentagon had chosen a rescue staging area approximately 200 miles south of Tehran that had an ideal landing surface capable of supporting the large C-130 transport aircraft and support helicopters to be used in the rescue mission. The force assembled for the Iranian rescue attempt was a composite one, comprising army, navy, Marine Corps, and air force elements. Known as Joint Task Force 1–79, U.S. Army units included the 1st Special Forces Operations Detachment or "Delta" Force along with a Special Assault Team from the 10th Special Forces Group and a company of army rangers. The combined force of marine and navy helicopters and pilots was complimented by navy surface ships and air force units.

The greatest problem faced by the military planners was the enormous distance from either the sea or other countries to the center of Tehran. Instead of relying upon a host nation to permit an overflight or to base U.S. military elements for a rescue mission, U.S. military planners conceived of placing the rescue team aboard seven helicopters that would be prepositioned by an aircraft carrier group. The plan envisioned that the 90-man Delta rescue team, led by Col. Charles Beckwith, would be able to fly into Iran undetected to the abandoned airstrip and link up with the awaiting rescue helicopters and then rendezvous at a site near Tehran undetected. Surprise was the key factor in all of the planning. Carter insisted on tight control of the entire operation, a factor that some believe contributed to the mission's ultimate failure. In addition, the plan was extremely intricate and was predicated on too many "ifs," including Iran's military ineffectiveness and Saudi Arabia's willingness to let its territory be used during the rescue.

On April 23, President Carter passed the word to Colonel Beckwith's team that the rescue operation would go forward. From the start of the operation, however, things began going wrong. Helicopters were disabled by desert conditions, and the rescuers were seen by Iranian civilians. It was at this point that Carter, acting upon the recommendations of Gen. David Jones, chairman of the Joint Chiefs of Staff (JCS), ordered the mission be aborted. The mission commander, Colonel Beckwith, argued that the mission could have gone forward, but he was overruled by President Carter and the JCS. During the withdrawal eight U.S. soldiers died in a helicopter accident.

In the end, however, political restrictions and constraints forced the termination of what could have been a successful rescue operation. Despite Carter's contention that cancellation of the mission was "caused by a series of mishaps," the mission could have succeeded had better planning and preparations been taken before the rescue attempt. Better coordination among the military services would have enhanced the probability of success. In the end, President Carter assumed full responsibility for the failed Iranian rescue attempt.

Bibliography: Carter, Jimmy, *Keeping Faith: Memoirs of a President* (Bantam, 1982); Kyle, James H., *The Guts* *to Try: The Untold Story of the Iran Hostage Rescue Mission by the On-Scene Commander* (Orion Books, 1990); McManus, Doyle, *Free At Last!* (Los Angeles Times Press, 1982).

Leo J. Daugherty III

DESERT SHIELD/DESERT STORM
(August 1990–March 1991)

U.S. military operation against Iraq, initiated after Iraq invaded the state of Kuwait on Aug. 2, 1990, in order to gain control of substantial oil reserves and monetary assets. In a well-coordinated attack, the Iraqi government, led by Pres. Saddam Hussein, annexed Kuwait on August 8 and renamed it "Province 19." Iraqi forces systematically looted the country and terrorized its citizenry.

An intense diplomatic effort by Pres. George Bush resulted in the formation of a wide coalition against Iraq. The United States reacted early by deploying air, land, and sea forces on August 6 in an operation called "Desert Shield." This began the start of a massive buildup of military forces against Iraq, with troops representing 33 countries. The U.S. Army's Gen. Norman Schwarzkopf assumed command of the multinational force in his position as the theater commander of the U.S. Central Command. On August 7, the United Nations (UN) voted to place an economic embargo on Iraq and occupied Kuwait and freeze all Kuwaiti assets. Reports of Iraqi army misbehavior in Kuwait and the Iraqi decision to hold foreign civilians hostage focused attention on Iraqi ruthlessness, thereby promoting the U.S. effort to rally participatory opposition to Saddam Hussein.

The Iraqi army seemed a potent threat to any defense of Saudi Arabia. Combat-experienced after the recently ended eight-year Iran-Iraq War, the Iraqi army possessed more than 4,700 tanks, 3,200 artillery pieces, 500 combat aircraft, and extensive chemical warfare capabilities. The Republican Guard, elite units loyal to Saddam Hussein, concerned coalition military planners. After seizing Kuwait, these units redeployed to counterattack positions astride the northwestern Iraq-Kuwait border while the rest of the army fortified the Kuwait-Saudi border. These defenses included numerous strongpoints, minefields, and antitank ditches filled with flammable liquids.

Strategic Options. Saddam Hussein promised a bloody and protracted war—the "mother of all battles"—that would sap U.S. and coalition willpower. He hoped to break the tenuous bonds forging the allied coalition.

Allied options were more varied. The UN and the coalition did implement economic sanctions and a blockade of Iraq. The opinions on how long sanctions would take varied greatly, the general consensus being 12–18 months. The option to use military force seemed the only means of insuring Iraq's withdrawal.

American soldiers from the 82d Airborne Division conduct reaction drills in Saudi Arabia (1990) in preparation of Operation Desert Storm. (U.S. Air Force)

Coalition and U.S. advantages lay in air and sea power, high-technology precision-guided weapons, command and control procedures, and superbly trained troops. By the time warfare started on Jan. 17, 1991, the coalition had deployed more than 443,000 troops and 3,500 tanks against Iraq. The coalition campaign plan sought a rapid, decisive victory through the destruction of Iraqi combat forces.

Decision for War. President Bush consistently stated that Iraq must withdraw from Kuwait. After an initial groundswell of support in the United States, some complained that any conflict would be a "war for oil," not a moral war to free a democracy. Bush countered that the stability of this region was a vital U.S. interest and that the blatant Iraqi violation of international law had to be answered. Bush also expressed concern over the Iraqi development of chemical and nuclear weapons.

By late October 1990, Iraq still remained firmly ensconced in Kuwait. In early November, the United States announced the deployment of 200,000 more troops to Saudi Arabia. These reinforcements provided the coalition with an offensive capability previously not possessed. These additional forces deployed and were in place by early February 1991. The UN kept up the pressure on Iraq by authorizing, on Nov. 29, 1990, military action to expel Iraqi forces from Kuwait, setting the deadline for the withdrawal as Jan. 15, 1991. In early January 1991, the U.S. Congress authorized President Bush to use force to enforce the UN resolution. Last-minute negotiations between the United States and Iraq failed to achieve any settlement.

Air Campaign. Early on January 17, allied aircraft and cruise missiles began the attack against targets in Iraq and Kuwait, bombing Iraqi weapons facilities, command control sites, power plants, and other military targets. Aircraft also bombed the Iraqi army and Republican Guard ground units in order to damage their capabilities prior to the start of the ground campaign.

The air campaign achieved great success as allied pilots flew more than 62,000 combat missions. Precision-guided munitions and all-weather and night bombing capabilities allowed pinpoint attacks against Iraqi targets. The Iraqi air force fled to northern Iraq and to Iran in order to avoid destruction by allied aircraft. Suppression of Iraqi air defense systems and the overmatched Iraqi air force insured allied air supremacy.

Immediately after the war began, Iraq retaliated with the first of 91 militarily insignificant launches of Scud surface-to-surface missiles against Saudi Arabia and Israel. These attacks failed to achieve their objective of provoking Israel into attacking Iraq.

Coalition Deception Plans. The initial deployment of the U.S. ground forces insured the defense of Saudi Arabia. The allies later formulated a strategic deception plan that tricked the Iraqis into believing the main attack would come north into the Iraqi defenses along the Kuwait-Saudi border.

During January and February, the U.S. Army's VII and XVIII Corps redeployed from their initial assembly areas in northeastern Saudi Arabia. These units moved west over 150–250 kilometers, undetected, into their final attack positions, totally outflanking Iraqi fortifications.

The Iraqis conducted the first major ground operation on January 29, attacking south at four points on the Kuwait-Saudi border. Allied air and ground forces counterattacked and easily destroyed the Iraqi columns.

Ground Campaign. The allied ground offensive began on February 24. Two U.S. Marine divisions reinforced by a U.S. Army armored brigade launched secondary attacks along the main road from Saudi Arabia to Kuwait City. Arab forces attacked along the western Kuwait-Saudi border in order to fix Iraqi defensive forces. U.S. Marine Corps amphibious units remained offshore to pin down Iraqi forces deployed on the Kuwaiti coast.

The U.S. VII Corps conducted the main attack. This tank and mechanized infantry force of five and a half divisions attacked north into Iraq, outflanking Iraqi fortifications. Its ultimate objective was the destruction of the Republican Guard units. Further west, the U.S. XVIII Corps conducted an immensely successful secondary attack, which struck deep to the Euphrates River, thereby severing all Iraqi supply lines into the Kuwaiti theater of operations.

On February 25, Baghdad Radio announced that the Iraqi Army was withdrawing "in an organized manner" from Kuwait. U.S. reconnaissance detected this withdrawal, which was anything but organized. The VII Corps quickly turned east in order to trap and destroy the Republican Guard. During an all-night attack on February 26–27, the VII Corps fought the largest tank battles since World War II. More than 600 U.S. tanks destroyed elements from at least 12 Iraqi divisions as the VII and XVIII Corps pursued them into western Kuwait and southeastern Iraq.

The coalition, disturbed by the slaughter taking place against a retreating Iraqi army, declared a unilateral cease-fire, which took effect at 8:00 A.M., February 28, 100 hours after the start of the ground offensive. By the time of the cease-fire, allied forces had liberated Kuwait and severed nearly all Iraqi lines of communications between Baghdad and southern Iraq. Some Iraqi army units did escape from Kuwait due to the timing of the cease-fire. In addition, the Iraqi army blew up more than 1,000 Kuwaiti oil wells, which caused severe ecological damage to the region.

Operation Desert Storm ranks as the most one-sided victory in U.S. military history. American troops killed in action numbered 123, while Iraqi military losses have been estimated as high as 100,000 killed in action and 80,000 taken prisoner. Iraq lost more than 75 percent of its armored vehicles and field artillery pieces.

Aftermath. Under the cease-fire terms, the Iraqi government agreed to destroy its nuclear and chemical weapons plants, allow access to UN inspection teams, and pay reparations to Kuwait. After the war ended, Iraq resisted fulfilling the agreement. Coalition forces occupied southern Iraq until mid-April. Around the periphery of these positions, however, Saddam Hussein used his surviving Republican Guard units to suppress revolts against his regime. These units committed numerous, well-documented atrocities against Iraqi citizens. In northeastern Iraq, the UN and the U.S. military conducted extensive relief operations to assist the Iraqi Kurdish population that was being persecuted by the government.

Operation Desert Storm achieved the coalition objective of liberating Kuwait. Coalition forces triumphed due to a combination of U.S. military prowess and Iraqi ineptitude. In using air power to isolate the battlefield and weaken the Iraqi army, the coalition set the stage for the decisive ground operation by the VII and XVIII Corps.

Bibliography: DuBois, Thomas R., "The Weinberger Doctrine and the Liberation of Kuwait," *Parameters* (winter 1991–92); Freedman, Lawrence, and Efraim Karsh, "How Kuwait was Won," *International Security* (fall 1991); ———, The Second Gulf War (Princeton Univ. Press, 1992); Freidman, Norman, *Desert Victory: The War for Kuwait* (Naval Inst. Press, 1991); Szafranski, Richard, "Desert Storm Lessons from the Rear," *Parameters* (winter 1991–92); U.S. News and World Report Staff, *Triumph Without Victory: The Unreported History of the Persian Gulf War* (Random House, 1992).

Maj. Kevin McKedy

DISTANT EARLY WARNING LINE

System designed to provide radar and other electronic surveillance of the Soviet Union in order to monitor technological progress and, more important, any possible hostile actions against the United States and its allies. The Distant Early Warning (DEW) Line was created beginning in 1954 across the most northerly practicable part of North America. The capability of this string of listening posts across the Arctic was to be 100-percent detection for all weapons up to 100,000 feet in altitude, which would include ballistic missiles. The United States provided the funding and supervision of the construction, and Canada, with a similar system already in place in certain parts of its nation, would link with the DEW Line for an unbroken surveillance sequence in the Arctic. This system was constructed quickly in the next two years and served its purpose throughout the Cold War.

Bibliography: Watson, Robert J., *The Joint Chiefs of Staff and National Policy, 1953–1954* (Historical Div., Joint Chiefs of Staff, 1986).

Roger D. Launius

DOMINICAN REPUBLIC INTERVENTION
(April 1965–June 1966)

U.S. military response to a volatile situation in the West Indies. After the assassination of repressive dictator Raphael Trujillo Molina in 1961, the Dominican Republic, one of the poorest nations in the Western Hemisphere, entered into a prolonged period of political instability. In 1962, the reform-minded Juan Bosch was elected president. He fell from power in September 1963 in a coup d'etat orchestrated by a right-wing military clique, which failed to gain the loyalty of the Dominican people. On Apr. 24, 1965, pro-Bosch forces, including a number of leftist groups sympathetic to Fidel Castro's regime in Cuba, launched their own coup and toppled the government led by Donald Reid Cabral the following day. Full-scale civil war broke out, as army and navy units remaining loyal to the Cabral government—and under the command of Gen. Elias Wessin y Wessin—struck hard at rebel forces dug in at critical points in Santo Domingo, the capital, including the Presidential Palace and the Duarte Bridge leading into the city.

The administration of Pres. Lyndon B. Johnson, fearing for the safety of Americans in Santo Domingo, ordered U.S. Marines into the city. The first contingent, some 405 marines, landed by helicopter on April 28. As the fighting continued, the United States became increasingly fearful that the pro-Bosch faction was being taken over by leftists, and additional U.S. troops were deployed over the strenuous objections of most members of the Organization of American States (OAS), which was seeking (without much success) to bring about a negotiated settlement. Elements of the 82d Airborne Division were flown into Santo Domingo, and more marines were brought ashore from ships anchored just off the coast of the island nation.

U.S. troops first engaged rebel snipers near the U.S. Embassy on April 29. The nature of their mission changed somewhat on April 30, as the Johnson administration decided to separate the warring factions—a decision, in the words of one historian, that "in effect favored the military right-wingers." The marines moved eastward through the narrow streets of Santo Domingo, linking up with elements of the 82d Airborne Division and thereby separating the warring parties and establishing an "international security zone." The Pentagon announced on May 5 that U.S. forces in the Dominican Republic consisted of some 12,500 army troops and 6,900 marines. On that same day, an OAS-sponsored truce was signed, but fighting resumed on May

13 and continued until May 19. By that point, 19 U.S. servicemen had lost their lives in the confused fighting in and around Santo Domingo.

On May 23, an OAS-sponsored inter-American armed force took over the peacekeeping role the U.S. forces had performed unilaterally. Sporadic fighting continued until after the election of Pres. Joaquin Balaguer in June 1966. The U.S. contingent in the OAS force, some 6,000 officers and men, began to withdraw from the Dominican Republic at the end of June 1966.

Bibliography: Palmer, Bruce, Jr., *Intervention in the Caribbean: The Dominican Crisis of 1965* (Univ. of Kentucky Press, 1989).

James A. Warren

DOOLITTLE BOARD (1946)

Board created in March 1946 by Sec. of War Robert P. Patterson and chaired by Lt. Gen. James H. Doolittle, to study officer-enlisted relationships. In investigating the complaints of incompetent leadership and abuse of privilege by officers in the World War II era, the Doolittle Board found that the rapid expansion of the army between 1939 and 1945 had indeed created unprecedented personnel and morale problems. Many citizen soldiers disliked the regimentation and hierarchical structure of the armed forces. Poor leadership and a system that encouraged a wide social gap between commissioned and enlisted personnel had contributed to inequities in the management of enlisted soldiers and the abuse of privilege during the war. To create an army better attuned to democratic values, the board recommended improved selection and training of officers, more equitable treatment of enlisted personnel with respect to pay and access to facilities, and the amendment or elimination of many laws, regulations, and customs that unfairly discriminated against enlisted personnel. The board also recommended closer integration of the military with surrounding civilian communities.

Lt. Col. (Ret.) Charles R. Shrader

FIGHTER AIRCRAFT: F-86, F-14, F-15, F-16

Four classifications of U.S. combat planes. Essentially, the role of fighter aircraft is to seek and destroy enemy planes in flight and to protect bomber aircraft.

The F-86 "Sabre Jet," a straight-wing plane, was flight-tested in 1947 and entered air force front-line service in 1949. It was deployed to the Korean War theater in 1950 with the Air Force 4th Fighter-Interceptor Group to challenge the Soviet-built MG-15, which had been harassing U.S. B-29 bombers over North Korea. The F-86 began escorting B-29 bombers and quickly established air superiority for the United States. The F-86 went through six versions, the last of which, the F-86L, was flown into the early 1960s by National Guard air units. The first models weighed 16,000 pounds and carried four .50-caliber machine guns; the F-86D was the first aircraft to employ air-to-air missiles rather than machine guns.

The F-14 "Tomcat" was flight tested in 1970 and entered service in 1972 as a navy squadron fighter. Built with a swing wing configuration, armed with one 20-millimeter cannon and four mounted missiles, and flown at speeds up to 1,500 miles per hour, the F-14 consistently proved itself to be decisive in air combat, especially when it was used

An F-16C fighter plane, nicknamed the "Fighting Falcon," is equipped with AIM-9 Sidewinder missiles and Mark 84 2,000-pound bombs on a mission over Iraq during Operation Desert Storm. (U.S. Air Force)

during an air strike over Libya in 1986 and in the Persian Gulf region during Operation Desert Storm in 1991.

The F-15 "Fighting Eagle" was first produced in 1972 and, although initially designed as an air interceptor, proved just as effective as a fighter-bomber. Equipped with one six-barrel 20-millimeter gun and eight air-to-air missiles, its capabilities range from taking the lead in an air superiority role to flying ground support missions. Capable of carrying a heavy (16,000-pound maximum) payload, it can attain a speed of 1,678 miles per hour and has a combat range of 2,385 square miles.

The F-16 "Fighting Falcon" possesses a combat radius of more than 575 square miles and can carry a payload of up to 14,220 pounds. It is armed with one six-barrel 20-millimeter gun (500 rounds) and two air-to-air missiles, mainly for self protection.

Leo J. Daugherty III

FLEXIBLE RESPONSE

U.S. defense policy initiated by Pres. John F. Kennedy. By the end of the Eisenhower administration, the accepted concept of "massive retaliation" had been questioned by military leaders, civilian theorists of strategy and deterrence, and U.S. allies. Many questioned whether the United States would risk nuclear war with the Soviet Union for any challenge less than an invasion of America. During the election campaign of 1960, defense policy became a major issue. The Kennedy campaign insisted that the existing defense policy had to be replaced with a new strategy called "flexible response."

As soon as he entered the White House in 1961, Kennedy scrapped the concepts of the "New Look" and massive retaliation. He stated that the United States would return to a rational strategy and an ability to fight limited wars. The United States would choose how and where to retaliate, and the U.S. response would be appropriate to the type of aggression faced. One of the key reasons for the change was that Kennedy no longer believed the major threat to the United States was a general war with the Soviets. He believed that proxy wars and wars of national liberation would be the primary types of future conflicts. In such wars, the threat of massive nuclear attack would not be believed and, in fact, would never deter an aggressor from acting. The United States had to recast its military system into a credible conventional one.

The change from the armed forces of the massive retaliation era to a credible conventional military was not immediate. During the Berlin Crisis of 1961–62, the president still had limited options and was forced to call up reserve forces to maintain a strategic reserve. During the Cuban Missile Crisis of 1962, the regular army forces that mobilized had a wide range of personnel shortages, poorly trained units, and catastrophic maintenance failures. All of these could be attributed to the neglect of the New Look

period. However, increased defense spending slowly rebuilt the military.

Two other issues took even longer to resolve. First, flexible response needed smaller and more accurate missiles and nuclear warheads. The U.S. nuclear missile force could not be so large as to invite a Soviet first strike. The U.S. nuclear force also had to be carefully managed to be seen as a credible first strike force while having the small size and accuracy required to support a conventional war. The second issue concerning flexible response was its acceptance by the North Atlantic Treaty Organization (NATO). During the massive retaliation period, NATO had questioned if the United States was willing to defend Europe if faced with nuclear war. These doubts continued into the 1960s as European allies questioned the U.S. commitment to such circumstances. NATO did not accept flexible response as official policy until 1967. Approval was not gained until after the United States made concrete steps to increase its conventional forces.

By 1967, the United States had increased and modernized its units. The army reorganized its divisions, increased aviation assets, and introduced the air cavalry divisions. The navy increased its aviation assets and increased the Marine Corps, while the air force created more tactical air wings. In all these changes, the United States was declaring its willingness to fight at any level required to counter aggression. Flexible response has remained the military policy of the United States and NATO into the 1990s.

Bibliography: Hagan, Kenneth, and William Roberts, *Against All Enemies* (Greenwood Press, 1986); Millet, Allan, and Peter Maslowski, *For the Common Defense* (Free Press, 1984); Weigley, Russell, *The American Way of War* (Indiana Univ. Press, 1977).

Maj. George B. Eaton

FORWARD AIR CONTROLLER

Military pilot charged with directing air strikes, particularly when they are delivered in the near proximity of friendly troops. Forward air controllers (FACs) may conduct their duties while flying or they may be on the ground. They generally are experienced fighter-bomber pilots who return to their normal assignments after performing FAC duties. In some instances, the FACs live with the ground unit they support, becoming familiar with the terrain, the supported unit, and local conditions. During the Vietnam War, most FACs flew light, propeller-driven aircraft that had the capability to stay aloft for extended periods. They would effect radio contact with the ground unit, use smoke rockets to mark targets, and then communicate with incoming attack aircraft.

Bibliography: Robbins, Christopher, *The Ravens* (Crown, 1987).

Col. (Ret.) Rod Paschall

FRAGGING

Term used during the Vietnam War to describe the murder of U.S. officers and noncommissioned officers (NCOs) by disgruntled U.S. soldiers. The word "fragging" evolved from the practice of hurling fragmentation hand grenades into the sleeping quarters of the victims. These incidents were aimed at intimidating officers and NCOs who were too aggressive in carrying out dangerous tactical operations or in enforcing regulations against the use of drugs. The widely publicized antiwar statements of numerous U.S. government officials, including several senators, caused a sharp decline in discipline and morale, which fueled the fraggings. Of the 126 fraggings reported in 1969, 37 resulted in fatality. Fragging incidents increased over the next two years, with 271 cases reported in 1970 and 333 in 1971.

Brig. Gen. (Ret.) Theodore C. Mataxis

FREE-FIRE ZONE

Term used to denote an enemy-dominated region where it is permissible to bomb, strafe, or use artillery. The term was most used during the Vietnam War, where it was often necessary to secure the permission of Vietnamese government officials prior to subjecting an area to firepower. Unlike the lack of controls during the two world wars and the Korean War, these procedures were used in Vietnam so as keep to a minimum the alienation of the local population toward allied troops. Because Communist forces had managed to take control of certain uninhabited, heavily forested regions of South Vietnam, there were areas that were continuously subjected to allied firepower. In these free-fire zones, any suspicious movement or sighting was likely to be struck at any time.

Bibliography: Lewey, Guenter, *America in Vietnam* (Oxford Univ. Press, 1978).

Col. (Ret.) Rod Paschall

GAITHER COMMITTEE (1957)

U.S. committee (also known as the Security Resources Panel of the Office of Defense Management), headed by H. Rowan Gaither, Jr., that submitted to Pres. Dwight D. Eisenhower and to the National Security Council a formal report on the status of the U.S. nuclear deterrence program and on the estimated growing threat presented by the Soviet Union. The report contended that the Soviets would gain on and eventually lead the United States in the number of intercontinental ballistic missiles (ICBMs) manufactured and that it was time to negotiate for control. The report urged the administration to strengthen U.S. nuclear retaliatory capability and to begin a nuclear fallout shelter construction program.

Leo J. Daugherty III

GENEVA CONFERENCE (1954)

Co-chaired by Britain and the Soviet Union, the Geneva Conference of 1954 brought the era of French colonialism in Indochina to an end. Nations represented at the conference included the People's Republic of China, France, the United States, the Republic of Vietnam (South Vietnam), the Democratic Republic of Vietnam (North Vietnam), Cambodia, and Laos. The actual terms of the agreement were largely hammered out between the Chinese and the French. Although being acknowledged as independent, the newly formed states of Indochina were not wholly in agreement with the final product. The terms established a demilitarized zone between the two Vietnams, provided for the evacuation of French forces, called for supervised elections in 1956, and established a period for repatriation. Some of the agreements, such as the demilitarized zone and the elections, were later violated or ignored.

Bibliography: Gardner, Lloyd C., *Approaching Vietnam: From World War II through Dienbienphu* (Norton, 1988).

Col. (Ret.) Rod Paschall

GENEVA CONVENTIONS

Various international agreements, signed in Geneva, Switzerland, and designed to prevent or end war. The conventions of 1949 resulted from the revulsion at the horrors of World War II. The most important agreements set standards for the treatment of civilians and prisoners of war. Although most countries have accepted the conventions, belligerents often accuse each other of violating them during war.

The Geneva Conference of 1954 resulted in agreements to establish peace in Indochina, signed by France, Great Britain, the Soviet Union, the United States, and the Asian countries of China, North and South Vietnam, Cambodia, and Laos. Other conferences associated with Geneva include the 1955 summit conference among the United States, the Soviet Union, France, and Great Britain and the 1958 conference among the United States, the Soviet Union, and Great Britain on banning nuclear weapons testing.

Stephen Robinson

GRENADA, INVASION OF
(October 25–November 3, 1983)

U.S. military action against revolutionary forces in the West Indian nation of Grenada. Nicknamed "Operation Urgent Fury," it was a hastily conceived, yet essentially successful, rescue mission. On Oct. 19, 1983, a violent feud between leaders of Grenada's Marxist-oriented New Jewel party led to the execution of Prime Minister Maurice Bishop and seven associates. A revolutionary military council chaired by Gen. Hudson Austin declared martial law.

The U.S. government was initially concerned for the safety of several hundred U.S. and other foreign nationals, primarily students at Grenada's medical school. In the long run, however, the Ronald Reagan administration sought to limit Cuban influence in Grenada, an influence symbolized by the Cuban workers building the Salines airfield on the southwestern tip of Grenada. Thus, while the initial response on October 20 was the diversion of the 22d Marine Amphibious Unit (MAU) southward for a possible evacuation of noncombatants, U.S. officials soon sought to eliminate the Marxist government. This planning was encouraged by the Organization of Eastern Caribbean States.

Plans.   The marine forces could eventually have conquered any resistance on the island. However, their ships could not arrive off Grenada until October 24. In addition, U.S. planners wanted to use sudden, overwhelming force to avoid a prolonged struggle. These considerations prompted a piecemeal expansion of the intervention force.

The U.S. Atlantic Command (LantCom) gave overall control of the operation to Joint Task Force (JTF) 120, under Vice Adm. Joseph Metcalf III. While the marines secured the northern end of the island, the main tasks of seizing the Salines airfield, freeing the British governor general, and evacuating the foreign medical students fell to JTF 123, under Maj. Gen. Richard A. Sholtes. The navy's sea-air-land (SEAL) teams were assigned to free the British governor general from house arrest while the 1st and 2d battalions, 75th Ranger Regiment, seized Salines by low-level parachute assault and then evacuated foreign nationals. A task force of army special forces and rangers would free political prisoners at the Richmond Hill prison. By the time the press arrived, the marines held the northern end of the island while elements of the 82d Airborne Division mopped up resistance in the south.

From its inception, however, the planning and execution of Operation Urgent Fury had significant flaws. First, the plan grew gradually between October 20 and 23, with additional forces being added incrementally, often using these forces in impractical ways. The 82d Airborne Division, for example, was included in the plan without its parent XVIII Airborne Corps, which normally provided significant support for the division. Moreover, Metcalf chose not to use the joint, multiservice staff that was supposed to conduct such a large operation. Instead, he took only a "flyaway staff" of 20 naval officers. The commander of the 24th Infantry Division, Maj. Gen. H. Norman Schwarzkopf, was belatedly detailed to accompany this staff as a liaison officer. These planning problems should not be exaggerated, of course. Metcalf relied heavily on Schwarzkopf both as an adviser and a deputy joint commander. In addition, the XVIII Airborne Corps commander, Lt. Gen. Jack V. Mackmull, informally provided his experience and support to the deploying airborne division. Still, Admiral Metcalf's staff lacked the size and expertise necessary to coordinate all four armed services in such a complicated, high-risk operation.

Assault.   Only the 22d MAU landed on schedule on the morning of October 25, seizing the smaller airfield at Pearls without incident. To the south, the special operations forces ran into a series of delays. A SEAL team made its way to the governor general's house but was pinned down by defending forces. Delayed en route, the heliborne assault on Richmond Hill prison arrived in broad daylight and was driven off.

Given insufficient aircraft, and then delayed by a navigational failure, the two ranger battalions arrived over Salines airfield after sunrise on October 25. Antiaircraft fire caused the two units to become intermingled as they parachuted onto the field. Still, within four hours, the rangers had secured the field and located 138 U.S. students at the nearby True Blue campus of St. George's Medical School. Only then did they learn that an even larger group of students was at the previously unknown Grand Anse campus, farther north.

Buildup and Sweep.   The unexpected resistance, in conjunction with the need to secure Grand Anse, transformed the plan into a formal occupation of the island to forestall a prolonged guerrilla struggle. The 82d Airborne, originally assigned only a minor role in the invasion, had to conduct this sweep.

The 82d, however, was operating under numerous disadvantages. Atlantic Command planners had insisted that the 82d truncate its preparations to avoid a public signal that the United States was preparing to attack. This change, plus the absence of the XVIII Airborne Corps staff that normally assisted in such deployments, caused considerable bottlenecks when the paratroops finally assembled. Marine personnel who were supposed to coordinate naval fire support for these paratroops arrived without correct radio call signs. Meanwhile, JTF 120 had only one common satellite network for coordination.

The 82d had to build up its combat and logistics structure from nothing, using only the half-completed Salines airfield, which could accommodate only one aircraft at a time. Consequently, the 82d Airborne Division's leading brigade required 31 hours to assemble on the island. The 82d was also called upon to guard and feed prisoners of war, evacuate medical students, and support the forces provided by neighboring governments. Thus, contrary to the public image of a massive U.S. force being held at bay by a few hundred defenders, the actual number of rangers and paratroops available to fight during the first three days was never more than 1,500.

The limited U.S. forces available succeeded in breaking Grenadan resistance, however. Late on October 25, the 22d MAU skillfully landed a small force on the western shore of the island, and on the following morning, this unit cleared the capital and freed the governor general. That next day, marine helicopters transported army rangers to evacuate successfully the Grand Anse campus. On October 27, a series of errors caused a U.S. aircraft to attack mistakenly the command post of the 2d Brigade, 82d Airborne Division, wounding 17 soldiers.

Conclusion. After the fact, many observers criticized the high cost, lack of coordination, and apparently ponderous execution of the operation. Certainly, the U.S. forces suffered from the inevitable problems of hasty planning under extreme, and ultimately unsuccessful, requirements for secrecy. Despite these initial problems, the commanders on the scene worked together effectively, improvising solutions that accomplished the mission.

Bibliography: Adkin, M., *Urgent Fury: The Battle for Grenada* (Free Press, 1989); Dunn, P. M., and B. W. Watson, eds., *American Intervention in Grenada: The Implications of Operation Urgent Fury* (Westview Press, 1985); Metcalf, J., "Decision Making and the Grenada Rescue Operation," *Ambiguity and Command,* ed. by J. G. March and R. Weissengen-Baylon (Ballinger Publishers, 1987); Vessey, J. W., "JCS Responds to Criticism of Grenada Operation," *Army* magazine (Aug. 1984).

Jonathan M. House

GROUND ATTACK AIRCRAFT

Military planes utilized for air-to-surface assaults. Following World War II, U.S. ground attack aircraft largely continued to be wartime designs, such as the A-1 "Skyraider," or fighter-bombers pressed into the role. After the Korean War, however, the navy developed a series of jet-powered bombers capable of acting in a ground attack role. Designed to attack either naval or land targets, the A-4 "Skyhawk" and A-6 "Intruder" both proved valuable during the Vietnam War. The air force did not have a purpose-built ground attack plane, but relied instead on fighter-bombers. These planes, however, were vulnerable to groundfire, and their high speeds often affected their bombing accuracy. Therefore, both services supplemented their fighter-bombers with older designs, such as the A-1, and armed trainers, such as the A-37 "Dragonfly." The air force also purchased the A-7 "Corsair II," the navy's replacement for the A-4.

In the late 1960s, both the air force and marines began looking for new ground attack aircraft. The air force envisioned its new plane, the A-10 "Thunderbolt II," as a flying tank destroyer and built it around 30-millimeter Gatling-type cannon. Designed to operate at low altitude, the A-10 featured heavy armor and a wide variety of missiles and bombs in addition to its cannon. The marines, on the other hand, intended their A-8 "Harrier" to provide general ground support from rough forward airfields. Conventionally armed, the A-8 featured an innovative "vectored thrust" system that allowed the plane to take off and

land vertically. Both services began deploying these planes in the mid-1970s. The navy's subsequent decision to buy the F/A-18 "Hornet," a conventional fighter-bomber intended to replace the A-7, forced a cutback in marine purchases of the A-8.

Bibliography: Mrozek, Donald J., *Air Power and the Ground War in Vietnam* (Pergamon-Brassey's, 1989).

Richard F. Kehrberg

GULF OF TONKIN INCIDENT
(August 2–4, 1964)

Naval incident off the coast of North Vietnam that brought the United States directly into the Vietnam conflict. On July 30, 1964, South Vietnamese commandos accompanied by U.S. advisers raided two islands in the Gulf of Tonkin. From mid-July, the U.S. destroyer *Maddox* had been conducting surveillance operations in international waters in the gulf. On August 1, the *Maddox* hailed South Vietnamese gunboats returning commandos to Da Nang, and on the following day, the *Maddox* cruised close to offshore islands that were again subjected to South Vietnamese commando raids. The North Vietnamese government alleged that the destroyer had "protected" these commando attacks.

Later on August 2, three North Vietnamese patrol boats repeatedly approached the *Maddox,* which responded by opening fire. Only at this stage did the patrol boats retaliate by launching torpedoes, which missed. Having sustained gunfire damage, the patrol boats retired. Hanoi subsequently claimed that the incident was in response to the raids of July 30 and August 2. Although both sides agreed that the engagement took place, they disagreed about motivation. U.S. assistant secretary of state William P. Bundy announced that the *Maddox* had been "well off the coast of North Vietnam" and that its presence was unrelated to the South Vietnamese raids. Thus, the U.S. version of events claimed that the North Vietnamese boats had launched an "unprovoked" attack against a U.S. warship engaged in "routine" patrol.

Pres. Lyndon B. Johnson personally ordered the destroyer *Turner Joy* to reinforce the *Maddox* in the gulf in order to "assert the right of freedom of the seas." Concurrently, South Vietnamese commandos returned to the gulf, attacking mainland coastal fortifications. While the United States again denied any connection between the two incidents, Hanoi interpreted the U.S. response as deliberate provocation.

On August 4, the United States alleged that North Vietnamese torpedo boats had again attacked the *Maddox* and *Turner Joy,* 65 miles off the North Vietnamese coast. The destroyers claimed to have repulsed the attack, possibly destroying several attacking craft. Hanoi, however, vehemently denied that the attack ever occurred, and the incident remains obscure. The destroyers believed that they saw numerous torpedo tracks on radar, but no actual torpedoes or vessels were observed. More sober assessments after the initial alarm questioned whether an attack had taken place at all. However, just 13 hours after the alleged attack, at 11:30 A.M. on August 4, President Johnson informed the U.S. public that retaliatory air strikes were already underway, and on the following day, Congress passed the Gulf of Tonkin Resolution, which escalated U.S. military involvement in Vietnam.

Bibliography: Young, Marilyn B., *The Vietnam Years 1945–1990* (HarperCollins, 1991).

Russell A. Hart

GULF OF TONKIN RESOLUTION
(August 1964)

Proposal put before Congress by Pres. Lyndon B. Johnson on Aug. 5, 1964, in reaction to alleged unprovoked attacks by North Vietnamese torpedo boats on U.S. destroyers in the Gulf of Tonkin during August 2–4. Its stated purpose was to approve and support the president's determination to take all necessary measures to repel an armed attack against U.S. forces and to prevent further aggression. It declared that the maintenance of international peace and

Sen. Wayne Morse of Oregon, firmly against U.S. involvement in the Vietnam War, was one of only two congressional opponents (with Sen. Ernest Gruening of Alaska) of the 1964 Gulf of Tonkin Resolution. (National Archives)

security in Southeast Asia was vital to American interests. The resolution passed both houses of Congress on August 7, with only two dissenting votes. The resolution was later criticized as a congressional blank check for the president to wage war and was subjected to a Senate investigation.

Russell A. Hart

HAIPHONG, MINING OF (May 1972)

Mining of a vital North Vietnamese port by U.S. forces during the Vietnam War. Haiphong, about 10 miles inland from the Gulf of Tonkin, was North Vietnam's most important port and was connected to the capital of Hanoi by rail line. The North Vietnamese were receiving up to 85 percent of their imported supplies through the facility. Throughout the war, the U.S. Joint Chiefs of Staff had advocated the disabling of the Haiphong harbor, but prior to 1972, U.S. presidents were fearful of Chinese and Soviet countermoves if Haiphong's sea approaches were mined. Frustrated over Hanoi's intransigence at peace negotiations, Pres. Richard M. Nixon gave the order to mine the port, with those ships already in the harbor given a period of time to withdraw. The operation was conducted by naval aircraft and was a success. The mines were self-actuating. After the 1973 peace agreement, the harbor was cleared of mines by the U.S. Navy.

Bibliography: Marolda, Edward J., and G. Wesley Pryce III, *A Short History of the United States Navy and the Southeast Asian Conflict* (Naval Hist. Center, 1984).

Col. (Ret.) Rod Paschall

HAMBURGER HILL, BATTLE OF
(May 8–20, 1969)

Noted battle fought by elements of the U.S. 101st Airborne Division early in the "Vietnamization" phase of the Vietnam War. Originally launched as a brigade-size heliborne operation into the A Shau Valley to eliminate enemy base area 611, elements of the "Screaming Eagles" 3d Brigade discovered a large enemy force entrenched on Ap Bia Mountain (Hill 937). The 101st's efforts to dislodge the determined North Vietnamese Army (NVA) forces on Hill 937 led to some of the bloodiest combat of the war. Both U.S. and NVA losses soared as additional U.S. forces and firepower were thrown into the battle. When the North Vietnamese were finally driven off the mountain on May 20, more than 400 U.S. soldiers had been killed or wounded with the NVA suffering more than 600 killed. This grisly battle set off a political firestorm in Washington and led to the abandonment of the strategy of attrition.

Bibliography: Karnow, Stanley, *Vietnam: A History* (Viking, 1983); Zaffiri, Samuel, *Hamburger Hill* (Presidio, 1988).

Capt. Leslie Howard Belknap

HO CHI MINH TRAIL

The major infiltration route of the North Vietnamese Army (NVA) into South Vietnam during the Vietnam War. Work on the Ho Chi Minh Trail began as early as 1959, when NVA general Vo Bam was ordered to expand the network of old trails leading from southern North Vietnam into the Laotian panhandle and down the eastern edge of Cambodia. By 1967, the trails had been transformed into a vast network of paved and dirt roads carrying troops, ammunition, food, and other supplies essential to the Communist war effort. The trail branched eastward into critical areas of South Vietnam—including the A Shau Valley in I Corps, the Ia Drang Valley in II Corps, and War Zone C in the III Corps region—and connected base camps, supply depots, and hospitals.

In 1965, the U.S. Air Force began a long campaign to interdict the flow of troops and matériel into South Vietnam along the Ho Chi Minh Trail. Although the bombing of the trail network exacted a heavy toll on the NVA, it never succeeded in shutting off the flow entirely. Hanoi simply stepped up the pace of resupply to compensate for the losses. As early as 1967, Gen. William Westmoreland requested permission to cut North Vietnam's lifeline with a ground assault, but Washington was reluctant to grant his request, as it would have widened the war and violated the neutrality of Laos and Cambodia. The Army of the Republic of Vietnam (ARVN) conducted a raid on the trail network in February 1971, but with its lifeline threatened, the NVA committed a large force of regulars and tanks to the fight, inflicting heavy casualties on the ARVN forces.

Bibliography: Summers, Harry G., Jr., *Vietnam War Almanac* (Facts On File, 1985).

James A. Warren

HOOVER COMMISSIONS
(1947–1949, 1953–1955)

Two post-World War II commissions on organization of the executive branch of the U.S. government, the Hoover Commissions were headed by former president Herbert Hoover and were aimed at improving the efficiency of the government, especially that of the Department of Defense. The findings and recommendations of the first Hoover Commission (1947–49) led directly to the amendment in 1949 of the National Security Act of 1947. The so-called National Military Establishment was replaced by a Department of Defense; the powers of the secretary of defense were strengthened, and he was given a deputy and three assistant secretaries, including a comptroller. A nonvoting chairman was provided for the Joint Chiefs of Staff, and the service secretaries lost their cabinet status and seats on the National Security Council.

Although both commissions advocated greater integration and central control of defense activities, the second Hoover Commission (1953–55) focused in particular on defense logistical and financial management. The commission's report on business organization of the Department of Defense recommended various measures to improve management in the department, which ultimately led to the creation of the Defense Supply Agency and other integrated defense logistical activities.

Bibliography: *Department of Defense Comments on the Hoover Commission Report on Business Organization of the Department of Defense* (Dept. of Defense, Mar. 1956); *Digests and Analyses of the Nineteen Hoover Commission Reports* (Citizens Committee for the Hoover Report, 1955); Hewes, James E., Jr., *From Root to McNamara: Army Organization and Administration, 1900–1963* (Center of Military History, U.S. Army, 1975).

Lt. Col. (Ret.) Charles R. Shrader

HUE, BATTLE OF
(January 31–March 2, 1968)

Very bloody, month-long battle during the Vietnam War in which U.S. forces recaptured the ancient Vietnam capital city of Hue from North Vietnamese and Viet Cong forces. Although the U.S. command was conscious of the necessity of preserving ancient Hue, at battle's end, the vicious fighting had destroyed much of the city. Marines were forced to rout the enemy house by house, using flamethrowing tanks. An all-out assault was launched against the Citadel (the walled-in part of the city containing the ancient imperial palace and government buildings), as both U.S. Army and South Vietnamese forces blocked the enemy's supply routes into the city. The North Vietnamese lost almost 5,000 troops, while the United States and South Vietnam lost 142. It was later revealed that North Vietnam and Viet Cong "death squads," in their campaign for Hue, had murdered approximately 6,000 South Vietnamese civilians; the discovery of some 2,800 bodies of such victims buried in mass graves shocked the world.

Leo J. Daugherty III

HUNGNAM, EVACUATION OF
(December 11–24, 1950)

The withdrawal of U.S. troops and Korean civilians from a North Korean port district during the Korean War. During the two weeks prior to Dec. 11, 1950, the five divisions of Maj. Gen. Edward Almond's X Corps withdrew under adverse conditions from widely separated forward positions in eastern North Korea to a 20-mile perimeter around the port of Hungnam and the nearby city of Hamhung. Redeployment to more strategically valuable areas of Korea then commenced. Some elements of Almond's corps had already debarked from Wonsan and Songjin. Waiting to withdraw the men and their equipment from Hungnam was Task Force 90, organized around transport and amphibious ships. The battleship *Missouri*, two heavy cruisers, and smaller ships provided gunfire support. Air cover was furnished by seven fleet and escort carriers. On December 24, the evacuation was completed. More than 100,000 military personnel and nearly as many Korean refugees had been embarked.

Bibliography: Appleman, Roy E., *Escaping the Trap: The U.S. Army X Corps in Northeast Korea, 1950* (Texas A&M Univ. Press, 1990); Cagle, Malcolm, and Frank A. Manson, *The Sea War in Korea* (Naval Inst. Press, 1957).

Lloyd J. Graybar

IA DRANG VALLEY, BATTLE OF THE
(July–November 1965)

Vietnam War action in which elements from U.S. Special Forces, South Vietnamese units, and the 1st Cavalry Division, a U.S. division equipped with 470 aircraft, mostly helicopters, fought and defeated a North Vietnamese division-size unit in the central Highlands of South Vietnam. The battle, actually a lengthy campaign, raged over a wide area of the Ia Drang River valley. It was one of the first major encounters between U.S. and North Vietnamese ground forces.

North Vietnamese leaders ordered a major campaign in Pleiku Province during the latter half of 1965. It involved three of the five North Vietnamese regiments entering South Vietnam. These units, the 32d, 33d, and 66th regiments, were under a veteran officer, Brig. Gen. Chu Huy Man, whose mission was to inflict maximum casualties on the Americans and South Vietnamese and seize both Pleiku and Kontum cities. Chu Huy Man's concept was first to eliminate the two U.S. Special Forces bases on the region's western limit.

As soon as the lead North Vietnamese regiment, the 32d, arrived in South Vietnam, it was committed against the U.S. Special Forces camp at Duc Co. Led by Col. To Dinh Khan, the regiment surrounded the camp at the end of July and began to probe the perimeter. However, the colonel's primary scheme was the old Viet Minh "bait and trap" idea: feign an all-out attack on the objective, ambush the relief force, then consolidate all forces for the final assault on the first objective. The 32d Regiment—about 2,200 strong with heavy mortars, antitank weapons, and 12.5-millimeter antiaircraft guns—was more than a match for Capt. R. B. Johnson's Special Forces detachment of 12 Americans and the roughly 200 lightly armed mountain tribesmen. However, Johnson successfully used close air support from the Vietnamese and U.S. air forces. It was not until August 9 that the ground relief force (an AVRN [Army of the Republic of Vietnam] battalion-size armor column), reinforced with infantry, began cautiously approaching the camp on National Route 19. The battle-wise ARVN tankers were fully expecting an ambush. The Communists failed in their ambush and left more than 100 bodies behind at the ambush site. The siege of Duc Co raged

on for 30 more days, but Johnson and his camp survived.

By September, the second North Vietnamese regiment, the 33d, arrived in Pleiku Province, and Chu Huy Man decided to take on the other outlying Special Forces base, Plei Me. This time, two regiments would be used, as well as a local Viet Cong main force battalion, in a bait-and-trap plan. The 33d Regiment was to attack Plei Me, and the battle-weary 32d was to ambush the relief force.

The situation at Plei Me was much the same as it had been at Duc Co. When the camp was attacked on October 19, the Special Forces commanded at Plei Me immediately called for air support. The overall U.S. Special Forces commander in Vietnam ordered Special Forces Operational Detachment Delta—15 Americans and about 150 Vietnamese rangers—to reinforce the camp. Also, the ARVN armor task force started its march to Plei Me. Once again, the South Vietnamese tankers rode into the ambush, this time their commander actually predicting where it was going to occur. As soon as the first shots were fired, the tank crews immediately spun their vehicles to the right and left of the road in a prearranged pattern and opened up with 76-millimeter canister rounds. After two hours of bloody fighting, the 32d Regiment once more broke contact and withdrew. While Special Forces took some casualties, two of the three North Vietnamese 32d Regiment's battalion commanders died and about one-half of the unit's 2,200 soldiers were killed or wounded. The Communists set out for the Cambodian border to reorganize.

The 1st Cavalry Division's artillery had gotten into the fight for Plei Me during the last few hours, and one of the division's brigades was ordered to hunt down and destroy the retreating Northern units. Over the next 30 days, alternating brigades of the division would move battalions by helicopter 22 times and displace artillery batteries by the same means 66 times. Some of these moves were for as long as 75 miles. One of the first contacts resulted in 11 Americans being killed and 51 wounded. The North Vietnamese had left a total of 99 bodies and 44 soldiers who were captured; they also left a highly informative map, one that detailed their trails from Cambodia to Plei Me.

During the next few days, the cavalrymen used their newly acquired information to great advantage. On November 3, the 1st Squadron, 9th Cavalry, set an ambush along a main infiltration trail, not far from the Cambodian border. A large column of North Vietnamese marched into the ambush and were promptly taken under fire. The Americans killed 72 members of the North Vietnamese 8th Battalion, 66th Regiment, the last of Gen. Chu Huy Man's units to arrive. The Americans lost 4 killed and 25 wounded during the hurried withdrawal. Within three more days, several other contacts had resulted in about 100 more North Vietnamese deaths.

In early November, only the 66th Regiment and the Viet Cong main force battalion remained somewhat intact and fully available to Chu Huy Man. The 32d Regiment had suffered through the poundings of sustained allied air attacks at both Duc Co and Plei Me as well as the two failed ambushes of ARVN armor forces. Of its original 2,200 men, the 33d Regiment had lost 890 killed in action and counted another 100 as missing. Additionally, the 33d had lost 70 percent of its heavy weapons. In contrast, the 1st Cavalry Division had lost 59 killed and 196 wounded.

On November 14, the 1st Battalion, 7th Cavalry, landed on the eastern slope of the Chu Pong Massif, a mountainous area along the Cambodian border. Using an artillery preparation on the landing zone, the battalion was soon searching out the area. It was the area where the newly arrived North Vietnamese 66th Regiment was concentrating and where the remnants of the bloodied 33d Regiment were recuperating. Suddenly, the Communists attacked the arriving Americans. The battle was joined and would be named for the code designation of the landing zone, "LZ X-Ray." The battle continued until Communist forces withdrew on November 17. They left 834 bodies, 139 weapons, and 6 prisoners. The Americans lost 79 killed and 121 wounded. The U.S. ground relief units encountered only light resistance. The cavalrymen returned to their base camp by helicopter, while the relief units were instructed to sweep to the north and reach designated pickup zones for eventual return to their base camps by helicopter.

One of the U.S. units making its way north to rendezvous with transport helicopters at landing zone "Albany" was surprised and assaulted by the North Vietnamese 8th Battalion, 66th Regiment. The assault by the Communists on the unwary cavalrymen was devastating. Control and, in some cases, discipline in the U.S. column disappeared. Gradually, order was achieved, and air power concentrated on the attacking forces. After the North Vietnamese broke contact the next day, the Americans claimed that about 400 of the Northerners had been killed. American losses also were high: 151 killed, 121 wounded, and 4 missing.

Three days later, on November 20, the bloodied 32d North Vietnamese Regiment was located, this time by elements of the ARVN Airborne Brigade sweeping south from Duc Co. With the help of U.S. firepower, 127 more Northerners were killed. General Chu Huy Man then ordered what was left of the three regiments to withdraw from South Vietnam for the safety of Cambodia. Hanoi's ambitious 1965 campaign to conquer the Central Highlands was at an end.

Bibliography: Coleman, J. D., *Pleiku: The Dawn of Helicopter Warfare in Vietnam* (St. Martin's Press, 1988); Stanton, Shelby, *Anatomy of a Division: The First Cav in Vietnam* (Presidio, 1987).

Col. (Ret.) Rod Paschall

ICBM (*see* **Intercontinental Ballistic Missiles**)

INCHON LANDINGS (September 15, 1950)

Major U.S. amphibious offensive during the Korean War. While the U.S. 8th and Republic of Korea (ROK) armies battled to defend the Pusan perimeter, Gen. of the Army Douglas MacArthur, who was in overall command in the Far East, began to consider ways to gain the upper hand. MacArthur concluded as early as June 29, 1950, that an amphibious landing at Inchon, or some other place on the Korean west coast would be needed to defeat the North Koreans. (This was, actually, an element of Pentagon War Plan SL-17, which had been distributed on June 19.) The plan assumed an invasion of South Korea by North Korean forces.

As envisioned by MacArthur's chief of staff, Maj. Gen. Edward D. Almond, and the Far East General Headquarters, the U.S. 24th and 25th divisions would deploy to South Korea to help defend Pusan, while the 1st Cavalry Division launched an amphibious landing at Inchon. This plan, implementing SL-17, was called Operation Bluehearts. The swift movement of the North Korean army quickly overtook Bluehearts.

MacArthur's plan, which had to await the availability of troops, equipment, and adequate naval support was named Operation Chromite. In spite of SL-17, there were many opponents to any landing at Inchon. Army Chief of Staff J. Lawton Collins, Chief of Naval Operations Adm. Forrest P. Sherman, and Rear Adm. James H. Doyle, who would command the operation, all had reservations. Indeed, the drawbacks were varied and numerous: (1) Inchon could be reached only by a narrow, treacherous, and easily mined channel; a single disabled ship could block it. (2) Tides ranged close to 32 feet, and at low tide, the harbor became a 3-mile-wide mud flat; there would be only two hours of full tide, and then only on September 15 and 27 or October 11. (3) There was no gradual beach, and landing areas could be overlooked by steep hills rising near the water. (4) The landing would have to take place during the typhoon season. (5) Inchon was a great distance from the Pusan perimeter; if the U.S. forces were repelled or pinned down on the Inchon beaches for very long, it would spell defeat for the Americans. (6) The landing would have to be made directly into the heart of a city, possibly forcing a slow, bloody house-to-house fight. (7) The invaders would have to reach and cross the broad Han River early in the battle, requiring landing craft and bridging. MacArthur, acknowledging all the inherent obstacles, felt that surprise would be his primary weapon to overcome these problems.

On September 1, naval lieutenant Eugene Clark, in Operation Trudy Jackson, was landed on a small island off Inchon. From there, he gathered valuable intelligence for the landing. As anticipated, a typhoon did batter the armada of ships converging on Inchon, but little damage was sustained. The fleet mustered 260 vessels, carrying nearly

70,000 men (including 37 landing ships manned by Japanese crews). The landing itself was carried out by the 1st Marine Division. The 7th Army Division landed later.

The objectives were three beaches: Green, Red, and Blue. Green Beach was against the small island of Wolmi-do, north of Inchon's inner harbor. The 3d Battalion, 5th Marines (Lt. Col. Robert D. Taplett), was assigned there. The remaining two battalions of the 5th (Lt. Col. Raymond L. Murray) came in on Red Beach, over a sea wall, and into Inchon itself, north of a causeway leading to Wolmi-do. Cemetery, Observation, and British Consulate hills all overlooked this landing area. Blue Beach, south of Inchon, was assigned to the newly formed 1st Marines (Col. Lewis B. Puller).

At midnight on September 14–15, a 19-ship force proceeded to its station at the entrance of Flying Fish Channel, leading to Inchon. It was guided, unexpectedly, by light from the lighthouse on Palmi-do. On his own initiative, Lieutenant Clark had gone to that island and turned on the light.

Green Beach. At 5:20 A.M., the first marines were embarked for Wolmi-do. Ten minutes later, the island was smothered by naval gunfire and rockets, followed by bombing and strafing by Corsair aircraft. At 6:33 A.M., the 3d Battalion came ashore. Within an hour and a half, Wolmi-do was secured, and a smaller island, South Wolmi-do, was taken by noon. Seventeen marines had been wounded. Of the enemy, 136 had been captured, 108 killed, and some 150 more buried in the rubble of their bunkers.

Red Beach. The assaults on both Red and Blue beaches were scheduled for 5:30 A.M. that day. Rain squalls, heavy smoke, and haze hampered visibility. The attack on Red Beach was supported by the 1st Battalion, 5th Marines, on Wolmi-do. A three-hour naval bombardment and air attacks preceded the attack. Company A, 1st Battalion, on the left and Company E, 2d Battalion, on the right led the assault, using scaling ladders to go over the sea wall. The going was easy in the south (right) zone, but the enemy fought hard in the north. More men were landed, and Cemetery Hill was taken without opposition. More men came ashore. By midnight September 15–16, all objectives, except Observatory Hill, belonged to the marines.

Blue Beach. The 2d and 3d battalions, 1st Marines (Lt. Col. Allan Sutler and Lt. Col. Thomas L. Ridge), began the assault on Blue Beach at 5:32 P.M. Blue Beach was wide, requiring speed to cross the initial beachhead against the advancing dusk. It had also to be approached over a 2.5-mile stretch of mud flats involving a 45-minute run to land the troops. The landing area was dominated by an abrupt hill only a few yards inland. To the hill's right was a wide, muddy, ill-smelling ditch, which divided the beach into two sectors (Blue 1 and Blue 2). South of the

landing area was the sharp promonotory of Tok Am. The assault forces would also be forced to scale a rock sea wall with ladders.

Blue Beach, like the others, was plastered by naval gunfire, rockets, bombing, and strafing. Smoke from this bombardment, mixed with the smoke drifting down from Inchon, made observation very difficult. Then the landing craft encountered an unexpected 3.5-knot current, making it difficult to stay on course for the correct landing site. As a further complication, some landing craft drivers were not adequately trained. Also, there were only 4 navy guide boats available to handle 25 boats waves, when the naval beach control officer thought there should have been 32 guide boats.

In spite of these adverse conditions, the 2d Battalion landed without opposition and the 3d Battalion encountered only moderate fire. An officer of the 3d Battalion found another suitable landing area in a cove to the right of the battalion's beach. The new area was promptly used to expedite the landing. At 1:30 A.M. on September 16, Puller reported that the beach had been taken. Because of the darkness, smoke, and chaos in the area, his reserve battalion, the 1st (Lt. Col. Jack Hawkins), was landed more than two miles to the left of the beaches, on the outer sea wall of Inchon's tidal basin. Hawkin's men set out overland, rejoining the regiment early on September 16.

By the end of the first day, 13,000 marines had been put ashore, with the loss of 21 servicemen dead, 174 wounded, and 1 missing. By evening, the marines were firmly in control of Inchon and were on the outskirts of Ascom City, about six miles inland from Inchon. Within two weeks, the marines, with elements of the 7th Army Division, had recaptured Seoul.

Bibliography: Appleman, Roy E., *U.S. Army in the Korean War. South to the Naktong, North to the Yalu* (Dept. of the Army, 1961); Heinl, Robert Debs., Jr., *Victory at High Tide* (Lippincott, 1968); Langley, Michael, *Inchon Landing: MacArthur's Last Triumph* (Times Books, 1979); Montross, Lynn, and Nicholas A. Canzona, *U.S. Marine Operations in Korea 1950–1953; Vol. 2: The Inchon-Seoul Operation* (Hist. Branch, U.S. Marine Corps, 1957).

Brig. Gen. PNG (Ret.) Uzal W. Ent

INTEGRATION OF THE ARMED FORCES

Federally mandated program of racial desegregation of the U.S. armed services. In 1946, the Gillem Board conducted an army-wide review of segregation policies and recommended a 10-percent quota for black recruits, smaller black units, and more black officers, with integration as a long-term goal. Pres. Harry S Truman signed Executive Order No. 9981 on July 26, 1948, directing equal treatment within the armed services—that is, integration, not segregation, would constitute the norm. In addition, the order created the President's Committee on Equality of Treatment and Opportunity in the Armed Services, better known as the Fahy Committee.

Personnel demands of the Korean War transformed integration from a gradual issue into one of immediacy. In the interest of efficiency, the armed forces integrated basic training by March 1951. Moreover, Far East Commander Matthew Ridgway sought to integrate combat forces in Korea totally no later than the summer of 1951. "Project Clear," a study conducted by the Operations Research Office (ORO) of Johns Hopkins University, reported that black soldiers performed better in integrated units and that attitudes reflected acceptance rather than opposition. The ORO study further recommended that "the Army should commit itself to a policy of full and complete integration to be carried out as rapidly as operational efficiency permits."

Desegregation began throughout the U.S. military in late 1951, and each service achieved total integration by 1954. In 1963, Sec. of Defense Robert McNamara attempted to extend equal treatment beyond military installations, thus setting the stage for the Civil Rights Act of 1964.

Bibliography: Bogart, Leo, ed., *Social Research and the Desegregation of the U.S. Army* (Markham, 1969); Dalfiume, Richard M., *Desegregation of the U.S. Armed Forces* (Univ. of Missouri Press, 1969); MacGregor, Morris J., Jr., *Integration of the Armed Forces, 1940–1965* (Center of Military History, U.S. Army, 1989); Nalty, Bernard C., *Strength for the Fight* (Free Press, 1986); Stillman, Richard J., *Integration of the Negro in the U.S. Armed Forces* (Praeger, 1968).

Maj. James Sanders Day

INTERCONTINENTAL BALLISTIC MISSILES

Guided long-range missiles, the development of which revolutionized the potential for nuclear warfare following World War II. Although research into rocket propulsion had taken place before World War II, the war truly altered the course of rocket development and made possible the development of intercontinental ballistic missiles (ICBMs) that could deliver nuclear warheads, weapons from which there was virtually no defense. During the war, almost every belligerent was involved in developing some type of rocket technology. Germany, however, had the greatest success in developing an operational missile capability and laid the foundations of the postwar ICBM program.

The critical German breakthrough was the V-2 rocket, developed by the Peenemünde rocket team under the leadership of Wernher von Braun. A true ballistic missile, this weapon was the immediate antecedent of ICBMs developed for the United States in the 1950s. A liquid propellant missile rising 46 feet in height and weighing 27,000

pounds, the V-2 flew at speeds in excess of 3,500 miles per hour and delivered a 2,200-pound warhead to a target 500 miles away. First flown in October 1942, it was employed against targets in Europe beginning in September 1944, and by the end of the war, 1,155 had been fired against England and another 1,675 had been launched against Antwerp, Belgium, and other continental targets. The guidance system for these missiles was imperfect, and many did not reach their targets, but there was no defense against them.

Project Paperclip. Clearly the technology employed in this weapon was worthy of U.S. study, and as the war was being concluded, captured V-2s were brought back to the United States. Along with them—as part of a secret military operation called Project Paperclip—came many of the scientists and engineers who had developed these weapons, most notably von Braun and several members of his rocket development team from the Peenemünde Experimental Center. They were installed at Fort Bliss in El Paso, Texas, and launch facilities for the V-2 test program were set up at nearby White Sands Proving Ground, New Mexico. Later, in 1950, von Braun's team of more than 500 people was moved to Redstone Arsenal near Huntsville, Alabama, to concentrate on the development of new missiles for the army.

Meantime, the first successful U.S. test firing of the captured V-2s took place at White Sands on Apr. 16, 1946. Immediately thereafter, an experimental program was instituted to learn more about rocket technology. Throughout the late 1940s and early 1950s, ever more demanding test flights were conducted. One of the most important series was Project Bumper, which mated a smaller army Wac Corporal missile to a V-2 as a second stage to obtain data on higher altitudes and on the principles of two-stage rockets. The only fully successful launch, which took place on Feb. 24, 1949, reached an altitude of 244 miles and a velocity of 5,150 miles per hour.

These flights led directly to the army's development of the Redstone (sometimes known as the Jupiter) rocket during this period. Built under the direction of von Braun and his German rocket team, the first Redstone was launched from Cape Canaveral, Florida, on Aug. 20, 1953. An additional 36 Redstone launches were executed through 1958. This new rocket was developed as a short-range ballistic missile to deliver a nuclear warhead on a battlefield, and its capability for this mission was tested on May 16, 1958, when combat-ready troops fired the rocket in a test. The Redstone was placed on active service with U.S. units in Germany the next month.

Interservice Rivalries and ICBMs. During this same period, each of the armed services worked separately toward fielding ICBMs that could deliver warheads to targets half a world away. To streamline this effort, Sec. of Defense Charles E. Wilson issued a decision on Nov. 26,

1956, that effectively took the army out of the ballistic missile business and assigned responsibility for land-based systems to the air force and for sea-launched missiles to the navy. The navy immediately stepped up work on the development of the submarine-launched Polaris ICBM, which was first successfully fired in January 1960.

The air force did the same, and its efforts were already well developed at the time of the 1956 decision. The Atlas ICBM program had begun in 1953; it received high priority from the White House and hard-driving management at the top from Brig. Gen. Bernard A. Schriever, a flamboyant and intense air force leader. The first Atlas rocket was test-fired on June 11, 1955, and the system continued to be improved thereafter. A later-generation Atlas was placed into operational status in 1959. These systems were followed in quick succession by the Titan ICBM and the Thor intermediate-range ballistic missile.

ICBM Strategy.   By the late 1950s, therefore, rocket technology had developed sufficiently for the creation of a viable ballistic missile capability. This was a revolutionary development that gave humanity for the first time in its history the ability to attack one continent from another. It effectively shrank the size of the globe, and the United States, which had been protected from outside attack by two massive oceans, could no longer rely on that natural boundary. Its own capability, additionally, signaled for the rest of the world that the United States could project military might anywhere in the world.

Bibliography: Beard, Edmund, *Developing the ICBM: A Study in Bureaucratic Politics* (Columbia Univ. Press, 1976); Emme, Eugene M., ed., *The History of Rocket Technology* (Wayne State Univ. Press, 1964); Neufeld, Jacob, *Ballistic Missiles in the United States Air Force, 1945–1960* (Office of Air Force History, 1990).

Roger D. Launius

JOLLY GREEN GIANT

Nickname given to a model of U.S. helicopter developed during the Vietnam War for rescue missions. During the 1960s, the U.S. Air Force's increasing involvement in the air war over Southeast Asia led to the development of specially equipped helicopters for rescuing downed fliers. The CH-3 were among the first helicopters fitted out for these missions. Redesignated the HH-3E and named "Jolly Green Giants" because of their size and garish green and brown camouflage, they began arriving in Vietnam in 1965. These machines generally performed well but had difficulty hovering at treetop level in Vietnam's mountains and suffered from limited armor and firepower. Therefore, in 1967, the air force turned to the HH-53 "Super Jolly Green Giant." The "Super Jolly" had better protection and more power, although its larger size was a disadvantage. Nevertheless, the strengths of the HH-3 and HH-53 de-

signs helped make successful aircrew rescues the rule rather than the exception in Southeast Asia.

Bibliography: Tilford, Earl H., Jr., *Search and Rescue in Southeast Asia, 1961–1976* (Office of Air Force History, 1980).

Richard F. Kehrberg

JUNCTION CITY, OPERATION
(February 22–May 14, 1967)
Multidivision Vietnam War offensive launched in early 1967 by U.S. and ARVN (Army of the Republic of Vietnam) forces to destroy Viet Cong bases in War Zone C near the Cambodian border and, if possible, to capture enemy headquarters of the Central Office for South Vietnam. The units participating in Junction City approached War Zone C from three sides, forming a large horseshoe-shaped array designed to crush the enemy. The largest American offensive operation up to that time, it was executed by two U.S. infantry divisions, five additional infantry brigades, and an armored cavalry regiment. Together, they engaged enemy units from February 22 to May 14. The North Vietnamese Army and Viet Cong lost more than 2,700 killed, as well as a number of base camps and supply caches destroyed.

Bibliography: Rogers, Bernard, *Cedar Falls-Junction City: A Turning Point* (U.S. Govt. Printing Office, 1974).

Capt. Leslie Howard Belknap

JUST CAUSE, OPERATION
(December 1989)
Culmination of a two-year attempt by the United States to oust Panamanian leader and strongman Gen. Manuel Antonio Noriega, who had been indicted (1988) by a U.S. federal grand jury for drug trafficking. Both the Ronald Reagan and George Bush administrations sought initially to pressure the dictator into resigning through a combination of economic and diplomatic sanctions.

The deployment of additional marine units in the spring of 1989 and the addition of army and air force units to U.S. installations in Panama ultimately failed to impress Noriega, as did diplomatic efforts designed to isolate Panama via the Organization of American States and economic sanctions that crippled Panama's economy. In October 1989, a coup attempt by members of the Panamanian army to depose Noriega was thwarted by troops loyal to him.

Immediately prior to what was code-named Operation Just Cause, several precipitating events—including some incidents of harassment against U.S. citizens and a Panamanian "declaration against the United States"—had occurred. Relations between Noriega and the United States hit rock bottom when Panamanian soldiers killed an off-duty U.S. Army officer. On Dec. 19, 1989, an alternative government led by Pres. Guillermo Endara was sworn in by a Panamanian judge at a U.S. military base and was immediately recognized by the United States.

Invasion.   Operation Just Cause officially began in the early morning hours of December 20, when U.S. forces in F-117 Stealth fighters bombed the Panamanian Defense Force (PDF) barracks. Just Cause involved the coordination of both an airborne and a land assault. It not only was the testing ground for the F-117 Stealth fighter, but also was the baptism of fire for the army's new light infantry and special operations forces (rangers) that had been created earlier for just such an operation. While the operation was basically an all-army affair, 24,000 troops from all branches of the armed forces—including navy SEAL (Sea-Air-Land), air force, and air National Guard units—performed vital missions.

The army's primary mission was to capture General Noriega; the marines, carrying the code name of Task Force Semper Fidelis, were assigned to guard the entrances to the Panama Canal and other U.S. defense sites that are located in the Canal Zone. Army rangers and other special task forces were dropped by army "Apache" attack helicopters over key points in the Canal Zone. Troops aboard M-113 armored personnel carriers emerged from Fort Sherman and rumbled through the streets of Panama City, engaging in battle those members of the PDF they found along the way. As the army rangers, reinforced by marines, moved toward the central Canal Zone, they attacked the Commandancia, the headquarters of both General Noriega and the PDF.

Meanwhile, other task forces were assigned to guard the western entrances of the Panama Canal opposite Balboa and Panama as well as other U.S. defense sites located in the Canal Zone. They were directed to prevent the PDF from infiltrating the Canal Zone and from moving reinforcements from Panama City. Orders included the apprehension of the "Dignity Battalion," who, as members of Noriega's personal militia, were well-trained in acts of terrorism and sabotage. These task forces also were ordered to seize and hold Torrijos International Airport, a staging area for PDF reinforcements based outside of Panama City; the Bridge of the Americas; and Rio Hato airfield, 90 miles south of Panama City. A task force secured all U.S. military bases, and another freed prisoners taken by the PDF. The U.S. Air Force and Air National Guard provided continuous close-air support.

Women soldiers, acting as police personnel, also played an important role during the actual operation. They helped to patrol Panama City, keeping check on the looting of the already destroyed shops and aiding in the apprehension and jailing of members of Panama's Dignity Battalion.

Mopping Up.   Noriega, now considered a fugitive, disappeared from sight. For the first time in its history, the Panama Canal was shut down and remained closed until December 21. The fighting raged on for five days as the

On Dec. 20, 1989, U.S. Marines enter the town of Arrijan, Panama, as part of Operation Just Cause, a U.S. military action that ousted Panamanian dictator Manuel Noriega. (U.S. Marines)

marines, abandoning traditional combat techniques of frontal assaults and vertical envelopments, waged a low-intensity conflict, conducting a relentless house-to-house, urban manhunt for PDF soldiers and the elusive Noriega.

Several days after the invasion, the remaining elements of a civil-affairs rangers battalion were flown into Panama City where they were to assist in the establishment of law and order by Endara's government. They were also charged with creating an entirely new police force, the Panama Public Force, to preserve civil order, especially after U.S. troops withdrew. Meanwhile, Noriega sought refuge in the Vatican embassy in Panama City. It was not until January 1990 that he was flushed out of hiding, arrested, and transported to the United States for trial.

By the time the fighting had ended, 314 PDF soldiers had been killed, 124 wounded, and 5,313 taken prisoner. An estimated 72,000 PDF weapons and 33 PDF armored vehicles had been captured. On the U.S. side, 19 soldiers were killed and 303 were wounded.

Operation Just Cause contained many valuable lessons for the U.S. armed forces. It proved a testing ground for low-intensity conflict in urbanized areas and for new equipment such as light armored vehicles. It stressed the importance and value of armor, light tanks, and air-droppable artillery; of small-unit leadership; of physical fitness; and of precise coordination of joint operations.

Leo J. Daugherty III

KANSAS-WYOMING LINE

Korean War battle line. By July 1951, United Nations forces occupied a defense line designed to maintain contact with the enemy and to provide a defensible battle line, international border, and demilitarized zone. Line Kansas ran generally northeast from the mouth of the Imjin River to the 38th parallel, turned eastward toward the Hwach'on Reservoir, then continued northeastward to the east coast. Wyoming, an outpost line extending to the southern base of the Iron Triangle, North Korea's logistical and communication hub, looped northeastward from the mouth of the Imjin toward Ch'orwon, then eastward to Kumwha, and finally southeastward to rejoin the Kansas line near the Hwach'on Reservoir. After armistice negotiations began, the 8th Army improved the Wyoming; it became the main line of resistance on July 30, 1951.

Maj. James Sanders Day

KEY WEST CONFERENCE
(March 11–14, 1948)

Post-World War II meetings held at the direction of Sec. of Defense James V. Forrestal, for which the Joint Chiefs of Staff and other military leaders convened in Key West, Florida, in mid-March 1948. There, they reached several critical agreements that guided the Department of Defense thereafter. These were outlined in a fundamental statement, "Functions of the Armed Forces and the Joint Chiefs of Staff." After additional meetings on March 20, Forrestal was able to issue this document as official policy.

The statement delineated the roles and missions of each service. It affirmed the army's responsibility to organize, train, and equip forces for sustained combat on land; the navy's primacy for seaborne combat; the Marine Corps' mission of amphibious operations; and the air force's charge to conduct strategic air warfare, U.S. air defense, and air and logistics support of ground forces. More important, the conference reached an accord over certain fringe areas that were being contended for by the various services. Notably, all services wanted some part of the airpower mission, and overlapping roles had to be resolved. The solutions reached in this conference were later tested in actual crisis situations and modified.

Bibliography: Rearden, Steven L., *History of the Office of the Secretary of Defense: The Formative Years, 1947–1950* (Office of the Secretary of Defense, 1984).

Roger D. Launius

KHE SANH, SIEGE OF
(January 21–April 7, 1968)

A 77-day battle between North Vietnamese Army (NVA) troops and U.S. Marine Corps elements, and one of the Vietnam War's most controversial episodes. In the summer of 1967, Gen. William Westmoreland ordered that the marine combat base near the western edge of the demilitarized zone (DMZ) be reinforced by the 26th Marine Regiment and by additional marine and South Vietnamese battalions as a springboard for a possible invasion into Laos to interdict NVA troops moving along the Ho Chi Minh Trail. In the late fall, radio transmissions and NVA troop dispositions pointed to a possible assault of the base. An estimated 15,000–20,000 battle-hardened enemy troops were believed to be in the area. The relative isolation of the base—the NVA controlled Route 9, the only road leading to Khe Sanh—prompted analogies to Dien Bien Phu, the 1954 battle in which the Viet Minh had successfully crushed besieged French forces, thus ending the First Indochina War. Pres. Lyndon B. Johnson was so unnerved at the prospect of the base falling to the enemy that he asked for (and received) a written guarantee from the Joint Chiefs of Staff that the base could be held.

The first of many NVA attacks came on Jan. 21, 1968, as the 6,000 American marines manning Khe Sanh were hit with both rockets and artillery fire from the big Soviet and Chinese guns hidden in the surrounding hills. One rocket set the marines' main ammunition dump ablaze, forcing a dramatic aerial resupply effort. Tensions mounted after the North Vietnamese overran the nearby U.S. Special Forces camp at Lan Vei on February 6 with infantry and tanks. Meanwhile, the marines inside the base continued to take steady fire from the NVA guns and to repulse NVA ground assaults on their positions. To take pressure off the base, Westmoreland ordered B-52 bomber strikes against suspected NVA troop positions. By the end of March, enemy activity in the area had diminished markedly. Relief of the beleaguered marine garrison began on April 1, as elements of the U.S. Army's 1st Cavalry Division fought their way into the area. With plans for the invasion of Laos shelved, the Khe Sanh combat base was abandoned in June 1968. Approximately 10,000 NVA soldiers lost their lives in the battle, while 205 marines died.

The significance of the battle and its outcome are still debated. Some historians see the NVA troop concentration in the area as a successful ruse, designed to draw allied troops away from the cities that were the object of the Tet Offensive that began on Jan. 30, 1968. Others have depicted the battle as a very costly loss that discouraged Hanoi from massing troops near U.S. bases for the remainder of the war.

Bibliography: Pisor, Robert, *The End of the Line: The Siege of Khe Sanh* (Norton, 1982).

James A. Warren

KILLER/RIPPER, OPERATIONS (February 21–March 21, 1951)

Tandem U.S. offensives against Communist forces in South Korea during the Korean War. Operation Killer was a limited-objective offensive mounted on Feb. 21, 1951, by eight divisions of Lt. Gen. Matthew Ridgway's 8th Army. The 1st Marine Division (IX Corps) made the main attack northeast of Wonju toward Hoengsong. West of the marines, the British Brigade and the 1st Cavalry and 24th Infantry divisions (also IX Corps) struck north from Yoju and Chip'yong. To the east of the marines, the X Corps (Republic of Korea [ROK] 3d and 5th Infantry and the U.S. 2d and 7th Infantry divisions) attacked north toward Pangnim from near Chechon. Farther west, the ROK 1st Infantry and the U.S. 3d and 25th Infantry divisions held the Han River and feinted large-scale river crossings.

The offensive was plagued by unseasonable warming and torrents of rain that significantly slowed the advance. Bridges were washed out, and roads became quagmires, slowing resupply efforts. Further, there was a shortage of ammunition. In spite of these adverse factors, the attack maintained the initiative and "offensive spirit" of the 8th Army. During the offensive, Maj. Gen. Bryant E. Moore, IX Corps commander, died of a heart attack after his helicopter crashed. Although the offensive did not live up to its "Killer" name (few of the enemy were killed), it did achieve one of its objectives by restoring the 8th Army's line east of Yangpyong through Hoengsong to Pangnim.

Killer led into Operation Ripper, which Ridgway launched across a 55-mile front on March 7. Ripper was designed to inflict maximum punishment on the enemy, disrupt enemy plans for a new offensive, and retake Seoul. An elaborate deception plan began on February 28, featuring a simulated amphibious invasion of Chinnampo and a maneuver by the ROK 1st Division to make the Chinese believe that it was crossing the river northwest of Kimpo Airfield.

On March 7, the 25th Infantry Division did cross the Han, west of Seoul, outflanking that city in the process. Meantime, the 1st Cavalry, 1st Marine, and 2d Infantry divisions also attacked north. The attacks went well, but troops in the X Corps (U.S. 2d and 7th divisions and ROK 5th Division) were slowed by the extremely rugged terrain. However, by March 15, the 1st Cavalry and 1st Marines had reached Hongch'on, some 12 miles from their starting line, while the U.S. 3d Division and ROK 1st Division entered Seoul on March 16, unopposed. The 1st Cavalry captured Ch'unchon on March 21. All along the line, the 8th Army advanced with little opposition. The enemy gave ground without much of a fight. All of Ripper's objectives were attained. The crowning achievement had been the bloodless recapture of Seoul.

Bibliography: Blair, Clay, *The Forgotten War* (Time Books, 1987); Mossman, Billy C., *U.S. Army in the Ko-* *rean War. Ebb and Flow: November 1950–July 1951* (Center of Military History, U.S. Army, 1990).

Brig. Gen. PNG (Ret.) Uzal W. Ent

KIT CARSON SCOUTS

Name given to Viet Cong defectors who joined the allied effort during the Vietnam War. In 1963, the South Vietnamese government instituted the Chieu Hoi ("Open Arms") program to offer amnesty to Viet Cong soldiers who wanted to defect. Some of the men who came in under this program, the *hoi chanhs* ("ralliers"), volunteered to fight against their former comrades. In 1966, several *hoi chanhs* began serving with American army and marine units. Marine Maj. Gen. Herman Nickerson, a Western history buff, renamed them the Kit Carson Scouts after the famous army guide, and a screening and orientation process soon emerged to select and train prospective scouts. In addition to their psychological and propaganda effect, the scouts proved invaluable in the field. Their knowledge of Viet Cong tactics and methods helped uncover numerous ambushes and weapons caches. Moreover, they were often able to identify Viet Cong soldiers and political cadres among local villagers.

Richard F. Kehrberg

KOJE-DO, PRISONER OF WAR RIOTS AT (May 1952)

Uprising by Communist prisoners of war (POWs) at Koje-do, an island off the southern coast of South Korea, during the Korean War. The demonstration, designed to undermine the argument of the United Nations Command (UNC) for voluntary repatriation of POWs, achieved some success and forced the UNC to revamp its procedures.

Overcrowding had created adverse situations, and unrest increased when the UNC began screening prisoners for voluntary repatriation. Riots in February and March had left 89 POWs dead and 166 wounded. Camp commandant Brig. Gen. Francis T. Dodd spoke frequently with Communist leaders in an attempt to ease tensions. On May 7, several Communist prisoners seized the camp commander, holding him hostage. Brig. Gen. Charles F. Colson, I Corps chief of staff, assumed command and demanded Dodd's release. On May 9, while Colson waited for armored reinforcements, the POWs held court to try Dodd on several counts of abuse. Colson issued a statement responding to POW demands on May 10 and secured Dodd's freedom that evening.

Colson's message admitted nothing directly but implied that the UNC habitually treated POWs inhumanely. Consequently, Brig. Gen. Haydon L. Boatner, assistant division commander of the 2d Division, replaced Colson and immediately relocated prisoners, dispersing them throughout Korea. Also, with Department of the Army approval, Gen. Mark Clark, commanding general of the Far East Command, recommended reductions in grade for both Dodd and Colson and an administrative reprimand for Brig. Gen. Paul F. Yount, commander of the 2d Logistical Command.

Bibliography: Hermes, Walter G., *Truce Tent and Fighting Front* (Center of Military History, U.S. Army, 1988).

Maj. James Sanders Day

KUNU-RI, AMBUSH AT
(November 29–30, 1950)

Surprise assault by the Chinese on U.S. forces in North Korea during the Korean War. Extreme pressure from a Chinese offensive in November 1950 forced the U.S. 8th Army to order a general withdrawal. The U.S. 2d Infantry Division defended north and east of Kunu-ri against the Chinese 38th and 40th armies. Two roads were available from Kunu-ri. The northern road ran west along the Ch'ong-chon River to Sinanju. The second road ran south to Ch'unch'on. Confused reports concerning the availability of the northern route led Maj. Gen. Laurence B. Keiser to select the southern road for his 2d Division's withdrawal. His 23d Infantry Regiment, reinforced, was the rear guard.

The Chinese 113th Infantry Division, unknown to Keiser, had organized a series of roadblocks along three miles of the withdrawal route, capped by a major block in a pass. Chinese machine guns, mortars, small arms fire, and grenades poured into the troops on the road. Repeated attempts by the Americans to dislodge the enemy were thwarted. Artillery pieces, trucks, and other equipment were destroyed or abandoned as the division made its slow, bloody way southward. Wrecked vehicles blocked the pass. The U.S. division suffered an estimated 3,000 casualties and lost 54 artillery pieces and hundreds of vehicles. Coupled with previous losses, the 2d Division was short by more than 8,000 of its authorized strength of 18,931 men. Less than a month latter, it was reequipped and ready for battle.

Bibliography: Blair, Clay, *The Forgotten War* (Times Books, 1987); Marshall, S. L. A., *The River and the Gauntlet* (Morow, 1953); Mossman, Billy C., *U.S. Army in the Korean War. Ebb and Flow: November 1950–July 1951* (Center of Military History, U.S. Army, 1990).

Brig. Gen. PNG (Ret.) Uzal W. Ent

LAM SON 719, OPERATION
(February–March 1971)

Code name of a large-scale Vietnam War raid launched in February 1971 by the Army of the Republic of Vietnam (ARVN) against the Ho Chi Minh Trail in southern Laos. The purpose of the operation was to disrupt North Vietnamese supplies coming down the trail into South Vietnam and to put the North Vietnamese Army (NVA) on the de-

fensive. Since Congress forbad U.S. ground forces from entering Laos, only ARVN units would be used across the border. On February 8, 16,000 ARVN troops began fighting their way up Route 9 toward the Laotian town of Tchepone. Within three days, the South Vietnamese reached the halfway point. On February 11, however, the weather turned bad. Close air support and aerial resupply became difficult, and Route 9 turned into a morass.

Its principal supply line threatened, the NVA rushed 36,000 troops into the region. As the weather cleared, U.S. air strikes helped hold off the NVA, and on March 6, ARVN forces captured Tchepone. On March 9, the ARVN began a hard-fought two-week-long withdrawal from Laos. Casualties in the raid had been heavy. The ARVN lost 2,000 killed or missing and more than 5,500 wounded. U.S. air crews suffered 55 killed, 34 missing, and 178 wounded. The NVA, however, lost more than 16,000 killed. The results of Lam Son 719 were mixed. The NVA's main supply route had been disrupted and the time-table for its next offensive upset, but the ARVN's performance had been uneven and revealed serious problems in command and control. Nevertheless, these same ARVN units would turn back the NVA's Easter Offensive the following year.

Bibliography: Nguyen Duy Hinh, *Lam Son 719* (Center of Military History, U.S. Army, 1979); Palmer, Bruce, Jr., *The Twenty-Five Year War: American's Military Role in Vietnam* (Univ. Press of Kentucky, 1984).

Richard F. Kehrberg

LEBANON, INTERVENTION IN
(July–October 1958)

Intervention of U.S. military forces in response to a perceived Soviet threat to both Jordan and Lebanon in the aftermath of the Suez Crisis of 1956. The U.S. government felt that indirect Soviet influence and the threat of Arab nationalism (personified by Egyptian leader Gamal Abdel Nasser) warranted military aid to Lebanon. Seeking to forestall Nasser, the western powers, most notably the United States and Great Britain, proceeded to form an "anti-Nasser" coalition by supporting the Baghdad Treaty countries of Lebanon, Jordan, and Iraq. This support took the form of an open declaration by the Dwight D. Eisenhower administration and the announcement of the Baghdad Pact, which, led by Sec. of State John Foster Dulles, offered both financial and military support. The Eisenhower Doctrine (1957) stated that the independence of Middle East nations was vital to U.S. interests and to world peace.

The Soviet-backed alliance of Egypt and Syria (the United Arab Republic, formed in January 1958) had already put such western-friendly countries as Lebanon, Jordan, Turkey, and Iraq in jeopardy, and the overthrow of King Faisal of Iraq by army officers allied with the United

Arab Republic brought the situation in the Middle East to a head.

The Iraqi revolution of 1957 signaled the beginning of the attempt on the part of the leaders of Egypt and Iraq to initiate the destabilization of Jordan and Lebanon. Both arms and men began flooding into both Middle East countries at an alarming rate, prompting Lebanon's president, Camille Chamoun, whose country was plagued by rebel guerrilla fighters, and Jordan's King Hussein to invoke the clauses of the Eisenhower Doctrine.

In 1957—with the approval of the U.S. Congress and the British House of Commons—U.S. Marines, a full U.S. Army brigade, and a British regiment were sent to protect King Hussein's government. During 1957, the U.S. Joint Chiefs of Staff had warned Adm. James L. Holloway, commander in chief, Eastern Atlantic and Mediterranean, that the possibility of intervention in both Jordan and Lebanon was real. Holloway had begun to prepare for this possibility, and three marine battalions had been brought together for possible operations. Reconnaissance of potential landing sites in Lebanon had been conducted and a strategic plan formulated. At the time of the overthrow of King Faisal in Iraq, the U.S. Army had already set in motion a plan that foresaw the airlifting of an entire army task force that could be deployed immediately for battle.

Intervention and Stability. On July 15, 1958, marines attached to the Mediterranean fleet began landing on Khalde (Red) Beach. They were joined the next day by other marine troops that had been airlifted to Lebanon, and Army troops arrived three days later. Initial reaction to the arrival of U.S. forces in Beirut, Lebanon's capital, was mixed. Many greeted the Americans as friends, and the U.S. troops met no significant resistance other than occasional harassment from local snipers and overzealous Lebanese army patrols. The relations between U.S. and Lebanese army officers were tense at first, but gradually improved as the specific mission of U.S. forces was defined in consultation with the Lebanese government. Integrated U.S.-Lebanese troops patrolled the strife-torn areas of Beirut.

Also on July 15, President Eisenhower called upon the United Nations (UN) to intervene and to send a peacekeeping force to safeguard Lebanese integrity. This, he felt, would enable the United States to withdraw its military forces. When the Soviets vetoed the resolution brought before the UN Security Council, Eisenhower dispatched Deputy Undersec. of State Robert D. Murphy to Lebanon to bring all the warring factions to the bargaining table in hopes of stabilizing the situation and enabling the United States to withdraw its forces.

Meanwhile, a tenuous cease-fire was in place, despite the constant harassing sniper fire from Lebanese rebels and several more serious incidents. By the end of the month, however, a 20-mile defensive perimeter that protected Bei-

rut from attacks from any direction had been established.

The main mission of the U.S. military was to prevent either a Syrian or a Syrian-sponsored government from ousting President Chamoun from office. During negotiations, Murphy had been able to convince all factions that new elections were imperative in order to end the rebellion. In September, elections brought Gen. Faud Chehab, Chamoun's original successor, to power. As he was inaugurated on Sept. 23, 1958, the withdrawal of U.S. troops began; it was completed several days later.

Sending U.S. troops to Lebanon was a bold but necessary move on the part of President Eisenhower—necessary in order to avoid Soviet influence and to provide a stabilizing influence amid political chaos. It not only executed the commitment of the Eisenhower Doctrine, but also showed the military preparedness of the United States and proved its resolve to defend its allies.

Ironically, despite their repeated protests, the Soviets could have done little to stop U.S. intervention in Lebanon. Although the Soviet Union had 10 well-trained airborne divisions and the aircraft necessary for power projection, it lacked an effective power-projection doctrine since its post-World War II efforts had emphasized the application of airborne forces on the nuclear battlefield.

Bibliography: Ferrell, Robert H., *American Diplomacy: A History* (Norton, 1975); Fisher, Sidney Nettleton, *The Middle East: A History,* 3d ed. (Knopf, 1979); Millett, Allan R., *Semper Fidelis: The History of the United States Marines Corps* (Macmillan, 1980).

Leo J. Daugherty III

LINEBACKER, OPERATION (1972)
Two intense bombings ordered during the Vietnam War by Pres. Richard M. Nixon in hopes of forcing the North Vietnamese to the peace table. After three North Vietnamese Army (NVA) divisions poured across the DMZ (demilitarized zone) into South Vietnam on Mar. 30, 1972, Nixon responded with Operation Linebacker I, which unleashed bombers against invasion routes and military targets inside North Vietnam. The next months, aircraft dropped mines at the entrances of North Vietnamese ports to cut off the flow of foreign supplies. After 9 months of bombing, the North Vietnamese indicated a willingness to talk, which led to an October 22 bomb halt. Talks disintegrated, however, so Nixon ordered Linebacker II, an 11-day bombing blitz of North Vietnam begun on December 18. When North Vietnam agreed to negotiate, the bombings stopped on December 29. By Jan. 23, 1973, a cease-fire agreement was reached.

Bibliography: Berger, Carl, ed., *The United States Air Force in Southeast Asia, 1961–1973* (U.S. Govt. Printing Office, 1977); Morrocco, John, *The Vietnam Experience: Rain of Fire* (Boston Pub. Co., 1985).

John F. Wukovits

LONG BINH

One of the four main supply and maintenance depots set up for the U.S. Army in South Vietnam during the Vietnam War. Located near the city of Bien Hoa, 20 miles north of Saigon, Long Binh also served as the headquarters of II Field Force Vietnam and the III ARVN (Army of the Republic of Vietnam) Corps and housed the stockade named by soldiers as the "LBJ"—Long Binh Jail. In addition to containing huge ammunition and supply depots, the installation also served as the processing center for numerous incoming and outgoing U.S. soldiers. At its height, more than 43,000 Americans lived at Long Binh, and more than 20,000 Vietnamese eventually worked at the complex. Viet Cong forces assaulted the center during the 1968 Tet Offensive as well as during the following year.

Bibliography: Sheehan, Neil, *A Bright Shining Lie* (Random House, 1988); Stanton, Shelby, *The Rise and Fall of an American Army* (Presidio, 1985).

John F. Wukovits

M-1, M-14, AND M-16 RIFLES

Three models of U.S. military shoulder arms. During the 1930s, the U.S. Army adopted the .30-caliber, semiautomatic M-1 rifle, and it served as the standard-issue shoulder arm into the 1950s. After Korea, however, the army changed to the M-14. The M-14 represented a compromise between the army's traditional emphasis on long-range marksmanship and a new trend toward using automatic fire at short ranges. The new rifle fired a 7.62-millimeter round, had a large magazine, and could be used as either a semiautomatic or an automatic weapon. In Vietnam, the M-14 proved heavy to carry in the field and difficult to control when fired on automatic. Therefore, the military moved to replace it with the smaller, lighter 5.56-millimeter M-16. After some initial problems, the M-16's ability to deliver high volumes of fire at short ranges recaptured its popularity with the troops. Improved versions continued to be used by the military into the 1990s.

Bibliography: Ezell, Edward C., *The Great Rifle Controversy* (Stackpole Books, 1984).

Richard F. Kehrberg

MacARTHUR, RELIEF OF
(April 11, 1951)

The relief from command, by Pres. Harry S Truman, of Gen. of the Army Douglas MacArthur during the Korean

The M-16A1 rifle, an improved model of the M-16, is used during a navy sea-air-land (SEAL) tactical warfare training operation during the 1980s. (U.S. Navy)

War. At the time, MacArthur was Supreme Allied Commander; commander in chief, United Nations Command (UNC); commander in chief, Far East; and commanding general U.S. Army, Far East. Truman's action shocked the American people, but the decision marked the culmination of events that had frustrated the president in dealing with his military commander in the Far East. After receiving an unprecedented visit from Emperor Hirohito, MacArthur left Japan and flew to San Francisco via Hawaii. He addressed a joint session of Congress on Apr. 19, 1951, and enjoyed parades in both Washington, D.C., and New York City.

Background.   Conflict between Truman and MacArthur began in August 1950 concerning the Nationalist Chinese regime in Taiwan. MacArthur, at Truman's suggestion, conferred with Nationalist Chinese leader Chiang Kai-shek, but the secrecy surrounding his meeting fostered unpopular speculation. In response to an invitation to speak at the 51st National Encampment of the Veterans of Foreign Wars in Chicago, MacArthur wrote a letter criticizing Truman's policy toward Nationalist China and challenging Communist China's role in the Far East. MacArthur's opinion, leaked and printed in late August, forced Truman to demand a retraction and to fire Sec. of Defense Louis Johnson, an ardent MacArthur supporter.

At Wake Island, Truman and MacArthur met for the first time on Oct. 15, 1950. In response to Truman's query, MacArthur assured the president that the Chinese Communists would not intervene in Korea. Meanwhile, as United Nations (UN) forces moved north of the 38th parallel, MacArthur continually violated directives from the Joint Chiefs of Staff (JCS). He extended his limit of advance ever closer to the Yalu River (the boundary between North Korea and the Manchuria region of Communist China) and used non-Korean forces along the Manchurian border. After the Chinese intervention in the Korean War in November, MacArthur used public statements to excuse himself while openly criticizing the administration's policy to limit the conflict to the Korean peninsula.

In early December, MacArthur again berated the Truman administration in an interview with the magazine *U.S. News and World Report* and in a letter to the United Press. Advocating attacks on Chinese planes and airfields, MacArthur prompted Truman to issue a directive on December 5 (received by MacArthur on December 6) that all public information be "accurate and fully in accord with the policies of the United States Government." Moreover, Truman's policy directed overseas officials to clear all statements through the U.S. State and Defense departments and to refrain from discussing military or political issues with the media.

After visiting the front in February 1951, MacArthur violated Truman's directive four times in as many weeks. He continued to advocate bombing the Chinese mainland and blockading the China coast while Truman considered a negotiated settlement. In fact, as UNC forces approached the 38th parallel in the spring of 1951, the president decided to issue an appeal for negotiations to the Chinese. MacArthur, on the other hand, issued a communique implying the imminent use of military force and suggesting a complete surrender of Chinese forces. MacArthur's hawkish message compromised Truman's conciliatory stance, thereby postponing any overtures for peace. Truman termed the affront "deliberate, premeditated sabotage of U.S. and UN policy."

Relief from Command.   At this point, Truman began the process that led to MacArthur's relief. Meanwhile, MacArthur continued his bombastic indiscretions. Writing to House minority leader Joseph Martin of Massachusetts, MacArthur challenged Truman's policies while stating that "there is no substitute for victory." Martin, believing the American people had a right to know, read MacArthur's letter on the House floor on April 5. Another critical statement appeared in *Freemen* on April 7 as Truman discussed MacArthur's fate with Sec. of Defense George Marshall, Sec. of State Dean Acheson, Chairman of the JCS Omar Bradley, and Special Assistant Averell Harriman. Bradley conferred with the service chiefs, who unanimously supported MacArthur's relief. With the approval of his military and civilian advisers, Truman decided on April 9 to relieve MacArthur.

Marshall would inform MacArthur of the president's decision by forwarding a coded message via State Department channels through Ambassador John Muccio to Sec. of the Army Frank Pace. Pace, on a routine visit to Korea, would notify MacArthur personally. A power outage precluded efficient transmission to Korea, however, and Truman ordered a retransmission in the clear. The original notification plan failed, and MacArthur's aide, Sidney L. Huff, hearing the news on Tokyo radio, informed his boss.

After his return to the United States and his speech to Congress, MacArthur testified before the Senate Foreign Relations and Armed Services committees. He testified for three days beginning on May 3, espousing his mission to clear, unify, and liberalize North Korea; to counter the growing threat of Communist China; to win Asian support for the democratic cause; and to offer greater protection and security to Europe. He distinguished between loyalty to the nation and the Constitution and to those who temporarily hold its power—that is, the Truman administration. MacArthur admitted to Sen. Brien MacMahon, however, that his role as theater commander prevented him from having a global perspective on foreign policy. In addition, the investigative committee listened to 30 days of testimony from Marshall, Bradley, the service chiefs (Gen. J. Lawton Collins, Gen. Hoyt S. Vandenberg, Adm. Forrest P. Sherman), Acheson, Gen. Albert Wedemeyer, and former secretary of defense Johnson. The JCS did not support

MacArthur's position, but advocated limiting the war to the Korean peninsula, based on global perspective and practicability. In the final analysis, the committee upheld Truman's actions, determining that MacArthur's removal lay within the constitutional powers of the president.

Bibliography: Schnabel, James F., *Policy and Direction: The First Year* (Center of Military History, U.S. Army, 1988); Spanier, John W., *The Truman-MacArthur Controversy and the Korean War* (Norton, 1965).

Maj. James Sanders Day

MACV (*see Military Assistance Command Vietnam*)

MARKET TIME, OPERATION

Joint, U.S.-South Vietnamese effort to arrest North Vietnamese infiltration of weapons, ammunition, supplies, and personnel to South Vietnam during the Vietnam War. The operation was initiated in March 1965 and included both surface and air surveillance and interception. Eventually, U.S. participation included both the navy and the Coast Guard. Market Time was preceded by a number of similar attempts. Initially, in the early 1960s, the U.S. Navy assisted Saigon's naval arm by outfitting fishing junks with powerful engines and armament to catch unwary Northern infiltration craft. Since the Communists often used innocent-looking fishing craft for their illegal shipments and since there were thousands of such craft along the coast, identification was a major problem. Additionally, the use of wooden infiltration craft reduced the utility of radar. In one form or another, interdiction along South Vietnam's coast continued throughout the war.

Bibliography: Marolda, Edward J., and G. Wesley Pryce, III, *A Short History of the United States Navy and the Southeast Asian Conflict* (Naval Hist. Center, 1984).

Col. (Ret.) Rod Paschall

MARSHALL PLAN

First outlined by Sec. of State George C. Marshall at a commencement speech at Harvard University on June 5, 1947, the Marshall Plan sought to establish a framework through which U.S. economic aid could be channeled to war-torn countries in Europe in the aftermath of World War II. Also called the European Recovery Program, the plan went into operation in 1948 and provided more than $13 billion to Europe's successful recovery before its completion in 1952. The Marshall Plan was seen as a threat to Communism by the Soviet Union and its allies and was a key economic outgrowth of the Truman Doctrine and the containment of Communist influence in Europe.

Stephen Robinson

MASSIVE RETALIATION

Military strategy corollary to Pres. Dwight D. Eisenhower's "New Look." The New Look's call for increased use of nuclear weapons and reduced manpower levels and defense expenditures led to a concentration on strategic nuclear weapons. "Massive retaliation" became military strategy as a part of the Basic National Security Policy, approved in October 1953.

The policy of massive retaliation was publicly defined and explained in Sec. of State John Foster Dulles's Jan. 25, 1954, "massive retaliation" address to the Council on Foreign Relations. Dulles stated that the United States should no longer overextend itself in countering Soviet expansion. U.S. ground troops were not to be stationed permanently in Asia but should be returned to the United States to constitute a strategic reserve. Troop levels in Europe should also be cut. For economic as well as foreign policy reasons, the United States could not completely support other nations but had to make them rely on themselves for conventional defense. The Eisenhower solution to providing maximum deterrence for minimum cost was to rely on nuclear weapons and declare that the United States would "respond vigorously at places and with means of its own choosing."

The Strategic Air Command was the primary fighting force of massive retaliation. The air force increased the number of strategic bomber wings, developed the B-52 Stratofortress bomber, and developed nuclear-capable missile systems. Plans for conventional warfare were limited. While the air force was expanding its strategic wings, this growth came at the expense of its own transport and troop carrier wings. The navy and army were drastically reduced and searched for new nuclear weapons so they could demand some portion of the shrinking defense budget. Continental air defense systems were developed, especially after the Soviets developed their own intercontinental bombers and missiles.

The shortcomings of massive retaliation were readily apparent to the army and navy. In addition, the Soviet Union and other Communist forces, as well as U.S. allies, soon realized that the U.S. policy was not effective. By depleting its conventional forces and increasing nuclear forces, the United States prepared itself for a type of warfare it was unwilling to conduct. As military leaders had warned, the Soviets soon had their own strategic nuclear forces, and U.S. allies had to question American willingness to meet defense obligations. Would the United States risk nuclear war to stop limited Soviet expansion? American allies, especially in Europe, also feared that U.S. forces had become tripwires and that the only possible U.S. military response to Soviet aggression would be to use nuclear weapons and destroy the free societies the United States was pledged to defend. The Eisenhower administration and the world realized the limitations of U.S. military power when Eisenhower did not have the conventional forces to assist the French during the Battle of Dien Bien Phu (on the North Vietnamese-Laotian border) in 1954. The same dilemma presented itself in Beirut, Lebanon, in 1958. Nuclear weapons were not effective in a limited war. With John F. Kennedy's presidential election in 1960, massive retaliation gave way to "flexible response."

Bibliography: Hagan, Kenneth, and William Roberts, *Against All Enemies* (Greenwood Press, 1986); Millet, Allan, and Peter Maslowski, *For the Common Defense* (Free Press, 1984); Weigley, Russell, *The American Way of War* (Indiana Univ. Press, 1977).

Maj. George B. Eaton

MAYAGUEZ, RECOVERY OF THE
(May 12–15, 1975)

Recovery by force of the U.S. container ship *Mayaguez,* seized by the newly installed government of Cambodia, the Khmer Rouge. On May 12, 1975, soldiers from a Khmer Rouge gunboat boarded the *Mayaguez,* towed it to port, and forcibly removed Capt. Charles T. Miller and his crew. The *Mayaguez*'s distress message was received in Jakarta, Indonesia, and in Manila, the Philippines.

U.S. President Gerald R. Ford consulted with the National Security Council and sent the aircraft carrier *Coral Sea* into the area of Koh Tang Island. He ordered several battalion landing teams of marines to Okinawa to prepare for a probable recovery mission. The *Mayaguez,* followed since its seizure by P-3B Orion turboprop aircraft, was reported dead in the water north of Koh Tang Island. Intelligence forces believed the crew to be still aboard.

President Ford issued the final orders for the assault on Koh Tang Island, and the first wave of marines landed as air force and navy jets streaked overhead, providing air support. As the "Jolly Green Giant" helicopters attempted to land troops, Khmer Rouge defenders opened up against the marines; 2 helicopters, 10 marines, 2 navy corpsmen, and 1 air force pilot were lost. Meanwhile, marines under

On May 14, 1975, U.S. Marines storm aboard the Mayaguez, *a U.S. merchant ship that two days earlier had been seized by Khmer Rouge soldiers.* (U.S. Navy)

the command of Capt. Walter J. Wood boarded the *Mayaguez,* only to find it abandoned. Unknown to those involved in the attack, the crew of the *Mayaguez* had already been released by the Cambodians.

Fighting continued on the island and quickly escalated into full combat. After several enemy assaults, three platoons of marines had been able to carve out a defensive perimeter ringed with mortars. On May 15, the marines were able to beat back an enemy counterattack, thus insuring the incoming second wave of an adequate landing zone. However, the news that the *Mayaguez* crew had been released finally reached the troops, and preparations were made to evacuate Koh Tang Island. As evacuation took place, the enemy continued to fire, and rescue attempts had to be curtailed until darkness had set in. Air force and navy jets continuously pounded the Cambodian positions, and, finally, an orderly evacuation took place. The *Mayaguez* incident proved that, despite the lack of communication, poor intelligence, and a confused chain of command, the marines possessed both resourcefulness and the ability to repel repeated enemy assaults.

Leo J. Daugherty III

MILITARY ASSISTANCE COMMAND VIETNAM (MACV)

U.S. advisory/support group established in late 1961 under Gen. Paul D. Harkins to direct American assistance to anticommunist activities in Vietnam. It supervised the existing U.S. Military Assistance Advisory Group Vietnam, commanded by Maj. Gen. Charles Timmes. By late 1963, MACV comprised 11,000 U.S. advisers. In June 1964, Gen. William C. Westmoreland took command. With the direct commitment of U.S. ground forces in 1965, MACV adopted a liaison role. In 1967, MACV introduced the CORDS (Civil Operations and Revolutionary Development Support) scheme in a renewed attempt at pacification. In July 1968, Gen. Creighton W. Abrams succeeded Westmoreland, and after the adoption of "Vietnamization," MACV improved South Vietnamese combat effectiveness. The command of MACV passed to Gen. Frederick C. Weyand in June 1972, just seven months before the group disbanded.

Russell A. Hart

MILITARY-INDUSTRIAL COMPLEX

Term popularized by Pres. Dwight D. Eisenhower's January 1961 farewell address, which warned against the conjunction of interest and the growing political influence wielded by a military establishment linked to a large and increasingly influential arms industry. Since then, the term essentially has been understood to encompass the deleterious effect defense spending has had on the U.S. economy, and on social and welfare programs. It also refers to the entangled relationship between government and corporations in the acquisition of new equipment and technology. However, the term remains ill-defined and loosely applied. The "military-industrial complex" is generally understood to include the Department of Defense, defense industries, certain influential members of Congress (especially those who sit on the armed services committees), private research institutions, scientists, and technologists. Associated with the term has been the concept of a "revolving door" in which thousands of Defense Department personnel have taken jobs with defense contractors. Another concern has been the growing influence of the Department of Defense in university research programs, many of which appear to have little direct relevance to military needs.

Russell A. Hart

MISSILE GAP

Term coined by John F. Kennedy during the 1960 presidential campaign. The implication of the "missile gap" was that the United States was especially vulnerable to a Soviet surprise missile attack due to a supposed numerical superiority enjoyed by the Soviets. In 1962, when the Soviet Union tried to place missile-launching facilities in nearby Cuba, U.S. fears were sparked again. Although the Cuban crisis ended peacefully, the Kennedy administration's defense positions were bolstered, and Congress was ready to respond to the missile gap. In an attempt to lessen the possibility of worldwide nuclear annihilation, a nuclear test-ban treaty between the Cold War powers was signed in 1963. By the late 1960s, changing attitudes toward war, especially the Vietnam War, brought a rejection of the missile gap theory.

M. Guy Bishop

MOBILE RIVERINE FORCE

U.S. joint task force of the Vietnam War, comprised essentially of the army's 2d Brigade, 9th Infantry Division, and the navy's Task Force 117 (Riverine Assault Force) and SEAL (Sea-Air-Land) teams. This unique force went into action in June 1967 and operated in the rivers and canals of the Mekong Delta, effecting an unusual means of battlefield mobility against the Viet Cong.

The Mobile Riverine Force (MRF) had a base at Dong Tam in the upper delta. Often acting in conjunction with South Vietnamese army, marine, and naval forces, the MRF was capable of riverine movements of 150 miles in 24 hours. Upon reaching a destination, the MRF could engage in combat almost immediately.

The MRF had two co-equal commanders and staffs, one army and the other navy. Although both sides learned to cooperate effectively, the force never had a mutually agreed doctrine for its employment, and the parallel chains of command stretched as far as the joint U.S. commander in Vietnam and, for some questions, to the commander in chief for the entire Pacific region. The MRF was especially

effective in its early operations, before the Viet Cong began to evolve means to warn themselves and slow the advance of these amphibious forces. In April 1971, in accordance with the "Vietnamization" program, the MRF ceased to exist as a U.S. command and became part of South Vietnamese forces.

Jonathan M. House

MUTUAL DEFENSE ASSISTANCE ACT
(1949, 1950)

The Mutual Defense Assistance Act, passed by Congress in 1949 and extended for one year in 1950, was an outgrowth of the Truman Doctrine and the Truman administration's containment policy against the spread of Communist power. The act authorized specific amounts of military aid to certain countries, primarily for North Atlantic Treaty Organization (NATO) members that asked for such aid. Greece and Turkey, the beneficiaries of the Truman Doctrine, received substantial amounts in each year, with other NATO countries, South Korea, and the Philippines receiving most of the balance. Congress limited President Truman's options by specifying the eligible countries and complicated the political issues by earmarking funds for China.

Stephen Robinson

MY LAI MASSACRE (March 16, 1968)

Atrocity committed by U.S. forces upon a South Vietnamese civilian village. Lt. Gen. William R. Peers investigated the incident and concluded that a massacre of at least 175 and perhaps more than 400 Vietnamese took place in the course of Operation Son My, conducted by the U.S. troops of Task Force Baker in March 1968. The commander's orders and the associated intelligence estimates were embellished as they were disseminated down the chain of command and presented the individual soldier with a distorted picture of the area as an armed camp devoid of civilians. Artillery and air strikes were conducted in a manner clearly indicating that the hamlets were enemy positions, and troops entered the area by combat assault. Even this background fails to explain the kind of killing frenzy that followed. Murder, rape, and maiming took place, as did the killing of livestock, the destruction of crops, the closing of wells, and the burning of dwellings. Much of the barbarism was conducted under the supervision of officers and noncommissioned officers as groups of old men, women, and children were taken to ditches and shot.

The Peers Report concluded that a series of inadequate responses from company to division levels of command proved that an attempt at cover-up was made; knowledge of the extent of the incident existed at the company level, among the key staff officers and commander at the Task Force Baker (battalion) level, and at the 11th Brigade command level. Knowledge at the Americal Division level was not complete, but attempts were made to conceal what was thought to be the killing of 20-28 civilians. The battalion commander, Lt. Col. Frank Barker (later killed in action), knew that a war crime had been committed and deliberately concealed the fact from higher authority. The division conducted superficial investigations, thus suppressing information about the incident.

On Nov. 24, 1969, Army Chief of Staff William C. Westmoreland directed Peers "to explore the nature and scope of the original investigation(s) of the alleged My Lai operation." Peers confirmed that there was a massacre and an attempt to cover it up. Of 13 men suspected of committing war crimes, charges were dismissed in 8 cases, 5 were tried, and only Lt. William L. Calley was convicted of murder. Others were given administrative punishment, such as reduction to permanent rank or revocation of awards and decorations.

Bibliography: Peers, W. R., *The My Lai Inquiry* (Norton, 1979).

Col. (Ret.) Henry G. Gole

NATIONAL SECURITY ACTS (1947, 1949)

The National Security Acts, passed after World War II to coordinate and unify the U.S. armed forces, essentially overhauled how the military forces were organized, in terms of responsibility. Supporters of a unified armed forces believed that interservice bickering would lessen and that both cost and military efficiency would improve.

The National Security Act of 1947 established the National Military Establishment as an umbrella organization headed by a secretary of defense, who would have cabinet rank and would coordinate planning. The individual armed services—the army, the navy (including the Marine Corps), and the newly created air force—operated as executive departments within the National Military Establishment; their secretaries did not have cabinet rank. This structure represented a compromise between those who wanted a single unified military force, expected to be dominated by the army and its air force allies, and those who wanted to maintain totally independent services, which would allow the navy greater freedom. The Joint Chiefs of Staff were given formal recognition by the act, and the National Security Council, the Central Intelligence Agency, and other agencies were established by the act.

The operation of the National Military Establishment proved unwieldy, and following the Hoover Commission report in 1949, Congress passed at President Truman's request the National Security Act of 1949. It amended the 1947 act by eliminating the National Military Establishment by name and by creating in its place the Department of Defense (DOD) as an executive department that had the separate service departments squarely under the DOD's authority. This reorganization had the effect of diminishing the power of the separate service secretaries and of giving the defense establishment a unified voice.

Stephen Robinson

NATO (*see* North Atlantic Treaty Organization)

NEW LOOK

Term coined by Pres. Dwight D. Eisenhower to describe his 1953 reassessment of the U.S. military budget. When Eisenhower won the 1952 presidential election, the U.S. military establishment expected that it had a firm ally in the White House. However, one of the president's first official acts was to direct a review of national security policy. Eisenhower was looking for a way to cut the defense budget, which he believed was so large that it was fueling inflation and driving the nation into bankruptcy. The results of the review, the "New Look," were recorded in NSC-162/2 in October 1953. The basic assumption of NSC-68 (that the Soviets were bent on global domination and all further expansion had to be contained) remained. Eisenhower knew that personnel costs were the largest part of the defense budget. The New Look proposed a military policy more dependent on technology than manpower and announced a heightened emphasis on nuclear weapons and machines to deter the Soviets. Eisenhower considered nuclear weapons as available as other weapons, and the resulting corollary to the New Look was the doctrine of "massive retaliation."

The new emphasis on technology benefited the air force. New Look depended on the strategic ability to deliver nuclear weapons. The Strategic Air Command (SAC) was the centerpiece of New Look, and the number of air force wings increased. However, the army and navy were cut and had to search for ways to employ nuclear weapons in order to retain a sizable percentage of the defense budget. The army continued work on missile development while also developing tactical nuclear weapons. The navy developed the Polaris missile system as well as nuclear-capable carrier-launched bombers. Technology was also used to improve U.S. intelligence gathering. During the period of the New Look, spy satellites were developed, and the U-2 spy plane was built to fly over the Soviet Union.

The New Look also emphasized reorganization and increased efficiency as a way to cut the defense budget. Eisenhower believed that the army and air force should depend on the National Guard and reserves for most of their manpower. At the same time, he encouraged the decrease in support and logistics units. The army developed the Pentomic Division, which had fewer men and was designed for the nuclear battlefield. The United States also announced that it expected its allies to provide the ground troops to fight proxy wars and other conventional battles while the United States would provide a nuclear guarantee.

The New Look had important ideas and a significant impact on the United States and its allies. The Department of Defense was forced to develop better and more efficient ways of meeting missions. West Germany and Japan rearmed in order to provide means of conventional warfare. However, there were as many if not more disadvantages to the New Look. Interservice rivalry increased as the armed forces competed for dwindling funds. Instead of promoting global stability, the New Look encouraged Soviet adventurism. Neither the Soviets nor U.S. allies believed that the United States would risk nuclear war unless the United States was directly threatened. Conventional military units in the army, navy, and air force were gutted as spending flowed to strategic systems. By the end of the Eisenhower period, the United States was unable to counter global Communist expansion.

Bibliography: Hagan, Kenneth, and William Roberts, *Against All Enemies* (Greenwood Press, 1986); Millet, Allan, and Peter Maslowski, *For the Common Defense* (Free Press, 1984); Weigley, Russell, *The American Way of War* (Indiana Univ. Press, 1977)

Maj. George P. Eaton

NORTH ATLANTIC TREATY ORGANIZATION (NATO)

Collective security pact established Apr. 4, 1949, by representatives of 12 Western European nations plus the United States and Canada, and later joined by Greece and Turkey (1952), West Germany (1955), and Spain (1982). NATO was designed primarily to deter potential Soviet aggression in Europe. However, it was also supposed to promote political, economic, and social ties among members. NATO's chief policymaking body is the North Atlantic Council, whose permanent representatives meet weekly.

The Defense Planning Committee of the North Atlantic Treaty Organization meets in Brussels, Belgium, in 1975. (NATO)

However, NATO had no formal military structure before the Korean War (1950–53), which was widely perceived as heralding a worldwide Communist offensive. Gen. Dwight D. Eisenhower became the first Supreme Allied Commander, Europe, in December 1950. In 1966, France withdrew from NATO's integrated military structure.

Conflicts within the alliance have arisen in four main areas: problems associated with the balance of forces between the Warsaw Pact and NATO; questions of strategic doctrine, notably the credibility of nuclear deterrents and the employment of tactical nuclear weapons; issues of military standardization; and political disputes among members (for example, Greece and Turkey). The 1983 deployment of U.S. intermediate-range missiles in Europe caused unprecedented dissension within NATO. In the 1990s, the collapse of Communism and the Warsaw Pact in Eastern Europe renewed the debate over NATO's fundamental role.

Russell A. Hart

NORTH VIETNAMESE ARMY (*see* Viet Minh/Viet Cong/North Vietnamese Army)

NSC-68 (April 1950)

Document of U.S. military policy drafted just prior to the Korean War. Immediately after World War II, the United States drastically reduced its armed forces from wartime levels to levels considered appropriate for peace. In the months after the war, the United States felt secure against any future threat because of its monopoly of nuclear power. However, by 1947, the Soviet Union was seen as a threat to national security and global stability. Different groups within the Harry S Truman administration and Congress began to be openly critical of U.S. policy toward the Soviets.

In 1949, the USSR exploded its first atomic bomb, and in early 1950, President Truman authorized the development and building of the hydrogen bomb. As a part of this decision, Truman also ordered a reappraisal of U.S. foreign and military policy and strategy. He was particularly concerned with the assessment of the Soviet threat and ordered a joint State Department and Defense Department board to prepare a new policy statement. This joint board was chaired by Paul Nitze, while Sec. of State Dean Acheson oversaw the process and presented the document to Truman in April 1950. The National Security Council (NSC) discussed the findings and proposals included in the study and approved the document on Apr. 25, 1950, as "NSC-68." Due to the outbreak of the Korean War in June, Truman did not formally approve NSC-68 until October.

Background. Prior to 1949, the United States had tried to minimize differences with the Soviets. Truman attempted to reestablish global stability and wanted to convince the Soviets that cooperation was better than confrontation. Many members of the State Department considered Soviet security concerns valid. In 1947, after the publication of State Department policy-planner George Kennan's ideas on "containment," more and more members of the Truman administration saw Soviet expansion as an ideological and economic threat to the United States, democracy, and free trade. Kennan had argued that all measures short of war had to be used in an attempt to blunt Soviet expansion and induce a change of government while increasing the morale of the West. Kennan also argued that the United States could not be strong everywhere and had to delineate between vital and peripheral interests. Kennan's proposals prevailed until the Soviets exploded their first atomic bomb.

Assumptions. While the drafters of NSC-68 began from the basic concept of Kennan's containment policy, some of their basic assumptions and conclusions were vastly different. The primary difference in assumptions was that the drafters of NSC-68 saw Americans and Soviets in a basic conflict of aims. While the United States wanted a global community where free societies could flourish, the USSR was bent on world domination. While the United States had been able to keep the USSR in check in the five years after the war, the NSC-68 drafters expected that unless the United States changed policy, the USSR would have—and use—overwhelming military force to achieve control over whatever portion of the globe it desired. In a fundamental difference from Kennan, the drafters of NSC-68 believed that they could not allow the USSR any further expansion anywhere, that there were no longer peripheral interests, only vital interests. They also believed that there was a monolithic Communism controlled by the USSR and that, therefore, any Communist expansion was controlled by the Soviets. They thought that the United States had to achieve a position of strength before the USSR would be willing to negotiate and change behavior. Like Kennan, the NSC-68 drafters agreed that isolationism was not an option. They also rejected appeasement and viewed preventive nuclear war as repugnant. The conclusion was that the United States would again have to rely on conventional forces.

Emphasis and Impact. NSC-68 was seen by Dean Acheson as a tool to "bludgeon the mass mind of top government" to make the decisions required to meet the Soviet threat. NSC-68 was not a detailed plan for changes in defense or diplomatic policy but a "ponderous expression of elementary ideas" about Soviet intentions on domination and the need for a change in U.S. response. Like Kennan, NSC-68 demanded economic, military, political, psychological, and cultural means to counter the Soviets, but in NSC-68, the emphasis was primarily on the military. If all interests were now vital, then the United States could no longer rely solely on a nuclear response to Soviet expan-

sion. Thus, NSC-68 called for the ability to escalate the military response to Soviet actions from small-scale conventional response, through full-scale conventional war, to nuclear warfare. NSC-68 did not discuss cost nor resources. However, a basic economic assumption of the drafters was that the national economy was expandable and could accept a tripling of defense spending while simultaneously increasing the standard of living.

NSC-68 may have languished in obscurity had it not been for the outbreak of the Korean War. The Communist invasion of South Korea in June 1950 reaffirmed the conclusions of NSC-68 and was a catalyst to change in U.S. military policy. The defense budget was increased from around $13.5 billion to more than $50 billion per year. This spending was more than enough to cover the costs of the Korean War, and all three services increased the size of its forces while embarking on modernization drives. The army was the big winner as the Defense Department realized that the air force could not win conventional wars solely through air power. The navy also was able to increase at the expense of the air force.

The primary flaws of NSC-68 were that it concentrated too heavily on military response to Soviet expansion while ignoring the diplomatic, economic, and cultural tools available. In addition, by concentrating on Soviet actions, NSC-68 gave the initiative to the Soviets. Soviet actions suddenly defined U.S. interests. Finally, NSC-68 focused on Soviet capabilities rather than on Soviet intentions. Despite these flaws, the basic conclusion of NSC-68—that the Soviets were bent on world domination and the destruction of free societies—remained the blueprint for national strategy for the next two decades.

Bibliography: Acheson, Dean, *Present at the Creation* (Norton, 1969); Gaddis, John Lewis, *Strategies of Containment* (Oxford Univ. Press, 1982); LaFeber, Walter, *America, Russia and the Cold War,* 5th ed. (Knopf, 1985); Mr. X (Kennan, George), "The Sources of Soviet Conduct," *Foreign Affairs* (July 1947).

Maj. George B. Eaton

OREGON, TASK FORCE

Division-size U.S. Army task force formed in 1967 to replace the Marine Corps units in the southern part of the I Corps Tactical Zone during the Vietnam War. Task Force Oregon deployed to south of Da Nang in late April 1967 in response to increased North Vietnamese Army activity near the demilitarized zone. Under the command of Maj. Gen. William B. Rosson, the 1st Brigade, 101st Airborne Division; the 196th Light Infantry Brigade; and the 3d Brigade, 25th Infantry Division, constituted the major units of this task force. After deploying to I Corps in April 1967, Task Force Oregon was redesignated as the 23d (American) Division in September 1967.

Bibliography: Ott, David E., *Field Artillery, 1954–1973* (U.S. Govt. Printing office, 1975); Pearson, Willard, *The War in the Northern Provinces, 1966–1968* (U.S. Govt. Printing Office, 1975).

Capt. Leslie Howard Belknap

PANMUNJOM PEACE TALKS (1951–1953)

Negotiations held in North Korea for the purpose of ending the Korean War. On June 23, 1951, Soviet deputy foreign minister Jacob Malik intimated that a negotiated settlement of the Korean conflict would be possible. Consequently, liaison teams met at Kaesong, near the South Korean border, on July 8, and full negotiations began two days later. Problems arose, however, as the United Nations Command (UNC) exerted military pressure on the battlefield while the Communists sought political advantage at the negotiating table. For example, the UNC delegation initially sat facing south, the victor's position according to Korean custom. Moreover, white flags on UNC vehicles provided propaganda value for the Communists. Chair size, size and height of flags, and violations of the neutral zone around the negotiating site added to the list of grievances. Nevertheless, on July 26, the delegates approved the topics to be discussed, consisting of: (1) the agenda, (2) a line of demarcation, (3) enforcement of armistice provisions, (4) prisoner of war (POW) exchange, and (5) general recommendations to the governments involved.

The UN delegates outrightly refused to reestablish the international border at the 38th parallel. The UNC sought a line that provided for a demilitarized zone and long-term defense. Reaching an impasse over the demarcation line and frustrated by numerous neutral zone violations, the Communists broke off negotiations on August 23.

Frustration extended to the UNC as well, and UNC commander Matthew Ridgway insisted on a new negotiation site. After much diplomatic maneuvering, talks resumed on October 25 at Panmunjom, a village just east of Kaesong. The UNC agreed to a line of demarcation along the current battle line as long as other issues were resolved within 30 days. This hiatus, from November 27 through December 27, allowed the Communists to reinforce the main line of resistance, however, and the UNC forfeited its military leverage.

In January 1952, the UNC proposed the concept of voluntary repatriation for all prisoners. The Communists countered with POW riots, accusations of chemical and biological warfare, and charges of inhumane treatment. Meanwhile, the delegates agreed on item 5 after only 11 days of deliberation. "Recommendations to the governments of the countries concerned on both sides," adopted on February 17, provided for a conference within three months of armistice to settle matters involving foreign presence in Korea, Korean unification, and other political issues. Negotiations continued with major issues limited to

the rehabilitation of North Korean airfields, the Soviet Union's status as a belligerent or neutral, and voluntary repatriation of POWs. Chief UNC delegate Adm. C. Turner Joy presented a package proposal on April 28 that made no mention of airfield rehabilitation, excluded the Soviet Union from the Neutral Nations Supervisory Commission, and advocated voluntary repatriation. Accepting compromise on the first two counts, the Communists refused to budge on the repatriation issue.

As a result, negotiations stalled in the summer of 1952, and the UNC delegation walked out on October 8. The war continued with no diplomatic progress until the death of Soviet premier Joseph Stalin on Mar. 5, 1953. Communist negotiators seemed more eager to achieve a settlement thereafter, and the delegates signed the armistice agreement at Panmunjom on July 27, 1953.

Maj. James Sanders Day

PARIS PEACE ACCORDS (1973)

Officially titled the agreement on Ending the War and Restoring the Peace in Vietnam, the Paris Accords were signed in Paris, France, on Jan. 27, 1973. Like the Geneva Agreement of 1954, the 1973 version neither ended the war nor restored peace in Vietnam.

Serious efforts to obtain a negotiated settlement among the governments in the United States, South Vietnam, and North Vietnam had been in progress for at least five years when the Paris ceremony was finally concluded. The negotiating partners were the United States and three main governments plus the Provisional Revolutionary Government (PRG) of Vietnam (Viet Cong). The PRG was supposed to represent South Vietnamese Communists who were claimed by Hanoi as being independents. In reality, the PRG was under the tight control of North Vietnam.

The terms of the agreement included a return of all prisoners, a cease-fire, and an International Commission of Control and Supervision (ICCS). The ICCS was to investigate cease-fire violations and disputes and to recommend means of peaceful resolution to the signatories. Additionally, the terms included a withdrawal of all U.S. forces, which followed quickly. The agreement did not, however, require a withdrawal of North Vietnamese troops from South Vietnam, and therein lay a serious dispute between U.S. president Richard M. Nixon and South Vietnamese president Nguyen Van Thieu. Prior to the agreement, the U.S. and South Vietnamese position had been that North Vietnam must withdraw its forces. The North had been holding considerable parts of some of South Vietnam's uninhabited border regions since the Easter Offensive of 1972. Heavy U.S. bombing of North Vietnam, including the use of B-52s in the Hanoi region and the mining of Haiphong's harbor during December 1972, brought the North to the bargaining table, but Hanoi's leaders consistently refused to withdraw their troops from South Vietnam. In exasperation, the U.S. negotiator, Henry Kissinger, recommended signing the agreement in spite of Hanoi's refusal. In the words of one U.S. diplomat, "we bombed them into accepting our concessions." President Thieu's approval of the agreement was bought only by President Nixon's threat of suspending all U.S. aid and heavy assurances that if the Communists violated the cease-fire, the United States would resume combat operations in Southeast Asia.

Both South Vietnamese and North Vietnamese forces broke the Paris Accords by a resumption of fighting. The ICCS proved to be an impotent body, incapable of proving that one side or the other violated cease-fire directives. To monitor the tense situation, the United States maintained a headquarters in nearby Thailand and a defense attaché's office in Saigon. Both reported steadily increasing combat operations, and the headquarters in Thailand made contingency plans for a return of U.S. combat forces. But there was no will in the United States for a resumption of fighting. When North Vietnamese tank columns poured into South Vietnam in the spring of 1975, U.S. political leaders ignored Saigon's pleas for help. The 1973 agreement was little more than a dignified way out of the war for the United States.

Bibliography: Dillard, Walter Scott, *Sixty Days to Peace* (U.S. Govt. Printing Office, 1982); Goodman, Allan E., *The Lost Peace: America's Search for a Negotiated Settlement of the Vietnam War* (Hoover Inst. Press, 1978); Nguyen Tien Hung and Jerrold L. Schecter, *The Palace File* (Harper & Row, 1986).

Col. (Ret.) Rod Paschall

PENTAGON PAPERS, THE
The documents popularly known as the Pentagon Papers consisted of excerpts from a top-secret, 47-volume Department of Defense study on the Vietnam War, prepared by order of Sec. of Defense Robert S. McNamara in 1967–69. The text traced the history of U.S. involvement in the war, and the published excerpts convinced the American public, especially antiwar activists, that the government had been misleading about U.S. policy in Vietnam. The Pentagon Papers were leaked to *The New York Times, The Washington Post,* and other newspapers by Daniel Ellsberg, a Rand Corporation employee who had previously worked for McNamara and who hoped that publication would increase antiwar feelings. Excerpts from the study were first published on June 13, 1971. In a landmark decision, *New York Times v. United States,* the U.S. Supreme Court ruled that a federal government suit to prevent further publication was a violation of the First Amendment. Ellsberg and an associate, Anthony Russo, were brought to trial on a variety of charges in 1973, but the judge ultimately dismissed the case because of "im-

proper government conduct." This included clandestine examination of Ellsberg's psychiatrist's patient files.

Bibliography: Herring, George C., ed., *The Secret Diplomacy of the Vietnam War: The Negotiating Volumes of the Pentagon Papers* (Univ. of Texas Press, 1983); *Pentagon Papers* (Bantam Books, 1971).

Stephen Robinson

PHOENIX PROGRAM
Most controversial of all the pacification programs during the Vietnam War, the Phoenix Program commenced shortly after the 1968 Tet Offensive as part of the Accelerated Pacification Program initiated by South Vietnamese president Nguyen Van Thieu in July 1968. Known to the Vietnamese as "Phung Hoang" ("all seeing bird"), Phoenix was the element of the efforts of the U.S. program CORDS (Civil Operations and Revolutionary Development Support) to destroy the Viet Cong infrastructure (VCI) and its inherent politico-military apparatus in the countryside.

In spite of official U.S. and South Vietnamese efforts, Phoenix was soon labeled by the media and critics of the war as an assassination program at a time when U.S. domestic support for the war was rapidly eroding. Historians still argue about Phoenix's overall effectiveness. Clearly, the VCI was weakened in the years following Tet and played an increasingly less important role within South Vietnam. From 1968 to 1971, nearly 17,000 VCI participants sought amnesty, almost 28,000 were captured, and another 20,000 were killed. From the enemy's perspective, Phoenix was responsible for wiping out many Viet Cong bases throughout the Vietnamese countryside. However, widespread abuse and corruption by the local Vietnamese security agencies carrying out Phoenix, plus the poor intelligence generated by Phoenix informants, allow many historians to criticize the Phoenix Program. Critics charge that the program alienated more Vietnamese peasants than it won by the elimination of the VCI.

Bibliography: Blaufarb, Douglas, *The Counterinsurgency Era: U.S. Doctrine and Performance* (Macmillan, 1977); Karnow, Stanley, *Vietnam: A History* (Viking, 1983); Lewy, Guenter, *America in Vietnam* (Oxford, 1978).

Capt. Leslie Howard Belknap

PORK CHOP HILL, BATTLE OF
(April 16–18, 1953)
One of the final U.S. battles of the Korean War. A U.S. unit, the understrength Company E., 31st Infantry Regiment, occupied Hill 255 (known as "Pork Chop Hill" for its shape), an outpost in North Korea of bunkers enclosed by barbed wire. On the night of Apr. 16, 1953, the Chinese attacked, gained entry into the position, and soon decimated the garrison. For two days, a bitter, bloody

struggle between U.S. and Chinese forces took place for the hill. Seven of eight U.S. rifle companies were chewed up in the battle. Both sides plastered the tiny position with thousands of artillery and mortar rounds. The Americans finally prevailed. In July, however, the hill was abandoned to the Chinese, who had again initiated a bloody battle of possession. Two weeks later, Pork Chop Hill became part of the demilitarized zone when the armistice agreement was signed on July 27.

Bibliography: Hermes, Walter G., *U.S. Army in the Korean War: Truce Tent and Fighting Front* (Office of the Chief of Military History, U.S. Army, 1966); Marshall, S. L. A., *Pork Chop Hill* (Morrow, 1956).

Brig. Gen. PNG (Ret.) Uzal W. Ent

POST-TRAUMATIC STRESS DISORDER

Clinical term used to indicate the response of some soldiers to the physical and psychological stresses of combat. Known in earlier times as neurasthenia, shell shock, or combat fatigue, post-traumatic stress disorder (PTSD) has become a favored explanation for aberrant behavior by some veterans of the Vietnam War. Alcoholism, drug dependency, hallucinations, and other psychiatric problems as well as a wide range of physical ailments have been attributed to the delayed effects of combat stress.

The treatment of PTSD has varied widely over the years. Even after the phenomenon became widespread and well-studied during World War I, the usual response was to treat the victim of PTSD as a coward or slacker, and disciplinary action was often prescribed as the cure. Gen. George S. Patton, Jr.'s slapping of a soldier hospitalized in Sicily for combat fatigue during World War II is a well-known example. However, it became generally recognized in World War I that the stress of prolonged combat could indeed cause very real physical and psychological disability and various "scientific" treatments were prescribed, including such drastic regimes as ice-water baths and electric shock. In World War II and the Korean War, good results were obtained by providing the victim with a short rest in a safe environment with warmth and good food. A high percentage of the soldiers receiving such basic treatment were quickly returned to duty. Curiously, among Vietnam veterans, the symptoms of PTSD seem to have remained latent until well after the events that are alleged to have caused the condition. Drug therapy and psychiatric counseling are now the preferred treatments.

Bibliography: Spiller, Roger J., "Shell Shock," *American Heritage* (May–June 1990).

Lt. Col. (Ret.) Charles R. Shrader

PRISONERS OF WAR

One of the most bitterly debated issues of the Vietnam War. There has been little complaint from Hanoi about the treatment of its soldiers and agents who were held captive by the government of South Vietnam during the war because the Northerners largely denied the existence of its citizens and soldiers in the South. And, since the government of South Vietnam no longer exists, there have been few complaints about the treatment of Saigon's troops in Communist prisons, even though many languished in harsh captivity 15 years after the war's end. The great bulk of the dispute concerns the treatment of U.S. prisoners under Northern control and the possibility there may still be U.S. citizens held by the Socialist Republic of Vietnam.

Despite being a signatory to the Geneva Convention of 1949 on the care and treatment of prisoners of war (POWs), North Vietnam condoned the murder of some of its U.S. captives, and Communist authorities supervised the torture of U.S. prisoners. Additionally, in violation of the Geneva Convention, the Northerners placed their U.S. captives on display for propaganda purposes, parading them in the streets and exposing them in humiliating circumstances for the benefit of reporters. With the help of some U.S. collaborators and extreme physical abuse, Hanoi elicited "confessions" of war crimes from some of the Americans. These long-remembered incidents inflamed the U.S. public and were responsible for much of the bitterness directed at Hanoi years after the conclusion of war. Between February and April 1973, the North Vietnamese released 591 U.S. POWs. Another 68 Americans stranded in Southeast Asia after war's end were subsequently turned over to U.S. authorities.

The most inflammatory issue between Washington and Hanoi, however, is the matter of Americans missing in action (MIAs), who might have been POWs. During the war, there were more than 2,400 Americans classified as MIAs in Vietnam, Laos, and Cambodia. There have been a number of reports from those who claim they have been captive Americans, captives Hanoi denies it holds. The U.S. government has been unable to substantiate the claims but continually presses Vietnam to divulge information on undisclosed U.S. prisoners. Additionally, there have been numerous joint searches for the remains of Americans, especially around airplane crash sites, and the U.S. armed forces have established a laboratory containing the medical records of American MIAs. In the early 1990s, Vietnam became much more cooperative about the MIA issue.

The MIA issue has been the most important bar to normal diplomatic relations between Hanoi and Washington, eclipsing the issue of Vietnamese refugees. Families of the missing have organized political pressure groups, and their efforts have been supported by U.S. veterans organizations. Together, these groups demand a full accounting of all Americans who were held by Hanoi, and their message to U.S. politicians has been to withhold U.S. recognition of Vietnam until that accounting is delivered.

U.S. prisoners of war, being repatriated in 1973 during the Vietnam War, are assembled by their North Vietnamese captors. (Na-tional Archives)

Bibliography: *POW and MIA Fact Book* (Dept. of Defense, 1985); Garrett, Richard, *P.O.W.* (David & Charles, 1981).

Col. (Ret.) Rod Paschall

PUEBLO INCIDENT (January 23, 1968)

Seizure of a U.S. naval vessel by North Koreans that resulted in the 11-month imprisonment of its crew and an ongoing public controversy. The USS *Pueblo* weighed anchor at Sasebo, Japan, on Jan. 11, 1968. The ship's complement of 6 officers, 74 enlisted men, and 2 civilian oceanographers embarked on their first elint (electronic intelligence) mission. The crew sought to gather elint and oceanographic data on seawater temperature, salinity, depths, and currents off the Korean coast. On January 23, North Korean patrol boats and fighter planes fired on the

Pueblo; later, North Koreans boarded the ship and escorted it to Wonsan harbor.

Accusing the *Pueblo* crew of espionage, the North Koreans gained a confession from Cmdr. Lloyd M. Bucher in which he admitted violating North Korean territorial waters and spying for the Central Intelligence Agency. The United States ruled out force as a countermeasure and resorted to diplomatic negotiations at Panmunjom. Ultimately, the United States admitted to the spy charges and apologized publicly to the North Korean government. The U.S. delegation repudiated a written confession, but then signed the document to secure the release of the prisoners. Thus, on Dec. 23, 1968, the *Pueblo* crew regained its freedom.

A U.S. Navy court of inquiry—convened on Jan. 20, 1969, and adjourned on March 13—recommended trial by general court-martial for Commander Bucher, listing five alleged offenses. In addition, the court suggested a general court-martial on three charges against Lt. Stephen R. Harris, the officer in charge of the research detachment. Recommendations for nonjudicial punishment included a letter of admonition for the executive officer, Lt. Edward R. Murphy, Jr., and letters of reprimand for Rear Adm. Frank L. Johnson, commander of naval forces in Japan, and for Capt. Everett B. Gladding, director of the Naval Security Group, Pacific. In turn, the commander in chief of the U.S. Pacific Fleet modified the court's recommendations, and the chief of naval operations concurred with the modifications. A review by Sec. of the Navy John H. Chafee determined that all charges should be dropped. In his words, "they have suffered enough, and further punishment would not be justified."

Further research by Robert A. Liston discounts the official report, however. He contends that the *Pueblo* surrender represented a covert intelligence operation by the National Security Agency. In fact, the United States planted a code machine on-board in order to entice the North Koreans to use it, thereby assisting U.S. codebreakers in deciphering a secret Soviet code. The *Pueblo* intercepted a Soviet message, however, that revealed a plan to attack China. Thus, the Chinese, not the North Koreans, captured the *Pueblo* in an attempt to seize the message, and the Soviets fired on the U.S. ship to prevent the Chinese takeover. When the Chinese discovered no message, they turned the ship over to the North Koreans who used the coding machine as originally designed.

According to Liston, the *Pueblo* surrender (1) helped prevent a U.S. defeat in the Tet Offensive in Vietnam in 1968, (2) enhanced relations between China and the United States, and (3) compromised Soviet intelligence efforts that resulted in détente. Indeed, Liston considered the *Pueblo* incident "the greatest intelligence coup of modern times."

Bibliography: Armbrister, Trevor, *A Matter of Accountability: the True Story of the Pueblo Affair* (Coward-McCann, 1970); Brandt, Ed., *The Last Voyage of USS Pueblo* (Norton, 1969); Bucher, Lloyd M., *Bucher: My Story* (Doubleday, 1970); Liston, Robert A., *The Pueblo Surrender* (M. Evans, 1988); Schumacher, Frederick Carl, and George C. Wilson, *Bridge of No Return: the Ordeal of the U.S.S. Pueblo* (Harcourt Brace Jovanovich, 1971).

Maj. James Sanders Day

PUSAN PERIMETER, BATTLES OF THE
(August–September 1950)

Early Korean War engagements at the so-called Pusan perimeter, a battle line enclosing a rectangular area about 100 air miles from north to south and some 50 miles from east to west, protecting the port of Pusan in southeast South Korea. United Nations forces, primarily U.S. and South Korean, had been driven into this small area by the North Korean attacks launched in June 1950. On the ground, the line was some 300 miles long, forcing the understrength U.S. and Republic of Korea (ROK) divisions to hold frontages of 30–40 miles each (U.S. Army doctrine specified a maximum front of 6–8 miles). As a result, principal river crossing sites, key hills, and road junctions were outposted, and counterattacks by reserves were employed to repel the enemy.

There were four main avenues of attack into the perimeter. In the south, it was the main road to Masan; in the center, through a large loop in the Naktong River; in the north, through the city of Taegu; and in the east, down the coastal road.

The Naktong formed a natural moat along almost three-quarters of the defense line. Utilizing this natural barrier, Lt. Gen. Walton H. Walker deployed the U.S. 25th Infantry Division in the south, then the U.S. 24th Infantry and 1st Cavalry divisions, with the ROK 1st Division extending the line north of the river to the town of Naktong-ni. The ROK 6th, 8th, Capital, and 3d divisions carried the perimeter east from Naktong-ni to the sea.

North Korean August Attacks. The most serious threat was in the south, where the 27th Regiment fortuitously had uncovered the approach of the North Korean (NK) 6th Division. Walker decided to attack there with the 25th Division (less the 27th Regiment, in 8th Army reserve), the 5th Regimental Combat Team, and the 1st Provisional Marine Brigade. The attack, launched Aug. 7, 1950, ran into an attack by the enemy. Although the marines drove deep into enemy territory, the North Koreans got into U.S. rear areas, and a bloody, confused battle ensued. Pressure on other sectors of the perimeter forced Walker to call off the attack.

The NK 4th Division had crossed the Naktong on August 5, driving deep into the 24th Division in the Naktong Bulge. The Marine Brigade and elements of the 27th Infantry reinforced the 24th. The 27th recaptured ground on the division southern flank, and the marines and 24th Division troops counterattacked. The line was restored along the Naktong by August 18.

Between August 4 and 6, the NK 13th and 1st divisions attacked the ROKs troops farther north. They were joined by the tank-led NK 15th Division. Although the ROK fought stubbornly, by mid-August, the enemy was rapidly approaching the last mountain ranges protecting the vital city of Taegu. The 27th Infantry was sent north to bolster that front. The 27th Infantry and the ROK 1st Division attacked on August 18. After a short gain, they established defenses in and overlooking a long, flat, narrow valley. That night and for six more nights, the NK 13th Division unsuccessfully attacked the 27th Infantry. On August 19, elements of the 23d Infantry were sent to backstop the 27th.

On the night of August 8, the NK 3d Division's 7th Regiment crossed the Naktong against the 1st Cavalry Division, seizing Hill 268 ("Triangulation Hill"). The other two regiments of the 3d were largely destroyed. By August 12, the cavalry had driven out the 7th Regiment and restored its lines.

On August 11, the NK 10th Division attacked across the river into the cavalry's southern sector, seizing two commanding hills, but further crossings were thwarted. Early on August 14, the North Koreans crossed the river north of the cavalry, attacked south through the ROK faction, and seized Hill 303 in the cavalry zone near Waegwan. When the hill was retaken two days later, the survivors of two rifle companies and the bodies of 26 members of a mortar platoon who had been murdered by the enemy were discovered.

On August 8, the NK 8th Division attacked the ROK 8th Division, but it was stopped. Meantime, the NK 12th Division headed for P'chang-ni, on the east coast. The NK 5th Division pinned the ROK 3d Division to the coastline, forcing its evacuation on August 17. Walker eventually had to commit the ROK Capital Division; four ROK regiments; three separate battalions; the 3d Battalion, 9th U.S. Infantry Regiment; and artillery, mortar, and tank units to repel the enemy in this sector. On the southern flank, the NK 6th and 7th divisions struck the 25th Division on August 17 and 18, but they succeeded only in taking one position.

Heavy casualties in 8th Army and the lack of replacements reduced front-line units to less than half strength. Between August 20 and early September, Koreans were systematically assigned to U.S. Army divisions. These soldiers—known as "KATUSAs" (Korean Augmentation to the U.S. Army)—comprised as much as 30–50 percent of some rifle companies.

September Attacks.   The enemy planned five new assaults to be made between August 27 and September 2. This coordinated offensive was designed to deny Walker the opportunity to commit reserves everywhere and almost assured a breakthrough somewhere.

The NK 12th Division attacked the Capital Division on August 27, driving it back five or six miles. Although the U.S. 21st Regiment, the 3d Battalion, 9th Infantry, and most of a tank battalion were sent to help, the ROKs refused to counterattack. Walker then sent the newly created ROK 7th Division to the scene. The ROK 3d Division, under pressure from the NK 5th, also refused to counterattack. Finally, after the 24th Division was ordered in, the combined U.S.-ROK force, in savage fighting, forced the enemy back. Meantime, the ROK 6th Division beat the NK 8th, but the NK 15th drove back the ROK 8th.

Reinforced by two ROK regiments, the ROK 8th then destroyed the NK 15th.

On September 3, an attack by the NK 3d, 1st, and 13th divisions penetrated the rear of the 1st Cavalry and forced the evacuation of Waegwan. The division was forced to withdraw. Although the enemy was deep in its rear areas, cavalry counterattacks threw the enemy back by September 14. Matters were so critical in early September that Walker seriously considered withdrawing farther south to a previously reconnoitered defensive position.

Assaults on the 25th Division on the night of August 31 by the NK 6th and 7th divisions penetrated the 24th and 35th regiments. Counterattacks by the 1st Battalion, 27th Infantry, and the 35th Infantry restored the line, but three NK battalions had slipped into rear areas. The 2d and 3d battalions, 27th Infantry, joined later by the 1st, ejected these infiltrators, killing 2,000 of them. But the enemy held fast on Battle Mountain in the 24th Regiment's area.

On August 31, the NK 2d, 9th, and 10th divisions attacked the U.S. 2d Division, precipitating the Second Battle of the Naktong Bulge. (This was the same area that had been occupied by the 24th Division.) The NK 10th Division gained one hill mass and stayed there until withdrawn. The NK 2d and 9th divisions, meantime, split the 24th Division. The marines were again committed, joining counterattacks with army units, until withdrawn from the perimeter to prepare for the Inchon landing.

When the U.S. X Corps landed at Inchon on September 15, the ROK troops and 8th Army were still locked in battle with the North Koreans. Both sides had suffered heavily. U.S. battle casualties to September 15 numbered 19,165 (4,599 dead, 12,058 wounded, 401 captured, and 2,107 missing). The successful defense of the Pusan perimeter paved the way for the landing at Inchon and the subsequent ejection of North Korea from the South.

Bibliography: Appleman, Roy E., *The U.S. Army in the Korean War. South to the Naktong, North to the Yalu* (Dept. of the Army, 1961); Blair, Clay, *The Forgotten War* (Times Books, 1987).

Brig. Gen. PNG (Ret.) Uzal W. Ent

RANGER INFANTRY

Specialized U.S. army units. During the Korean War, ranger units were organized and trained along conventional lines and were utilized primarily as scouts, long-range penetration units, and small commando-type units that destroyed installations and weapons caches behind enemy lines. They were formed and trained at Fort Benning, Georgia, in 1950 and 1951. Training of these specialized units continued through the 1960s and early 1970s when, primarily during the Vietnam War, Rangers were utilized in a long-range reconnaissance and deep interdiction role.

After the Vietnam War, existing Ranger units were reactivated and strengthened, namely the 1st Battalion and 2d Battalion, 75th Rangers, at Fort Lewis, Washington, and the 3d Battalion, 75th Rangers, at Fort Benning. With a psychological operations unit and a civil affairs battalion added, they became the 1st Special Operations Command with the purpose of being deployable to any crisis area that threatened vital U.S. interests worldwide. The 75th Special Forces were used in Grenada in 1983 and in Panama in 1989. During Operation Desert Storm (1991), the rangers conducted reconnaissance and sabotage missions against Iraqi lines of communication and munition storage dumps and searched for mobile Scud launchers.

Leo J. Daugherty III

REFORGER EXERCISES

Part of the annual NATO (North Atlantic Treaty Organization) exercises that were designed to prove U.S. ability to move conventional military forces rapidly from the continental United States to Central Europe. The first "Reforger" (*return of forces to Germany*) exercise was 1963's Operation Gyroscope. Gyroscope was intended to demonstrate the U.S. shift to a policy of flexible response and resolve to use conventional land, air, and sea forces to defend Europe from Soviet aggression. The exercises rapidly became an annual event and were used to exercise the NATO command structure, transportation systems, local logistic support of U.S. units, and issue and maintenance procedures for military stocks prepositioned in Europe.

Maj. George B. Eaton

RIBBON CREEK INCIDENT (April 8, 1956)

The drowning of six marine recruits during a disciplinary march through a tidal estuary at Marine Corps Recruit Depot, Parris Island, South Carolina. Staff Sgt. Matthew C. McKeon, the drill instructor who ordered the march on the evening of Apr. 8, 1956, for his "unruly" and "undisciplined" unit, was indicted on charges of manslaughter and negligent homicide. In July, he was found guilty of negligent homicide and of drinking on duty. He was fined and sentenced to nine-months hard labor and a dishonorable discharge. The sentence was later lightened by the secretary of the navy. As a result of this incident, the marine training program was revamped to include new teams of command, extended supervision of and better qualified drill instructors, increased attention to physical fitness, and special training platoons to provide individual attention to recruits.

Leo J. Daugherty III

ROLLING THUNDER, OPERATION (1965–1968)

Name given to a series of U.S. air operations against North Vietnam, which were designed to make the North pay a heavy price for its support of Viet Cong activities in the South. It was promoted by Pres. Lyndon B. Johnson and Sec. of Defense Robert S. McNamara, who overruled the Joint Chiefs of Staff's advocacy of an immediate heavy retaliation in favor of a gradual approach in which the bombing commenced in a limited manner, halted for a time to give North Vietnam a chance to begin negotiations, then resumed on an escalated scale when the North failed to cease its operations.

The program started in March 1965 when U.S. aircraft bombed North Vietnamese supply routes to the South. When the campaign failed to reduce the flow of enemy supplies, military leaders again pressured Johnson and McNamara to give them a free rein, and after a pause from Dec. 24, 1965, to Feb. 1, 1966, failed to draw a response from the North, target selection was broadened to include North Vietnamese ammunition dumps and oil facilities.

On June 29, 1966, navy and air force fighter-bombers hit oil storage sites in the Hanoi-Haiphong region. Throughout July and August, U.S. planes blasted other storage areas throughout North Vietnam, but again achieved little success since the North Vietnamese had dispersed much of its oil and supplies. After this phase of the bombing, McNamara commissioned a study of Rolling Thunder by the Institute for Defense Analysis, an independent group of eminent scientists. Their report concluded that Rolling Thunder had failed to interdict North Vietnamese supply routes and would most likely not succeed with future escalation. McNamara now began to support a total cessation.

Rolling Thunder expanded into its most intensive phase in the spring of 1967 after a second pause brought no response from the North. Planes hit previously exempted targets, dropped mines into harbors, and bombed close to the Chinese border. Once more, the campaign proved ineffective, a fact made bluntly obvious by North Vietnam's surprisingly strong and widespread Tet Offensive in early 1968. Combined with major political turmoil in the South Vietnamese government, Tet shocked President Johnson into ordering another bombing halt in April 1968, followed by a gradual deescalation until Rolling Thunder was halted in November.

Although 643,000 tons of bombs were dropped in the 44-month campaign, Rolling Thunder failed to achieve its objectives. North Vietnamese supplies continued to pour down infiltration routes to the South, and rather than harming morale in the North, the bombing appeared to solidify the people's determination to fight. More than 900 U.S. aircraft costing $6 billion were lost during Rolling Thunder, and the captured pilots handed North Vietnam an important bargaining chip for future negotiations. Rolling Thunder also gave the North a major propaganda edge in world opinion in that a small nation withstood an intensive bombing campaign mounted by the world's mightiest superpower. In the United States, antiwar critics used this to intensify their attacks on the conflict.

Bibliography: Berger, Carl, ed., *The United States Air Force in Southeast Asia, 1961–1973* (Office of Air Force History, 1977); Davidson, Phillip B., *Vietnam at War* (Presidio, 1988); Morrocco, John, *The Vietnam Experience: Thunder From Above* (Boston Pub. Co., 1984).

John F. Wukovits

ROLLUP-REBUILD, OPERATIONS (1945–1952)

Post-World War II U.S. operation in which surplus war matériel was collected and transported to Japan for reconditioning. Following the surrender of Japan, large amounts of surplus military property, such as vehicles and weapons, remained at U.S. bases throughout the Pacific. Much of that stock became part of Rollup. Once the items were in Japan, Operation Rebuild took over. Making use of Japanese labor, they were refitted and made serviceable for use by U.S. forces in the Far East. The value of these programs to U.S. forces during the Korean War is inestimable. Stock from Japan, salvaged as part of Rollup/Rebuild, furnished virtually all of the ammunition requirements during the early months of the war.

Bibliography: Farmer, W. C., "Operation Rebuild," *Military Review* (Feb. 1953); Japan Logistical Command, Operation Rollup, *Operation Rebuild (14 August 1945–30 June 1952)* (1952).

David Friend

SALT

Acronym for "Strategic Arms Limitation Treaty," the name of two preliminary nuclear-control agreements between the United States and the Soviet Union. By the mid-1960s, the U.S. strategic triad of land-based intercontinental ballistic missiles (ICBMs), submarine-based sea-launched ballistic missiles (SLBMs), and long-range bombers was roughly matched by Soviet strategic forces. Differences in the systems made the establishment of equivalence exceedingly difficult, but recently developed techniques to monitor the other side—called "national technical means" (NTM)—permitted verification.

SALT I (1969–72) ended with an Interim Agreement on Strategic Offensive Arms. Among the provisions were (1) freezing the number of ICBM and SLBM launchers, (2) reducing reliance on land-based systems, (3) formalizing the principle of verification by banning both deliberate interference with NTM and hiding from NTM forces limited by the agreement, and (4) establishing a joint U.S.-Soviet Standing Consultative Commission to deal with any questions of treaty implementation and compliance that might arise. The agreement expired on Oct. 2, 1977, but both sides continued to observe it as negotiations for SALT II went on from 1972 until 1979.

U.S. systems were forward-based, meaning that relatively short-ranged U.S. systems could hit the Soviet Union. Soviet "heavy" ICBMs were capable of carrying either enormous warheads or multiple independently targetable reentry vehicles (MIRVs), units composed of a number of smaller warheads capable of hitting a number of various targets. The Soviet Union had no nuclear-armed allies and had to worry about China, Britain, and France as well as the United States. The Soviets were concerned with U.S. air-launched cruise missiles (ALCMs); the United States wanted to count the "medium" Soviet Backfire as a "heavy" bomber because it could reach the United States. Despite these asymmetries, the parties agreed on an extremely detailed and technical document designed to close loopholes and clarify ambiguities. SALT II set limits on the aggregate number of ICBMs, SLBMs, and heavy bombers; established ceilings on MIRV systems; included limits on heavy bombers; and provided for verification of compliance by NTM. The Soviet occupation of Afghanistan in 1979 resulted in U.S. nonratification of the treaty, but the United States remained in technical compliance until 1986, when modifications to B-52 aircraft put the United States over certain limits. Evidence indicates that the Soviet Union remained within the limits of the treaty.

Bibliography: *Arms Control and National Security, An Introduction* (Arms Control Association, 1989).

Col. (Ret.) Henry G. Gole

SCAP

Acronym for both "Supreme Commander for the Allied Powers" (the office of military administrator established in Tokyo in September 1945, at the time of the Japanese surrender) and for the commander of the office. SCAP nominally reported to two agencies that represented the 11 nations that had participated in the war against Japan. The United States had veto power over both agencies, so in practice, SCAP implemented American policy for the governing and reconstruction of Japan. As SCAP, Gen. Douglas MacArthur organized his command into a dozen sections, some performing traditional military functions, the rest paralleling the ministries of the Japanese cabinet. The office of SCAP introduced many changes to Japan in regard to land ownership, education, and other aspects of Japanese life and along with the economic stimulus of the Korean War is often credited with bringing about the rapid reconstruction of the Japanese economy and other institutions.

Bibliography: Schaller, Michael, *The Occupation of Japan: The Origins of the Cold War in Asia* (Oxford Univ. Press, 1985).

Lloyd J. Graybar

SEARCH AND DESTROY TACTICS

Operations conducted by the U.S. Armed Forces during the Vietnam War in order to engage and, ultimately, to destroy or to neutralize elusive enemy forces. These operations consisted of sweeps throughout the countryside to track down and destroy enemy units that had sought to avoid contact with better-equipped U.S. forces. Advocated by Gen. William Westmoreland, these aggressive patrolling and offensive operations were designed to keep the enemy off balance and to bring about defeat by depriving the enemy of supplies and a firm base from which to conduct operations. The helicopter was a valuable aid in conducting search and destroy missions.

Leo J. Daugherty III

SHAPE

Acronym for "Supreme Headquarters Allied Powers, Europe." In December 1950, when the Korean War had taken an ominous turn and fears about the security of Western Europe were high, the United States announced that General of the Army Dwight D. Eisenhower would be Supreme Allied Commander, Europe, with instructions to establish an appropriate headquarters (SHAPE) and command structure for the North Atlantic Alliance that had been founded in 1949. Eisenhower flew to Frankfurt, West Germany, toured the NATO (North Atlantic Treaty Organization) capitals, and named a deputy supreme commander. He also established regional headquarters in Oslo, Norway; Fontainebleau, France; and Naples, Italy. SHAPE offices were temporarily located in Paris while more suitable facilities were under development near Versailles, France. On Apr. 2, 1951, Eisenhower declared SHAPE operational. Headquarters were moved to Belgium in 1967.

Bibliography: Kaplan, Lawrence S., *NATO and the United States: The Enduring Alliance* (Twayne, 1988).

Lloyd J. Graybar

SMITH, TASK FORCE (July 1950)

First U.S. ground force to oppose the North Korean army during the Korean War. Task Force Smith (named for its commander, Lt. Col. Charles B. Smith) consisted of Companies A and B, 21st Infantry Regiment; Battery A, 52d Field Artillery Battalion; and headquarters and service units (all from the 24th Infantry Division). It defended a position two miles north of Osan, South Korea. On July 5, 1950, elements of the North Korean 4th Infantry Division, with more than 30 tanks, attacked, and a desperate battle ensued. Outflanked and about to be overwhelmed, Smith withdrew, having held for seven critical hours. He lost more than 200 of his 540 men. The enemy lost 4 tanks and approximately 120 men.

Bibliography: Appleman, Roy E., *The U.S. Army in the Korean War: South to the Naktong, North to the Yalu*

(Dept. of the Army, 1961); Blair, Clay, *The Forgotten War* (Time Books, 1987).

Brig. Gen. PNG (Ret.) Uzal W. Ent

SON TAY RAID (November 21, 1970)

U.S. joint operation to rescue prisoners of war (POWs) deep in North Vietnam by an Army Special Forces ground element supported by air forces and a navy air diversion near Haiphong. This imaginative and daring mission—personally approved by Pres. Richard M. Nixon after consultation with senior advisers—failed because the American POWs thought to be held at Son Tay, 23 miles west of Hanoi, had been relocated some four months earlier. The overall mission commander was air force brigadier general Leroy J. Manor. The ground assault commander was army colonel Arthur D. Simons.

Bibliography: Schemmer, Benjamin F., *The Raid* (Harper & Row, 1976).

Col. (Ret.) Henry G. Gole

SPECIAL OPERATIONS FORCES

Operationally controlled by the U.S. Special Operations Command (USSOCOM), U.S. special operations forces include units from three of the armed services. They are capable of combat and combat support and are characterized by high levels of training, unique and varied skills, and light armament and equipment. The U.S. Army's special operations forces include Special Forces, psychological operations units, civil affairs units, Rangers, and special operations aviation units. The U.S. Air Force employs several special operations squadrons. The U.S. Navy has Sea-Air-Land (SEAL) forces.

Army. The army has the widest array of special units. Formed in 1952, Special Forces had the original mission of supporting and directing indigenous guerrilla forces. In the last stages of the Korean War, Army Special Forces were employed with Korean partisan units located on many of the small islands off the North Korean coasts. Their tasks there were to advise and assist some of the 22,000 partisans fighting Kim Il Sung's Communist regime. In the early 1960s, Special Forces missions were expanded to include counterinsurgency (sometimes called foreign internal defense) and reconnaissance. Special Forces were used in Laos from 1960 until 1962, training and assisting the Royal Lao Army and two indigenous Laotian minorities, the Hmong and Kha peoples. These units were employed extensively during the Vietnam War, mostly advising and assisting the South Vietnamese in remote and vulnerable locations. In the early part of the war, Special Forces absorbed the largest numbers of casualties on a per capita basis of any of the U.S. military organizations.

At the same time, Special Forces units were busy in Latin America and were responsible for training the Bolivian units that eventually brought down the Communist guerrilla leader Che Guevara. Special Forces units were used during the Persian Gulf War of 1991 in a reconnaissance capacity, deep behind Iraqi lines. There they reported on Iraqi movements, a critical activity since during the allied attack, Gen. H. Norman Schwarzkopf's left flank was exposed and lightly defended. When the shooting stopped, Special Forces units were involved with setting up refugee camps for the Kurdish people in Iraq.

Psychological operations units were organized at about the same time as the army's Special Forces with a mission of modifying the behavior of enemy forces and foreign populations through psychological campaigns using broadcast, leaflet, and other means of communications. Mostly, U.S. psychological operations units have been used in an advisory capacity in Third World settings.

Ranger units were briefly recreated during the Korean War, disbanded, and once again resurrected during the 1970s. Ranger units are superbly trained light infantry specializing in raids and reconnaissance. Like members of Special Forces, Rangers are parachute-qualified. They were used most prominently during the rescue operation on the island of Grenada in 1983 and in the invasion of Panama in 1989.

Civil affairs units are primarily composed of reserve component personnel and are capable of advising and assisting indigenous governments in all types of civil administration, including law enforcement and public works. They were extensively used in northern Iraq among the Kurds after the cease-fire ending the Gulf War of 1991.

The army's special operations aviation units are largely equipped with helicopters that are modified for precision night flying. Typically, the aviation units clandestinely put Special Forces and Ranger units in place; however, some of these aircraft are armed. In the late 1980s, armed army special operations helicopters equipped with night-vision equipment were used by the U.S. Navy in the Persian Gulf to thwart raids by small, fast Iranian patrol boats.

Air Force. The air force's special operations forces were originally labeled "air commandos" when they were created in the early 1960s. There had been an air commando organization during World War II, but the concept for that organization was different than what was envisioned in the early John F. Kennedy administration. Initially, air commando missions involved advising and assisting indigenous air forces in developing nations. However, by the mid-1960s, language training and technology transfer skills began to wither away. Most of these forces were being employed in South Vietnam, where they were increasingly involved in direct combat and combat-support activities. In the early 1960s, the air commandos were often using World War II-vintage airplanes, but they eventually employed modern U.S. Air Force planes.

By the 1990s, air force special operations aircraft in-

Special operations forces train for quick-reaction combat during a Special Operations Command exercise. (U.S. Air Force)

cluded long-range helicopters with highly accurate navigation equipment, long-range transport aircraft with extensive penetration aids, and gunships, which were transport aircraft armed with automatic cannons and equipped with sophisticated sighting equipment. In the 1960s, gunships were likely to be modified older aircraft such as C-47s or C-119s. Later, the larger, more modern C-130 aircraft were used in this role. Gunships were used extensively in the 1983 rescue operation on Grenada and in the 1989 invasion of Panama. Their sensors were developed to include low-light television and infrared detection gear. Their employment usually depends on a high degree of air control if not absolute air superiority. During the Gulf War, air force special operations crews dropped giant fuel-air bombs on Iraqi defenses and minefields, transported U.S. Special Forces units, and performed many other tasks.

Navy. The navy's SEAL forces were created in the early 1960s and were given commando-type missions: reconnaissance and raiding. They were equipped with light, speedy watercraft used for infiltration but were also capable of being transported and delivered by submarine. They were used in the Mekong Delta during the Vietnam War and, like the army's Special Forces, in reconnaissance roles outside South Vietnam. During the rescue operation in Grenada, they experienced a high casualty rate, and the same fate awaited them in a raid on an airport a few years later in Panama.

USSOCOM. The U.S. Special Operations Command was created in the late 1980s in response to congressional demands that U.S. special operations forces be better represented and looked after by the nation's military and naval leaders. Commanded by a full general and having its own budget hearings on Capitol Hill, USSOCOM oversees the training, supply, and equipment development programs. Additionally, the command can employ these forces.

Bibliography: Barnett, Frank R., et al., eds., *Special Operations in U.S. Strategy* (National Defense Univ. Press, 1984); Marolda, Edward J., and G. Wesley Pryce, *A Short History of the United States Navy and the South-*

east Asian Conflict (Naval Hist. Center, 1984); Paddock, Alfred H., Jr., *U.S. Army Special Warfare: Its Origins* (National Defense Univ. Press, 1982); Paschall, Rod, *LIC 2010: Special Operations and Unconventional Warfare in the Next Century* (Brassey's, 1990); Stanton, Shelby, *The Green Berets at War* (Presidio, 1985).

Col. (Ret.) Rod Paschall

STEALTH AIRCRAFT

Combat airplanes designed to be nearly invisible to radar. Beginning at least by the 1970s, the U.S. Department of Defense undertook a program to develop stealth aircraft. The ability to sneak through enemy defenses, proponents argued, was the next logical step for military aircraft development. Research programs were conducted under tight security, but at least one leak and a spy scandal led to a public disclosure of the program. The F-117A fighter, however, was built, tested, and fielded without public knowledge.

The 37th Tactical Fighter Wing, based near Tonapah, Nevada, received the only F-117s built. In 1989, the air force made public the existence of the F-117s; they were employed in Panama in 1989 and with excellent effect during the 1991 Persian Gulf conflict.

The B-2 Stealth bomber had a more difficult time. The existence of the aircraft was made known during its development phase, and it has been the subject of intense budget battles ever since. The bombers cost $520,000,000 each, and the Defense Department decided to reduce its proposed purchase of 132 aircraft. At most, a much-reduced number of B-2s will be fielded in the post–Cold War era.

Bibliography: Dornheim, Michael A., "USAF Display of F-117A Reveals New Details of Stealth Aircraft," *Aviation Week & Space Technology* (Apr. 30, 1990); Easterbrook, Gregg, "Sticker Shock: The Stealth Is a Bomb," *Newsweek* (Jan. 23, 1989); Lenoritz, Jeffrey M., "F-117s Drop Laser-Guided Bombs in Destroying Most Baghdad Targets," *Aviation Week & Space Technology* (Feb. 4, 1991); Palmer, Elizabeth A., "The Nine Lives of the B-2," *Congressional Quarterly* (Oct. 13, 1990).

Roger D. Launius

STRANGLE/SATURATE, OPERATIONS (1951–1952)

Effort of the United Nations Command (UNC) to interdict Communist lines of communication and logistic support during the Korean War. Operation Strangle, begun in August 1951, concentrated on cutting rail lines throughout North Korea. Every day, a specified 15–30-mile rail length was targeted and attacked twice. By December, Communist repair crews were restoring the damage almost as fast as it was being delivered.

The spring thaw of 1952 brought a new plan, codenamed Saturate, under which one specific stretch of roadbed received round-the-clock saturation bombing. During bad weather and night bombing lulls, repair crews were able to keep the railroads operative. The bombing campaign did prevent the Communists from stockpiling supplies at the front and from building up their artillery capability.

Bibliography: Futrell, Robert F., *The United States Air Force in Korea, 1950–1953* (Office of Air Force History, 1983).

David Friend

U.S. Air Force F-117 Stealth fighters, almost undetectable by radar, return from a mission during Operation Desert Storm (1991). (U.S. Air Force)

STRATEGIC AIR COMMAND (SAC)
One of the major field commands of the U.S. Air Force, the Strategic Air Command is a long-range force with nuclear strike and nuclear defense capabilities. SAC has combat-ready aircraft available at all times and is responsible for intercontinental ballistic missiles. Organized in 1946, SAC elements participated in many non-nuclear engagements, including the Korean and Vietnam wars and Operations Desert Shield/Desert Storm. With the end of the Cold War in the early 1990s, the future necessity of SAC for the defense of the United States became an issue.

Stephen Robinson

STRATEGIC ARMS LIMITATIONS TREATY (*see* SALT)

STUDIES AND OBSERVATION GROUP
Element of the U.S. Military Assistance Command Vietnam (MACV), the Studies and Observation Group (SOG) conducted special operations in Southeast Asia during the Vietnam War. It was a highly secretive organization, and some of its exploits remain classified. At its greatest strength, it was composed of about 2,000 personnel, most from U.S. Army Special Forces, SEAL (Sea-Air-Land) navy commandos, Air Force 90th Special Operations Wing, and Marine Corps reconnaissance. In addition to the Americans, the unit trained and employed indigenous personnel. Some of its tasks were accomplished in North Vietnam, but most were conducted in Laos and Cambodia. Primarily, the organization was concerned with reconnaissance and interdiction operations against the North Vietnamese Army. Based in Saigon, SOG managed outlying facilities in Kontum, Da Nang, and Ban Me Thout.

Bibliography: Stanton, Shelby, *Green Berets at War* (Presidio, 1985).

Col. (Ret.) Rod Paschall

SUPREME COMMANDER FOR THE ALLIED POWERS (*see* SCAP)

SUPREME HEADQUARTERS ALLIED POWERS, EUROPE (*see* SHAPE)

SURFACE-TO-AIR MISSILES
Military weapons launched from the ground to targets in the atmosphere. In 1953, the U.S. Army deployed its first antiaircraft missile system, the Nike. The Nike depended on ground-based radar and computers to plot interceptions and required a hefty amount of support equipment. Meanwhile, the army also began developing a mobile, medium-range missile to protect forward bases and units. Fielded in 1960, the Hawk ("*h*oming *a*ll the *w*ay *k*iller") relied on reflected radar energy to home in on its target. While the

Nike system disappeared by the mid-1970s, the Hawk has been modernized periodically and is still in service. During the 1970s, the army developed the Patriot to replace eventually both Nike and Hawk. Highly automated and shielded against electronic countermeasures, the Patriot provides protection against aircraft and tactical ballistic missiles. First used in combat during the Persian Gulf War in 1991, the Patriot gained acclaim for destroying a number of Iraqi Scud missiles.

Richard F. Kehrberg

TACTICAL MISSILES
Projectile weaponry used in nuclear warfare. During the Korean War of 1950–53, the United States began developing tactical missiles that could be easily transported and launched in combat situations. With the air force controlling the skies, the army developed tactical missiles that could be used on the battlefield. Discussed here are the seven U.S. missiles known as Corporal, Sergeant, Honest John, Little John, Pershing, Davy Crockett, and Lance.

The Corporal, developed in 1951 and contracted by the Jet Propulsion Laboratory (JPL) of California Institute of Technology was the first U.S. tactical ballistic guided missile. It was transported by several mobile vans equipped with radar guidance. With a weight of 5 tons and a length of 45 feet, the Corporal was vertically launched and had a range of 50–150 miles.

The Sergeant, developed in 1955 by JPL, was transported by three semitrailer trucks and thus had to be assembled at its launch site. The Sergeant was approximately 35 feet long, weighed nearly 5 tons, and had a range of 28–87 miles.

The Honest John, built by Douglas Aircraft Company beginning in 1957, was a short-range artillery ballistic rocket. It was fired from mobile launchers with no in-flight guidance. It weighed approximately 3 tons, was 27 feet long, and had a range of 30 miles.

The Little John, a smaller version of Honest John, was developed for use with the army's airborne units and was carried by light vehicles, including helicopters. Known as the "318-millimeter rocket," it was 12 feet long and had a range of 20 miles.

The Pershing, developed in 1957 by the Martin Company, was a two-stage missile transported by four tracked vehicles. It was approximately 35 feet long, weighed 5 tons, and had a range of 100–460 miles. Later developments to the Pershing included the automatic azimuth reference adapter and radar guidance systems.

The Davy Crockett, developed in 1962, was the smallest and by far the most mobile missile. It was spin-stabilized, with a solid-fuel motor that was fired from a titanium tube. It was transported by a two- or three-man crew on a utility jeep equipped with a launcher and recoil-canceling rear nozzle.

The Lance, developed by the Vought Corporation beginning in 1962, replaced the Honest John and the Sergeant. It could be carried by a M-113-type amphibious tracked vehicle, or could be heliported or paradropped. The Lance used the M-752 erector launcher and M-680 with a resupply of two additional Lances. Running on liquid fuel with an on-board gas generator, it was approximately 20 feet long, weighed 1.7 tons, and had a range of 45–75 miles.

As of 1991, the Lance and Pershing missiles were phased out through U.S. and Soviet treaties. Thereafter, the U.S. Army continued to move in the direction of phasing out all tactical nuclear missiles.

Bibliography: Bergaust, Erik, *Rockets and Missiles* (Putnam's, 1957); Gaston, Bill, *The Illustrated Encyclopedia of the World's Rockets and Missiles* (Salamander Books, 1979).

Byron Hayes

TAEJON, BATTLE OF (July 16–20, 1950)

Korean War engagement in which North Korean forces took Taejon (100 miles south of Seoul), a major South Korean city and the command center of the U.S. 24th Infantry Division. On July 16, 1950, two North Korean divisions crossed the Kum River and prepared to attack remnants of the 24th Division at Taejon. Consequently, Maj. Gen. William Dean, commander of the 24th, revised his initial defense plan to a 48-hour delay to facilitate the commitment of the 1st Cavalry Division.

On July 19, the North Koreans attacked from the north and west while establishing roadblocks to the south and east. Continuing the assault of the following day, the North Koreans forced a U.S. withdrawal. The 24th Division accomplished its delaying mission, but at a cost of 30-percent casualties. In addition, Dean, cut off during the confused withdrawal, fell into the hands of the North Korean People's Army after 36 days of evasion.

Bibliography: Appleman, Roy E., *South to the Naktong, North to the Yalu* (Center of Military History, U.S. Army, 1986).

Maj. James Sanders Day

TANKS

Caterpillar-treaded armored combat vehicles. In 1951, the U.S. Army moved to improve its tank arsenal by introducing the M-48 "Patton." Rushed into production during the Korean War, the M-48 suffered a number of design problems, including complicated maintenance requirements and short range. Its main failing, however, was its weak 90-millimeter gun. The army overcame this problem in 1960 by introducing the M-60, which featured a 105-millimeter gun. Thereafter, the army periodically upgraded both tanks with improved mechanical systems and enhanced electronics. Upgrades could do only so much, however, and the army sought to develop a new vehicle that would be faster,

The M-60A1 tank served as a versatile weapon with American ground units. (U.S. Army)

better protected, and more heavily armed. The result was the M-1 "Abrams," which featured ceramic armor, a gas turbine engine, and advanced fire-control systems. In the 1980s, the army deployed the M-1, which evolved into the M-1A1, the tank that solved the armament problem by being equipped with a 120-millimeter gun.

Bibliography: Hunnicutt, R. P., *Abrams* (Presidio, 1990); ———, *Patton* (Presidio, 1984).

Richard F. Kehrberg

TAN SON NHUT AND BIEN HOA

Two major facilities that housed substantial U.S. Air Force units and served as headquarters locations for a number of American organizations during the Vietnam War. Of the two, Tan Son Nhut was by far the more important air base. Both installations were vital Communist objectives during the 1968 Tet Offensive, and both were spared from protracted fighting by rapid-moving U.S. Army armor and mechanized units.

Headquartered at Tan Son Nhut were the U.S. Military Assistance Command Vietnam (MACV), the U.S. 7th Air Force, and the South Vietnamese Air Force. U.S. air units located there included the 834th Air Division, the 460th Tactical Reconnaissance Wing, the 3d Aero Rescue and Recovery Group, the 315th Troop Carrier Group, and the 505th Tactical Control Group. Tan Son Nhut also handled commercial flights and Air America flight operations.

Bien Hoa occupants included the U.S. Air Force 3d Tactical Fighter Wing. The U.S. II Field Force headquarters, Long Binh Depot, and the South Vietnamese III Corps Headquarters were located nearby.

Bibliography: Dunn, Carrol H., *Base Development, 1965–1970* (U.S. Govt. Printing Office, 1972).

Col. (Ret.) Rod Paschall

TET OFFENSIVE (January–February 1968)

Widespread surprise attacks by the North Vietnamese and Viet Cong against U.S. and South Vietnamese forces during a holiday-observation cease-fire in the Vietnam War. Significantly consequential to all belligerent parties, the Tet Offensive became the turning point of the war. The offensive destroyed the Viet Cong as a viable insurgency movement, galvanized South Vietnamese opposition to Communist aggression, and inspired a new level of professionalism from the Army of the Republic of Vietnam (ARVN). However, the scope of the offensive, mounted by a foe supposedly near defeat, shattered U.S. domestic support for the war. As a result, the United States shifted its focus from prosecuting a costly war of attrition to extricating itself from South Vietnam.

Origins of the Offensive. In April 1967, the North Vietnamese Politburo issued Party Resolution 13. The resolution stipulated that a protracted guerrilla campaign against South Vietnam was no longer appropriate. Instead, an overwhelming conventional assault was now necessary. North Vietnam's Gen. Vo Nguyen Giap subsequently planned the assault and based it on five critical assumptions: (1) U.S. troop strength would remain constant, regardless of a Communist offensive; (2) Pres. Lyndon B. Johnson's administration would maintain strategic restraints on the U.S. military, again despite Communist aggression; (3) a large-scale attack would trigger a spontaneous uprising by the South Vietnamese people against the regime of Nguyen Van Thieu; (4) the ARVN would disintegrate when confronted by a Communist attack and a popular insurrection; and (5) the realization of assumptions 1–4 would increase antiwar sentiment in the United States and thus ensure the departure of U.S. troops. Ultimately, Giap's assumptions were only partially correct. U.S. troop ceilings and operational restraints remained in force, and a psychological withdrawal by the United States did occur. However, a popular uprising and the collapse of the ARVN did not occur, and thus contributed to the military failure of the Tet Offensive.

Giap's Plan. In response to Party Resolution 13, General Giap formulated a three-phase plan. It was similar to the successful one he had used against the French in 1953–54, but it also had significant differences. In phase one, the North Vietnamese Army (NVA) would attack enemy outposts in the remote border regions of South Vietnam and thus draw allied defenders away from critical population centers. The attacks began in October 1967 and triggered a series of bloody confrontations throughout South Vietnam. The battles exacted a heavy toll on the NVA and failed to disperse helicopter-supported allied forces. However, the engagements did capture the imagination of military intelligence analysts, who anticipated a climactic contest similar to the 1954 Battle of Dien Bien Phu. As a result, all eyes turned to Khe Sanh, a marine outpost located in the demilitarized zone (DMZ) and encircled by two NVA divisions, one of which had fought at Dien Bien Phu. The Johnson administration became obsessed with defending Khe Sanh and failed to recognize that the siege was largely another diversion.

Phase two of Giap's plan would not be a climactic battle, given allied superiority in conventional warfare. Instead, the Communists would unleash a surprise offensive throughout South Vietnam, which would incite a popular uprising by the South Vietnamese people. However, Giap knew that the South Vietnamese would not revolt if the NVA conducted the offensive. As a result, local Viet Cong cadres, many of which had long operated in secret, would now surface, infiltrate urban areas and wait to implement Plan TCK-TKN, also known as the "General Offensive-General Uprising." At the appropriate time, Viet Cong units would simultaneously seize radio stations, police headquarters, and other symbols of government authority. They would declare a new coalition government, extend

MACV commander Gen. William Westmoreland (second from left) inspects damage during the surprise Tet Offensive against U.S. and South Vietnamese forces in early 1968. (National Archives)

amnesty to dispirited ARVN soldiers, and coordinate the people's revolt. In phase three, rested and resupplied North Vietnamese troops would attack from their enclaves and ensure final victory. The final phase of Giap's plan never transpired, at least not in 1968.

The Offensive. The three-day celebration of the Vietnamese lunar new year ("Tet") for 1968 began on January 30. Shortly after midnight, despite a previously announced cease-fire by both sides, the Tet Offensive was launched. During the first two days of the assault, the Communists attacked 21 South Vietnamese provinces. Bac Lieu, the last province attacked, came under assault on February 10. In the interim, an estimated 85,000 Communist troops attacked or harassed 36 of 44 provincial capitals, 64 of 242 district capitals, 5 of 6 autonomous cities, and 50 hamlets. However, despite achieving strategic surprise and some control over 10 South Vietnamese provincial capitals, the Communist offensive quickly collapsed. Within 10 days, an estimated 30,000 Viet Cong died, as did the insurgency movement they had faithfully served.

Consequences. There were multiple reasons why the Tet Offensive was a military failure. By attacking everywhere, the Communists had superior strength nowhere. As a result, weak commanders were not supported and performed poorly. Further, faulty coordination and too much secrecy prevented the Communists from executing a truly simultaneous series of nationwide strikes. Instead, uncoordinated attacks occurred over several days, and thus permitted harried allied units to regroup, corner their foes, and prevent reinforcement. Nor did the ARVN or the South Vietnamese people aid the Communists—both opted to resist rather than revolt.

However, the offensive was successful enough to unnerve permanently the Johnson administration and the American people. For example, Viet Cong Sapper Battalion C-10 penetrated the grounds of the U.S. Embassy. Although the Viet Cong caused only minor damage, erroneous press reports announced that the embassy had been captured and that South Vietnam was near collapse. Worse yet was the Battle of Hue. Communists held portions of the city until February 25. They executed 3,000 people and conducted an urban campaign that left another 116,000 homeless. Such setbacks disillusioned the American people, who previously had believed the Johnson administration's claims of imminent victory. A "tidal wave of defeatism" followed and led to a reversal in American policy—the United States would henceforth prepare the South Vietnamese to defend themselves while also seeking peace.

Bibliography: Herring, George, *America's Longest War* (Wiley, 1979); Karnow, Stanley, *Vietnam: A History* (Viking, 1983); Krepinevich, Andrew, *The Army and Vietnam* (Johns Hopkins Univ. Press, 1986); Palmer, Bruce, *The 25-Year War* (Simon & Schuster, 1984); Palmer,

Dave Richard, *Summons of the Trumpet* (Ballantine Books, 1978).

Maj. Peter R. Faber

TRANSPORT AIRCRAFT

Military airplanes designed to transport heavy cargo under conditions requiring immediacy and maneuverability. The three principal U.S. transport aircraft of the Cold War era were the Lockheed-built C-130 "Hercules," the C-141 "Starlifter," and the C-5 "Galaxy."

The C-130, a turboprop aircraft, first appeared in 1951; more than 900 were purchased by the air force. Ideally functional as a tactical airlifter for the delivery of combat forces onto a battlefield, it has been adapted for many other uses: rescue, reconnaissance, gunships, weather reconnaissance, ski operations, electronic surveillance, drone launching, airborne operations, and satellite recovery. The C-130 has been flown by 45 other nations.

The C-141 became the workhorse of the air force's strategic airlift fleet in 1965, when it first entered service, and has remained such. The first jet transport specifically designed for military operations, the C-141 could project 67,000 pounds of cargo for 4,000 miles at speeds of 500 miles per hour. It provided the capability to project military presence virtually anywhere in the world within hours.

The giant C-5 became operational in December 1969 and demonstrated a capability to move more than 160,000 pounds of cargo anywhere in the world on numerous occasions. It also has been a mainstay of the strategic airlift force available to the Department of Defense.

Bibliography: *Anything, Anywhere, Anytime: An Illustrated History of the Military Airlift Command, 1941–1991* (Office of Military Airlift Command History, 1991); Burkard, Dick J., *Military Airlift Command Historical Handbook, 1941–1984* (Office of Military Airlift Command History, 1984); Launius, Roger D., and Betty Kennedy, "A Revolution in Air Transport: Acquiring the C-141 Starlifter," *Airpower Journal* (fall 1991); McGowan, Sam, *The C-130 Hercules: Tactical Airlift Missions, 1958–1975* (Aero Books, 1988).

Roger D. Launius

TRUMAN DOCTRINE

The American foreign policy stance known as the Truman Doctrine was formulated by Pres. Harry Truman in a speech to the U.S. Congress on March 12, 1947. At the time, Greece was fighting Communist insurgents and Turkey was being heavily pressured by its neighbor, the Soviet Union. Truman's request that Congress vote a $400 million aid package to support Greece and Turkey was part of a broader policy to support "free peoples" who were resisting armed attacks and those who were attempting to establish governments free of outside influences. Truman's policy of containing Communism became a foundation of subsequent programs, such as the Marshall Plan and the

North Atlantic Treaty Organization, and helped to establish his reputation as a decisive and forceful leader.

Stephen Robinson

TUNNEL RATS

Name given to specially trained U.S. Army units who undertook the hazardous task of following Viet Cong and North Vietnamese Army forces into extensive tunnel systems that honeycombed certain areas of South Vietnam during the Vietnam War. Led by Capt. Herbert Thornton, tunnel rats normally worked in small teams and disappeared into underground complexes, each man armed with only a flashlight, a handgun, and a knife to kill or flush out the enemy. Although their heroism was undeniable, success against the elaborate tunnel systems—stretching for hundreds of miles and containing enemy workshops, supply dumps, headquarters, medical facilities, cooking areas, and sleeping quarters—remained elusive throughout the war. Especially challenging were the tunnels at Cu Chi, approximately 25 miles northeast of Saigon.

Bibliography: Mangold, Tom, and John Penycate, *The Tunnels of Cu Chi* (Random House, 1985); Page, Tim, and John Pimlott, eds., *Nam: The Vietnam Experience, 1965–1975* (Mallard Press, 1988).

John F. Wukovits

UNIFIED AND SPECIFIED COMMANDS

Two types of major commands, within the U.S. Department of Defense, that are established to perform broad and continuing missions under the direction of the president and the secretary of defense. A unified command has forces assigned from two or more of the different armed services, while a specified command generally includes forces of only one service. The most obvious example of a specified command is the Strategic Air Command (SAC), created in 1946 to control nuclear-armed bombers (and later missiles) of the U.S. Air Force.

Although the unified commander is provided by one armed service, his staff normally includes members of all services involved. Below this joint commander and staff, service forces are administered by "component command" headquarters. Pres. Harry S Truman approved the first Unified Command Plan on Dec. 14, 1946, but in most instances, the joint commands of World War II carried over into peacetime. Thus, Douglas MacArthur's Southwest Pacific theater became the Far East Command in Japan.

Truman's 1946 plan included this headquarters and six others—for the Pacific, Alaska, the U.S./Canadian Northeast, the Atlantic, the Caribbean, and Europe (SAC was created by a separate executive decision). The concept of

U.S. Army "tunnel rats"—each armed with only a flashlight, a handgun, and a knife—descended into enemy tunnels during the Vietnam War. (National Archives)

unified commands was included in the National Security Act of 1947.

Beginning with the Korean War, each U.S. conflict or other major military operation has been supervised by the unified commander with planning responsibility for that area of the world. This joint commander is often described as the "supported commander in chief" because he receives units, supplies, transportation, and other reinforcements from other or "supporting" commanders in chief.

Bibliography: Reardon, S. J., *History of the Office of the Secretary of Defense; Vol. 1: The Formative Years, 1947–1950* (U.S. Govt. Printing Office, 1984).

Jonathan M. House

UNIFORM CODE OF MILITARY JUSTICE

Enacted by Congress in 1950 under the provisions of the Constitution of the United States, the Uniform Code of Military Justice (UCMJ) is a single code of military law that governs the conduct of U.S. armed forces. Several subsequent revisions streamlined the military justice system and made it more responsive to commanders while retaining the fundamental rights of service members. During the Vietnam War, the military used the provisions of the UCMJ to uphold discipline and punish UCMJ violators, including war criminals. The court-martial of Lt. William L. Calley, Jr., for his actions at My Lai was the most notable example of the usage of the UCMJ in Vietnam to prosecute such offenders.

Capt. Leslie Howard Belknap

UNITED NATIONS COMMAND (UNC)

Collective military force empowered by the United Nations (UN) Charter to carry out the specific enforcement of a UN mandate: As stated in articles 45–51 of the charter, UN members may take collective military action if so approved by the Security Council, which is comprised of the five permanent members—United States, Great Britain, France, Russia, and China. A UN military staff committee, comprised of the chiefs of staff of the five permanent members, is empowered to direct strategy. Two examples of a United Nations Command occurred in the Korean War (1950–53) and in Operation Desert Storm (1990–91).

Leo J. Daugherty III

UNIVERSAL MILITARY TRAINING/ SERVICE, DEBATE OVER

Longstanding U.S. military issue born of the political controversy over conscription. In the first half of the 20th century, advocates of universal military training (UMT) sought a form of conscription that, in their minds, was the most American and democratic alternative to a large standing army.

Terminology. "Universal military training" meant just that—mandatory participation of all physically qualified men in a military system designed to provide a vast pool of trained soldiers, who would return to civilian life as soon as their training was completed. Such training was to be conducted on a regular basis in peacetime, rather than waiting until war provided a sudden demand for soldiers. Advocates of UMT frequently cited the Swiss example in this regard, arguing that such a pool of trained manpower would allow the United States to reduce its professional armed forces to the bare minimum necessary for training reservists, planning for war, and providing immediate-response units in a crisis. UMT would fill the ranks of reserve and National Guard organizations in peacetime, reducing the time-consuming and often painful process of mobilization that the United States has frequently experienced. In practice, however, most proposals for UMT have been aimed at creating a federal reserve force. As a result, many advocates of a state-oriented, volunteer National Guard have viewed UMT as a threat to their own beliefs.

By contrast, U.S. conscription has always been in the form of selective service (SS) or universal military service (UMS). The primary purpose of such conscripted service was to provide manpower for the immediate needs of the active armed forces, and not to train men for a future emergency. The military drafts of 1863, 1917, and 1940 were all intended to provide such manpower for current active service.

Origins. The Spanish-American War (1898) clearly outlined both a new, larger world role for the United States and a variety of military weaknesses, including a shortage of trained reserves. However, the debate on UMT first came to a head during the period of U.S. neutrality (1914–17) prior to entry into World War I.

Gen. Leonard Wood, who had retired as chief of staff in 1914, openly advocated national conscription in 1915 and helped found the National Association for Universal Military Training. Its members included former secretaries of war Elihu Root and Henry Stimson. Preparedness, and with it UMT, became a bitter partisan issue that eventually produced the compromise National Defense Act of 1916. This act envisioned a combination of active, National Guard, and reserve forces based on volunteers.

Despite the partisan nature of the debate, Wood's successor as chief of staff, Maj. Gen. Hugh Scott, helped convince Sec. of War Newton Baker to support UMT, and the General Staff drafted a UMT bill in January 1917. The Selective Service Act of 1917 was hastily drafted and was then modified by the astute politician Baker to include local selection boards, thus placating congressmen who supported the National Guard. This bill was intended solely to meet the enormous manpower needs of World War I, and it expired almost as soon as the fighting stopped.

U.S. commander Gen. H. Norman Schwarzkopf (front left) *visits troops from other countries under the umbrella of the United Nations Command in 1990 during Operation Desert Shield.* (U.S. Army)

Interwar Period. When Congress sought to codify the experience of that fighting, however, the advocates of UMT again intervened. Indeed, their influence may have been decisive in Sen. James Wadsworth's decision to ask Lt. Col. John M. Palmer to help draft what became the National Defense Act of 1920. In 1917, Palmer had participated in the General Staff planning for a stillborn UMT law.

Based on the World War I experience, Palmer and Wadsworth sought to create a reserve component structure based on UMT, a concept unsupported by a war-weary public and political opponents. When finally passed, the National Defense Act of 1920 contained the outline for a reserve component structure of both National Guard and federal Organized Reserve forces. Without mandatory UMT, however, this structure withered rapidly to little more than cadre strength. Palmer and others campaigned tirelessly for a citizen armed force without conscription. Once World War II loomed, however, Palmer and other advocates returned to the familiar theme of UMT.

World War II. The immediate justification for the Selective Service Act of 1940, the first peacetime conscription in American history, was the prospect of war. Once the United States actually entered that war, however, advocates of UMT saw another opportunity to implement their plan. Stimson, one of its earliest proponents, was again secretary of war, and Chief of Staff George C. Marshall had long admired Palmer's arguments. Marshall recalled Palmer from retirement and placed him in charge of planning the postwar defense structure while the fighting was still going on.

To be completely equitable, Palmer argued, UMT should grant no exemptions or deferments, even for R.O.T.C. (Reserve Officers Training Corps) students in college. After much prodding, Pres. Franklin Roosevelt endorsed the concept of a compulsory year of training.

In January 1945, however, Stimson advised Roosevelt to defer discussion of the proposal in order to concentrate public energies on the war effort. As in 1919, this delay doomed any chances for peacetime military training. Roosevelt's sudden death in April 1945 deprived Palmer of his strongest backing, as succeeding president Harry Truman lacked the political authority to implement such a sweeping change in American lifestyles. The advent of atomic weapons allowed critics to argue that UMT, which was designed to provide the manpower for mass armies, had been rendered obsolete. The War Department published Palmer's detailed plan for a peacetime military system in November 1945, but UMT was virtually dead. Instead, the army concentrated on demobilization and budget cutting.

Postwar Policy. Except for a brief lapse in 1947, the United States continued selective-service conscription until 1973. Without an exorbitant increase in military pay and benefits, the government saw no alternative to provide the manpower necessary for the worldwide commitments of the Cold War.

The Korean and Vietnam conflicts called for rapid expansion of the draft. At such times, the draft deferments and exemptions that Palmer had opposed contributed even more to a public perception that selective service was arbitrary and unpredictable, rather than an inevitable part of growing to maturity. Palmer and his supporters had intended that UMT would provide the United States with a source of trained military manpower without the inequities that in practice doomed selective service.

Bibliography: Crossland, Richard B., and James T. Currie, *Twice the Citizen: A History of the United States Army Reserve, 1908–1983* (U.S. Govt. Printing Office, 1984); Holley, I. B., Jr., *General John M. Palmer, Citizen Soldiers, and the Army of a Democracy* (Greenwood Press, 1982); Palmer, John M., *America In Arms,* ed. by Richard H. Kohn (1941; reprint Ayer, 1979).

Jonathan M. House

UNSAN, BATTLE OF (November 1–2, 1950)

First U.S. battle with the Chinese Communist Forces during the Korean War. The sector near Unsan (a village in west-central Korea) was defended by the U.S. 8th Cavalry Regiment and the Republic of Korea (ROK) 15th Infantry Regiment. At dusk on November 1, the Chinese mounted an attack by two full divisions (some 20,000 men) against the two regiments. Blowing bugles, whistles, and horns, the Chinese swarmed over the defenders. Within two hours, the ROK 15th Regiment collapsed. Their supporting U.S. tanks and artillery retreated in disorder. The 1st and 2d battalions of the 8th Cavalry were forced from their positions, and the 3d Battalion was attacked. Survivors fought hand to hand as the regiment lost 800 men. Counterattacks by the rest of the 1st Cavalry Division failed to restore the line.

Bibliography: Appleman, Roy E., *The U.S. Army in the Korean War: South to the Naktong, North to the Yalu* (Dept. of the Army, 1961); Blair, Clay, *The Forgotten War* (Time Books, 1987).

Brig. Gen. PNG (Ret.) Uzal W. Ent

URGENT FURY, OPERATION (see Grenada, Invasion of)

VIET CONG (see Viet Minh/Viet Cong/ North Vietnamese Army)

VIET MINH/VIET CONG/NORTH VIETNAMESE ARMY

Various factions of Communist and/or Nationalist forces operating in Vietnam during the latter half of the 20th century. For Americans trying to fully understand U.S. involvement in the Vietnam War during the 1960s and 1970s, the terminology used to identify the enemy was often ambiguous and imprecise.

During the First Indochina War (1946–54), Communist forces were generally referred to as "Viet Minh," a contraction of "Vietnam Doc Lap Dong Minh" (League for Vietnamese Independence). Ho Chi Minh's Viet Minh forces fought in Laos, South Vietnam, and Cambodia against the French but were located mainly in the northeastern part of Indochina. The term largely disappeared with the French departure and the independence of the four former colonies.

In the aftermath of the First Indochina War, when the Republic of Vietnam (South Vietnam) was created, the term "Viet Cong" arose and could be ascribed to a political adherent of South Vietnam's National Liberation Front, to a tax collector for the front, or to an armed Communist soldier in South Vietnam. It was a loose, largely derogatory name for Saigon's opponents and was used by supporters of the Republic of Vietnam.

South Vietnamese villagers, such as this man taken into custody near Da Nang in 1965, were often suspected of being Viet Cong sympathizers or agents. (National Archives)

The "North Vietnamese 'Army'" (NVA) was largely an Americanized designation for what was officially the "People's Army of Vietnam" (PAVN), Hanoi's primary combat force from 1944. Between the years 1964 and 1974, the NVA was transformed from a modestly equipped army of 250,000 (augmented by some 30,000 Viet Cong guerrillas) to a 570,000-man force armed with a modernized weapons system. In the 1980s and early 1990s, the PAVN ranged between the third and the fourth largest army in the world.

Bibliography: Pike, Douglas, *People's Army of Vietnam* (Presidio, 1986); ———, *Viet Cong: The Organization and Techniques of the National Liberation Front of South Vietnam* (MIT Press, 1966).

Col. (Ret.) Rod Paschall

VIETNAMIZATION

Term coined by U.S. Sec. of Defense Melvin Laird, "Vietnamization" was the war-abatement policy officially proclaimed by Pres. Richard M. Nixon on June 8, 1969. It comprised a phased withdrawal of U.S. ground combat forces from South Vietnam and a return to training/advisory/logistical support of the South Vietnamese forces backed by continued air bombardment missions. It thus represented a progressive transfer of the burden of combat to an increasingly augmented and better equipped South Vietnamese army. By August 1972, all U.S. combat troops had withdrawn leaving a total of 74,000 army support, naval, and air force personnel. By Jan. 27, 1973, when the United States signed the Vietnam Peace Accord, this total had fallen to 24,000. The last U.S. troops left South Vietnam in April 1973.

Russell A. Hart

WAKE ISLAND MEETING
(October 15, 1950)

The Wake Island Meeting, held as the UN forces in Korea seemed to be on the brink of victory, had UN commander Gen. Douglas MacArthur and Pres. Harry Truman (who had called the conference) as its primary participants. Truman, who initiated the meeting, had never met MacArthur. Truman was accompanied by Gen. Omar Bradley, Sec. of the Army Frank Pace, and other officials. While reviewing the military situation in Korea, MacArthur stated his belief that Communist China would not intervene in the conflict and that U.S. troops could soon be withdrawn from Korea. Although the short meeting was amicable and was given wide positive publicity, it was eclipsed by early November by the news that the Communist Chinese had attacked in force and that UN forces were retreating.

Stephen Robinson

WAR CRIMES TRIALS (NUREMBERG AND TOKYO)

Post-World War II trials conducted by international military tribunals against alleged violators of recognized ethics of wars. War consists of acts that would be criminal if performed in peace; from ancient times the warrior has been generally immune from prosecution for performing those acts in war. But this immunity is limited by the laws of war flowing from medieval ideas of chivalry, by the concept that the ravages of war should be mitigated, and in more recent times by religious humanitarianism and the opposition of merchants to unnecessary interruption of commerce. The 20th-century series of treaties known as the Hague and Geneva conventions declared that the rights of belligerents to injure the enemy are limited. These laws of war are stated as general principles; neither the means of enforcement nor the penalties for violation are specified. The substance of their provisions, however, has been taken into the military law of many countries—including the United States—in the form of general orders, manuals, and other official documents.

The trials in Nuremberg, (West) Germany, and in Tokyo, Japan, brought something new to the laws of war and to the governments and peoples around the world: affirmation of the individual's obligation to comply with internationally recognized standards of conduct, enforcement of the concept of crimes against peace, and expansion of the area of criminal liability for violations of the laws of war. Simply expressed, these trials said that a citizen must *not* go along with policies he believes to be wrong.

From Nov. 20, 1945, to Oct. 1, 1946, an international military tribunal at Nuremberg tried 24 principal Nazi offenders of crimes against peace, humanity, and the laws of war, sentencing 12 to be hanged. In addition, 836,000 lesser former Nazis were tried in the U.S. zone, of whom 503,360 were convicted and punished by fines, performance of community work, short terms in labor camps, property loss, or denial of the right to hold public office.

From June 3, 1946, to Nov. 12, 1948, an international military tribunal for the Far East in Tokyo tried high Japanese civilian and military officials for the same categories of crimes as in Nuremberg. Seven of the accused were hanged, 16 were given life sentences, and others were given long prison sentences. In addition, other special tribunals both in Japan and in areas of Japanese wartime operations convicted 4,200 army and navy officers, of whom 720 were executed.

Bibliography: Taylor, Telford, *Nuremberg and Vietnam* (Quadrangle Books, 1970).

Col. (Ret.) Henry G. Gole

WAR POWERS RESOLUTION

U.S. congressional act passed in November 1973 over the veto of Pres. Richard M. Nixon. The War Powers Resolution requires the president to inform Congress if members of the U.S. armed forces are placed in situations where combat is expected. After this notification, the president may keep U.S. soldiers, airmen, sailors, and marines in combat for a period of 60 days, with the possibility of a 30-day extension, if the safety of the U.S. forces is in question before Congress is obliged to vote on a declaration of war or some other such resolution or legislation.

This measure was the direct result of the 1964 Gulf of Tonkin Resolution that authorized Pres. Lyndon B. Johnson to use what force was necessary to protect U.S. troops. Many congressmen believed the 1964 measure was used by the president to conduct a war without adhering to the U.S. Constitution's requirement to refer matters of war and peace to the Congress. Opponents of the War Powers Resolution pointed out that Congress could have debated the U.S. involvement in Southeast Asia at any time during the long war and could have refused to fund U.S. military and naval expenditures in that area. The War Powers Resolution was therefore considered by many to be superfluous. Proponents countered that the resolution did require Congress to act, eliminating the situation that occurred all during the Vietnam War where senators and representatives did not have to vote for or against the war. Under the resolution, Congress may have to decide on funding for a military action if that action continues for 90 days.

Many have challenged the constitutionality of the measure, saying that the resolution degrades the president's responsibilities as commander in chief as enumerated in Article 2 of the Constitution. Others claim that the Founding Fathers intended the president and not the Congress to conduct foreign affairs. Mostly, presidents have complied with the notification provision of the resolution without acknowledging its legality. There was little practical effect of the resolution during U.S. military operations in Grenada in 1983, in Panama in 1989, and during the 1991 Persian Gulf War. The legislation has inhibited some types of military action, such as secret military operations where combat is expected.

Bibliography: Committee on International Relations, U.S. House of Representatives, 94th Congress, *The War Powers Resolution* (U.S. Govt. Printing Office, 1975).

Col. (Ret.) Rod Paschall

WHITE STAR MOBILE TRAINING TEAMS (1959–1961)

U.S. Special Forces personnel sent to Laos in July 1959. After the 1954 Geneva Accords, the U.S. Department of State established a Program Evaluation Office to handle military supplies furnished to the Royal Lao government. When the North Vietnamese violated the cease-fire by furnishing 10,000 troops to the Communist Pathet Lao, the United States responded by sending a number of Special Forces mobile training teams (White Star) to assist the Laotian military. Concurrently, a Military Advisory Assistance Group was established to manage the increased commitment. This stabilized the situation, and the United States and the Soviet Union agreed to accept a coalition government. After a Protocol on Neutrality was signed in

Geneva in July 1962, the White Star teams were withdrawn before the deadline of October 1962.

Brig. Gen. (Ret.) Theodore C. Mataxis

WOMEN IN THE ARMED FORCES

By the end of World War II, more than 350,000 women had served in the uniformed armed forces—army/WAC (Women's Army Corps); navy/WAVES (Women Accepted for Volunteer Emergency Service); marines/Women Marines; Coast Guard/SPAR ("Semper Paratus—Always Ready")—including nurses in the army and navy. It was questionable, however, whether the postwar Congress would authorize the services, all of which approved, to include women in their regular and reserve components. But, after two years of debate, Congress in 1948 (1947 for army and navy nurses) authorized the integration of women into the regular and reserve components of the army, navy, marines, and air force. Congress established the air force in 1947; thus, Women in the Air Force (WAF) was included in the women's integration bill. Women were limited to positions exclusive of combat duties and were further limited in numbers (two percent of each service's total regular strength), in promotions (none above lieutenant colonel or commander except for one woman colonel or captain per service), and in claiming dependents. Because the SPAR reverted to Treasury Department control at war's end (and later to the Department of Transportation), it did not attain regular status until much later—1974.

Korean and Vietnam Wars. Army nurses landed in Pusan, Korea, on July 5, 1950, just 10 days after the Korean War began. Along with other army medical personnel, they moved forward in MASH (mobile army surgical hospital) units to give prompt emergency care to U.S. combat troops. The nurses later served in evacuation, field, and station hospitals and hospital trains in South Korea. More than 540 army nurses served in Korea between 1950 and 1953. Navy nurses served on hospital ships in nearby waters, and air force nurses served on planes evacuating wounded to military hospitals in Japan and the Philippines. In 1952, after most ground fighting had ended and peace negotiations had begun, about 10 WAC officers and enlisted women served in South Korea in administrative positions and as interpreters. Wacs and women in the navy, air force, and Marine Corps served in Japan, Okinawa, Hawaii, the Philippines, and throughout the United States in support of the combat operations in Korea. At the onset of the war, 22,069 women were on active duty. Although the war did inspire many women to enlist, the services were forced to recall women reservists on active duty involuntarily. By war's end (June 1953), the strength of women in the armed services had grown to 45,485 (including nurses).

During World War II, women had served in both traditional and nontraditional jobs. But recruiting in the 1950s

The number of military women in nontraditional roles, such as this helicopter mechanic, has climbed sharply since the Vietnam War. (U.S. Army)

and 1960s was directed away from women oriented to blue-collar jobs and toward women seeking business and technical careers in the services. Thus, during and between the Korean and Vietnam wars, women continued to serve primarily in administrative, medical, and communications positions, traditional jobs for women in and out of the armed forces.

In 1965, Gen. William C. Westmoreland, commander of U.S. Forces in South Vietnam, requested the assignment of WAC officers and enlisted women to fill traditional jobs in major headquarters within his command. About 20 Wacs arrived that year; the next year, a WAC detachment was established at the Ton Son Nhut air base. It later moved to Long Binh. Approximately 600 WAC officers and enlisted women served in Vietnam between 1965 and 1973. Arriving later were a small contingent of Women Marines, one WAVES officer per year, and many WAF officers and enlisted women (500–600 WAFs served in Vietnam from 1967 to 1973). Army nurses were assigned to field, station, and evacuation hospitals; air force nurses were sent to aeromedical evacuation groups and hospitals; most navy nurses served on the hospital ships *Repose* and *Sanctuary*. Six female and 2 male army nurses died in Vietnam, one of the women as a result of enemy fire. Approximately 5,000 army, 600 navy, and 450 air forces nurses served in Vietnam between 1965 and 1973.

Post-Vietnam Era. The withdrawal of the United States from South Vietnam signaled the beginning of many changes in the services that had a great impact on women in uniform. Congress discontinued the draft and directed the establishment of an all-volunteer armed force. To encourage the enlistment of women, the services opened most military specialties to them; they allowed women to become pilots and military police, to receive weapons training, to serve in combat support and combat service support units, and to serve on noncombat ships and planes but not on those likely to be involved in combat. Mandatory discharge for pregnancy was discontinued in 1975, and women received the same allowances for dependents as men. In 1976, women were authorized to enter all the military academies and R.O.T.C. (Reserve Officers Training Corps) units.

In 1976, Congress eliminated major inequities between men and women serving in the armed forces. It passed a law that removed promotion and retirement restrictions on women officers, permitted women to serve in the National Guard, and eliminated the two-percent restriction on women in the regular services. The law that restricted women to noncombat duties was retained. The positions of director in each of the women's services were eliminated between 1976 and 1978 as were all separate units, branches, and corps for women. The last to go was the Women's Army Corps, disestablished in October 1978. As the inequities were removed, the strength of women in the services rose from 55,402 in June 1973 to 197,878 in September 1983.

Service in the 1980s and 1990s. No longer restricted to traditional jobs, women now served in combat support and combat service support units. During the U.S. invasion of Grenada in 1983, intervention in Panama in 1989, and the Persian Gulf War in 1990–91, women served as helicopter pilots, air transport pilots, refueling tanker pilots, truck mechanics, military police, ammunition specialists, and officers and crew on naval supply and repair ships, as well as in many other noncombat positions. More than 30,000 women served in the Persian Gulf War; 2 army women were taken prisoner and later rescued, and 13 army women lost their lives, 4 from enemy fire.

The women's performance in Grenada, Panama, and the Persian Gulf helped convince Congress to remove the ban on women serving on combat ships and planes. On Dec. 5, 1991, Pres. George Bush signed the bill that removed the statutory provisions that restricted women from serving in combat roles. By the end of 1990, 226,937 women were serving on active duty in the army, navy, air force, and Marine Corps. Another 2,564 were on duty with the Coast Guard.

Bibliography: Hancock, Joy Bright, *Lady in the Navy* (Naval Inst. Press, 1984); Holm, Jeanne M., *Women in the Military: An Unfinished Revolution* (Presidio, 1982); Morden, Bettie J., *The Women's Army Corps 1945–1978* (Center of Military History, U.S. Army, 1990); Shields, Elizabeth A., *Highlights in the History of the Army Nurse Corps* (Center of Military History, U.S. Army, 1981); Stremlow, Mary V., *A History of the Women Marines, 1946–1977* (Historical Div., U.S. Marine Corps Hdqrs., 1986).

Col. (Ret.) Bettie J. Morden

Bibliography

Chapter 1. The Organization of Military Forces: 1945–1992
and
Chapter 2. The Cold War: 1945–1960

Arkin, William M., et al., *Encyclopedia of the U.S. Military* (Harper & Row, 1990).

Armed Forces Information School, *The Army Almanac* (U.S. Govt. Printing Office, 1950).

Armed Forces Staff College, *The Joint Staff Officer's Guide 1988* (1990).

Army Focus—June 1991 (Dept. of the Army, 1991).

Brodie, Bernard, and Fawn M. Brodie, *From Crossbow to H-Bomb,* rev. ed. (Indiana Univ. Press, 1973).

Brophy, Arnold, *The Air Force: A Panorama of the Nation's Youngest Service* (Gilbert Press, 1956).

Coletta, Paolo Enrico, *The American Naval Heritage in Brief* (Univ. Press of America, 1978).

Crocker, Lawrence P., *Army Officer's Guide,* 45th ed. (Stackpole Books, 1990).

Department of the Army, *American Military History, 1607–1958,* ROTCM 145-20 (July 1959).

———, *The Army* (1978).

———, *Army Heritage,* pamphlet 355-27 (Aug. 7, 1963).

———, *Status of the Army HQ Reorganization* (1987).

Department of the Navy, *The United States Navy* (Naval History Div., 1969).

Depuy, R. Ernest, *The Compact History of the United States Army,* rev. ed. (Hawthorn Books, 1961).

Fact Sheet: Atlantic Command (CINCLANT Public Affairs Office, 1983).

Fact Sheet: U.S. Atlantic Fleet (CINCLANTFLT Public Affairs Office, 1983).

Glines, Carroll V., Jr., *The Compact History of the United States Air Force,* rev. ed. (Hawthorn Books, 1973).

Goldich, Robert L., "Historical Continuity in the U.S. Military Reserve System," *Armed Forces and Society,* 7, no. 1 (fall 1980).

Hagan, Kenneth J., ed., *In Peace and War: Interpretations of American Naval History, 1775–1978* (Greenwood Press, 1978).

Hinter, Edna J., "Combat Casualties Who Remain at Home," *Military Review* 60, no. 1 (January 1980).

House, Jonathan M., *Toward Combined Arms Warfare: A Survey of 20th Century Tactics, Doctrine, and Organization,* CSI research survey no. 2 (Combat Studies Inst., August 1984).

Howarth, Stephen, *To Shining Sea: A History of the United States Navy, 1775–1991* (Random House, 1991).

International Institute for Strategic Studies, *The Military Balance, 1990–1991* (1990).

Kruzel, Joseph, ed., *1990–1991 American Defense Annual* (Lexington Books/The Mershon Center, 1990).

Mason, Herbert Malloy, Jr., *The United States Air Force: A Turbulent History* (Mason/Charter, 1976).

Matloff, Maurice, ed., *American Military History* (Office of the Chief of Military History, U.S. Army, 1969).

Millett, Allan R., *Semper Fidelis: The History of the United States Marine Corps* (Macmillan, 1980).

Millis, Walter, *Arms and Men: A Study of American Military History* (Mentor Books, 1956).

Ney, Virgil, *The Evolution of Military Unit Control, 500 BC–1965 AD,* memorandum CORG-M-217 (1965).

Ney, Virgil, *Evolution of the US Army Division, 1939–1968,* memorandum CORG-M-365 (Technical Operations, Inc., January 1969).

Parker, William D., *A Concise History of the United States Marine Corps, 1775–1969* (Historical Div., U.S. Marine Corps Hdqrs., 1970).

U.S. Army Air Forces, *AAF: The Official World War II Guide to the Army Air Forces, A Directory, Almanac and Chronicle of Achievement* (Bonanza, 1988).

Weigley, Russell F., *The American Way of War: A History of United States Military Strategy and Policy* (Macmillan, 1973).

———, *History of the United States Army* (Macmillan, 1967).

Chapter 3. The Korean War: 1950–1953

Appleman, Roy E., *Disaster in Korea: The Chinese Confront MacArthur* (Texas A&M Univ. Press, 1989).

———, *East of Chosin: Entrapment and Breakout in Korea, 1950* (Texas A&M Univ. Press, 1987).

———, *Escaping the Trap: The US Army X Corps in Northeast Korea, 1950* (Texas A&M Univ. Press, 1990).

———, *Ridgway Duels for Korea* (Texas A&M Univ. Press, 1990).

———, *South to the Naktong, North to the Yalu (June–November 1950): United States Army in the Korean War* (Office of the Chief of Military History, U.S. Army, 1961).

Blair, Clay, *The Forgotten War: America in Korea, 1950–1953* (Times Books, 1987).

Condit, Doris M., *History of the Office of the Secretary of Defense; Vol. 2: The Test of War, 1950–1953* (Office of the Secretary of Defense, 1988).

Futrell, Robert F., *The United States Air Force in Korea, 1950–1953,* rev. ed. (Office of Air Force History, 1983).

Hermes, Walter G., *United States Army in the Korean War: Truce Tent and Fighting Front* (Office of the Chief of Military History, U.S. Army, 1966).

Hoyt, Edwin P., *The Pusan Perimeter* (Stein and Day, 1985).

Montross, Lynn, and Nicholas Canzona, *The U.S. Marine Operations in Korea, 1950–1953,* 4 vols. (U.S. Govt. Printing Office, 1957).

Schnabel, James F., *United States Army in the Korean War: Policy and Direction: The First Year* (Office of the Chief of Military History, U.S. Army, 1972).

Chapter 4. Vietnam—From Discord to War: 1954–1964

Davidson, Phillip B., *Vietnam at War: The History, 1946–1975* (Presidio, 1988).

Democratic Republic of Vietnam, *30 Years of Struggle,* book 1 (Foreign Languages Publ. House, 1960).

Fall, Bernard B., *Hell in a Very Small Place: The Siege of Dien Bien Phu* (Vintage, 1962).

———, *Street Without Joy: Indochina at War, 1946–1954* (Stackpole Books, 1961).

Hammond, William M., *The United States Army in Vietnam: The Military and the Media* (Center of Military History, U.S. Army, 1988).

Hannah, Norman B., *The Key to Failure: Laos and the Vietnam War* (Madison Books, 1987).

Ho Chi Minh, *Ho Chi Minh on Revolution: Selected Writings, 1920–1966* (New Amer. Library, 1967).

Karnow, Stanley, *Vietnam: A History* (Viking, 1983).

Lansdale, Edward G., *In the Midst of Wars: An American's Mission to Southeast Asia* (Harper & Row, 1972).

Mao Tse Tung, *On Protracted War,* 3d ed. (Foreign Languages Press, 1967).

Nolting, Frederick, *From Trust to Tragedy: The Political Memoirs of Frederick Nolting* (Praeger, 1988).

Patti, Archimedes L. A., *Why Vietnam?: Prelude to America's Albatross* (Univ. of California Press, 1980).

Pike, Douglas, *PAVN: People's Army of Vietnam* (Presidio, 1986).

———, *Viet Cong: The Organization and Techniques of the National Liberation Front of South Vietnam* (MIT Press, 1966).

Rust, William J., *Kennedy in Vietnam: American Policy, 1960–1963* (Scribner's, 1985).

Sharp, U.S. Grant, *Strategy for Defeat: Vietnam In Retrospect* (Presidio, 1978).

Sheehan, Neil, ed., *The Pentagon Papers* (Bantam Books, 1971).

Socialist Republic of Vietnam, *Lich Su Tam Muoi Nam Chong Phap/A History of 80 Years Resistance to French Rule* (Hanoi, 1958).

Taylor, Maxwell D., *Swords and Plowshares* (Norton, 1972).

Tran Van Don, *Our Endless War: Inside Vietnam* (Presidio, 1978).

Truong Chin, *Primer For Revolt* (Praeger, 1963).

U.S. Congress, Senate, Committee on Foreign Relations, 98th Congress, 2nd session, *The U.S. Government and the Vietnam War, 1945–1961* (U.S. Govt. Printing Office, 1984).

U.S. Department of State, *Foreign Relations of the United States: Indochina, 1952–1954*, vol. 13 (U.S. Govt. Printing Office, 1982).

Vo Nguyen Giap, *People's War, People's Army* (1959).

Westmoreland, William C., *A Soldier Reports* (Doubleday, 1976).

Chapter 5. Vietnam—A Decade of American Commitment: 1965–1975

Basel, G. I., *Pak Six: The Story of the War in the Skies of North Vietnam* (Jove Books, 1987).

Cao Van Vien, *The Final Collapse* (Center of Military History, U.S. Army, 1983).

Clarke, Jeffrey J., *The U.S. Army in Vietnam: Advice and Support: The Final Years* (Center of Military History, U.S. Army, 1988).

Colby, William, *Honorable Men: My Life in the CIA* (Simon & Schuster, 1978).

Coleman, J. D., *Pleiku: The Dawn of Helicopter Warfare in Vietnam* (St. Martin's Press, 1988).

Cook, John L., *The Advisor* (Bantam Books, 1987).

DePuy, William E., *Changing an Army: The Oral History of General William E. DePuy* (Center of Military History, U.S. Army, 1986).

De Silva, Peer, *Sub Rosa: The CIA and the Uses of Intelligence* (Times Books, 1978).

Donovan, David, *Once a Warrior King: Memoirs of an Officer in Vietnam* (Ballantine Books, 1985).

Dorr, Robert F., *Air War Hanoi* (Blandford Press, 1988).

Eschmann, Karl J., *Linebacker: The Untold Story of the Air Raids Over North Vietnam* (Ivy Books, 1989).

Halberstam, David, *The Making of a Quaqmire* (Ballantine Books, 1989).

Heiser, Joseph M., Jr., *Vietnam Studies: Logistical Support* (Dept. of the Army, 1974).

Johnson, Lyndon Baines, *The Vantage Point: Perspectives of the Presidency, 1963–1969* (Holt, Rinehart & Winston, 1971).

LeGro, William E., *Indochina Monographs: Vietnam From Cease Fire to Capitulation* (Center of Military History, U.S. Army, 1981).

Mahler, Michael D., *Ringed in Steel: Armored Cavalry in Vietnam, 1967–1968* (Jove Books, 1987).

McChristian, Joseph A., *Vietnam Studies: The Role of Military Intelligence, 1965–1967* (Dept. of Army, 1974).

Momyer, William W., *Airpower in Three Wars* (U.S. Govt. Printing Office, 1978).

Ngo Quang Troung, Lieutenant General, *Indochina Monographs: The Easter Offensive of 1972* (Center of Military History, U.S. Army, 1980).

Nguyen Khac Vien, ed., *Vietnamese Studies No. 20: American Failure* (Xunhasaba, 1968).

Nguyen Tien Hung, and Jerrold L. Schecter, *The Palace File* (Harper & Row, 1986).

Nichols, John B., *On Yankee Station: The Naval Air War Over Vietnam* (Naval Inst. Press, 1987).

Nolan, Keith W., *Into Laos: The Story of Dewey Caynon II/Lam Son 719* (Presidio, 1986).

Palmer, Bruce, *The 25 Year War: America's Military Role in Vietnam* (Univ. of Kentucky Press, 1984).

Peers, W. R., *The My Lai Inquiry* (Norton, 1979).

Pisor, Robert, *The End of the Line: The Siege of Khe Sanh* (Ballantine Books, 1982).

Sak Sutsakhan, *Indochina Monographs: The Khmer Republic and the Final Collapse* (Center of Military History, U.S. Army, 1984).

Sheehan, Neil, *A Bright and Shining Lie: John Paul Vann and America in Vietnam* (Random House, 1988).

Stanton, Shelby, *Anatomy of a Division: The First Cav in Vietnam* (Presidio, 1987).

———, *Green Berets at War: U.S. Army Special Forces in Southeast Asia, 1956–1975* (Presidio, 1985).

———, *The Rise and Fall of an American Army: U.S. Ground Forces in Vietnam* (Presidio, 1985).

Terzani, Tiziano, *Gia Phong!: The Fall and Liberation of Saigon* (St. Martin's Press, 1976).

Thayer, Thomas C., *War Without Fronts: The American Experience in Vietnam* (Westview Press, 1985).

Tran Dinh Tho, *Pacification* (Center of Military History, U.S. Army, 1979).

Tran Van Tra, *Vietnam: History of the Bulwark B 2 Theater, Concluding the Thirty-Year War* (trans. Foreign Information Broadcast Service, 1982).

Trotti, John, *Phantom Over Vietnam* (Presidio, 1984).

Van Tien Dung, *Our Great Spring Victory: An Account of the Liberation of South Vietnam* (Review Press, 1977).

West, F. J., Jr., *The Village* (Harper & Row, 1972).

Chapter 6. The Era of Flexible Response: 1961–Present

Addington, Larry, "The Nuclear Arms Race and Arms Control," *War and Society* (May 1983).

Adkin, Mark, *Urgent Fury: The Battle for Grenada* (Lexington Books, 1989).

Allison, Graham T., *Essence of Decision: Explaining the Cuban Missile Crisis* (Little, Brown, 1971).

Blaufarb, Douglas, *The Counterinsurgency Era* (Free Press, 1977).

Bolger, Daniel, *American at War, 1975–1986* (Presidio, 1988).

———, *Scenes from an Unfinished War: Low-Intensity Conflict in Korea, 1966–1969*, Leavenworth paper no. 19 (Fort Leavenworth, 1991).

Bornet, Vaughn Davis, *The Presidency of Lyndon B. Johnson* (Univ. of Kansas Press, 1983).

Brzezinski, Zbigniew, *Power and Principle* (Farrar, Straus & Giroux, 1983).

Bundy, McGeorge, *Danger and Survival* (Random House, 1988).

Chang, Laurence, and Peter Kornbluh, eds., *The Cuban Missile Crisis, 1962* (New Press, 1992).

Daugherty, Robert A., *The Evolution of U.S. Army Tactical Doctrine, 1946–76*, Leavenworth paper no. 1 (Fort Leavenworth, 1979).

Donnelly, Thomas, Margaret Roth, and Caleb Baker, *Operation Just Cause: The Storming of Panama* (Lexington Books, 1991).

Frank, Benis M., *U.S. Marines in Lebanon 1982–1984* (History and Museums Div., U.S. Marine Corps, 1987).

Gaddis, John Lewis, *Strategies of Containment* (Oxford Univ. Press, 1982).

Garthoff, Raymond L., *Detente and Confrontation* (Brookings Inst., 1985).

Hilsman, Roger, *To Move a Nation* (Doubleday, 1967).

Insight Team of the London Sunday Times, *The Yom Kippur War* (Doubleday, 1974).

Isaacson, Walter, *Kissinger* (Simon & Schuster, 1992).

Johnson, Lyndon Baines, *The Vantage Point: Perspectives of the Presidency, 1963–1969* (Holt, Rinehart & Winston, 1971).

Kissinger, Henry, *White House Years* (Little, Brown, 1979).

———, *Years of Upheaval* (Little, Brown, 1982).

Kyle, James H., *The Guts to Try: The Untold Story of the Iran Hostage Mission by the On-Scene Commander* (Orion Books, 1990).

Martin, David C., and John Walcott, *Best Laid Plans: The Inside Story of America's War Against Terrorism* (Harper & Row, 1988).

Odom, Thomas P., *Dragon Operations: Hostage Rescues in the Congo, 1964–1965*, Leavenworth paper no. 14 (Fort Leavenworth, 1988).

Parmet, Herbert S., *JFK: The Presidency of John F. Kennedy* (Dial Press, 1983).

Pastor, Robert, *Condemned to Repetition: The United States and Nicaragua* (Princeton Univ. Press, 1987).

Rosen, Stephen Peter, "Vietnam and the American Theory of Limited War," *International Security* (fall 1982).

Rusk, Dean, *As I Saw It* (Norton, 1990).

Slusser, Robert M., *The Berlin Crisis of 1961* (Johns Hopkins Univ. Press, 1973).

Smith, Gaddis, *Morality, Reason and Power: American Diplomacy in the Carter Years* (Hill & Wang, 1986).

Sorensen, Theodore C., *Kennedy* (Harper & Row, 1965).

Vance, Cyrus, *Hard Choices* (Simon & Schuster, 1983).

Woodward, Bob, *The Commanders* (Simon & Schuster, 1991).

Wyden, Peter, *Bay of Pigs* (Simon & Schuster, 1979).

Yates, Lawrence A., *Power Pack: U.S. Intervention in the Dominican Republic, 1965–1966,* Leavenworth paper no. 15 (Fort Leavenworth, 1988).

Chapter 7. The Gulf War: 1990–1991

Bullock, John, and Harvey Morris, *Saddam's War: The Origins of the Kuwait Conflict and the International Response* (Faber & Faber, 1991).

Chadwick, Frank, *DESERT SHIELD Fact Book* (GDW, Inc., 1991).

———, *The Gulf War Fact Book* (GDW, Inc., 1991).

Dorr, Robert F., *Desert Shield: The Build-Up: The Complete Story* (Motorbooks Inter., 1991).

Friedman, Norman, *Desert Victory: The War for Kuwait* (Naval Inst. Press, 1991).

Friedrich, Otto, ed., *Desert Storm: The War in the Persian Gulf* (Time Warner, 1991).

Miller, Judith, and Laurie Myhoie, *Saddam Hussein and the Crisis in the Gulf* (Times Books, 1990).

Ridgeway, James, ed., *The March to War* (Four Walls Eight Windows, 1991).

Schwarzkopf, H. Norman, with Peter Petre, *It Doesn't Take a Hero* (Bantam Books, 1992).

Index

Boldface numbers indicate main essays;
italic numbers indicate illustrations.

Moore, Bryant E. 281
Moorer, Thomas Hinman
(1912-) **210–211**
Morse, Wayne *272*
Muccio, John 285
Multiple independently
targetable reentry vehicles
(MIRVs) 24, 128, 130
Murphy Jr., Edward R. 296
Murphy, Robert D. 283
Murray, Raymond L. 276
Murrow, Edward R. *64,* 128
Mutual Defense Assistance Act
288
My Father, My Son (Elmo
Zumwalt Jr. and Elmo
Zumwalt III) 245
My Lai massacre 106–107,
288–289

N

Nam Tha 73
Nasser, Gamal Abdel 41, 123,
282
National Guard 5, 7, 10–11,
19–20
National Liberation Front 71
National Security Acts of
1947/1949 6–7, 28, 29, 53,
273, **289**
National Security Agency 7,
296
National Security Council
Cold War document
formulated by (NSC-68) 4,
36, 48–49, 115, **290–291**
development of 7, 28, 53,
289
in Korean War 57
NATO *See* North Atlantic
Treaty Organization
Nautilus (submarine) 22
Navy, U.S.
active forces 13–14
in Cuban blockade 120
in Gulf War 143, 145, 148,
149, 158–159
interservice coordination
144, 145
in Korean War 62
missile technology 24, 278
nuclear propulsion 22
nuclear strategy 35
organizational structure 6,
13, 15, 28
reserve forces 14–15
role of 13, 28, 280
sealift resources 14, 15
special operations forces 301
tactical doctrine 15
Task Force 155 *139, 146*
in Vietnam War 84
women in 5
Neither Liberty Nor Slavery
(Nathan Twining) 234
Netherlands 33, 34, 64
Neutron bomb 24

New Look strategy 38, *38,*
42–45, 260, 286, **289–290**
New York Times (newspaper)
293
New Zealand 37, 64, 249–250
Ngo Dinh Diem (1901-1963)
182–183
coup against 81, 83
government of 71, 72, 76,
80, 251
suspicious of ARVN 251
U.S. assessment of 66–67,
69, 178
U.S. support of 70, 71,
80–82, 83
Ngo Dinh Nhu 77, 78, 80, 81,
82
Ngo Quang Truong 163
Nguyen Be 86, 97
Nguyen Cao Ky (1930-) 90,
99, **199**
Nguyen Chi Than 87, 91, 96, 97
Nguyen Van Linh 86, 87
Nguyen Van Ngan 112
Nguyen Van Thieu 90, *90,* 108,
109, 111, 112, 114, **231–232,**
292
Nicaragua 132
Nickerson, Herman 281
Nike-Ajax missile system 21,
303
Nimitz (aircraft carrier) *131*
Nimitz, Chester William
(1885-1966) **211**
Nitze, Paul Henry (1907-) **211,**
244
Nixon, Richard Milhous
(1913-1994) **211–212,** *212,*
242
and Acheson 165
anticommunism of 115
Cambodian incursion 108,
170
China policy 125–126
foreign policy altered
approach 125
and Haig 190
Middle East policy 127–128
pursuit of détente 126
resignation of 128
Vietnam policy 89, 105–
106, 110, 272, 283, 292,
293, 300, 311
Nixon Doctrine 125
Noriega, Manuel Antonio
134–136, *136,* 144, 278, 279
Norstad, Lauris (1907-1988)
212
North Atlantic Treaty
Organization (NATO) **290**
and flexible response strategy
268
Kennedy administration
approach 118–119
and Korean War 36–37, 57
origins of 33–34, 290
Reforger exercises **298**

Supreme Allied Commander
300
Goodpaster as 188
U.S. troops removed from
Germany (in Gulf War
buildup) 148
weaponry 20, 118–119
North Korea
in Korean War *See* Korean
War
Pueblo seizure 124–125,
171, **295–296**
North Vietnam *See* Vietnam
War
North Vietnamese Army (NVA)
311
Norway 64
Nuclear Test Ban Treaty 121
Nuclear weapons
Air Force tactical doctrine 20
artillery 21
in China 121
conventional force strategy
39–40
Cuban missile crisis
119–121, **260–262**
defense spending 6
deterrence strategy 3, 4,
38–39
Eisenhower policy 38, 260
evolution of strategy 3–4,
34–35
first postwar test of
(Operation Crossroads)
(1946) 259
flexible response strategy
116, 261, 268
ICBMs 24, 43, 116, **277–278**
mutual deterrence 44, *45*
mutually assured destruction
126
and NATO 118–119
research and development
24, *34,* 36, 121, 259
SALT negotiations 124,
126–127, 128, 130, **299**
in Soviet Union 3, 124
START negotiations 132
Nuremberg trials (for war
crimes) **311**
NVA *See* North Vietnamese
Army

O

O'Daniel, John Wilson
(1894-1975) **212**
O'Donnell Jr., Emmett
(1906-1971) **212–213**
Oil embargo 112
Olds, Robin (1922-) **213**
On Watch (Elmo Zumwalt) 245
Operations, military *See also*
Desert One; Grenada, invasion
of; Just Cause, Operation
Gulf War
Desert Shield/Desert Storm
142–143

Korean War
Big Switch and Little
Switch 255
Bluehearts 275
Chromite 275
Killer/Ripper 281
Strangle/Saturate 302
Trudy Jackson 275
Vietnam War
Attleboro 95, 252–253
Birmingham 95
Cedar Falls 95, 256
Francis Marion 95
Junction City **278**
Lam Son 719 108–110, 282
Linebacker 110–111, 283
Market Time **286**
Masher/White Wing 95
Paul Revere 95
Rolling Thunder 298–299
Sam Houston 95
Oregon, Task Force **291–292**
Organization of American
States 123
Organized Reserve Corps 10

P

Pace Jr., Frank (1912-1988)
213, 285
Pacific Command 8
Pakistan 41, 256
Palestinians 127, 134, 140
Palmer Jr., Bruce (1913-) **213**
Palmer, John C. 309
Panama
Canal Treaties 130
U.S. invasion (1989) 4,
134–136, 144, **278–280,** 313
Panmunjom Peace Talks
60–61, **292**
Paris Peace Talks **292–293**
Partridge, Earle Everard
(1900-1990) **213–214**
Pate, Randolph McCall
(1898-1960) **214,** 227
Patriot (surface-to-air missile)
21, 150, *150,* 156, 303
Patterson, Robert Porter
(1891-1952) **214,** 267
Patton, George S. 163, 170, 294
Paul Revere, Operation 95
PAVN *See* People's Army of
Vietnam
Peers, William Raymond
(1914-1984) **214,** 288
Peng Teh-huai 60
Pentagon Papers **293**
People's Army of Vietnam
(PAVN) **311**
Pershing (tactical missile) 303
Persian Gulf *See* Gulf War
Pham Ngoc Thao, Albert 71, 85
Phan Viet Dung 105
Philippines 37
Phoenix Program 98, **293**
Poland 41